John MacEvilly

An exposition of the epistles of St. Paul,

And of the catholic epistles - Vol. 2

John MacEvilly

An exposition of the epistles of St. Paul,
And of the catholic epistles - Vol. 2

ISBN/EAN: 9783337730901

Printed in Europe, USA, Canada, Australia, Japan

Cover: Foto ©ninafisch / pixelio.de

More available books at **www.hansebooks.com**

OF THE

EPISTLES OF ST. PAUL,

AND OF

𝕿𝖍𝖊 𝕮𝖆𝖙𝖍𝖔𝖑𝖎𝖈 𝕰𝖕𝖎𝖘𝖙𝖑𝖊𝖘;

CONSISTING OF

AN INTRODUCTION TO EACH EPISTLE, AN ANALYSIS OF EACH
CHAPTER, A PARAPHRASE OF THE SACRED TEXT,

AND A

COMMENTARY,

𝕰𝖒𝖇𝖗𝖆𝖈𝖎𝖓𝖌 𝕹𝖔𝖙𝖊𝖘, 𝕮𝖗𝖎𝖙𝖎𝖈𝖆𝖑, 𝕰𝖝𝖕𝖑𝖆𝖓𝖆𝖙𝖔𝖗𝖞, 𝖆𝖓𝖉 𝕯𝖔𝖌𝖒𝖆𝖙𝖎𝖈𝖆𝖑,

INTERSPERSED WITH MORAL REFLECTIONS.

BY HIS GRACE THE MOST REV. JOHN MacEVILLY, D.D.,

𝕬𝖗𝖈𝖍𝖇𝖎𝖘𝖍𝖔𝖕 𝖔𝖋 𝕿𝖚𝖆𝖒.

"All Scripture, inspired of God, is profitable to teach, to reprove, to correct, to instruct in justice. That the
man of God may be perfect, furnished to every good work."—2 TIM. iii. 16, 17.
" Understanding this first, that no prophecy of Scripture is made by private interpretation."—2 PETER, i. 20.
I believe " that the Holy Apostolic See and the Roman Pontiff have the Primacy over the entire earth, and that
the Roman Pontiff is the successor of the Blessed Prince of the Apostles and the true Vicar of Christ.....and that
to Him was given, in the person of the Blessed Peter, by our Lord Jesus Christ, full power of feeding, ruling, and
governing the Universal Church."—COUNCIL OF FLORENCE.

VOL. II.

FOURTH EDITION, ENLARGED, REVISED AND CORRECTED.

DUBLIN:

M. H. GILL & SON, 50 UPPER O'CONNELL STREET.

BENZIGER BROTHERS,
NEW YORK, CINCINNATI AND CHICAGO.

1891.

WORKS BY SAME AUTHOR:

AN EXPOSITION

OF THE

GOSPELS OF SS. MATTHEW AND MARK.
THIRD EDITION, ENLARGED.

AN EXPOSITION

OF THE

GOSPEL OF ST. LUKE.
SECOND EDITION, ENLARGED.

AN EXPOSITION

OF THE

GOSPEL OF ST. JOHN,
ETC.

DUBLIN:
PRINTED BY SEALY, BRYERS AND WALKER,
94, 95 AND 96 MIDDLE ABBEY STREET.

THE EPISTLE

OF

ST. PAUL TO THE PHILIPPIANS.

———◆———

Introduction.

The history of St. Paul's arrival and preaching at Philippi is recorded at full length in the Acts of the Apostles (xvi. 6–40). When at Troas, he was divinely admonished to pass over to Macedon, to preach the Gospel there. A man of Macedon stood before him in a vision at night, and besought him to pass over to his country and help them. Accordingly, setting sail from Troas, he reached Neapolis on the following day accompanied by Timothy, Silas, and Luke; and from thence they came to Philippi, so called from Philip, the father of Alexander the Great, by whom it was enlarged and fortified against the incursions of the Thracians. Here, having preached the Gospel with success, both himself and Silas were scourged and cast into prison, upon the doors of which being miraculously thrown open, the gaoler, with all his family, were converted. The Philippians, although very poor, were liberal in aiding the Apostle out of their temporal substance; they sent him pecuniary aid when at Thessalonica, and they were the only Church that did so. Hearing of the Apostle's imprisonment, they sent Epaphroditus (who, according to some, was their Bishop), to carry relief to him in his necessities. Epaphroditus, falling sick, was brought to the very verge of the grave. Upon his recovery, the Apostle sent this Epistle by him to the Philippians.

Its Object was—To thank them for their charity towards him, and to inform them how matters stood with him; to congratulate them on the patience which they exhibited under affliction, and, at the same time, to encourage them to persevere. He charges them, in a particular manner, to distrust the false teachers, whose morals he depicts, and denounces as "dogs," as "enemies of the cross of Christ," &c. The false teachers in question were the same that he combated in his Epistle to the Galatians—viz., the *Judaizantes*, or Jewish zealots, whose leading error was that the observances of the Mosaic law should be necessarily united with the Gospel, in order to obtain justification.

Its Language, Greek.

Its Canonicity, never questioned in the Church.

Time and Place of.—Written by St. Paul in chains, (as is generally supposed), during his *first* imprisonment, from which he expected to be liberated. He was not liberated from his *second* imprisonment. It was written about the year **62**.

THE EPISTLE

OF

ST. PAUL TO THE PHILIPPIANS.

CHAPTER I.

Analysis.

The Apostle commences this Epistle with the usual form of salutation (1, 2). He next declares his affection for the Philippians, which he shows, by thanking God for the gift of beneficent generosity, conferred on them, towards the ministry of the Gospel (3–8); and by fervently begging of Him to grant them an increase of knowledge and charity, and also to enable them to persevere in the performance of good works (8–12). And as the Philippians sent Epaphroditus for the purpose of knowing how matters fared with the Apostle in prison, and also the effect of his imprisonment on the cause of the Gospel, he informs them, that his imprisonment rather served the cause of the Gospel than otherwise : since it had the effect of making the Gospel more extensively known (13), and of inspiring others with greater courage in preaching it (14). And although, in the preaching of it, some might be actuated by unworthy motives, still, he is delighted to find that, be their motives what they may, the truth of the Gospel is preached (12–20.) He is indifferent about what may befall himself, provided in every contingency the glory of Christ be promoted. He cares not whether he die or live ; as, in either case Christ will be glorified (20, 21). He is perplexed which course to adopt, whether to die, and enjoy Christ, or remain longer in life, to promote the good of others. As, however, his continuance in life is useful to the Philippians and all Christians, he resolves his doubt, and determines to continue in life, and to visit the Philippians (20–26). He exhorts them to steadfast co-operation in the cause of the Gospel, and to patience under the persecutions they may have to endure (26–28). He tells them it is a great gift from God to be accounted worthy of suffering for Christ's sake.

Text.

1. PAUL and Timothy, the servants of JESUS CHRIST ; to all the saints in Christ JESUS, who are at Philippi, with the bishops and deacons.

2. Grace be unto you and peace from God our Father, and from the Lord JESUS CHRIST.

Paraphrase.

1. Paul and Timothy, servants of Jesus Christ, (salute) all the faithful of Philippi, who are sanctified through the merits of Jesus Christ, and incorporated with him in baptism, as also the Bishops and Deacons.

2. May you enjoy the abundance of all spiritual gifts, together with their undisturbed enjoyment, from their efficient cause, God the Father, and their meritorious cause, our Lord Jesus Christ.

Commentary.

1. "Paul and Timothy." He adds "Timothy" in the salutation, because he was greatly beloved by the Philippians. "Servants of Jesus Christ." He refers to the special engagement in the duties of preaching the Gospel. And he uses "servants" in preference to Apostles, because the former was a title common to himself with Timothy ; and, moreover, his Apostleship was never questioned by the Philippians, so that there was no necessity for asserting it.

"To the Bishops and Deacons." It may be asked, what is become of the "PRIESTS"*

Text.

3. I give thanks to my God in every remembrance of you,

4. Always in all my prayers making supplication for you all, with joy;

5. For your communication in

Paraphrase.

3. I always return thanks to God, whenever the remembrance of you occurs to my mind.

4. And in all my prayers I always pray to God for you with joy.

5. On account of the pecuniary aid which you have

Commentary.

Some Interpreters join the words "Bishops and Deacons" with the words "Paul and Timothy"—thus, "Paul and Timothy with the Bishops and Deacons" (who are at Rome) "salute all the saints who are at Philippi." This, however, is commonly rejected as a very forced and unnatural construction. Hence, others reply to the question thus :—They say the word "Bishops" includes the clergy of the second order, and means both Priests and Bishops ; for the same office of *watching* over the spiritual interests of their flocks (which the word, επισκοπος, or "bishop," implies) was exercised by Priests of the second, as well as by those of the first order. And they have many duties in common, such as absolving from sin, offering sacrifice, &c. In the infancy of the Church, Bishops and Priests observed no distinction in the discharge of ecclesiastical functions—(those of course, excepted, that exclusively belong to Bishops)—until, in consequence of the insolent demands of some of the Priests, the Bishops, "*in order*," as we are told by St. Jerome (*Commentar. in Titum*, and *Ep. ad Evagrium*, "*to remedy schism*," were forced to assert the superiority which, faith tells us (*Concil. Trid. SS.* 23, Can. vii.) they possess over the clergy of the second order. According, then, to these Expositors of SS. Scripture, under the word "Bishops" are included *Priests*, as under "Deacons" are included, *Subdeacons*.

Some Expositors of Scriptures understand the word "Bishops," of the Priests of the second order exclusively.—(*See* Beelen *in hunc locum*, and Acts, xx. 17-29). These maintain that in the New Testament, the words *episcopus* and *presbyter* were indiscriminately employed to designate the clergy of the second order, while in the Apostolic age, they were called *Apostoli*, not only who were proximately sent by God, as in the case of the twelve, but those also who were proximately instituted by man, and vested with the Episcopal character.

Others, taking the word "Bishops" in its ordinary ecclesiastical acceptation, understand it of the clergy of the first order only ; and, although in conformity with the discipline of the Church, and the Apostolical canons, there could be only *one* Bishop at Philippi ; still, as this Epistle was intended as a circular for the neighbouring Churches, it is most likely, the Apostle includes the Bishops of these places. The omission of the Priests may be easily accounted for on the ground, that the Bishop alone, aided by the Deacons, in consequence of the paucity of the faithful in these Churches, performed all the requisite priestly functions. St. Gregory Thaumaturgus had only seventeen souls under his charge when he entered on his Episcopal office—(*See* 1 Tim. iii. 8, 9; Titus, i. 6). The Apostle places Bishops and Deacons last among those whom he salutes. Although included in the entire Church, which he addressed in the first instance, he now, by way of special honour, addresses them in particular—(*See* 1 Tim. iii. 8).

3, 4. The Apostle thanks God for the graces they received and the good works they performed from the very beginning of their conversion, and prays for their perseverance unto the end; for, "he that shall persevere unto the end, the same shall be saved." Some Interpreters include verse, 4, in a parenthesis, and connect verse, 3, with the following verse, 5. Others give the passage a continuous meaning, thus :—I give thanks to God as often as the recollection of you occurs to my mind, and that happens always in my prayers. "Making supplication for you all with joy." These latter words, which form a portion of verse 4, are, according to them, nothing more than a repetition of the former verse, as if he said, with thanksgiving praying to God; for the subject of his joy and thanksgiving was the same—viz., their charity and generosity, referred to in next verse.

5. "Communication" refers to the pecuniary aid which they sent him. This is the usual meaning of the corresponding Greek word, κοινωνια, in the Epistles of St.

Text.

the gospel of Christ from the first day until now.

6. Being confident of this very thing, that he, who hath begun a good work in you, will perfect it unto the day of Christ Jesus.

7. As it is meet for me to think this for you all: for that I have you in my heart; and that in my bands, and in the defence, and confirmation of the gospel, you all are partakers of my joy.

8. For God is my witness, how I long after you all in the bowels of Jesus Christ.

9. And this I pray, that your

Paraphrase.

generously furnished towards the propagation of the gospel of Christ, and that, not on one occasion merely, but constantly, from the very first day of your conversion to the faith.

6. Firmly trusting and feeling a moral persuasion that God will perfect the good work which he hath begun in you unto the day of judgment, when the Judge, Jesus Christ, will reward you according to your works.

7. It is but just for me to entertain this firm hope and confidence that you will receive from God the gift of perseverance; because I love you most tenderly, and you are always present to my mind, as sharers in the joy which I feel and the grace which I possess in my chains, and in the defence of myself and confirmation of the truth of the gospel.

8. For, I call God to witness the tender and deep love which I entertain for you, a love similar to that with which Jesus Christ has loved you.

9. And this I beg of God—viz., that your charity

Commentary.

Paul—viz., iv. 14, of this Epistle; Rom. xii. 13; Hebrews, xiii. 16; Gal. vi. 6. Again, if we compare this phrase with chapter iv. verse 15, where this signification of the word is more clearly expressed, the same will appear. Moreover, one of the objects of this Epistle was to thank the Philippians for their generosity. "In the gospel of Christ." The Greek reading omits, *Christ*.

6. "Being confident;" πεποιθὼς, expresses only a hope and moral certainty. The word does not by any means imply, that St. Paul believed, as a matter of faith, that all the faithful at Philippi would persevere. He says, "who hath begun a good work in you, will perfect it," rather than, *you who began will perfect it*, to commend the efficacy of divine grace, to which our salvation from beginning to end is principally to be ascribed. The "good work" refers to the good work of contributing to the support of the ministers of the gospel; or, it may refer to a good life in general. "The day of Christ Jesus," refers to the Day of Judgment, whether particular, when every one will be rewarded according to his works; or general, when the sentence passed at the particular will be solemnly ratified; the Apostle wishes us to keep this continually in mind, the better to prepare for it.

7. He states the grounds of his confident hope of their receiving the gift of perseverance. He ardently wishes for it on account of his great affection for them. "He has them in his heart," and constantly before his mind, and he keeps always in mind, that they are partners of his joy, &c. "In the defence," may also refer to the defence of the gospel. The sense amounts to the same, since the reasons adducible by him in his own defence and apology, would serve to defend and confirm the gospel.

"Of my joy." The Greek is, *of my grace*. The similarity of both words in the Greek, χάριτος and χαρᾶς, would account for the mistake; both come, however, to the same; since, it was a source of "joy" for them to suffer for Christ, and "a grace" to be able to do so (verse 29). (Both meanings are united in the Paraphrase.) Some Interpreters join the words, "in my bands," with the preceding. It is better, however, place the words, "partakers of my joy," between them (as in Paraphrase).

8. He explains the word, "I have you in my heart." "In the bowels of Jesus Christ," may also mean that his love for them is not a carnal, but a pure Christian love. They express the excess of the Apostle's love for his spiritual children. His own heart being incapable of loving them with the fulness and intensity he would wish, he recurs to the Sacred Heart of Jesus Christ, and enters it. In the tepidity of our love for God and our neighbour, let us unite our love to that of Jesus Christ, and offer it to God in union with the ardent, pure love of Jesus.

9. "In knowledge and all understanding." These qualities are requisite, lest,

Text.

charity may more and more abound in knowledge and in all understanding :

10. That you may approve the better things, that you may be sincere and without offence unto the day of Christ.

11. Filled with the fruit of justice through JESUS CHRIST, unto the glory and praise of God.

12. Now, brethren, I desire you should know, that the things which have happened to me have fallen out rather to the furtherance of the gospel.

13. So that my bonds are made manifest, in Christ, in all the court, and in all other places :

14. And many of the brethren in the Lord, *growing* confident by my bands, are much more bold to speak the word of God without fear.

15. Some indeed even out of envy and contention : but some also for good-will preach Christ :

16. Some out of Charity : know-

Paraphrase.

may daily more and more increase, according to the rules of Christian knowledge and discernment.

10. That you may be able to choose and discern what is better and more useful, and may be free from the admixture of false doctrines, and persevere in a blameless course until the coming of Christ to judgment ;

11. Abounding in good works, which both confer and preserve justice and sanctification, through Jesus Christ, unto the glory and praise of God.

12. Now, brethern, I wish you to know that the persecutions which have befallen me have rather advanced, than retarded the propagation of the gospel.

13. So that my chains and imprisonment for Christ have become known not only in the palace of Nero, but also in other parts of Rome.

14. Another advantage is, that many of our brethren in the Lord, strengthened by the happy fruits and success that have resulted from my chains, are inspired with courage to preach the word of God fearlessly and with greater confidence.

15. Some, indeed, preach Christ from motives of envy (seeing me occupy the first place), and of contention (being anxious to obtain that place and the glory attached thereto, themselves, now that I am in prison), but some, with a sincere desire of promoting the glory of Christ.

16. And some preach from a feeling of charity and

Commentary.

through the indiscriminate exercise of charity towards the teachers of error, as well as towards the Apostles of truth, their charity would be injurious, and cease to be virtuous.

10. "That you may approve," &c. So as to be able to discern the true gospel from false teaching, and promote the former, and thus be preserved from the leaven of the latter. "Sincere," may also mean, free from all sin in the sight of God, and "without offence" before men. "The day of Christ," virtually commences at death, when the particular judgment takes place, of which the general will only be a solemn and public ratification.

11. "Fruit." In Greek, *fruits*. The Vulgate reading is, however, supported by the best Manuscripts and Versions. "Justice" may also mean, eleemosynary good works, as in the gospel of St. Matthew (c. v.)

12. The Philippians dreaded lest his imprisonment might obstruct the extension of the gospel, and probably wished that Epaphroditus would inform them on this subject.

13. As it was known, that St. Paul was cast into chains for no other crime save the preaching of the gospel of Christ, many of the courtiers, as well of the other inhabitants of Rome, were induced on this account to inquire about the nature of Christianity, of which they would otherwise know nothing ; and some, in consequence, were converted (iv. 22). This was an advantage resulting from his chains. "And in all other places." The Greek is, *and to many others*, which may refer to persons as well as places.

14. "In the Lord," is connected by some Interpreters with "confident," *i.e.*, growing confident in the Lord, owing to my chains. The Paraphrase is preferable, "brethren in the Lord," or Christian brethren. "The word of God." *Of God*, is not in the Greek.

15, 16. "Some out of charity." They preach Christ from kind feelings, knowing

Text.

ing that I am set for the defence of the gospel.

17. And some out of contention preach Christ not sincerely : supposing that they raise affliction to my bands.

18. But what then ? So that by all means, whether by occasion, or by truth, Christ be preached : in this also I rejoice, yea, and will rejoice.

19. For I know that this shall fall out to me unto salvation, through your prayer, and the supply of the Spirit of JESUS CHRIST.

20. According to my expectation and hope : that in nothing I shall be confounded, but with all confidence, as always, so now also shall Christ be magnified in my body, whether *it be* by life, or by death.

21. For to me, to live is Christ : and to die is gain.

Paraphrase.

kindness towards me, knowing that I am destined by Christ for the preaching and defence of the gospel (which office they now discharge, in order to gratify me, who am prevented by chains from performing it myself).

17. Others announce Christ from corrupt motives, from motives of contention, thinking that they will add the inward torture of envy to the chains with which I am bound—judging of me from themselves.

18. What are their motives and intention to me? Provided Christ is in any way announced, and his true doctrine preached, whatever may be their intention, whether they act from corrupt motives and under the pretext of piety, or from the pure and true motive of charity, I rejoice and will always rejoice at the fact.

19. For, whatever may be their motives, I know that all this will contribute to my salvation, through the assistance of your prayers, and the abundance of the grace of the Holy Ghost, which you will obtain for me.

20. It will contribute to my salvation, conformably to my ardent expectation and firm hope; that in nothing that may happen, shall I be confounded or frustrated in my hope of advancing the cause of Christ; so that by preaching the gospel intrepidly and fearlessly now, as well as hitherto, Christ will be magnified and glorified in my body, whether I be permitted to live, or be put to death, for his sake.

21. For if I live, my life will be for Christ, and will be devoted to his service ; and my death will be to me gain, by uniting me immediately with Christ, and freeing me from the miseries of this life.

Commentary.

that nothing could be so gratifying to the Apostle as the advancement and furtherance of the gospel, this being the post assigned him by Christ.

17. Verses 16 and 17 are in inverse order in the Greek ; but the Vulgate order is generally supported by ancient MSS. "Supposing that they raise affliction to my bands." (For, "raise," the Greek has, *add*). By this, some Expositors understand a more speedy punishment from Nero, whom they intended to exasperate against St. Paul by their preaching the gospel. However, this is an improbable exposition, as in that case they themselves would not escape punishment. Moreover, the meaning in the Paraphrase is more in accordance with what follows.

18. He is not concerned about the intention with which they preached; he rejoices at the success that attends them ; the fact of their preaching, without minding their intention makes him rejoice. From this it appears that these preachers, whose motives were corrupt, were not either Simonians, or Judaizantes, or heretics of any other class ; because, surely, the Apostle would not rejoice at the preaching of Christ by heretics; since they would only involve the Pagans in a worse and more dangerous kind of infidelity, viz., Heresy. He speaks of orthodox teachers, who preached from corrupt motives.

19. "Through your prayer." In this, he tacitly calls for the assistance of their prayers.

20. According to my expectation." The Greek word, αποκαραδοκιαν, means, *ardent expectation*. These words are to be connected with the words "shall fall out to me unto salvation" (as in Paraphrase). "Christ will be magnified in my body, whether it be by life or by death ; in the former case, by labouring to convert souls ; in the latter, by furnishing the most distinguished testimony of the truth of the gospel, sealing it with his blood.

21. The interpretation in the Paraphrase connects this verse with the words of

Text.

22. And if to live in the flesh, this is to me the fruit of labour, and what I shall choose I know not.

23. But I am straitened between two; having a desire to be dissolved and to be with Christ, a thing by far the better.

24. But to abide still in the flesh, is needful for you.

25. And having this confidence, I know that I shall abide, and continue with you all, for your furtherance and joy of faith:

26. That your rejoicing may abound in Christ JESUS for me, by my coming to you again.

27. Only let your conversation be worthy of the gospel of Christ:

Paraphrase.

22. But, if to live in this mortal body be attended with fruit for the glory of Christ, resulting from my laborious exertions in his service, and (if to die be immediate gain to myself) I am perplexed what choice to make, whether to live or die.

23. I am constrained on two sides. I wish, on the one hand, to have the union between my soul and body dissolved, and be with Christ, which in itself is incomparably the better choice.

24. But it is necessary, on the other, for your salvation that I should live and continue in this mortal body.

25. And firmly persuaded of the fact that I am necessary for you, I feel morally certain, and I firmly trust and hope, that I shall remain, and that for a long time with you, for your spiritual advancement, and to procure for you that holy joy which can come from faith alone.

26. So that by my arrival amongst you again, you may have more ample matter for congratulating yourselves and glorying at my restoration to you in Christ Jesus, who will have liberated and preserved me for your sakes.

27. This only attend to, that your lives be in accordance with the gospel of Christ, so that whether I

Commentary.

verse 19, "shall fall out to my salvation," and this connexion accords better with what follows.

Others connect it with the last words of the preceding verse—"by life or by death," which latter words, according to them, are explained in this verse—"for, whether I live or die, Christ is my gain;" *i.e.*, my life and death will gain for Christ. If I live, by converting souls; if I die, by bearing testimony to his truth. These transpose the words thus—"Christ to me both to live and to die (*i.e.*, by living and dying), is gain," or is a gainer both by my life and death.

22. "And what I shall choose I know not." The particle "and" has caused some difficulty in the construction of this verse. It more probably is joined to a second member of the sentence, which in his doubt and perplexity is not expressed by the Apostle, and may be easily inferred from the preceding verse, "*and* (if to die is gain for me,") I am perplexed what choice to make. St. Chrysostom is of opinion that the Apostle had it in his power either to continue in life for the salvation of souls, or to die in order to enjoy Christ; but, that he prefers the former. What an example for those charged with the care of souls! Woe to them, if seeking their own ease, their own gain in everything, they are indifferent to the salvation of those committed to them! It is recorded of St. Ignatius, the founder of the great society of the Jesuits, that were certain salvation offered to him, he would still prefer to remain on earth, uncertain of salvation, to labour for souls.

23. "Having a desire to be dissolved," *i.e.*, the union between soul and body to be dissolved, this union being the only obstacle to being with Christ. This dissolution has been desired by many of the Saints, and it is desirable; because, *it frees us from grief, sin, and dangers*, says St. Bernard. This passage furnishes a satisfactory proof that the souls of the saints, who depart this life without sin, are instantly admitted to bliss before the general resurrection; otherwise, the Apostle's earnest wish "to be dissolved and be with Christ," *i.e.*, to enjoy Christ and the Beatific Vision of God, the principle of heavenly bliss, would be unmeaning.

24. He feels that his continuance in life is necessary for the good of the Philippians, and all the faithful.

25. And hence he resolves his doubt, and determines on remaining for the good of souls. This he judges preferable to the immediate enjoyment of Christ.

Text.

that, whether I come and see you, or being absent may hear of you, that you stand fast in one spirit, with one mind, labouring together for the faith of the gospel.

28. And in nothing be ye terrified by the adversaries, which to them is a cause of perdition, but to you of salvation, and this from God :

29. For unto you it is given for Christ, not only to believe in him, but also to suffer for him.

30. Having the same conflict as that which you have seen in me, and now have heard of me.

Paraphrase.

come to see you or not, I may hear of your perseverance in one spirit of concord, and of your labouring with one mind to advance the faith of the gospel.

28. And, that I may also hear, that you are no way terrified or shaken by the persecution and opposition of the enemies of our faith, which opposition will cause their damnation, and will be the occasion of your salvation, according to the holy disposition of God.

29. For to you is given the grace not only of believing in Christ, but also of suffering for his sake.

30. Engaged in a contest similar to that which you saw me undergo (Acts, xvi. 22), and to that which you hear of my being now engaged in at Rome.

Commentary.

"And having this confidence," *i.e.*, firmly persuaded that I am necessary for you. "I know." This word expresses only a morally certain conviction.

30. "Having the same conflict as that which you have seen in me." He was scourged and cast into prison at Philippi.—(Acts, xvi. 22). "And now have heard." In Greek, *hear.*

CHAPTER II.

Analysis.

In this chapter, the Apostle fervently exhorts the Philippians to the exercise of mutual concord, fraternal charity, and humility, both interior and exterior (1-4). And in order to urge them the more to practise both humility and charity, he proposes the example of Christ, who, although he was God, possessing the divine essence, still, for love of us, took upon himself the form of a slave ; nay, humbled himself to the death of the cross ; in reward of which humiliation, God exalted him in this assumed nature above all other creatures (4-11). He exhorts them to work out their salvation with fear and trembling, and by the splendour of their virtues, to shine forth, as brilliant luminaries, in the midst of Pagan darkness and infidelity. Should the effusion of his blood be necessary to complete the sacrifice of their sanctification, which he began in their conversion, he is ready and willing to pour forth his blood, as a libation, on their sacrifice (12-18). He promises to send them Timothy and Epaphroditus, with whose praises and commendation the remainder of the chapter is almost taken up (19-30).

Text.

1. IF there be therefore any consolation in Christ, if any comfort of charity, if any society of the spirit, if any bowels of commiseration ;

Paraphrase.

1. If, then, you wish to afford me, a prisoner for the faith, any spiritual consolation becoming a Christian ; any solace dictated by charity ; if you have any union of soul with me ; any feeling of sincere, heartfelt compassion (as I am firmly persuaded you have) :

Commentary.

1. "If," far from expressing doubt, is here strongly affirmative. It is a form of obtestation not unusual with the most eminent classical writers, and means : if you wish to afford me any consolation, &c. (as I know you do). The words within the

Text.

2. Fulfil ye my joy, that you be of one mind, having the same charity, being of one accord, agreeing in sentiment.

3. Let nothing be done through contention, neither by vain-glory : but in humility, let each esteem others better than themselves :

4. Each one not considering the things that are his own, but those that are other men's.

5. For let this mind be in you, which was also in Christ JESUS :

Paraphrase.

2. I entreat you to complete the joy which your conversion and charitable contributions have afforded me, by agreeing in the same doctrine and feelings, by entertaining mutual charity for one another, by being of one mind and soul, having the same wishes and sentiments.

3. Do nothing from a spirit of contradiction, or of ambitious affectation of superiority ; but through the spirit of humility, let each one esteem his neighbour better than himself.

4. Let no one selfishly seek his own advantages merely ; but let him rather consult for the interests of others.

5. Let the same feeling be cherished by you for one another that was entertained by Christ Jesus :

Commentary.

parenthesis affect each member of the sentence. The meaning of the entire verse comes to this : in the name of the duties of charity, which religion prescribes, and which I know you faithfully to discharge.

"If any society of the spirit." In Greek, *any communion of spirit*, "any bowels of commiseration." *i.e.*, any tender feelings of interior and heartfelt compassion. "Any bowels of commiseration." In Greek, *any bowels and commiseration.*

2. "Fulfil ye my joy," &c. In the name of all the foregoing duties which you owe me, I entreat of you to complete my joy, by being "of one mind," *i.e*, by holding the same faith, and entertaining the same feelings and wishes. This is more clearly expressed in the following—"agreeing in sentiment." This member of the sentence differs from the first, "be of one mind," in this respect only, that it is a stronger expression of concord and harmony, as appears from the Greek, το ἐν φρονουντες.

3. "Let each esteem others better than themselves." How can men do this, in all cases, consistently with truth ? According to some, in this way ; because no matter how grievous the crime of our neighbour, although you may be conscious to yourself of nothing, there may be still some unknown spiritual sin, which may render you more disagreeable in God's sight than he is, and may be the source of your damnation. Again, we may say with truth, that if our neighbour, no matter how great a sinner, received the graces conferred on us, he might be better than we ; and if we were in his circumstances, with only the same graces he had, we might have done worse. Again, St. Thomas and others say, we can regard our neighbour as better than ourselves, by looking to ourselves, without regarding the graces and gifts we have from God, and looking only to the gifts of others, in which sense, he explains the following verse. At all events, what is here inculcated is a practical exhibition of humility, by honouring all as our betters, which may be done in the exercise of true humility, although, in point of fact, we might chance to be better than they.

4. According to the exposition in the Paraphrase, the Apostle censures that spirit of selfishness, which is the greatest obstacle to fraternal charity, and the source of dissensions. Others interpret the verse, thus—not looking to the gifts we have, but to those which others have, which is a great means of exercising true humility. Commentators here remark that St. Paul prescribes its proper remedy for each of the four causes of dissension. To an excessive desire of maintaining our own opinion, he opposes, submission of our own judgment, "agreeing in sentiment ;" secondly, to vain glory—contempt for glory ; to the third cause—a desire of domineering—humility of heart, "but in humility," &c. ; to the fourth source of discord, undue selfishness—a disregard for self interests, "but those that are of other men."

5. In order to excite them to the exercise of the last-mentioned dispositions of humility and disinterestedness, he adduces the example of Christ. Pride being the greatest obstacle to fraternal charity ; he, therefore, inculcates humility, as the most efficacious means of promoting and preserving it.

Text.	Paraphrase.
6. Who being in the form of God, thought it not robbery, to be equal with God :	6. Who, pre-existing in the form of God, possessing the divine nature, and essence, and attributes, did not still tenaciously retain this equality with God, as is done by those who unexpectedly obtain some booty or emolument.
7. But emptied himself, taking the form of a servant, being made in the likeness of men, and in habit found as a man.	7. But, far from this; by taking upon him the form of a slave, he voluntary debased himself, having become like a man, by becoming really and in nature such, and in external appearance and habits of life found as a man.
8. He humbled himself, becoming obedient unto death : even to the death of the cross.	8. Nay, he humbled himself still more, having become obedient unto death—and that a death of no ordinary kind—but the ignominious death of the cross, the instrument of torture for malefactors and slaves.
9 For which cause God also hath exalted him, and hath given him a name which is above all names :	9. In reward for this humiliation God exalted him by raising him from the dead, and placing him at his right hand above all creatures, and gave him a name, which is above all names.

Commentary.

6. "Who being in form of God, *i.e.*, having the real essence and nature of God. The Greek word for "form," μορφῇ, has been interpreted by the Holy Fathers to denote, *the Divine Nature, the perfect equality of the Son with the Father, the Divine Majesty, the image of God the Father.* "Thought is not robbery to be equal to God." The interpretation of these words, found in the commentary of *Theodore Beelen*, seems the most probable, the only one which accords best with the context. According to him, the words convey a proverbial meaning, and have reference to those who tenaciously keep and grasp whatever emolument or prize they may unexpectedly fall in with. So, the words here mean, in regard to Christ, that he did not with eager tenacity retain the external form and equality with God the Father, which he possessed ; but, by taking on himself human nature and the appearance of man, veiled his Divine glory and Majesty ; thus humbling himself, which is a powerful motive for humiliation on our part. The Greek word "for robbery," ἁρπαγμον, favours this interpretation. It means, not the *act* of rapine, but the *thing itself* eagerly seized on, and tenaciously retained. Nouns ending in, μος, sometimes bear this meaning. Independently of the context, inculcating humility, the antithesis "*but* debased himself," shows this to be the true interpretation.

7. Christ debased himself, because, without undergoing any change whatever in his nature or attributes, which are immutable and essential, he put on externally human nature, which was to the eyes of men an annihilation of himself. The phrase, "and in habit found as a man," by no means implies that he was not really a man ; because, "as," *as it were*, and other adverbs of similitude, are found to express reality, "*as it were*, of the only begotten of the Father."—(Gospel St. John, i. 14). Christ was like a man. Who can be so like a man, as another man ? "In habit," in his external actions and manner of life he "was found" to act and live like other· men. The example of Christ not greedily grasping and retaining his equality with God, which he had before the world began, but rather externally divesting himself of it, is a powerful motive for us to exercise humility. Hence, this interpretation accords best with the context.

8. What a prodigy of humility ! A God, eternal and omnipotent, expiring on an ignominious gibbet ! What intense charity, prodigious disinterestedness—the Creator submitting to death for the sake of the creature ! From this example of Christ, concealing his divinity, a lesson of humility is inculcated not to glory in the gifts of nature, grace or fortune, the ordinary incentives to pride.

9. "Exalted." In Greek, *superexalted.* The Apostle refers to this as an incentive to stimulate the Philippians to acts of humiliation in hopes of like exaltation with Christ. "And gave him a name." By "name," is understood the name of "God," or "Son of God," as made known after his Resurrection and Ascension, under which name and character God made his Son to be adored and acknowledged by all nations. This name is said to be given him after his death and humiliation; because, then it

Text.

10. That in the name of JESUS every knee should bow, of those that are in heaven, on earth, and under the earth.

11. And that every tongue should confess that the Lord JESUS CHRIST is in the glory of God the Father.

12. Wherefore, my dearly beloved, (as you have always obeyed) not as in my presence only, but much more now in my absence with fear and trembling work out your salvation.

13. For it is God who worketh in you both to will and to accomplish according to *his* good will.

14. And do ye all things without murmurings and hesitations :

Paraphrase.

10. So that the person expresssed by the name of Jesus being recognised throughout creation as the Son of God, should receive the homage and adoration of creatures, whether in heaven, on earth, or under the earth, in hell, or purgatory.

11. And every tongue, whether in heaven, on earth, or under the earth, should confess, that the Lord Jesus Christ possesses glory equal to that of God the Father.

12. Wherefore, my dearly beloved, as you have always obeyed since your conversion ; so now obey, or, do now, as you have done since your conversion, work out your salvation with interior dread, and exterior lowliness and bodily uneasiness, not only in my presence, but also in my absence, in order to prove how purely you act for God's sake only.

13. For it is God who worketh in us the good will, and the accomplishment of that good will, according to his good pleasure.

14. Do all things without murmuring against the mandates of your superiors, and without hesitation or reluctance, comply with their orders.

Commentary.

was that it was publicly made known regarding him. Others understood it of the fame of his Divinity, which comes to the same with the former interpretation. Others, again, understood it of the Adorable Name of Jesus, which although given from his conception, was still given in consideration of the future redemption effected by his passion and death.

10. "In the name of Jesus." "Name," is used for the person expressed by it. The words, "every knee would bend," express adoration of the divine Person of Jesus. "And under the earth," whether in purgatory or hell ; the damned adoring him from co-action, and the others, voluntarily. The word "Jesus" is taken not for the sound expressed, but for the person whom it designates. The usage of the Church, as appears from the words of Gregory the Great, has sanctioned a relative worship to be paid to the very name of Jesus, *ad nomen Jesu omnes flectent genua cordis sui, quod vel capitis inclinatione testentur.* The Council of Lyons, as Navarre relates, commanded all to bow the head at the name of Jesus, and Catharinus cites a decree of a Roman Pontiff to the same effect. As to the etymology of the word "Jesus ;" it is derived from the Hebrew root, *jascha, i.e., he has saved.* Hence the word *Jeschua,* Latin, "Jesus," *i.e.,* Saviour. It is the proper name of the Word Incarnate, and is said by many to be superior to the name of God, as superadding the idea of ransom and redemption, in which that of Creator is implied ; whereas, the name of God conveys the idea of Creator alone, without that of Saviour.

11. "And every tongue should confess that the Lord Jesus," &c., which some interpret thus, and every tongue should confess that our Lord Jesus Christ is unto the glory, &c., *i.e.,* that Jesus Christ is supreme Lord unto the glory of God the Father; because, the exaltation of the Son confers glory on the Father. This interpretation is conformable to the Greek. St. Bernard found no pleasure in any writings that were not seasoned with this sweet name of Jesus. How often do we not hear this sacred name blasphemously invoked in the most shocking imprecations, without feeling the slightest emotion !

13. In this verse is assigned a reason why they should tremble, &c. Because, as their salvation does not depend on themselves, but principally on God's grace, they should tremble, lest God, in punishment of their sins, would withhold his grace, and leave them to their ruin. In this verse is contained a proof of the amissibility of grace. He says, "that it is God that worketh," because the grace of God is the principal

Text.

15. That you may be blameless and sincere children of God, without reproof, in the midst of a crooked and perverse generation : among whom you shine as lights in the world,

16. Holding forth the word of life to my glory in the day of Christ, because I have not run in vain, nor laboured in vain,

17. Yea, and if I be made a victim upon the sacrifice and service of your faith, I rejoice and congratulate with you all.

18. And for the self same thing do you also rejoice, and congratulate with me.

19. And I hope in the Lord Jesus to send Timothy unto you shortly, that I also may be of good comfort, when I know the things concerning you.

20. For I have no man so of the same mind, who with sincere affection is solicitous for you.

Paraphrase.

15. That you may be exempt from blame or reproach, free from all guile and deceit, and be immaculate sons of God, in the midst of a crooked and perverse generation of unbelievers, who narrowly watch and scrutinize your actions, among whom you should shine as so many heavenly luminaries placed to enlighten the world ;

16. Preserving and increasing in yourselves the light of vivifying faith, wherewith you may also enlighten and inflame others, so that I may have cause for glorying in you on the day of judgment, as not having laboured in vain, by preaching the gospel among you.

17. But should it be necessary that my blood be poured out as a libation over the acceptable sacrifice of your faith, which I have presented to God, I rejoice at the prospect of so great an advantage, and rejoice with you, who have been already offered up as an agreeable offering.

18. You also should rejoice on account of the advantage you already possess, and rejoice together with me on account of the hope I have of being offered up as a victim.

19. I hope in the Lord Jesus to be able to send Timothy to you, for your consolation, that I myself may also be consoled and cheered in my captivity, on learning the happy state of your affairs.

20. For, I have no one who is so much of one mind with me, so attached to me, or in whom I can repose such confidence as Timothy, or who will so heartily concern himself in regard to your interests.

Commentary.

cause in the production of good works, although human liberty also has its share, and it is usual in Scriptures to ascribe an effect to the *principal* cause, although *subordinate* causes also may concur in its production. That human liberty is not here denied is clear from the exhortation of the Apostle in the preceding verse ; for, why *work* out their salvation with fear and trembling, if in the *work* they had no *free* agency ?

15. From the Greek it is quite clear that the words, "sincere" and "blameless," are not to be joined to "children of God," but the words, "without reproof," should be joined thus : "children of God without reproof," τεκνα Οιου αμωμητα, *i.e.*, irreprehensible and immaculate sons of God.

16. "Holding forth," &c., as men hold forth a lantern, or as the heavenly bodies display their light. The meaning in the Paraphrase is preferable.

17. The words may also mean : if I were to pour out my blood by martyrdom, to present your faith as an agreeable sacrifice, I rejoice, &c. The words, "made a victim," mean "made a libation," referring to the libation, which in the sacrificial act was poured on the victim. Their faith was the sacrifice, and his blood the libation used in perfecting the sacrifice. "And service" means the legitimate sacerdotal act of offering up sacrifice. In Greek, *liturgy*.

18. He assuages their sorrow in case he should be put to death by Nero, and says, that instead of mourning, both they and he ought to rejoice, should such an event take place.

19. The Philippians had sent Epaphroditus to relieve St. Paul ; hence, he promises to send them in turn, for their consolation, Timothy, who was greatly beloved by them. Nothing should be omitted by a superior that can be legitimately employed to conciliate the good will and affection of those under him.

Text.	Paraphrase.
21. For all seek the things that are their own ; not the things that are Jesus Christ's.	21. For almost all seek their own interests, and prefer them to the glory of Jesus Christ. Hence, it is, that I could not find any one else, so disinterested as he, in undertaking a laborious journey, without some motive of personal advantage.
22. Now know ye the proof of him, that as a son with the father, so hath he served with me in the gospel.	22. But if you wish for any proof of his worth, I can only adduce the fact, that a child could not manage the concerns of a parent, or serve him with greater fidelity and fondness than has been exhibited by him towards me in preaching the gospel.
23. Him, therefore, I hope to send unto you immediately, so soon as I shall see how it will go with me.	23. Such, then, is the man whom I hope to send you, as soon as I see the result of my chains, and the events that await me.
24. And I trust in the Lord, that I myself also shall come to you shortly.	24. I trust, however, in the Lord, that I myself will be soon able to see you personally
25. But I have thought it necessary to send to you Epaphroditus my brother and fellow-labourer and fellow-soldier, but your Apostle and he that hath ministered to my wants.	25. But in the mean time, I have judged it necessary to send to you Epaphroditus, who is my Christian brother ; my co-operator in preaching the gospel ; my fellow-soldier in the war in which we are engaged for the gospel, under the banner of the cross ; he is also your Apostle ; and has likewise ministered to my wants and necessities.
26. For indeed he longed after you all : and was sad, for that you had heard, that he was sick	26. For, indeed, he has been eagerly longing to see you all, and it was a source of much trouble to him to learn, that you heard of his sickness, which he knew would cause you pain and uneasiness.
27. For indeed he was sick nigh unto death : but God hath mercy on him : and not only on him, but on me also, lest I should have sorrow upon sorrow.	27. For, in truth, he was sick to such a degree as to be on the very verge of dissolution ; but God took pity on him, by rescuing him from the jaws of death, and on me also, lest to the affliction of my chains would be added the further affliction of being the occasion of the death of a friend who came to minister to my wants.
28. Therefore I sent him the more speedily : that, seeing him again, you may rejoice, and I may be without sorrow.	28. I have, therefore, dispatched him with all haste in order that you may rejoice at his return, and that my sorrow may be lessened and alleviated from knowing that you are in joy.
29. Receive him therefore with all joy in the Lord : and treat with honour such as he is.	29. Receive him, therefore, with sincere Christian affection, and with great spiritual joy, and honour such persons, by contributing to their maintenance and support.

Commentary.

21. "For all seek their own," &c. He speaks of those about him, whom he could think of sending to them. It means : almost all seek their own, &c. It is, however, true of all men, and at all times. Timothy, then, was the only person disinterested enough to undertake so perilous and laborious a journey, without any regard to his own private interests.

24. From this verse it appears St. Paul expected to be liberated from his present imprisonment. He was liberated from his first, but not from his second. The words "to you" are not in the Greek. They are, however, in the Alexandrian and Vatican manuscripts.

25. "Your Apostle." Some say Epaphroditus was Bishop of Philippi.

29. "Receive him in the Lord," *i.e.*, with sincere Christian affection, "with all joy." "In the Lord" is to be joined with the words, "receive him." "And treat with honour." "Honour" means support, sustenance, as in the passage, "Honour

Text.

30. Because for the work of Christ, he came to the point of death : delivering his life, that he might fulfil that which on your part was wanting towards my service.

Paraphrase.

30. For, he was brought to the very brink of the grave, while engaged in the work of Christ (by administering to me during my incarceration, for the cause of Christ), exposing his life to imminent danger, in order that he might in person perform towards me, on your behalf, these kind services, which absence prevented yourselves from personally discharging.

Commentary.

widows who are really widows" (1 Tim. verse 3); and also, "worthy of double honour" (1 Tim. verse 17); in both places, it means sustenance or support.

30. "Delivering his life." Probably, he was attacked on the way with some malady, which he disregarded from anxiety to fill his commission ; and this, it might be, that had nearly proved fatal to him at Rome.

CHAPTER III.

Analysis.

In this chapter, after briefly referring to the subject matter of the preceding, and inviting the Philippians to rejoice at the news which he communicated therein (verse 1), *cautions them against certain false teachers, most likely the Judaizantes, whom he designates as "dogs," falsely circumcised, because only circumcised in the flesh ; whereas, the true circumcision is the Christian circumcision of the heart* (1–3). *He shows that he could himself glory in more external privileges conferred by the Mosaic law, than could any of the false teachers. He enumerates those external advantages* (4–7). *But these legal privileges, as well as all temporal advantages whatsoever, he has valued as nought in comparison with the exalted knowledge of Christ* (8); *and he has sacrificed all, and submitted to suffering, in order to gain Christ, and be rendered a sharer in his merits, and at a future day, in the glory of his resurrection* (8–11).

In referring, however, to his sacrifice for Christ, he is not to be understood as wishing to convey, that he had already attained to Christian perfection; he is only, by constant and unceasing efforts, endeavouring to attain the summit of this perfection, and to secure the prize held out in the stadium of Christian virtue. He exhorts the Philippians to do the same (11–16). *He invites them to imitate himself rather than the false teachers, whose conduct and unhappy end he describes* (17–19). *With these he contrasts the God-like conduct of the followers of Christ, and the glorious consummation in store for them.*

Text.

1. AS to the rest, my brethren, rejoice in the Lord. To write the same things to you, to me indeed *is* not wearisome, but to you *is* necessary.

Paraphrase.

1. (Whereas, then, my chains, far from injuring, have on the contrary, served the cause of the gospel, and Epaphroditus is recovered, and Timothy is to be shortly amongst you), it only remains for you brethren, to rejoice in a manner becoming Christians. And to me it is not wearisome to write the same things upon which I had formerly spoken to you ; because, such a course is a necessary, or at least, a very useful means of keeping you in the faith.

Commentary.

1. "For the rest," may be understood (as in Paraphrase) to have reference to the preceding chapter, or, the words may be regarded as a familiar kind of transition,

Text.	Paraphrase.
2. Beware of dogs, beware of evil workers, beware of the concision.	2. Beware of those teachers, who, like unclean dogs, are placed outside the pale of the Church, or, rather, like snarling dogs, endeavour to devour the true preachers of the gospel ; beware of those engaged in the wicked work of destroying the gospel ; beware of the falsely circumcised, those scarred merely in the flesh.
3. For we are the circumcision, who in spirit serve God: and glory in Christ JESUS, not having confidence in the flesh.	3. For we, Christians, are the true circumcised, who serve God, not in these mere external rites, that have been abolished; but, with that spiritual, reasonable service, which comes from the heart ; and we glory in JESUS CHRIST, placing all our hopes of salvation in his merits, and not relying on the external advantages resulting from the Mosaic law.
4. Though I might also have confidence in the flesh. If any other thinketh he may have confidence in the flesh, I more,	4. At the same time, if the possession of all the external advantages of the Jewish religion could furnish any grounds for boasting or confidence, I should have greater cause than those who make such advantages the subject of boasting.

Commentary.

from one subject to another, common with the Apostle. "To write the same things," may mean, the same things of which he discoursed among them, or the same things he had written to others, (*v.g.*) the Galatians, &c., whom he cautioned against the false teachers (as in next verse).

2. "Dogs," a term of reproach which he applies to the false teachers, on account of their impudence and their endeavours to destroy the preachers of the gospel. It may be also, that he called them "dogs," to convey that they were unclean and not belonging to the holy people of God. For, the Jews, by whom dogs were reckoned among the unclean animals, applied this opprobrious epithet to the idolatrous Gentiles, to denote that they were not belonging to the people of God, as being profane and impure. "Concision." It is thus he reproachfully designates their circumcision, which was no longer the religious and honourable rite it formely was, having now become a mere cutting of the flesh. The abstract term "concision," is employed for the concrete, *circumcised*. The Apostle designates the same class of false teachers in the words "dogs," "evil workers," and " concision," and the repetition of the word "beware," shows the strong feelings from the impulse of which the Apostle denounces them.

It may be asked to what class of heretics does the Apostle refer ? Some say, he refers to those who were known under the general denomination of *Gnostics*, of whom one class—the followers of Cerinthus and others—taught, that Christ never died on the cross, and that the Son of God left the son of Mary at the crucifixon. Hence, he calls them "enemies of the cross," and "dogs," on account of their immoral teaching and conduct. Others, however, think, with more probability, that he refers to the *Judaizantes*, or Jewish zealots, who crept in, and were privately sowing the seeds of Judaism, maintaining the necessity of observing the Mosaic law, for justification. The motives adduced here by the Apostle in refutation of their errors, favour this latter opinion. These motives regard circumcision, his extraction, the justice of the law, which latter error constituted them "enemies of the cross." For, "if justice be from the law, then Christ died in vain."—(Gal. ii. 4). Then, the "scandal of the cross is made void.'—(Gal. v. ii). Moreover, the teachers in question gloried in the same things, as appears from the words of the Apostle here, that the Judaizantes are charged (2 Cor. xii.) with making a subject of boasting.

3. Although the external sign of circumcision is abolished, still the thing signified, viz., the cutting away the vices of the heart, exists. "In the flesh," means the external advantages of the Jewish religion, such as circumcision, being a Pharisee, &c., as appears from next verse. The words might also be understood of the works performed by the aid of the law without grace.

4. Lest any person should, for an instant, suppose that he depreciates and rejects the Mosaic ceremonial law from feelings of envy, in consequence of not possessing

Text.

5. Being circumcised the eighth day, of the stock of Israel, of the tribe of Benjamin, an Hebrew of the Hebrews ; according to the law, a Pharisee.

6. According to zeal, persecuting the church of God : according to the justice that is in the law, conversing without blame.

7. But the things that were gain to me, the same I have counted loss for Christ.

8. Furthermore I count all things to be but loss, for the excellent knowledge of Jesus Christ my Lord : for whom I have suffered the loss of all things, and count them but as dung, that I may gain Christ :

9. And may be found in him not having my justice, which is of the

Paraphrase.

5. Being circumcised on the eighth day, an Israelite by birth, and of the tribe of Benjamin (the only tribe which, with Juda, remained faithful, and joined not in the schism of Jeroboam), a Hebrew of the Hebrews—all my ancestors being Hebrews—and, according to religious profession, a Pharisee.

6. And so zealous for the Jewish religion, as to endeavour to destroy everything opposed to it, even to persecute the Church of Christ, thinking that I was thereby doing a service to God, and in the observance of legal justice, free from reproach or censure of any kind.

7. But these prerogatives, which I before regarded as the greatest gain, I afterwards rejected as loss for Christ.

8. But not only these, but all the other goods of this life do I regard as quite useless, as mere nothing, in comparison with the eminence, the exalted advantage of the knowledge of Jesus Christ, my Lord, on whose account I have cheerfully parted with all things else as loss, and have reputed all their advantages as filth and ordure, that I may gain Christ.

9. That I may be found ingrafted, as a living member, on his mystic body, not having my own justice, the justice arising from my own natural works aided

Commentary.

such privileges himself, as men often undervalue in others the accomplishments which they have not themselves, he says that in his case no such feelings can exist. "Though I might also." "*Also*," is not in the Greek.

5. "Being circumcised on the eighth day," shows that he was not a Jewish proselyte, like many of the Jewish zealots, who, as mere proselytes, received circumcision only after arriving at maturer years. He received it on the eighth day, like Isaac and his descendants. "Of the stock of Israel." Neither was he descended of parents merely, as proselytes, admitted into the Jewish religion, but, not of the race of Israel. "Of the tribe of Benjamin," which was the only tribe with Juda that did not apostatize under Jeroboam. "An Hebrew of the Hebrews." All his ancestors were Jews, or, it might mean, as some understand it, a Hebrew in language, retaining the knowledge of this sacred tongue, which many of the Jews, scattered, as his parents were, among the Gentiles, had altogether lost. These four prerogatives just mentioned were not his own, but were derived from birth, and were common to him with many others. The three following are of his own choice ; and hence, a matter of greater commendation for him. "According to the law," by religious profession. "a Pharisee," the most respectable religious sect among the Jews, and externally the most observant of the law.

6. "According to zeal, persecuting the Church of God." So ardently zealous in defence of the laws and institutions of his fathers, that he persecuted everything opposed to them, even the Church of God, from a false and erroneous conscience, thinking he was thereby advancing the cause of God.

7. "The things that were gain to me." Some Expositors understand these words to mean, *these things which might be a recommendation to honour, preferment, and emolument.* "I counted as loss for Christ." I rejected as noxious and injurious, as obstacles in the way of my salvation, which comes from Christ.

8. "For the excellent knowledge." In Greek, *for the excellence of the knowledge, i.e.,* in comparison with the excellence, &c. "For whom I have suffered the loss of all things," may also mean, that he deprived himself of all earthly advantages for Christ, to become partaker of his grace and merits.

9. "In him," may also signify, that I may be found in his judgment, who judges

Text.

law, but that which is of the faith of Christ JESUS, which is of God, justice in faith :

10. That I may know him, and the power of his resurrection, and the fellowship of his sufferings, being made conformable to his death.

11. If by any means I may attain to the resurrection which is from the dead,

12. Not as though I had already attained, or were already perfect : but I follow after, if I may by any means apprehend, wherein I am also apprehended by Christ JESUS.

Paraphrase.

by the lights derived from the Mosaic law ; but that real justice gratuitously coming through faith in Christ—that justice which comes from God and is based on faith.

10. All these advantages I have renounced, that I may know him, and the great effort of omnipotent power exerted in his resurrection (the same that will also raise us to the like glorious state), and the partnership in his passion and sufferings, of which I shall have an experimental knowledge, by becoming conformed to his death, by actual sufferings.

11. If by any means I may attain to the perfect, glorious resurrection of the dead.

12. In recounting the sacrifices which I made for Christ, and the advantages accruing to me therefrom, I by no means wish to imply that I have already attained the summit of Christian knowledge and perfection ; but, I eagerly aspire after it, that I may in some way secure that prize, on account of which I was forcibly seized upon by Christ in his mercy and pressed into his service.

Commentary.

truly. This verse does not prove the sufficiency of faith for justification. All that follows from it is, that faith is one of the disposing causes for justification. The Apostle is only opposing the system of justification, of which faith is the foundation, to the system of justification through natural works, or works performed by the aid of the Mosaic law devoid of faith, which faith the unconverted Jews, continuing in their unbelief, could not have. "But that which is of the faith of Christ," *i.e.*, that justice which is gratuitously acquired through the faith of Christ, which justice "is of God," comes from God the Father, as its efficient, from Christ, as its meritorious cause, and is infused by the Holy Ghost—hence, altogether divine, and founded and based on the faith of Christ as its foundation.

10. This verse is more probably connected with verse 8, I have sacrificed all wordly advantages, &c., "That I may know him," *i.e.*, all things appertaining to his nature, all his mysteries, but particularly the power of his resurrection, that glorious state of Christ resuscitated, to which we will be likened in our resurrection to glory, and know this practically at a future day, "and the fellowship of his sufferings," and that I may know by experience how sweet and meritorious it is to suffer in union with Christ and for his sake, "being made conformable," &c., by conforming myself to his sufferings and death, by my own actual sufferings.

11. "The resurrection from the dead." The word "resurrection," in the Greek, εξαναστασιν, means a *complete, perfect resurrection*, that glorious resurrection which will be followed by no evils, and which is in store for the just. The Apostle almost invariably forbears referring to the resurrection of the reprobate, which is rather a misfortune than an advantage. "If by any means I may attain to the resurrection," &c. Then, St. Paul was not quite sure of his salvation. He feared also lest he should become a reprobate (1 Cor. ix.) and if he was not certain, although "a vessel of election," who else can be secure ?

12. This verse is to be connected with the passage, where the Apostle speaks of the sacrifices which he made for Christ, and the advantages he received therefrom. He does not wish to imply, by saying these things, that he attained the goal of perfection in this life, or acquired a perfect degree of knowledge and Christian virtue, but he is eagerly stretching forward to arrive at it ; for, it was for this end that Christ, by the abundance of grace, almost forced him into his service, on his way to Damascus ; on which occasion he exclaimed : "Lord, what wilt thou have me to do?" In the Greek

Text.	Paraphrase.
13. Brethren, I do not count myself to have apprehended. But one thing *I do:* forgetting the things that are behind, and stretching forth myself to those that are before,	13. Brethren, I do not yet suppose that I have attained the perfection to which I am called. One thing I endeavour to do, never to regard what I have passed over and left behind me, but only to look forward to what lies before me.
14. I press towards the mark, to the prize of the supernal vocation of God in Christ JESUS.	14. I exert my utmost might to reach the goal in order to obtain the prize to which God invites me from heaven, through the merits of Christ JESUS.
15. Let us therefore, as many as are perfect, be thus minded : and if in any thing you be otherwise minded : this also God will reveal to you.	15. Let us, therefore, who are better instructed and practised in the principles of our faith than others, be of the same opinion, viz., that we have not yet attained perfection in this life ; and should you have formed a different opinion on the subject, I hope that God will remove this error, and open your eyes to the light of truth.
16. Nevertheless whereunto we are come, that we be of the same mind, let us also continue in the same rule.	16. But, waiving the subject of the degree of perfection at which we may have severally arrived, this much at least should be to us a matter of solicitude, viz., to be united in charity, and firmly to adhere to the same rule of faith and doctrine, which is one and unchangeable.
17. Be followers of me, brethren, and observe them who walk so as you have our model.	17. Be imitators of me, brethren, and attentively observe (for the purpose of imitation) those who take me for their model.

Commentary.

word for "apprehended," κατελήφθην, there is an allusion to the practice of pressing soldiers and sailors into service.

13. One thing he endeavours to do, like men engaged in a running match, never to look to the part of the course he has gone over, but only to look to the part that yet lies before him. There is an allusion in the words of the Apostle to the exercise of the race course, with which he frequently compares our passage through this life towards the goal of eternity, where the prize is held out by God himself inviting us to struggle earnestly in pursuit of it. The words of the Apostle in this verse show, that in the performance of good works, that is to say, in running the course of the Christian *stadium,* we should not be puffed up with our past merits, but should only look forward to the future, and fear for our final perseverance in reaching the goal ; hence, no one can stand still in the way of Christian perfection ; not to advance is to lose ground, and recede farther from the goal.

14. "The mark," *i.e.,* the goal or winning post, at which God, the master of the race, holds out the prize, and invites me from heaven to secure it, by running in the race, as I should. It is to be obtained through the merits of Christ.

15. As many as are perfect," may also mean : as many as aspire to perfection. But even in the sense given in the Paraphrase, there is no opposition between this and the preceding, in which he speaks of himself as not being perfect ; because, here he speaks of a lower degree of perfection, which both he and they attained ; whereas, in the preceding, he speaks of a more exalted degree of perfection in this life, perfection being quite a relative thing. The word "perfect," has the same meaning here that it has in the First Epistle to Corinthians (c. ii.): "We speak wisdom among the perfect," *i.e.,* those who are well instructed in the faith. "God will reveal," implies merely the ordinary exercise of the intellect aided by divine grace ; it does not imply any extraordinary revelation.

16. Others, with St. Chrysostom and Theophylact, interpret this verse thus : In the meantime (πλὴν) let us in our onward course proceed according to the mode of perfect life at which we have arrived, and not deflect from it in any way.

Text.

18. For many walk, of whom I have told you often (and now tell you weeping) that they are enemies of the cross of Christ ;

19. Whose end is destruction : whose god is their belly : and *whose* glory is in their shame : who mind earthly things.

20. But our conversation is in heaven : from whence also we look for the Saviour, our Lord JESUS CHRIST.

21. Who will reform the body of our lowness, made like to the body of his glory, according to the operation whereby also he is able to subdue all things unto himself.

Paraphrase.

18. For many live and act quite differently, whom I frequently designated in your presence and cautioned you against (and now I repeat the same with tears), as enemies of the cross of Christ.

19. Whose end is eternal perdition, whose God is their belly, or, the gratification of their sensual appetites, whose glorying has for object those deeds of wickedness, which should rather be a cause of shame ; who are wholly engrossed with earthly things, without feeling any concern for the heavenly.

20. But we pass through this life as citizens of heaven, whence we expect also our Saviour the Lord Jesus Christ.

21. Who will transform this vile, earthly body of ours, and conform it unto a likeness with his glorified and resplendent body, and that by an efficacious effort of that power, by which all things are subject to his supreme will.

Commentary.

18. The reason why he tells them to imitate himself is, because many who affect to labour for Christ and preach his gospel act a part wholly unsuited to their profession. " Enemies of the cross." This has been already explained of the Jewish zealots, and it has been shown how they are enemies of the cross. Others, however, understand the words to refer to their immoral lives, so opposed to mortification and the self-denial pointed out by the cross.

19. Far from being wholly engrossed with earthly things, our conversation, or manner of living, is such as becomes men aspiring after heaven ; our citizenship is there ; as free citizens of heaven, we are engaged only about heavenly things. How few, even of those engaged in God's service, can say this of themselves !

21. He refers to our bodies committed to the earth, and to the glorified property of clarity.—(*See* 1 Ep. to Cor. xv. 42, 43, 44).

CHAPTER IV.

Analysis.

In this chapter, the Apostle exhorts the Philippians to persevere in Christian virtue (1); to practise concord and charity (2, 3); to rejoice always, notwithstanding their afflictions (4); to display a mild evenness of conduct, free from all extremes of passion (5); in every occurrence, to exercise acts of petition to God for future blessings, and thanksgiving for the past (6). He wishes them an increase of interior peace and joy (8). He sums up all his moral precepts, and exhorts them to the practice of everything good and praise-worthy (8–10). He commends their past and present liberality towards himself, and this he values not so much on account of being placed thereby beyond the reach of want, as on account of the charity manifested on their part; for, as to himself, he was enabled by God's grace, to accomodate himself to every turn of fortune, as well in enduring want and privation, as in enjoying abundance (11–17). He concludes with the usual salutation, wishing them the full enjoyment of all spiritual blessings.

Text.

1. THEREFORE, my dearly beloved brethren, and most desired, my joy and my crown: so stand fast in the Lord, my dearly beloved.

2. I beg of Euodia, and I beseech Syntyche to be of one mind in the Lord.

3. And I entreat thee also, my sincere companion, help those women that have laboured with me in the gospel with Clement and the rest of my fellow-labourers, whose names are in the book of life.

Paraphrase.

1. Wherefore, my brethren—whom I love affectionately, and am most anxious to behold, who are the subject of my joy and the occasion of the crown to be given me for having effected your conversion—persevere steadfastly, my dearly beloved, in the Christian faith, as I have pointed out to you, both by example and teaching,

2. I entreat Euodia, and Syntyche, laying aside all differences, to have but one mind and will, to live in charity and concord for the sake of the Lord.

3. And I entreat thee also, my sincere and faithful colleague, to assist these women (either in administering to their temporal support, or in bringing about a reconciliation), who, with Clement and my other fellow-labourers, whom I cannot here enumerate, but whose names are enrolled in the book of life, have laboured with me in promoting the cause of the gospel.

Commentary.

1. "Therefore," since such great glory, both as to soul and body, is promised you by Christ. "So stand fast to the Lord;" persevere in a Christian life, following me, and those who imitate me, as models. "My joy and my crown." For every Prelate and Pastor his people must be the source of his joy and crown, or, of his sorrow and damnation.

2. These were two women of quality residing at Philippi, who had rendered great service to the Apostle in the work of converting the Philippians. From this verse it appears that there must have been some misunderstanding between them at this time. In place of feelings of estrangement, he Apostle, however, beseeches them to substitute charity and unanimity.

3. "Book of life," means the catalogue of those predestined for grace or glory—which catalogue is treasured up in the prescience of God. This book of life is referred to by Moses (Exodus, xxxii. 22)—and David says, "may they be blotted out from the book of the living."—(Ps. lxviii.) It is most probable that he refers to the predestination of these to grace, in which case, their names are inscribed in an incomplete, conditional

Text.

4. Rejoice in the Lord always; again, I say, rejoice.

5. Let your modesty be known to all men. The Lord is nigh.

6. Be nothing solicitous; but in every thing by prayer and supplication with thanksgiving let your petitions be made known to God.

7. And the peace of God, which surpasseth all understanding, keep your hearts and minds in Christ Jesus.

8. For the rest, brethren, whatsoever things are true, whatsoever modest, whatsoever just, whatsoever holy, whatsoever lovely, whatsoever of good fame, if there be any virtue,

Paraphrase.

4. Rejoice always in the Lord, notwithstanding your persecutions and losses—again, I say, rejoice.

5. Let, however, your dignified Christian bearing and deportment, free from all extremes of passion, whether of joy or sorrow, be known to all men, so as to edify both the faithful and the unbelievers; for, the Lord is near.

6. Therefore, be not over anxious for the concerns of this world, but in every occurrence, by fervent supplications and entreaties for future blessings, as well as by acts of thanksgiving for the past, let your petitions be offered up in such a way as to please God, and cause him to lend an ear to them.

7. And may the interior tranquility and consolation of God's spirit, consequent on the performance of good actions, which surpasses all understanding, guard your wills, your intellects and entire hearts, against all fears and anxieties whatever, that might lead you astray from virtue and the service of Christ Jesus.

8. To bring to a conclusion, and sum up in a word all my moral precepts, whatever things are true—either as opposed to falsehood in language or dissimulation in action—whatever things are brave, becoming, and honourable in conduct; whatever things tend to estab-

Commentary.

way; when there is question of predestination to glory, their names are inscribed absolutely and completely. "My sincere companion" ($\sigma\acute{\nu}\zeta\upsilon\gamma\epsilon\ \gamma\nu\acute{\eta}\sigma\iota\epsilon$), probably refers to the Bishop of Philippi, who may have been Epaphroditus. Some Protestants refer it to St. Paul's wife, but in the 7th chap. 1st Ep. to Cor., St. Paul equivalently asserts that he was unmarried. Again, the words are masculine in the Greek, and although, by an Attic turn, they might have a feminine signification, still, it is improbable that St. Paul, not well versed in the Greek tongue, wrote in the Attic dialect. All the Fathers (with the exception of Clement of Alexandria, who holds that the Apostle, though married, was still continent), concur in saying that St. Paul was unmarried. Besides, to use the reasoning of Œcumenius, can we suppose that in a letter addressed to the entire Church, St. Paul would address his wife?—why leave her at Philippi?—why not leave her at Tharsis, or Jerusalem, and not be bringing her about with him—a thing he expressly denies his having done in reference to any woman?—1st Cor. ix. Hence, the word "companion," in Greek, *yoke-fellow*, is metaphorically understood of some faithful co-operator in planting the gospel.

5. "Modesty;" your even mildness of conduct, free from all extremes of passion. "The Lord is nigh." The Apostle usually proposed the near approach of judgment, which with all men virtually commences at death, as the great leading motive of perseverance in good works, which will then receive a reward, and for patiently enduring crosses and miseries of every kind, which will then cease, and will ensure "an eternal weight of glory." Oh! if we kept the judgment of God always before our eyes, how different would our conduct be from what it is! How patiently would we submit to God's holy will in sufferings—how fervently would we advance in the way of perfection, could we but frequently reflect that "the Lord is nigh!"

6. Since the Lord is shortly to come from heaven to judge us, and to crown our patience, we should betray no excessive solicitude as regards the sufferings of this life, The words of this verse are a consequence of the words of the preceding verse: "the Lord is nigh," as he is soon to come to judge us, we should show no excessive anxiety for the things of this life.

8. He sums up all his precepts in this one, which is a most comprehensive precept of morality. "Whatsoever modest." In Greek, $\sigma\epsilon\mu\nu\alpha$, *grave*, or *venerable*. "Whatsoever holy." In Greek, $\acute{\alpha}\gamma\nu\alpha$, the meaning of which is, *chaste*. For it, probably ("$\alpha\gamma\iota\alpha$,")

i. any praise of discipline, think on these things.

lish and preserve the relations of justice towards our neighbour; whatever things are chaste and pure from all carnal defilement; whatever things tend to beget the love and well-grounded esteem of others: whatever things are calculated to insure a good reputation; if there be anything that is regarded as virtuous and good; any mode of living that is praiseworthy; make these things the subject of your consideration, so that you may know how to practise them, with the greatest advantage, in proper time and circumstances.

9. The things which you have both learned, and received, and heard, and seen in me, these do ye, and the God of peace shall be with you.

9. Whatever things you have learned from me when instructing you, or received from me by writing, or heard of me when absent, or seen done by me when present; do these things, and the God of peace will be always with you—imparting and communicating his blessings to you.

10. Now I rejoice in the Lord exceedingly, that now at length your thought for me hath flourished again, as you did also think : but you were busied.

10. I have rejoiced exceedingly, with a truly Christian and spiritual joy, that the solicitude you formerly felt for me, though relaxed for some time, has again revived. However, as an apology for this remission, it can be said, that you have always the will and the affection, but had no opportunity of manifesting it (either from want of means, or of a trusty messenger by whom to send your aid).

11. I speak not as it were for want. For I have learned, in whatsoever state I am, to be content therewith.

11. The subject of this joy is not so much on account of your having relieved my want (as on account of the charity which you manifest). For, I have learned to be contented with whatever may befall me in the different circumstances in which I may chance to be placed.

12. I know both how to be brought low, and I know how to abound : (every where, and in all

12. I know how to use with moderation every turn of fortune—both to bear the want of the necessaries of life, or to turn them to account when they abound.

Commentary.

"holy," might have been inserted., "Of good fame." The first of earthy goods is a good reputation, "habe curam de bono nomine."—Eccles. xli.

9. The things that I have preached, written, spoken, and exemplified in my conduct, these things do.

10. Some Expositors say that he does not imply in this verse, that their attention and solicitude for him had relaxed; that the meaning of the verse is—your solicitude for me has revived; according to the feelings of your heart, it is now manifested; and it was only the want of opportunity that prevented you from manifesting it earlier. It would seem, however, that there is a silent reproach conveyed in this verse, for which he makes the best excuse that could be made, "*a want of opportunity*," as is explained in Paraphrase, the meaning also of the Greek word, ἠκαιρεῖσθε δέ.

11. He removes all suspicion of his having felt this joy in consequence of being relieved from want. He rejoiced at the succour sent him, not so much on account of its having placed him beyond the reach of want, as on account of the charity which it displayed on their part. As for himself, he learned from experience to be content with whatever might befall him.

12. "I know both how to be brought low," *i.e.*, to be in want; for, it is opposed to I know **how to abound.**" "Suffer need," is opposed to "abound," in the end of this **verse.** Hence, the word "brought low," means to be brought low by want. ("Everywhere and in all things I am instructed.") The Greek for "instructed," μεμύημαι, means to be, *initiated in mysteries ;* hence, it means here to be initiated and practised in the exercises of a Christian and Apostolic life. These words are commonly read within

Text.

things I am instructed) both to be full, and to be hungry; both to abound, and to suffer need.

13. I can do all things in him who strengtheneth me.

14. Nevertheless you have done well, in communicating to my tribulation.

15. And you also know, O Philippians, that in the beginning of the gospel, when I departed from Macedonia, no church communicated with me concerning giving and receiving, but you only :

16. For unto Thessalonica also, you sent once and again for my use.

17. Not that I seek the gift, but I seek the fruit that may abound to your account.

18. But I have all, and abound; I am filled, having received from

Paraphrase.

For, I have been fully initiated and practised in the Christian exercise of endurance under all circumstances—to be satiated with abundance of food, or to suffer hunger—to abound in the other necessaries, or bear the want of them.

13. I can do all these things and everything else required of me, not through any power of my own, but through the grace with which Christ interiorly strengthens me.

14. Still, you have done well in relieving my distress by contributing out of your temporal substance for that purpose.

15. And you know also, O Philippians ! and you could bear witness to the fact, that when I first preached the gospel to you, and afterwards departed from Macedonia (to go into Achaia), no other Church, except your own, contributed anything that I could place to the account of given and received.

16. For you repeatedly administered to my wants, when I was at Thessalonica.

17. This I do not say as if I were anxious for gifts ; what I am anxious about is, the abundant gains resulting from them to your credit.

18. I have received all your presents, and in consequence abound in the means of subsistence.   I have

Commentary.

a parenthesis.   There is no necessity, however, for such a construction.   They may be connected with the following words, thus :—In all things have I been initiated and instructed, both to be full, and to be hungry, *i.e.*, to be content when I have a sufficiency of food, and when I suffer hunger.   "To abound and suffer need," are more extensive in their signification than the preceding—they denote the want of clothing and of other necessaries, as well as that of food.

13. Lest in the preceding he might appear to be attributing too much to himself, he corrects any such false conception, and ascribes all to the power of God.   "*I can do all in Christ corroborating me,*" is the Greek reading.

14. He adds this, lest they might imagine that he did not duly appreciate their goodness, by saying that their generosity did not afford him joy in consequence of relieving his wants, because he is content under all circumstances, whether of plenty or want ; he, therefore, praises them for their generous charity.

15. The circumstance of their's being the only Church to relieve him, tends more to their praise, and at the same time, clears him from every charge or suspicion of avarice ; for, no other Church contributed, and he would not receive aid from some particularly from the Churches of Achaia.

"As concerning giving and receiving."   In this, he alludes to the account-books of merchants, wherein are entered separately the sums expended and the sums gained in trade.   The Philippians had given *temporal* goods, and reaped *spiritual* blessings. Hence, alms-deeds, and contributions towards the support of those engaged in preaching the gospel, may be regarded in the light of a lucrative traffic, in which spiritual and heavenly blessings are purchased by temporal goods,   This, of course, is not to be understood in a mercenary or simoniacal spirit.—(*See* 1 Cor. ix. 11.)

17. He still alludes to the account-books of the merchants.   Temporal alms purchase eternal glory.   The alms-giver keeps a book of account with God, and lends to the Lord, who will pay him back with great interest.

18. "An odour of sweetness."   Alms-deed is an incense of most sweet fragrance— it is even "a sacrifice"—an offering most pleasing to God.

Text.

Epaphroditus the things you sent, an odour of sweetness, an acceptable sacrifice, pleasing God.

19. And may my God supply all your wants according to his riches in glory in Christ JESUS.

20 Now to God and our Father be glory world without end. Amen.

21. Salute ye every saint in Christ JESUS.

22. The brethren, who are with me, salute you. All the saints salute you; especially they that are of Cæsar's household.

23. The grace of our Lord JESUS CHRIST be with your spirit. Amen.

Paraphrase.

a sufficient supply of the necessaries of life, having received from Epaphroditus the gifts you sent by him as a sacrifice of sweet odour, an offering acceptable and pleasing to God.

19. And I pray that my God may supply you with all things of which you stand in need, according to the abundance of his riches, and may these temporal goods lead to your eternal glory through Christ Jesus.

20. But to God, who is also our Father, be glory for ever and ever.—Amen.

21. Salute every Christian who has been sanctified in Christ Jesus.

22. The brethren, who visit me and minister to me in prison, salute you. So do all the Christians here; but especially such of them as belong to the household of the Emperor, Nero.

23. The grace of our Lord Jesus Christ be with your spirit. Amen.

Commentary.

19. The Greek readings vary, as regards the word "want." Some read "grace;" others, "joy." Ours is, however, the most probable. "According to his riches in glory," &c., which some interpret "*the riches of his glory.*"

22. From this verse, it appears, that St. Paul had converts even among the courtiers of Nero.

The common Greek subscription has: "*Written to the Philippians from Rome, through Epaphroditus.* The *Codex Vaticanus* has: "*Written to the Philippians from Rome.*"

THE EPISTLE

OF

ST. PAUL TO THE COLOSSIANS.

Introduction.

WHO WERE THEY?—The Colossians, to whom this Epistle was addressed, are supposed by many to have been the people of the Island of Rhodes, called by the name of Colossæ, owing to the famous colossal statue of the sun which stood there, reckoned as one of the seven wonders of the world. This opinion is, however, generally rejected as improbable; and the Colossians are commonly believed to have been a people of Phrygia, in Asia Minor. The city of Colossæ was not far distant from Laodicea and Hieropolis, as appears from Chap. ii. 1; iv. 16, 17, &c., of this Epistle. It is most likely, nay, almost certain, that St. Paul was never at Colossæ. This is clearly inferred from Chap. ii. 1, and from the fact, that, throughout the entire Epistle, he never makes the most remote allusion to the exercise of his Apostleship there, which he ordinarily does, when addressing those whom he himself converted. On the contrary, he ascribes their conversion to Epaphras (i. 7). The common opinion, then, is, that Epaphras was the first who preached the Gospel to the Colossians. But, although St. Paul did not in person preach to them; still, in character of Apostle of the Gentiles, having "the solicitude of all the churches," he feels himself called upon to address them on subjects of faith, regarding which the weight of his Apostolic authority might be required to secure them against the wiles and snares of the false teachers. And although he was not the founder of their Church, immediately, still he might be regarded as such in a certain sense, inasmuch as the Gospel came to them at least mediately through him.

OCCASION OF.—The occasion of this Epistle was to guard the Colossians against the false teachers, who endeavoured to introduce corrupt doctrines amongst them. The heresies which St. Paul combats in all his Epistles might be classed under two heads. To the first, belonged the heresies of the *Judaizantes*. These were certain Jewish fanatics, who ascribed too much efficacy to the ceremonial law of the Jews, and while admitting Christ to be a model of virtue and the consummator of faith, still maintained that the observance of the Mosaic law was necessary to confer justice, and should be associated with the Christian religion. Against this class the Apostle specially directs his Epistles to the Romans, Galatians, Philippians, and Hebrews. Under the second, were comprised the errors of the *Gnostic* heretics, who wished to join the Platonic system of philosophy with the Christian religion.   To these belonged Simon Magus, Ebion, Cerinthus, Valentinus, and the Manichees.   Against this class were specially directed the Epistles to the Colossians, Ephesians, Timothy, Jude, and Second of St. Peter.   It was to guard the faithful of Colossæ against this latter class of false teachers, St. Paul, in character of Apostle of nations, wrote this Epistle.

The second part of this, as in the case with all the Epistles of St. Paul, is chiefly employed in inculcating several duties of Christian morality.

WHEN AND WHERE WRITTEN.—It is generally supposed to have been written from Rome.   The subscription of the Greek copies asserts, that it was sent by Tychicus and Onesimus, whom St Paul had converted when in chains.   It is supposed to have been written during his first imprisonment, about the year 62, and to have been conveyed to its destination, by the bearers of the Epistles to the Ephesians, Philippians, and also of that to Philemon.

THE EPISTLE

OF

ST. PAUL TO THE COLOSSIANS.

CHAPTER I.

Analysis.

*The Apostle commences this Epistle with the usual form of Apostolical salutation (1, 2).
In the next place, he gives thanks to God for the gifts of grace and the divine virtues of
faith, hope, and charity, bestowed on the Colossians (3–5). These gifts and virtues were
to terminate in the enjoyment of the future blessings promised in the Gospel. From the
mention of the Gospel, he takes occasion to confirm the doctrine preached to them by
Epaphras, as a faithful minister of the Gospel. He prays that the Lord would grant.
them a more perfect knowledge of his holy will, and strength and power to lead lives
worthy of God, in the performance of good works, and the patient endurance of
sufferings for his sake (6–12).*

*The Apostle then renders thanks to God for the grace of faith, and the other blessings of
redemption bestowed on all Christians ; and from this, takes occasion to point out the
attributes of Christ, and his superior excellence over the angels. He claims for him,
in a special way, the prerogatives of Creator and Redeemer, of which the heretics wishes
to deprive him, by transferring them to the angels. The apostle, therefore, asserts, that
he is the image of the invisible God—the Creator of all things, the angels included—
the preserver, by his Providence, of all things created—the Redeemer of all men, Jews
and Gentiles—the head of the Church—the reconciler of offended heaven with sinful
man—the very fulness of the Divinity (12–21.)*

*He says that the Colossians will be partakers of the blessings of Redemption, provided
they persevere in the faith announced to them, which is the same with that preached
throughout the rest of the world. He declares himself to be appointed by the will of
God a minister of the Gospel, in order to announce to the Gentiles a mystery hitherto
concealed from them—a mystery for the fulfilment or accomplishment of which among
the Gentiles, he cheerfully submits to suffering and privations of every kind.*

Text.	Paraphrase.
1. PAUL an apostle of JESUS CHRIST, by the will of God, and Timothy a brother :	1. Paul, an Apostle of Jesus Christ, by the will and authority of God, and Timothy a brother :
2. To the saints and faithful brethren in CHRIST JESUS who are at Colossæ.	2. (Salute) the Christians of Colossæ, who are sanctified in Christ Jesus : who believe in him and faithfully serve him.

Commentary.

1. "By the will of God." At the very outset, the Apostle asserts his divine
commission, in opposition to the false teachers, who usurped the office of preaching
without any divine mission or warranty whatever from God.

"And Timothy." He mentions him, because known to the Colossians and beloved
by them.

2. The three words, "saints," "faithful," "brethren," denote the same, viz., the
Christians of Colossæ. They are termed "Saints," because called to a state of sanctity,

Text.

3. Grace be to you and peace from God our Father, and from the Lord Jesus Christ. We give thanks to God, and the Father of our Lord Jesus Christ, praying always for you:

4. Hearing your faith in Christ Jesus, and the love which you have towards all the saints.

5. For the hope that is laid up for you in heaven, which you have heard in the word of the truth of the gospel,

6. Which is come unto you, as also it is in the whole world, and bringeth forth fruit and groweth, even as it doth in you, since the day you heard and knew the grace of God in truth.

7. As you learned of Epaphras, our most beloved fellow-servant, who is for you a faithful minister of Christ Jesus.

Paraphrase.

3. May you enjoy the abundance of all spiritual gifts from their efficient cause, God the Father, and their meritorious cause, our Lord Jesus Christ. We always give thanks to God the Father of our Lord Jesus Christ, and always pray for you.

4. After we heard of your faith in Christ Jesus, and of the charity which you exercise towards all the faithful.

5. In the hope of securing these future blessings, treasured up for you in heaven ; these blessings of the life to come, you have heard announced and promised to you, by the preaching of the gospel of truth.

6. Which gospel has come to you, as it was preached all over the earth, where it fructifies and is become extended, as it has fructified and become extended among you, from the first day you heard it, and knew the true doctrine regarding the gratuitous goodness of God, in reference to man's redemption.

7. According as you learned it from Epaphras, my fellow-servant and co-operator in preaching the gospel, who is most dear to me, as he is also the faithful and sincere minister of Christ Jesus for our good.

Commentary.

and also, because they were satisfied in baptism, having been incorporated with Christ and engrafted on him ; "faithful," true sons of the faithful Abraham, and heirs of his promises ; "brethren," both of Christ and of one another. Hence, the necessity of brotherly union. These three are distinctive epithets of all Christians. "In Christ Jesus." The word " Jesus," is not in the Greek, but it is found in several MSS.

3. " Grace," &c., the ordinary Apostolic form of salutation. The words, "and the Lord Jesus Christ," are wanting in many MSS. and rejected by modern critics. They are found in the Armenian and Coptic versions. "We give thanks to God," &c. The Apostle usually commences his Epistles with acts of thanksgiving and prayer. He gives thanks for past favours, and prays for their future continuance. "To God and the Father," Τῷ Θεῷ καὶ πατρί. For this St. Chrysostom reads, *To God the Father*, &c.

4. "Hearing," ἀκούσαντες, *i.e., having heard*, or, after we heard of your faith, &c.

5. This love of their brethren they exercised in the hope of the future rewards, &c. "In the word of the truth of the gospel," *i.e.*, in the word of the most true gospel in which there is contained no falsehood. Hence, it is a laudable thing, to propose the rewards of the life to come, as the motive of our good works.

6. The words "and groweth," are not in the Greek, Their genuineness is now admitted, being found in the ancient MSS., in that used by St. Chrysostom among the rest. "Knew the grace of God in truth," may also mean, have known the grace of God truly and without any admixture of error. In this verse, the Apostle wishes to remove any erroneous impressions, which the false teachers might endeavour to create in their minds, regarding the imperfection of the gospel preached to them, compared with that preached by the Apostles, probably with the view of making their own erroneous doctrine, the complement of the gospel preached to the Colossians.

7. This gospel which has been preached by the Apostles throughout the earth, has been preached to you without any error by Epaphras. This the Apostle adds, to guard them against the wiles of the false teachers, who endeavoured to persuade them, that the gospel preached by Epaphras was defective, and that this defect could be supplied only by admitting the points of doctrine preached by themselves. From this it is commonly inferred, that St. Paul was never at Colossæ ; otherwise, he should have referred to the doctrines which he himself preached. Hence, he advances the

Text.

8. Who also hath manifested to us your love in the spirit.

9. Therefore we also, from the day that we heard it, cease not to pray for you, and to beg that you may be filled with the knowledge of his will, in all wisdom, and spiritual understanding :

10. That you may walk worthy of God, in all things pleasing; being fruitful in every good work, and increasing in the knowledge of God :

11. Srengthened with all might according to the power of his glory, in all patience and long-suffering with joy,

12. Giving thanks to God the Father, who hath made us worthy to be partakers of the lot of the saints in light,

Paraphrase.

8. Who has made known to us your spiritual and pure love, not only for us, but also for all the saints (4).

9. Therefore, as soon as we heard of your faith and charity, we ceased not praying to God for you, and supplicating him to fill you with a more perfect knowledge of his holy will, by bestowing upon you the gifts of all knowledge and spiritual understanding.

10. That you may live in a manner becoming sons of God and followers of Christ, so as to please God in all things, producing the fruit of every kind of good works, and advancing and progressing more and more in the knowledge of God.

11. That strengthened with perfect power, which came from the operation of his glorious omnipotence alone, you may endure all crosses with patience, with long-suffering, and with joy.

12. We give thanks to God the Father, who, of his pure mercy and grace, has vouchsafed to make us sharers by the light of faith in the inheritance of the saints, which consists in light, or the beatific vision of God.

Commentary.

full weight of his Apostolic authority in support of the truth of the gospel preached to them by Epaphras. Epaphras is generally supposed to have been the first teacher of the Colossians; most probably sent to them by St. Paul while visiting the other cities of Phrygia; they, now, in turn, deputed him to visit the Apostle and minister to him in prison.

8. This Epaphras, who had been ministering to him in his chains, made known to him their love for him. " In the spirit," means spiritual, unlike the carnal love of the Gnostics ; or, it may mean, proceeding from the Holy Ghost.

9. " With the knowledge of his will," may mean, the general will of God, regarding them, the great rule to which they should conform their lives ; or " the will of God," in reference to the mode in which he has been pleased to save man, viz., by the death of his Son, and not by angels. And this extended knowledge they will acquire more perfectly by "spiritual wisdom," *i.e.*, by knowing the mysteries of faith on principles of faith, and "understanding," knowing them by human illustrations ; or "wisdom," may mean the speculative knowledge of the truths of faith, and "understanding," the knowledge of applying these truths and principles to the practical detail of their lives.

10. " Worthy of God." In Greek, *worthy of the Lord.* " In all things pleasing," in Greek, *unto all pleasing.* He explains in the following words, how they will walk worthy of God and please him : it is by omitting no opportunity of performing good works, which he calls "fruitful," because as the fruits of the earth preserve our temporal life, so do good works ensure our eternal life.

11. He also prays without ceasing, that fortified with perfect spiritual strength, through the glorious power of God, they would be patient and forbearing in adversity, and even receive it with joy, "according to the power of his glory," *i.e.*, his glorious power. *God's omnipotence is never so glorious as in rendering those omnipotent who hope in him,* says St. Bernard. " Patience " is exercised in bearing those afflictions which we cannot revenge ; "longanimity," in bearing with those which we can punish. " With joy." The patient endurance of crosses is more magnanimous than the performance of the most heroic actions. " *Romanorum est fortia facere, Christianorum fortia pati,*" but to bear severe trials, not only with patience but with joy, is peculiarly Christian.

12. " Giving thanks to God the Father." The Greek omits, *God.* Some persons connects this verse with verse 9, thus : "we cease not praying God to grant you this grace also of thanking him for having called you," &c. According to the connexion in the Paraphrase, a new sentence is commenced, and St. Paul having concluded his

Text.

13. Who hath delivered us from the power of darkness, and hath translated us into the kingdom of the Son of his love,

14. In whom we have redemption through his blood, the remission of sins;

15. Who is the image of the invisible God, the first-born of every creature:

16. For in him were all things created in heaven and earth, visible, and invisible, whether thrones; or dominations, or principalities, or powers; all things were created by him and in him:

17. And he is before all, and by him all things consist:

Paraphrase.

13. Who has rescued us from the power of darkness, i.e., of demons and infidels, and translated us to the kingdom, i.e., the Church of his beloved Son here. which is the portal to the kingdom of heaven hereafter.

14. Through whom we have obtained redemption, which consists in the remission of our sins, and which he effected by giving his blood by way of ransom or price for us.

15. Who is the perfect image of the invisible God (having the same identical nature with Him), existing before any creature, having been begotten of the Father by an eternal generation.

16. For by him were all things created in heaven and earth, both visible and invisible, men and angels of every rank and order—whether thrones or dominations, or principalities or powers, all things were created by him and unto him, i.e., for his glory.

17. And he is before all creatures, and in him, and through him, all things subsist and are preserved.

Commentary.

petitions in the preceding verse, now thanks God for the benefits here enumerated. "The lot of the saints," τοῦ κλήρου τῶν ἁγ.ων. Eternal life is called a "lot," to express its gratuitousness, and the absence of strict claim on our part signified by the absence of a claim on the part of those who gain a thing by casting lots. And though we merit eternal life; still, it is primarily founded on grace. *In crowning our merits, he only crowns his own gifts.*—St. Augustine. "In light." The light of faith here, or the light of glory hereafter, by which we shall see God, face to face. "It may, however, denote both, as in Paraphrase.

13. "Darkness," taken in a moral sense in SS. Scripture, denotes evil; hence, it means here, the power of the devil, the prince of darkness. "The Son of his love," a Hebraism, for *his most beloved Son.*

14. In the following verses the Apostle claims for Christ, the titles of Creator and Redeemer, the two grand prerogatives of which the Simonians attempted to deprive him, and which they wished to transfer to angels. In this verse, he claims for Him the title of Redeemer, upon which he dilates more fully at verse 20—after claiming for him the title of Creator in the intervening verses, 16, 17, 18, 19. The words "through his blood," are not in the Rhemish Version, made from the Sixtine Edition of the Vulgate, nor in the *Codex Vaticanus*, nor in MSS. or Versions generally.

15. Before asserting that he is Creator, the Apostle first claims for Christ the supreme attribute of Divinity, and the eternal Sonship of God. Others say, that the object of the Apostle in this verse is, to show the great benefits of Redemption from the exalted nature of the person by whom it was effected. Christ is the perfect delineation of that invisible God whom no one ever saw, and exhibits the perfect image which the person possessing the nature of God could alone exhibit. He was begotten of God by an eternal generation; hence, as far anterior to the Eons of the Gnostics in time, as he is superior to them in causality, which latter is shown in the following verse.

16. In this verse is refuted the false doctrine of the Gnostics, who asserted that this material visible world was created by the ministry of angels. "Through him and in him." In Greek, *unto him, i.e.,* unto his glory.

17. In this verse, the Apostle refers to the Divine attribute of Providence, whereby all created things are preserved. From this and the preceding verses, it is clear, that the "image," εἰκών, referred to in verse 15, must regard the substantial image of God, and the possession of the divine nature; since of God only could it be said that all things were created "by him," and "in him," or *unto him,* as in the Greek, i.e., for his glory, as also that by his providence all things subsist and are preserved. And it was this God—

Text.

18. And he is the head of the body, the church, who is the beginning, the first-born from the dead : that in all, things, he may hold the primacy :

19. Because in him, it hath well pleased the Father, that all fulness should dwell :

20. And through him to reconcile all things unto himself, making peace through the blood of his cross, both as to the things on earth, and the things that are in heaven.

21. And you, whereas you were some time alienated and enemies in mind, in evil works :

22. Yet now he hath reconciled in the body of his flesh through

Paraphrase.

18. And this same person of whom we are treating as God, is, as man, the head of the Church, which is his mystical body ; he is the principle and author of the resurrection, and is himself the first born, or first fruits of the dead, consecrating the resurrection of all by raising himself from the grave. So that whether viewed as God, or as man, he holds pre-eminence over all things created.

19. For, it has pleased God the Father, that in Christ, all fulness, all perfection of power necessary for him as head, to govern, and of grace, to vivify his body, should permanently and inseparably dwell, and essentially reside.

20. And it hath pleased the Father, to reconcile all things to himself through him—making peace, by the blood which he shed on the cross, between the angels in heaven and men on earth, between whose union under one common head, sin stood as an obstacle.

21. And you, when you were alienated at one time from God—nay, enemies in your hearts and minds, offending him by your evil deeds, by your wicked and impious lives :

22. He has reconciled now by death, endured in his natural body of flesh, that he might exhibit you to his

Commentary.

born of the Father before all ages, begotten by eternal generation—his substantial image, by whom all things were made and are still preserved—that submitted to the ignominious tortures of the cross, for what?—to make atonement for the sins of his own creatures—the sins by which he himself was offended. He, though God, submits to tortures, which he could not merit, to free us, worms of earth, from the eternal tortures of the damned which we justly deserved. What excessive love ! *Sic amantem quis non redamaret.*

18. He now treats of him, as man ; as such, he is the head of his mystical body, the Church—towards her, he exercises all the duties, which the relation of head imposes on him, governing and vivifying her by the continual influx of his graces. He is "the beginning," which appears from the Greek, ὅς ἐστιν ἀρχὴ, to refer to the words immediately following, viz., "the first born from the dead." Hence, it means, "he is the principle and author of the resurrection."

19. "All fulness," *i.e.,* all perfection of wisdom, grace, power, befitting him, as head of the Church. He has the fulness, not only of grace, but of divinity. "Should dwell," perpetually, inseparably, and essentially. All grace befitting him as head, dwelt in him in the sense already explained, in order that from the head it would descend to the members, and that each might derive from him, as source, the graces necessary for his state and place in the body. The Greek word for "fulness," πλήρωμα, had a special significance, in the false system of the *Gnostics*.

20. The Apostle again refers in this verse to the other great prerogative of Christ, viz., that of Redeemer, to which he alluded before (verse 14). "The things on earth, and the things in heaven." He reconciled men and angels, and united them, hitherto so far dissevered from each other, under one common headship, having destroyed, by the blood which he shed on the cross, the chiefest obstacle to this union, viz., sin.

21. He now in a special manner applies to the Colossians what he had spoken generally in reference to all. They were aliens to the divine promises and benefits, and enemies to God in their minds, by their own wills, which was shown by their bad works, and their wicked lives.

22. "In the body of his flesh," not in his mystical body. Hence, their reconciliation was not effected by angels, as the *Gnostics* affirmed; but by the death of Christ endured

Text.

death, to present you holy and, unspotted, and blameless before him:

23. If so ye continue in the faith grounded and settled, and immoveable from the hope of the gospel which you have heard, which is preached in all the creation that is under heaven, whereof I, Paul, am made a minister.

24. Who now rejoice in my sufferings for you, and fill up those things that are wanting of the sufferings of Christ, in my flesh for his body, which is the Church;

25. Whereof I am made a minister according to the dispensation of God, which is given me towards you, that I may fulfil the word of God.

Paraphrase.

Father as holy and blameless, free from censure before men, and irreproachable before God himself.

23. You will be thus holy and irreproachable, provided, however, you remain firm and unshaken in your faith, and persevere unchangeably in the hope of the good things promised by the gospel, which you heard preached amongst you, the same that is preached to every creature under heaven, whether Jew or Gentile, of which gospel, I, Paul, am constitued by God the minister.

24. Who now rejoice in the sufferings, which I endure for your sake and for your good, because, by them I fill up and complete in the place of Christ these sufferings which he left to be endured for his mystical body, which is his Church.

25. Of which mystical body, or Church, I am made a member, according to the wise dispensation of God, by which I am constituted the Apostle of you, Gentiles, and fulfil the promise of God regarding your vocation to the faith.

Commentary.

in his body of flesh; or, natural body. These words clearly refute the class of early heretics who asserted that Christ assumed not a real but a fantastical body.

23. He will exhibit them as holy and irreproachable, provided they hold to the faith, and persevere in the hope of heavenly blessings, promised to them by the gospel preached throughout the world. He adds this, probably, in order to disprove the calumnious charge which the false teachers made against Epaphras, whose gospel they asserted to be different from that preached by the Apostles. St. Paul, in character of Apostle, and with the full weight of Apostolic authority, asserts, in refutation of this calumny, that the gospel preached by Epaphras, and by the Apostles all over the earth, perfectly coincided.

24. "And fill up those things that are wanting of the sufferings of Christ." In this, it is by no means implied, that anything was wanting to the sufferings of Christ, as a *sufficient* atonement. This would be heretical; for, Christ made not only a sufficient, but also a superabundant atonement. But although Christ did this, and would even wish to submit to every kind of suffering, necessary for the formation and perfection of his Church; still, it was the will of God, that to his Apostles and the ministers of the gospel he would leave much to be endured for his Church, and that in his own place, as the Greek for "fulfil," ἀνταναπληρω, implies. So that "wanting," (ὑστερήματα, *shortcomings*), does not regard "the sufferings of Christ," but wanting on the part of St. Paul to be endured for the Church. He, then, rejoices in having to undergo what was wanting to himself, or, on his own part, of the sufferings he was to have undergone for the Church, in quality of minister of Christ. Others, by "the sufferings of Christ," understand the sufferings which St. Paul himself underwent. These he calls "the sufferings of Christ," because Christ regards the sufferings of his members as his own, since they are parts of his mystical body. It was in this sense, he said to Saul, when persecuting his followers: "Saul, why persecutest thou *me?*" (Acts, xi. 24). Hence, as Christ, while here on earth, suffered in his natural body; so, now in heaven will he suffer in his mystical body, in order to apply to us the fruits of his passion. In this interpretation, "the sufferings of Christ," mean the sufferings which Christ endures in the members of his mystical body. This latter is the common interpretation; the former, nevertheless, appears the more probable.

25. He is constituted a minister of the Church by the wise distribution of the great Father of the family, who has allotted to him the task of preaching the gospel to the Gentiles, so as to fulfil the promise of God, &c.—*See* Paraphrase. Others, by "fulfilling the word of God," πληρῶσαι τὸν λόγον τοῦ Θεοῦ, understand, that he was appointed to preach the word of God fully, so as that there would be no nation left, to which the gospel would not be preached. This interpretation accords well with what follows.

Text.

26. The mystery which had been hidden from ages and generations. but now is manifested to the saints,

27. To whom God would make known the riches of the glory of this mystery among the Gentiles, which is Christ, in you the hope of glory,

28. Whom we preach admonishing every man and teaching every man in all wisdom, that we may present every man perfect in Christ Jesus.

29. Wherein also I labour, striving according to his working which he worketh in me in power.

Paraphrase.

26. Which vocation of the Gentiles is the mystery that has been hidden from all past ages and generations of men, but is now manifested to the Apostles and faithful of the new law.

27. To whom God wished to make known how vast are the riches and the glory of this great secret which is accomplished among the Gentiles, which has for object, Christ, who is the cause of your hope of eternal glory.

28. Whom we announce, rebuking every man living in ignorance and sin, and instructing every man in the perfect knowledge of God and of his mysteries, wherein consists true wisdom, so as to exhibit every man as possessing a perfect knowledge of the faith and gospel of Christ.

29. In discharging this duty I labour strenuously, exerting myself according to the strength which Christ powerfully exercises in me.

Commentary.

26. For the full meaning of this verse, see third chapter to the Ephesians.

27. "The riches of the glory of this mystery," is fully expressed in the passage referred to, viz., that the Gentiles were to be made "fellow-heirs of the same body, and co-partners of his promise," &c. (iii. 6), "which is Christ," which mystery, or, great secret has for object, all the leading events of our Blessed Redeemer's life, death, and resurrection. He is the cause and fountain of our hope.

28. "Admonishing every man," &c., i.e., every man that we can admonish, excluding no man, so as to be able to have every man within our reach, perfectly instructed in the mysteries of God. Happy the pastor of souls, who at judgment can exhibit those committed to his charge instructed in the necessary truths of faith ! But how few are there who can meet death with this confidence—how many are there whose little ones cry for bread, without one to break it for them !

29. "Which he worketh in me in power," may mean, which he worketh, or which is worked in me, by the power of performing miraculous wonders, confirmatory of the doctrine preached, or, the strong internal virtue conferred on him by divine grace.

CHAPTER II.

Analysis.

The Apostle commences this chapter by expressing his anxious solicitude for the Colossians, as also the object of this solicitude, which was to afford them the consolation that would result from their close union in the bonds of charity, and their perfect knowledge of the leading truths of Christian faith (1, 2).

He next cautions them against the deceitful wiles of the false teachers, both Gentiles and Judaizers. Against the former, he shows that Christ is the great fountain of all knowledge (3.) He encourages the Colossians to guard against their false reasoning, and by closely adhering to Christ, to persevere in the faith and Christian life, which they had embraced (4–8). He points out the means which the Gnostics would employ to seduce them from the faith, viz., false and erroneous philosophy, opposed to the true principles of Christian faith. These false principles of Pagan philosophy, they should reject, and have recourse to Christ, in whom, as God, was eminently contained all knowledge, who is also the ruler of all the hosts of angels, and, therefore, to be adored before them (8–10). Against the Jewish zealots, who proclaimed the necessity of circumcision, and the legal ceremonies, he reminds the Colossians that the circumcision which they received in baptism as far surpassed that of the Jews, as the reality exceeds the sign (11, 12).

He ascends to the source of their spiritual blessings, viz., redemption through Christ, and graphically describes the mode in which redemption was accomplished, and the triumph which Christ achieved over the whole hosts of demons, driving them before his triumphal car, as so many trophies of victory (13, 14, 15). From the foregoing he infers, that the Colossians should pay attention neither to the Judaizers, who endeavoured to turn them aside from these real blessings to vain, empty shadows (16, 17), nor to the Simonians or Gnostics, who encouraged the false worship of angels (18)—and adhered not to Christ, the head of the Church, from whom she derived all graces (19). He concludes the chapter, by mildly rebuking the Colossians for attending to the false teaching of either the Gnostics or Judaizers.

Text.

1. FOR I would have you know, what manner of care I have for you and for them that are at Laodicea, and whosoever have not seen my face in the flesh :

Paraphrase.

1. For, I wish to make known to you my anxiety and solicitude for you and the people of Laodicea, and for all others, who, as well as you, have never seen me.

Commentary.

1. "For" is a connecting link between this and the last verse of the preceding chapter, as if he said : I have made mention of my labours and exertions, because I wish you to know the struggle I sustain for you.

"What manner of care." In Greek, ἀγῶνα, *what a struggle or contest*. From this verse, it is commonly inferred that St. Paul, although he visited some part of Phrygia, had never been at Colossæ. Theodoret, however, comes to an opposite conclusion ; but, his inference is very improbable.

Text.

2. That their hearts may be comforted being instructed in charity, and unto all riches of fulness of understanding, unto the knowledge of the mystery of God the Father and of Christ Jesus:

3. In whom are hid all the treasures of wisdom and knowledge.

4. Now this I say, that no man may deceive you by loftiness of words.

5. For though I be absent in body, yet in spirit I am with you; rejoicing, and beholding your order, and the steadfastness of your faith which is in Christ.

6. As therefore you have received Jesus Christ the Lord, walk ye in him,

Paraphrase.

2. The object of my labours, and anxious solicitude both for you and them is, that your hearts may be filled with spiritual consolation, having been firmly united by the bond of charity, and furnished with the most perfect and valuable knowledge, and firm persuasion regarding those truths, that appertain to the mysteries of the Trinity and the Incarnation of our Lord Jesus Christ.

3. In whom—the man God—are concealed, in such a way as never to be communicated to creatures, all the treasures of wisdom and knowledge.

4. Now, I make mention of this great wisdom and knowledge of Christ, as a caution to you not to be deceived by the false and persuasive reasonings of others, who affect wisdom and knowledge.

5. For, though personally absent, still, I am present with you in heart and soul, rejoicing, when I see your orderly conduct, and the firmness and constancy of your faith in Christ Jesus.

6. As, then, you have been instructed in Christ Jesus; so persevere in his doctrine and in the observance of his precepts;

Commentary.

2. The end and object of his anxiety was, to procure for them true spiritual consolation, which is acquired by being united in charity (for "intructed in charity," the Greek is, συνβιβασθεντων, *united*, *compacted*, as joints are in a body); and also, by being *introduced to, or furnished with,* "all riches of fulness of understanding," *i.e.*, the fullest and most perfect knowledge and persuasion. The words, *furnished with, introduced to,* or some such expression, must be understood, to make full and perfect sense; it is implied in the foregoing Greek participle. "Unto the knowledge of the mystery of God the Father," who is the principle of the Godhead, one in nature, and three in persons; "and of Jesus Christ;" in other words, regarding the two grand, fundamental mysteries of the Trinity and Incarnation—the two great points in which the Gnostics wished to corrupt the faith of the Colossians. *charity* and *perfect knowledge* are means to obtain *consolation*. "Of God the Father," &c. In Greek, *of God and of the Father, and of Christ.*

3. "In whom are hid all the treasures of wisdom and knowledge." "In whom," as God and man. As God, his knowledge is infinite; and as man, he has the most perfect finite knowledge. "Are hid;" *hid* (ἀπόκρυφοι), is an adjective. "All the treasures" express the great abundance of this knowledge, &c. Nothing can escape him. In him they are "hid." No creature can fully know them. The finite share which we are capable of comprehending, is known to us from revelation. From Christ, then, is to be obtained all that knowledge of which the Gnostics boasted, as their *name* implies, and for which they wished that recourse should be had to other sources than Christ.

4. The Apostle now enters on the object of the Epistle, viz., to guard them against the imposing reasoning of the Gnostics. "Deceive," in Greek, παραλογιζηται, means, to *deceive by false reasoning, or sophistry.* "Loftiness of words," in Greek, πιθανολογια, *plausible or smooth language.*

5. He is present in "spirit," by his anxiety and Apostolic care in watching over their faith, and spiritual interests. "Absent in body," &c. Similar is the form of words (1 Cor. verse 3).

6. "Jesus Christ the Lord." In Greek, *Christ Jesus the Lord.* He tells them to persevere in the faith of Christ, taught them by Epaphras, at their conversion.

Text.

7. Rooted and built up in him, and confirmed in the faith, as also you have learned, abounding in him in thanksgiving.

8. Beware lest any man cheat you by philosophy, and vain deceit according to the tradition of men, according to the elements of the world, and not according to Christ.

9. For in him dwelleth all the fulness of the Godhead corporally:

Paraphrase.

7. Having been engrafted on him as the stock and root, and reared on him as the foundation, and confirmed in the faith which you have learned ; nay, advancing in grace and faith, with thanksgiving for so many distinguished favours.

8. (Since, then, by ceasing to be in connexion with Christ, you would be as so many trees without roots, edifices without foundations) ; Take care, lest any person deceive you, and rob you of your faith, by the display of false philosophy, which is no better than empty fallacy, calculated to impose upon us ; the teachings of which are not derived from the authority of God, but founded on the corrupt and false opinions of men, and grounded on elementary principles either false in themselves, or falsely applied, and altogether at variance with the doctrine of Christ, and, therefore, to be rejected.

9. Let no one seduce you from Christ ; for, in him, the entire plenitude of the Godhead dwells, really and substantially, or personally, in a manner somewhat resembling the dwelling of the soul in the body.

Commentary.

7. Under a twofold similitude of a tree, and of an edifice, the Apostle represents their close connexion with Christ. He is the foundation ; they, the superstructure. He is the root, and the stock ; they, the tree or branches. This verse is connected with the preceding, thus : persevere in his doctrine, &c., having been ingrafted on him, &c., so as to increase and advance in faith and grace with thanksgiving.

"Abounding in him." In Greek, *abounding in it.* The Vulgate reading is found in some of the chief manuscripts.

8. The philosophy condemned here by the Apostle is not the *science* of philosophy, the knowledge of human things derived, by legitimate reasoning, from certain fixed principles ; he only condemns the false and erroneous systems of Pagan philosophy, wherein were contained the most monstrous errors in matters appertaining to God and religion. It was a philosophy which, in reference to religion, was nothing but "vain deceit," which inculcated systems of belief, founded only on the corrupt inventions of men, transmitted from generation to generation ; founded on elementary axioms, either false or falsely applied, and outstripping the proper limits to which they could be applied. See, for example, the abuse which they made of the logical axiom, *quæ sunt eadem uni tertio, sunt eadem inter se,* in reference to the mystery of the Trinity. See, also, the moral axiom current with the philosophers, *expedit populos decipi in negotio religionis.* The "elements of the world," may, according to some, refer to the carnal outward precepts of the ceremonial law of the Jews, in which sense, the word "elements" is employed, chapter iv. verse 3, of the Epistle to the Galatians ; in this interpretation, he is here alluding, partly, to the errors of the *Judaizantes.*

"But not according to Christ." In this, he condemns the system of religion introduced by the *Gnostics* and *Judaizantes* ; because, they were opposed to the purity of the gospel.

"Beware lest any man cheat you." The Greek for "cheat," συλαγωγων, means, to *despoil,* or *lead away captive.*

9. The Apostle assigns the reason, why they should follow Christ, as teacher, in preference to those opposed to him, viz., because he is God : and hence, in him are all the treasures of wisdom and knowledge. He adds this rather than repeat the third verse, because it is the truth announced in this verse, viz., that Christ is God, which verifies verse 3. Hence, no other is to be heard before him. "Corporally," *i.e.,* personally. The divine Person has really assumed the human nature of Christ, so that the divine Person is alone the Person of his perfect humanity.

Text.

10. And you are filled in him, who is the head of all principality and power :

11. In whom also you are circumcised with circumcision not made by hand in despoiling of the body of the flesh, but in the circumcision of Christ :

12. Buried with him in baptism, in whom also you are risen again by the faith of the operation of God, who hath raised him up from the dead.

13. And you, when you were dead in your sins, and the uncircumcision of your flesh; he hath quickened together with him ; forgiving you all offences :

14. Blotting out the hand-writing

Paraphrase.

10. And you are abundantly filled by him with all gifts and knowledge necessary for salvation without recurring to the law of Moses or the philosophy of the Gnostics. And he is the head, the ruler and master of all the angels, and hence, to be adored in preference to them.

11. In whom, also, you have received circumcision, not like the Jewish circumcision, made by hands consisting merely in taking away the foreskin from the body of the flesh, but a spiritual circumcision, consisting in the destruction of sin, and of sinful passions, of which the circumcision among the Jews was but a mere type or figure.

12. You received this spiritual Christian circumcision, when in receiving baptism you were buried, and consequently dead to your sins, with Christ, in which baptism also, while emerging from its waters, you rose to a new spiritual life of grace, of which spiritual resurrection, faith in the omnipotence of him who raised Christ from the dead is required as a necessary condition.

13. And you, when dead in your sins, both actual and original, together with the passions flowing from orginal sin, were raised by him to spiritual life, by an effort of the same power by which he raised Christ from the dead, pardoning all your sins, through his merits.

14. Having first blotted out and abolished the

Commentary.

10. "Who is the head of all principality and power." He is the head of all the good angels, represented by the two orders referred to, inasmuch as he is their Lord, and rules them, to promote their happiness. This is added by the Apostle in opposition to the Gnostics, who inculcated the adoration of angels. This verse is more fully expressed (Ephesians, i.)

11. He cautions them against the Jewish zealots, who endeavoured to superadd the rite of circumcision to the Christian religion, and says, we have a circumcision which as far surpasses that in use among the Jews, as the reality, or thing signified, exceeds the sign and the figure. In the Greek, the particle, "but," is omitted, and the word "sins," added to the preceding clause, thus : *in despoiling of the body (of the sins) of the flesh, in the circumcision of Christ ;* a reading, according to which, the entire verse is understood without any antithesis of the circumcision of Christ, thus : by whom you were circumcised with a circumcision not made by hands, which consists in putting off the body of the sins of the flesh, in other words, in entirely laying aside the old man of sin, which is the circumcision of Christ, and not of Moses. This is a very probable interpretation.

12. He shows how this circumcision is effected by baptism. The immersion in baptism—the form, in which it was conferred in the time of the Apostle—is a type of our burial, and consequently of our death to sin, which death to sin it also operates as well as signifies ; and the emersion from the waters of baptism is also a type of our spiritual resurrection to a life of grace, which resurrection it also effects, requiring as a condition, faith in the omnipotence of him who raised Christ from the dead.

13. When they were dead in their actual and original sins as well as in all the evils flowing from original sin, he raised them spiritually, with Christ, and made them desert their former vicious ways, and live to God, "and the uncircumcision of your flesh," the sign, for the thing signified, the foreskin, for original sin, and the evils following from it.

14. In this verse, some Expositors say, there is reference to the abolition of the

Text.

of the decree that was against us, which was contrary to us. And he hath taken the same out of the way, fastening it to the cross :

15. And despoiling the principalities and powers, he hath exposed them confidently in open shew, triumphing over them in himself.

16. Let no man therefore judge you in meat or in drink, or in respect of a festival day, or of the new moon, or of the sabbaths,

Paraphrase.

sentence of eternal death, which had been recorded against us all, by the decree of God after the sin of Adam, and the same sentence he took out of the way and annulled, by nailing it to his cross, *i.e.*, destroying it, by the atonement and satisfaction which he made on the cross.

15. And stripping the entire host of infernal spirits, who were to be the executioners in carrying out this decree, of the dominion and power they had over man, he exposed them publicly to the gaze and derision of men and angels, triumphing over them thus prostrate and vanquished, by his own power.

16. Such, therefore, being the blessings purchased for you by Christ, have no fears about being condemned by any one for neglecting the Mosaic ceremonies, either in matters appertaining to meat or drink, whether clean or unclean, or in reference to festival days, whether annual, monthly, or weekly.

Commentary.

obligation which every Jew had contracted to observe the law of Moses. Hence, by "handwriting" they understood the liability to observe "the decree," or Mosaic law. Others, following the Greek reading, which is, τοῖς ζόγμασιν, *by decrees*, understood it to have the same meaning that it has in the passage to the Ephesians (ii. 15), "the law of commandments in decrees," which refers to the abolition of the ceremonies of the Mosaic law, and the substituting of "the decrees," or precepts of the Christian faith, in their stead. This interpretation, however, does not well accord with the next verse ; for, how can it follow from his abolishing the Mosaic ceremonial law, that he was "despoiling principalities," &c.? (15). Besides, the Mosaic law is never called a "decree ;" and if we desert the Vulgate reading, to which the Ethiopic version is conformable, and read, "by decrees," we must confine it to the Jews ; whereas, it is clear that the Apostle refers to all, by saying, "you," verse 13, "us," this verse. Hence, the common interpretation is far the more probable, which makes "handwriting" refer to the liability to eternal death pronounced against us by the "decree" of God after the sin of Adam, of which, by an unsearchable judgment of God, we were all made sharers ; and this liability or sentence is called "a handwriting," either because we ourselves, by actual sin, subscribed to the justice of this sentence of punishment, or probably, to signify that it is as certain against us as is the debt against the debtor, whose bond or note of hand is in the possession of the creditors. "Fastening it to the cross ;" this refers to the ancient custom of annulling bonds or covenants, by driving a nail through them. Hence, the words may be translated, *driving a nail through it by his cross*, *i.e.*, by the satisfaction made on the cross. All this, therefore, refers to the atonement which Christ made for the sins of all mankind, by his death on the cross.

15. These words are very expressive of Christ's triumph over his prostrate enemies ; he first stripped them of the power which they had over mankind, during the time that this sentence of death was hanging over their heads. He afterwards publicly exposed them to derision, dragging them after his triumphal car, or rather driving them before it, as so many trophies of victory. This public exposure of the devils is now made before angels and men, who see it by faith ; but it will be evidently seen, on the great day of judgment. The two orders, of "principalities" and "powers," are put for all the orders of demons. There is but one word in the Greek corresponding with the words "confidently" and "open show," εν παρρησια. The word, however, bears both the significations, given to it in our English version, after the Vulgate.

16. Having shown the excellence of our baptism beyond circumcision, and having pointed out the cause of its efficacy, viz., the redemption of Christ, the Apostle resumes the subject of the Mosaic rites, and cautions the Colossians against practising them. "In respect of," *i.e.*, in reference to, or in the matter of, a "festival day," &c.,

Text.	**Paraphrase.**
17. Which are a shadow of things to come, but the body *is* Christ's.	17. For, all these were but mere shadows of future things, and the reality, of which they were the figures, or rather, the body, of which they were the shadows, is Christ. Having, then, the reality, what need have we to preserve the shadows?
18. Let no man seduce you, willing in humility, and religion of angels, walking in the things which he hath not seen, in vain puffed up by the sense of his flesh,	18. Be not defrauded of the prize, for which you are striving, by any one wishing to inculcate prostrate humiliations before the angels and the religious adoration of them, intermeddling in things which he hath not seen, or pretending to visions and knowledge beyond his reach; inflated and puffed up without any cause or grounds for it, by his own carnal conceptions and ideas, as if they were revealed by God.

Commentary.

i.e., festival days observed among the Jews, in compliance with the ceremonial law of Moses.

18. "Let no man seduce you." In the Greek it is, καταβραβευέτω, *let no man defraud you of the prize*, or reward, for which you are striving. "Willing;" this word is connected, by some, with the foregoing word, "seduce," thus: let no man seduce you, however anxiously and studiously he may exert himself for that purpose. Others more probably connect it with the following words, "humility and the religion of angels," *i.e.*, affecting humility, or, wishing to make it appear, that he is consulting for the dignity of Christ, by denying that redemption came through him; and, hence, wishing that you should adore, and have recourse to angels. This is the interpretation given of the passage by those who maintain that the error which St. Paul is combating in this Epistle, is the error of those heretics who asserted that it was beneath Christ to undertake the office of mediator and redeemer; and hence, they assigned this office to angels. It would not appear, however, that this opinion is borne out by the scope and context of the Apostle. On the contrary, it would seem from the Apostle's proving in this, as well as in some of his other Epistles, the superior excellence of Christ, that his arguments are entirely directed against the class of heretics, who lowered the dignity of Christ too much, by placing the angels above him. It is, therefore, more likely, that the Apostle here refers to the errors of the *Platonists*, who extolled the angels above Christ. They believed in the existence of a sort of minor gods or angels, who, according to them, created the world, inspired the prophets of old, purified and redeemed the souls of men; one of these angels gave the law on Sinai, and was the God of the Hebrews. This latter error was maintained by Cerinthus; he also held, that at the time of the passion, the Son of God left the son of Mary and Joseph, and returned to heaven. Hence, they asserted that Christ was unworthy of being the mediator between God and man; and that this office, therefore, devolved on the angels, who should be adored by a more perfect and excellent rite than was due to Christ. [Ireneus, Theodoret, and Epiphanius record these errors of Cerinthus in their dissertations on Heresies.] That this was the class of heretics to whom the Apostle here refers, seems very likely, if it be borne in mind that at Laodicea, which was contiguous to Colossæ, there was a sect who propounded such doctrines, which were condemned, in the 35th canon of the Council of Laodicea. The words, then, mean, as in Paraphrase; inculcating humble prostrations before angels, and adoring them. "Walking in things," &c., prying into and intermeddling in things which they could not know, and pretending to visions beyond their reach.

OBJECTION.—How reconcile this with the Catholic practice of worshipping and invoking angels?

RESP.—There is no necessity for reconciling it, if we look to what the Catholic practice is. The worship paid by Catholics to angels is an inferior worship, *cultus duliæ*, which tends to the glory of God, in the same way, as the civil respect shown a viceroy tends to the honour of the sovereign, whom he represents. But, we never pay them the supreme worship, or, as it is termed, *cultus latriæ*, due to God alone. Now,

Text.

19. And not holding the head, from which the whole body, by joints and bands being supplied with nourishment and compacted, groweth unto the increase of God.

20. If then you be dead with Christ from the elements of this world; why do you yet decree as living in the world?

21. Touch not, taste not, handle not:

22. Which all are unto destruction by the very use, according to the precepts and doctrines of men.

23. Which things have indeed a shew of wisdom in superstition and humility, and not sparing the body, not in any honour to the filling of the flesh.

Paraphrase.

19. Not adhering to the head of the Church, Christ, from which the entire body of the Church, or of the faithful, supplied with life and animation, and compactly joined and fitted together, by the various joints, sinews, and arteries, grows with a divine increase.

20. If, then, by becoming Christians, you have altogether renounced all connexion whatever with the errors of Pagan philosophy, or, with the heavy and intolerable yoke of the Mosaic ceremonial precepts, why should you any longer submit to have these precepts taught you, and dictated to you, as if you were still to live up to such elementary principles?

21. Such are, for instance, do not touch, or taste, certain meats or drinks, and have nothing to do with marriage.

22. All such precepts as these serve only, in use, to the destruction of those who adopt them, having been enacted according to the doctrines and ordinances of men.

23. Such ordinances have, indeed, the appearance of true wisdom, as manifested in arbitrary, self-imposed practices of devotion—practices that have not the sanction of superior authority—in a spurious, false humility, which is but the sign of pride; in macerations of the flesh both unmeaning and excessive, and in the subtraction of the just refection and proper sustenance of the body.

Commentary.

in this passage, the Apostle manifestly contemplates the worship being paid to them which robs God of his glory, as appears from the entire context, and particularly from the words of the following verse—"not holding the head."

19. "Not holding the head." From this it appears clear that they rejected the true worship of God. From whom, as head, the entire body of the faithful were furnished with life and animation (of course, in the mystical body, he refers to the graces of Christ).—*See* Epistle to the Ephesians, iv. 14.

20. "The elements of this world," with which they now hold no more connexion than the living hold with the dead, are understood by some of the errors of Paganism; by others, of the precepts of the ceremonial law of the Jews. "Why do you decree," may also mean, *why are you decreed, i.e.,* why do you submit to be taught these precepts, as if you were to live according to them, and not according to the doctrine of Christ? The Greek word for "decree," δογματιζεσθε, will admit of either an active or passive signification. It may mean either *to dogmatize,* or *to be dogmatized.*

21. He probably refers to the errors, of which he treats in his Epistle to Timothy, "forbidding to marry, to abstain from meats," (iv. 3). We know, that some of the Gnostics held that certain meats were *in se* bad; also that marriage was *in se* evil.

22. This refers to the precepts, verse 21. The Apostle is here condemning those ordinances in reference to religion, that have no authority from God, or from the rulers of his Church—that are purely human, and, as in the present case, opposed to the commands of God. He regards either the ceremonial law of the Jews or the errors of the Platonists; but he by no means condemns the salutary laws of God's Church, of whose authority he is so jealous, "*qui vos audit, me audit.*"

23. The Apostle by no means condemns the fasting prescribed by the Church, and which Christ our Lord has sanctioned, "but you when you fast," &c.—(Matt. vi. 17). Our fasts are regulated by prudence; and instead of being commanded, fasting is prohibited, whenever it would interfere with our duties in life. It is a "reasonable service,"

Commentary.

as enjoined by the Church. This very passage is an argument in favour of the Catholic practice ; for, these practices must be true wisdom, the appearance of which the others affected. If they were not regarded as good and praiseworthy, even in the days of the Apostle, why should the heretics affect them, in order to appear more holy? And why should the Apostle say, that they had the appearance of wisdom? Was it not because their prudent and proper exercise was true and solid wisdom, perfectly in accordance with the Gospel?

CHAPTER III.

Analysis.

The Apostle had made a twofold assertion in verses 12 and 13 of the preceding chapter, viz., that the Colossians were buried with Christ in baptism, and had also risen with him. This twofold assertion he makes the ground of a twofold conclusion. Having already pointed out the conclusion to be drawn from their death in baptism from verse 20 of preceding chapter, he points out in this, the moral conclusion to be drawn from their spiritual resurrection, viz., that they should devote their entire thoughts to the things of heaven, and despise the things of earth (1, 2). They should despise earthly things, because dead to them, and love heavenly things, because raised to a heavenly life (3). He points out the glory which is to be the reward of this life of sanctity (4). In order to secure this heavenly glory, they should, therefore, mortify all the members of the old man of sin, all the vicious inclinations of the flesh, the heart, or the tongue, in one word, they should strip themselves of the old man with his deeds (5-9).

They should, after putting off the old man, put on the new man with all his virtues, which relates to God, their neighbour, and themselves. With reference to God, they should conform to his image, by being renewed in the knowledge and love of him, in which spiritual renovation there is no distinction whatever of persons, or, conditions in life recognised by the Lord (10, 11). With reference to their neighbour, they should exhibit the new man in the most tender feelings of mercy—in bearing with his infirmities, in pardoning offences, and above all, in cultivating charity and peace (12-15). With reference to the duties they owed themselves, they should, by sedulous attention to the word of God, fill their minds with true wisdom ; they should express their inward joy and preserve spiritual unction, by piously singing canticles and spiritual songs, rendering thanks to God, and referring all their actions to his glory through Christ (15, 16, 17). He concludes by pointing out to several parties—viz., wives, children, and slaves, the duties of obedience which devolve upon them ; while on husbands, parents, and masters, he enjoins also their correlative and reciprocal obligations.

Text.	Paraphrase.
1. THEREFORE, if you be risen with Christ, seek the things that are above ; where Christ is sitting at the right hand of God :	1. Since, therefore, by baptism you have risen with Christ to a spiritual resurrection, seek and love the things that are above, that appertain to heaven, where Christ, after rising from the dead, is sitting at the right hand of God.

Commentary.

1, 2. "If you be risen," means : *whereas,* you are risen with Christ. In this verse the Apostle draws his moral conclusion from their spiritual resurrection out of the grave

Text.	Paraphrase.
2. Mind the things that are above, not the things that are upon the earth.	2. Have your minds and your thoughts fixed upon the things of heaven and not upon the things of earth.
3. For you are dead; and your life is hid with Christ in God.	3. You should have no concern about earthly things, on the contrary, you should undervalue them, because you renounced all connection with them in baptism. But you should regard heavenly things, because by baptism you have received a heavenly life—a life now indeed unperceived by men, and hidden with Christ in God; but, it shall be seen at a future day.
4. When Christ shall appear, who is your life; then you also shall appear with him in glory.	4. When Christ, in whom and of whom we hold this spiritual life, shall appear and shall manifest his glory, then, you shall appear glorious with him, and then this life, which is now hidden, shall be conspicuous to all.
5. Mortify therefore your members which are upon the earth,	5. Mortify, therefore, the members, the depraved and wicked inclinations of your earthly and sinful man,

Commentary.

of sin, of which their emersion from the waters of baptism was a type. It is this: that they should bestow their entire care and affections, and all their thoughts, on the things of heaven.

"Where Christ is sitting on the right hand," &c. These words simply mean, that whereas Christ, as God, is equal to the Father; as man, he holds the most honourable place in heaven, being next to God in honour and glory, which is expressed by the Scripture, in accommodation to human conceptions, in the words—"Sitteth at the right hand of God."

3. In the foregoing verses, the Apostle made two assertions—viz., that the heavenly things were to be cared for, and the earthly, undervalued. He now assigns a reason for both. The immersion practised in baptism was a type of their burial, and consequently death to sin and the passions, which it effected at the same time, after the model of Christ's death and burial. They, therefore, should have no more connexion with "the things upon the earth," i.e., either the "elements of this world," or the vices of the earth, which he enumerates (verse 5), or perhaps both, than the living have with the dead.—Secondly, the emersion from the waters of baptism was a type of their spiritual life and resurrection, which it also effected, after the model of Christ's resurrection from the grave; hence, they should mind the things of heaven. But this spiritual life received by them in baptism is "hidden" from the eyes of worldlings "with Christ in God;" it shall, however, be manifested when Christ shall come to judge the world. How calculated are not these words of the Apostle to stimulate us to labour and suffer for eternal life, and have our thoughts fixed on heaven! We are called to eternal life; to the things that are above: our final resting-place, our country is heaven, we are enrolled, as citizens of heaven, where our fellow-citizens are waiting for us. Why, then, keep our thoughts fixed on this earth, this place of passage!—why, mere travellers, centre our affections on this inn, in which we are for a short time to reside, during the time that we are tending towards the lasting habitation, reserved for us in the vast and magnificent palaces of the King of Glory? "O Israel! how great is the house of God, and how vast the place of his possessions."—(Baruch, iii. 24). How frequently in our passage through life, during our sojourn in this land of banishment, should we not look forward to our lasting home, our true country in eternity, to which every moment brings us nearer, and how earnestly should we not labour to secure it!

4. Christ is both the efficient—the meritorious—the exemplary—and the final cause of our life of grace here, and of glory hereafter, and when he shall come to judge the world, then we shall appear glorious like him. "Your life." In Greek, our life. The Vulgate is, however, supported by many manuscripts and Fathers, among the rest, by Saint Chrysostom.

5. In order to appear one day thus glorious, "mortify your members which are upon earth." In his Epistle to the Romans, the Apostle calls all sins taken collectively, the

Text.   Paraphrase.

Text.	Paraphrase.
fornication, uncleanness, lust, evil concupiscence, and covetousness, which is the service of idols.	which are, fornications, uncleanness, obscene passion, all wicked desires, and especially avarice, which is the worship of idols.
6. For which things the wrath of God cometh upon the children of unbelief.	6. On account of which crimes the heavy anger and vengeance of God is in store for, and will at a future day be inflicted on, those who have no faith and disobeys the commands of God, prohibiting such crimes.
7. In which you also walked some time, when you lived in them.	7. Which crimes you also committed formerly, when you lived in the habitual indulgence of your wicked passions.
8. But now lay you also all away; anger, indignation, malice, blasphemy, filthy speech out of your mouth.	8. But now lay aside not only these more grievous crimes, but also these others of lesser enormity, which you have also committed—viz., all angry excitement, all desires of revenge, all evil dispositions to injure your neighbour, all reproachful and insulting language towards him, all obscene and immodest expressions.
9. Lie not one to another : stripping yourselves of the old man with his deeds,	9. Lay aside all lies in your language, and all fraud in your dealings with one another. Entirely put off the old man with his wicked deeds.
10. And putting on the new, him who is renewed unto knowledge, according to the image of him that created him.	10. And put on the new man with his virtues, I say, that new man, who by the knowledge of revealed mysteries and of spiritual things, is renewed according to the image of God his Creator.

Commentary.

"body of sin" (vi. 6), and verse 11 of the preceding chapter of this Epistle, "the body (*of the sins*) of the flesh," as also "the old man," because as man, or the body of man, consists of different members ; so, is the body of sin made up of different kinds of sin, as of so many members. He calls them "upon the earth," because they fix our desires on earth, and withdraw us more from God. To the same he refers in verse 2 :—"Not the things that are on the earth." "Uncleanness," all kinds of unclean acts ; "lust," every kind of abominable passion ; .... "avarice." There is the same diversity of opinion regarding the meaning of this word here as in the Epistle to the Ephesians (chap. v. verse 6).

6. See chapter v., verse 6, to the Ephesians.

7. "Walked," and "lived," differ in this, that the former refers to acts ; the latter, to the habitual commission of such sins.

8. "But now lay you also away ;" lay aside the following sins of lesser enormity, as well as the preceding more grievous ones ; or "also," may mean, lay aside these other sins in which you also lived. Both meanings are united in the Paraphrase..............

"Blasphemy," here means, insulting and opprobrious language towards our neighbour. "Blasphemy," strictly speaking, which is committed against God, is a most grievous crime, and would have been classed with the preceding.

9. Lay aside all lying in your words, all frauds and circumvention in your dealings with each other. "Stripping yourselves of the old man with his deeds." In the Greek, ἀπεκδυσάμενοι, *having stripped yourselves*, &c., which may mean, cast away the foregoing vices which are members of the old man of sin whom you have put away at your baptism ; or, as in Paraphrase, it may be the commencement of a new sentence, thus :—In a word, I exhort you to put off the old man with his acts.

10. "And putting on the new." There is the same diversity in the Greek in this as well as in the preceding verse—"*And having put on the new.*" "Who is renewed into knowledge," *i.e.*, which new man receives a new existence, after the image of God, his Creator ; for, as man was naturally created after the likeness and image of God, which consisted in his intellect and will ; so, in his second birth, or creation by grace, he is formed after the image and likeness of God, which image of grace consists in sanctity and justice.—(Ephes. iv. 24). For the meaning of "old man" and "new man," and "putting on" the one, and "putting off" the other.—(*See* Ephesians. iv. 22-25.)

Text.

11. Where there is neither Gentile nor Jew, circumcision nor circumcision, Barbarian nor Scythian, bond nor free. But Christ is all, and in all.

12. Put ye on therefore, as the elect of God, holy, and beloved, the bowels of mercy, benignity, humility modesty, patience:

13. Bearing with one another and forgiving one another, if any have a complaint against another. Even as the Lord hath forgiven you, so you also.

14. But above all these things have charity, which is the bond of perfection:

15. And let the peace of Christ rejoice in your hearts, wherein also you are called in one body: and be ye thankful.

16. Let the word of Christ dwell

Paraphrase.

11. In which affair of spiritual renovation, there is no distinction of Gentile or Jew, circumcised or uncircumcised, of barbarian or—of worse than barbarian—of Scythian, of slave, or freeman, but Christ confers all Christian blessings, grace, sanctification, &c., on every description of men without distinction.

12. Wherefore, as men elected by God, sanctified by Christ, and loved by him from eternity—put on the most lively feelings of compassion for your brethren, gentleness and sweetness of disposition, humility, modesty, patience.

13. Bearing with each other's weakness and imperfections, pardoning and remitting to each other the injuries which you may have mutually to sustain, after the example of God, who has pardoned us our manifold sins and transgressions against him.

14. But above all things, have charity or love for one another, which is the most perfect bond of union.

15. And may the peace of God, to which you were called, when you became one body, victoriously exult in your hearts, and be ye grateful for the past benefits of God.

16. Let the doctrine of Christ permanently reside

Commentary.

11. "Where," *i.e.*, in which affair of spiritual renovation, or, in which new man, there is no regard paid to the circumstances of birth, nation, dignity, &c.; because Christ is all in all; he is justice, sanctity, and everything good in all who are thus renewed. The only thing regarded in it is, how far you have communicated with Christ. In this new man, the circumstances of country and condition are confounded; in him Christ alone is to be attended to. "Nor Scythian;" the most barbarous of the barbarians. The antithesis between "Scythian" and "barbarian," is not between barbarism and civilization, but between a lesser and greater degree of barbarism—the Scythians being reputed, in the days of St. Paul, the greatest barbarians. Others maintain the reverse, and contend that the Scythians were the most polished and civilized among ancient peoples. In this latter opinion, the force of the atithesis is quite clear.

12. As Christ alone is to be considered in this new man, the Apostle shows the duties they owe each other, and the acts of the new man whom he wishes them to put on. "The bowels," *i.e.*, the most tender feelings "of mercy." In Greek, *of mercies.* The Vulgate is, however, generally adopted by critics.

14. "Which is the bond of perfection," *i.e.*, the most perfect bond of union. All other bonds of human society are imperfect and easily broken by the slightest provocation; charity is eternal and indissoluble.

15. "Of Christ." In Greek, *of God.* "Rejoice." The Greek word for which, βραβευέτω, means either to gain the prize of victory, or to award it : in the former acceptation, it refers to the persons engaged in the contest ; in the latter, to the judges, who are to decide the struggle and award the prize. Here, then, according to this twofold acceptation, the words may mean :—May the peace which Christ brought from heaven, and to which the unity of the Church, of which we are members, obliges us, obtain the victory over all the adverse passions in your hearts. This is the more probable meaning. They may also mean : In all your differences may the decision be, not according to the dictates of passion, but of the peace of God. "Be ye thankful," besides the meaning in the Paraphrase, may also mean, according to some Expositors — Be ye kind, courteous, and civil to one another ; as this contributes much to peace. The Greek word, εὐχάριστοι, will admit this latter meaning, which also accords with the context.

16. He says that the doctrine and gospel of Christ should be engraved on our

Text.

in you abundantly, in all wisdom: teaching and admonishing one another in psalms, hymns, and spiritual canticles, singing in grace in your hearts to God.

17. All whatsoever you do in word or in work, all things *do ye* in the name of the Lord JESUS CHRIST, giving thanks to God and the Father by him.

18. Wives, be subject to your husbands, as it behoveth in the Lord.

19. Husbands, love your wives, and be not bitter towards them.

20. Children, obey your parents in all things. for this is well pleasing to the Lord.

21. Fathers, provoke not your children to indignation : lest they be discouraged.

22. Servants, obey in all things your masters according to the flesh, not serving to the eye, as pleasing men, but in simplicity of heart, fearing God.

Paraphrase.

in you, so as that you may be filled with the abundance of all spiritual wisdom, teaching and instructing each other in psalms, hymns, and spiritual canticles, singing the praises of God with joyous and grateful hearts.

17. Direct all your words and actions to the glory of God, invoking the name of our Lord Jesus Christ, and rendering thanks to God the Father through him.

18. Women, be subject to your husbands, according to the will of God, and as far as the law of Christ permits.

19. Husbands, love your wives, and be neither morose towards them, nor provoking them to bitterness.

20. Children, obey your parents in all things ; for such is the good will and pleasure of God.

21. And parents, do not, by undue and untimely severity, provoke to anger or exasperate the minds of your children, lest, falling into despondency, they cease to perform anything good.

22. Servants, obey your earthly masters in all things lawful, not merely serving to please them when they are present and their eyes are fixed upon you, as those do who merely wish to please men, but with good faith, with a sincere and upright mind, like men fearing God, whose eye is always upon us, and who sees the innermost thoughts of the heart.

Commentary.

hearts, so as to dwell there and fill us with the abundance of true wisdom, which we may dispense to others. Hence, the word of God is to be read, not with hurry or precipitancy, but with reflection and meditation on its sacred truths, so as that it may "dwell" in us, and not rarely, but frequently, "abundantly." Would to God, the meditation on the SS. Scriptures was substituted in place of those light and frivolous works of fancy, which poison and corrupt the mind ! "Teaching......in Psalms," &c. *See* chapter v. verses 19 and 20, Epistle to the Ephesians. "Singing in grace," may either mean with thanksgiving, or in an agreeable, pleasing manner, so as to excite feelings of devotion "in your hearts." In Greek, *in your heart.*

17. "To God." In Greek, *to the Lord*. This verse contains a negative precept prohibiting us from offering our actions to God through angels, according to the corrupt notions of the heretics, who prefer them to Christ, as has been already explained, or from giving thanks through them, and indirectly commanding us to do so through Christ. He is the meritorious cause of the benefits which we enjoy, and through Him thanks should be given ; it also contains a positive precept of referring our actions, occasionally, by a direct intention to God. The practice of referring them as frequently as possible is very commendable. For the rest—*see* chap. x. 31, 1st Epistle to the Corinthians.

18. "To your husbands." In the Greek, *to your (own) husbands*, as if to withdraw their attention from any other men.

20. "In all things," not prohibited by the law of God. "For this is well pleasing to the Lord," that is, this is pleasing to God as being his own precept.—(*See* Epistle to Ephes. chap. vi.)

22. He here addresses slaves, or those engaged in a state of slavery.—*See* Ephes. vi. where he uses the same forms of expression employed by him in this passage.

Text.	**Paraphrase.**
23. Whatsoever you do, do it from the heart as to the Lord, and not to men :	23. Whatever you do, perform it with cheerfulness, as if it were the Lord and not men you were serving.
24. Knowing that you shall receive of the Lord the reward of inheritance. Serve ye the Lord Christ.	24. Knowing from the unerring principles of your faith, that you shall receive a surpassing great reward, the inheritance of eternal life ; therefore, in serving your masters, offer the services to Christ the Lord, who will bestow on you the recompense of eternal life.
25. For he that doth wrong, shall receive *for* that which he hath done wrongfully, and there is no respect of persons with God.	25. But whosoever does an injury, whether it be the slave who is unfaithful to his master, or the master who is harsh and cruel towards his slave, will receive the punishment of his unjust conduct. For, God regards not the face or person of any man.

Commentary.

24. "The reward of inheritance." On this earth, slaves receive but a very trifling *recompense* from their earthly masters—the *inheritance* is reserved for the children. The Apostle, in order to render the slaves more prompt and willing in the performance of their duties, promises them, on the part of their heavenly father, an abundant reward, even the eternal, undying inheritance of children. "Serve ye the Lord Christ ;" for which we have in the Greek, *for, ye serve the Lord Christ,* as if assigning a reason why they should receive this eternal recompense. They would receive it, because in serving their temporal masters in a pious and Christian manner, they were serving Christ himself. The Vulgate reading in the imperative is well supported by manuscripts and versions.

25. "For he that doth wrong." In Greek, *but he that doth wrong.* Some understand this of the faithless slave ; others, of the harsh masters ; it may be better, however, understand it of both. "And there is no respect of persons with God." God will not regard the person of the master any more than that of the slave ; he will reward or punish both, according to their deserts. The words, "with God," are not in the Greek ; they are, however, found in several ancient manuscripts and versions.

CHAPTER IV.

Analysis.

After pointing out in the first verse of this chapter, to masters, the treatment which they were to give their slaves (verse 1), the Apostle, in the next place, points out some duties common to all Christians ; and first, he exhorts them to the duty of prayer in general, the conditions of which he marks out (2), and of prayer for himself in particular, in order that he might be enabled to preach the word of God with success (3, 4). He enjoins upon them to observe circumspection and wise discretion in their intercourse with the Pagans (5, 6).

He refers them for information regarding the state of his affairs to Tychicus, the bearer of this Epistle, and to Onesimus, whom he sent to bear him company (7, 8, 9). He conveys the salutations of several parties who were with him at Rome (10–14). He conveys his own salutation also to the Church of Laodicea, and enjoins on them to have the Epistle, which he sent to the Laodiceans, read in their Church at Colossæ ; and to have this read in the Church of the Laodiceans (15, 16). He admonishes Archippus to attend to the ministry entrusted to him, and concludes by subscribing his own salutation with his own hand, and by wishing them to be mindful of his chains.

Text.	Paraphrase.
1. MASTERS, do to your servants that which is just and equal, knowing that you also have a master in heaven.	1. Masters, treat your slaves with justice and humanity ; knowing that you also have a master in heaven.
2. Be instant in prayer, watching in it in thanksgiving.	2. Persevere in prayer, and be vigilant in exercising it with thanksgiving.
3. Praying withal for us also, that God may open unto us a door of	3. Pray also for us, that God, removing every obstacle, may enable us to announce boldly and

Commentary.

1. "Masters," &c. Several Commentators say, this verse should be joined to the preceding chapter, with which it is immediately connected in sense, and these make verse (2) the commencement of this chapter. "That which is just," by supplying them with clothes, food, and other necessaries. "And equal," by treating them with feelings of kindness and humanity, neither overburdening them with labour, but assigning to each one the duties he can perform; nor exacting the performance of the tasks assigned them with too much rigour, which is expressed—(Ephesians, vi. 9)—by these words, "forbearing threatenings." Others, by "equal," understand showing equal regard for all, so as to give occasion of jealousy to none.

"Knowing that you also have a master in heaven," a master, too, with whom there is no exception of persons, and who will treat them, as they treat their slaves, whom they should regard as fellows in servitude, and as having the same master in heaven.

2. In this verse, the Apostle points out a duty common to all Christians, the duty of prayer, the conditions of which he enumerates :—first, it should be persevering and urgent—"be instant," &c.; secondly, it should be performed with vigilance, attention, and devotion, "watching in it ;" thirdly, offered in a spirit of humility and grateful remembrance of past favours, "with thanksgiving." Gratitude for the past, and confidence of obtaining future favours, are the surest means of rendering our prayers efficacious.

3. "Would open to us a door of speech," by which some understand : Would remove all obstructions and impediments to our opening our mouth, and afford us an

Text.

speech to speak the mystery of Christ (for which also I am bound.)

4. That I may make it manifest as I ought to speak.

5. Walk with wisdom towards them that are without, redeeming the time.

6. Let your speech be always in grace seasoned with salt : that you may know how you ought to answer every man.

7. All the things that concern me Tychicus, our dearest brother, and faithful minister, and fellow servant in the Lord, will make known to you.

8. Whom I have sent to you for this same purpose, that he may know the things that concern you, and comfort your hearts.

9. With Onesimus, a most beloved and faithful brother, who is one of you. All things that are done here, they shall make known to you.

Paraphrase.

intrepidly the mystery of man's redemption through Christ (for the preaching of which mystery I am now in chains).

4. And that I may announce it in due and proper circumstances, so as to produce the full effect.

5. Behave with prudence and circumspection in your intercourse with the infidels, who are outside the Church, making good use of the opportunity which the present time affords you.

6. Let your language be agreeable, calculated to conciliate the good will of those who hear you, but let it be, at the same time, seasoned with wisdom and sound discretion, so that you may be able to accost and answer each person as may be fit and proper.

7. Tychicus, my dearest brother, who serves the Lord with me, and is his faithful minister, will inform you of the state of my affairs.

8. I have sent him for the purpose of knowing all about you (and of bringing me an account), and also for the purpose of consoling you.

9. I have sent him, with Onesimus, a most beloved and faithful brother, who is also a Colossian ; they will make known to you all things regarding myself and the faithful, and the progress of the gospel here.

Commentary.

opportunity "to speak the mystery of Christ," &c. "By a door of speech," some understand simply, the mouth ; that he would open my mouth, to speak and announce openly the mystery of human redemption. ("For which," &c.), some understand to mean : for which mystery. Others more probably, for announcing which mystery, &c., I am now in chains.

4. Two things are required for a true preacher of the word, to announce wholesome truths, and to do so in proper circumstances, as regards the time, the manner of announcing them, &c., both of which he should beg of God's Holy Spirit, who alone can open the hearts of the audience, and the mouth of the preacher, with effect.

5. "Redeeming the time," by which some understand, making good use of the present opportunity, which you have, of giving the infidels good example to the glory and edification of the church. Others understand them to mean : purchasing an exemption from persecution, by making good use of the present opportunity, which you have, of acting prudently in regard to the unbelievers. The Greek word for "time" καιρὸν will likewise mean, *opportunity.* The words may also mean : by redoubled exertions, redeeming and making up for the past time, which was squandered so foolishly, and even employed in offending God (*see* Ephesians, verse 16), where the same words are used.

6. He tells them that their language should be pleasing and agreeable, not too austere, as it might be otherwise repulsive, and might deter the infidels from embracing the faith. This, however, should not degenerate into levity or dissoluteness, but it should be seasoned with wisdom, of which "salt" is the emblem, so that in their discourse would be accommodated to the dispositions, circumstances, and inclinations of their hearers—a different mode of speaking is to be employed towards different persons.

9. Commentators here admire the prudence of St. Paul : he sends Tychicus to console and teach them ; but Onesimus who, from being a fugitive slave, became a Christian, receives no other commission except that of giving them all the necessary

Text.

10. Aristarchus my fellow-prisoner saluteth you, and Mark, the cousin-german of Barnabas, touching whom you have received commandments: if he come unto you, receive him:

11. And Jesus that is called Justus: who are of the circumcision: these only are my helpers in the kingdom of God: who have been a comfort to me.

12. Epaphras saluteth you, who is one of you, a servant of Christ JESUS, who is always solicitous for you in prayers, that you may stand perfect and full in all the will of God.

13. For I bear him testimony that he hath much labour for you, and for them that are at Laodicea, and them at Hierapolis.

14. Luke, the most dear physician, saluteth you; and Demas.

15. Salute the brethren who are at Laodicea; and Nymphas, and the church that is in his house.

16. And when this epistle shall have been read with you, cause that it be read also in the church of the Laodiceans; and that you read that which is of the Laodiceans.

Paraphrase.

10. Aristarchus, who is in prison with me, salutes you; so does Mark, the cousin-german of Barnabas, concerning whom you have received commendatory letters; receive him with kindness, should he come to you.

11. So does Jesus, who is called Justus. These three are Jews, and they alone are wont to assist me in preaching the kingdom of God, and they have been a great source of comfort to me.

12. Epaphras, a Colossian, a servant of Jesus Christ salutes you; he, also, assiduously and anxiously offers up his prayers for you, that you may fully and perfectly fulfil in everything the will of God.

13. For, I bear testimony regarding him, that he has much zeal for you, and for those who are of Laodicea and Hierapolis.

14. Luke, the most dear physician, salutes you, and so does Demas.

15. Salute the brethren who are at Laodicea, and Nymphas, and the Church, which is in his house.

16. And when this Epistle shall have been read amongst you, see that it be also read in the Church of the Laodiceans, and see that the Epistle to be sent to you from the Laodiceans be read in your church in turn.

Commentary.

information regarding St. Paul. They also admire the humility of the Apostle, this great vessel of election, snatched up to the third heavens, calling slaves by the name of "most beloved and faithful brethren."

10. Aristarchus was a Macedonian of Thessalonica. He suffered much in Asia with the Apostle, and he set out with him, when taken captive, to Rome (Acts, xix. 21–27). "And Mark, the cousin-german of Barnabas." This is the John Mark, referred to (Acts, xii.) on whose account St. Paul and Barnabas separated (Acts, xv. 39). "Touching whom," *i.e.*, John Mark, "you received commandments," or commandatory letters. Barnabas was too well known all over the church to require such; probably it was from Barnabas he received those letters, and St. Paul now adds his own recommendation, to show that he held him in esteem.

12. "A servant of Christ Jesus." The word, "Jesus," is omitted in the Greek. "Solicitous," in Greek, αγωνιζομενος, *suffering agony*.

13. "Much labour." In Greek, *much zeal*. "Hieropolis," a city of Phrygia.

15. "And Nymphas." This word is of the masculine gender, as appears from the Greek.

16. "And when this Epistle shall have been read with you, cause that it be read also in the Church of the Laodiceans, and that you read that which is of the Laodiceans," or (as in the Greek, τὴν ἐκ Λαοδικείας, *which is of Laodicea*.

It is a subject of much controversy, whether the Apostle, in the latter words of this verse, refers to an Epistle addressed to him by the Laodiceans, which he wishes to be read at Colossæ, or, to an Epistle written by him to the Laodiceans, but now lost. St. Chrysostom and others are of the former opinion; St. Gregory the Great, St.

Text.

17. And say to Archippus : Take heed to the ministry which thou hast received in the Lord, that thou fulfil it.

18. The salutation of Paul with my own hand. Be mindful of my bands. Grace be with you. Amen.

Paraphrase.

17. And say to Archippus, attend to the ministry, which thou hast received from the Lord, that thou mayest diligently fulfil it.

18. I subscribe my own salutation with my own hand. Be mindful of my chains, so as to pray for me, and receive strength and courage after my example. Grace be with you. Amen.

Commentary.

Thomas of Aquin, St. Anselm, and others, are of the latter. Before we embrace or reject either opinion, it is to be observed, that there is no doubt whatever entertained of the spuriousness of the Epistle published by Sixtus Senensis, under the title of "the Epistle to the Laodiceans," as it is agreed on all hands, that it is not the Epistle here referred to, supposing the opinion of St. Thomas to be the correct one. This Epistle is given by A'Lapide, in his commentary on this verse. It bears evident internal marks of spuriousness. It is shorter than the Epistle to Philemon, and is nothing more than a collection of expressions used by the Apostle in his several Epistles, particularly in his Epistles to the Ephesians and Philippians, strung together by some impostor. Nor, is there question of an "Epistle to the Laodiceans" in circulation in the days of St. Jerome, which he, as well as Theodoret, assures us, was exploded by all, "*ab omnibus exploditur*" (Hieron. in Catalog.), and of which the seventh General Council says, *Epistolam ad Laodicenses Apostolo adscriptam, patres nostri, tanquam alienam, reprobaverunt.* Whether this latter Epistle be the same with the one now in circulation, published by Sixtus Senensis, is a matter of doubt ; it is quite certain, however, that the latter is, like the former, spurious and supposititious.

The question, therefore, is : Did the Apostle write an Epistle to the Laodiceans, which must consequently have been lost ? The opinion of St. Thomas, who maintains that he did, and that reference is made to the same in this verse, seems the more probable. This is inferred in the first place, from the absence of all probability, that the Laodiceans, who had never seen St. Paul, would have written to him ; and even supposing them to have done so, what reason can there be why St. Paul would call on the Colossians to have that letter read in their own church in the same way as this letter of his own to the Colossians was to be read in the Church of Laodicea ? The reason given by Estius, viz., that the Epistle of the Laodiceans to St. Paul had contained an illustrious testimony of their faith and charity, which, being made known at Colossæ by the reading of this letter, would stimulate the Colossians to the practice of the same virtues, cannot be considered as having any weight ; because, Colossæ and Laodicea being scarcely three leagues asunder, the Colossians needed not to be informed from Italy, whence St. Paul wrote this Epistle, from his prison at Rome, of what was going on in their vicinity among the brethren in the faith.

Again, is it to be supposed, that St. Paul, who expressed so much anxiety for the Laodiceans, in common with the other churches which were never favoured with his personal presence, would omit sending them an Epistle in reply to the one which they are supposed in the other opinion to have sent him, particularly when he had written to so many churches, from which he received no previous communication at all ?

Moreover, unless St. Paul had written to the Laodiceans in some form or other, telling them to send their Epistle to be read at Colossæ, as is here enjoined on the Colossians regarding them, they, surely, would not have sent it of their own accord, or, if they had already sent it, of their own accord, what necessity was there for the Apostle to admonish the Colossians to read an Epistle which had been already sent for that purpose. Hence, in any supposition, the Apostle must have written an Epistle to the Laodiceans. The Greek text, then, upon which the advocates of the opposite opinion chiefly rely, *that from Laodicea*, must mean, "the Epistle (*to be sent you*) *from Laodicea.*" The evident motive of the Apostle's injunction was this : Laodicea and Colossæ were neighbouring cities, troubled by the same false teachers. It is likely, that in his Epistle

Commentary.

to the Laodiceans, the Apostle treated of matters of which he made no mention in that addressed·to the Colossians, or, at least, that he had treated of the same matter differently in both.   Hence, by having the two Epistles read in both churches, the faithful of each would have a more complete exposition of faith and morals, and stronger motives for perseverance in the faith, and in the performance of good works.   And the fact of the Apostle telling the Colossians to have the Epistle of the Laodiceans read in their church, in the same way as this was to be read in the church of the Laodiceans, would evidently imply that the reading of both would be attended with results equally beneficial, which could hardly be said, if there were question in one case, of an Epistle, written by the Laodiceans to him.   These are the reasons for the opinion of St. Thomas, as given by Mauduit.   It must, however, be admitted, that the opinion of St. Chrysostom is the more common with both ancient and modern Expositors of SS. Scripture.

FIRST EPISTLE

OF

ST. PAUL TO THE THESSALONIANS.

Introduction.

THESSALONICA—now called Salonica—was the Capital of Macedonia. The history of St. Paul's arrival at Thessalonica, of the success of his preaching there, is recorded in the Acts of the Apostles (chap. xvii.) After leaving Philippi, the Apostle, accompanied by Silas, came, about the year 50, to Thessalonica, and preached, for three sabbath days, in the Jewish synagogue. The fruit of his preaching was the conversion of some among the Jews, and of a great multitude of the Gentiles, among whom were many women of quality. This excited the envy of the Jews; and in consequence, tumults were excited by them over the whole city; the Apostle was, therefore, forced to fly to Berea. Having preached there for some time with success, he was obliged to depart, owing to the same spirit of jealousy; he then came to Athens. The Thessalonians were, in the meantime, subjected to much persecution, and had to endure many privations for the faith. The Apostle, having been informed of this, began to entertain fears and anxiety for their perseverance; and in consequence, sent Timothy from Athens to console and confirm them in the true doctrine of Christ. Timothy, after discharging the duties of his mission, returned to St. Paul, who was now at Corinth (for he remained but a very short time at Athens), and bore a most consoling and satisfactory testimony regarding the unshaken firmness of their faith.

Hence, the OCCASION OF THIS EPISTLE.—In the three first chapters, the Apostle congratulates the Thessalonians on their unshaken constancy and firmness in the faith; and brings forward the most engaging motives to encourage them to persever- ance. In the two remaining chapters, he inculcates certain duties of morality, particularly in regard to chastity and the marriage bed; he also treats of the general resurrection and other subjects, regarding which it would appear, as he had been informed by Timothy and Silas, erroneous notions were entertained at Thessalonica.

TIME AND PLACE OF.—It is asserted by the subscription of the Greek copies, that this Epistle was written at Athens. But the more common, as well as the more pro- bable, opinion held by Baronius and others is, that it was written at Corinth; for, Timothy had returned before it was written (chap. iii.) Now, it was to Corinth, and not to Athens (where St. Paul's stay had been very short), Timothy had returned from his mission, as is clear from chap. xxiii. of the Acts of the Apostles; hence, the date of this Epistle is fixed about the year 52. St. Paul preached at Thessalonica about the year 50; and that it was the first written by St. Paul seems clear, as we have no account of any other written at an earlier period.

FIRST EPISTLE

OF

ST. PAUL TO THE THESSALONIANS.

CHAPTER I.

Analysis.

In this chapter, the Apostle, after the usual form of Apostolical salutation (verse 1), *informs the Thessalonians that he never omits praying for them, whenever he addresses his petitions to God, to whom he returns thanks for the abundant gifts of grace bestowed upon them, as manifested in their faith, their patience, and operative charity. From these gifts, as well as from those displayed in their conversion to the faith, the Apostle infers their election to grace and their segregation from this wicked world ; and for this he renders thanks to God* (2–6). *He commends their constancy in the faith ; in this respect, serving as a model not only to Macedonia, but to the entire province of Achaia* (7). *For, the edifying account of their faith has been spread abroad, both in these places, and in every other place, with which they were in communication* (8). *He exhorts them to persevere in the same firmness and edifying constancy, in the expectation of the coming of Jesus Christ to judge the world.*

Text.

1. PAUL and Sylvanus and Timothy : to the church of the Thessalonians, in God the Father, and in the Lord JESUS CHRIST.

2. Grace be to you and peace. We give thanks to God always for you all ; making a remembrance of you in our prayers without ceasing.

3. Being mindful of the work of your faith, and labour, and charity,

Paraphrase.

1. Paul and Sylvanus (or Silas) and Timothy (salute) the assembly of the faithful at Thessalonica, called to grace here and glory hereafter, by the mercy of God the Father, and through the merits of our Lord Jesus Christ.

2. Grace to you and peace. We always give thanks to God for the favours bestowed on you all ; and we also, in our prayers, petition him for their increase and continuance.

3. Always mindful before God our Father of the works of your lively and operative faith, and of the

Commentary.

1. "Sylvanus," a Latinized form for Silas. The same who was chosen by St. Paul to be the companion of his travels, after the departure of Barnabas (Acts, xv. 40).

The Apostle unites him and Timothy with himself in this salutation, because, as sharers in his Apostolical labours at Thessalonica, they were beloved by the Thessalonians.

2. "Grace to you and peace ;" to which are added in the Greek, "*from God our Father and the Lord Jesus Christ.*" These words are not found, however, in the Vatican Manuscript, nor in the ancient versions. "Without ceasing," is commonly connected with the next verse ; because "always" affects both parts of this verse.

3. "Labour and charity." "And" is not in the Greek. The words mean, *the labour of your charity;* charity must therefore be operative, and must brave all difficulties. Reference is probably made to their labours, in rescuing himself in the tumult

Text.

and of the enduring of the hope of our Lord JESUS CHRIST before God and our Father.

4. Knowing, brethren, beloved of God, your election:

5. For our gospel hath not been unto you in word only, but in power also, and in the Holy Ghost, and in much fulness, as you know what manner of men we have been among you for your sakes.

6. And you became followers of us, and of the Lord; receiving the word in much tribulation, with joy of the Holy Ghost.

7. So that you were made a pattern to all that believe in Macedonia and in Achaia.

8. For from you was spread abroad the word of the Lord, not

Paraphrase.

labours which your charity prompted you to undergo, and of your patient endurance of afflictions and persecutions, under which you were supported by your hopes in the Lord Jesus Christ.

4. We give thanks to God, knowing your election by God to grace and to his Church here, and to glory hereafter, should you persevere.

5. Because our preaching of the gospel among you was not confined to mere words, but was sanctioned by miracles, by the plentiful and abundant diffusion of the gifts of the Holy Ghost, and by a multitude of other motives, calculated to convince you of the truth of the doctrine preached, as you yourselves know what manner of men we have been among you, having in view your conversion to the faith.

6. (Nor was this exhibition of zeal on our part without success); for, you became faithful imitators of me and of the Lord. You received the gospel, though attended with much suffering and persecution to you, with the joy of the Holy Ghost.

7. So that you have become a model, in this respect, to all the faithful, not only of Macedonia, but also of Achaia.

8. For, from you the word of the Lord has been proclaimed, not only in Macedonia and Achaia, but

Commentary.

excited against him at Thessalonica. "Before God," is by some connected with the words "faith, labour," &c.; and then it would express the characters of their faith, &c., and mean the sincere workings of their faith, &c. The connexion in the Paraphrase is more probable.

4. The reason why he gives God thanks is, because he knows, from what he says (verse 5), that they are predestined by God; and as this decree, predestining them, together with the spiritual graces bestowed on them in consequence, whereby they were enabled to perform good works (verse 3), were all gratuitous gifts of God, He should, therefore, be thanked for them, and the glory of them referred to Him.

5. The reasons from which their election was inferred by the Apostle are these, viz., the miracles ("but in power also"); the gifts of the Holy Ghost ("and in the Holy Ghost"); such as tongues, prophecy, &c., which accompanied the preaching of the gospel among them, as well as the multitude of other motives, calculated to produce conviction in their minds, "and in much fulness." This "fulness," which may refer either to the strong interior conviction of the truth of the gospel; or, as we have understood it, to the additional motives for producing this conviction, may have been founded on the Apostle's own conduct, his disinterestedness, his heroism in exposing himself to danger without any hope of temporal compensation, &c. All this, joined to the sanction lent by God himself, was calculated to produce the most firm conviction of the truth of the gospel preached. This conjecture is rendered very probable by the following words—"as you know what manner of men," &c., which show, that, in the preceding, he was referring to his own conduct among them.

6. They were imitators of our blessed Lord and of St. Paul, because our Lord preached his gospel, and submitted to insults and persecutions with joy and gladness, for the salvation of his people; and so did the Apostle.

7. They were a model to their own countrymen; and to those of Achaia, where St. Paul then was.

8. The words "spread abroad," not only mean that the fame of their faith was rumoured abroad, but also that it sounded forth in such a way as to serve as an example for imitation with all men, both believers and unbelievers. For, though he preached at Philippi before he preached at Thessalonica; still, his preaching in the

Text.	Paraphrase.
only in Macedonia and in Achaia, but also in every place, your faith which is towards God, is gone forth, so that we need not to speak anything.	also in every place with which you are in communication, has the rumour of your faith in God been spread, so that it is unnecessary for me to say anything regarding it.
9. For they themselves relate of us, what manner of entering in we had unto you; and how you turned to God from idols, to serve the living and true God.	9. For all to whom we converse regarding you, anticipate us in speaking of our advent amongst you, and of the success that attended us, and of your conversion from worshipping inanimate and senseless idols to serve and adore the living and true God.
10. And to wait for his Son from heaven (whom he raised up from the dead) JESUS, who hath delivered us from the wrath to come.	10. And to expect from heaven his Son Jesus (whom he raised from the dead), and by whom we have been delivered from the wrath to come.

Commentary.

latter place was more noted and more successful. "In every place," must be understood of those places only with which Thessalonica was in communication, owing to its extensive relations of commerce.

9. "To serve the living God:" unlike the inanimate blocks you heretofore adored, and "*true* God," unlike the false gods of the Pagans, either men ranked among the gods, or demons. *Omnes dii gentium dæmonia.*—(Ps. xcv. 5).

10. "Whom he raised from the dead." This being an act of power, is, by appropriation, ascribed to God the Father. The Apostle refers here to their faith in the second coming of God to judge the world. And although the dead who have long since slept in the Lord will accompany him from heaven; still, they may be said to be expecting him on earth, as their bodies are there. "Who hath delivered us from the wrath to come." From this the Apostle wishes them to infer, that those thus favoured beyond the unbelievers, who remain subject to eternal death, should persevere in this state of security, to which God has gratuitously called them.

CHAPTER II.

Analysis.

In this chapter, the Apostle adduces a variety of motives for consoling the Thessalonians, and confirming them in the faith—viz., the success of his preaching in the midst of persecutions—the nature of the doctrine preached (1–3)—the purity and disinterestedness of motive which actuated him (4–9)—and the sanctity of his life and conduct among them (10, 11). He praises them for the zeal with which they received the word of God, and the constancy with which they persevere therein (13). Finally, he expresses his great affection for them.

Text.

1. FOR yourselves know, brethren, our entrance in unto you, that it was not in vain :

2. But having suffered many things before, and been shamefully treated (as you know) at Philippi, we had confidence in our God, to speak unto you the gospel of God in much carefulness.

3. For our exhortation was not of error, nor of uncleanness, nor in deceit,

4. But as we were approved by God that the gospel should be com-

Paraphrase.

1. But I need not refer to my advent amongst you to preach the gospel, and the success which attended it, as a motive to confirm you in the faith ; you yourselves are aware that it was not without fruit.

2. You are aware of the difficult and trying circumstances under which we went to you. Although we suffered much persecution and were ignominiously scourged at Philippi, still we assumed courage, relying on the grace and power of the Lord, to announce to you the Gospel of God, with great personal fear and uneasiness.

3. (And not without cause have we trusted in the Lord, being fully conscious) that the doctrine we preached was not false or deceitful, neither did it announce obscene or impure things, nor was it in connexion with deceit or hypocrisy of any kind.

4. But like men whom God reputed worthy of the high commission of preaching the gospel, and, rendered

Commentary.

1. "In vain." By which some understand—*without tribulation;* because, it is of his tribulation that the Apostle is treating in the entire chapter. However, the interpretation in the Paraphrase is the more probable : this being the usual signification of the word in the writings of St. Paul (1. Cor., xv.), and in this Epistle (iii., 5). Moreover, in the preceding chapter, with which this verse is clearly to be connected, the Apostle is treating of his success in the preaching of the gospel among them.

2. After referring to the fruit which God accorded to his labours, he refers to the trying circumstances under which he went to them "in much carefulness." The Greek is ἐν πολλῷ ἀγῶνι, "*in much struggle,*" referring to the struggle he had with his enemies, or to his uneasiness of mind.

3. According to the Vulgate reading, the Apostle refers to the subject matter of his preaching as opposed to that preached by the philosophers : his doctrine was not false, calculated to lead himself or others into error, nor was it "in deceit," *i.e.,* a doctrine deluding others; such was the maxim of the philosophers : *that the people should be led astray in matters of religion.* According to the Greek reading, ἐκ πλάνης, *from error,* &c., the Apostle refers in this verse rather to the motives of his preaching. He did not preach with a view of leading them into error, nor with the impure motive of self-interest, nor of circumventing or deceiving them.

4. The Apostle preached the Gospel in a manner becoming men whom God judged

Text.

mitted to us : even so we speak, not as pleasing men, but God, who proveth our hearts.

5. For neither have we used, at any time, the speech of flattery, as you know ; nor taken an occasion of covetousness, God is witness :

6. Nor sought we glory of men, neither of you, nor of others.

7. Whereas we might have been burdensome to you, as the apostles of Christ : but we became little ones in the midst of you, as if a nurse should cherish her children :

8. So desirous of you, we would gladly impart unto you not only the gospel of God, but also our own souls : because you were become most dear unto us.

9. For you remember, brethren, our labour and toil : working night

Paraphrase.

fit for such a commission, we announced it with all sincerity and truth, not caring to please men but God, who searches the heart.

5. Nor did we at any time adopt the language of adulation, as you yourselves know. And God is the witness that we did not make the gospel the occasion of gratifying avarice.

6. Nor did we preach it with a view of gaining or seeking glory or esteem from you, or from any man living.

7. (And that we had no motives of avarice or ambition, is clear from the fact), that while we might, like the other Apostles of Christ, be a burthen to you for our support, or by exercising authority over you, we became like children amongst you, mild, unassuming, unconscious of our rights, like a mother nursing her own children, accommodating ourselves, to your temper and habits.

8. Thus having feelings of the liveliest affection towards you (as the mother has towards her offspring), we eagerly longed to impart to you not only the gospel of God, but also our very souls, if necessary, from no other motive except that of the purest love and affection for you.

9. (And how far we accommodated ourselves, like a nurse, to your weakness, you yourselves know). For

Commentary.

and rendered fit for so high a commission—in its pure, unadulterated truthfulness ; wishing to please God only, the Searcher of hearts.

5. He was wholly exempt from the vices of all those teachers, who, by adulation, please men and wish to make the gospel the means of accumulating wealth and promoting their own glory. The nature, then, of the doctrine preached, or rather the disinterested purity of his motives in preaching it, under such circumstances (2, 3), together with the total absence of any impure or sinister motive on his part (4, 5, 6), should be a strong argument of its truth, and a strong motive to induce them to persevere.

7. "Burdensome to you," refers to his right to receive maintenance from them ; or, according to others, to the right of exercising authority over them. This latter interpretation is followed ·by the Greeks ; the former is, however, the more probable. "Little ones," in the present Greek version is *νήπιοι, mild, gentle*—but the meaning is still the same. "As if a nurse should cherish her children"—in the Greek, *τὰ ἑαυτῆς her own children.* The Apostle opposes humility to the pride of false teachers. He employs a twofold metaphor, to express the feelings displayed by him in preaching the gospel to the Thessalonians. Some Expositors, in order to avoid a confusion of metaphor, connect the latter part of this with the following verse.

8. "So desirous of you ;" *i.e.*, as desirous of you, as the nurse is of her children. He opposes charity to cupidity. What a lively picture is given here of the true Pastor of souls—at one time, clothing himself, through a spirit of accommodation to the weakness of his people, with the simplicity, humility, and meekness of children, apparently claiming no authority ; at another, displaying the lively affection of a tender mother, dispensing the milk of holy doctrine in such a way, as to be prepared to give his life, and that from no motive of lucre, but purely from love and charity, co-operating with Christ in the salvation of those souls for whom our blessed Lord gave up his life.

9. The Apostle toiled at manual labour, for the purpose of procuring the necessaries of life, at the very time he was announcing the gospel to them.

Text.

and day lest we should be chargeable to any of you, we preached among you the gospel of God.

10. You are witnesses, and God *also*, how holily, and justly, and without blame, we have been to you that have believed :

11. As you know in what manner, entreating and comforting you, (as a father doth his children.)

12. We testified to every one of you that you would walk worthy of God, who hath called you unto his kingdom and glory.

13. Therefore we also give thanks to God without ceasing : because that when you had received of us the word of the hearing of God, you received it not as the word of men, but (as it is indeed) the word of God, who worketh in you that have believed.

14. For you, brethren, are become followers of the churches of God which are in Judea, in Christ JESUS: for you also have suffered the same things from your own countrymen, even as they have from the Jews.

15. Who both killed the Lord

Paraphrase.

you remember how we laboured and toiled, working day and night to gain sustenance, while at the same time we preached the gospel of God to you ; and this labour and toil we underwent to gain a livelihood, lest we should in any way be a burthen to you.

10. I call both you and God to bear testimony to the sanctity towards God, the justice towards our neighbour, the irreprehensibility towards all, that marked our conduct amongst you.

11. You also know how we entreated each of you (with the feelings of a father towards his children) to persevere firmly in the faith.

12. How we consoled you in your difficulties, and earnestly besought you to lead lives worthy of the God who called you to his kingdom and his glory.

13. Therefore (owing to our success amongst you), we give God thanks without ceasing, that when you received from us the word of God which we preached to you, you received it not as the doctrine of men, but (what it really is) as the doctrine revealed by God, who, by the power of his grace, wrought in you the conviction of faith.

14. It was owing to the power which God worked in you, that you embraced all the tribulation which you had to endure in consequence ; on account of which you are faithful imitators of the Christian Churches of Judea ; for, you suffered from your fellow-countrymen the same persecution, they had to endure from their Jewish brethren.

15. Who killed the Lord Jesus and their own

Commentary.

10. "Holily," may also mean, in doctrine and life ; "justly," without injury of exaction ; "without blame," causing no scandal to the weak.

11, 12. The Vulgate reading of these two verses is rather obscure. "As you know," *i.e.*, you also know, how we entreated each of you (as a father entreats his children), and comforted each of you, &c. The word "you" is redundant after "comforting," in the construction adopted in the Paraphrase ; a construction which, however, accords best with the Greek. Who hath called you unto his kingdom ;" *i.e.*, his Church, where they received the Holy Ghost as a pledge of glory to come, the hopes of which should encourage them under afflictions and persecution. In the Greek version, "testified" is read in a participial form, *testifying*.

13. "Therefore," all this being premised regarding his advent and success amongst them, and the purity of motive with which he preached, the Apostle now returns thanks to God for his success, and shows that his advent was not "in vain ;" as he asserted (verse 1). "When you had received of us the word of the hearing of God," *i.e.*, the word of God which you heard from our preaching it to you. "You received it not as the word of men ;" because, under the circumstances of persecution with which it was attended, they would certainly have rejected it, had they regarded it as emanating from man ; but they received it as "the word of God," who, by his grace, worked in them and made them receive his word with a firm faith. "Who worketh," may, in the Greek construction, ὃς καὶ ενεργεῖται, be also rendered *which works*, or *is worked in you*, &c. There is, however, but little difference of signification between it and our Vulgate.

14. Had they not received it as the word of God, and had they not been strengthened by him, they would never have submitted to so many persecutions on account of it.

15. The unbelieving Jews were the principal agents in exciting disturbances against

Text.

JESUS, and the prophets, and have persecuted us, and please not God, and are adversaries to all men,

16. Prohibiting us to speak to the gentiles that they may be saved to fill up their sins always: for the wrath of God is come upon them to the end.

17. But we, brethren, being taken away from you for a short time, in sight, not in heart, have hastened the more abundantly to see your face with great desire.

18. For we would have come unto you, I Paul indeed, once and again: but Satan hath hindered us.

19. For what is our hope, or joy, or crown of glory? Are not you, in the presence of our Lord JESUS CHRIST at his coming?

20. For you are our glory and joy.

Paraphrase.

prophets, and also persecuted us, Apostles; who, moreover, are hated by God, and opposed to all men whose salvation they wish to prevent.

16. While endeavouring to prevent us from announcing to the Gentiles the truths of faith wherein they may be saved, it comes to pass that they fill up the measure of their sins; for, the vengeance of God, which is to remain upon them for ever, is come upon them.

17. But we, brethren, separated from you, although only for a short time in sight and bodily absence, not, however, in affection, (for we cherish you in our hearts), have used our utmost endeavours in consequence of the great wish we have for you, to see you as soon as possible.

18. In consequence of this desire which we have of seeing you, we wished to come to you, and I, Paul, in particular, desired this; but Satan (our chief adversary) prevented me.

19. (And what wonder that we should eagerly long to see you?) For are not you, owing to your firmness in the faith, the subject and occasion of our hope, of our joy, and of our crown of glory, before our Lord Jesus Christ, when, at his second coming, he shall judge the world?

20. In truth, you are our glory and our crown.

Commentary.

the Apostle. Hence, the unsparing severity dealt out against them in this verse. He also wishes to impress the Thessalonians with the belief, that their patient endurance of persecutions will make them sharers in the sufferings of the Lord, of the Prophets, and Apostles. "And the Prophets." In Greek, *and their own Prophets.*

16. "To fill up their sins always;" as if he said, from this it follows as a consequence, that they fill up the measure of their sins. Hence, there is a certain measure of guilt, after which God will inflict summary vengeance on both individuals and entire nations. This passage also confirms the opinion of these Divines, who maintain, that there is a certain number of sins, after the commission of which God will not pardon the sinner. This, of course, will not arise from a *defect* of power in the Church to absolve him, but from the *want* of proper dispositions on his part, in consequence of the withholding of God's grace from him, in such circumstances. "For the wrath of God is come upon them to the end." The Greek reading is, *for the wrath of God has surprised them,* or, *come beforehand on them.* The perfect is put for the future tense, on account of the certainty of the event. The words may refer to the temporal destruction of Jerusalem under Titus, which was an image of the eternal destruction of the wicked;—"Unto the end;"—or, to the punishment of individual Jews in the hardness and impenitence of their hearts; for, with respect to the Jews as a body, it is the common opinion that at the end of the world they will be converted. "And so all Israel should be saved, as it is written: *There shall come out of Sion, he that shall deliver, and shall turn away ungodliness from Jacob.*"—(Romans, xi. 26).

17. "Being taken away from you." The Greek word, ἀπορφανισθέντες, means, *left in a state of bereavement.*

18. The devil prevented the accomplishment of the Apostle's wishes, by exciting the wicked passions of men against him.

20. Hence, looking to SS. Scripture, there is nothing objectionable in our invoking the Blessed Mother of God, as "*our life, our sweetness, and our hope;*" since, St. Paul here calls his own spiritual children, "his hope." Of course, if no such expression ever occurred in SS. Scripture, the Catholic prayer to the Blessed Virgin could be

Commentary.

explained in the only true sense attached to it—viz., the sense of intercession for us, since God has been pleased to dispense all his graces through her hands : *omnia voluit nos habere per Mariam,*" says St. Bernard ; and the same is the common opinion of Divines after him. Hence, she is termed "*omnipotent*" by some of the Fathers, without the slightest outrage to Christian faith or piety ; for, she is truly omnipotent, in the sense in which they employ the word, inasmuch as she *can obtain from her Divine Son,* who by nature is Omnipotent, all our requests. Happy he, who by the exhibition of a tender and filial devotion to our sweet Mother during life, shall have secured the patronage, at the hour of death, of this *powerful Virgin,* in whom no one ever confided and was confounded ! Jesus, alone, being God, is omnipotent by *Nature*—it would be the rankest blasphemy to predicate this of any mere creature, however exalted— Mary is omnipotent by *grace,* in the sense already explained

CHAPTER III.

Analysis.

In this chapter, the Apostle expresses his affectionate solicitude for the Thessalonians, in consequence of which he sent Timothy to ascertain their steadfastness in the faith after having been tested in the severe ordeal of persecution (1–5). He expresses the intense joy, which the cheering accounts regarding them brought back by Timothy had caused him (6–8). He returns thanks to God, the source of these blessings. He prays that it may be granted him to visit them once more, in order to complete the system of religious teaching, which he had commenced amongst them (9–11). He prays, that God may grant them abundant increase of faith and charity, together with the grace of persevering in sanctity, unto the end (12, 13).

Text.	Paraphrase.
1. FOR which cause forbearing no longer, we thought it good to remain at Athens, alone.	1. On this account, being no longer able to bear up against the desire with which we eagerly longed to see you, and being prevented from visiting you in person, we thought fit to employ the services of our dearest friends for that purpose, and remain alone, deprived of their society, at Athens.
2. And we sent Timothy our brother, and the minister of God in the gospel of Christ, to confirm you and exhort you concerning your faith.	2. And we sent Timothy, our brother, (although very necessary for us), being the minister of God, and our co-operator in preaching the gospel of Christ, to confirm you in the faith, and by his consoling exhortations, to animate you to perseverance.

Commentary.

1. " For which cause " has reference to the state of bereavement in which he was, and his anxious desire to pay them a visit, from which he was prevented by the wiles of Satan (ii. 18.)

" We thought it good." He employs the plural, " we," although he is speaking of himself, as appears from verse 5.

2. " The minister of God " to which the Greek adds, *and our fellow-labourer*), " in the gospel of Christ." " For your faith." In Greek, *concerning your faith.*

Text.

3. That no man should be moved in these tribulations : for yourselves know, that we are appointed thereunto.

4. For even when we were with you. we foretold you that we should suffer tribulations, as also it is come to pass, and you know.

5. For this cause also I, forbearing no longer, sent to know your faith ; lest perhaps he that tempteth, should have tempted you, and our labour should be made vain.

6. But now when Timothy came to us from you, and related to us your faith and charity, and that you have a good remembrance of us always, desiring to see us, as we also to see you :

7. Therefore we were comforted, brethren, in you, in all our necessity, and tribulation, by your faith,

8. Because now we live, if you stand in the Lord.

9. For what thanks can we return to God for you, in all the joy wherewith we rejoice for you before our God,

Paraphrase.

3. Lest any of you should be moved or terrified by those afflictions which have befallen you ; for, you know that, by our call to Christianity, we are destined to undergo suffering.

4. For, when amongst you, we predicted that we would endure the sufferings, which you know have since befallen us.

5. Wherefore, no longer able to bear up against our ardent desire of seeing you, and of knowing all regarding you, we sent to know, how your faith held out ; for, we feared, lest Satan, taking occasion from the sufferings you had to undergo, would tempt you, and that thus our labour amongst you would be rendered fruitless.

6. But now, after the return of Timothy, and the cheering account which he has given us of your faith and charity, and of the kind remembrance which you always make of us, and of your ardent desire of seeing us, which we in turn reciprocate :

7. From these joyous tidings we derived such consolation, in the midst of all the perils and tribulations to which we were subjected, as to forget them all, on account of your steadfastness in the faith.

8. For (although we are dying daily), we still are kept alive, and in joy, if you persevere in the faith.

9. For, what thanks can we return to God, for your firmness and stability in the faith, and for the very great joy, which we feel in God's presence on your account?

Commentary.

3. "In these tribulations," are understood by some of the Apostle's own sufferings. "I will show him how great things he must suffer for my name sake" (Acts ix.); by others, more probably, of the sufferings of the Macedonians, as these would be more apt to stagger their faith. "By many tribulations we must all enter the kingdom of God."—(Acts, xiv.) "And all who will live piously in Christ Jesus, must suffer persecution."—(2 Tim. iii. 12).

"We are appointed." In Greek, κείμεθα, *we lie*, which probably conveys a military allusion to sentinels at their posts.

4. In this verse, reference is made to the Apostle's own sufferings also. The greater the glory destined for us, the greater must our sufferings be. Hence, Apostolic men suffer more than others. The momentary and light sufferings of the present life will hereafter work in us an eternal weight of glory.

5. "Wherefore I also," &c. He now employs the singular number, to express the same thing for which he already had employed the plural ; verses 3, 4, being parenthetical, he resumes the subject, of which he had been treating in verses 1, 2.

6. "Related." In Greek, *evangelized*, conveyed good news.

7. The effect of the good news conveyed to him by Timothy was, "in all necessity," *i.e.*, perils and danger, and in "all tribulation," to forget all his sufferings on account of the abundance of the consolation which their faith afforded him.

8. Although the Apostle was daily in the midst of the perils of death (1 Cor. xv.) ; still, he valued these perils as nought, and he felt the joy of a man perfectly secure, as long as his converts persevered. So closely did he connect his own welfare, nay, his life, with their perseverance, that without it, he would not value existence.

9. "In all the joy," *i.e.*, the exceeding great joy. The second effect which the good news brought by Timothy had on him was, to make him render God thanks for it.

Text.

10. Night and day more abundantly praying that we may see your face, and may accomplish those things that are wanting to your faith?

11. Now God himself and our Father, and our Lord JESUS CHRIST direct our way unto you.

12. And may the Lord multiply you, and make you abound in charity towards one another, and towards all men : as we do also towards you,

13. To confirm your hearts without blame, in holiness, before God and our Father, at the coming of our Lord JESUS CHRIST with all his saints. Amen.

Paraphrase.

10. Constantly and most earnestly do we beseech God to enable us to see you, and thus complete the system of Christian faith, by either disclosing new truths, or more fully explaining those you already know; the suddenness of our departure prevented us from doing so.

11. May God himself, who is our Father, and our Lord Jesus Christ, direct our journey to you.

12. May the Lord increase the number of the faithful amongst you, and make you advance in mutual charity towards one another, and towards all men, as I abound in charity towards you and all mankind.

13. I also pray, that he may confirm your hearts in exterior edification, so as to be blameless before men, and in true interior sanctity in the sight of God and our Father, and that, on the day on which our Lord Jesus Christ will come, with all his saints, to judge the world. Amen.

Commentary.

10. "And may accomplish those things that are wanting to your faith." There were a good many points which the Apostle did not, in all probability, propound to them, or, at least, fully explain, in consequence of being obliged to leave suddenly, and or this sudden departure he would make up, by visiting them again. He might refer to the article of the resurrection of the dead, and of the day of judgment, regarding which he afterwards instructs them more fully. The Greek word for "accomplish," καταρτισα, conveys the idea of filling up the joints, wanting in a human body. Hence, he refers to a body or system of faith.

11. It is uncertain whether he went to them or not. It is more probable, however, that he did, as appears from the 20th chapter of the Acts, in which account is given of his second journey to Macedonia.

12. "And may the Lord multiply you," *i.e.*, increase your number, so that a greater number would embrace the faith. In Greek, *may the Lord make you to increase and abound in love.*

13. "Without blame," irreprehensible and free from all complaint before men, and "in holiness before God and our Father," *i.e.*, true and real holiness, "at the coming," &c., and this with constancy and perseverance, to the end. "Amen" is not in the Greek. It is, however, found in several ancient versions, and in some of the chief manuscripts.

CHAPTER IV.

Analysis.

In this chapter, the Apostle encourages the Thessalonians to perseverance (1); *he delivers a precept regarding the practice of purity, and the avoidance of adultery, and he adduces several motives to stimulate them to fidelity in this matter* (3–8). *He praises their charity, and encourages the poor to engage in some honest employment, so that by this means they would not abuse the liberality of the rich* (9, 10, 11). *Finally, he assuages their excessive grief for their departed friends, by propounding the doctrine of the general resurrection, the order and manner of which he describes* (12–17).

This and the following chapters are employed in such subjects of morality, as the Thessalonians, according to the information furnished by Timothy, needed instruction in

Text.	Paraphrase.
1. FOR the rest therefore, brethren, we pray and beseech you in the Lord JESUS, that as you have received of us, how you ought to walk and to please God, so also you would walk, that you may abound the more.	1. For the rest, therefore, brethren, we implore and exhort you in the name of our Lord Jesus Christ, that as you have received precepts from us, by word of mouth when amongst you, regarding the manner of living and of pleasing God, you would so live, as to observe these precepts, and by advancing in perfection, please him more and more.
2. For you know what precepts I have given to you by the Lord JESUS.	2. I have said, *as you have received from us.* For, you know what precepts of a holy life we delivered to you, in the name, and by the authority of the Lord Jesus.
3. For this is the will of God, your sanctification : that you should abstain from fornication.	3. Now, this is a summary of God's precepts, or the expression of his will, that you should lead a life of sanctity, a life free from all sins, but particularly from sins of impurity, or unlawful sensual pleasures.
4. That every one of you should know how to possess his vessel in sanctification and honour.	4. So that every one of you should be able to master and keep under subjection his own body, in sanctification and honour.
5. Not in the passion of lust, like the gentiles that know not God :	5. And not be the slave of the strong, impulsive motions of concupiscence, like the Gentiles that know not God.

Commentary.

1. " For the rest "—a form of transition usual with the Apostle, particularly at the close of his Epistles. The Greek copies want the words "so also you would walk ; " according to the Greek, the words, "that you may abound the more," will signify, that, not contenting themselves with mere precepts, they ought to practise matters of counsel.

4. By "vessel" some persons understand, the wife of the married husband. However, as St. Paul refers to the sins of luxury, as well in the unmarried as in the married state, it is better to refer it to the body of each person ; of course, not excluding those engaged in marriage ; and this meaning of "vessel" is common in SS. Scripture (1 Kings, xvi. 5), and also with profane writers ; because, the body is the receptacle of the soul, or the instrument through which the soul acts. "Possess" is frequently used to signify, holding the mastery over, and is here opposed to the dominion which lust, or his lustful body, exercises over the voluptuous man. " Honour " is opposed to those pollutions and defilements by which the Gentile philosophers (Romans, i.) are said to dishonour their bodies.

5. He shows, by the contrary, what "honour" is.

Text.

6. And that no man over-reach, nor circumvent his brother in business : because the Lord is the avenger of all these things, as we have told you before, and have testified.

7. For God hath not called us unto uncleanness, but unto sanctification.

8. Therefore he that despiseth these things, despiseth not man but God : who also hath given his holy Spirit in us.

9. But as touching the charity of brotherhood, we have no need to write to you : for yourselves have learned of God to love one another.

10. For indeed you do it towards all the brethren in all Macedonia, but we entreat you, brethren, that you abound more.

11. And that you use your endeavour to be quiet, and that you do your own business, and work with your own hands, as we commanded you : and that you walk honestly towards them that are without ; and that you want nothing of any man's.

Paraphrase.

6. And let no one exceed the limits of justice or circumvent his brother in this matter, by indulging in unlawful pleasures in violation of the rights of the father or husband ; for, the Lord is the avenger of all these crimes, as we foretold, and solemnly assured you, when present amongst you.

7. For in calling us to Christianity, the Lord has called us not to a state, or to the practice of impurity, but to a state, and to the practice of purity and sanctity.

8. Wherefore, whosoever despises these precepts, despises not man who propounds them, but God himself, from whom they emanated, who has given us, Apostles, his holy spirit, authorizing us to announce such precepts.

9. In reference to the subject of fraternal charity, unlike the preceding one, it is unnecessary to say anything regarding it : for, God himself, by the law of Christ, and the internal inspiration of his grace, has instructed you in this love towards one another.

10. For, you fulfil this precept, by excercising fraternal charity towards all the brethren throughout the entire of Macedonia, but we entreat you to make still greater progress in this brotherly love.

11. And to use your best exertions to be quiet, and not be interfering with the peace of others, also to mind your own business, and engage in manual labour, according to the instructions received from us, when amongst you ; also to live in such a way in your intercourse with the Pagans as to be without reproach, and not to covet the property of any one.

Commentary.

6. Some Commentators understand this of real property, and of injustice committed in business transactions. The article prefixed to the word "business" shows, however, that he is referring to the matter of chastity, or the exercise of marriage. Besides, "business" has this meaning frequently with profane writers. He assigns a reason why they should exercise justice in such matters, because God will avenge such crimes, "as we have told and testified." This solemn assurance was required, because the Pagans made light of crimes against chastity.

7. The second motive by which he deters them from the commission of impurities, is the reason upon which the menace on the part of God is grounded, viz., that by calling them to Christianity, he called them to a state of purity and sanctity which they desert, and not to the state of impurity, which they indulge in against his will and ordinances.

8. The third motive is, because such sins of impurity are committed as acts of contempt against God himself. These words, "who also hath given his holy spirit in us," may also mean, that these impurities committed against God's precepts, besides the contempt against God, from whom these precepts emanated, also involve a special contempt of the Holy Ghost, who dwells in the bodies of the baptized, as in his temple.

9. The words, "have learned of God," are expressed by one word in the Greek, θεοδίδακτοι and signify, that special unction of divine grace, inclining their wills to the practice of this precept.—(*See* 1 John, ii. 27.) "We have no need." In Greek, *ye have no need.* The *Codex Vaticanus* supports the Vulgate reading.

11. The Apostle now cautions them against idleness and curiosity. It would appear that some persons amongst them were going about indulging in idleness and curiosity,

Text.

12. And we will not have you ignorant, brethren, concerning them that are asleep, that you be not sorrowful, even as others who have no hope.

13. For if we believe that JESUS died and rose again, even so them who have slept through JESUS will God bring with him.

14. For this we say unto you in the word of the Lord, that we who are alive, who remain unto the coming of the Lord, shall not prevent them who have slept,

Paraphrase.

12. In reference to the dead, brethren, I will not that you should be ignorant of their condition, in order that you may cease from indulging in the immoderate excessive grief, in which the Pagans, who have no hope of a future resurrection, are wont to indulge.

13. For, if we believe (as we really do) that Christ has died and risen from the dead, so (ought we likewise believe) that he will resuscitate with him, and evoke from their graves, those who have died in the faith, and bring them to eternal life.

14. For, this I tell you, on the authority of the word of God, or of divine revelation, that such of us as will be left in life, or shall be alive at the coming of the Lord, will not anticipate in the glory of the resurrection, those who died before us.

Commentary.

searching into the concerns of others, to the total neglect of their own business, and while able to work, contenting themselves with begging, to the great disgust of the Gentiles, and the injury of the faith. Nothing could be so disgusting to the infidels as to see able bodied men going about as mendicants, when they might work, and this they would be apt to attribute to the Christian religion. The Apostle witnessed this irregularity himself, and he was informed by Timothy of its continuance. He treats of the subject more fully in the 3rd chapter of 2nd Epistle. "Use your endeavour," the Greek word, φιλοτιμεῖσθαι, conveys an allusion to the diligent exertions employed by the ambitious, in pursuit of honours and self-advancement.

12. It appears that the Thessalonians had indulged in immoderate and excessive grief at the death of their near relations, and deplored it as bitterly as they had done when in a state of Paganism, and when they regarded them as lost for ever. The Apostle proposes as a remedy for this abusive practice, the doctrine of the future resurrection of the dead—a doctrine already propounded to them, as appears from his referring to it at the end of the 2nd and 3rd chapters of this Epistle ; but they practically forgot it ; and hence, he takes occasion here to inculcate it anew and propound it more fully. The Apostle is by no means to be understood as censuring all grief for the dead, as had been done by the Stoic philosophers. Our Redeemer wept for his friend Lazarus, and among the crimes of the Pagans (Romans, i.) the Apostle reckons the want of "affection ;" and he himself would have sorrowed for the death of Epaphroditus (Philippians, ii. 27). He only censures that excessive grief which would argue ignorance, at least practical ignorance, of the doctrine of the resurrection. "We will not." In Greek, *I will not.* The *Codex Vaticanus* has "*we.*"

13. The connexion between the resurrection of Christ, and the general resurrection of all, is clearly pointed out by the Apostle (chapter xv. of his 1st Epistle to the Corinthians). It is worthy of remark, that in speaking of the death of Christ, he says, " Jesus died," lest there might be any mistake about the reality of his death, as if it were merely apparent ; whereas, speaking of our death, he says, "those who have slept," to console those in sorrow, whose friends were not lost to them for ever, but were merely in the condition of persons asleep, to be again roused and resuscitated ; and in SS. Scripture, death is frequently termed "sleep."—(Daniel, xii. 2 ; St. John, xi. 11). Hence, the usual form among Christians of saying, *he slept in the Lord,* to express, that a person *died,* because death is but a mere protracted sleep, as sleep is but a short death. For the same reason, churchyards are termed *cemeteries,* or sleeping places.

14. "We who live." He speaks in the person of those who are to be alive at the day of judgment. In this verse, the Apostle meets an error existing in the minds of the Thessalonians regarding the manner of the resurrection ; they did not imagine that it would occur " in a moment, in the twinkling of an eye."—(1 Cor. xv.) They thought there would be in it a succession of time, and that those whose bodies were corrupted would be resuscitated more slowly ; and hence, that they would see their deceased

Text.

15. For the Lord himself shall come down from heaven with commandment, and with the voice of an arch-angel, and with the trumpet of God : and the dead who are in Christ, shall rise first.

16. Then we who are alive, who are left, shall be taken up together with them in the clouds to meet Christ, into the air, and so shall we be always with the Lord.

17. Wherefore comfort ye one another with these words.

Paraphrase.

15. For the Lord himself (and not an angel, as on Sinai), after issuing his order to the angels to attend his descent, and after the archangel, in a voice louder than the loudest trumpet, shall have evoked the dead from their tombs, shall descend from heaven ; and those who died in the faith shall rise in the first place.

16. And after that, such of us as shall live till then, shall be instantaneously drawn up with them in the clouds to meet Christ, into the air, and thus we shall be always with the Lord (and enjoying his glory).

17. Wherefore, console each other in your grief for departed friends by this announcement regarding the resurrection.

Commentary.

friends more tardily in glory. He removes this erroneous impression in this verse. He says, "we who are alive," not but he knew well, that he would not live till the day of judgment ; but, he wishes to teach us by his own example, always to keep in view and prepare for this great day, which virtually happens at our death.

15. He now describes the glorious coming of the Judge, and mentions some circumstances calculated to give us an exalted idea of the glory and majesty that will attend him. "With commandment." The Greek word, κελεύσματι, properly signifies the shout of sailors or soldiers rushing in concert to battle, or of labourers encouraging each other to some common exertion. The Greeks retain the idea of command, and say, it refers to the command of God, ordering all the angels to be ready. "The trumpet of God," by a Hebrew phrase, means *the loudest trumpet* (*v.g.*) "The cedars of God," mean, *the tallest cedars.* It refers to the same thing with the "voice of the archangel." Whether the archangel shall use a trumpet or not is disputed. The more probable opinion is, that by the agitation or commotion of the air, he will cause a tremendous sound louder than thunder, like that caused by the loudest trumpet, which shall reach the dead in their graves ; this by the power of God, they shall hear. Hence, it is called in the gospel, "the voice of the Son of God." St. Thomas says it shall have an instrumental efficacy in resuscitating by its very announcement. It is commonly supposed, after St. Jerome, that it shall distinctly sound forth these words : *surgite mortui et venite ad judicium.* "And the dead who are in Christ will rise first." All the dead will rise at the same time, but the Apostle omits all mention of the resurrection of the reprobate, as it would not serve to console those who were in mourning. "First" does not mean that there will be any priority of time in the resurrection of the dead among themselves ; it only means, as the Greek word, πρῶτον, shows, *in the first place.* This event of their resuscitation shall take place before that mentioned in the next verse, that is, before they are drawn into the clouds.

16. "Then," *i.e.*, after the resurrection. The order which shall take place in the resurrection, though instantaneous, is conceived in the following way :—The Lord Jesus, accompanied with all his angels, whom he shall command to be ready, will descend from Heaven. He shall issue his command to the archangel, who, with a loud voice, like that of a trumpet, shall sound the signal of the resurrection. At this sound, all the dead shall arise—those who are then alive shall be changed—all the just shall be caught up into the air to meet the Judge, while the reprobate shall be at his left hand on the earth. The other circumstances are more fully recorded in the 1st Epistle to Cor. xv., and by our Redeemer—Matthew, xxiv. 29, &c. ; xxv. 31, &c. From this verse, some persons infer that the men living at the day of judgment will be changed into a state of immortality, without suffering death. This is the opinion of the Greeks, who understand the words of the Apostles' creed, *to judge the living and the dead,* in the same sense. Others say, that their death will take place *in raptu,* or, while they are being caught up

Commentary.

into the clouds. The more common opinion, however, is, that they shall die on the earth, probably, by the agency of the fire of conflagration, and that after death, which shall be only momentary, they shall, in common with those, whose bodies were long before corrupted and for ages mouldering in their graves, and who now have come forth from heaven or purgatory to resume them, be caught up into the air, to meet Christ in the clouds. This he says in order to show that the living will not be glorified in their bodies before the dead, and that this shall occur to all at once, " in the twinkling of an eye."—(1st Epistle to Cor. xv.) They shall all, in the first place, arise ; after that, they shall be taken up into the air to meet the Judge : he says, " they shall be taken up ; " for, although they can go there of themselves by the quality of *agility*, with which they shall be clothed ; still, they shall go thither, owing to a kind of draw or moral attraction to meet their Lord.

CHAPTER V.

Analysis.

After having pointed out in the foregoing chapter, the order and several other circumstances of the Resurrection, the Apostle tells the Thessalonians in this, that there is one circumstance of the General Resurrection, which it is neither necessary nor possible for them to know at present ; that circumstance is, the precise time at which it will occur (1). They know from faith, that it will come unexpectedly, and will bring sudden destruction on the wicked ; but it will not surprise, nor will it come unawares upon, the just, so as to find them unprepared, since, as children of light, they are always on the alert, always employed in the works of light, in hopes of the Lord's coming (2–8). He exhorts them to correspond with the designs of God in their regard, putting on the breast-plate of faith and charity, and the helmet of hope—to live in the expectation of salvation from the goodness of God, who gave us his Son for Saviour (9, 10, 11).

He inculcates, with regard to the people, the necessity of discharging certain duties towards their Pastors ; while, to the latter, he points out the duties which they in turn owe their people (12–15).

He enjoins on all the faithful to cultivate and exhibit spiritual joy—to practise assiduous prayer—to employ the gifts of the Holy Ghost with profit and discernment, and to abstain from all appearance of evil (16–22).

Finally, he beseeches God to grant them the gift of perfect sanctity both of soul and body, and recommends himself to their prayers ; he salutes them all, and adjures them to have this Epistle read to all the brethren. He concludes with the usual form of Apostolical benediction.

Text.	Paraphrase,
1. BUT of the times and moments, brethren, you need not that we should write unto you.	1. But as to the periods of time or precise moments at which this great event shall take place, it is not necessary (nor indeed is it possible) that I should write to you.

Commentary.

1. The word " times," denotes longer periods, such as years ; "moments," shorter terms, such as months, days, hours.

" You need not that we should write to you," as if to say, it was necessary for your

Text.	**Paraphrase.**
2. For yourselves know perfectly, that the day of the Lord shall so come, as a thief in the night,	2. For you know yourselves full well, from the principles of your faith, that the day of the Lord shall come suddenly and unexpectedly, like a thief in the night.
3. For when they shall say, peace and security; then shall sudden destruction come upon them, as the pains upon her that is with child, and they shall not escape.	3. For when the impious shall say, peace and security, *i.e.*, all things are quite secure; then, shall sudden and unexpected destruction come upon them, as the throes of child-birth come upon a woman with child, from which they will not be able to escape.
4. But you, brethren, are not in darkness; that that day should take you as a thief.	4. But although this day may come unexpectedly, like the approach of the nightly thief, still, it will not surprise you unawares, who are not unprepared for it, having been enlightened by faith, and free from the darkness of infidelity and sin.
5. For all you are the children of light, and children of the day; we are not of the night nor of darkness.	5. For, how could you be in darkness, you, who are the sons of light and the sons of day? For, we Christians, are not the children of night nor of darkness.
6. Therefore let us not sleep as others do: but let us watch and be sober.	6. Let us, therefore correspond with our calling, and not be, like the infidels, engaged in the works of darkness, regardless of the coming of our Lord; but, like men who are called to the works of light, let us be on the alert, and let us be sober.
7. For they that sleep, sleep in the night; and they that are drunk, are drunk in the night.	7. For the time suited for sleep and drunkenness is the night; hence, those who indulge in sleep and those who indulge in drunkenness, do so in the night (we should, therefore, not indulge in sleep or drunkenness, which are unsuited to our vocation, or to the time of our actions, *i.e.*, the day).

Commentary.

consolation, that we should explain to you the order and the other circumstances of the Resurrection referred to already; but the time you need not, nay, you cannot know.

2. *He shall come unexpectedly.* This is true of the death of each one, when the day of judgment for him shall have virtually arrived; and, although Antichrist will precede it, this, however, shall not be a sign so much of the precise time of Christ's coming, as of the approaching end of the world; and so far as the signs in the sun and in the moon, &c., are concerned, these may occur, probably on the very day of Judgment.

3. "For when they," the impious, "shall say peace," &c., because as it happened in the days of Noe, so shall men be eating and drinking, &c., at the coming of the Lord. —(Matthew, xxiv. 37).

"For," is omitted in the Greek. The example of the woman with child is frequent in the SS. Scripture. As she knows that she is to bring forth, but knows not the moment in which she may be suddenly seized with the throes of child-birth, so neither will the wicked know when the final destruction shall come upon them.

4. "Overtake," *i.e.* catch by surprise, so as to be unprepared for it.

5. "Children of Light," *i.e.*, called to perform good works, suited to appear in open light, and not followers of the works of darkness. "Light" and "darkness" are frequently used in the SS. Scripture, to signify *good* and *evil*. Christians are called "children of light," in allusion to the light of faith which they received, and because they are called to good works, forsaking the darkness of infidelity and sin.

6. From the metaphors of *light* and *darkness*, the Apostle takes occasion to exhort them to good works, to live up to their Christian profession, which will avail them nothing, but rather deepen their damnation, if, like Pagans, they indulge in the works of darkness. "Sleep as others do." The Vulgate has *sicut et ceteri*, "*even* as others do."

7. We should watch and be sober, in consequence of being children of light, because the opposite characteristics—viz., sleep and drunkenness—are peculiar to the

Text.

8. But let us, who are of the day, be sober, having on the breast-plate of faith and charity, and for a helmet, the hope of salvation.

9. For God hath not appointed us unto wrath, but unto the purchasing of salvation by our Lord JESUS CHRIST,

10. Who died for us; that, whether we watch or sleep, we may live together with him.

11. For which cause comfort one another: and edify one another, as you also do.

12. And we beseech you, brethren, to know them who labour among you, and are over you in the Lord, and admonish you:

13. That you esteem them more abundantly in charity for their work's sake Have peace with them.

14. And we beseech you, brethren, rebuke the unquiet, comfort the

Paraphrase.

8. Let us, therefore, who belong to the day (abstaining from these deeds which are signified by sleep and drunkenness), be vigilant and sober, putting on faith enlivened by charity, as a breast-plate, and the hope of salvation, for a helmet.

9. I say, we should put on the helmet of hope. For, God has not destined us for damnation, but for eternal salvation, to be acquired through the merits of our Lord Jesus Christ.

10. Who died for us, in order that, whether living or dead, we may live with him here a life of grace, and hereafter a life of eternal glory.

11. In consequence, then, of these cheering motives of your hope—viz., the death of Christ to bestow on us eternal life, continue to console one another, to edify one another, by word and deed, as indeed, you are already doing.

12. But we implore of you to reverence and respect those who are labouring amongst. you in preaching the gospel, and who preside over you in a spiritual capacity, and admonish you of your duties.

13. And treat them with more abundant honour by administering to their support in consequence of their labours amongst you, and this from a feeling of charity. Be at peace with them.

14. But, we entreat you, brethren, who preside, to correct the disorderly, who are causing disturbances,

Commentary.

night. On this account it is that men select the night for indulging in sleep and drunkenness. Hence, as these deeds are unsuited to our calling, or to the time of our action, we should wholly abstain from the works signified by them.

8. We should, therefore, as children of the day, perform the works represented, or signified, by vigilance and soberness; but, in order to do so, we should be cased in the Christian panoply; for otherwise, although sober and vigilant, we will not be able to make a stand against the powerful enemies with whom we have to contend. "The breast-plate of faith and charity." In the panoply of the Christian soldier (Ephes. vi.) The Apostle calls "justice" the "breast-plate," but it does not differ from this—for, faith animated by charity is "justice." "And hope of salvation for helmet;" since hope will raise and elevate our thoughts on high. Three things are necessary for us—vigilance, sobriety, and armour. St. Chrysostom excites to vigilance in the narrow way of salvation, which is beset on all sides with dangers and precipices, by the example of rope-dancers, and of those who walk on the brink of precipices, all whose senses are awake and on the alert; so ought it be with us in the way of salvation. We ought to be sober, free from all vicious affections; and for armour we should have faith, hope, but especially active, operative charity towards our neighbour.

10. "Watch," in this verse, means to be in this life, and "sleep," to be dead; hence, they have a signification different from that which they have in the preceding verses.

11. "Edify one another;" for the meaning of this word, *see* 1st Epistle to Cor. viii. 1. "As you also do," he adds these words of well-timed praise with a view of rendering his exhortation more agreeable.

12. He here addresses the people, and inculcates reverence and respect for their prelates and the ministers of the gospel.

13. "Have peace with them," *i.e.*, have no difference with your pastors. In the Greek it is, *have peace among yourselves;* a reading which is preferred by some, Estius among the rest.

14. He now addresses those who preside: "Be patient towards all men," whether they be "unquiet," "feeble-minded," or "weak."

Text.	Paraphrase.
feeble-minded. support the weak, be patient towards all men.	to console the faint-hearted under afflictions, to prop up the weak who may be easily scandalized, accommodating yourselves to their weakness, and to be patient towards all.
15. See that none render evil for evil to any man : but ever follow that which is good towards each other, and towards all men.	15. Take care that no one, in a spirit of vengeance, render evil for evil to any man, but always endeavour to do good to all men whomsoever, whether brethren or unbelievers.
16. Always rejoice.	16, 17. Under all circumstances spiritually rejoice. Pray without ceasing.
17. Pray without ceasing.	
18. In all things give thanks : for this is the will of God in CHRIST JESUS concerning you all.	18. Give thanks to God in all things (whether in prosperity or adversity), for, this is the will of God, that you should all do so, through Jesus Christ.
19. Extinguish not the spirit.	19. Do not extinguish the Holy Ghost in his gifts, by altogether prohibiting the exercise of spiritual gifts.
20. Despise not prophecies.	20. But especially do not despise the useful gifts of prophecy.
21. But prove all things : hold fast that which is good.	21. But examine all matters proposed to you by those who have the gift of prophecy, and retain what is good.
22. From all appearance of evil refrain yourselves.	22. Fly everything that has even the appearance of evil.
23. And may the God of peace himself sanctify you in all things : that your whole spirit, and soul and body, may be preserved blameless in the coming of our Lord JESUS CHRIST.	23. May God, the author of peace, perfectly sanctify you, so that your entire being, your soul, considered both as to its sensitive and rational part, and your body, may be preserved without reproach, at the coming of our Lord Jesus Christ, when he shall render to every one, according to his works.

Commentary.

15. "But ever follow towards all men." This is perfectly conformable to the precept of our Lord in the gospel, commanding us to love all men, not excepting our very enemies.

17. "Pray without ceasing." This, of course, is to be understood in this sense, that we should frequently and at certain times pray, and that the intervals of labour should be consecrated to God by prayer, and that our actions should be of such a nature as to be referrible to his glory.

18. "This is the will of God ;" is referred by some to the three preceding precepts of spiritual joy, prayer, and thanksgiving ; by others, it is confined to the precept of thanksgiving.

19. It appears that many pretended to the gifts of the Holy Ghost, prophecy, miracles, &c., who had them not, and that to prevent altogether, any such practices of imposition, the heads of the Church wished to prohibit the exercise of these gifts, in every instance. Of this the Apostle disapproves. Others interpret the verse, do not expel from you the Holy Ghost ; thus, as far as you are concerned, destroying him. The word "extinguish" has reference to the form in which the Holy Ghost is frequently exhibited in SS. Scripture—viz., that of fire.

20. For the meaning of "prophecies," *see* chapter xix., 1st Epistle to Corinthians.

21. There is question here of *private* prophecies, and of doubtful matters, which had not been defined by competent authority,— and the Apostle is addressing the rulers, whom he authorizes to judge of such matters, and reject or retain them, as they may think fit. Hence, this passage contains no argument against the *Dogmatic Decrees* of Councils ; for, in them, there is question of quite a different matter altogether, a matter defined by a competent authority.

23. "Your whole spirit and soul." He considers the human soul under two different respects, and as exercising different faculties. "Spirit, is the rational soul guided in its judgment by reason, and exercising the higher faculties of intellect and

Text.	Paraphrase.
24. He is faithful, who hath called you, who also will do *it*.	24. God, who called you to sanctity, is faithful, and he will perfect what he has begun, by giving you the grace of perseverance.
25. Brethren, pray for us.	25. Brethren, pray for us.
26. Salute all the brethren in a holy kiss.	26. In my name, salute all the brethren in a holy kiss, the symbol of charity.
27. I charge you by the Lord that this epistle be read to all the holy brethren.	27. I conjure you in the name of our Lord Jesus Christ, to have this Epistle read in a public assembly of all the faithful.
28. The grace of our Lord JESUS CHRIST be with you. Amen.	28. The grace of our Lord Jesus Christ be with you. Amen.

Commentary.

will. " Soul," the sensitive, concupiscible part, guided by sensation, common to us with the beasts. So that your mind, your will, and all your senses, external and internal, be preserved from the stain of sin.

The Greek subscriptions add : *The First to the Thessalonians was written from Athens.*"

SECOND EPISTLE

OF

ST. PAUL TO THE THESSALONIANS.

——◆——

Introduction.

THIS Epistle is nothing more than a supplement to the preceding, from which it appears that the Apostle had anxiously desired to visit Thessalonica, "to accomplish the things that were wanting to their faith."—(Chap. iii. 10). This was to be effected by a fuller exposition of the several points of Christian doctrine. Having been prevented from the accomplishment of this his anxious desire, he writes this Epistle to answer all the ends he proposed to himself by a personal visit. Before writing, however, a second time, he wishes to ascertain what effect the former Epistle had produced on them, and finding that some portions of it, particularly the part relating to the resurrection, had been misunderstood, and that his exhortation to the poor, to shun a life of idleness, and to refrain from undue curiosity, had been attended with no effect, he now writes to instruct them more fully, on those points. Certain false and erroneous notions respecting the near approach of the day of General Judgment, to which his own words (iv. 14–16 of the preceding Epistle) had given some colour of truth, had been industriously circulated among the people by the false teachers, who, in support of their own views, produced counterfeit Epistles of the Apostle, to the same effect. The consequence was, that many among the Thessalonians became quite unconcerned regarding their temporal interests, and the duties they owed society.

The Apostle employs the first chapter in pointing out the glory, which was one day securely treasured up for the faithful, and in denouncing the heavy vengeance of God, against their persecutors. The second chapter he employs in removing the false notions that were afloat respecting the near approach of the great day of judgment; and for this end, he minutely describes the character of Antichrist, whose coming must precede the day of judgment. The third chapter is chiefly employed in pointing out the necessity, on the part of the disorderly, of shunning idleness, and of devoting themselves to a life of labour.

TIME AND PLACE OF.—This is generally supposed to have been written a few months after the date of the preceding Epistle. The Greek subscriptions say, it was written from Athens. But, more probably, it was written from Corinth, where the Apostle remained for eighteen months, after leaving Athens.—(Acts, xviii.)

SECOND EPISTLE

OF

ST. PAUL TO THE THESSALONIANS.

—◆—

CHAPTER I.

Analysis.

In this chapter, the Apostle, after the usual Apostolic salutation, returns thanks to God for the exalted virtues of faith and charity which his grace enabled the Thessalonians to display in the midst of sufferings and persecution (1–5). He consoles them, in the next place, by pointing to the rich rewards in store for them—to attain which, however, suffering is necessary—and to the heavy anger reserved, as is meet, for their persecutors, on the day of judgment, when Christ will come in majesty to judge the world (5–8). He describes the coming of the Judge for the twofold purpose of punishing his enemies, and rewarding his faithful servants, in whose exaltation, after suffering persecutions and humiliations, he shall be glorified, and his power and goodness rendered conspicuous—(8–10). Lastly, he prays God to grant the Thessalonians perseverance, and the grace to perform good works worthy of their vocation.

Text.

1. PAUL and Sylvanus and Timothy, to the Church of the Thessalonians in God our Father, and the Lord JESUS CHRIST.

2. Grace unto you and peace from God our Father and from the Lord JESUS CHRIST.

3. We are bound to give thanks always to God for you, brethren, as it is fitting, because your faith groweth exceedingly, and the charity of every one of you towards each other aboundeth :

Paraphrase.

1. Paul, and Silas, and Timothy (salute) the Church or congregation of the faithful at Thessalonica, established by the power of God our Father, and by the merits of the Lord Jesus Christ.

2. Grace to you, and peace from God our Father, and from the Lord Jesus Christ.

3. We are bound always to give thanks to God for you, brethren, as is meet and just, because your faith is greatly augmented and confirmed, and the charity of each of you towards his neighbour, more and more enlarged and intensified.

Commentary.

1. " In God our Father." This shows the dignity of our vocation, which renders us the adopted sons of God, and brethren of Christ, his Son by nature.

2. The usual form of Apostolical salutation. The opening of this is the same as that of the first Epistle, except in the words, "our Father" (verse 1), which in the first Epistle is, "the Father."

3. "As it is fitting," *i.e.*, meet and due, as an obligation of justice, "your faith groweth," both in fervour and intensity, as was proved by their constancy in enduring persecution on account of it. And "their charity abounded," as their kindness to one another had shown. In the first Epistle, the Apostle recommended the Thessalonians for their faith and charity. In this, he commends them for the increase of both, "of every one of you." In Greek, *of every one of you all*.

Text.

4. So that we ourselves also glory in you in the churches of God, for your patience, and faith, and in all your persecutions, and tribulations, which you endure.

5. For an example of the just judgment of God, that you may be counted worthy of the kingdom of God, for which also you suffer.

6. Seeing it is a just thing with God, to repay tribulation to them that trouble you :

7. And to you that are troubled, rest with us when the LORD JESUS shall be revealed from heaven with the angels of his power :

Paraphrase.

4. So that we ourselves make you the subject of our boasting with the other churches of God, on account of your faith, and of your patience, under persecutions and tribulations.

5. Which you endure, and which God permits to befall you, to serve as a demonstrative proof beforehand, that he will one day exercise just judgment upon your enemies ; and that you may be rendered worthy of the kingdom of God, for which you suffer (and which no man shall ever enter, according to the decrees of God, without suffering).

6. I said, *as a proof that he will one day exercise just judgment on your enemies*), since it is just before God, that those who unjustly afflict you should, in turn, be visited with affliction themselves.

7. And it is also just, that rest and respite should be given to you who are thus unjustly troubled, with us, Apostles, when the Lord Jesus Christ shall appear glorious, on his coming to judgment, and shall descend from heaven, accompanied by the angels, the ministers of his power :

Commentary.

4. Instead of regretting and bewailing the tribulations of the Thessalonians, he thanks God for them, and makes these tribulations the subject of his boasting with the other Churches, to whom he proposes the Thessalonians, as models for imitation in this respect. He joins "faith" to "patience," because nothing so strongly animates us to endure the evils of this life with patience, as the faith of Christ, and the hope of future goods. "And in all our persecutions," &c. "And" is wanting in the Greek.

5. "For an example of the just judgment of God." "For" is wanting in the Greek, which runs thus : *an example of the just*, &c. There is a diversity of opinion regarding the meaning of the word "example." If we look to the meaning of the Greek word, Ἐνδειγμα, it means *a demonstration or proof beforehand*, as if the Apostle meant to convey that the sufferings referred to were permitted by God for a twofold end : first, that these sufferings, or the men themselves thus afflicted, might serve as a convincing demonstration or proof even beforehand, that God would, one day, exercise a just judgment on their persecutors. For, "if such things are done in the green wood, what shall be done in the dry ?" And if judgment has been thus severely dealt out on the house of God—1 Peter, iv.—what shall be the rigours of the punishment which awaits the impious ?—and secondly, that by their suffering, they might render themselves worthy of the kingdom of God, since, according to the decrees of Providence, in the present order of things, no one can enter glory but as Christ did, *i.e.*, by suffering. This is the interpretation which best accords with the following verses "worthy of the kingdom of God." The Vulgate is, "worthy *in* the kingdom of God."

6. He shows how far the first object of God would be secured by permitting their suffering and persecutions; because if natural equity and justice demands, even with men, that those who persecute and afflict others unjustly, should themselves be punished, and that those who are punished unjustly should obtain rest and peace, how much more so is it required with a just God ?

7. He shows how the second end is accomplished, since it is just that those who are unjustly persecuted should obtain rest. Hence, eternal life is given as a reward, due as a matter of justice—a justice, however, ultimately founded on God's liberal and gratuitous promise. Who, therefore, would not patiently receive all injuries and sufferings from the hand of God, knowing that he permits them in order to give us a title to eternal life ?

Text.

8. In a flame of fire yielding vengeance to them who know not God, and who obey not the gospel of our Lord JESUS CHRIST.

9. Who shall suffer eternal punishment in destruction, from the face of the Lord and from the glory of his power :

10. When he shall come to be glorified in his saints, and to be made wonderful in all them who have believed : because our testimony was believed upon you in that day.

11. Wherefore also we pray always for you ; that our God would make you worthy of his vocation, and fulfil all the good pleasure of his goodness and the work of faith in power.

12. That the name of our Lord JESUS may be glorified in you, and

Paraphrase.

8. In the midst of a flaming fire, to take vengeance on those who have not known God, and on those who obey not the gospel of our Lord Jesus Christ.

9. Who shall suffer punishment, eternal destruction, in that dying life, or living death, which shall never end ; this sentence the mouth of the Lord, while his countenance shall be resplendent with majesty, shall announce, and his glorious and terrible omnipotence shall execute.

10. When he shall come to be glorified in his saints, and to show himself worthy of admiration for the superior excellence with which all his faithful and obedient believers shall be clothed, and you, among the rest, since you have believed the gospel preached by us amongst you, as the testimony of God, regarding that day, or, in hopes of remuneration, to be received by you on that day.

11. Wherefore, we always pray for you, that our God may render you worthy of his call (to this glory) by giving you perseverance to the end of your life, and so may fulfil the benevolent designs of his will (in electing you), and perfect by his all-powerful grace the work of your faith (by consummating it in glory).

12. And that our Lord Jesus Christ may be glorified in you, and you may in turn be glorified, and this

Commentary.

8. " In a flame of fire." The Greek of which is, Εν πυρι φλογος, *in a fire of flame,* *i.e.,* a fire which will burn and cause torture by its very light. There are two classes of men on whom the Lord will, on that day, wreak his vengeance, viz., those who know not God, and those who, knowing him, have failed to serve him, offending him by their evil deeds, and by disobeying his gospel.

9. "Who shall suffer eternal punishment in destruction." In the Greek, *who shall suffer punishment, eternal destruction,* or the punishment of eternal death ; they shall suffer the agonies of death for ever, and yet shall never cease to exist—shall never obtain a respite from the excruciating tortures. O God, we deserved those tortures, as often as we committed mortal sin. May not our sins equal in number the hairs of our head : and still, in thy goodness, thou hast stretched forth thy hand and rescued us from the jaws of the abyss. *Nisi Deus adjuvit me, paulo minus habitasset in inferno anima mea.* Be thou blessed for ever for thy infinite charity ! " From the face of the Lord," *i.e.,* a sentence which shall be uttered by the mouth of the Lord, while his face shall be resplendent with glory, the very sight of which shall torture the reprobate ; hence, they shall call on the mountains to fall upon them, and upon the hills to cover them from it.

10. In the two preceding verses, the Apostle shows how the judgment of their persecutors, of which he has beforehand given us a proof (verse 5), shall take place. In this and the following verses, he refers to the glory, of which their suffering will render them worthy (verse 5). God shall then be glorified in his saints, and rendered worthy of admiration for the exalted glory to which he shall have raised those who, in this life, were wretched and despised—*hi sunt quos habuimus in derisum,......ecce nunc computati sunt inter filios Dei, et inter sanctos sors illorum est.*— (Sap. v.)

11. " Wherefore," *i.e.,* in order that you may arrive at this exalted glory. We pray him so to perfect in you the work of faith, &c. " Of his vocation." In Greek, *of the vocation,* referred to.

12. " Jesus Christ may be glorified in you." The final end of his prayer is, that Christ would be glorified in them ; and the secondary end is, that they would be

Text.	Paraphrase.
you in him, according to the grace of our God, and of the Lord JESUS CHRIST.	owing to the gratuitous goodness of our God, and the merits of the Lord Jesus Christ.

Commentary.

glorified in Christ, as the glory and dignity of the master tends to render the servant exalted and glorious.

"According to the grace of our God," &c., lest they might attribute anything to themselves, the Apostle refers all the praise of these blessings and favours to the gratuitous bounty of God.

CHAPTER II.

Analysis.

It appears, that certain expressions employed by the Apostle in chapters iv. v., of the preceding Epistle, as implying the near approach of the day of judgment, produced feelings of terror and alarm in the minds of the Thessalonians. They, in consequence, became indifferent about their temporal concerns and their duties to society. This state of feeling had been artfully employed by the false teachers, to confirm them in these erroneous impressions; these also alleged certain expressions and epistles as emanating from the Apostle, to the same effect. To remedy this state of things, the Apostle beseeches them to be no way affrighted, and to pay no attention to any assertion or epistle purporting to emanate from himself, on this subject (1, 2).

In the next place, he gives two precursory signs, that are to usher in the day of judgment, viz., a general apostacy, and the coming of Antichrist (3). He describes the sacrilegious impiety and wicked morals of Antichrist, and reminds the Thessalonians of his oral instructions on the subject, when amongst them; and also of the cause which, he told them, was to retard the public appearance of this impious man, who, at present, works clandestinely and privately by means of his wicked precursors, until the obstacle to his public appearance is removed (4–8). But when this obstacle, whatever it be, is removed, then, this wicked impostor will appear, performing wonders and prodigies, and leading into error those who, in punishment of their resistance to God's light, will be delivered over by him to the spirit of error (9–11).

He calms any apprehension which the character given of Antichrist might be apt to beget in the minds of the Thessalonians, by assuring them, that there is room for dread on the part of the incredulous, but none whatever as regards those, who are the first fruits of the faithful, or of God's elect (12, 13). He exhorts them to persevere and firmly hold to the traditions which they have learned (14). He, finally, wishes them perseverance in grace and good works (15, 16).

Text.	Paraphrase.
1. AND we beseech you, brethren, by the coming of our Lord JESUS CHRIST, and of our gathering together unto him;	1. We earnestly beseech you, brethren, by the coming of our Lord Jesus Christ (which you dread so much), and by our gathering together unto him;

Commentary.

1. "And of our gathering together," &c.—(*See* First Epistle, ii. 26). "We shall be taken up into the clouds to meet Christ." To this, reference is made in the present verse.

Text.

2. That you be not easily moved from your mind, nor be frighted, neither by spirit, nor by word, nor by epistle, as sent from us, as if the day of the Lord were at hand.

3. Let no man deceive you by any means : for unless there come a revolt first, and the man of sin be revealed, the son of perdition,

4. Who opposeth, and is lifted up above all that is called God, or that is worshipped, so that he sitteth in

Paraphrase.

2. Not to be easily moved from the settled faith and persuasion of your mind (and among other points, regarding the day of judgment), nor to be seized with terror or perturbation, either by any person pretending to a spirit of prophecy, or by any words or Epistle said to emanate from us to the effect, that the day of the Lord was at hand.

3. Let no person, then, succeed in deceiving you by these or any other means whatsoever ; for, the day of the Lord will not come, until there first takes place a general defection and apostasy from the faith, and the unity of the Church ; and until Antichrist, that most sinful of men, who, consequently, is deserving of eternal perdition, shall have, publicly and openly, made his appearance.

4. That most wicked of men, I say, who is the adversary of God, and shall be raised above all that is called God, or is worshipped as such (*i.e.*, every

Commentary.

2. "As if the day of the Lord." In Greek, *the day of Christ*. The Vulgate is preferred by critics generally.

3. The Apostle gives two precursory signs, the revolt, and the coming of Antichrist. "For, unless there come," &c., as if he said—"for (*the day of judgment will not arrive*) unless there come a revolt first." The words in the parenthesis are understood to complete the sense, and they are clearly inferred from the concluding words of verse 2.

What is meant by this "revolt?" Some understand by it, a revolt and departure from subjection to the Roman empire, which shall, in consequence, suffer dismemberment; this, they say, the Apostle expresses, in an obscure manner, through dread of offending the Romans, who regarded the stability of their empire, as eternal. This opinion, however, is quite improbable : for, the temporal empire of Rome has long since passed away, and Antichrist has not yet made his appearance. Besides, Christ has not annexed the flourishing condition of his Church to the flourishing temporal condition of the Roman empire. The far more probable opinion is that, which understands it of a departure from the unity of the Church and the centre of Catholic communion, in a general way, similar to the partial defections caused by Luther, Calvin, &c. The article in the Greek, which means, *the revolt*, or, *apostacy*, shows that it shall be a *general* apostasy. Some persons, with St. Augustine, read for revolt, or apostacy, *the apostate*, or, *revolter*, making it the same with "the man of sin," &c. ; but, our reading, according to which the apostasy is to precede and make way for the coming of Antichrist, is the more common. "The man of sin," *i.e.*, the most sinful man. "The son of perdition ;" or, he that, in consequence of his sinfulness deserves, and is marked out for, eternal perdition. This man is commonly understood by the Holy Fathers and Commentators, to refer to Antichrist, whose reign is to precede the second coming of the Redeemer, and whose persecution shall be the most dreadful of those, which the Church had ever before to encounter. His morals are here described by the Apostle. Hence, he shall be a man, and not a demon, as some imagine. There is reference also to an individual, as appears clearly from the Greek article, "THE *Man of Sin*, THE *Son*," &c., and not to a series of individuals, as is asserted by some crazed fanatics, who wish to affix this opprobrious epithet, on the sainted and glorious rulers of God's Church, who sit in the chair of Peter.

4. His impiety and pride are here described—"Or that is worshipped," includes everything to which religious or divine honour is paid ; so that he shall be raised above every God, whether true or false, and will abolish all divine worship, which he shall have transferred to himself. By the "temple of God," some understand the temple of Jerusalem, which he will rebuild ; this is, however, an erroneous opinion, because such a temple would not be, "the temple of *God*." Hence, it more probably refers to the Christian temples in being at his coming. "So that he sitteth in the

Text.

the temple of God, showing himself as if he were God.

5. Remember you not, that when I was yet with you, I told you these things?

6. And now you know what withholdeth, that he may be revealed in his time.

7. For the mystery of iniquity already worketh : only that he who now holdeth, do hold, until he be taken out of the way.

8. And then that wicked one

Paraphrase.

God, whether true or false, and who will, consequently abolish every kind of divine religious worship, which he will have men pay to himself), so that he shall sit in the temple of God, showing himself as God, and claiming for himself divine honour.

5. (What cause of disturbance can you have?) Do you not recollect, that when I was amongst you, I told you all these things, and explained them to you?

6. And (from what you then heard) you know the cause why his coming is delayed, in order that he may openly and publicly appear in his own time.

7. I said *openly* appear ; for as to the private and clandestine commission of iniquity, it is already accomplished by his precursors, who clandestinely carry out the iniquity, which he will publicly and openly profess at the end of the world, when the obstacle that now detains him shall have been entirely removed : in other words, he worketh iniquity privately in the persons of his precursors, until such time as he will appear himself, when the obstacle to his coming shall have been removed.

8. And then, after the removal of this obstacle

Commentary.

temple," &c. The Greek has, *So that he sitteth (as God) in the temple*, &c. This reading is rejected by critics generally.

5. Hence, many things were left by the Apostles with the faithful, to be transmitted either by oral or written tradition ; which, although forming a part of the deposit of faith, were never intended to be conveyed by the inspired writings of the SS. Scripture.

6. What this obstacle to the more speedy advent of Antichrist is, was known to the Thessalonians at the time ; but, unknown to us : the more probable conjecture is, that it refers to the steady profession of the Catholic faith by individuals, and the reverence and submission of Catholic princes to the Apostolic See. If this be not it, we can only say, with St. Augustine, *ego prorsus, quid dixerit, fateor me ignorare.—(De Civitate Dei*, c. 29, Book 20).

7. The precursors of Antichrist are the heretics, the enemies of the faith and of obedience to lawful authority. In them is accomplished, clandestinely and privately (this is the meaning of "mystery,") the iniquity which Antichrist will openly profess and confirm with false signs, at the end of the world. They carry out, in a concealed, private way, however, under the guise of truth, and with an affected zeal for religion, the impiety which he will openly profess. The word "worketh," may also be taken in an active signification, thus : for he already worketh and carries out in the person of his precursors, privately, and under the appearance of truth, the same iniquity which he will publicly avow. "Only that he who now holdeth, do hold," &c. The word "hold," in the second place, is not found in the Greek ; it is, however, understood. These words some understand thus : but whilst this iniquity is only privately carried on, let him who holds the faith, hold it firmly, until Antichrist is publicly segregated from the faithful, and raises his standard against the Church. The interpretation in the Paraphrase, referring "he who holdeth" to the obstacle by which Antichrist is detained, is the one that accords best with the following verse. The other interpretation, however, derives great probability, from the masculine article prefixed in the Greek to the words, *he that now holdeth*, ὁ κατέχων as also, from the common acceptance of the words, "taken out of the way," ἐκ μέσου γένηται, which mean, *to be segregated, to go out from*.

8. "And then," *i.e.*, after the removal of this obstacle, or after the great apostasy, "shall be revealed that wicked one," or, as the Greek has it, ὁ ἄνομος, *the lawless one*.

Text.

shall be revealed, whom the Lord JESUS shall kill with the spirit of his mouth : and shall destroy with the brightness of his coming ; him,

9. Whose coming is according to the working of satan, in all power, and signs, and lying wonders,

10. And in all seduction of iniquity to them that perish : because they received not the love of the truth that they might be saved. Therefore God shall send them the operation of error, to believe lying :

Paraphrase.

shall be publicly revealed that wicked, lawless man, whom the Lord Jesus will kill by his sole command, and will destroy by some of these bright signs, which are to announce his coming.

9. This lawless man, on attaining power, will perform, by the operation of Satan, all sorts of false miracles, or manifestations of great power, signs, and wonders.

10. And not only will he have recourse to miracles, but he also will have recourse to all other means of seducing into iniquity, viz., riches, honours, pleasures, blandishments, &c., those who are to perish, through their own fault, because they did not receive and embrace the truth, which had a great claim on their love and affection, and by which they would be saved. In punishment of their sins and of their rejecting the truth which they should love, God will send them the operation of error and imposture, so that they may believe falsehood.

Commentary.

The Greek article clearly shows, that here, as well as in verse 3, the Apostle refers to an individual. "The Lord Jesus." "JESUS" is not in the Greek. "With the spirit of his mouth," *i.e.*, his sole word ; or, as St. Thomas says, *by his command ; because*, says the saint, *by the command of our Lord, Michael will kill Antichrist on Mount Olivet.* St. Thomas, with many other divines, states, that the army of Antichrist being destroyed by fire from heaven (Apocalypse, xx. 9, 10), he will take to flight, and conceal himself in some solitary part of Mount Olivet, where he shall be discovered by Michael the Archangel, and slain, or, rather, precipitated from that spot into hell with his false prophet, in which descent, downwards, they shall both die. This perfectly accords with the text of the Apocalypse (xix. 20), wherein it is said, "they will be cast alive (*i.e.*, but dead for a very short time) into the pool of fire."

9. "And lying wonders." The word "lying" is understood of his miracles, as regards their object and effect, which are, to lead men astray and confirm error. Because a miracle as such, or as viewed in the light of a testimony, is a seal of the truth of things, which it is adduced to confirm. Now, the miracles of Antichrist shall be adduced in confirmation of falsity and error ; and hence, in a moral sense, may be termed "lying." But whether the devil can operate miracles *proprie dicta*, or not, is another question, which cannot be decided one way or the other from this passage. For a truly admirable dissertation on the subject of miracles, *see* Murray's (Very Rev. Dr.) Annual Miscellany, vol. ii.

10. Because they received not the love of the truth, *i.e.*, they embraced not the truth of God, which had great claims on their love and affection. In punishment of their sins and of their rejection of the truth, God will send this impious man, who will perform deeds of deception, by which they shall be led astray, so as to embrace lying falsehoods.

"Therefore, God shall send them the operation of error." When God is said to *deceive men*, to *tempt them*, to *harden their hearts*, we are not to understand this, as if he *positively* produced these sinful effects. He does so, *negatively*, by withdrawing his lights and graces from men in punishment of their sins ; upon the withdrawal of which, men shall as infallibly be *deceived*, *hardened*, and *tempted*, as if God had done so in a positive way. So far as the effects of deception and obduration are concerned, God acts *negatively ;* but, he, sometimes, acts *positively*, in a certain sense also, by throwing in their way, occasions not necessarily inducing to sin, but which will infallibly lead to sin in such as are bereft of God's lights and graces.

"To believe lying." The result of this operation of error shall be, that men will believe lying ; or, the end of this seduction on the part of Antichrist is, to compel them to believe lies and falsehood.—(*See* Romans, i. 24, ix. 18). The most fearful judgment of God is, when in punishment of sin he gives man over to a reprobate sense, to a

Text.

11. That all may be judged who have not believed the truth, but have consented to iniquity.

12. But we ought to give thanks to God always for you, brethren beloved of God, for that God hath chosen you first-fruits unto salvation, in sanctification of the spirit, and faith of the truth:

13. Whereunto also he hath called you by our gospel, unto the purchasing of the glory of our Lord JESUS CHRIST.

14. Therefore, brethren, stand fast; and hold the traditions which you have learned, whether by word, or by our epistle.

Paraphrase.

11. And thus they shall be all inexcusable and justly condemned, who have not believed the truth but have consented to error and iniquity.

12. (The impious have just grounds to be alarmed at such announcements), but as for us, we are bound to give God thanks always for you, brethren, beloved by God, because he has elected you, as first-fruits for salvation, sanctifying you by his Holy Spirit, and inspiring you with the faith of the truth.

13. To which faith and sanctification he has called you through our preaching of the Gospel, so that you may acquire the glory of our Lord Jesus Christ.

14. Wherefore, brethren, persevere steadfastly in the faith, to which God has called you, and faithfully observe and adhere to the traditions which you have been taught by us, whether orally, or by our Epistles.

Commentary.

blindness and insensibility of heart, the assured forerunner of final impenitence "God delivered them up to a reprobate sense."—(Romans, i. 24).

11. They believed not in Christ the truth, operating true miracles; but adhered to Antichrist seducing them, and for this end performing lying wonders.

12. The vivid description given by St. Paul of Antichrist, and of the judgment of God on his followers, was calculated to create alarm. With a view of dispelling these vain fears from the minds of the Thessalonians, the Apostle says, that such apprehensions may concern the incredulous, but as for them, they are "the first-fruits," whom God has marked out "for salvation." "The first-fruits," because they were among the first to whom the Apostle preached. While the infidels shall be condemned for not believing the truth and consenting to error, the Thessalonians are marked out for salvation, on account of the faith of truth and the practice of sanctity; and for those, as pure gifts of God, the Apostle gives thanks. "First-fruits," in Greek, *from the beginning.* There is but very little difference in the sense supplied by both.

13. "Unto the purchasing of the glory," &c., may also mean, in order that you may become the glorious purchaser; or, the glorious purchased people of our Lord Jesus Christ. "Whereunto," for which the Vulgate reading is, *wherein.*

14. By "tradition," he means doctrines and institutions of the Christian religion, whether appertaining to faith or discipline. Of the latter kind he spoke—chap. xi. Ep. 1 to Cor.—"*Cetera, cum venero, disponam.*" From this latter verse it is clear, that Tradition was intended to be a channel of divine revelation no less than the sacred Scriptures. Traditions may be committed to writing in after times; but still they are said to be the *unwritten* word of God, because, not written by the Apostles, like the SS. Scriptures, but merely delivered by the word of mouth. If the SS. Scriptures were the only channel intended by God to convey to us his divine revelations, why make the writing of these Scriptures dependent on the most casual circumstances? If the disputes, the ignorance, the abuses, the misconceptions, and efforts on the part of heretics to proselytize, &c., which elicited the several Epistles of St. Paul, did not exist; or, if the Apostle were himself on the spot, would we have the inspired doctrine, which they convey, committed by him to writing? What was the method of instructing men in the faith, for the first six years after the Ascension? What from the time of Adam to Moses? Surely, not the inspired Scriptures, but Tradition; and surely, no one will deny that the faith of men during this period was as strong as had been the faith of men in other ages. St. Iræneus tells us, that in his day, many tribes embraced the faith, who had neither ink nor paper. Hence, God wished that the great certain means of conveying his divine truth, independent of every species of casualty, was to be the tradition of his Church, which he has constituted the indefectible oracle of his heavenly truth, unto the end of time. On this account, it is, that the Gospel is called, a *testimony*, to be handed down by witnesses.

Text.

15. Now our Lord JESUS CHRIST himself, and God our Father, who hath loved us, and hath given us everlasting consolation, and good hope in grace,

16. Exhort your hearts, and confirm you in every good work and word.

Paraphrase.

15. But may our Lord Jesus Christ himself, and God the Father, who is our Father also, who hath loved us, and hath given us eternal consolation, by giving us his grace, through which we firmly hope to reap in the life to come these abundant blessings, of which grace is the seed ;

16. May he, I say, increase your consolation and strengthen your hearts (amidst the persecutions you endure), and confirm you in the belief of sound doctrine, and in the practice of all sort of good works.

Commentary.

15. The Apostle concludes his exhortation by a prayer. God, "who loved them," by electing them from eternity, and giving in time his grace, which is the seed of glory ; "and hath given everlasting consolation," by the hopes of future blessings, in giving them his grace in this life, which is an earnest or pledge of future glory.

16. May he "exhort your hearts." The Greek word for "exhort" (παρακαλέσαι), means also to *console*. Hence, it means, may he increase in your hearts that "eternal consolation," which in the preceding verse he says, has been already imparted to them.

"In every good work and word." The order is inverted in the common Greek, which runs thus : The *Codex Vaticanus* has the order of the Vulgate.

CHAPTER III.

Analysis.

The Apostle had been informed that, notwithstanding his instructions, when at Thessalonica, and his injunctions conveyed in his former Epistle, some able-bodied men among the Thessalonians continued to go about, begging, when they might procure means of support by manual labour; indulging in idle curiosity, prying into the concerns of others and neglecting their own, to the great disedification and estrangement of the unbelievers. Hence, in this chapter, after recommending himself to their prayers (1, 2); and promising them the aid of the Almighty (3); and praying to God in turn for them (4, 5); he repeats his former injunctions on this important subject, and conjures these disorderly men, in the most solemn manner, to devote themselves to a life of labour.

He quotes himself as an example in this matter, and refers to the laborious life which he led amongst them; but should any person, after this admonition, continue refractory, he enjoins on the rulers of the Church to separate such a one from the society of the faithful. He tells them that severity should, however, be blended with tenderness and brotherly compassion (6–15). He concludes, by wishing them the abundance of peace and grace.

Text.

1. FOR the rest, brethren, pray for us, that the word of God may run and may be glorified even as among you :

2. And that we may be delivered from importunate and evil men : or all men have not faith.

3. But God is faithful, who will strengthen and keep you from evil.

Paraphrase.

1. For the rest, brethren, pray for us (ministers of the Gospel), that the word of God, the true doctrine of Christ, may be successfully propagated by our ministry, and may be received with reverence and honour elsewhere, as it has been with you.

2. Pray, therefore, that we may be delivered from the annoyance caused us by importunate and wicked men, who everywhere oppose us, and resist the progress of the Gospel; and no wonder, for all men to whom the Gospel is preached, do not believe; or, all who profess the faith, do not in reality believe.

3. (Still, notwithstanding the many domestic and foreign enemies whom the faith has to encounter, you should not be afraid), for God is faithful to his engagements, and will confirm you in the faith, and deliver you from the power of the wicked adversary (Satan).

Commentary.

1. "For the rest." A form of transition from one subject to another, usual with the Apostle.

2. "Importunate." The Greek word, τῶν ἀτόπων, *unsteady; remaining in no one place.* He probably alludes to the Jews, his chief adversaries, who persecuted him from place to place, and everywhere excited commotions against him. Others understand him to refer to the *Judaizantes* and false Christians, by whom the name of Christ was brought into disrepute.

"For all men have not faith." If we understand the word "importunate," of the obstinate and unbelieving Jews; then, these words mean, all to whom the Gospel is preached, do not believe : if, of bad Christians, then, they mean, all who profess the faith externally, have not faith in reality.—(*Vide* Paraphrase).

3. "God is faithful." In Greek, *the Lord is faithful.* God will perfect what he

Text.

4. And we have confidence concerning you in the Lord, that the things which we command, you both do, and will do.

5. And the Lord direct your hearts, in the charity of God, and the patience of Christ.

6. And we charge you, brethren, in the name of our Lord JESUS CHRIST, that you withdraw yourselves from every brother walking disorderly, and not according to the tradition which they have received of us.

7. For yourselves know how you ought to imitate us: for we were not disorderly among you:

8. Neither did we eat any man's bread for nothing, but in labour and in toil, we worked night and day, lest we might be chargeable to any of you.

Paraphrase.

4. But we have the greatest hopes regarding you, and we trust, that aided by God's grace and succour, you fulfil, and will continue to fulfil, the precepts which we have given you.

5. But may the Lord direct your hearts unto the love of God, and the patient expectation of Christ's coming.

6. But we command you, in virtue of the authority given us by our Lord Jesus Christ, to shun familiar intercourse with every brother, who follows a disorderly and turbulent life, and lives not according to the instructions which we inculcated both by word and example.

7. For you yourselves know what example we gave you, and how deserving we were of imitation; for we did not lead a disorderly life amongst you; we were neither idle nor turbulent;

8. Nor did we receive the necessaries of life from any of you without paying for them, but in labour and toil, we exerted ourselves unceasingly for that end; lest we might be a burden to any of you.

Commentary.

began in those whom he has elected to salvation: hence, as each one should hope, that God has predestined him, so ought he trust that God will strengthen him in faith, guard him from the wiles, and protect him from the power of Satan, the evil one, by nature.

4. But, nevertheless, all does not rest with God, human co-operation is required; hence, we should not grow idle or apathetic, in reference to our salvation. "You do," shows that their co-operation is required; and "will do," shows that they must co-operate perseveringly, to the end of life. "In the Lord," *i.e.*, by the aid of God's grace and succour, "we command." In Greek, *command you*.

5. He again recurs to God, the source of all justice and the author of our salvation; and he prays him to grant them, to arrive straightway at salvation, by observing God's precepts, which is the test of the "love of God," and by patiently enduring the evils of this life, after the example of Christ. "Patience of Christ," probably means the patient expectation of Christ's coming to remunerate us. In this, however, patient suffering of evils is implied; so that the meaning is the same, whether we make it the patience of Christ in enduring suffering, or the patient expectation, &c. (as in Paraphrase), "in the charity of God." In Greek, *unto the charity*, &c.

6. "In the name," &c., *i.e.*, by the authority, "of our Lord," &c. The Apostle instructed the superiors of the Church at Thessalonica to correct the disorderly, who neglecting all the rules of Christian propriety, were following their own whims and humours. He now, on finding that the practices he then prohibited were persevered in, and that some of the able-bodied went about begging, indulging in an undue spirit of curiosity, prying into the affairs of others, and neglecting their own, calls upon the faithful to shun the company and society of such persons. This is a sort of *minor* excommunication, whereby civil intercourse is prohibited. It is not, however, that dreadful punishment of *major* excommunication, by which the delinquent "is handed over to Satan."—(1 Cor. v. 5). Nor is it, strictly speaking, what is now termed *minor* excommunication, which only excludes from intercourse with the faithful in the reception of the sacraments. "They received." In Greek, *he received*. The Vulgate is suported by the chief manuscripts.

7. He gave them an example for imitation.

8. "Neither did we eat." In some Greek copies, *neither did we receive;* which

Text.

9. Not as if we had not power; but that we might give ourselves a pattern unto you, to imitate us.

10. For also when we were with you, this we declared to you : that, if any man will not work, neither 'et him eat.

11. For we have heard there are some among you who walk disorderly, working not at all, but curiously meddling.

12. Now we charge them that are such, and beseech them by the Lord Jesus Christ, that, working with silence, they would eat their own bread.

13. But you, brethren, be not weary in well-doing.

14. And if any man obey not our word by this epistle, note that man,

Paraphrase.

9. Not that we had not a strict right to support from you, but, we had foregone that right, in order, by working hard, to exhibit ourselves to you as a model for imitation.

10. (We are inculcating nothing new at present), for when we were amongst you, we enjoined the duty of labouring contained in the adage : the man who does not wish to work, is not deserving of the food he eats.

11. For we have heard, that some amongst you are still leading a disorderly life, doing nothing, wholly engaged in curiosity, and in prying into the affairs and concerns of others.

12. But we command such persons, and we also entreat and conjure them by the Lord Jesus Christ, to lead a quiet, unobtrusive life, to engage in manual labour, and thus provide themselves with the means of subsistence, and not be depending on the charity of others.

13. But you, brethren, (although others are undeserving of support), be not, however, weary of performing acts of charity and beneficence.

14. But if any person refuses to obey this our precept signified to him in this Epistle, mark that man,

Commentary.

differs little in signification from ours ; for it was to be eaten that it was received. "For nothing," *i.e.*, without paying for it. "But in labour and toil." He laboured at the trade of a cabinet-maker, in order to procure the means of subsistence, and that assiduously. "Day and night," means continually. What an example of Apostolic independence is here furnished by the Apostle! The minister of the Gospel, who is anxious for the gifts of his people, and is the slave of avarice, can never enjoy that freedom and bold independence of mind, so necessary for the impartial discharge of his duties. The Apostle, also, by his example, teaches us to devote all our time to some useful occupation. What a picture ! the teacher of the entire world labouring, as a mechanic, to procure a livelihood !

9. He had a right to support.—1 Cor. ix. 14, &c.

10. He announced to the Thessalonians, prone to idleness, the precept of labouring, which he confirmed by many examples and adages ; among the rest by this : "the man who does not wish to labour, should not eat." He says, "will not work ;" *wishes not* to work (οὐ θέλει), because, some are not able to do so ; but all should be disposed to do so.

11. His reason for dwelling on this subject arose from his having heard that some among them were living in a disorderly manner, since it is against the ordination of God for men to lead a life of idleness, of indolence, and ease. For idleness begets curiosity ; curiosity begets turbulence and inquietude, which destroys discipline and causes disorder. The idle and the curious go about intermeddling in the concerns of others, and thus disturb peace and social order.

12. "By the Lord Jesus Christ." In Greek, *by our Lord Jesus Christ.* The Vulgate is supported by the chief manuscripts. He joins earnest entreaty, lest the repetition of the command might savour of harshness or undue severity. "Working with silence." He opposes "silence" to curiosity, to going about and creating disorder by prying into the concerns of others ; and "working" he opposes to idleness.

13. But though the idle beggars be unworthy of support, still, that is no reason why the others should cease from deeds of charity ; charity relieves good and bad, after the example of the Father of charity, who "makes his sun rise on the good and the bad, and rains on the just and the unjust."

14. This penalty of noting the contumacious and refractory, which the Apostle

Text.

and do not keep company with him, that he may be ashamed.

15. Yet do not esteem him as an enemy, but admonish him as a brother.

16. Now the Lord of peace himself give you everlasting peace in every place. The Lord be with you all.

17. The salutation of Paul with my own hand : which is the sign in every epistle. So I write.

18. The grace of our Lord JESUS CHRIST be with you all. Amen.

Paraphrase.

and hold no intercourse with him ; that thus he may feel shame, and return to his duty.

15. Do not, however, regard him as an enemy, nor treat him harshly, but correct and admonish him kindly, as a brother.

16. But may the Lord, the author of peace, grant you unceasing peace, at all times and in all places. May the Lord, by his grace, be with you all.

17. The salutation which I, Paul, subscribe with my own hand, and which, written with my own hand, is a sign that the Epistle to which it is attached is mine is to the following effect :

18. The grace of our Lord Jesus Christ be with you all. Amen.

Commentary.

directs the heads of the Church to inflict, is a sort of excommunication. The threat or admonition ("note him,") should precede the infliction of punishment.

15. He wishes them to temper the severity of inflicting punishment with tenderness and brotherly compassion, for the delinquent party.

16. "In every place." The present Greek reading is, ἐν παντὶ τρόπω, *by all means.* The reading adopted by the Vulgate is supported by MSS. and Fathers. He prays for that measure of peace at all times and places, which can be enjoyed in this life, as *perfect* peace can be found only in heaven.

17. His subscribing, with his own hand, the salutation contained in verse 18, is the mark given by the Apostle that the Epistle is genuine. This was necessary, because many epistles were represented as coming from St. Paul, which were spurious and supposititious.--Chapter ii. 2.

18. This is the salutation written with his own hand ; the rest of the Epistle was written, at his dictation, by an amanuensis. He commenced this Epistle with wishing them the abundance of grace, the greatest of all blessings ; he concludes with the same.

The Greek subscription has the following :—" *The Second to the Thessalonians was written from Athens.*" It is supposed, however, to have been written from Corinth.— (*See* Introduction).

FIRST EPISTLE

OF

ST. PAUL TO TIMOTHY.

Introduction.

TIMOTHY, the beloved disciple and faithful follower of St. Paul, was a native of Lystra, in Lycaonia. His father was a Gentile, and his mother, a converted Jewess. He was educated in the Christian faith, from his infancy, and well versed in the SS. Scriptures. The high repute in which he was held, and the great esteem entertained for him by his fellow-citizens, induced the Apostle, on the occasion of his visit to Lystra, after parting with Barnabas, to adopt him, as the companion of his travels, and as his colleague in preaching the Gospel.—(Acts. xvi. 3).

Wherever the Apostle refers to him in his sacred writings, he speaks of him in terms of the greatest affection and commendation. He styles him "his beloved (or genuine) son" (Chap. i. 2, of this Epistle); the "*man of* God," (vi. 11). See also Chap. ii. 20, 21, &c., to the Philippians. The Apostle's confidence in him was unbounded. To him he entrusted commissions in the sacred ministry, requiring consummate zeal and fidelity; and finally created him Archbishop of Ephesus, and Primate of all Asia. To him the Apostle addressed two Pastoral Epistles.

THE CANONICITY AND LANGUAGE of this first Epistle were never a subject of controversy. It is universally admitted, that it is an inspired writing, written in the Greek language.

OBJECT AND OCCASION OF.—St. Paul, on leaving Ephesus, ordained Timothy Bishop of that city; and now writes to him this Epistle, as is generally supposed, from Macedonia, to instruct him in the discharge of his pastoral duties. The Epistle is principally devoted to doctrinal matters, in treating of which the Apostle cautions Timothy against the poisonous errors of the heretics, then, as well as at all subsequent periods of the Church, endeavouring to sap the immovable foundations of Catholic faith and morality. The heretics to whom he particularly alludes are the *Judaizantes* or Jewish zealots, and the *Gnostics*, or early illuminati, of whose errors an account has been given in some of the preceding Epistles. He dwells, at full length, on several of the Episcopal functions, and treats of some points of discipline and of Church Government, on which account, this, as well as the second Epistle to Timothy, and the Epistle to Titus, are called, HIERARCHICAL, having for object to instruct the members of the hierarchy in their respective duties. Hence it is, that St. Augustine recommends every ecclesiastic to keep these Epistles constantly before his eyes, to make them the subject of his constant reading and meditation, and to regard them as written for himself exclusively.—(*De Doc. Christiana*, lib. iv. c. 16).

TIME AND PLACE OF.—The subscription of the Greek copies asserts that this Epistle was written from Laodicea. The common opinion, however, is, that it was written from Macedonia.

The date of it is referred by some to the year, 57. The more common opinion refers it to the year, 64; while some, and among the rest, Mauduit say, that the year 66 was its probable date.

FIRST EPISTLE

OF

ST. PAUL TO TIMOTHY.

CHAPTER I.

Analysis.

In this chapter, the Apostle, after the usual Apostolical salutation, renews (verse 3) the instructions which he gave Timothy, on leaving Ephesus, to denounce certain false teachers, who had altogether mistaken the aim and object of the law, of which they constituted themselves the expounders (5, 6, 7). He guards against the calumny, with which he was often charged, of being the enemy of the law itself (8), and points out the end for which the law was given (9, &c.) He gives thanks to God for having called him to the sacred ministry, notwithstanding his unworthiness (12, 13, 14, &c.) And, finally, he recommends Timothy to attend to the precepts contained in the entire chapter (18, &c.)

Text.

1. PAUL an apostle of JESUS CHRIST, according to the commandment of God our Saviour, and of Christ JESUS our hope:

2. To Timothy his beloved son in faith. Grace, mercy, and peace from God the Father, and from Christ JESUS our Lord.

3. As I desired thee to remain at Ephesus when I went into

Paraphrase.

1. Paul an Apostle of Jesus Christ, by the authority and commission of God the Father, who has saved us through his son, whom he sent, and of Jesus Christ, who is both the meritorious cause and object of our hope.

2. (Writes) to Timothy his genuine son in the faith. Grace, mercy, and peace be to you from God the Father, and from Jesus Christ our Lord.

3. *I once more repeat the earnest entreaty* which I formerly addressed to thee, when I was leaving for

Commentary.

1. "According to the commandment of God our Saviour," *i.e.*, God the Father, because the mission of an Apostle being, what is usually termed, an *actus ad extra*, is common to the Trinity. Hence the acts of the Holy Ghost, "Separate unto me Saul and Barnabas," &c. (Acts, xiii. 2), as also of the Son, "For unto the Gentiles afar off will I send thee," (Acts, xxii. 21), are the acts of God the Father also.

"And of Christ Jesus." In Greek, *and of the Lord Jesus Christ.* The word "Lord," is rejected by critics generally.

2. "His beloved son." In the Greek, it is, γνησίῳ τέκνῳ, *his genuine son ;* he may be called the son of St. Paul in the faith ; because, although Timothy had learned the faith from his infancy, and before the arrival of St. Paul at Lystra ; still, the Apostle more fully developed the truths of faith ; and confirmed him in it. Again, he might be called "his son," from the assiduity and fidelity with which he served him in preaching the gospel (Philippians, ii. 22) ; and because he so perfectly imitated the Apostle, as to reflect in himself most perfectly his life and morals. "Mercy ;" the fountain of "grace" and "peace ;" or, it may mean, merciful meekness and clemency—a gift so necessary for a young Prelate. "From God the Father." In Greek, *our father.* The Vulgate reading is commonly preferred, although St. Chrysostom has the Greek reading.

3. This verse is evidently elliptical, and is generally filled up, as in Paraphrase. The

Text.	Paraphrase.
Macedonia, that thou mightest charge some not to teach otherwise,	Macedonia, to remain at Ephesus, and to command certain false teachers to cease from propounding erroneous doctrines opposed to those of the Apostles.
4. Nor to give heed to fables and genealogies without end : which minister questions rather than the edification of God which is in faith.	4. And also to cease from devoting their entire time and attention to idle fables, and endless genealogies, which have the effect of raising useless, foolish disputations, rather than of advancing true sanctification, which proceeds from active, operative faith.
5. Now the end of the commandment is charity from a pure heart, and a good conscience, and an unfeigned faith.	5. Now, the scope and end of the divine law, both in the Old Testament and in the New, for which these teachers affect so much zeal, is to bring men to charity, the characteristics of which are, that it proceeds from a heart pure and free from guilt, a clear conscience, and sincere faith.
6. From which things some going astray, are turned aside unto vain babbling :	6. Which charity, as well as its accompanying virtues, certain persons missing, as their proper aim, have turned aside to foolish babbling.

Commentary.

word for " desired," παρεκαλεσα will signify either a *request* or *command*. The first thing he requests or commands Timothy to do is, " to remain at Ephesus ;"— *residence* being the first and chief duty obligatory on a Pastor charged with the care of souls (*see* Council of Trent, ss. 23, c. I., *de Reform.*), and also to denounce such as taught doctrines " otherwise " than as the Apostles taught. Besides the evidence of the fact supplied by these Epistles, we have the authority of Eusebius (lib. 3, c. 4, of his history), asserting that St. Paul ordained Timothy Bishop, or rather, Archbishop of Ephesus, since he orders him to ordain and appoint Bishops throughout the other cities of Asia Minor ; the Apostle now reminds him of the charge which he gave him, when leaving Ephesus.

4. " To fables," which word probably refers to the fabulous traditions of the Jewish Rabbins, many of which are to be seen in the Talmud. " And endless genealogies," which are understood by some of the *Eons* of the Gnostics. They are, however, more commonly understood to refer to the Jewish practice of enumerating their ancestry, and claiming a descent from Abraham, as if a carnal descent from that Patriarch were sufficient to make them heirs of his glorious promises, an error which the Apostle ably refutes, chap. ix. of his Epistle to the Romans. St. Chrysostom understands it to refer to the heathenish fables respecting the origin of the Pagan divinities. " The edification of God," *i.e.*, true piety, whereby our souls, which are so many temples of the Holy Ghost, are advanced in the knowledge and love of God, and thus his glory promoted. This piety is founded on, and perfected by faith, animated with charity. Instead of " edification of God," some Greek copies have, *the economy of God.* According to this reading, the Apostle refers to the economy or design of God in bringing man to salvation through faith, and not through the observance of the ceremonial precepts of the Mosaic law, or, by the force of human reasonings.

5. The Apostle in this verse shows, that the teachers to whom he refers, have erred from the end and scope of the law of God, by teaching vain and useless things, because these things never conduce to charity. The marks given by him of this charity distinguish it from the impure love and profane affection which associates in crime may entertain for each other. The teaching of these men does not beget " faith," or the knowledge of God, nor does it stimulate to good works, which alone beget a conscience free from guilt or remorse, nor does it conduce to that purity of heart, that destruction of the passions, which are the marks of charity, the end of the law. By " end" some understand, the *fulfilment*, of the law; because, the abstract and compendium of the entire law is the love of God and of our neighbour.

6. " Going astray." The idea conveyed by the Greek word, αστοχησαντες, is allusive to marksmen who miss their aim.

QUERITUR.—Do not St. Matthew and the Book of Paralipomenon recount genealogies? Yes; because such were then useful to know the rights and privileges of each

Text.

7. Desiring to be teachers of the law, understanding neither the things they say, nor whereof they affirm.

8. But we know that the law is good, if a man use it lawfully :

9. Knowing this, that the law was not made for the just man, but for the unjust and disobedient, for the ungodly and for sinners, for the wicked and defiled, for murderers of fathers and murderers of mothers, for man-slayers,

Paraphrase.

7. While they ambition the honour and title of teachers of the law, they neither understand the law, nor the scope of the law of which they speak, nor do they know the persons in regard to whom they confidently assert the law and its ceremonies to be so necessary.

8. (While thus censuring the wrong and abusive application of the law, I am not to be understood as finding fault with the law itself). For, I well know and admit, that the law itself, both in its nature and end is excellent, provided it be applied agreeably to its object.

9. Knowing this, in the first place, that the law was not given to restrain the just, but the unjust and disobedient, the ungodly and sinners, the wicked and defiled, murderers of fathers, and murderers of mothers, manslayers,

Commentary.

man in the Land of Promise, and St. Matthew wished to show that Christ was descended, according to promise, from David. Whereas, now, since the time of Christ, they are quite useless, and only tend to divert and distract the mind from the necessary and useful duties of religion.

7. These men vainly ambition the title and dignity of teachers of the law, and yet are ignorant of the scope of the law, and of the persons to whom the legal ceremonies ought to be applied. Hence, they stray far from the end or scope of the law, which is Christ and charity, the *legalia* being no longer applicable to Christians, for whom these false teachers hold them to be necessary. How many vain and foolish preachers are there now-a-days, who aspiring after the empty bubble of fame and human applause, incur the reproach of the Apostle, understanding not the aim nor the object of all Christian preaching, which is "charity," *i.e.*, the advancement of the glory of God and the good of our neighbour.—(*See* Council of Trent, c. 2, ss. 5, *de Reformatione*, both as to the manner and matter of preaching).

8. The Apostle guards against a calumny frequently charged upon him, of being an enemy to the law. Hence, he says, that while denouncing the abuses and misapplication of the law, he by no means finds fault with the law itself. The law itself is "good," commanding good, prohibiting evil, and leading us by the hand to Christ. But this law, in itself good, is to be used for the purposes which it was intended to°subserve—namely, to bring them to charity and to Christ. The false teachers had perverted it to quite different purposes.

9. "Knowing this, that the law is not made for the just man," &c. No matter how zealous the Jew may be for the law—no matter how much he may boast of it, he should still, for his humiliation, bear in mind, that the law is but a proof of the prevarications of the Jewish people, since its *minatory* precepts would have never been imposed, had the Jews not been guilty of the crimes, which these precepts are intended to prevent and punish. The law has a triple object—to oblige, to direct, to punish. With the two former, requisitions of the law, the just, spontaneously and through the love of justice, comply. In the latter respect of punishing, under which the Apostle considers it here, "the law was not made for the just." It was not held as a terror over them ; since the just man may set its threats and menaces at defiance. ("Against such there is no law."—Gal. v. 23). By this, the Apostle confounds the vain glorying of the Jews in the law, which should be to them a source of confusion, as furnishing a proof of their own prevarications, as well as those of their fathers ; for had they lived in innocence, like the Holy Patriarchs, the law, with its threats and menaces, would never have been imposed, "but for the ungodly," &c.

Text.

10. For fornicators, for them who defile themselves with mankind, for men-stealers, for liars, for perjured persons, and whatever other thing is contrary to sound doctrine,

11. Which is according to the gospel of the glory of the blessed God, which hath been committed to my trust.

12. I give him thanks who hath strengthened me, *even* to CHRIST JESUS our Lord, for that he hath counted me faithful, putting me in the ministry.

13. Who before was a blasphemer and a persecutor and contumelious. But I obtained the mercy of God, because I did it ignorntly in unbelief.

14. Now the grace of our Lord hath abounded exceedingly with faith and love which is in CHRIST JESUS.

Paraphrase.

10. Fornicators, those who defile themselves with men, men-stealers, liars, perjurers, and in general all these sinners whose lives are opposed to the sound doctrines of faith and morals;

11. Which sound doctrine of faith and morality is in perfect accordance with the glorious gospel of the sovereignly happy God, the preaching of which gospel is divinely intrusted to me.

12. I give thanks to our Lord Jesus Christ, for having strengthened me by his grace for so arduous an undertaking, and for having confided to me so important a ministry, one of the chief requisites of which is, fidelity.

13. Who, before, had been a blasphemer, and a persecutor, and a contumelious enemy of God. But God took compassion on me, because I acted from ignorance, while I was yet in the darkness of unbelief.

14. He not only pardoned me, but the grace of our Lord superabounded in me, so as to overcome my perversity in a signal degree, by conferring on me the fruits of Christian faith and love.

Commentary.

10. "And whatever other things is contrary to sound doctrine." Under this general head the Apostle comprehends all sinners whose lives, may, in any other way, not included in the foregoing, be opposed to the sound doctrine of faith and morals. The Apostle insinuates against the Jews the charge of having committed the foregoing crimes, as it was to restrain these, and the like, that the law was given.

11. The gospel is the rule of true doctrine, and so perfect a rule is it, that anything opposed or conformable thereto, is opposed or conformable to sound doctrine. This verse is an explanation of the preceding, showing what is meant by sound doctrine—viz., that which is conformable to the gospel, or, it may mean, that in this the law and gospel agree. "The gospel of the glory," *i.e.*, the glorious gospel, or the gospel which promotes the glory of God, and promises eternal glory to us.

12. The mention of the gospel ministry intrusted to him, puts the Apostle in mind of his former sins and unworthiness. He renders thanks to God for his special goodness towards him, which his former sinfulness and unworthiness render the more illustrious. "For he that had counted me faithful, putting me in the ministry," is a phrase signifying, that God called him to his sacred ministry, wherein the chief requisite is fidelity, which must be secured by his own grace. It by no means signifies that God was moved by the provision of fidelity and of the good use of grace in St. Paul, as a motive for calling him to the ministry. This would savour of semi-Pelagianism.

13. He recounts his former sinfulnes for the purpose of displaying in a stronger light, the infinite goodness of God towards him, and of exciting himself to more intense feelings of gratitude. He was a "blasphemer" by words, a "persecutor" by his deeds, and he was a "contumelious" enemy by the unjust violence to which he had resorted. But he "obtained mercy," because his ignorance was an extenuation of his guilt, and he placed a lesser obstacle to grace, than if he had sinned knowingly, through malice. Others interpret the words, "because I did it ignorantly in unbelief," thus: because the greatness of my misery and spiritual blindness was such as to render me a fit subject for the exercise of divine mercy; sins of ignorance constitute, above all others, the greatest misery. Of course, the Apostle by no means insinuates that his ignorance and spiritual misery was anything else than the occasional cause of his justification, the mercy of God being the real cause.

14. "Hath abounded exceedingly," *i.e.*, the grace of God far exceeded his iniquity. God not only pardoned him, and showed him mercy, but he also bestowed on him the

Text.

15. A faithful saying, and worthy of all acceptation, that CHRIST JESUS came into this world to save sinners, of whom I am the chief.

16. But for this cause have I obtained mercy: that in me first Christ JESUS might shew forth all patience, for the information of them that shall believe in him unto life everlasting.

17. Now to the king of ages, immortal, invisible, the only God, be honour and glory for ever and ever. Amen.

18. This precept I commend to thee, O son Timothy: according to the prophecies going before thee, that thou war in them a good warfare.

Paraphrase.

15. It is a certain, undoubted truth, and worthy to be received with all thankfulness and gratitude, that Christ Jesus came into this world for the purpose of saving sinners, of whom I am the greatest and most unworthy.

16. But it was on account of this very excessive unworthiness and sinfulness, that Christ Jesus showed mercy to me, selecting me as a great object of mercy, for the purpose of displaying in me, the most unworthy of sinners, his great patience and compassion, and with a view of making me serve as a great exemplar and model for all future penitents who are to believe in him, and by this means, expect eternal life.

17. For this, may eternal honour and glory be rendered to the one only true God, the immortal and invisible King of ages.

18. The entire preceding doctrine, or the precepts contained in this chapter, I commend to you, my son, Timothy, according to the prophecies which had preceded your ordination, so that corresponding with them, thou mayest fight the good fight.

Commentary.

gifts of his grace and its fruit—"faith," which was opposed to his former incredulity, and "love," to his former hatred of Christ.

15. He says, this mercy shown himself, should inspire all other sinners with hope, and hence he announces a general and important proposition on the subject. "Of whom I am the chief." This he might say, looking to himself, and abstracting from the sins of others—or, by looking to his own nature without grace, there was no sin ever committed, that he too might not commit, if left to himself.—(*See* Philip. ii. 3).

16. "For the information of them that shall believe," &c. The Greek for "information," ὑποτυπωσιν, means, *to serve as a type or model*, so that, after his example, all future sinners who are to believe in God, would have recourse to the divine clemency, and learn to hope in God, and thus gain eternal life. As a physician, for the purpose of rousing the drooping and desponding spirits of his patient, points to some instance of recovery from a similar and almost incurable disease ; so, had God placed St. Paul, whose blindness and obstinacy were apparently incurable, as a model, an example to animate other sinners to hope for forgiveness in the depth of their miseries and sins.

17. God is by nature "immortal," and incorruptible, and "invisible," he cannot be seen by the aids of nature,—even in the life to come the saints require the *lumen gloriæ* to see him as he is, "face to face."—(*See* 1 Cor. xiii. 12). "Only God." In Greek, *only wise God*. The epithet, *wise*, is, however, wanting in the oldest manuscripts and versions, and generally rejected by critics.

18. "This precept," is referred by some to the precept of denouncing false teachers (verse 3), and these say, the ellipsis observable in verse, 3, is filled up here. "As I desired thee," &c. (verse 3)..........verse 18, "this precept I commend to thee, O Timothy." By others it is referred to the following words :—"War a good warfare." Others refer it to the precept of preaching the truth enunciated, verse 15. It more probably regards the precepts of faith contained in the entire chapter. "According to the prophecies," &c. It is likely, that St. Paul was induced to consecrate Timothy, owing to the revelations from the Holy Ghost regarding his zeal and fitness. Others, by "prophecies," understand, the hopes and expectations given of him by his fellow-citizens. "That thou war in them," or, in correspondence with these prophecies, "a good warfare." The life of a pastor of souls, is a life of labour, vigilance, and warfare, against the visible and invisible enemies of the salvation of his people. By taking on himself voluntarily the charge of souls, he enters into an implicit contract with God

Text.	Paraphrase.
19. Having faith · and a good conscience, which some rejecting have made shipwreck concerning the faith.	19. Keeping a firm hold of the faith, and a good conscience, the result of a holy and upright life; owing to the loss of which pure conscience, or rather, to the crimes against morality which destroyed it, some persons have suffered a shipwreck of their faith.
20. Of whom is Hymeneus and Alexander, whom I have delivered up to Satan, that they may learn not to blaspheme.	20. Among whom are Hymeneus, and Alexander, whom by excommunication I handed over to Satan, to be tortured even in body, that thus they may learn to speak with more becoming reverence and respect of the holy things of God, and the unerring truths of faith.

Commentary.

. and the Church, to devote his entire energies to the sublime work of co-operating with Jesus Christ, in the salvation of his people. Woe, then, to him, if like the sluggish watchman in the house of Israel, he permit the wicked man, without being warned of it, to die in his sins !—or like the faithless pastors of Israel, he attend only to his own gain and emolument, without attending, as he is in duty bound, to the spiritual wants and necessities of his flock ! On the day of reckoning, he shall give life for life and blood for blood.—(Ezechiel, xxxiii. 6, &c., xxxiv. 4, &c.)

19. The arms of the Christian warfare, particularly in a pastor, are a firm faith, a pure and holy life. " Have made shipwreck concerning the faith." Hence, faith is not inamissible. How many melancholy instances does not history supply of men, who to gratify abominable lust, or avarice, have flung aside the livery of Christ and deserted to the camp of his enemies.

20. " Hymeneus " denied the Resurrection.—(2 Ep. ii. 17). " And Alexander," probably, the silver-smith, to whom he refers, chap. iv. of second Epistle. These he excommunicated by driving them out of the pale of the Church, and placing them in the kingdom of Satan, to be bodily tormented by him. Bodily afflictions by the demon, as we are informed by St. Chrysostom, Theodoret, &c., were one of the results of excommunication, in the early ages. These men, by being driven out of the Church, were placed in the kingdom of Satan, since his is the other kingdom that is arrayed against the Church, or kingdom of God. The end and object of this wholesome castigation was, by being excluded from all intercourse, they should cease from announcing heretical doctrines, which are so many blasphemies against God the sovereign truth.

CHAPTER II.

Analysis.

The Apostle, after instructing Timothy in the preceding chapter concerning the mode in which he should guard the purity of doctrine, devotes this chapter to his instruction, as regards the manner of arranging the public offices and prayers of the faithful. He points out the persons for whom prayers ought to be offered, and assigns the reason of praying for such (1–7). *He shows, in the next place, where it is, that prayer can be offered up* (8); *and he treats of the manner in which women should appear in the public assemblies of the faithful* (9–14). *Finally, he points out the occupations whereby women can save their souls* (15).

Text.

1. I DESIRE therefore first of all that supplications, prayers, intercessions and thanksgivings be made for all men,

2. For kings, and for all that are in high stations : that we may lead a quiet and peaceable life in all piety and chastity.

Paraphrase.

1. Therefore, I entreat and enjoin above all things that (in daily and public service) supplications, prayers, intercessions, and thanksgivings be made for all men,

2. But especially for kings, and for all who, placed, in elevated stations, have charge of the public weal, that (owing to their just and wise administration) we may lead a quiet and peaceable life, in the exercise of all the duties of piety, and in becoming sanctity and purity of morals.

Commentary.

1. "Therefore," shows the connexion of this chapter with the preceding. It may regard chap. i. 15, "Christ came to save sinners," or, verse 18, "that thou war in them a good warfare," or, more probably, both. "Therefore," in order to co-operate with Christ in saving sinners, and to "fight the good fight ;" in a word, in order to discharge the Episcopal functions, according to the prophecies made regarding thee. "I desire." The Greek word, παρακαλῶ, means either a wish, or a command. "First of all," because, all good things come to us through prayer ; and prayer is the principal duty of a bishop. "That supplications, prayers, intercessions," which some persons regard as a rhetorical amplification, signifying the same thing. They are commonly, however, supposed to bear different significations. Supplications, or, as the Greek has it, *deprecations*, prayers, offered for averting evils. "Prayers," or as the Greek has it, *obsecrations*, offered up for the purpose of obtaining blessings. "Intercessions," prayers for others, particularly for our enemies ; and "thanksgivings," for benefits received. All the Fathers and Commentators say, these are to be understood of the public prayers of the Church, and St. Augustine (59 *Ep. ad Paulinum*) and St. Thomas refer them to the Adorable Sacrifice of the Mass and its different parts, which shows the antiquity of the Mass, its different parts being, in the days of St. Augustine, the same as they are at the present day. "For all men," without exception, believers and unbelievers.

2. "For kings," even Pagans ; for, the kings then existing were Pagan, "and all that are in high stations," i.e., for their ministers, and all who have a share in the government of the state. The ministerial power is but an emanation of the regal dignity, which latter is a ray and participation of the divine Majesty. "That we may lead a quiet," &c. All Christians should pray that God would inspire their rulers with the spirit of wisdom and justice, because the peace of the Church depends on the wisdom of her temporal rulers. "In all piety and chastity," or, as in the Greek, σεμνότητι, *gravity*. This is the end for which we should desire peace, not to indulge

Text.

3. For this is good and acceptable in the sight of God our Saviour,

4. Who will have all men to be saved, and to come to the knowledge of the truth.

5. For there is one God, and one mediator of God and men, the man Christ Jesus:

6. Who gave himself a redemption for all, a testimony in due times.

Paraphrase.

3. For, to pray thus for all is in itself good, and acceptable to God our Saviour.

4. Who wishes that all men should be saved, and for this end, wishes that all should come to the knowledge of the truth, *i.e.*, to Christian faith.

5. (And no wonder) for there is but one God, who is equally the Creator of all men, and one Mediator of God and men, the Man-God, Christ Jesus.

6. Who delivered himself up to death, as a vicarious, substitutional ransom for all; this giving of himself for ransom was a splendid and undoubted testimony of his will that all should be saved, given at the time marked out by the ancient prophecies.

Commentary.

in luxury, but to practise with greater facility the duties of religion and morality, both of which are greatly injured during the calamities of war.

3. "For this," *i.e.*, to pray for all "is good" in itself, "and acceptable in the sight of God our Saviour," the reason of which he assigns next verse, because, in this, we conform to the will of God.

4. "Who will have all men to be saved." God wishes the salvation of all men without exception (for, "he is unwilling that any should perish"—St. Peter, 2 Ep. iii. 9.), "and to come to the knowledge of the truth," this being the necessary means for salvation.

5. In this verse is assigned a reason why God sincerely wishes the salvation of all, viz., because they are all equally his creatures, and he has given to all the same supreme Mediator, the Man-God, Christ, who uniting in himself the nature of God and man, can most efficaciously interpose with outraged heaven in behalf of sinful mortals. In this the Apostle strikes at the errors of Simon Magus, who asserted that it was through the angels, and not through Christ, we should approach God. These errors were circulated at Ephesus, of which Timothy was chief Pastor. It was for the same reason that the Apostle says in his Epistle to the Ephesians (iii. 12), that it is by Christ we have access to God, because he is our principal Mediator and Intercessor. It is needless to say, that there is not the shadow of objection here against the Catholic doctrine and practice on the subject of the invocation of saints. For, as is clear from the entire context, the Apostle speaks of Christ, as Mediator of *redemption ;* he paid the ransom and set us free, and he alone could do so. The saints, according to the teaching of Catholics, are only mediators of *intercession*, mediators in a secondary degree, subordinate to Christ, who alone is Mediator of Redemption."—(*See* 1 John, ii. 2).

6. The Greek word for "redemption," αντιλυτρον, means not only giving a price, but a *vicarious, substitutional* price, head for head and life for life. This clearly shows in what sense "Christ Jesus" is termed the "one Mediator" by the Apostle; it is as *Redeemer*, who ransomed us on the cross, and offered himself as a victim, *in our stead*, and to say there could be any other such Mediator, would be the rankest blasphemy. This, of course, is by no means opposed to—what is quite a different thing—the *mediation* of saints, according to Catholic doctrine. "A testimony in due times," is understood by some to mean, that this substitution of himself by Christ for us is the doctrine to be taught and preached—a doctrine to which testimony is to be borne in due time. The Apostle thus intimates through Timothy to all the Pastors of the Church what the great theme of their preaching should be, viz., "Christ crucified." The interpretation in the Paraphrase is the one more commonly received.

It would be out of place to enter here into a discussion of the several scholastic questions regarding the will of God to save all, which are raised by interpreters on the foregoing passage. Let it suffice simply to remark, that it is clear from the words themselves and the entire context, that God *sincerely* and *truly* wishes the salvation of all men (verse 5) without exception. For, the Apostle tells us to pray for *all men* without exception (verse 1). Why? Because, it is pleasing to God that we should do so (verse 3). And why is this pleasing to God? Because, it is conformable to his

Text.

7. Whereunto I am appointed a preacher and an apostle (I say the truth, I lie not) a doctor of the gentiles in faith and truth.

8. I will therefore that men pray in every place, lifting up pure hands without anger and contention.

9. In like manner women also in decent apparel: adorning themselves with modesty and sobriety, not with plaited hair, or gold, or pearls, or costly attire,

Paraphrase.

7. To announce which testimony regarding the will of God, I solemnly and sincerely declare, I am constituted the herald and divinely commissioned legate, as well as the teacher of the Gentiles in particular, who are to be instructed in the faith and truth of the gospel.

8. I wish, therefore, that the men should pray in every place suited for prayer, with consciences pure from guilt, and exempt from the vices peculiar to men, viz., anger and animosity.

9. In like manner, I wish that women should, besides possessing the foregoing dispositions, appear at prayer in decent becoming apparel, exhibiting a chaste and modest appearance, without any extravagant fineries of dress, in braidings of the hair, or in gold, or ornaments of precious stones, or costly splendid attire.

Commentary.

will, "since he wishes all to be saved" (verse 4). Now, unless he wished all to be saved without exception, it would not be conformable to his will, that we should pray for the salvation of all, without exception. In a word, the Apostle gives the will of God for the salvation of all, as the rule of our will in the same respect, and as a motive to induce us to will it. We have, moreover, the same truth announced in a *negative* form by St. Peter.—(2 Ep. iii. 9). "God is unwilling that any should perish." And here it is said that "he wishes all to be saved." Hence, any interpretation, that restricts this universal will in God, is to be rejected. The interpretation of Estius is quite opposed to the context. He maintains, that God wishes the salvation of all, because he inspires us with the wish, just as "the spirit asketh for us with unspeakable groans."—(Rom. viii. 26.) Because *he makes us* ask, &c. This interpretation is opposed to the context. For why should the Apostle exhort us to wish for the salvation of all, if God makes us wish for it already?

7. "Whereunto," *i.e.*, to preach which testimony regarding the will of God to save all, or, according to others, regarding "Christ crucified."......("I lie not, I say the truth"). The Greek adds, *in Christ.* These words are employed to silence the cavils of some who questioned his Apostleship. "Doctor of the Gentiles in faith and truth," may also mean a true and faithful doctor of the Gentiles.

8. Having pointed out, verse 1, the objects of prayer, and verse 2, the persons for whom we should pray, he now, as Apostle of the Gentiles, points out the *place* where we are to pray, viz., "in every place" suited for public prayer, of which he here speaks. Hence, it is not confined to the Jewish synagogues, nor to the temple of Jerusalem. "Anger and contention," or animosity towards each other, are vices peculiar to men. "Pure hands," mean, consciences free from guilt. It is not so much physical or bodily ablutions, as moral purity he requires.

9. Besides the foregoing dispositions, purity of conscience, and charity; (for, these he requires in *women* as well as in *men*), the Apostle requires in women, modesty in dress, when they appear at public prayer—an excessive regard for the fineries of dress being a vice peculiar to women. He wishes them to appear in a modest, becoming dress, redolent of "modesty and sobriety." The words, "adorning themselves with modesty and sobriety," may also mean, putting on modesty and chastity as their chief ornaments and not indulging in extravagant topping of the hair, nor in golden headbands, armlets, ear-rings, &c., nor in the various ornaments of precious stones, &c. He plainly regards the attendance at public prayer. The ornaments and forms of female dress were, in the luxurious cities of Greece and Asia Minor, carried to great excess, and the converted females had indulged too far in this, to the scandal of the Pagans, and the injury of the faith. Hence, the severe strictures of the Apostle.—(See 1 Cor. xi.; 1 Peter, iii. 3). He by no means condemns those modest ornaments of female dress, suited to their dignity and station in life.—(See 1 Peter, iii. 3).

Text.	Paraphrase.
10. But as it becometh women professing godliness, with good works.	10. But let them be chiefly ornamented with good works, as become Christian women, making piety their profession.
11. Let the woman learn in silence, with all subjection.	11. Let the women learn in silence with the utmost submission.
12. But I suffer not a woman to teach, nor to use authority over the man : but to be in silence.	12. But the woman I do not permit to teach in the church, nor to exercise authority over the man. She should observe silence.
13. For Adam was first formed ; then Eve.	13. *She should exercise no authority over the man ,* for, the man is her superior, having been first created. And she was created after him, as a helpmate, subordinate to him.
14. And Adam was not seduced : but the woman being seduced, was in the transgression.	14. *She should not teach on account of her imbecility of intellect and liability to seduction, which appears from the fact,* that she alone was seduced by the serpent to violate God's precept. Adam was not seduced, but by weak compliance, yielded to the persuasion of his wife.
15. Yet she shall be saved through child-bearing : if she continue in faith and love and sanctification with sobriety.	15. Yet, she shall be saved through the pious education of her children, provided she persevere in faith, in charity, in sanctification, in becoming self-restraint and propriety of morals.

Commentary.

10. The verse may also be interpreted thus :—But let them wear such ornaments as suit Christian women professing piety, which is to be manifested really and sincerely by good works, and not merely in words.

11. A woman should be silent in the church.—(1 Cor. xiv.)

12. She should not teach in the church, nor exercise authority over the man.

13. This shows, that being an inferior to man, because created after him, and as a helpmate for him, bearing to him the relation of a means to an end, she should not exercise authority over him.

14. From this it appears, that she should not teach, on account of the weakness of her mind, and her liability to seduction. Hence it was, that the serpent, knowing the weakness of the female intellect, addressed himself to her ; she alone was deceived, since she alone believed the words of the serpent, uttered for the purpose of deception. Whereas, Adam prevaricated more from a weak compliance, than from any belief in the promises of the serpent, that he would become " like unto God, knowing good and evil." And this is quite apparent from his answer to God : " The woman gave me of the tree." Whereas, Eve said : " The serpent *deceived* me."—(Gen. iii. 12, 13.)

15. Although the woman be not allowed to speak in the church, yet she shall have a pious occupation at home in the education of her children, and thus be saved, provided she follow not the example of Eve, but persevere in faith, charity, sanctity of morals, joined with a legitimate restraint upon the passions, even in the exercise of marriage. " If she continue." In Greek, *if they continue.*

CHAPTER III.

Analysis.

On Timothy, as Archbishop of Ephesus, and Primate of Asia, devolved the duty of ordaining bishops and the other members of the hierarchy, and giving them charge over the several cities. Hence, the Apostle instructs him in this chapter, in the duties and qualities of bishops and others. And although, in the early ages, the bishops were the first victims marked out for persecution, and the Episcopal office, was the threshold to martyrdom; still, it would seem that many, dazzled by the exalted elevation, inordinately ambitioned the Episcopal dignity, even in the very midst of persecution. The Apostle had also, with a prophetic insight into futurity, clearly foreseen, that the Episcopacy would, in future ages, be an object of ambition, with many wholly unfit for its tremendous responsibilities and onerous duties, "too heavy even for the shoulders of angels to bear"—"Onus quippe angelicis humeris formidandum."—(Council of Trent, SS. vi. c. 1). Hence, he dwells in this chapter, in describing at full length the exalted virtues which should adorn a bishop (1–7). The same applies, to a certain extent, to the subordinate members of the hierarchy, charged with the care of souls (8–14). He, next, instructs Timothy regarding the manner in which he should govern the Church, "the pillar and ground of truth" (15); and, finally, he points out the leading truth, the foundation of all the others, of which the Church is the divinely appointed guardian, viz., the great mystery of the Incarnation (16).

Text.

1. A FAITHFUL saying. If a man desire the office of a bishop, he desireth a good work.

2. It behoveth therefore a bishop to be blameless, the husband of one

Paraphrase.

1. It is a saying deserving of the most undoubted belief, that if a man desire the office of a bishop, he desires a distinguished work, an honourable employment.

2. A bishop, then, should be a man of irreproachable life; he should not be the husband of more than

Commentary.

1. "A faithful saying." This is a form of expression usually employed by the Apostle, when about to announce any truth of great importance, such as the following regarding the Episcopacy. "He desireth a good work." He says, "work," to show that in the Episcopacy, we should regard its onerous duties and responsibilities more than the eminence or dignity it confers. It is a post of labour, of vigilant superintendence and inspection, as the word "bishop" (ἐπίσκοπος) implies, rather than of ease and indulgence. "Good," which some interpret, *honourable*, since its end is to bring men to salvation; others, by "good," understand, *arduous, difficult*. He does not say, that whosoever desires the office of bishop, has a good WISH. Because, according to St. Augustine (*de Civitate Dei*, lib. 19, c. 19), and St. Thomas (*2da dæ quæst.* 185)— no one could, without the greatest presumption, wish for the Episcopal office, unless in case of great and rare necessities of the Church, inasmuch as no one could, without presumption, look upon himself as possessing the superiority required for a bishop, or encounter the responsibilities which such exalted superiority, aided by God's grace, is alone competent to master. In this verse, then, the Apostle wishes us to know that in aspiring to the Episcopal office, it is its heavy duties and responsibilities, rather than its honours or emoluments, we should regard.

2. The Apostle now proceeds to enumerate the virtuous qualities which should

Text.	Paraphrase.
wife, sober, prudent, of good be- haviour, chaste, given to hospitality, a teacher :	one wife ; or, he should not be twice married. He should be a man of sobriety, and consequently vigi- lant, prudent, of composed, regular deportment, chaste, a lover of hospitality to strangers, capable of teaching and instructing ;

Commentary.

adorn a bishop. First, he should be "blameless," free from all vice, and adorned with every virtue, like the great Bishop of bishops, whose representative he is, so that by being thus irreprehensible himself, he may enjoy greater liberty in discharging the duty of reprehending offenders. "The husband of one wife." This does not regard *simultaneous* polygamy, since *simultaneous* polygamy, or the having of more than one wife *at the same time*, was never allowed among the Christians ; it was abolished among the Jews, and prohibited by the law of Rome even among Pagans ; there is no necessity, therefore, for the Apostle's referring to it here. The same is clear, from a similar expression regarding widows (verse 9), "the wife of one husband," which must evidently mean, *successively.* Hence, he prevents the consecration of a man, as bishop, who was twice married. *Successive* polygamy was thus early instituted as an irregularity, both for mystical causes and moral reasons, viz., the fears of incontinency.

This passage furnishes no argument against the Catholic discipline of clerical celibacy. The words merely convey a *negative* precept, or a prohibition to consecrate bigamists, as bishops ; but, by no means, a precept for bishops to marry ; otherwise, St. Paul himself would be the first to violate it (1 Cor. vii.), so likewise would Timothy and Titus, who never married. It is not easy to define the precise period at which celibacy was made obligatory on those engaged in holy orders. The Apostles we are told by Tertullian (*de Monogamia*), were all unmarried, except St. Peter, And, that such was the general opinion in the third century, appears from the sect which then sprang up, called "*Apostolici*," who renounced marriage, in order the more perfectly to imitate the Apostles. And that St. Peter left his wife, is clear from the words, "behold we have left all," &c. We have no instance on record in which *persons already in Holy Orders* were permitted afterwards to marry, and retain the exercise of their respective orders. There is but one exception wherein the contrary was allowed. In the Council of Ancyra (A.D. 315), it was allowed only to deacons, who, at their ordination, protested their unwillingness to abstain from marriage. However, even this exception was abrogated and annulled by a subsequent disposition of the Church. As to the law of celibacy, in reference to those who, *before their ordination*, had been married, it is the opinion of many, that in the *Western Church*, the law making it obligatory, on those engaged in holy orders, to abstain from all intercourse with the wives they had married, before ordination, was derived from St. Peter.—(*See* Perrone "*De Celibatu Ecclesiastico*"). Tertullian gave up his wife when he was ordained a priest, and he evidently insinuates that such was the custom throughout the African Church.—"*Se dicaverunt filios illius ævi, i.e., primitivi status Paradisi*" (lib. *de Exhortatione Castit*). Aurelius, primate of Africa, expresses the same in the second Council of Carthage, *quod Apostoli docuerunt......nos quoque custodiamus.* Hence it was, that Pope Siricius (A.D. 385) threatens with punishment, such as act otherwise. Innocent I., *Epistola 2da, ad Vitricium* (A.D. 404), and Leo the Great, *Ep.* 167, *ad Rusticum,* suppose the same law to exist. And several early Councils enjoin the same.

As for the *Eastern* Church, St. Jerome and St. Epiphanius assure us that in the East as well as in the West, the ancient discipline was the same in this respect.

QUERY.—How reconcile this with the account left by Socrates and Sozomen, both of whom assure us, that when in the Council of Nice, it was proposed to render the discipline of the Eastern Church conformable to that of the Western, by making it imperative on those engaged in holy orders to separate from their wives, Paphnutius, an Egyptian bishop, who himself led a chaste life, opposed it, as too arduous and difficult ?

ANSWER.—In the first place, many persons question this relation of Socrates, &c. (*Vide Cabassutium, Notitia Ecclesiastica,* Canon 3, Con. Niceni.) They say that St. Jerome and St. Epiphanius, who lived before Socrates, and spent a great part of

Text.

3. Not given to wine, no striker, but modest, not quarrelsome, not covetous, but

4. One that ruleth well his own house, having his children in subjection with all chastity.

5. But if a man know not how

Paraphrase.

3. Not given to wine, not violent in temper, nor ready to strike, but meek and gentle; not quarrelsome, nor given to disputes and wrangling; not fond of money;

4. But he should be a person who governs well his own household, keeping his sons subject and obedient to him, in all propriety of moral conduct, particularly in the practice of chastity.

5. For, if he cannot properly manage his own

Commentary.

their lives in the East, had a better right to know the state of discipline prevailing there than Socrates had. And even admitting that Paphnutius did oppose such a law, and that the Council came into his way of thinking, it might be reconciled with the account of St. Jerome, in this way : the discipline of the *Western* Church, in regard to celibacy, prevailed in the *great Churches* of the East ; a few obscure Churches, in which persons could not be found to receive holy orders, with the obligation of future continency, might have departed from this discipline, and in consideration for these, the Council did not enact a law on the subject. Moreover, such a law, emanating from the Council of Nice, might be distorted by the heretics, who denounced marriage as *in se* evil, to favour their own views.

Be the truth or falsity of this narration of Socrates what it may, it is now certain that since the Council of Quinisextum or Trullanum (so called from being held in one of the halls of the imperial palace at Constantinople, called " *Trullus*," A.D. 692), the discipline of the Greek Church permits *deacons* and *priests* to cohabit with the wives they had married, *before* ordination ; the same indulgence was denied to *bishops*. This discipline, although introduced by an uncanonical synod, was afterwards permitted by the universal Church.

" Sober," a very necessary quality for him who, in virtue of his office, and as his name implies, is supposed to be a vigilant superintendent.

" Prudent," the Greek word means, *one who keeps his passions under thorough control.* " Of good behaviour," *i.e.*, of composed, regular deportment. On clerics in general, the Council of Trent enjoins, " *nihil nisi grave, moderatum et religione plenum præ se ferant.*"—(SS. 22, cap. 1). " Chaste, for which there is no corresponding word in the Greek. It must be, then, that the Vulgate interpreter gave the word for " prudent," σωφρονα, a twofold translation, to mean both " prudent " and " chaste." " Given to hospitality." " Hospitality "—a term so often abused and perverted to serve the worst purposes of reckless dissipation and dishonest extravagance—means, a love for strangers, whom a bishop should entertain at his house. Owing to the want of accommodation, and the spirit of persecution, many of the early converts were thrown on the charity of others, and the bishop, as their spiritual father, was therefore bound to be the first in attending to their wants. " A teacher." Teaching and preaching the divine word is the first duty of a bishop.—(Council of Trent, SS. 24, c. 4).

3. " Not given to wine," a disgraceful vice in a pastor of souls ; the Apostle refers to it here, because the Asiatics were not remarkable for their habits of temperance. A Pastor of souls should be a model of self-denial to his flock, especially in the matter of abstinence from intoxicating drinks. " No striker," not ready of hand to strike. In the Greek copies are to be found the words, μὴ αἰσχροκερδῆ, *not greedy of filthy lucre.* These are not found, however, in the works of St. Chrysostom, nor in any of the old Greek or Latin versions ; hence, it is probable they were introduced into the present Greek reading from a corresponding passage (chap i. 8) of Titus, in which they are read ; for, the last words of this verse, in our version " not covetous," express the same thing. " But modest," merciful, mild. " Not quarrelsome," not fond of disputes. " Not covetous," fond of money, " the root of all evils "—(chapter vi. of this Epistle.)

4. From the proper management of his own household, is inferred the fitness of a bishop to govern the Church.

5. The inference is quite clear : if a man cannot manage his own domestic little

Text.

to rule his own house, how shall he take care of the church of God?

6. Not a neophyte : lest being puffed up with pride, he fall into the judgment of the devil.

7. Moreover he must have a good testimony of them who are without : lest he fall into reproach and the snare of the devil.

8. Deacons in like manner chaste, not double-tongued, not given to much wine, not greedy of filthy lucre :

Paraphrase.

family, how can it be expected that he will properly manage the Church of God, composed of so many families?

6. Not a man lately converted to the faith and baptized, lest, dazzled by the dignity to which he is raised, he should grow proud, and thus incur the same condemnation, which a similar sin of pride brought on the devil.

7. He ought, likewise, be a person to whose integrity even the infidels could bear testimony, lest otherwise he fall into disgrace, by being reproached with his own crimes, while correcting others, and so fall into the snare of the devil, by deserting the faith, in a fit of despair.

8. Deacons, in like manner, should be distinguished for a becoming propriety of morals, particularly in the matter of chastity, not deceitfully saying one thing and thinking another, or saying one thing to one party, and a different thing to another ; not addicted to indulge over much in wine ; not avaricious in the pursuit of filthy lucre.

Commentary.

Church, how can he manage the larger Church of God? If he cannot manage private affairs, how can he be trusted with public concerns?

6. "Not a neophyte." The word νεόφυτον, literally means, *one newly planted ;* in allusion to our being engrafted by baptism on the body of Christ, and incorporated with him.—(Romans, vi. 5). Hence, the word "neophyte" means, one lately converted and baptized. Among the many reasons which might be adduced for the exclusion of such a person from the Episcopal office, the Apostle only adduces one, viz., lest, dazzled by his exalted position, and not sufficiently versed in the principles of faith, he would attribute all to his own merits, and thus incur the same judgment of condemnation which the devil, as yet "a neophyte" in heaven, had incurred for a similar sin of pride. As for cases of the ordination of neophytes, (*v.g.*) St. Ambrose, &c. ; these were exceptive cases, in which the precept of the Apostle was dispensed with, because the reason lest, "being puffed up," &c., was not apprehended ; but, on the contrary, a great good was likely to result to the Church.

7. There are two reasons why he should be a man of good character, even among the Pagans: first, "lest he fall into reproach," by being reproached with his former deeds of sin, and thus his authority necessarily diminished ; and secondly, "fall into the snare of the devil," *i.e.*, into anger, hatred, impatience ; or, finally, into despair, by being reproached with his former sins. Hence, the caution observed in all ages by the Church and by ecclesiastical superiors, in the advancement of men to Holy Orders, and to the awful responsibilities of the sacred ministry.—(*See* verse 22).

8. "Deacons in like manner should be chaste." The Greek word for "chaste," σεμνούς, means *grave, i.e.,* remarkable for moral propriety in general. The nature of his duties, viz., ministering at the altar, attending the bishop, dispensing the Holy Eucharist, &c., required in the deacon great purity of soul and body. "Not double-tongued," a most disgraceful vice in a man, whose tongue should be the organ of the Holy Ghost. "Not given to much wine ;" indulgence in wine weakens the faculties of the soul. "Not greedy of filthy lucre," a virtue most necessary for deacons, to whom were given in charge the treasures of the Church.

The Apostle passes here at once from the bishops to the deacons. Hence, it is asked, what is become of the second order of the clergy? Some divines, and among the rest, St. Thomas and St. Anselm, say, that the term, *Episcopus,* or bishop includes "priests," because priests, too, had to discharge the office of superintendent, or bishop, in a subordinate way. This opinion is rejected by others, who deny that *Episcopus,* or bishop, was ever used to designate a priest of the second order. They say, that in

Text.

9. Holding the mystery of faith in a pure conscience.

10. And let these also first be proved : and so let them minister, having no crime.

11. The women in like manner chaste, not slanderers, but sober, faithful in all things.

12. Let deacons be the husbands of one wife: who rule well their children, and their own houses.

13. For they that have ministered well, shall purchase to themselves a good degree, and much confidence in the faith which is in Christ JESUS.

Paraphrase.

9. Firmly adhering to and guarding Christian faith, or faith in the mysteries of the Christian religion, with a conscience pure and free from reproach.

10. And let these, too, be first proved and subjected to a rigorous trial for a long time, and after that, if no crime can be alleged against them, let them be admitted to the sacred ministry of serving.

11. The woman should, in like manner, be distinguished for moral propriety, particularly in the matter of chastity ; not given to calumny or detraction, and faithful in all things.

12. The deacons should be husbands of one wife, and also should have their sons and their entire household well regulated.

13. Those who will have well served in the office of deacon will merit for themselves an honourable post, and earn for themselves much confidence and freedom of speech in preaching the faith of Christ Jesus.

Commentary.

ecclesiastical usage, it always designated the chief pastor of a Church, and here the word "bishop" is used in the singular number (verse 1), while "deacons" is used (verse 8) in the plural, as if to show that, when speaking of bishops, the Apostle referred to that order of pastors, only one of whom can be found in any city ; whereas, *presbyteri* or priests were many in one Church, "*inducat presbyteros ecclesiæ.*"—(James v.) St. Epiphanius says—the reason why he makes no mention of priests is, because in the primitive ages, the public functions of the Church were discharged by the bishop, assisted by the deacons : hence, the ministrations of priests in many instances were not required, because the number of the faithful in several cities was very small. Of this, the city of Neocesarea, of which St. Gregory Thaumaturgus was bishop, furnishes an example. It may be given as a general answer, that the very great similarity between the functions of the bishops and priests, (*v.g.*) conferring sacraments, consecrating the Eucharist, celebrating Mass, &c., made it quite unnecessary for the Apostle to refer to the priests, as a distinct order ; whereas, the functions of the *deacons* were quite distinct, under whom he includes the *sub-deacons*, on account of the similarity of functions also.—(*See* Philippians, i. 1 ; Titus, i. 5).

9. "The mystery of faith," may also mean : the obscure truths of faith unknown to the common faithful. Some understand by it, the Eucharist, the distribution of which was one of the principal functions of the deacons ; according to them the meaning is, distributing the adorable Eucharist—which in the very words or consecration is termed "*mysterium fidei,*"—with a clean conscience.

11. By "women," some, with St. Chrysostom, understand deaconesses, or religious females, who were deputed by the bishops to perform certain functions in the Church. (*Vide* Epistle to the Romans, xvi.) Others understand by them, the wives of the deacons, whose faults might be injurious to religion and chargeable on the deacons themselves, in the same way as the bishop would be charged with the irregularity of his own household (verse 5). Both meanings might be united, as, probably, the wives of the deacons might have discharged the functions of deaconesses.

"Not slanderers," this is a vice to which women are very subject. "Faithful in all things ;" if this regard deaconesses, it has reference to the dispensing of the contributions among persons of their own sex, to whom men had no access, according to the custom of the Greeks ; if it regard the wives of the deacons, it means, that they should be faithful to the marriage contract (and not be adulteresses), and in the management of their domestic concerns.

12. This verse is explained in the same way as the second.

13. "A good degree," according to some, means the office of presbyter or bishop ; according to others, the highest grade of glory in eternal life, for their humble services

Text.

14. These things I write to thee, hoping that I shall come to thee shortly.

15. But if I tarry long, that thou mayest know how thou oughtest to behave thyself in the house of God, which is the church of the living God, the pillar and ground of the truth.

16. And evidently great is the mystery of godliness, which was manifested in the flesh, was justified in the spirit, appeared unto Angels,

Paraphrase.

14. These things I write to thee, hoping to come to thee shortly.

15. But should any unforeseen accident retard me longer than I expect, I write in order that thou mayest learn from the instructions given, how to conduct thyself in managing and regulating the affairs of the house of God, which is the Church of the living God —the pillar and the ground of truth.

16. And confessedly, beyond all question, the truth of which I speak, and which is the foundation of all Christian faith, is a great mystery, hidden during all past ages from the world—a truth calculated to beget

Commentary.

in the functions of deacon. "Much confidence in the faith which is in Christ Jesus," *i.e.*, much confidence in admonishing and correcting others relative to their Christian duties. This will be the result of their own personal irreprehensibility.

15. "The house of God," in which, as in a well regulated household or family, all the members have their proper functions and duties, "which (house) is the Church of the living God," to distinguish it from the churches, or rather temples of false gods, who, as such, *i.e.*, as vested with divinity, have no existence whatever. This Church "is the pillar and ground of truth ;" because, as the pillar supports the superstructure, so does the Church preserve and guard inviolate the deposit of faith left by God to the world. Hence, in matters of faith, the Church can never err, otherwise she could not be termed "the pillar of truth." She must, therefore be gifted with *infallibility*, of which the promises of Christ are the guarantee ; for, unless she were vested with this supernatural gift, she could never support or guard the faith against the insidious assaults of her manifold enemies ; nor could she define points, the most minute and difficult, surpassing the human understanding (such as many points of faith are), with the accuracy required to furnish, in all cases, sufficient grounds or motives of credibility, for the firm assent of faith. How could it be expected that the learned and inquisitive portion of mankind would embrace truths incomprehensible to reason (as many of the truths of faith are), unless they had a sufficient security that the authority which propounded them was infallible in so doing ? If the propounding authority were not infallible, the precise point of faith, which men would be called upon to believe unhesitatingly, might not really be revealed at all. The fact, therefore, of the Church being constituted "the pillar of truth," proves her *infallibility*. Hence, it appears, that God would not have propounded sufficient motives of credibility for bringing *all classes* of men to faith, and consequently to salvation, unless he left some infallible means of arriving at the knowledge of his divine revelation. As, then, he has constituted the Church, "the pillar of truth," of course, in reference to *all classes of men, and all classes of revealed truth*, he must have gifted her with infallibility—the only motive accommodated to the learned—otherwise, she might be the bulwark of error. This passage also proves the *visibility* of the Church ; since the duties marked out for Timothy could not be performed in an *invisible* Church ; and as the precepts given to Timothy apply to all bishops, at all times ; hence, the Church must be, at all times, *visible*.

16. The truth, of which the Church is the guardian and depositary, has for its basis and foundation, the great fundamental article of Christ's Incarnation, and the other mysteries of his life, death, and resurrection, which flow therefrom. These are the foundation of all Christian faith. The Apostle calls this Incarnation of the Son of God, a "great mystery," because it was concealed during all past ages (Ephesians, iii.), and was only revealed of late. It is a "mystery of godliness," because calculated to promote the worship and glory of God. The Apostle refers to it particularly here, because it was a fundamental truth regarding which many of the early heretics had erred. The Greek reading of this verse runs thus : *and, confessedly, it is a great mystery of piety, God has been manifested in the flesh, has been justified in the spirit, appeared to angels*, &c. This reading is found in St. Chrysotom. The Vulgate reading of this verse

Text.

hath been preached unto the gentiles, is believed in the world, is
taken up in glory.

Paraphrase.

feelings of piety towards God ; and it is this—viz.,
that God—or the Word of God—of his own nature,
invisible, has been manifested and rendered visible in
human flesh, has been justified from the calumnies
of the Jews and proved, what He declared himself
to be—viz., the natural Son of God—by the stupendous
miracles which He performed, and by the gifts of the
Holy Ghost visibly poured forth upon Him ; was seen
by angels, who ministered to Him repeatedly, adoring
Him at his Nativity, Resurrection, &c. ; was preached
to the Gentiles, who were before permitted to walk in
their own ways ; was believed in the world, after He
was preached there ; and was assumed gloriously into
heaven.

Commentary.

is supported by the Syriac, Ethiopic, and Armenian versions, and by the Latin Fathers
generally. The Greek reading more clearly and explicitly conveys the meaning which
is commonly given to our Vulgate reading, as in the Paraphrase. The words are understood of the mystery of the Incarnation, and of the other mysteries of our blessed
Saviour's life and death, which flow from the Incarnation.

"Which was manifested in the flesh," means, that God, as the Greek expressly has
it, who was heretofore invisible, became visible in human flesh, which he assumed at
his Incarnation. "Justified in the spirit ;" "justified" has frequently, in the SS.
Scriptures, the meaning given it here, viz., declared and proved to be just, &c. ;
"appeared unto angels," who adored him at his Nativity, Resurrection, &c., and
frequently ministered to him ; he was seen by them now in a new form, and
his multifarious wisdom, hitherto unknown, was now clearly seen by them.—
Ephesians, iii.

CHAPTER IV.

Analysis.

The Apostle, having before established the unerring authority of the Church, in guarding the deposit of revealed truth against the encroachments and insidious attacks of error, now asserts in this chapter, that certain destructive errors shall soon spring up (1-5). Against these he admonishes Timothy, to guard the flock confided to his charge, by instructing them in sound doctrine (6). He exhorts him to works of piety (8) ; by the gravity of his conduct to merit public respect (12) ; and by keeping in mind the exalted gift conferred on him (14), to live in such a way as to insure his own salvation and that of his people (16).

Text.	Paraphrase.
1. NOW the spirit manifestly saith, that in the last times some shall depart from the faith, giving heed to spirits of error, and doctrines of devils,	1. Now, the Holy Ghost openly and clearly reveals to me, that in the times immediately approaching some will apostatize from the faith, giving heed and attention to erring, deluded men, and to diabolical doctrines advanced by them.
2. Speaking lies in hypocrisy, and having their conscience seared,	2. Men who, putting on the appearance of sanctity, propound false doctrines, which appear to be holy, whose consciences are callous to every feeling of remorse or compunction, in the commission of deeds of iniquity,
3. Forbidding to marry, to abstain from meats, which God hath	3. Prohibiting marriage and (*commanding*) men to abstain from certain kinds of food, which God created

Commentary.

1. "In the last times." The word "last," as it appears from the Greek, ὑστέροις, means times immediately approaching : the Apostle, in speaking thus, wishes to intimate to Timothy, that he will himself have to encounter these errors, and, therefore, must use the utmost diligence. "Will depart." In Greek, ἀποστήσονται, *will apostatize.* "Spirits of error." A Hebrew form of expression for *erring spirits ;* "doctrines of devils," by a similar idiom means, *devilish,* or *diabolical doctrines*—doctrines of which the devil is the author and suggester.

2. "Speaking lies in hypocrisy." This is connected with the preceding verse ; attending to diabolical doctrines advanced by men, speaking lies, &c. "In hypocrisy," may either affect the doctrines which have the appearance of holy doctrines, viz., the prohibition to marry, has the appearance of recommending chastity ; and abstinence from meat, the appearance of temperance ; or, the men who, while they publicly pretend to lead lives of sanctity, in private, indulge in every species of immorality. "And having their conscience seared." In the word "seared"—the Greek of which, κεκαυτηριασμενων, means, *cauterized*—there may be an illusion to a brand of infamy stamped on criminals. In that case, the words mean, that, notwithstanding their external profession of sanctity, their souls contain the certain seeds, the undoubted marks of corruption, arising from their bad habits. As a bodily sore is the source of bodily corruption ; so, is their former immorality the source of fresh deeds of sin ; or, the allusion contained in the word "seared," may refer to the cauterizing of mortified flesh, sometimes resorted to by surgeons. In this case, the meaning is that given in the Paraphrase—that their consciences are steeled against every feeling of remorse or compunction, in the commission of iniquity.

3. He instances one or two of their diabolical doctrines, prohibiting marriage (*com-*

Text.

created to be received with thanks-giving by the faithful, and by them that have known the truth.

4. For every creature of God is good, and nothing to be rejected that is received with thanksgiving:

5. For it is sanctified by the word of God and prayer.

Paraphrase.

for the purpose of being used with thanksgiving by the faithful and by those who have known the truth.

4. For, it is a certain truth, which they should know, that, of its own intrinsic nature, everything created by God is good; and, therefore, that nothing deserves to be rejected as evil of itself; but that every gift of God should rather be used and received with thanksgiving.

5. Moreover, the use of it is sanctified by the word of God and prayer.

Commentary.

manding), to abstain from certain kinds of food. The word, *commanding*, is evidently understood to fill up the sentence. "Which God hath created to be received," &c. The Apostle passes by the first error, as too patent to need refutation; and the second error regarding abstinence from certain sorts of food, as of themselves evil, he refutes, first, from the intention of God in creating them, which was, that "the faithful," or "those who have known the truth," would use them with thankfulness. God has destined these kinds of food for the use of unbelievers also; but they deprive themselves of the legitimate use of them frequently, as in the present instance, from false and superstitious notions. It is only the faithful that use them properly; and it is for the faithful in a particular way, that all things were destined by God.

4. And among the truths which all the faithful should know is, this proposed by Moses in Genesis, that "God saw, that all things which he created were good," and hence it follows, that no food deserves to be rejected, of its own nature, (such is the force of the Greek word, απoβλητον, corresponding with "to be rejected,") but that all kinds of food should be received and used with thanksgiving. The second argument, then, is derived from the authority of God asserting that all things created by him were good.

5. Again, he says, that any injurious tendency which might be attached to food, owing to the power which, after man's transgression, "Satan obtained over earthly things, is removed, and this power, counteracted by the "word of God;" which either means the words taken from SS. Scripture, employed in the blessing of food; or, faith, which comes from the word of God, and is the word believed. "And prayer," which we offer to God to remove all injurious tendency from food. Hence, the custom of *grace* at meals so early as the day the Apostle, as also of exorcisms and benedictions of bread, wine, &c., to repress the power, which the demon has, of effecting evil, by means of material things.

In this entire passage there is no ground whatever for argument against the celibacy of the clergy, or the fasts of the Catholic Church. Surely, the Apostle does not mean to assert, that it is "the doctrine of devils," to forbid marriage in certain instances, (*v.g.*) when the parties are bound by vows, or in case of other impediments; if so, he was himself the first to practise the doctrine of devils (chap. v. 11.) Nor can he call the precept of abstaining from certain kinds of food, in some cases, the doctrine of demons; for so, would not God himself, in forbidding Adam to eat the fruit in Paradise, be guilty of sanctioning such a doctrine?

To what then does the Apostle refer? He refers to the errors broached by the ancient heretics, Ebion, Saturninus, the Encraticæ, the Marcionites, the Manichees, and the whole tribe of the early *illuminati* or Gnostics, who forbade marriage, and the use of certain food, wine, &c., as *in se* evil, and proceeding from an evil principle. That such doctrines were held by the heretics in question we have the authority of the ancient Fathers. This is asserted by St. Ignatius in his Epistle to the Philadelphians regarding the Ebionites; by St. Iræneus (Lib i. c. 22), and by Theodoret regarding Saturninus; by St. Chrysostom regarding the Encraticæ and Marcionites; by St. Augustine, St. Jerome, and St. Epiphanius regarding the Manichees. Such were the doctrines denounced by the Apostle as "the doctrines of devils." The same is clear from the line of argument adopted by the Apostle in refutation of them. He maintains

Text.

6. These things proposing to the brethren, thou shalt be a good minister of Christ Jesus, nourished up in the words of faith and of the good doctrine which thou hast attained unto.

7. But avoid foolish and old wives' fables : and exercise thyself unto godliness.

8. For bodily exercise is profitable to little : but godliness is profitable to all things, having promise of the life that now is, and of that which is to come.

Paraphrase.

6. By expounding these things to your brethren, you will prove yourself to be a good minister of Christ, and you will show how well educated and nurtured you have been in the faith and in sound doctrine, which you have perfectly learned and followed up.

7. But avoid and despise foolish and old woman's stories, but exercise yourself in solid piety, attending to these actions of morality, that advance the worship of God which faith alone points out to us.

8. For the corporal exercise of the gymnasium profits only in a trifling degree and but for a short time ; whereas, piety, or the exercise of the spiritual gymnasium, is useful for securing all sorts of blessings, having annexed to it the promise of present and future goods.

Commentary.

that every creature of God is *in se* good, and that nothing of itself deserves to be rejected (verse 4). The heretics, to whom he refers, must, therefore, have maintained the opposite. Do Catholics prohibit marriage as evil *in itself?* Certainly not. They maintain it to be, *of itself,* good, even one of the Seven Sacraments of the New Law. But, this would not warrant marriage in every case. The heretics themselves, who assail the Catholic discipline, would not allow marriage between persons within the prohibited degrees of kindred, nor between two persons, one of whom was already married ; until lately, marriage was interdicted by them to the Fellows of Trinity College, and at this very moment, it is interdicted to policemen, until after certain terms of service ; and still they would not have it said, that they are acting against the doctrine of the Apostle. How absurd and inconsistent, therefore, is their charge against the Church of God, on this score ? Do Catholics, in forbidding certain meats on fast days, forbid them, as evil of *themselves?* Certainly not. It might as well be made a charge against a physician, who prohibits the use of certain meats to his patients, that he acts against the doctrine of the Apostle, as charge it upon the Catholic Church. She enjoins abstinence from certain meats and certain quantities of food, for spiritual reasons, as spiritual efficacious medicines, to cure the maladies of the soul ; for, " there are certain devils, which can be cast out only by prayer and fasting."

6. By expounding these things to your brethren, and cautioning them against the opposite errors, you will prove yourself a good minister of Christ, and show how well nurtured you had formerly been in " faith and doctrine," *i.e.,* in the knowledge of your practical duties. " Nourished," may also mean, being nourished and supported by the constant reflection on faith, &c. (ver. 15). " Meditate on these things, &c. The word " nourished," ἐντρεφόμενος, being, in the Greek, a middle verb, may also have an active signification, thus: " bringing them up and forming them in the summary of your faith," &c. The Greek word for "minister," διάκονος, literally means, *a deacon.*

7. He probably alludes to the stories of the heretics, particularly of the Simonians, who, as we are informed by St. Epiphanius and Augustine, forged long and foolish tales, regarding the good and evil principles, the fight of the angels, &c.

8. Having alluded in the words, " exercise thyself," to the athletic exercises of the gymnasium, so common among the Greeks, he shows the advantages of the spiritual gymnasium over the corporal, so much prized and practised amongst them. The corporal exercise has but a trifling temporary result ; it produced bodily health and vigour, and gained a mere corruptible crown, which lasted but a short.time (1 Cor. ix.); whereas, the spiritual gymnasium, *i.e.,* piety, is useful for all things, for obtaining all sorts of blessings, temporal and spiritual, having annexed to it the promise of the goods of this life and of the life to come. " Seek first the kingdom of God and his justice, and all these things will be added unto you."—(Matt. vi. 33). And although men the most holy are, oftentimes, in this life visited with afflictions, they shall be fully compensated with a higher order of goods, (*v.g.*) patience, spiritual joy, &c., in this life, and eternal glory in the life to come.

Text.

9. A faithful saying and worthy of all acceptation.

10. For therefore we labour and are reviled, because we hope in the living God, who is the Saviour of all men, especially of the faithful.

11. These things command and teach.

12 Let no man despise thy youth: but be thou an example of the faithful, in word, in conversation, in charity, in faith, in chastity.

13. Till I come, attend unto reading, to exhortation, and to doctrine.

14. Neglect not the grace that is in thee, which was given thee by

Paraphrase.

9. This assertion regarding the good effects of piety is a true saying, worthy of entire, unqualified acceptance.

10. For, we willingly submit to the labours and miseries of this life, and we patiently bear the reproaches and persecutions of men on this account, because we hope in the living God, who is the Saviour of all men, especially of the faithful.

11. Teach all these things with the authority of a bishop.

12. In order that no one shall despise thee on account of thy youth, be the model of the faithful in the gravity and prudence of your words, in the sweetness and amiability of your external intercourse with them, in the expression of ardent charity, of lively faith, and in the purity of morals, particularly in chastity.

13. Until I come to you, diligently attend to reading the SS. Scriptures, to exhorting the faithful to continue in the practice of the virtues which they already know, and to the instruction of the ignorant in the duties and truths of religion.

14. Do not suffer the grace to lie dormant, which had been conferred on thee, when, in accordance with

Commentary.

9. He adds this on account of the importance of our keeping in mind the rewards attached to the service of God, as a stimulus for us to attend to our religious duties. We may fairly attribute our indifference and spiritual indolence to our forgetfulness of these exalted rewards.

10. In this verse, is found an argument similar to that in favour of the resurrection (1 Cor. xv.) derived from the labours, perils and bad treatment which the Apostles endured. They submitted to all, because they hoped in the living God, who is Saviour of all men, whom he furnishes with the *necessary* means of salvation, but chiefly of the faithful, whom he furnishes with still more *special* and *efficacious* helps, and whose temporal wants he will not neglect, so far as the, conduce to the great end of their eternal salvation. "We labour," &c. In Greek, κα κοπιῶμεν καὶ ὀνειδιζόμεθα, *we both labour and are reviled. Both*, is wanting in the chief manuscripts.

11. He tells Timothy, to teach these things, regarding "the great mystery" (iii. 16), heresies, piety, &c., with the authority of a bishop; for, although young, he was still a bishop, and, therefore, vested with authority.

12. Timothy was a young prelate; hence, to conciliate the respect due to his station, the Apostle tells him to supply, by the gravity of his manners and the maturity of Episcopal virtue, what was wanting to his years. "Be an example of the faithful in word." Let your words be grave and prudent. The words, "in conversation," refer to his conduct and external intercourse with the people, which should be marked by sweetness and amiability. "In charity." In the manifestation of your love of God and your neighbour. In the Greek are added here, the words, *in the spirit*, expressive of the fervour of God's spirit working in him. These words are not in the chief Manuscripts, nor in the Fathers generally. "In faith,"......"in chastity." Hence, Timothy must have led a single life; otherwise, how could he be the model of chastity to others? and the Greek word, ἁγνείᾳ, expresses chastity of the highest order, virginal chastity.

13. "Attend unto reading." He refers to reading the SS. Scriptures, which St. Ambrose calls, *Liber Sacerdotalis*, and from which the Pastor of souls will derive matter for "exhortation and doctrine," that is for private ("exhortation") and public instruction. ("Doctrine.")

14. "Neglect not the grace that is in thee," &c. What this "grace" refers to is much controverted. Some, adhering to the meaning of the Greek word, χαρισμα, which

Text.

prophecy, with imposition of the hands of the priesthood.

15. Meditate upon these things, be wholly in these things; that thy profiting may be manifest to all.

16. Take heed to thyself, and to doctrine: be earnest in them. For in doing this thou shalt both save thyself and them that hear thee.

Paraphrase.

the revelation of God, the priests (of the first order) imposed hands on thee.

15. Make these things the subject of repeated meditation. Be constantly engaged in them, so that your advancement, both in piety and knowledge, may be clearly seen by all men.

16. Attend to your own sanctification, and to the instruction of your flock; persevere in these two things; for, thus, you will save both yourself and those who hear you.

Commentary.

means, a *gratia gratis data*, or a gratuitous gift, given for the benefit of others, and not necessarily supposing the sanctification of the subject on whom it is conferred, understand it of the Episcopal order conferred on him, and enabling him to exercise certain functions. Others understand it, of the gratuitous gift necessary for discharging the pastoral duties conferred on him at ordination, viz., the gift of teaching, exhorting, &c., which, although possessed by Timothy before his ordination, was still confirmed and increased at his consecration, when he also received sanctifying grace; and this is the gift which St. Paul tells Timothy to reduce to practice, by exhorting and teaching. It seems very likely, that "grace" means also, *sanctifying* grace of a specific kind, which, together with a right to *actual* graces, when necessary in due time, for the discharge of certain specific duties and the exercise of certain functions, is conferred in the sacraments. This sanctifying grace, joined to the *actual* graces referred to, is, what Divines call, *sacramental grace*, and to this St. Paul here refers; for, the Greek word in many places denotes, *sanctifying grace*, (*v.g.*) Rom. v. 15, vi. 23. *Sacramental grace*, as it is called, is not, as a habit, really distinct from sanctifying grace in general. It is only a new intrinsic permanent modification, a special vigour superadded to sanctifying grace, which is also the principle of actual graces, to be conferred in due time and circumstances.—Billuart. "Which was given thee by prophecy, with the imposition," &c., *i.e.*, which was given thee, when, by divine revelation, the bishops, or priests of the first order, imposed hands on thee. That he refers to the bishops, is clear, because he says (2 Ep. i. 6), that he himself imposed hands on him, being the principal person employed in his consecration. The only ceremony which he refers to in the ordination of Timothy is the "imposition of hands;" because this was a ceremony common to many other things, and served to conceal the knowledge of the sacred mysteries and the arcana of the faith from the infidels.

16. "Attend to thyself and to doctrine." A most useful exhortation for such as are engaged in the exalted duties of saving the souls of their brethren. While ministering to others, they may neglect their own sanctification, and while saving thousands of others, they should take care to escape damnation by attending to themselves. This all-important work of self-sanctification, the Pastor of souls will promote most effectually by constant meditation on the great truths of eternity. In such meditation, the fire of divine charity, and a burning thirst for his own perfection, will spring forth. In truth, it is not too much to say, that without a proper attention to this holy exercise of mental prayer in some form, the salvation of a Pastor of souls is *morally impossible;* in other words, he will scarcely be saved without it. He will also promote his sanctification by securing for himself, through a filial devotion to the glorious Queen of Heaven, the powerful protection of this Most Chaste Virgin and Mother, in whom no one ever confided and was confounded. *Memorare, O piissima Virgo Maria,* &c. A Pastor desirous of his own sanctification, and that of his people, should never fail to recommend himself and them to the powerful protection of St. Joseph also. In all his necessities, he should have recourse to St. Joseph. "*Ite ad Joseph.*"— (Genesis, xli. 55).

"Be earnest in them." This is the one thing necessary for a Pastor of souls—his own sanctification and that of his people. This alone will form the subject matter of his

Commentary.

judgment when he shall stand before the tribunal of Jesus Christ. He shall have to render a most rigorous account of the means he employed for securing the faith and piety of his people. The more exalted his station, the heavier, the judgment of neglect, *judicium durissimum his qui præsunt.* Woe to the Pastor of souls, if embarking in affairs that do not concern either the temporal preservation, or, the sanctification and salvation of his people, he selfishly becomes wholly engrossed in personal, secular matters, at variance with the perfection of his state and opposed to his sublime calling!

CHAPTER V.

Analysis.

In this chapter, the Apostle instructs Timothy in the manner of admonishing and correcting both the young and the old (1–2). In the next place, he gives him instructions regarding the widows who were to be admitted among those supported by the Church, on a part of the offerings of the faithful. He points out the quality of such widows:—They should be really destitute (3); given to prayer (5); sixty years of age (9); of a good reputation (10). He then points out the class of widows who should not be admitted among this number (11, 12, 13).

He, in the next place, instructs him how he should treat his clergy, both in supporting them (17), and in receiving accusations against them (19, 20).

Finally, he implores of him to act the part of a just judge in deciding Ecclesiastical matters (21). Not to be rash or precipitate in admitting persons to Holy Orders, and to lead a life of chastity.

Text.	Paraphrase.
1. AN ancient man rebuke not : but entreat him as a father : young men, as brethren ;	1. Rebuke not with severity a person your senior in years, but admonish him with sweetness, so as to appear entreating him, like a son entreating his father, and sweetly exhort and admonish young men as brothers.
2. Old women, as mothers : young women, as sisters, in all chastity.	2. Aged women admonish, as mothers ; and the young, as sisters, guarding against everything either in the language of admonition, or its circumstances, that might endanger chastity (or lead to disedification).

Commentary.

1. "An ancient man," *i.e.*, your senior in years, "rebuke not." The Greek is, μὴ ἐπιπλήξῃς, *strike not;* it means, to rebuke in a harsh manner, "but entreat him as a father." The Greek word for "entreat," ταρακαλει, means, also, to *admonish.* This, of course, regards ordinary cases of delinquency; because if an old man commits grievous sin and gives scandal to the young, he forfeits the privileges of age, and should be rebuked with severity.—"Young men as brethren;"—*admonish*, understood.

2. "Young women, as sisters, in all chastity." Neither in the language addressed to them, nor in the circumstances of the time, place, &c., should there be anything that might endanger chastity, or, in any way, tend to disedification.

Text.

3. Honour widows, that are widows indeed.

4. But if any widow have children, or grand-children ; let her learn first to govern her own house, and to make a return of duty to her parents: for this is acceptable before God.

5. But she that is a widow indeed and desolate, let her trust in God, and continue in supplications and prayers night and day.

6. For she that liveth in pleasures, is dead while she is living.

Paraphrase.

3. Nourish and support the widows, who may truly be called such, in the strict sense of the word, *i.e.*, destitute of all aid.

4. But if any widow be not thus destitute—if she have children or grand children, let them learn, in the first place, to regulate their own house properly, by supporting their near friends and widowed domestics, and not throw them as a burden on the Church, and pay back to their parents the duty of support, which is due by them, for the care taken of them in their infancy ; for, this exercise of filial piety is pleasing and acceptable to God.

5. But let her, who is a widow indeed, that is to say, desolate and destitute of all aid, have recourse to God and hope in him, and devote her entire time, both day and night, to fervent prayers and supplications.

6. But the widow who lives a life of luxury and self-indulgence, although living and animated in body, is dead in soul, dead to God and to grace.

Commentary.

3. " Honour," *i.e.*, support. " Honour " has this meaning in many passages of SS. Scripture—(*v.g.*) Matthew, xv., also in verse 17, of this chapter. " That are widows indeed," *i.e.*, in the proper sense of the word ; for the Greek corresponding with widow, χηρας, is derived from a root, signifying, *to be destitute*.

4. " Let her learn." In the Greek it is, *let them learn*, &c. This latter reading is preferred in the Paraphrase, because it would appear, that the Apostle, having in the preceding verse referred to the widow, who is deserving of support, now shows who the widow is, that is not deserving of the public support. Again, the Greek word for " govern," ευσεβειν, means the exercise of that piety which children owe their parents. Moreover, the widow in question is supposed to have " grandchildren " also, and it could not be required of her " to make a return of duty to her parents," in reference to them, since she had done so already towards her children. Besides, the phrase, " make a return of duty to her children," would bear a very forced construction in the Vulgate reading ; whereas, according to the Greek, it runs quite smooth. Finally, the reason assigned, " for this is acceptable before God," is very like the reason given (Col. iii.), why children should obey their parents. This reading is adopted by St. Jerome, Œcumenius, &c., and preferred by Estius.

The Apostle here treats of Ecclesiastical widows, who were supported at the expense of the Church. In the infancy of the Church, some of these lived together in communities, and others, in their own houses. They made vows of chastity (verse 12), and devoted their entire time to works of piety (verse 5). From among them were taken the deaconesses, who were charged with the instruction of ignorant females, and with preparing them for baptism. They ought to be advanced in age, and were placed under the care of the Bishop ; hence, among the reasons assigned by St. Chrysostom for flying the Episcopal office, he assigns the duty of taking charge of widows (lib. 3, *de Sacerdotio*). In the time of St. Augustine, these had a distinct dress of black colour, as appears from the Council of Orange (c. 15) ; 4th Council of Carthage (c. 104) ; and St. Augustine's Ep. 199, *ad Ecdiciam*. The Apostle says nothing about honouring *virgins*, because the honour to which he refers is the honour of support, and the widows alone required this, the virgins being supported by their parents.

5. According to the Greek, in this verse he assigns some of the good qualities which should distinguish the Ecclesiastical widow. For, " let her trust in God," &c. ; the Greek is ηλπικεν, *she has trusted*, or, *trusts in God*. In our version, the words convey an exhortation. The Greek indicative form is read in St. Chrysostom.

6. This verse would favour the Greek reading in the preceding. The ecclesiastical widow, worthy of support, must be a person addicted to prayer, &c. ; for, as to those widows that lead a life of ease and indulgence, though their bodies be animated, their

Text.

7. And this give in charge, that they may be blameless.

8. But if any man have not care of his own, and especially of those of his house, he hath denied the faith, and is worse than an infidel.

9. Let a widow be chosen of no less than three-score years of age, who hath been the wife of one husband.

10. Having testimony for her good works, if she have brought up children, if she have received to harbour, if she have washed the saints' feet, if she have ministered to them that suffer tribulation, if she have diligently followed every good work.

11. But the younger widows avoid. For when they have grown wanton in Christ, they will marry:

Paraphrase.

7. Command and explain what I have said to all widows, that they may be free from all reproach, and that the Church may be saved from scandal.

8. But if any one neglect to make the necessary provision for his near relations, particularly those most closely connected with him, such a man, by unnatural conduct of this sort, has practically denied the faith, and is worse than an infidel.

9. A widow, in order to be enrolled on the catalogue of those to be supported by the Church, should have reached her sixtieth year, and not be married more than once.

10. She should have the reputation of practising good works, among the rest, of piously educating her children, and of exercising hospitality, according to her means, towards holy strangers, of washing their feet, according to the existing usage, of having afforded aid and consolation to the afflicted, and of having sought every occasion of doing good.

11. But younger widows do not admit on this catalogue; for, after having been supported at the expense of the Church, they will grow wanton, and recalcitrate against Christ, and indulge a wish to marry an earthly spouse:

Commentary.

souls are dead. The words of the gospel, "Suffer the dead to bury their dead," are similar in signification to the words, "she is dead, while living." Such a person is not a widow indeed; for, though bereft of her husband, she is not still desolate. She employs the means of livelihood which she possesses in purposes of self-indulgence, and not in the exercise of benevolence or charity.

7. These things, regarding the obligation of prayer, of avoiding luxurious living, &c., teach all widows, so that they may be free from reproach. "And this give in charge." In Greek, ταῦτα παράγγελλε, *and these things give in charge.*

8. Here he confirms, by a general assertion, what he applied to children and grand-children (verse 4), wherein he said, that if a widow have children, &c., they should pay back the reciprocal duty of support. Here, he goes farther, and asserts if any person, man or woman, neglects the care of his (or her) *own,* which is generally understood of such as have claims on them, on the grounds of consanguinity or marriage, "and especially those of his house," which is commonly understood of near relatives, parents, brothers, and such as generally live in the same house with a person, and form part of his family, such a one has, practically, and in deed, "denied the faith, and is worse than an infidel;" for, the infidels are not dead to these natural feelings.

9. The widow, to be enrolled on the Ecclesiastical catalogue, must be sixty years of age; because, then, she is unfit for labour, and not in danger of incontinence, to which younger widows would be exposed. At this time, such persons were not so securely enclosed, as the nuns are now within convents. She must be a person who was but once married, a mark of continency.

10. She must be a person, whom a character for exercising good works will pronounce deserving of support. He instances a few of these good works:—Bringing up her family in piety, exercising hospitality toward holy travellers, washing their feet, according to the custom then existing. The exercise of hospitality was, in the infancy of the Church, very necessary and meritorious, owing to the want of accommodation, and the danger of perversion at the Pagan places of entertainment. The poor widow should exercise it, according to her means and ability. "If she have diligently followed every good work," *i.e.,* lost no opportunity of doing good, and had the will and inclination, even when the power of doing good was wanting.

11. He tells him not to admit permanently, by religious vows, widows under sixty,

Text.

12. Having damnation, because they have made void their first faith.

13. And withal being idle they learn to go about from house to house; and are not only idle, but tattlers also, and busy-bodies, speaking things which they ought not.

14. I will therefore that the younger should marry, bear children, be mistresses of families, give no occasion to the adversary to speak evil.

15. For some are already turned aside after satan.

Paraphrase.

12. Thus incurring damnation for having violated and rendered void the promise which they made before, to their spouse Christ.

13. Another reason for their rejection is, that they are accustomed to go about, doing nothing, from house to house, and they are not merely idle, but they also indulge in garrulity and foolish talkativeness, and in curiously prying into the concerns of others, and engaging in conversations which are not becoming.

14. Considering all things, then, I prefer that, before engaging in vows of chastity, the younger widows should marry, bear children, and manage domestic concerns, and deprive the enemies of the faith of every opportunity of maligning our holy religion.

15. For, already some of them have deserted Christ, and have passed over to Satan.

Commentary.

because there is great danger that they will become wanton. The Greek word for "grown wanton in Christ," κατεστρηνιάσωσι τοῦ Χριστοῦ, conveys an allusion to cattle, that, through wantonness, throw off the yoke, and kick against their masters : so, these widows are apt to grow wanton against Christ, by whose Church they were to supported, and wish to marry an earthly lover to the injury of their heavenly Spouse, whom they were pledged by vow. "Wanton in Christ." In Greek, *wanton against Christ.*

12. "Having damnation," *i.e.*, rendering themselves, by this wish to marry, liable to damnation, "because they have made void their first faith," *i.e.*, *they rejected* (as in the Greek, ηθέτησαν) and consequently violated the promise or vow of chastity, which they formerly made to Christ. This is the interpretation given of this verse by all the Holy Fathers, and, in fact, none other can be admitted : for, all the interpretations given of it by heretics, who are opposed to vows, are manifestly opposed to the scope and words of the Apostle ;—he evidently says, that they have damnation, because they wish to marry. Now, if there were merely question of deserting the faith, and violating their promise at baptism—or of committing carnal sins, as some of them explain it— what would the wish to marry have to do with these?—and, manifestly, in the Apostle's mind, this wish to marry is the cause of their damnation. Surely, marriage is not opposed to baptismal faith, and it is one of the remedies against concupiscence. The "faith" here opposed to marriage is a vow of continency, and "faith" has often the meaning of promise (Rom. iii.; Gal. v.; 2 Tim. iv.); he calls it "first," *i.e.*, former, as in Apocal. ii. 4, 5—"*prima opera fac.*" "*Charitatem tuam primam reliquisti*," *i.e.*, *priorem*, also (Acts, i. 1), "*primum quidem sermonem*," *i.e.*, *priorem sermonem.*

13. Another reason for not admitting them. From idleness following gossiping, curiosity, garrulity, and other faults in women. "Speaking things which they ought not ;" perhaps, divulging secrets, or indulging in detraction, or improper language.

14. Weighing all things, he prefers that the younger widows should marry, sooner than make vows which they may be apt to violate. In his Epistle to Cor. vii., he prefers, viewing the matter absolutely, that they would be all like himself, *i.e.*, unmarried. There is no argument here against the profession of young females in convents. There is only question here of *widows*, and not of *virgins.* Moreover, at the time of the Apostle, those were not enclosed so strictly in convents, as consecrated virgins are now. Nor had they the extraordinary helps derived from, and merited by, the observance of strict discipline, nor the exact vigilance, such as the Church now practises, with such jealousy, towards the virgin spouses of Christ. Moreover, none are admitted to solemn vows, at present in convents, without being first, subjected, for a reasonable period of time, to a novitiate probation, to test their fitness and consult for their perfect liberty, in regard to their vows and the state of life which, of their own free will and consent, they mean to embrace.

15. Experience showed the evil effects of precipitancy in the admission of junior widows.

Text.

16. If any of the faithful have widows, let him minister to them, and let not the church be charged; that there may be sufficient for them that are widows indeed.

17. Let the priests that rule well be esteemed worthy of double honour: especially they who labour in the word and doctrine,

18. For the scripture saith: *Thou shalt not muzzle the ox that treadeth out the corn:* and the *labourer is worthy of his reward.*

19. Against a priest receive not an accusation, but under two or three witnesses.

20. Them that sin reprove before all: that the rest also may have fear.

21. I charge thee before God, and Christ Jesus, and the elect angels, that thou observe these things without prejudice, doing nothing by declining to either side.

Paraphrase.

16. If any Christian has widows who have any claims on him, let him support them, so that the Church may not be burdened with their maintenance, and that provision may be made for such widows as are really destitute, having neither friends nor connexions.

17. The priests who rule well, are deserving of a more liberal and abundant support, particularly such among them as toil at preaching the word of God.

18. For the SS. Scriptures, saith (Deut. xxi.) "*Thou shalt not muzzle the ox that treadeth out the corn,*" and "*the labourer is worthy of his reward.*"

19. Against a priest do not so much as receive an accusation, unless it be proved by two or three witnesses.

20. Those who sin in public, rebuke also in public, that the others, deterred by this example of severe correction, may be restrained within the bounds of duty.

21. I conjure thee in the presence of God and Christ Jesus, and his holy angels, to observe with exactness, what I have said regarding trials, to act the part of a just judge, without precipitancy, or without inclining the balance of justice through favour or affection to one side or the other.

Commentary.

17. He now passes from treating of widows, to treat of the manner in which Timothy is to act in reference to "Priests," which word, in this passage, is commonly supposed to include the priests of the first order, *i.e.*, Bishops, as well as those of the second. For, Timothy, as Primate of Asia, of which Ephesus was the metropolis, had to appoint Bishops throughout the different cities. The pastors, whether of the first or second order, "who rule well," are deserving of a more liberal support. Such is the meaning of "double," a meaning which it has in many parts of SS. Scripture, (*v.g.*) Jeremiah, chap. xvii., *duplici contritione contere eos;*" Proverbs, xli. 21; Isaias, xl. 2. "Especially they who labour in word and doctrine." No labour is more severe, according to St. Athanasius, than that of the preacher of the gospel.

18. In confirmation of this, he quotes the law of Moses (Deut. xxv. 14), and the natural law enunciated by our Redeemer (Mat. x. 10; Luke, x. 7). The meaning and application of the text from Deuteronomy are given, 1 Cor. ix. 9. Some persons say, the latter text is used by St. Paul himself; the gospel of St. Luke, in which it is found, not being written at this time. So that the words, "the Scripture saith," refer only to the first text from Deuteronomy.

19. The Apostle does not say: *Do not pass judgment*, on a priest, unless there be three witnesses; but do not even *receive* the charge, or proceed to try him, unless there be two or three witnesses. By the law of Moses, a person could not be *condemned* except on the testimony of two witnesses; but here, the Apostle commands, that against a priest, the accusation could not be *entertained*, unless first proved by two witnesses, both on account of his dignity, as also, because he is subject to envy and to enmities, owing to the duty which he has to exercise, of correcting and rebuking others.

20. But when the sins of men are public, they are to be rebuked publicly, not only for their own emendation, but for the honour of the Church, and for the purpose of deterring others from committing the like crimes.

21. He conjures him in the name of "God," from whom all power is derived, and of "Jesus Christ," the judge of all, and of "the elect [or holy] Angels," his ministers, "to observe these things," *i.e.*, these rules which he has laid down regarding ecclesi-

Text.	Paraphrase.
22. Impose not hands lightly upon any man, neither be partaker of other men's sins. Keep thyself chaste.	22. Do not, on light grounds, and without sufficient trial, impose hands on any man. And do not, by your precipitate admission of unworthy candidates to orders render yourself a participator in the sins of others. Keep thyself chaste, continue to lead a life of chastity.
23. Do not still drink water: but use a little wine for thy stomach's sake, and thy frequent infirmities.	23. Do not restrict yourself any longer to drinking mere water, but use a little wine mixed with it, on account of the weakness of your stomach, and your other frequent infirmities.
24. Some men's sins are manifest.	24. The sins of some persons are well known, even

Commentary.

astical trials—to act the part of a just judge, "without prejudice," which is commonly interpreted to mean, without precipitancy, not coming to a decision before the cause is fairly and fully examined, on both sides. "Doing nothing by declining to either side." There is an allusion in these words to the equilibrium of scales, when they are made the instrument of just weights and measures; if they incline to either side, fraud is committed. So is it with the judge, if he entertain favour for either party. Two faults are to be avoided by all judges—precipitancy, and favour or affection; which are the ordinary causes of unjust decisions. The Apostle cautions Timothy against the former, in the words, "without prejudice;" and against the latter, in the words, "doing nothing by declining to either side," holding, with a steady hand, the even balance of justice. In the person of Timothy, he admonishes all Prelates, under pain of incurring the wrath of God, the vengeance of Christ, and the indignation of his holy Angels, to act the part of just judges. The thought of God's presence, and of that Omniscient Judge, who will, one day, pass sentence on judges themselves, is the most efficacious restraint on the injustice of human tribunals.

22. Some refer to this to the Sacrament of Penance, and it is applicable to it. The consequences of precipitate absolutions are frightful; particularly, if absolution be conferred in the case of *proximate* occasion of sin; and especially of the external occasion of sins of impurity; or, of *relapsing* sinners. No doubt, the confessor is, in such cases, guilty of sacrilege, unless he adopt the proper precautions, and renders himself a participator in the future sins of his penitents. The words, however, more probably refer to the admission to Holy Orders, which are called "imposition of hands." This latter ceremony being used in the collation of orders, conveyed the proper idea to the mind of the faithful, while it left the unbeliever in the dark, as to the act itself. "Neither be partaker of other men's sins," shows the heavy responsibility with which those are charged, who are concerned in advancing men to Holy Orders. Hence, the exactness of the Council of Trent [SS. 23] on this subject, "Keep thyself chaste." The Apostle found Timothy chaste, and he now wishes that he should persevere; otherwise, he could not rebuke others transgressing in this most important, most essential, point of clerical morality.

23. It is clear that Timothy altogether abstained from the use of wine, and drank water only, knowing well how useful such abstinence was to preserve chastity— "*venter æstuans vino spumit in libidinem.*"—St. Jerome. The Apostle says, that although he exhorted him to perseverance in chastity, still, he did not wish he would continue to adopt means for that end, which would prove injurious to his health, such as *total* abstinence from wine. He tells him to "use a little wine," evidently insinuating, by the quantity recommended, that it would not be his sole drink, but only taken, when diluted with water. And from the example of Timothy, it is clear, if health did not interfere, that it would be far more perfect to *abstain from it altogether.* Temperance is a very necessary virtue for a pastor of souls, and should be earnestly recommended both by word and example. Considering the numbers of souls that excessive indulgence in intoxicating drinks sends daily to hell, and the danger there is of falling into this vice, by progressing gradually, *total abstinence*, when health permits it, is the safest antidote. It is sickening to hear it depreciated.

24. He returns to the subject of ordaining worthy persons, and instituting an inquiry

Text.

going before to judgment : and some men they follow after.

25. In like manner also good deeds are manifest : and they that are otherwise, cannot be hid.

Paraphrase.

previous to any judgment or inquiry regarding them ; whereas the sins of others are only known, after an inquiry regarding them is instituted.

25. In like manner, the good works of some persons are fully known, and need no inquiry ; and the good works of others are secret ; but these, in the course of trial cannot be concealed (and hence, in such a case, enquiry should be held, lest the deserving be rejected).

Commentary.

regarding them. Some persons are evidently unworthy ; the unworthiness of others will be known only after inquiry.

25. And others are evidently worthy, their good works being of themselves manifest. And the good works of others which are secret and not public, cannot be kept concealed after investigation ; and, then, they can be admitted to orders. In the preceding verse, he says, the evil works of some are private ; and hence, an examination should take place, less the unworthy be admitted. In this verse, he says, the good works of some are private, and unless examined, the worthy may be rejected. It is not sufficient, if after trial, their evil deeds are not known ; they must give proofs of a good life, before they can be admitted to orders. Woe to Superiors, if they are content with less ! Shall they not have to answer for the innumerable souls which the unworthy object of their careless choice, may be instrumental in damning ? It is recorded of St. Leo the Great, that he watched and prayed for forty days at the tomb of St. Peter, begging pardon for his sins through the Apostle's intercession ; and that after that term, St. Peter informed him in a vision : " Your sins are forgiven you by God, except those committed by you in conferring Holy Orders : of these you still remain charged to give a rigorous account."—(*See* Lives of Saints, April 11). It is much to be feared, that men, in other respects irreproachable, whether Ecclesiastical Superiors, who recommend to Holy Orders, or Prelates who rashly confer them, will answer, at their souls' peril, before the judgment seat of Christ, for their mistaken lenity, or rather *merciful cruelty* in advancing *even doubtful* subjects to Holy Orders—*cruelty*, to the *unhappy subjects* themselves, who might be useful members of society and saved in the world, but whom a melancholy experience proves, in almost *every instance*, to turn out unfortunately, in the sacred ministry—*cruelty* to the *Church*, that has to shed unavailing tears over their fall—*cruelty* to the *altar*, on which they again crucify and trample on the Son of God—*cruelty* to the *faithful*, whom, in many instances, they scandalize and ruin for ever ! In all cases of doubt, the doubt should be resolved in favour of the Church and the souls of the people.

CHAPTER VI.

Analysis.

As a Bishop is charged with the superintendence of his entire flock: hence, in this chapter the Apostle instructs Timothy in the duties he owes even the most destitute and lowly among his people, viz., the Christian slaves. He should instruct them in the duty of obedience, as well to their unbelieving, as to their Christian masters (1, 2). He denounces the men who taught a different doctrine (3); these he declares to be corrupt in heart, making piety the means for obtaining gain (5). He treats of the dangers of avarice (8, 9), and cautions Timothy, and through him, all the ministers of the Gospel, against this damning vice, and implores them to observe the precepts delivered in this Epistle (13, 14-16). He points out the duties of the rich (17-19), and finally, through Timothy, exhorts all Bishops to guard the deposit of faith, and fly foolish novelties originating in the vain opinion of false science.

Text.

1. WHOSOEVER are servants under the yoke, let them count their masters worthy of all honour: lest the name of the Lord and *his* doctrine be blasphemed.

2. But they that have believing masters, let them not despise them, because they are brethren, but serve them the rather, because they are faithful and beloved, who are partakers of the benefit. These things teach and exhort.

Paraphrase.

1. Whosoever are in the condition of slaves, under the yoke of servitude, let them regard their masters, although unbelievers, with feelings of reverence, serving them with prompt obedience, and respectful submission, lest, on account of their disobedience, the name of God be blasphemed and the doctrine of the gospel spoken ill of, as sanctioning this disobedience of slaves.

2. But such slaves as have Christian masters, far from showing them less respect and serving them with less promptitude, on account of being their brethren in Christ, should, on the contrary, redouble their zeal in serving them, because they are Christians, and they should become dear to them, as being sharers in the same benefits of Christianity with themselves. Do thou teach them, so that they may know these things, and exhort them to the practice of the same.

Commentary.

1. "Their masters." He speaks of unbelieving masters. In the next verse, he speaks of Christian masters. "Lest the name of the Lord (in Greek, *of God*) and his doctrine be blasphemed," lest these infidel masters should blaspheme the name of God and the doctrine of the gospel, as sanctioning rebellion on the part of slaves, and the dissolution of social order. This conduct on the part of the slaves would estrange the infidels from the faith; whereas, the Apostle tacitly conveys an admonition to slaves to render the faith commendable, by their obedience to their unbelieving masters, and thus induce them to embrace it.

2. "Because they are brethren," *i.e.*, because their masters are their brethren in Christ. This is no reason why they should, in a civil point of view, dispute their superiority, and refuse them obedience. On the contrary, it is an additional motive to serve them with greater zeal. "And beloved." The Greek, ἀγαπητοί, means, *and deserving to be loved*, because their masters are sharers with them in the same blessings of Christianity. Others make the words, "who are partakers of the benefit," refer to the slaves, as if he said, that the slaves are made partakers of the beneficence of their masters; the rigour of servitude being greatly relaxed under Christian masters, who also feed, clothe them, and allow the free exercise of their religious duties. "Teach these things" to the ignorant, "and exhort" those who already know them, to practise them.

Text.

3. If any man teach otherwise, and consent not to the sound words of our Lord JESUS CHRIST, and to that doctrine which is accorded to godliness,

4. He is proud, knowing nothing, but sick about questions and strifes of words : from which arise envies, contentions, blasphemies, evil suspicions,

5. Conflicts of men corrupted in mind, and who are destitute of the truth, supposing gain to be godliness.

6. But godliness with contentment is great gain.

Paraphrase.

3. But if any man teach otherwise than we have taught, and refuse assent to the salutary and wholesome words of our Lord Jesus Christ, and that sound doctrine of the gospel, which promotes true piety,

4. Such a man is inflated with empty pride, he knows nothing, but is sick (and raving) about futile questions, and mere verbal disputes, which are the source of envy, of contentions, wrangling, of reproachful invectives against man, as well as blasphemies against God, of evil suspicions, or perverse dogmas and opinions,

5. Of foolish and pernicious disputations of men corrupt in mind, who are deprived of the light of truth, making piety serve the purposes of gain and avarice.

6. And, truly, piety accompanied with contentment of mind, which it insures, and which the necessaries of life satisfy, is a great gain.

Commentary.

3. It appears, that certain false teachers, confounding the spiritual liberty into which Christ had asserted us with civil liberty, taught, that slaves, on becoming Christians, were freed from all human servitude. Such men are here denounced by the Apostle, as the enemies of the gospel and disturbers of social order ; while, at the same time, he denounces all teachers of error, as he had already done, chapter i. of this Epistle.

4. "He is proud," in the Greek, τετύφωται, *he is swollen*, the meaning of which is well conveyed in the words of the Vulgate, swollen and inflated with empty pride. The word also conveys an idea of the mental disease of the man, who recedes from the truth. The words of our Lord Jesus Christ are all sound ; they are the wholesome ailment of the soul ; whosoever refuses assent to them is sick in soul, of a distemper analogous to bodily swelling. "Knowing nothing." Such a person is destitute of all true and solid knowledge, being deprived of faith. "Sick about questions and strifes of words." In the Greek, *logomachies.* "From which arise envies." Every one of these affecting the mastery envies such as appear to excel him. "Contentions," verbal wranglings, having for object superiority rather than the discovery of the truth. " Blasphemies," *i.e.,* reproachful and injurious language both to God and man. " Evil suspicions." The Greek, ὑπόνοιαι πονηραί, also means, *pernicious opinions* or *dogmas.*

5. "Conflicts." The Greek word, παραδιατριβαί, means, *useless, noxious disputations.* St. Chrysostom and others give it another signification which the word bears, "*contagious communications* of men corrupted in mind." These persons communicate corruption and spiritual distemper to such as come in contact with them. "And who are destitute of truth." Such persons are corrupted in mind, because blinded, by being deprived of the light of truth, and corrupted in heart, as is proved from their making religion a matter of traffic, looking upon it in the light of a means to subserve the purposes of gain and avarice. In the Greek are added to this verse the words, ἀφίστασο ἀπὸ τῶν τοιούτων, *keep aloof from such persons.* These words were found in the version used by St. Chrysostom. It is likely that they were admitted into the text, from the margin, or, from some commentary on the passage.

6. This is a sort of rhetorical correction : the Apostle corrects himself and says, that piety is a great gain in quite a different sense from that in which these corrupt men viewed it ; it is a great gain joined to "contentment," by which is meant, a mind content with the necessaries of life. So, it implies both a contented mind, and also the supply of the necessary means of life, without which no man can be content ; piety insures this contentment ; for, the Apostle learned to be satisfied in whatever state he was (Phil. iv. 11), and it also secures the necessaries of life, having the

Text.

7. For we brought nothing into this world: and certainly we can carry nothing out.

8. But having food and wherewith to be covered, with these we are content.

9. For they that will become rich, fall into temptation, and into the snare of the devil, and into many unprofitable and hurtful desires, which drown men into destruction and perdition.

10. For the desire of money is the root of all evils; which some coveting have erred from the faith, and have entangled themselves in many sorrows.

11. But thou, O man of God, fly these things: and pursue justice, godliness, faith, charity, patience, mildness.

Paraphrase.

7. For it teaches us, that as we have brought nothing with us into this world, so, undoubtedly, we will carry nothing out of it.

8. Having, therefore, the necessary food and clothing, with these let us be content.

9. For, those who wish to become rich and indulge in the pursuits of avarice, fall into several temptations to sin, in which, as in so many snares, they are caught by the devil; and into many foolish and noxious desires, which involve men in miseries of all kinds.

10. For, the love of money is the root of all evils, and in consequence of eagerly indulging this passion, some persons have deserted the faith, and transfixed themselves with many sorrows.

11. But thou, O man of God, fly this vice of avarice, and all these other sins which follow in its train, and zealously cultivate Christian sanctity and its concomitant virtues, viz., piety, faith, love, patience, meekness.

Commentary.

promise of the life that now is, &c. (iv. 8). "Seek first the kingdom of God and his justice," &c. In a word, piety is a great gain *on account of the contentment*, &c., which it insures.

7. Piety is apt to beget this contentment, for, it teaches us, that "we brought nothing," &c.

8. And it enables us to draw infallibly this conclusion, that as we will take out of this world, when leaving it, none of our possessions, we should, therefore, be content with the necessaries of life, food, and clothing. The Greek word for "we are content," αρκεσθησόμεθα, shows that the word "contentment," in verse, 6, supposes a supply of the necessaries of life, without which, no one can be content, or life prolonged.

9. Another reason for avoiding the pursuits of avarice, "they that will become rich." He does not say, *they that are rich;* he only speaks of the inordinate desire of amassing riches—it is this that makes one avaricious, and not the actual possession. "Fall into temptation," of fraud, injustice, perjury, &c., "and into the snare of the devil." In the Greek, we have only the words, *into a snare.* The words, "of the devil," are wanting. They may have been introduced from chap. iii. 7, and they merely express the sense of the passage more fully. They are, however, found in several manuscripts, and in the several Greek and Latin interpreters. "And into many unprofitable and hurtful desires." In some Greek copies, the reading is, *unto many foolish and hurtful desires. Foolish,* because opposed to reason ; and *hurtful,* because they "drown men into destruction and perdition," *i.e.,* they involve them both in present misfortune and future misery. This is particularly true of the class whom St. Paul here instructs in the person of Timothy. The desire of amassing riches is seldom exempt from the sins and dangers here enumerated; hence the difficulty in the salvation of the rich.—(Luke, xviii.)

10. "For the love of money is the root of all evil," because, there is scarcely a sin which it would not impel a man to commit, such as perjuries, rapines, homicides, and even Deicide, as in the case of Judas. Pride is said to be "the beginning of all sin," (Eccles, x. 15), because it was the first sin ever committed ; hence, it is said of it in quite a different sense from that in which it is said of avarice here. "And have entangled themselves." In the Greek, "*and have transfixed themselves,*" &c., περιέπειραν. Hence, it is, even in this life, the source of countless miseries, as melancholy experience every day testifies.

11. "O man of God," Every minister of religion is like Timothy, "a man of God,"

Text.

12. Fight the good fight of faith : lay hold on eternal life whereunto thou art called, and hast confessed a good confession before many witnesses.

13. I charge thee before God, who quickeneth all things, and before Christ JESUS who gave testimony under Pontius Pilate, a good confession,

14. That thou keep the commandment without spot, blameless, unto the coming of our Lord JESUS CHRIST,

15. Which in his times he shall shew who is the Blessed and only

Paraphrase.

12. Engage bravely in the glorious struggle for the faith, grasp the prize of eternal life to which thou hast been invited, and in pursuit of which thou hadst made a glorious confession in presence of many witnesses.

13. I command and conjure thee before God, who vivifies all things, and before Christ Jesus who rendered publicly under Pontius Pilate a glorious testimony to truth,

14. To observe, in their full integrity, without any admixture of error, or without incurring any reprehension for their violation, all the precepts delivered to thee in this Epistle, until the final coming of our Lord Jesus Christ.

15. Which glorious coming of Christ, he shall display at the proper time, who alone is essentially happy,

Commentary.

wholly devoted to him, enlisted in his service, his representative before men, consequently, entitled to the utmost respect. But he should, at the same time, fly avarice and its attendant vices, so opposed to the exalted disinterestedness, which should distinguish the man who, at his first entrance into the sanctuary, had chosen God for his inheritance, and practise "justice," *i.e.*, Christian justice or sanctity, and its concomitant virtues of "piety" towards God ; "faith," which points out to us heavenly goods ; "charity" towards our neighbour, which inspires us with liberality towards him, so opposed to cupidity ; "patience," in adversity, and when in want of temporal goods ; "mildness," even when offended and maltreated by those, whom we served on former occasions.

12. In order to incite Timothy to labour with greater zeal in shunning vice, and practising virtue, the Apostle alludes to the Grecian exercises of the gymnasium, of which the people of Asia Minor were so fond, and particularly to the exercises of the racecourse, to which he so often assimilates the course of a Christian life (1 Cor. ix. ; Philip. i. 29 ; Hebrews xii. 1), and compares the struggle in which Timothy is engaged for the faith, in which struggle faith alone can insure success, to these different bodily exercises. "Lay hold on eternal life." This is the prize held out by God, as master of the course, to such as gain the victory. "And hast confessed a good confession before many witnesses," and in pursuit of which Timothy made this public confession, which some understand of the profession of faith, which he publicly made at his baptism ; others, of that which he made at Ephesus on the occasion of the tumult referred to (Acts, xix. 25) ; and a third class, of the public promise, which he made at his Episcopal consecration, of faithfully discharging the duties of a bishop.

13. He conjures him in the presence of God, who gives life to every creature that lives, and of Christ, who sealed with his blood the testimony which he bore to truth, and gave him the example of declaring the truth at the risk of his life.

14. "The commandment," is commonly understood of all the precepts given in this Epistle, "without spot," "blameless," can, according to the Greek, ἄσπιλον, ἀνεπίληπτον, affect either Timothy, or the commandment ; "without spot," is commonly understood of the precepts, which should be kept without the alloy of falsehood or error ; "blameless," of Timothy, who should not incur reprehension, by violating the commandments given him. "The coming (in the Greek, τῆς ἐπιφανείας, *unto the Epiphany or manifestation*) of our Lord Jesus Christ." Writing to Timothy, he wishes to instruct all bishops, that to the end of time these precepts are obligatory. And he also, by reference to the coming of Christ, which will virtually take place for all at the hour of death, wishes to remind Timothy and all bishops, that they will be judged for the observance of the precepts which he is after delivering.

15. "Which," *i.e.*, apparition or coming, "in his time," *i.e.*, at the period he has

Text.

Mighty, the King of kings, and Lord of lords.

16. Who only hath immortality, and inhabiteth light inaccessible, whom no man hath seen, nor can see, to whom be honour and empire everlasting. Amen.

17. Charge the rich of this world not to be high-minded, nor to trust in the uncertainty of riches, but in the living God (who giveth us abundantly all things to enjoy.)

18. To do good, to be rich in good works, to give easily, to communicate to others.

19. To lay up in store for themselves a good foundation against the time to come, that they may lay hold on the true life.

20. O Timothy, keep that which is committed to thy trust, avoiding

Paraphrase.

and alone enjoys of himself sovereign sway, the King of kings, and the Lord of those that rule.

16. Who alone is, of his own nature, unchangeably immortal, and inhabits light inaccessible to mortals, whom no man ever saw in this life, or ever can see by the sole aids of nature, to whom belong honour and empire for endless ages. Amen.

17. Charge those who possess the goods and riches of this life, not to indulge in feelings of pride, and not to place their trust in frail, fleeting, uncertain riches, but to place their entire trust and confidence in the ever living God, who abundantly furnishes us with all things necessary for use.

18. Charge them also to do good and grow rich in the fruits of good works, to be liberal to the poor, and to make the indigent and distressed sharers in their wealth.

19. To amass for themselves treasures of merit, which will serve as a secure and solid foundation in future, so as to insure for them the secure possession of eternal life.

20. O Timothy, carefully guard the treasure of sound doctrine, which, as a sacred deposit, has been

Commentary.

destined and decreed. "He shall show," i.e., openly and publicly reveal. "Who is the blessed and only Mighty," i.e., who is alone essentially happy, and alone, of his own nature, possesses absolute sway. "The King of kings, and the Lord of lords," who, of himself, enjoys absolute, independent authority, of which all created power is but a mere emanation and dependent participation.

16. "Who only hath immortality," i.e., has life essentially of himself, with perfect incorruptibility and immutability. "And inhabiteth light inaccessible," which light is God himself; for, God exists in himself. Hence, the words mean, that God is an uncreated, immense, infinite light, and so, "inaccessible" to mortals. "Whom no man hath seen or can see," i.e., in this life, or ever can see, since this vision of God is reserved as the great reward of the life to come; and even there, the sole aids of nature will not suffice, nor the grace of this life; the *light of glory* must elevate created faculties, to the power of seeing God. What an idea of God, alone immortal and invisible, alone sovereignly powerful, alone supremely happy! *To serve him is to reign.* He alone is capable of satisfying the desires of our hearts; *he has made us for himself, nor can our hearts find rest until they rest in him.*—St. Augustine.

17. Having spoken in very strong terms (verses 9, 10) of the dangers of riches, the Apostle now shows the rich in what manner they are to sanctify themselves, the vices they ought to avoid, and the virtues they ought to practise. They should not entertain thoughts of pride, which riches are apt to engender, nor place their confidence in riches, which are so frail and fleeting; but all their hopes should be in God, from whom proceeds every blessing, both in the order of nature and grace. God is "living," and a certain object of our confidence.

18. They should practise good works, and become rich in the treasures of merit. They should particularly be constant in the exercise of the good works of liberality towards the poor, and make the indigent and distressed sharers in their blessings. The goods of this life are intrusted to them as stewards to dispense them; the supreme dominion belongs to God.

19. They should lay a solid foundation in merit, particularly in alms-deeds, for that future edifice which they are building up for themselves in heaven. On works of charity is reared a spiritual structure, wherein are deposited true life and everlasting treasures, "which the moth does not consume," &c.—(S. Matthew, vi. 20).

20. "Keep that which is committed to thy trust." This is commonly understood of

Text.

the profane novelties of words, and oppositions of knowledge falsely so called :

21. Which some promising, have erred concerning the faith. Grace be with thee. Amen.

Paraphrase.

confided to thy keeping ; and, for this purpose, shun all vain novelties of words which profanely express doctrines at variance with those confided to you, and spurn the objections proposed to you by heretics, who falsely claim to themselves the character of possessing superior knowledge

21. Of which false knowledge certain persons making a profession have fallen away from the faith. Grace be with thee. Amen.

Commentary.

the doctrine of Christ, which is left, whole and entire, to the guardianship of the bishops of the Church, without admitting either of diminution or addition, to be handed down to their successors, to the end of time. The same is expressed by the Apostle (2 Epistle i. 14, 15, ii. 2), and he supposes here that it may be destroyed by "false science." Hence, he refers to *true science*, or, the doctrine of the gospel, as "the trust committed" to him. "Avoiding the profane novelties of words ;" that is to say, new words which express a new and false doctrine, such as *special faith, imputative justice, impanation,* &c., which alone can be called "profane," because they alone express doctrines at variance with the *sacred treasure,* or *deposit,* and hence, it would be *profane* to employ them. But words which express revealed doctrines with greater clearness and precision, and are virtually found in the SS. Scriptures, such as *Trinity, Incarnation, Transubstantiation,* &c., are not contemplated, since they help to guard the deposit against the refined subtleties of heresy. The Greek reading for "novelties of words," κενοφωνιας, means, *foolish terms.* The change in a single Greek letter causes the difference. The Vulgate interpreter must have read a Greek edition different from the present. The meaning, however, is the same ; for, the word "profane," shows that he refers to words, expressive of a new and false doctrine. "And oppositions," *i.e.,* objections proposed by men who falsely claim the repute of science, or, objections proposed from principles, which are falsely called principles of knowledge ; since truth cannot be opposed to truth, and no *true science* can be opposed to the truths of faith, which are of eternal, unchangeable verity. God, the source and fountain of all truth, whether natural or revealed, cannot be opposed to himself in the different orders which he himself has established. St. Chrysostom thinks that, in the preceding, the Apostle alludes to the *Gnostics.* It is likely, however, as the *Gnostics* were not known under this *name* (which implies superior knowledge) in the days of the Apostle, that he refers to all heretics, whose wonted boast it has always been, in imitation of the first blasphemer against God's truth, that they were the apostles of knowledge and enlightenment, and that they have been divinely commissioned to rescue men from the darkness and ignorance in which the Church has kept them. By telling him to "avoid the oppositions " or objections "of false knowledge," the Apostle does not prevent him from refuting the doctrine of heretics, when they require refutation, and in proper circumstances ; for, by requiring that a bishop should be a "teacher," chap. iii., and "be able to convince the gainsayers " (Titus, i.), he evidently requires of him sometimes to refute them. But there are certain false doctrines *assumed* by heretics, which they should prove before they can expect that the possessors of the ancient faith would undertake their refutation. The *onus probandi* devolves on them, as is here clearly insinuated.

21. Hence faith is not inamissible ; for these men fell away from the faith and deserted the Christian religion.

The common Greek subscriptions have—(*The first to Timothy was written from Laodicea, the metropolis of Phrygia Pacatiana.*) These subscriptions, however, are not always of undoubted authority. The common opinion is, that this Epistle was written from Macedon, whither St. Paul went after leaving Ephesus (Acts, xx.), and it is insinuated in chap. i. 3, of this Epistle, that he had been in Macedon while writing this. Moreover, it is certain that he had not been at Laodicea.—(*See* Epistle to the Coll. ii., written subsequent to this Epistle.)

SECOND EPISTLE

OF

ST. PAUL TO TIMOTHY.

Introduction.

THIS Epistle embraces subjects almost the same as those treated of in the preceding. It is principally devoted to instructing Timothy—and in his person, all the Pastors of the Church, to the end of time—in the nature of his pastoral duties, the virtues he should practise, and the faults he should avoid. The Apostle puts him on his guard against the errors which, even in his lifetime, were to assail the purity of Christian faith and morals. He particularly charges him to manifest great zeal in instructing the faithful, of every grade and order of life, in the truths of faith, and the duties of their respective calling ; and this, at all times, both "in season and out of season."

WHEN AND WHERE WRITTEN.—It is quite certain that this Epistle was written by St. Paul while imprisoned at Rome. This is agreed upon by all, and it is quite clear from chap. i. 16, 17 ; ii. 9. But, it is much controverted, whether this occurred during his first or second imprisonment. Almost all the ancient writers, and among the rest, Eusebius, St. Jerome, and St. Chrysostom, assert that it was written during the Apostle's second imprisonment. The same is asserted by the subscriptions of the Greek copies. The principal ground of this opinion are the words of the Apostle :—" I am now ready to be sacrificed, and the time of my dissolution is at hand " (iv. 6). Mauduit has written a lengthened and learned Dissertation in support of this opinion. In the Dissertation referred to, he shows, on very probable grounds, that Timothy had been a fellow-prisoner of the Apostle's, and had been brought to Rome with him on the occasion of his first imprisonment. It appears from the Epistles to the Philippians, Colossians, and Philemon—all written during his first imprisonment—that Timothy had been at Rome when they were written, for he is united with the Apostle in his concluding salutation in each of these Epistles ; and, from this, Mauduit infers, that it could not have been written during this imprisonment ; because St. Paul informs Timothy of many things which occurred during his voyage (iv. 20, 21, &c.), things with which Timothy himself must have been fully acquainted already, if the Apostle referred to the first voyage. Hence, he infers that the Apostle must refer to his second voyage, and that, consequently, this Epistle was written during his second imprisonment, which followed. The arguments adduced by the supporters of the other opinion, are refuted by him in the second part of the Dissertation.

Baronius, and others, assert, that it was written during his first imprisonment. Their principal argument is founded on the words :—" But the Lord stood by me,...... and I was delivered out of the mouth of the lion" (iv. 18). However, it will be shown, in the Commentary, how easily these words can be reconciled with the former opinion. The question, as to the precise year in which it was written, will altogether depend on the determination of the preceding.

SECOND EPISTLE

OF

ST. PAUL TO TIMOTHY.

CHAPTER I.

Analysis.

In this chapter, the Apostle, after the usual Apostolical salutation, expresses his great affection for Timothy, of which he gives a proof in his unceasing remembrance of him (1–3); and he shows how deserving Timothy was of this affection (4, 5). He, next, exhorts him to re-enkindle within him the grace which he received at his ordination. To preach the gospel with fortitude, and not to be ashamed of Christ crucified (8).

After having adduced several engaging motives for enduring sufferings and labour in the cause of the Gospel, he points out the manner of preaching, and the doctrine to be preached (9–14). He notes the defection of certain parties from the faith, and commends the charity of Onesiphorus towards himself in chains, for which he prays that he may be amply remunerated by God (15–18).

Text.

1. PAUL, an apostle of JESUS CHRIST by the will of God, according to the promise of life, which is in CHRIST JESUS.

2. To Timothy my dearly beloved son, grace, mercy, and peace from God the Father, and from CHRIST JESUS our Lord.

3. I give thanks to God, whom I serve from my forefathers with a pure conscience, that without ceasing I have a remembrance of thee in my prayers, night and day.

Paraphrase.

1. Paul, constituted an Apostle of Jesus Christ, by the will and authority of God, for the purpose of announcing to men the promise of eternal life, which is given to the believers through Christ Jesus.

2. (Salutes) Timothy, his beloved son. Grace, mercy, and peace be to thee from God the Father, and from Christ Jesus our Lord.

3. I give thanks to God, whom I have worshipped in the religion transmitted to me from my ancestors, with a sincere conscience, for having inspired me with an unceasing remembrance of thee, both day and night, in my prayers.

Commentary.

1. "According to the promise of life." The Greek word for "according," κατα determines the end of St. Paul's Apostleship: the end or purpose of it was, to announce this "promise of life."

2. (See 2nd verse of the 1st Epistle).

3. "Whom I serve." The Greek word, λατρευω, shows that this service means paying divine and supreme honour. "From my forefathers." This he adds in consequence of the calumnies of his enemies, who charged him with destroying the law and institutions of his ancestors. He was a Pharisee, of the tribe of Benjamin. Now, he says, he has been serving God by a religion which he derived, as if by inheritance, from his ancestors. Before his conversion, he was most zealous in observing the Jewish law, and now, after his conversion, he only embraced that form of religion, to which the old law, rightly understood, clearly conducted him. "With a pure conscience," i.e., a

Text.	Paraphrase.
4. Desiring to see thee, being mindful of thy tears, that I may be filled with joy.	4. I anxiously long to see thee, in order that I may be filled with joy and consolation at thy presence—mindful of the abundant tears thou didst shed on the occasion of my departure from thee.
5. Calling to mind that faith which is in thee unfeigned, which also dwelt first in thy grandmother Lois, and in thy mother Eunice, and I am certain that in thee also.	5. Calling to mind also the sincere faith that I witnessed in thee, which also firmly and perseveringly abode first in my maternal grandmother, Lois, and in thy mother, Eunice, and which I am morally certain and firmly persuaded, will perseveringly abide in thee.
6. For which cause I admonish thee, that thou stir up the grace of God, which is in thee by the imposition of my hands.	6. In order, then, to insure this perseverance in faith, I exhort thee to enkindle and resuscitate within thee the grace, which thou didst receive at thy ordination, conferred by me, through the imposition of hands.
7. For God hath not given us the	7. For, God has not conferred on us, Bishops,

Commentary.

sincere conscience; free from hypocrisy, for, even when persecuting the Church, he did so, thinking in his conscience, that he was serving the cause of God; or "pure," may mean, free from guilt or sin; because, he was most observant of legal justice, being by sect, a Pharisee. "That without ceasing," &c. This is the thing for which, as a gift of charity, he thanks God—viz., for inspiring him with a continual remembrance of his beloved disciple. Others make the preceding act of thanksgiving regard the benefits of God conferred on Timothy; and then, they understand the latter words thus:—"As I have constant remembrance of thee." The Greek, ὡς ἀδιάλειπτον ἔχω τὴν περὶ σοῦ μνείαν, will admit of it; the former is, however, the more probable construction; it is also the construction of St. Chrysostom, Theodoret, &c.

4. The hearts of the Apostles were not stony hearts. Among the crimes charged by the Apostle on the Pagan philosophers is, that they were "without affection," (Rom. i.)

5. Another cause of this affection and desire to see Timothy, was his sincere faith. Lois was Timothy's maternal grandmother; for, his father was a Gentile—(Acts, xvi.) Both she and his mother, Eunice, were converted to the faith before St. Paul's arrival at Lystra. The word "dwelt," by an Hebrew idiom means, firmly inhered and persevered until death. He commends Timothy for deriving piety and faith from his ancestors, in the same way as he himself—"served God from his forefathers." The piety of parents often serves as a great stimulus to children to imitate their good example. "And I am certain," &c., only expresses a firm conviction, a moral certainty.

6. "For which cause," *i.e.*, in order to persevere in the faith, "I admonish thee that thou stir up the grace of God." The Greek word for "stir up," ἀναζωπυρεῖν, means to *blow up the smouldering fire*, to which the grace of God is compared. "Which is in thee by the imposition of my hands." This shows that the grace to which he refers is of an *habitual, permanent* nature. "Which is in thee," refers to the *sacramental* grace of his ordination, which is an habitual sanctifying grace, like every *sacramental grace* producing certain specific effects, a certain aptitude for particular duties; and, moreover, conferring a *right*, founded upon God's gratuitous, but unerring promises, to the necessary actual graces that may, in due time, be required for the proper discharge of the duties of the state for which the sacrament fits us.—(*See* 1 Tim., iv. 14). St. Thomas says, that Timothy grew remiss in the discharge of his Episcopal functions, particularly that of preaching; and hence, the Apostle admonishes him to resuscitate the grace of his ordination. If this was necessary for Timothy—if tepidity and sloth were to be found in this Apostolic man—what cause have not others to tremble for themselves, and to adopt every means, prayer, meditation, and pious works, to revive the grace of their vocation?

7. "Hath not given us," *i.e.*, Bishops at our ordination, "the spirit of fear," *i.e.*, timidity and indolence, on account of which we would dread danger and death; "but

Text.

spirit of fear : but of power and of love, and of sobriety.

8. Be not thou therefore ashamed of the testimony of our Lord, nor of me his prisoner : but labour with the gospel according to the power of God,

9. Who hath delivered us and called us by his holy calling, not according to our works, but according to his own purpose and grace which was given us in Christ JESUS before the times of the world.

10. But is now made manifest by the illumination of our Saviour JESUS CHRIST, who hath destroyed death, and hath brought to light life and incorruption by the gospel :

11. Wherein I am appointed a preacher, and an apostle, and teacher of the gentiles.

Paraphrase.

at our ordination, the spirit of timidity or indolence, but the spirit of fortitude, and of love, and equanimity.

8. Be not, therefore, ashamed to bear testimony to our Lord Jesus Christ crucified, by preaching his Gospel ; nor be ashamed of me, a prisoner on his account ; but labour along with me in bearing the afflictions to which all the ministers of the Gospel are subjected, according to the strength given thee by God.

9. Who has saved us from sin and eternal death, and has, for this end, called us to a state of sanctity, not certainly in consideration of our works ; (for, they were evil), but out of his own liberal bounty, and gratuitous mercy, which was decreed from eternity to be given to us, in consideration of the merits of Jesus Christ.

10. But this gratuitous and merciful will of God in our regard, though hidden from eternity in God, has now been manifested by the advent and apparition of Jesus Christ our Saviour, who, indeed, by his passion destroyed the dominion of death, and brought into open light, immortal and incorruptible life, and afforded us a sure hope of enjoying it, by the preaching of his Gospel throughout the world.

11. To announce which Gospel I am constituted the herald, the divinely-commissioned legate, and the teacher of the Gentiles.

Commentary.

of power," *i.e.*, fortitude and intrepidity, so necessary for the leaders in the Christian warfare, to meet the enemies of God and of religion. "And of love," whereby, after the example of Christ, the Bishop would seek only the glory of God and the honour of his Church. "And sobriety ;" a certain equanimity of soul both in prosperity and adversity. This shows, that the grace to which he refers in the preceding verse is an interior, sanctifying grace, of which a Bishop stands no less in need for the discharge of his Episcopal functions, than he does of the "gratiæ gratis datæ."

8. The "testimony of Christ," may mean the gospel, which means a testimony handed down by witnesses, or rather the preaching of Christ crucified. "But labour with the gospel." The Greek, συγκακοπάθησον, means, *suffer together with the gospel.* This he ought to do, in virtue of that spirit of love and equanimity which he received. "According to the power of God ;" distrusting himself, he should repose all his hopes in God.

9. "Who has delivered us." (In the Greek, τοῦ σώσαντος ἡμᾶς, *saved us*), from sin and its consequences, temporal and eternal, "and called us by his holy calling." He saved us, by calling us to a state of sanctification. "According to his own purpose and grace, which was given," *i.e.*, given from eternity on the part of God, in virtue of his unchangeable decree, though it is only in time we could enjoy its effects.

10. "By the illumination," *i.e.*, the apparition and coming, as appears from the Greek, which literally is, *Epiphany.* "Who hath destroyed death," or, according to the Greek, καταργήσαντος μὲν τὸν θάνατον, *rendered void death,* by depriving it of its dominion over man, "and hath brought to light, life and incorruption, by the gospel." Christ did this in two ways—first, he showed incorruptible life in himself, for forty days after his Resurrection ; secondly, by the preaching of the gospel, throughout the world, he gave us a certain hope of one day enjoying the same incorruptible life.

11. St. Paul is constituted the herald, Apostle, and teacher of the Gentiles, particularly in the preaching of this gospel.

Text.

12. For which cause I also suffer these things : but I am not ashamed. For I know whom I have believed, and I am certain that he is able to keep that which I have committed unto him, against that day.

13. Hold the form of sound words, which thou hast heard of me in faith, and in the love which is in Christ Jesus.

14. Keep the good thing committed to thy trust by the Holy Ghost, who dwelleth in us.

15. Thou knowest this that all they who are in Asia, are turned away from me : of whom are Phigellus and Hermogenes.

16. The Lord give mercy to the house of Onesiphorus : because he hath often refreshed me, and hath not been ashamed of my chain.

17. But when he was come to Rome, he carefully sought me, and found me.

Paraphrase.

12. On account of which also I now suffer in chains ; but I am not ashamed of them. For, I know who it is, to whose safe keeping I have entrusted myself, and I am quite certain, that he is able to guard inviolate the treasure of merits and sufferings which I deposited with him, until the great day of final recompense.

13. Let the sound words, which you heard from me on subjects of faith and Christian love, be the pattern which you will follow, when treating on the like subjects.

14. Carefully guard the precious deposit of sound doctrine confided to your keeping, by the grace of the Holy Ghost dwelling in us (and imparted to us at our ordination).

15. You cannot but be aware, that all the Asiatics at Rome have forsaken me, and among the rest, Phigellus and Hermogenes.

16. Onesiphorus is to be excepted, and may the Lord show mercy to his family, for he has often consoled and relieved me, and has not been ashamed of my chains.

17. Moreover, having come to Rome, he anxiously made search for me from prison to prison, nor did he relinquish his search, until he found me.

Commentary.

12. "For which cause," on account of exercising the function of herald, Apostle, and teacher of the Gentiles, in preaching the gospel, he is subjected to sufferings ; but he is not ashamed of them ; for he knows who it is to whom he has given in charge both himself and the treasure of merit resulting from his sufferings ; his depositary is an omnipotent, infinitely veracious God, faithful to his promises. "And he is able to keep that which I have committed unto him," &c. The Apostle makes no reference to the first quality required in a depositary—viz., fidelity, as being self-evident ; he asserts that God has the power of keeping inviolate the treasure of merit deposited with him. The deposits even fructify with him, in the eternal weight of glory, which they will secure with us.

13. He enjoins on Timothy, and through him on all preachers of the gospel, to make the language of the Apostle their pattern in preaching. Hence, vain novelties are to be avoided, in treating either of Christian faith or morality.

14. "The good thing committed to thy trust." This deposit which God has place in the hands of Timothy, is quite different from the deposit placed by Timothy in the hands of God (12). The deposit, in this verse, regards the sound doctrine of faith, which, according to the rules of a deposit, should be kept whole and entire, without increase or diminution. The Bishops are the depositaries of this divine treasure of doctrine in its unchangeable entirety, whether contained in the inspired SS. Scriptures, or Tradition.

15. All the Asiatics at Rome "are turned away from me." Whether it was that they deserted the faith, or merely forsook the Apostle in his perils, is not expressed. The former might in many cases result from the latter. Timothy heard all this by rumour. He mentions Phigellus and Hermogenes in particular, probably, because they signalized themselves in this defection from the Apostle, of whatever kind it was, and also to caution Timothy and the faithful against holding any intercourse with them.

16. He excepts Onesiphorus ; he, though an Asiatic, often solaced and relieved the Apostle ; and for this, the latter begs of God to have mercy on his entire family.

Text.	**Paraphrase.**
18. The Lord grant unto him to find mercy of the Lord in that day. And in how many things he ministered unto me at Ephesus, thou very well knowest.	18. May the Lord grant him to find mercy with himself on the day of judgment; and as to the extent of the charities he administered to me at Ephesus, I shall forbear from referring to them; you, yourself, being better acquainted with them than I can be.

Commentary.

18. "The Lord grant unto him to find mercy of the Lord." A Hebrew idiom for, "*The Lord grant him to find mercy of himself;*" like the text in Genesis, xix. :—"The Lord rained sulphur upon Sodom from the Lord," *i.e.*, from himself. "On that day;" by excellence refers to the day of judgment. "Thou very well knowest," because Timothy was present, and could witness the many good offices, which he bestowed on the Church at Ephesus, and on the Apostle himself, in particular.

CHAPTER II.

Analysis.

In this chapter, the Apostle exhorts Timothy, to display the spirit of fortitude, in the discharge of his functions (verse 1); and, he adduces the several examples of soldiers, wrestlers, and husbandmen, for the purpose of stimulating him to the faithful, laborious, and exclusive performance of his Episcopal functions (2–7).

He proposes to him several motives of encouragement to suffer for the Gospel. First, the glory of Christ, resuscitated after a course of ignominious suffering (8). In the next place, the example of the Apostle himself, in submitting to suffering, and enduring evils for the dissemination of the Gospel (9, 10). And lastly, the eternal glory of martyrdom, for the attainment of which, a course of suffering, after the example of Christ, is an indispensable condition (11–13). He wishes that Timothy should instruct the faithful in these matters (14).

He next instructs him in the manner in which he is to please God, as minister of the Gospel. He should properly dispense God's holy word, and avoid profane and impious novelties, put forward by heretics, whose teaching spreads a deadly poison, and corrupts its way, like a gangrene or canker (15–18).

He tells him not to be disturbed at the defection of some. This defection will not become general; for, those on whom God has designs of salvation, will remain firm. The reprobate will remain associated with the elect in the "great house," or church of God (19, 20). Those who have fallen may be restored by penance (21). Resuming the subject referred to in verse 15, and interrupted at verse 16, he gives further instructions to Timothy, as to the manner in which he may become "a workman agreeable to God." He should shun the passions of youth, and practise the leading Christian virtues. He should avoid all foolish questions and wranglings, and administer correction, with meekness and gentleness.

Text.

1. THOU therefore, my son, be strong in the grace which is in CHRIST JESUS:

2. And the things, which thou hast heard of me by many witnesses, the same commend to faithful men, who shall be fit to teach others also.

Paraphrase.

1. Since, therefore, it was a spirit of fortitude that God bestowed on us (i. 7), do thou, my son, display this fortitude by the grace of Christ Jesus, which thou hadst received at thy ordination.

2. And what things you heard from my lips, publicly and before many others, who may be witnesses of the same, do thou, in turn, commit to trusty and faithful men, qualified and fit to teach the same to others.

Commentary.

1. He resumes the exhortation to firmness in the discharge of his functions, to which he had referred (i. 7). "Therefore," *i.e.*, whereas, God has given us, bishops, the spirit of fortitude at our ordination. "In the grace," &c., relying not on your own strength, but on the grace of God, conferred on you at ordination, and which he will bestow, whenever necessary, and when prayed to for it.

.. He not only charges Timothy to display fortitude in preaching the gospel, but also diligence and fidelity, in guarding the purity of the doctrine delivered to him. Oral tradition and verbal preaching were the first methods of propagating the gospel. "Preach the gospel to every creature," is the precept of our Lord. *Write the gospel*, is not commanded. It was orally, and not in writing, St. Paul taught Timothy, "which thou hast heard of me," &c. Hence, tradition was the first, and for some time, the only rule of faith; and although this is the last Epistle written by the Apostle;

Text.

3. Labour as a good soldier of CHRIST JESUS.

4. No man being a soldier to God, entangleth himself with secular business: that he may please him to whom he hath engaged himself.

5. For he also that striveth for the mastery is not crowned except he strive lawfully.

6. The husbandman that laboureth, must first partake of the fruits·

Paraphrase.

3. Submit to sufferings and privations on behalf of the gospel, like a distinguished soldier of Jesus Christ.

4. Bear in mind that no one who makes arms his profession, ever entangles himself with the duties of any other calling or profession in life for the purpose of securing a livelihood (but confines himself exclusively to his military duties), that he may please him to whom he engaged himself, that is to say, the general, who enolled him, among the soldiers.

5. Consider, also, that the man who contests the prize, at the public games, will not receive the crown, unless he fights and conquers, according to the laws prescribed for the combatants.

6. Reflect, too, that the husbandman, who toils in the cultivation of the earth, has the first and best right to partake of the fruits of his labour; or, that the husbandman, in order to be entitled to a portion of the fruits of the earth, must first toil and labour, in its cultivation.

Commentary.

yet still, it was not to his written Epistles he refers Timothy, as containing the deposit, but to his preaching. "Hold the form of sound words which thou hast heard of me" (i. 13.) Tradition was the primary rule of faith, according to the designs of God. The writing of the Scripture depended, in many cases. on mere accidental circumstances.

3. "Labour as a good soldier." In Greek, *labour thou, therefore, as a good,* &c. The Greek for "labour," κακοπαθησον, means, *endure hardship or suffering.*

4. "No man being a soldier to God," &c. The words "to God," are not found in the Greek, nor in all the Latin copies, and they appear, indeed, to be quite redundant, being unnecessary for conveying the meaning of the Apostle; for, he has recourse to three examples, drawn from the conditions of soldiers, wrestlers, and agriculturists, to stimulate Timothy to activity, and exclusive devotion to the duties of his calling. It is likely that the words, "to God," were added by some persons who thought their addition requisite to complete the sense; and, thus, the addition crept into a good many copies. Their addition only expresses by anticipation the application of the simile, which the Apostle left to be merely inferred—"understand what I say" (verse 7). "Entangleth himself." In the Greek, εμπλεκεται ταις του βιου πραγματειαις, *is entangled in secular business.* By "secular business," is meant a profession in life, such as merchandise, agriculture, or any other calling for gaining a livelihood, from which the laws of military discipline exclude the soldier. This, of course, in its application to the ecclesiastic, who is enrolled in the service of Christ, shows, that the affairs of religion, and the things having reference thereto—viz., prayer, sacrifice, the care of God's house, the neatness of the sacred utensils and of the holy altar, the confessional, the instruction of every class in their respective duties, especially the catechetical instruction of such, as may be ignorant of the essential points of faith, the fearless and intrepid defence of the poor, and a paternal care of these, the dearest portion of the flock of Jesus Christ, regardless of self-interest, the assertion of their just rights, in a manner not unsuited to the clerical character, when they are trodden under foot from a hatred of the true religion—these and others such should form the great and exclusive occupation of the ecclesiastic. All things else not referrible to these, "entangle" and embarrass him.

5. "He that striveth for the mastery," has reference to the exercise of wrestling, running, leaping, &c., practised at the Grecian games. Such a person, in order to obtain the prize or crown, should comply with all the conditions of the games; so, in like manner, should Timothy not only struggle manfully in the pursuit of an incorruptible crown; but he should likewise follow the rules and laws prescribed for him by Christ.

6. This verse admits of a twofold interpretation (as in Paraphrase). The first

Text.

7. Understand what I say : for the Lord will give thee in all things understanding.

8. Be mindful that the Lord ·Jesus Christ is risen again from the dead, of the seed of David, according to my gospel.

9. Wherein I labour even unto bands, as an evil doer : but the word of God is not bound.

10. Therefore I endure all things for the sake of the elect, that they also may obtain the salvation,

Paraphrase.

7. Understand the application of the three parables which I am after proposing to you. I need not explain their import, for the Lord himself will give you understanding in all things (if you ask his aid by fervent prayer).

8. Bear in mind and frequently reflect, that the Lord Jesus Christ, who was born, and assumed flesh of the seed of David, had (after a course of suffering and death) risen glorious, according to the truth of the gospel, which I everywhere preach.

9. In the cause of which gospel I have gone through an ordeal of suffering, even unto chains and imprisonment, as if I were nothing better than a malefactor. But, though my body is bound in chains, still, the word of God is not in chains (for, from my chains I proclaim the gospel).

10. It is for this dissemination of the gospel, that I endure all these afflictions, in order that those who are elected by God to salvation, which is obtained through

Commentary.

(interpretation) supposes, that the Apostle proposes as a motive to Timothy, the reward which he is to receive, in the same way as the husbandman, according to the laws of justice and equity is the first to partake of the produce of the soil at which he toils ; so Timothy, by labouring here for the gospel, shall plentifully share hereafter, in the fruits of the spiritual blessings which he had sown. The second interpretation supposes that the Apostle exhorts Timothy to labour, otherwise he will be entitled to no reward, just as the husbandman should labour before he can claim any of the fruits of the earth ; and this latter interpretation is not opposed to the Greek ; in which, the word "first," πρωτον, may be an adverb.

7. Here he leaves to Timothy himself the conclusion or the application of the practical lessons, in which the three parables just mentioned are intended to instruct him. From the parable of the *soldier*, he should learn to endure patiently for the gospel, to devote himself exclusively to the duties of religion ; everything else will "entangle" him. From the case of the *wrestler*, he was to infer—that in all his functions he should, in order to merit the crown of glory, punctually follow the laws of God and his holy Church. And from the case of the *husbandman*, he should learn to labour before he could expect a recompense, or, to keep in view the recompense which he will be the first to obtain, if he labour for the glory of God, and the salvation of souls. In the Greek, for "the Lord will give," it is δῴη σοι, *may the Lord give thee understanding.*

8. The Apostle now proposes to Timothy the glory to which Christ was raised, after a course of ignominious suffering, as a motive to submit to suffering in the like cause, if he wish to be a sharer in the like glory. Probably, he proposes the article of the resurrection to Timothy, and wishes him to be zealous in inculcating it (verse 14), because it was questioned by many (verse 18), and because it is the foundation of all Christian faith. With this is joined another fundamental article of religion, regarding the Incarnation and the assumption of the real nature of man by Christ, which was also called in question, as appears from St. Augustine and St. Epiphanius. Simon Magus, and the Gnostics, maintained that he had not real, but fantastical, flesh ; while St. John tells us, "that there were seducers, who denied that Jesus came in the flesh."—(2nd Epistle, verse 7).

9. The Apostle proposes his own example, in suffering for the gospel, to stimulate Timothy. The Greek word for " I labour," κακοπαθω, means, *I suffer, or endure afflictions.* Though he is bound in body, still his tongue, his power of proclaiming the gospel, is not chained.

10. "Therefore," *i.e.*, in order that the gospel may be disseminated, and not kept captive, I endure all these evils, that the elect whom God has destined for salvation

Text.

which is in Christ Jesus, with heavenly glory.

11. A faithful saying. For if we be dead with him, we shall live also with him :

12. If we suffer, we shall also reign with him. If we deny him, he will also deny us.

13. If we believe not, he continueth faithful, he cannot deny himself.

14. Of these things put them in mind, charging them before the Lord. Contend not in words, for it is to no profit, but to the subverting of the hearers.

Paraphrase.

Christ, may obtain the life of grace here, and heavenly glory, hereafter.

11. It is an undoubted, unquestionable truth, that if we die with Christ, and for Christ, we will rise with him to a life of immortal glory.

12. If we suffer for him, we shall also reign together with him for eternity. If we deny him before men, he will deny us before his angels.

13. If we do not believe in his existence, or his words, he shall, nevertheless, remain the same in himself, faithful and veracious in his promises. He cannot deny himself, *i.e.*, he cannot lose his necessary existence, nor deny his words, by lying (hence, our denial of him, our incredulity will neither add to him, nor take from him).

14. Frequently admonish the faithful committed to your charge, of these things, earnestly appealing to the Lord as your witness, and the avenger of any disrespect shown him: Do not indulge in idle, verbal wrangling and disputation, which is not only useless, but even injurious, calculated to subvert and unsettle the faith of the hearers.

Commentary.

through our labours, may obtain here, the salvation of grace and faith, which comes from Christ Jesus, and heavenly eternal glory, hereafter.

11. "A faithful saying." These words are generally used by the Apostle as a preface to some important truth, like "Amen, Amen," in the Gospel. St. Chrysostom understands them to regard the preceding, as if the Apostle were referring to the salvation of the elect, and their participation in heavenly glory : and the construction of the following—"for if we be dead with him"—would favour this interpretation. It is, however, better refer it to the following, with St. Thomas : for, the entire scope of the Apostle is to excite Timothy to fortitude, by the hope of future glory. Hence, he announces it as an important truth, that if we die with Christ, and for him, we shall share in his glory. Then, "for" will have the meaning of, *because*.

12. If we deny him before men, he will deny us before his angels, and exclude us from his kingdom.

13. Our incredulity will in nowise affect him ; it will only injure ourselves, if we deny him and his promises ; nothing will be added to him, or taken from him, by this denial ; he will be what he was from eternity, an immutable God, and he is "faithful," *i.e.*, veracious, being truth itself. Hence, his promises will be always fulfilled. He is true to his words, faithful in his promises, terrible in his menaces.

14. "Charging them before the Lord," *i.e.*, invoking God, as the witness of the truth of your words, and the avenger of any disrespect or contempt shown them. "Contend not in words." According to this reading, this command regards Timothy himself. The Greek reading is an infinitive, μή λογομαχεῖν, *not to contend in words*, according to which, the command regards the people, whom Timothy is told "to charge before the Lord, not to contend in words." The Greek reading, however, will bear the former interpretation ; for, the Hebrews often use the infinitive mood, for the imperative. Our reading is the one adopted by St. Augustine, St. Ambrose, &c., and it is more probable, because the Apostle is here entering on a new topic. After his exhortation to fortitude, he now tells Timothy to render himself a worthy minister of the word of God ; and in order to become such, he should avoid certain defects, the first of which is contention in words. A person is said to contend in words, when it is not for the discovery of the truth, but for the vain repute of having obtained the mastery, that he is struggling. The Apostle by no means prevents disputation in proper circumstances.

Text.

15. Carefully study to present thyself approved unto God, a workman that needeth not to be ashamed, rightly handling the word of truth.

16. But shun profane and vain babblings: for they grow much towards ungodliness.

17. And their speech spreadeth like a canker: of whom are Hymeneus and Philetus:

18. Who have erred from the truth, saying that the resurrection is past already, and have subverted the faith of some.

19. But the sure foundation of God, standeth firm, having this

Paraphrase.

15. Studiously labour to render thyself a workman acceptable and pleasing to God, not ashamed of the reproaches of Christ, dispensing the word of truth in a proper manner, according to the wants and capabilities of your people.

16. But shun profane novelties of words; for they contribute much to engender impiety in the mind.

17. And the language of those who propound new and profane foolish expressions creeps like a canker, or gangrene, diffusing its poison more extensively. Of the number of such heretics are Hymeneus and Philetus.

18. Who have erred regarding the truth, saying that the resurrection has already taken place, and by their error have subverted the faith of many.

19. But, although some may fall away from the faith, this gangrenous corruption will not extend to the entire

Commentary.

15. "That needeth not be ashamed," may also mean, in a passive signification; of whom there will be no reason to be ashamed—of whom the Church need not feel ashamed. "Rightly handling the word of God." The Greek, ορθοτομουντα, literally means, *cutting straight* "the word of God." The idea, according to some, is borrowed from parents and nurses, who cut bread into small particles, accommodated to the wants of children, so that they may the more easily swallow and be nourished by them; or from cooks, who were wont to divide the portions marked out for each; or from the stewards at feasts, whose duty it was to cut for each guest the part most agreeable and best suited to him. So, in like manner, ought the preacher of God's holy word propose the true doctrine in a perfect, unmutilated form, distinguishing truth from falsehood, accommodating himself to circumstances, and to the capacities of his hearers, treating with the learned on learned subjects; proposing in all simplicity, the elementary truths of faith to the ignorant; not treating of virginity with the married, nor of marriage with virgins; not proposing alarming subjects to the timid, nor holding out promises of pardon to the obstinate in sin, unless they become converted. Others say, the allusion is to husbandmen, who are praised for cutting straight furrows, in cultivating their lands.

16. "But shun profane and vain babblings." The word "and" is not in the Greek; it is, *but shun profane vain babblings*. The expression is similar to that (1 Ep. vi. 20). The reading adopted by St. Chrysostom is, *shun profane novelties in words*. The sense will be the same in either reading; for, "profane" shows that the Apostle refers to words conveying a sense, which it would be profanation to mix up with the deposit of faith; the use of such profane language is another fault to be avoided by a preacher.

17. "Spreadeth like a canker." In Greek, γάγγραινα, *gangrene*. They communicate the virus of their errors to their neighbours, just as the canker feeds on and corrupts the surrounding flesh. "Philetus," &c.; these were the principal among those heretics.

18. "Who have erred from the truth." In the Greek, περὶ τὴν ἀλήθειαν, *regarding the truth*. They maintained, according to St. Thomas, that all things mentioned in the SS. Scripture, regarding the resurrection, are to be understood of the spiritual resurrection of the soul, by baptism and penance. They denied the resurrection of the body, but admitted a spiritual resurrection of the soul here, by grace, and hereafter, by glory. "And have subverted the faith of some;" because the article of the resurrection is the foundation of our faith. Hence, if it be rejected, faith is distroyed. From these words it follows, that faith is not *inamissible*.

19. In consequence of having said that the pernicious doctrines of heretics crept like a canker, and having instanced some who had fallen away from the faith, there might be reason to apprehend that the same might befall the entire body of the

Text.

seal: the Lord knoweth who are his; and let every one depart from iniquity who nameth the name of the Lord,

20. But in a great house there are not only vessels of gold and of silver, but also of wood and of earth: and some indeed unto honour, but some unto dishonour.

21. If any man therefore shall

Paraphrase.

body of the faithful: for, the predestined members of the spiritual edifice of God's Church, firmly founded on a rock, will remain firm and immovable, having as the authentic seal of their stability, the foreknowledge of the Lord, knowing from eternity, by a knowledge of predilection and love, who are his, which loving foreknowledge of God is made manifest, by their observing the precepts of avoiding evil and doing good, aided by the graces administered to them in consequence of this predilection.

20. (It is not to be wondered at. if in the Church there are sinful members, and weak members, liable to seduction); for, as in any spacious house, there are to be found not only vessels of gold, and vessels of silver, but also of wood and of earth, and some of each are used for honourable, and others for vile, purposes—(so it is in the great house of the Church).

21. Should any one, then, cleanse himself from the

Commentary.

faithful; and so, the Church might be destroyed. He says, no such danger is to be apprehended. Because "the sure foundation of God standeth firm," *i.e.*, the predestined members of God's Church, founded on a rock, will firmly persevere in the faith. "Having this seal." He alludes to the custom of placing certain sentences, sealed, under the foundation stone of buildings—a custom in use, even at the present day. They have impressed upon them the following character: "the Lord knoweth who are his." The word "knoweth," means, to know so as to love, a signification it has in many passages of SS. Scripture. And the consequence of this foreknowledge, and love of God, is, first, the ministration of the grace of faith, signified by "naming the name of the Lord" (for one invokes the name of the Lord, because he believes and trusts in him)—and secondly, the grace to avoid evil and do good, "depart from iniquity." The character impressed is one, "this seal," comprising these two sentences, "the Lord knoweth," &c., and "let everyone depart," &c., one of which is the result and the manifestation of the other. The decree and predestination of God preceded; faith and good works—the fruits of the graces of this predestination—are the manifestation of this seal, on the part of God. The first part—viz., the decree, it is, that guarantees infallibly the second—viz., the grace of faith and good works; and the second, which is, properly speaking, the character impressed, it is, that manifests the first. The words "The Lord knoweth who are his," are generally supposed to be taken from Numbers, xvi. 5, according to the Septuagint version. There is, however, some slight change in the Vulgate version by St. Jerome; "let every one depart," &c., is taken from Numbers xvi. 26. "Who nameth the name of the Lord;" in Greek, *the name of Christ.* The Vulgate is supported by manuscripts generally.

20. "The great house" is commonly in its application understood of the Church, which is called, "the house of God."—(1 Tim. iii. 15). In it are to be found, "vessels of gold and silver," *i.e.*, men of high accomplishments, of great spiritual gifts, eloquent and learned bishops, priests, deacons, &c., and "vessels of wood and earth;" such as the common order of Christians, gifted with no exalted privileges; and of each class, some are destined for the honourable purposes of salvation; and others, for the vile purposes of damnation. Hence, sinners and reprobates may be in the Church. What a subject of alarm is conveyed in this passage to such as occupy, by their learning and station, the place of "vessels of gold and silver," in God's Church! The higher their station, the greater their responsibility, and the deeper their damnation, should they deserve to be rejected. "*Judicium durissimum his, qui praesunt.*" They should, therefore, with fear and trembling, take care, lest in the end it may be found, that they are among the *some* marked out for "dishonour" and eternal reprobation.

21. The Apostle here says that such persons as have contracted the defilements of sin or error may be purged and cleansed from them, and thus become vessels of

Text.

cleanse himself from these, he shall be a vessel unto honour, sanctified and profitable to the Lord, prepared unto every good work.

22. But flee thou youthful desires and pursue justice, faith, charity, and peace with them that call on the Lord out of a pure heart.

23. And avoid foolish and unlearned questions, knowing that they beget strifes.

24. But the servant of the Lord must not wrangle : but be mild towards all men, apt to teach, patient,

25. With modesty admonishing them that resist the truth : if peradventure God may give them repentance to know the truth.

26. And they may recover themselves from the snares of the devil, by whom they are held captive at his will,

Paraphrase.

sordid stains of his sins, aided by God's grace, he shall become a vessel of honour, consecrated, accommodated to the uses of the Lord, prepared and fitted for every good work.

22. But do thou avoid the desires to which young men are subject, and eagerly pursue sanctity of life, faith, charity, and concord with all true and sincere Christians.

23. And reject frivolous questions, and such as nowise contribute to true wisdom, knowing that these questions beget strifes.

24. But the servant of our Lord should, like the Lord himself, not wrangle; but he should be mild towards all, ready to instruct them; patient in enduring adversity and opposition.

25. Instructing and administering paternal correction, with mildness, to such as resist the truth, in the hope that God would inspire them with a spirit of penance, to come to a knowledge of the truth.

26. And thus recover themselves out of the snares of the devil, by whom they were held captive, so as to be the slaves of his will, in the commission of sin.

Commentary.

honour, "sanctified" by the grace of God, "profitable" for the purposes of the Lord, "and prepared unto every good work." The grace which he will receive at his conversion will enable such a person to practise all virtues, and perform every good work which the will of God may require of him. "Cleanse" means to cleanse thoroughly. He says, "if any man shall cleanse," thereby assigning to free will its share, although grace shall be the principal cause.

22. The Apostle had been exhorting Timothy to become a "workman approved unto God" (verse 15), and to avoid the profane novelties of words, while he introduced other things incidentally. He now resumes his subject, and proceeds to show, how Timothy is to become "a workman" of this sort : viz., by "shunning youthful desires," not only the passions of lust and intemperance—for Timothy was chaste and abstemious—but, principally, the spiritual interior sins of vanity, ambition, boasting, &c., to which young men, like Timothy, are subject. "Pursue justice," *i.e.*, Christian justice or sanctity of life. "Faith," may regard truth and sincerity in his language. "Charity" towards all, and concord with all true and sincere Christians. What a description of Christian virtues obligatory on all ; but particularly so, on the minister of religion !

23. He should reject foolish and unlearned questions no way contributing to true knowledge or wisdom. The Apostle may probably be referring to some of the foolish questions of the Simonians.

24. "The servant of the Lord" should imitate the Lord himself, and therefore not indulge in wrangling. By "servant of the Lord," may be meant, every Christian, but in particular, the minister of religion, in a special manner devoted to his sevice. "Mild towards all." This does not interfere with the exercise of stern correction, when necessary. "Apt to teach," fit and prepared to instruct all persons requiring instruction. "Patient" of reverses and opposition offered him.

25. "With modesty." In Greek, ἐν πραότητι, *with meekness*, "admonishing them that resist the truth." The word "admonish" may also mean, *instructing*, and combine both, so as to mean, giving instructive admonition. "The truth." These words are not in the Greek.

26. "At his will," are understood by some, of the will of God ; these men are held captive by the devil, as long as God wills it. The Greek word for "his," ἐκείνου, would appear to warrant this interpretation. The Paraphrase is, however, the more probable, because "the devil" is the word immediately preceding, and these men are made the instruments of the devil, by performing freely whatever crimes he wishes them to perpetrate.

CHAPTER III.

Analysis.

In this chapter, the Apostle predicts the rise of false teachers, at no very distant period, and minutely describes their corrupt morals (1–5). He exhorts Timothy to shun them; for some of them had already made their appearance, who, although they may meet with partial success, shall ultimately, like the Egyptian Magicians who opposed Moses, be discomfited, and their imposture similarly exposed (5–9). He exhorts Timothy to preserve the doctrine which he himself had transmitted to him, and to take his own conduct, particularly in patiently enduring persecutions, as the model for imitation; for, all the just are doomed to endure persecution (10–15). Finally, he exhorts him to continue the study of the SS. Scripture, as most useful to supply the minister of the Gospel, with the abundant means of performing every good work, connected with his duties of teaching, reproving, correcting, and instructing (15–17).

Text.	Paraphrase.
1. KNOW also this, that in the last days, shall come on dangerous times.	1. Be assured of this also, that hereafter shall come on difficult times, seasons of danger.
2. Men shall be lovers of themselves, covetous, haughty, proud, blasphemers, disobedient to parents, ungrateful, wicked,	2. (They shall be rendered such) by men who shall arise, wholly engrossed with their own selfish interests, fond of money, boastful and haughty in their expressions, proud in their exalted ideas of their own superior claims and excellence, blasphemers, rebellious against their parents, ungrateful, perpetrators of every species of wickedness,
3. Without affection, without peace, slanderers, incontinent, unmerciful, without kindness,	3. Devoid of every feeling of natural affection, perfidious (or implacable), calumniators, voluptuaries, indulging in sensual pleasures, savage and inhuman, enemies and haters of all good men,

Commentary.

1. The Apostle, in order to remove any feelings of wonder on the part of Timothy at the defection of Hymeneus and Philetus, and also with a view of stimulating him to greater vigilance in combating them, predicts the rise of false teachers, at no distant period. "In the last days," means, hereafter. It is not confined to the period of Antichrist's coming; for, St. Paul tells Timothy to avoid them (5). The period of the Christian Law is frequently termed in SS. Scripture "the last hour," as it is not to be succeeded by any other form of Religion. "Dangerous." In Greek, καιροὶ χαλεποί, *hard*, or, *difficult times*.

2. "Men shall be lovers of themselves," &c. In Greek, *and men shall be lovers*, &c. *i.e.*, "*for* men shall be," &c.; *and*, is by a Hebrew idiom often employed to signify, *for*; "lovers of themselves," referring all things to themselves, as the last end; inordinate self-love is the root of all our corrupt passions. "Covetous," he enumerates the branches of this corrupted root of self-love. The first is avarice, the desire of money, and of rendering all external advantages subservient to our own ease and pleasure. "Proud," valuing themselves above others and despising them. "Blasphemers," may refer to those using injurious language either against God or man.

3. "Without peace," in Greek, ασπονδοι, not observant of compacts or treaties of peace, may either mean, violators of pacts and treaties, or implacable, never reconciled to any one. "Incontinent," indulging in lust and intemperance. "Without kindness," (ἀφιλάγαθοι, *enemies to good men*.)

Text.	Paraphrase.
4. Traitors, stubborn, puffed up, and lovers of pleasures more than of God :	4. Traitors towards their associates (petulant) or hasty and precipitate), swollen from the vain conceit of their own excellence, more attached to their pleasures than to God ;
5. Having an appearance indeed of godliness, but denying the power thereof. Now these avoid.	5. Bearing externally the mask—the mere appearance—of piety and of reverence towards God, but abjuring and denying, by their works, its truth and reality. Such persons repel far from you and endure them not.
6. For of these sort are they who creep into houses, and lead captive silly women loaden with sins, who are led away with divers desires :	6. For of these there are some who cunningly insinuate themselves into private families, and obtain such control over silly, foolish women, as to hold them insnared by their false doctrine ; prepared to follow their teaching in all things—women already loaded with the heavy weight of sins, and driven and led about by the various impulses of concupiscence ;
7. Ever learning, and never attaining to the knowledge of the truth.	7. Always seeming desirous of learning, but never arriving at the knowledge of the truth.
8. Now as Jannes and Mambres resisted Moses, so these also resist the truth, men corrupted in mind, reprobate concerning the faith.	8. But, as Jannes and Mambres resisted the divine power displayed by Moses, so also do these men now resist the Gospel truth—men corrupted in heart and mind, and therefore, erring regarding the faith.

Commentary.

4. "Stubborn," may also mean, precipitate or rash, "lovers of pleasure," &c., making a god of their bellies "more than of God." The Greek has "*more than lovers of God.*" "Lovers of pleasures," &c., φιλήδονοι μᾶλλον ἤ φιλόθεοι.

5. "Having an appearance of piety." The Greek word for "appearance," μόρφωσιν, may also mean having the *forming*, or, *inculcation* of piety which they teach to others, but by no means practise themselves. "Denying the power," *i.e.*, the truth and reality of piety, by the immorality of their lives. "Now these avoid," or (as the Greek, ἀποτρέπου, implies) *repel far from you*, of course, after having first "admonished them with modesty," (ii. 25). It is deserving of remark, that only few agree in the rendering or exposition of the several words of the preceding verses. The most probable exposition seems to be that given above.

6. Some of these impostors, after having obtained admission into private families, artfully succeed to inveigling foolish, "silly women," τὰ γυναικάρια, in the meshes of their erroneous teachings, and obtain such control over their minds as to make them their disciples and followers ; "loaded with sins," committed during their former sinful lives, which predispose them to abandon the faith (1 Tim. i. 19) ; or, "loaded with sins" by their teachers, who corrupt them with their errors, "led away" like brute beasts, by the impulse of their different passions. St. Jerome observes that it was by women, all heresies began to be propagated. It is also to be remarked, that these false teachers were faithful imitators of the father of lies in addressing first the weak intellects of women.

7. "Ever learning," &c., from the Greek, μανθάνοντα. It appears that this refers to the deluded women, ever anxious to acquire learing, but "never attaining to the knowledge of the truth," because, in punishment of their sins, and their undue curiosity in recurring to other sources of religious instruction than the true Apostles of Christ, they are delivered over to blindness of heart, and having consulted teachers of falsehood, they can never learn from them anything else than falsehood.

8. No wonder that the truth is now opposed ; it was opposed at all times. "Jannes and Mambres" were the two magicians, who were principally engaged in opposing the miracles of Moses by like miracles, until, overcome in the plague of sciniphs, they cried out, "this is the finger of God."—(Exodus, vii. 19). "Mambres," in the Greek *Jambres.* Our reading, however, is the one conformable to the Hebrew Talmud. St. Jerome gives both readings in his exposition of Hebrew words. The names of the

Text.

9. But they shall proceed no farther; for their folly shall be manifest to all men, as theirs also was.

10. But thou hast fully known my doctrine, manner of life, purpose, faith, long-suffering, love, patience.

11. Persecutions, afflictions: such as came upon me at Antioch, at Iconium, and at Lystra: what persecutions I endured, and out of them all the Lord delivered me.

12. And all that will live godly in Christ Jesus, shall suffer persecution.

13. But evil men and seducers shall grow worse and worse; erring, and driving into error.

Paraphrase.

9. But they shall not succeed long in their work of seduction; for, their folly and imposture shall be exposed, before all men, to their confusion, as happened the Magicians referred to.

10. (But thou being my constant companion, knowest well that I am not such), thou hast fully known my doctrine, my morals, my purpose, or the end I had always in view, the sincerity of my faith, my lenity towards all, my charity, my patience.

11. You have seen the persecutions and miseries I underwent. You have known my sufferings at Antioch, Iconium, and Lystra, which, together with other persecutions equally severe, I endured, but out of all the Lord delivered me.

12. But why speak of my own case? Since all who wish to lead a holy and pious life, according to the precepts of Christ, shall suffer persecution.

13. But wicked men and impostors will, without molestation, be permitted to progress in the indulgence of their corrupt passions, becoming worse and worse every day, seducing others, and seduced themselves.

Commentary.

magicians are not given in SS. Scripture. Hence, St. Paul must have had them from tradition or the inspiration of the Holy Ghost. "Men corrupted in mind;" corruption of heart predisposes for a shipwreck of faith.

9. They shall not long succeed in seduction, without exposure and discomfiture from the teachers of truth, or, "proceed no farther" may mean, that they shall have no influence over the predestined members of the Church, the "sure foundation of God," though they may succeed with the corrupt of heart, with silly women, weak in intellect.

10. To the teachings and corrupt morals of the heretics, he opposes his own doctrine and morals; these were the pattern for Timothy's imitation. Timothy, being his constant companion in preaching the Gospel, was fully acquainted with the Apostle's "doctrine," his "manner of life," the purity of his morals, his "purpose," the end which he proposed to himself in all his actions, viz., the glory of God and the salvation of the neighbour, his "long suffering," his lenity towards his enemies, which was also exercised in bearing the infirmities of his brethren; his "love" towards all, his "patience" under adversity. Such are the virtues the Apostle teaches every minister of the Gospel to practise.

11. He reminds Timothy of the afflictions and persecutions he underwent for the Gospel, at Antioch of Pisidia (Acts, xiii. 45 and 50), Iconium (Acts, xiv. 28, 2, 45), Lystra, (Acts, xiv. 18). "What persecutions I endured." You know how I endured these and other persecutions, "and out of all these," &c. This he adds, to give Timothy confidence, because the same Providence will be exerted for his deliverance also, if necessary.

12. "And all that will live godly," &c., i.e., all, or, *mostly* all. This was literally verified in the days of the Apostle, when the sword of persecution was openly unsheathed against the faithful. It is true of all times; the pious will have something to bear from the heretics and unbelievers, or from the envious and wicked, whose lives suffer in the contrast; sometimes, from friends and relatives; sometimes, from God himself, to try them and perfect their virtue; sometimes, from themselves and their own thoughts; sometimes, from the devil. "The life of man is a state of warfare on earth," and unless we take up our cross and follow him, we cannot be disciples of Christ.—(*See* the last chapter of the 2nd Book of the Imitation of Christ, for a beautiful Dissertation on this subject).

13. While the godly and pious shall be persecuted, the wicked and corrupt livers

Text.

14. But continue thou in those things which thou hast learned, and which have been committed to thee; knowing of whom thou hast learned *them;*

15. And because from thy infancy thou hast known the holy scriptures, which can instruct thee to salvation, by the faith which is in Christ Jesus.

16. All scripture, inspired of God, is profitable to teach, to reprove, to correct, to instruct in justice.

Paraphrase.

14. But do thou persevere in believing and preaching the things which thou hast learned from me, and which have been confided by me to thy safe keeping, mindful of the master, by whom thou wert taught them.

15. Bearing also in mind, that from thy infancy thou hast learned the SS. Scripture, which can instruct thee unto salvation, through the faith of Christ Jesus to which they conduct thee.

16. For all Scripture inspired by God is profitable both for the purposes of instructing the ignorant in the truths of faith, of rebutting the contrary errors, of correcting and rebuking corrupt morals, and of instructing and forming men to sanctity of life.

Commentary

and "seducers," γόητες, *jugglers,* will progress in vice and unlawful indulgence without being molested by any one; they will progress in "erring" themselves, "and driving into error," leading others astray after them. The Greek reading runs thus—"*seducing and seduced;*" as if their own progress in error was the punishment of their seducing others; "shall grow worse and worse" is not opposed to verse 9, "shall proceed no farther," because this latter is understood of their not undermining the elect members of the Church. Moreover, it can be said that there is question of different persons in both passages: in verse 9, of the heretics who were to arise in the days of Timothy; were, of the wicked in general, whose treatment is contrasted with that of the good in general, verse 12.

14. "And which have been committed to thee." Referring to the deposit of faith. "Knowing of whom thou hast learned them." He assigns two reasons why Timothy should continue faithful: the first is derived from the authority of his teacher, no other than an Apostle of Christ, carried up to the third Heaven.—(2 Cor. xii. 2).

15. The second is derived from the long period of his education in the Christian religion. From his very infancy, he was taught the SS. Scripture under the pious care of his mother, Eunice, and his grandmother, Lois; for, his father was a Pagan, and would not permit him to be circumcised. "Which can instruct thee," in the Greek, τὰ δυναμενα σε σοφίσαι, *which can render thee wise, i.e.,* render you learned, "unto salvation." "By the faith which is in Christ Jesus." The proper reading of the SS. Scripture would lead to Christ; for, "the end of the law is Christ"—or, the words may mean, that in order to derive the proper wisdom and instruction from the SS. Scripture, we should proceed to read them under the guidance of the faith of Christ.

16. In the Greek it is, πᾶσα γραφὴ, θεόπνευστος, καὶ ὠφελιμος πρὸς διδασϙαλίαν, &c., *all Scripture inspired of God and useful for doctrine,* &c. According to which, the word "*is*," is understood so as to convey two assertions: first, all Scripture is inspired of God; and secondly, Scripture thus inspired is also useful for the purposes of instruction, &c. According to our Vulgate reading, there is only one assertion conveyed, viz., that all Scripture that is inspired of God, is profitable for instructing the ignorant in the truths of faith, for refuting the errors opposed to sound doctrine, for rebuking men of corrupt principles and morals, and for forming men to sanctity and Christian justice. These are the four great duties of a minister of religion, and for these the SS. Scripture is profitable. It is quite evident that this passage furnishes no argument whatever that the SS. Scripture, without Tradition, is the *sole rule of faith;* for, although SS. Scripture is *profitable* for these four ends, still it is not said to be *sufficient.* The Apostle requires the aid of Tradition (2nd Thessalonians, ii. 15). Moreover, the Apostle here refers to the Scripture which Timothy was taught from his infancy. Now, a good part of the New Testament was not written in his boyhood; some of the Catholic Epistles were not written even when St. Paul wrote this; and none of the Books of the New Testament were then placed on the canon of the Scripture books. He refers, then, to the Scriptures of the *Old* Testament; and if the argument from this passage proved anything, it

Text.

17. That the man of God may be perfect, furnished to every good work.

Paraphrase.

17. So that (by the diligent and attentive study of the SS. Scripture) the minister of the Gospel becomes perfect, completely furnished with the means of performing every good work connected with the discharge of his sacred duties.

Commentary.

would prove too much, viz., that the Scriptures of the *New* Testament, not yet written, were not necessary for a rule of faith.

It is hardly necessary to remark that this passage furnishes no proof of the inspiration of the several books of SS. Scripture, even of those admitted to be such. According to the Vulgate reading of this verse (16), which Bloomfield assures us is adopted by all the most eminent critics after Theodoret, there is nothing said of the inspiration of any part of Scripture; all that is stated is simply this : that every portion of inspired Scripture is profitable for teaching, reproving, &c., without determining what these inspired Scriptures are. Nor is the question determined by the Greek reading either. For we are not told what is meant by "every Scripture," of which it is said, according to this reading, that it "is inspired," or what the Books or portion of "inspired Scripture" are.

Neither is there any argument here in favour of the indiscriminate reading of the Holy Scriptures. For, the advantage of reading them is here spoken of in reference to the ministers of the Gospel, which no one questions. Of these alone mention is made. "It is profitable" (verse 16). For whom? "That the man of God may be perfect," &c.—*See* Paraphrase.

17. So, "that the man of God," *i.e.*, the minister of the Gospel charged with the care of souls, "may be perfect," *i.e.*, prepared in all his duties, the meaning of which is more clearly expressed in the following words, "furnished to every good work," *i.e.*, supplied, from the study of SS. Scripture, with the abundant means of performing every work connected with the four great duties already mentioned. The study of the SS. Scripture is an imperative obligation on the Pastor of souls, in order to be furnished with the means of discharging all his duties. St. Paul exhorts Timothy to continue the study of them, although instructed in them from his infancy ; he tells him to attend "to reading" them (1 Tim. iv. 13), and if this was necessary for Timothy, instructed by the Apostle himself, how much more so must it not be for others. For the proper and effective application of SS. Scriptures, without which religious discourses or sermons would, in many instances, pass for mere philosophical disquisitions or moral essays, the constant study and attentive perusal of the Sacred Volume is necessary.

CHAPTER IV.

Analysis.

In this chapter, the Apostle earnestly conjures Timothy to apply himself to the zealous dis-charge of his duties, particularly that of preaching the word of God in all forms, and on all occasions. And he assigns as a reason for this earnest injunction, the near approach of corruption in morals, and instability of faith, among the faithful them-selves (1-5). He predicts that his own death shall occur at no distant period, and consoles Timothy, by telling him that he is only going to receive a crown of justice, in reward for his past works (5-9). He invites Timothy to come to him, and brings the Epistle to a close with the usual salutations.

Text.

1. I CHARGE thee before God and JESUS CHRIST, who shall judge the living and the dead, by his coming, and his kingdom :

2. Preach the word : be instant in season, out of season ; reprove, entreat, rebuke in all patience and doctrine.

Paraphrase.

1. I conjure thee before God the Father, and his Son Jesus Christ, who, in virtue of the power received from the Father, will judge all men, as well those who are living immediately before the judgment, as those long before dead, at his second coming, and at the final manifestation of his kingly and undisputed power.

2. (I conjure thee therefore), to preach the word of God, to attend to this duty constantly and sedulously, both in season and out of season ; to convince by arguments the gainsayers, to chide and rebuke the immoral, to entreat and exhort all to sanctity of life : and all this do with the utmost meekness and the most patient endurance, and the exhibition of sound doctrine.

Commentary.

1. Having referred, in the preceding chapter, to the four great duties of the Episco-pal office, he now earnestly conjures Timothy to devote himself to their fulfilment, and this obtestation is made in the most solemn form, invoking God the Father and his Son Jesus Christ (before "Jesus Christ," the words, *the Lord*, are placed in the Greek, to whom, as man, the "Father had given all judgment," and whom he constituted Judge of the living, &c.—Acts, x.)—as witnesses, who will also be one day the Judges of his fidelity or neglect. For the meaning of the words, "the living and the dead," (*see* First Epistle to Thessal. iv. 16.) "By his coming," &c. This is not to be joined to the words, "I charge thee," but to the words, "who shall judge," as appears from the Greek particle corresponding with "*by*," which signifies, that in this coming and manifestation of his glorious kingdom, when his enemies are trodden under foot, death among the rest (1 Cor. xv. 28), he shall judge all mankind. After the words, "I charge thee," the particle, *therefore*, is added in the Greek, but it is now rejected by critics.

2. This is what he thus solemnly conjures him to do :—It is, "preach the word" of God. "Be instant," *i.e.*, zealously discharge this sacred duty, "in season, out of season ;" which some understand to mean, constantly. The words also mean, that no opportunity, no matter how unseasonable or inconvenient to the minister of the Gospel himself, should be omitted, if there be a hope of advantage ; or even though it should be unseasonable for the hearer, as to time, if there be hope of advantage to him, the same is to be said, because even then the word itself is seasonable. "Reprove," "entreat," "rebuke," &c. In the Greek, "*rebuke*" is before "*entreat*;" thus :—"*Reprove, rebuke, entreat;*" expressing the four-fold duty for which he said, in the

Text.

3. For there shall be a time, when they will not endure sound doctrine; but according to their own desires they will heap to themselves teachers, having itching ears.

4. And will indeed turn away their hearing from the truth, but will be turned unto fables.

5. But be thou vigilant, labour in all things, do the work of an evangelist, fulfil thy ministry. Be sober.

6. For I am even now ready to

Paraphrase.

3. (It is not without a cause, I thus earnestly conjure thee). For, the time is approaching at no remote period, when the faithful themselves will not endure the sound doctrine of the gospel ; but, according to the corrupt desires of their own hearts, shall rashly select and multiply for themselves teachers, who shall propound principles pleasing to their passions ; and this, because they wish to hear things new and curious, soothing and agreeable to them.

4. Hence it is, that they shall turn away their hearing from the truth of the gospel, and shall attend only to idle fables.

5. But (in order to arrest the progress of these impending evils), be constantly on the alert, sustain all the evils to which you may be exposed, perform all the duties of an Evangelist, faithfully fulfil your ministry, and to do this, be sober.

6. (You cannot long enjoy the benefit of my coun-

Commentary.

preceding chapter, that the Scripture is profitable. "In all patience." The Greek is, *in all long suffering, i.e.,* with the most perfect meekness ; for, correction, or instruction, if appearing to emanate from passion rather than from charity, will lose all effect. "And doctrine ;" men wish to be convinced, and led by reason and argument. The great duty, then, of the minister of religion is, to "rebuke, and entreat," alternately, according to circumstances. Hence, the rigour with which the Council of Trent enjoins on Bishops, under the heaviest sanction of moral guilt, to discharge the great duty of preaching—(SS. v., 2, 2, and SS. xxiv., 4, *de Ref.*)

The common opinion of divines is, that a Pastor of souls who, without a justifying cause, omits the duty of instruction for one month, *continuously,* or *three* months of the year, *discontinuously,* is guilty of mortal sin. The conscientious zeal of Pastors cannot be too strongly stimulated in this matter.

3. "They will not endure sound doctrine ;" they will cast it away as an intolerable burthen. "They shall heap to themselves teachers." These words show that they will take to themselves, without any choice or prudent selection, and multiply teachers; just as men carelessly throw one stone over another in a heap. "Having itching ears." This refers to the people, and not to the teachers, as appears from the Greek, κνηθόμενοι τὴν ακοήν. "Itching ears," may either refer to their anxiety for hearing curious and new things, or things pleasing to their passions and corrupt inclinations. Such was the "itching of ears," among the Jews of old, when they listened to the eloquence of the prophet as "to a musical song ; they heard his words and did them not" (Ezechiel, xxxiii.) ; or when they called on the prophet—"Speak unto us pleasant things ; see errors for us."—(Isaias, xxx. 10).

4. The truth of the Gospel neither humours the whims, nor flatters the passions of any one ; hence, they will turn away from it and attend to "fables," *i.e.,* Jewish fables or, through insane curiosity, they will look after the fables of the heretics, viz., the Simonians, and others of the kind.

5. "But be thou vigilant, labour in all things." "All things" may affect either "vigilant" or "labour ;" the meaning of which latter word, according to the Greek κακοπάθητον, is, *endure hardships, i.e.,* manfully encounter all the evils that may befall thee in the discharge of thy duty. "Do the work of an evangelist," by preaching the gospel truth in its full integrity ; and from the pure motive of God's glory, "fulfil thy ministry," in all its parts ; neglect none of them. "Be sober." These words are not in the Greek, nor are they in all the Latin manuscripts. They have made their way into our Vulgate, owing to the signification of the Greek word corresponding with "be vigilant," νηφε, which also means, *be sober,* and hence, both significations may have been expressed in our version.

6. "I am now ready to be sacrificed." The Vulgate reading for "sacrificed," (*delibor*), and the Greek, σπενδομαι, clearly expresses that immediate preparation for

Text.

be sacrificed ; and the time of my dissolution is at hand.

7. I have fought a good fight, I have finished my course, I have kept the faith.

8. As to the rest, there is laid up for me a crown of justice, which the Lord the just judge will render to me in that day ; and not only to me, but to them also that love his coming. Make haste to come to me quickly.

Paraphrase.

sels), for, I am now subjected to the immediate process preceding my oblation as a victim, and the hour of my death is just at hand.

7. (This should be for you a subject of congratulation rather than of grief). For, I have fought a glorious fight, on behalf of the gospel and faith of Christ. I have successfully finished my course, and I have kept inviolable my promise of fidelity.

8. As to what remains, there is stored up and safely kept for me, now almost on the point of victory, the crown which I have justly merited, and which the Lord Jesus Christ, as a just judge, will award to me on the day of General Judgment ; and not only to me, but to all who expect and love his glorious coming. Hasten to come to me, without delay, to Rome.

Commentary.

sacrifice, consisting in pouring out a libation on the victim, as if he said : I am sprinkled with wine, as a libation preparatory to my immediate immolation as a victim. This he says with a view of stimulating Timothy to greater exertions, during the very short period of his own existence ; for, he will be immediately deprived of the benefit of his counsels.

7. "I have fought a good fight," *i.e.*, a glorious fight for the gospel ; "I have finished my course." In both these, he alludes to the athletic exercises of wrestling, and running, at the Olympic games. "I have kept the faith," commonly understood of his promise of fidelity, in allusion to the promise, which a soldier makes to his commander. It would be no great matter for him to glory in having kept the faith of Christ, or in not having become an apostate. Hence, the word "faith," refers to fidelity in the discharge of his Apostolic functions.

8. He continues his allusion to the Olympic games. As a prize-fighter, he had come off victorious in the glorious contest ; as a runner, he had reached the goal, observing all the rules of the race course. It remained, therefore, for him to receive from the master or judge of the games, the crown which he merited, *i.e.*, to receive from God the reward of eternal life, which is held out by our Lord Jesus Christ, to such as triumphantly struggle in the *stadium* of a Christian life. Then, this reward is not to be seen, but it is "laid up," and faithfully kept by God. It is "a crown of justice," or a crown justly merited ; eternal life is, therefore, to be the reward of merit. It is also a grace, because grace is indispensable for merit ; hence, as St. Augustine expresses it:—"*In crowning our merits, God only crowns his own gifts.*" And although eternal life be "a crown of justice," because due to our good works, owing to the liberal promises of God, it is also "a crown of *mercy*," because it is merited through the merciful grace of God, as being infinitely above the reach of our natural powers. "On that day," the day of General Judgment, when the soul and body shall be publicly glorified, though it virtually commences, on the day of particular judgment. "And not only to me," &c. It is a crown reserved for all Christians who shall finish their course well." "That love his coming," *i.e.*, who by good works are prepared for him, and show that they love his coming to reward them, as the faithful servant, who performs the wishes of his master, loves his coming.

What an exhortation this passage conveys to us to labour zealously for eternal life! The period of our exertions is but momentary ; to the man on the point of death, his past life, no matter how long, appears but a mere point. We have the judge of the games, the author and finisher of our faith, who is to be *judge* and *witness*, at the same time, holding out from heaven, the crown, that will never fade, and animating us by the sure prospect of enjoying it.

From the present passage, it appears quite clear, that this Epistle was written, when the Apostle was at the very point of death, which he knew, either from revelation or from circumstances, to "be at hand." The object of the Apostle in this passage is to excite Timothy to greater zeal, by telling him that these are the last written instruc-

Text.

9. For Demas hath left me, loving this world, and is gone to Thessalonica:

10. Crescens into Galatia, Titus into Dalmatia.

11. Only Luke is with me. Take Mark, and bring him with thee: for he is profitable to me for the ministry.

12. But Tychicus I have sent to Ephesus.

13. The cloak that I left at Troas with Carpus, when thou comest, bring with thee, and the books, especially the parchments.

14. Alexander the copper-smith

Paraphrase.

9. For, Demas, preferring the ease and pleasures of the world to a participation in my privations and dangers, has left me, and is gone to Thessalonica.

10. Crescens, at my instance, has gone to Galatia to preach the gospel, and Titus to Dalmatia.

11. Luke only remains with me. Take (John) Mark, and bring him with you, for, he is of service to me for the ministry of the gospel.

12. Tychicus I have sent to Ephesus (to supply your place).

13. Call on your way for the cloak, which I left with Carpus at Troas, and for the books also, but particularly the parchments.

14. Alexander, the copper-smith, has done me much

Commentary.

tions he will receive from him—for, that he is now in the position of the victim, on whose head is poured forth the preparatory libation, his death, just at hand. He removes the grief which this might naturally occasion Timothy, by telling him that he is about to enter on the possession of the crown of eternal life. Looking, then, to the plain, obvious meaning of the words, they can bear no other interpretation than that which fixes his death as instantly to occur. This Epistle was, therefore, written during his second imprisonment.

9. This Demas, afraid of sharing in the dangers of the Apostle, left him and went to Thessalonica. If neither the example, nor the miracles of the Apostle, could preserve this man, who is it that should not tremble for his own perseverance?

10. By "Galatia," some understand "Gaul," called "Galatia" by the Greeks. From the Ecclesiastical History of Eusebius (lib. 3, c. 4), as also from the Roman Martyrology (June 27), it appears that this Crescens, was Bishop of Vienne in Gaul. It might be that he came thither from Galatia, in Asia Minor.

11. Luke is the only person able to serve him; that the Apostle was not alone towards the end of his imprisonment—that he and St. Peter were both confined in the Mamertine prison, for nine months before their martyrdom, is the common tradition of the Romans, as we learn from Baronius (A.D. 69). "Mark," i.e., John Mark, the cousin of Barnabas, who was before rejected by the Apostle (Acts, xv. 27). After doing penance, the Apostle received him; he was before useless, but now of some service, while Demas becomes useless. The man who stands should not presume, nor should he who falls, despair.

12. He did not wish to leave Ephesus without a pastor during Timothy's absence; he, therefore, sends Tychicus to supply his place.

13. "The cloak." This was an outer garment, which the Apostle wished to have in prison, in order to keep off the cold, and not to be troublesome to others, in borrowing from them. His sending for it to so great a distance, shows his great poverty. "The books," long since written; probably the books of the Old Testament, and "the parchments," refer to the manuscripts lately written by himself. From this it appears, that though the Apostle was divinely inspired, and taught by Christ himself; still, he omitted no human labour or study for self-improvement. For the short time he had to live, he desired to engage in some useful occupation, and wished for these books to give them to the faithful. If the Doctor of Nations, taught by Christ himself, and after having discharged the Apostleship for so many years, wishes for books to read, how much more necessary must it be for us to make the SS. Scripture and pious books, the subject of our daily study and meditation!

14. "Alexander, the copper-smith." The same, probably, to whom reference is made (1 Tim. i.) Irritated at the excommunication with which the Apostle visited him, he resisted his preaching; he also, very likely, spoke of St. Paul to the friends of

Text.

hath done me much evil ; the Lord will reward him according to his works:

15. Whom do thou also avoid, for he hath greatly withstood our words.

16. At my first answer no man stood with me, but all forsook me : may it not be laid to their charge.

17. But the Lord stood by me, and strengthened me, that by me the preaching may be accomplished, and that all the gentiles may hear : and I was delivered out of the mouth of the lion.

Paraphrase.

evil : the Lord will inflict on him punishment proportioned to his misdeeds.

15. For fear of similar maltreatment, do you also shun him. For, he has offered very great resistance to our preaching.

16. The first time during this imprisonment, that I pleaded my cause before Nero, none of my friends stood by me, they all forsook me. May this not be imputed to them as a sin, i.e., may God forgive them for this desertion of me.

17. But the Lord did not abandon me, he stood by me, and supplied me with spirit and courage for my defence, in order that the preaching of the gospel would be accomplished by me, and that all nations might hear it, and, therefore, I was delivered out of the mouth of the lion.

Commentary.

Nero, as a seditious person, and an enemy of the Jewish religion, which was tolerated at Rome. "The Lord will reward him," &c. (In Greek, ἀποδῴη αὐτῷ ὁ Κύριος *may the Lord reward him*), which is a prophecy, joined with an approval, of the Divine vengeance with which he was to be visited.

16. "In my answer." (In Greek, ἀπολογίᾳ, *apology*), i.e., the first time he pleaded his cause during this second imprisonment, either before Nero, or before some subordinate judge. "No man" (of his friends), stood with him, "but all," i.e., almost all ; for, Luke and others did not desert him, but all who could be of any service to him in the court of Nero "forsook" him, from a dread of that Emperor's cruelty. "May it not be laid to their charge ;" may God forgive them, because they sinned only through weakness.

17. "The Lord stood by me ;" he was not altogether forsaken—the Lord stood by him, encouraging him. "And strengthened me ;" giving him strength and courage to go through his defence. Some persons interpret the Greek word corresponding with "stood by me," παρεστη, to mean, *appeared to me*, and by his presence refreshed me, giving me strength and confidence. "That by me the preaching may be accomplished ;" not that I deserved any such divine interposition ; but, the end for which he stood by me, and for which I wished to have my life prolonged, was, that the preaching of the gospel might receive its consummation through me, and that all the nations might hear it at the centre of the greatest power then existing—viz., at Rome, and even in the palace of Nero, to which many had flocked from all parts of the then known world. Hence, it came to pass, that in his second imprisonment, as well as in his first, "his bonds were made manifest in all the court, and to all the rest (Philip. i.) ; and, therefore, "he was delivered out of the mouth of the lion." Such was the appellation which Nero received for his savage ferocity and cruelty. He was delivered from Nero's grasp, and permitted to live some time longer, perhaps comparatively free, under the custody of a single soldier, as had been allowed him, during his first imprisonment. This passage furnishes no argument against the opinion of the ancients, that the present Epistle was written during the Apostle's second imprisonment. It is rather in favour of that opinion. Because, he says, that "in his first defence," or as in Greek, *apology*, "all had forsaken him," fearing the cruelty of Nero ; and he calls him the "lion," on account of his cruelty. Now, these expressions could not be used in reference to Nero during the Apostle's first imprisonment ; for, as Ecclesiastical writers tell us, St. Paul's first imprisonment occurred during the early part of Nero's reign, some say, in the second or third year of it. And it is quite certain that during the four first years of his reign, Nero was a most benevolent prince. So much so that Seneca declares, that when he was called upon to write the sentence for the execution of two robbers, he exclaimed, *would I never knew letters !* Why, therefore, should the faithful dread so clement and kind-hearted a prince ?—why call him "a lion" ? This would be true of

Text.

18. The Lord hath delivered me from every evil work : and will preserve me unto his heavenly kingdom, to whom be glory for ever and ever. Amen.

19. Salute Prisca and Aquila, and the household of Onesiphorus.

20. Erastus remained at Corinth. And Trophimus I left sick at Miletus.

21. Make haste to come before winter. Eubulus and Pudens and Linus and Claudia, and all the brethren salute thee,

22. The Lord JESUS CHRIST be with thy spirit. Grace be with you. Amen.

Paraphrase.

18. But as he has rescued me from the earthly lion so I hope he will rescue me from the spiritual lion— viz., from sin, and will preserve me unto his heavenly kingdom—to whom be glory for ever and ever. Amen.

19. Salute in my name, Prisca and Aquila, and the family of Onesiphorus.

20. Erastus remained at Corinth, on some business, but Trophimus I left sick at Miletus.

21. Hasten to come to me before winter. Eubulus, and Pudens, and Linus, and Claudia, and all the brethren salute thee.

22. May the Lord Jesus Christ be with you and all the faithful of your Church by his grace. Amen.

Commentary.

him only in the subsequent part of his reign, during the Apostle's second imprisonment. Then, he calls the defence his "first," because he was often interrogated during his second imprisonment.

18. "The Lord hath delivered (in Greek, ῥύσεται, *will deliver*) me from every evil work," from the incursions of the infernal lion, from all sin, and will grant me victory over all temptation, and transfer me to his heavenly kingdom.

19. "The household of Onesiphorus." Onesiphorus himself was at Rome, or, perhaps, dead.

20. Erastus was Treasurer of Corinth.—(Rom. xvi. 23).

21. This was written before winter, either in summer or autumn ; the Apostle was put to death, on the 29th of the following June. He was at least a year in his second imprisonment. And " all the brethren," *i.e.*, all the Christians at Rome " salute thee." "Grace be with you," *i.e.*, with you and all the faithful of your Church.

The Greek subscription is :—(*The Second to Timothy, ordained the first Bishop of the Church of the Ephesians, was written from Rome, when Paul stood a second time before Nero*).

These subscriptions are not always, however, of undoubted authority.

In the *Codex Vaticanus*, the subscription is merely : *The Second to Timothy.*

THE EPISTLE

OF

ST. PAUL TO TITUS.

Introduction.

TITUS was born of Gentile parents; it would appear, that he had been converted by St. Paul; for, he calls him his "beloved son" (chapter i. verse 4). He shared largely in the Apostle's confidence, and was entrusted by him with commissions of great importance. Among the rest, he was sent to Corinth, of which city many suppose him to have been a native, with full power to remedy the evils of that Church and put a stop to its dissensions. The Apostle finally appointed him chief Bishop of the Island of Crete (now called *Candia*), to perfect the work of the Gospel which the Apostle himself had first preached there on his return from Rome to the East, after being released from his first imprisonment.

Although the Apostle might have delivered orally all the instructions contained in this Epistle, at Nicopolis, where he instructed Titus to meet him, and spend the winter with him (chap. iii. 12), and, most likely, the latter was fully instructed in the matters it contained, and more, when he was appointed to govern the Church of Crete; still, he thought fit to commit them to writing on account of their very great importance, and for the instruction of all future Pastors of the Church. Hence it is, that St. Augustine (*de Doctrina Christ.*, c. 16) recommends to all the Pastors and teachers of the Church the constant perusal of this and the two Epistles to Timothy. The argument of the three Epistles is the same. They are chiefly employed in describing the duties of the chief Pastors of the Church, hence termed " Pontifical," or " Hierarchical."

This Epistle is nothing more than a compendium of the Epistles to Timothy. In the first chapter, Titus is instructed to appoint " Priests," *i.e.*, Bishops, as St. Chrysostom, St. Jerome, &c., interpret it, throughout the different cities of the island; in it also, the qualities necessary for a Bishop are briefly summed up. In the second, are marked out the duties which a Bishop should inculcate on persons in the different conditions of life, with due consideration for the several grades and ages in each. In the third, are marked out certain duties common to all the faithful, particularly that of due obedience and subjection, according to circumstances.

WHERE AND WHEN WAS THIS EPISTLE WRITTEN?—The Greek and Syriac versions testify, that it was written at Nicopolis. The same also appears from chap. iii. verse 12; but, it is disputed which Nicopolis is referred to; St. Jerome understands it of Nicopolis in Epirus; St. Chrysostom and others, of Nicopolis in Thrace.

It was written at a time that St. Paul was not in prison; for, in it, he makes no allusion to his chains; moreover, he says, " he is *determined* to winter at Nicopolis" (chap. iii. verse 12), which proves, he was then perfectly free. Baronius fixes its date before the Apostle's first imprisonment; St. Chrysostom, between his first and second imprisonment. The date of it is commonly referred to the year 64.

THE EPISTLE

ST. PAUL TO TITUS.

CHAPTER I.

Analysis.

In this chapter, the Apostle, after the salutation (1, 2–4), which is an epitome of the entire Epistle, reminds Titus of his command, when leaving him, to appoint Pastors over each city in Crete (5), and he describes the virtues which should distinguish a chief Pastor or Bishop (6–9). He assigns a reason why a Bishop should be learned (10), and particularly so, in dealing with the Cretans (12, 13). He refutes the errors of the Heretics, and describes their morals (15, 16).

Text.

1. PAUL, a servant of God, and an apostle of JESUS CHRIST, according to the faith of the elect of God and the acknowledging of the truth, which is according to godliness.

2. Unto the hope of life everlasting, which God, who lieth not hath promised before the times of the world:

3. But hath in due times manifested his word in preaching, which is committed to me according to the commandment of God our Saviour:

Paraphrase.

1. Paul, a servant of God, that is to say, an Apostle of Jesus Christ, sent for the purpose of announcing to the elect of God, the true faith whereby they may be brought to the knowledge of that saving doctrine which promotes the true worship of God.

2. Which imparts to us the hope of eternal life promised or decreed from eternity, to be given us by God, the unerring, unchangeable truth.

3. But this decree or promise of his, though hidden from eternity, God has made known at the period destined by him, through the ministry of preaching, which had been confided and entrusted to me by the delegation of God, our Saviour.

Commentary.

1. "A servant of God." This is a most honourable title, since "*to serve God is to reign.*" The following words, "and an Apostle," &c., clearly express the servitude to which he refers, that special engagement in his service, in quality of Apostle. "According to the faith," &c. The Greek word for "according," κατὰ, shows that the object of his Apostleship was to announce to the elect, the faith, which is expressed in other words. "The acknowledging of the truth," which truth is "according to godliness," *i.e.*, promotes the true worship of God. Wherefore, it excels philosophy, which only regards natural truths, but no way promotes the worship of God.

2. This piety or godliness has annexed to it the hope of eternal life, unlike the law of Moses, which held out only temporal hopes, "a land flowing with milk and honey." "Hath promised," *i.e.*, decreed. This decree is as certain in its actual execution, as would be the fulfilment of a promise on the part of one who would certainly accomplish it. On this account, this decree is called, a promise. "Before the times of the world," *i.e.*, before all ages, all time; hence, in SS. Scripture, it is used to denote, eternity.—2 Tim. i. 9.

3. "His word," refers to the promise or decree (verse 2). In Greek it means,

Text.

4. To Titus my beloved son, according to the common faith, grace, and peace from God the Father, and from Christ Jesus our Saviour.

5. For this cause I left thee in Crete, that thou shouldest set in order the things that are wanting, and shouldest ordain priests in every city, as I also appointed thee:

Paraphrase.

4. (Writes) to Titus, his genuine son, begotten by him spiritually, by imparting to him the faith common to both; grace and peace be to thee, from God the Father, and from Christ Jesus our Saviour.

5. My object in leaving thee in Crete, and giving thee charge over the entire island, was, that thou shouldst correct the things that remained to be corrected, and appoint pastors over each city, according to the rules which I had prescribed for thee.

Commentary.

" *his own word,*" τὸν λόγον αὐτοῦ, and the article prefixed to "word," shows that it refers to the preceding. The manifestation of his promise on the part of God challenges our eternal love and gratitude. This exordium is rather long, but it is an abstract of the entire Epistle and of all the duties of a pastor of souls, who should preach the word, and by this spiritual seed, beget faith (verse 1) hope (verse 2), charity (verse 3), in the souls of his people.

4. " My beloved (in Greek, γνησίω, *genuine, true*) son." He shows how he is his son, in having spiritually begotten him by imparting to him the faith common to them both. "Grace and peace." The present Greek copies add, *mercy*, but it is not found in the best manuscripts, nor in the Greek version of St. Chrysostom, nor in the ancient Greek or Latin Fathers. Hence, it was probably inserted from the Epistles of Timothy.

5. He now enters on the subject of the Epistle. "For this cause I left thee at Crete," making him chief Bishop, with jurisdiction over the entire island. "That thou shouldst set in order the things that are wanting." In Greek, ἵνα τὰ λείποντα ἐπιδιορθώσῃ, *that thou shouldst rectify the things which remained,* which were left to be rectified by the Apostle, for want of time to tarry there. The Apostles laid the foundations of the different Churches; the superstructure, in many cases, was to be reared by their disciples. "And appoint priests in every city." That under the word "priests" are included bishops, is clear from verse 7. The word "bishop," according to Apostolic and Ecclesiastical usage, refers to the first order of the clergy only, superior to the others, who are merely priests, both in point of orders and jurisdiction; while the word "*presbyteri,*" or "priests," comprises the clergy as well of the first, as of the second, order. It is likely, the word here extends to both, and that Titus was instructed to appoint pastors over each of the hundred cities of Crete (hence called " Hecatompolis "), priests over some, and bishops over others, according to their relative importance and the wants of the faithful. This commission given to Titus, shows, that from the very infancy of the Church, certain bishops in some localities enjoyed Primatial and Archiepiscopal jurisdiction over others. St. Jerome confines the meaning of "priests" to bishops only, who were to be appointed over the principal cities of the very populous island of Crete. It is an article of Catholic faith that bishops, who are the successors of the Apostles, are superior to priests.—(Council of Trent, SS. 23, cap. 4, canon 7.) Though not of faith, it is universally believed, that this superiority is of divine institution. In his commentary on this passage, and in his Epistle to Evagrius, St. Jerome would appear to hold, that this superiority was the result of Ecclesiastical usage or arrangement. All, however, that would follow, at most, from his words is, that the bishops, in course of time, vindicated the superiority which they had over the priests; and that, in order to put a stop to the insolent encroachments of some priests, the functions of the bishops came to be exercised more distinctly than before, when they governed the Church " *with common counsel.*" And in his Commentary on this passage, he employs a rhetorical hyperbole, when referring to the dignity of priests, in consequence of the tyrranical domination of some bishops over the priests; among other instances, John of Jerusalem treated St. Jerome himself and his followers with excessive severity. (*See* his Epistles, 60, 61, 62). In the Epistle to Evagrius, already referred to, St. Jerome asserts for the bishop alone the power of conferring orders.

Text.

6. If any be without crime, the husband of one wife, having faithful children, not accused of riot, or unruly.

7. For a bishop must be without crime, as the steward of God; not proud, not subject to anger, not given to wine, no striker, not greedy of filthy lucre :

8. But given to hospitality, gentle, sober, just, holy, continent :

9. Embracing that faithful word which is according to doctrine, that he may be able to exhort in sound doctrine, and to convince the gainsayers.

10. For there are many disobedient, vain-talkers, and seducers, especially they of the circumcision.

Paraphrase.

6. The qualifications necessary for the persons entrusted with pastoral charge are, to be irreprehensible, only once married ; as regards their children also, to be free from reproach, by having them brought up in the Christian faith, and of such temperate, sober habits, as not to be chargeable with luxurious excesses of any kind—obedient to their parents.

7. For, a bishop should be a man of blameless life, as becomes a steward, a dispenser of the treasures of God's household, he should be exempt from the vices of arrogance, anger, intemperance, violence, and base avarice ;

8. Adorned with the virtues of hospitality, benignity, or love for good men, sobriety in regard to himself, justice towards all men, sanctity and holiness in regard to God, continence.

9. He should tenaciously adhere to the faithful word which is comfortable to the sound doctrine of the Gospel, so as to be enabled by it to exhort the faithful to sanctity of life, and refute the heretical gainsayers.

10. For, there are many amongst them refractory, vain-talkers, and seducers, particularly the converted from among the Jews.

Commentary.

6. "Without crime." The Greek word, ἀνέγκλητος, means, *irreproachable*, not liable to be accused of serious crimes, and even irreproachable in his children whose vices might reflect discredit on their parents, who could not freely exercise the right of correction towards others, if their own household were disorderly. "Not accused of riot," *i.e.*, their children should not be chargeable with luxury either in the violation of temperance or chastity.

7. "For a bishop must be without crime." This shows, that in the word, "priests," verse 5, are included "bishops," which latter word is commonly confined to the clergy of the first order alone. "Without crime," as in verse 6.—(*See* also 1 Tim. chap. iii. verse 2). A bishop should be exempt from the vices here enumerated, so unbecoming his state ; "not given to wine ;" intemperance is opposed to chastity. *I shall never believe a drunkard to be chaste.*—St. Jerome. "Not proud," *i.e.*, not arrogantly adhering to his own opinion, which is the meaning of the Greek word, αυθαδη. No men inflict so much injury on the Church, or stand so much in the way of the salvation of souls, as those placed in high authority, when, from a spirit of pride, here condemned by the Apostle, they pertinaciously adhere to and carry out their own opinions, reckless of consequences, here and hereafter. The government of the pastors of the Church should not, in the remotest degree, savour of arrogance or domination. "The kings of the Gentiles lord it over them,......not so you."—(Luke, xxii. 25).

8. "But given to hospitality," (*see* 1 Tim. iii.) "gentle." The Greek, φιλαγαθον, means a friend or lover of good men. "Sober," σωφρονα, is rendered by some, *prudent*, by others, and among them, St. Jerome, *chaste*. "Continent," particularly refers to one who restrains the indulgence of all carnal lusts and passions.

9. "Embracing that faithful word," &c. It is not sufficient for a bishop to be pious, he must be also learned, to discharge properly his primary duties, of exhorting the faithful to piety and refuting the enemies of truth. The first and most indispensable duty of a bishop is to preach the word of God.—(Council of Trent, SS. 24, c. 4). It was to suffer no interruption in this holy employment, that the Apostles, whose successors they are, appointed the first deacons.—(Acts, vi. 4).

10. He shows the necessity of a bishop being learned, particularly in dealing with the Cretans. "For there are many disobedient," *i.e.*, refractory, impatient of Christian

Text.

11. Who must be reproved : who subvert whole houses, teaching the things which they ought not, for filthy lucre's sake.

12. One of them said, a prophet of their own, *The Cretans are always liars, evil beasts, slothful bellies.*

13. This testimony is true. Wherefore rebuke them sharply, that they may be sound in the faith.

14. Not giving heed to Jewish fables and commandments of men, who turn themselves away from the truth.

15. All things are clean to the

Paraphrase.

11. Who must be silenced by arguments; who pervert entire families by their errors, teaching false and erroneous doctrines, from the base motives of filthy lucre.

12. One of the Cretans themselves, well acquainted with them, one whose testimony they cannot question, for he was regarded as their own prophet, said of them, "the Cretans are always liars, evil beasts," ever ready to injure, "slothful bellies," ever addicted to sloth and gluttony.

13. This testimony (of the poet Epimenides regarding the Cretans) is true. Wherefore, admonish them severely, and rebuke them sharply for these vices, and see that they preserve intact the integrity of sound faith.

14. Not giving heed to Jewish fables and purely human traditions of men, who turn away from, and hate, the truth of the gospel.

15. All things are clean for Christians, no food is

Commentary.

doctrine and discipline among them. "Vain-talkers," teaching vain, fabulous trifles, &c. ; this especially applies to those converted from the Jewish faith.

11. "Who must be reproved." The Greek word, ἐπιστομίζειν, means, *to close their mouths,* of course, by argument. Our version expresses the meaning of the word ; hence, they should be treated with great severity, to serve as a caution to others whom they might seduce.

12. "A prophet of their own." He refers to the poet, Epimenides, who is called "a prophet of their own," because the Cretans regarded him as a prophet, and he also treated of oracles, and professed an acquaintance with secret things. "The Cretans are always liars," &c. These words are expressed by Epimenides in a single line of Greek hexameter verse. In them, the Cretans were charged with three vices for which they were notorious—viz., falsehood, ferocity, and sensuality. They were proverbial for their lying.

13. This testimony of the poet Epimenides, though before of human authority, is affirmed by the Apostle to be true ; and so, now, has the weight of divine authority, and entitled to the firm assent of faith. The same is to be seen (1 Cor. xv. 33), where the words of the poet Menander, before only conveying a natural truth, become, in consequence of being quoted by St. Paul, a portion of divine faith.

"Wherefore," as such are their dispositions, they must be rebuked with sharpness and severity. The Greek word for "sharply," ἀποτόμως, contains an allusion to the operations of surgeons cutting off putrescent flesh. Of course this is not opposed to his command to Timothy (2 chap. iii.), where a bishop is told to be mild in his rebuke ; because, he there only prescribes the disposition to lenity, while in reality, severity must sometimes be exercised, with which he himself menaces the Corinthians.—(1 Epistle iv.) "*Quid vultis, in virga veniam ?*"

14. "The commandments of men." By these are understood the false Jewish traditions, to an instance of which there is an allusion made, verse 15. In this, of course, there is nothing said derogatory to the precepts of fasting and abstinence, or of observing holidays, or the other ordinances of the Catholic Church. As well might you reject all civil laws, to which we are commanded by the Apostle to be obedient under pain of damnation (Rom. xiii.), and of the Church it is said, "he who hears you, hears me." The Apostle would, for the same reason, act wrongly in commanding the Gentiles to abstain from blood, &c.—(Acts, xv.) St. Paul here refers to false and corrupt commandments of men, "who turn themselves away from the (gospel) truth." —(*See* Coloss. ii. 22).

15. In this verse, the Apostle refutes one of the fables and purely human commands

Text.

clean: but to them that are defiled, and to unbelievers, nothing is clean; but both their mind and their conscience are defiled.

16. They profess that they know, God; but in their works they deny *him:* being abominable, and incredulous, and to every good work reprobate.

Paraphrase.

unclean for them, either of its own nature or in virtue of the prohibition of the law; but for the unclean and unbelievers, no food is clean, in consequence of their infidelity and erroneous conscience.

16. These profess that they know God, but they deny him by actions quite opposed to their verbal professions, being abominable on account of their immorality; incredulous, on account of their stubborn obstinacy; and, through their own fault, unfit for any good work.

Commentary.

of the false-teaching Jewish zealots. They inculcated the legal distinction between clean and unclean meats. The Apostle says there is no such distinction now, this as well as the other Jewish ceremonies having long since ceased; all meats are, therefore, clean, of themselves, and, so far as the law of Moses is concerned, perfectly indifferent for all Christians, who are cleansed in the blood of Christ and freed from the servitude of the law of Moses. "But to them that are defiled, and to unbelievers, nothing is clean," *i.e.*, no food is clean. He refers to the unbelieving Jews, of whom he has been speaking throughout; for them none of these meats prohibited by the law of Moses is clean; because, in partaking of them, they act against conscience, according to the dictates of which, although erroneous, they are bound to observe the law of Moses; and thus "their conscience is defiled," while in abstaining from them, they act against faith, and so " their mind is defiled," by infidelity.

16. They profess that they know and serve God, but their acts contradict their professions; they deny God by their actions, being "abominable" on account of their impurity; "incredulous," on account of their stubborn, obstinate indocility; and unfit for any "good work" conducive to salvation; since they reject Christ and his grace, the principle of every good work, and seek justice from a source that cannot confer it, viz., the law of Moses.

CHAPTER II.

Analysis.

In this chapter, the Apostle, after exhorting Titus to teach sound doctrine, points out to him what instructions he should deliver to persons of different ages and conditions in life (6). He admonishes him to show himself as a model in the practice of every virtue (7–10). He proposes the example of Christ, our Saviour, who appeared visibly in order to instruct all classes of men, both by word and example, as a motive to stimulate him to teach the same, with greater zeal (11). He shows what it is that Christ has taught us (12, 13). He points out the end and object of Christ's death (14). He, finally, wishes that Titus should authoritatively teach all these things (15).

Text.

1. BUT speak thou the things that become sound doctrine :

2. That the aged men be sober, chaste, prudent, sound in faith, in love, in patience.

3. The aged women, in like manner, in holy attire, not false, accusers, not given to much wine : teaching well.

Paraphrase.

1. (These wicked men may teach fables). But do thou (as a faithful minister of the Gospel) teach thy people the things that are in accordance with sound doctrine, either as regards the truths of faith or the principles of morality.

2. (Exhort) the aged men to practise sobriety, to observe becoming propriety of conduct, especially in matters of chastity, to exhibit prudence and moderation in their conduct, to be sincere in faith, in love, and in the patient endurance of adversity.

3. Aged women, in like manner (exhort) to observe in their whole exterior, in their gait, gesture, discourse, and dress, a modesty suited to Christian sanctity ; to guard against indulging in calumny or detraction ; not to indulge too much in wine ; teaching in their private instructions at home, both by word and by example, the things that are good and proper.

Commentary.

1. The Jewish zealots teach false doctrines, and prescribe practices purely human and opposed to the law of God—but Titus, as a faithful minister of the Gospel, should inculcate the truths of faith and sound principles of morals ; and because the Cretans were "slothful bellies," addicted to sensuality and intemperance, he should, therefore, inculcate the observance of temperance on all classes.

2. "That aged men be sober ;" the word "*exhort*," or some such, is understood, as appears from the Greek ; "sober," in the use of drink, particularly ; the moderate use of wine may be of use for old men—its excess, very injurious—and by observing sobriety themselves, they would serve as models for the young in this respect ; "chaste," the Greek word, σεμνους, means, *grave*, of composed, orderly habits ; "sound in faith," having no admixture of errors ; "in love," without dissimulation ; "in patience," suffering patiently the reverses of life for God's sake, with conformity to his will ; the chief prop of patience is the hope of future rewards ; hence, the words "the enduring of hope" (1 Thess. i.), so that the three Theological virtues of faith, hope, and charity, are here inculcated ; and, in the practice of these, the aged should serve as models to the young.

3. "Aged women, in like manner," encourage, "not false accusers," in Greek, μὴ διαβολους, *not devils*. The *devil*, was so called, in consequence of falsely accusing God, when tempting Eve. "Teaching well." In Greek, καλοδιδασκάλους, *teaching good things*, in their private instructions at home, teaching young females, not idle, old wives' tales, but what is virtuous and religious.

Text.

4. That they may teach the young women to be wise, to love their husbands, to love their children.

5. To be discreet, chaste, sober, having a care of the house, gentle obedient to their husbands, that the word of God be not blasphemed.

6. Young men, in like manner, exhort that they be sober.

7. In all things shew thyself an example of good works, in doctrine, in integrity, in gravity.

8. The sound word that cannot be blamed : that he, who is on the contrary part, may be afraid, having no evil to say of us.

9. *Exhort* servants to be obedient

Paraphrase.

4. Let them, therefore, teach the young women all the wisdom becoming their age, sex, and condition, viz., to love their husbands—to love their children.

5. To be prudent, chaste, sober, remaining constantly at home, and taking care of their domestic concerns, kind and gentle towards their domestics, obedient and subject to their (own) husbands ; so that the doctrine and gospel of Christ may not be brought into disrepute by them among the infidels.

6. Young men, in like manner, exhort to be sober and to govern their passions.

7. In all things, show thyself as a model in the performance of good works (in the practice of every virtue), in sound doctrine and the manner of propounding it, in purity of life, in the gravity of your government and holy conversation.

8. In teaching, employ language in accordance with sound faith, and which will not bring on you censure or contempt ; so that the adversary, be he Jew or Greek, may be ashamed to encounter us, not having it in his power to charge us with anything evil.

9. Exhort slaves to be subject to their masters, to

Commentary.

4. " That they teach the young women," &c. The duty of private instruction of the young women is committed to old women by the Apostle ; because, in regard to such, private interviews might not be edifying in Titus, he should address such persons only in public discourses. These are the things they shall teach them, viz., to love their husbands and their children.

5. To be " discreet," " sober." For both these words there is but one word in the Greek, σωφρονας, which bears both meanings—" obedient to their husbands," the Greek is, *to their own* (τοῖς ἰδίοις), husbands. " That the word of God be not blasphemed," as if it taught erroneous doctrine, or at least was of no advantage to its professors.

6. This is the fourth time he inculcates sobriety ; luxury had corrupted the young and old of both sexes in Crete ; and hence, his repeated inculcation of sobriety. The word for "sober," σωφρονεῖν, also signifies a restraint over the carnal passions, in which sobriety is of great advantage, nay, very necessary. Both meanings are united in the Paraphrase. It is needless to remark that sobriety is a necessary accompaniment of chastity. It is hard to conceive how an intemperate man can be chaste.

7. As example is far more powerful than precept ; hence, he requires of Titus to invite men to the practice of good works by the powerful force of example. This he enjoins on Timothy (1 Ep. iv. 12), and St. Peter enjoins the same (1 Ep. v.), " being made a pattern of the flock from the heart." The Apostle instances a few of the things in which Titus should particularly serve as a model, " in doctrine," &c. The Greek reading runs thus : " in doctrine (*exhibiting*) integrity, gravity," to which some copies add, *incorruptibility*, according to which reading, " integrity, gravity," &c., regard the doctrine.

8. " The sound word that cannot be blamed." According to the Greek construction, these words are a continuation of the preceding, and refer to " doctrine," depending on the word " exhibiting," *i.e.*, (*exhibiting also*) " the sound words which will not expose you to censure or contempt. Though their may be some diversity of construction in the passage, the meaning is quite clear. The Apostle exhorts Titus ,and through him, all bishops, to be the models of every virtue, to preach sound doctrine, without any admixture of error, grave doctrine, free from all futile vanities, conformable to sound faith, and beyond all reprehension or censure. " No evil to say of us ;" in Greek, *no evil......of you.*

9. Slaves will perform their duties towards their masters, if they reverence them for

Text.

to their masters, in all things pleasing, not gainsaying :

10. Not defrauding. but in all things shewing good fidelity, that they may adorn the doctrine of God our Saviour in all things.

11. For the grace of God our Saviour hath appeared to all men.

12. Instructing us that, denying ungodliness and worldly desires, we should live soberly, and justly, and godly in this world,

13. Looking for the blessed hope and coming of the glory of the great God and our Saviour JESUS CHRIST,

14. Who gave himself for us, that he might redeem us from all iniquity, and might cleanse to himself a people acceptable, a pursuer of good works.

Paraphrase.

be solicitous to please them in all things lawful, and not to disrespect or murmur against their commands.

10. Not defrauding, or privately stealing from them, but in all things practising the greatest fidelity, so that by this fidelity and obedience, they may render the Christian faith and doctrine commendable in the eyes of all, and thus become ornaments of the faith.

11. For the salutary beneficence of God's redemption has been made manifest to all classes of men without exception.

12. Instructing us to renounce impiety, and worldly corrupt desires, and to lead in this world a life of wisdom and temperance in regard to ourselves, of justice and equity towards the neighbour, and of piety and religion towards God.

13. Expecting eternal happiness, the object of our hope, and the glorious coming of our great God and Saviour Jesus Christ.

14. Who has delivered himself up to death for us, to redeem and purify us from all iniquity and from the stains of sin, and after thus cleansing us by his blood, to claim us as his peculiar people, his precious distinguished possession, a people exceedingly zealous for good works.

Commentary.

God, and look upon them as holding his place in their regard (*see* Ep. vi. 6 ; Colos. iii. 23) ; not gainsaying," *i.e.*, not replying disrespectfully to them or murmuring at their commands.

10. "Not defrauding." St. Jerome interprets it " *not stealing.*" It implies stealth, committed in taking property, as well as in squandering the time marked out for labour—"but in all things showing good faith." *i.e.*, by exhibiting perfect fidelity, both in reference to the substance of their masters, as well as in serving them, they would render the doctrine of Christ commendable, and not expose it "to blasphemy."— (1 Tim. vi.)

11. By "the grace of our Saviour," or (as in the Greek, ἡ χάρις ἡ σωτήριος,) *the salutary grace*, some understand, as in Paraphrase, the salutary benevolence of God displayed in the work of redemption (*see* 2nd Cor. vi. 1) ; others, Christ himself, the fountain of grace, the divine essential grace. This shows that as the benefit of redemption was displayed to all classes, men, women, slaves, &c. ; so, Titus should instruct every class, not excepting slaves.

12. "Impiety," *i.e.*, unbelief, "worldly desires," the corrupt passions of ambition, avarice, lusts, &c.—"we should live soberly, justly, and piously," by fasting, alms, deeds, and prayer ; these good works are specially recommended to all, specially opposed to the three enemies of salvation—the world, the flesh, and the devil ; and to the three great leading maxims of the world—"the concupiscence of the flesh, of the eyes, and the pride of life."—(John ii. 16).

13. "The blessed hope ;" "hope" means the thing hoped for, the object of hope. "The great God." The article in the Greek shows that by this is meant, *our Saviour Jesus Christ.* Besides, it is our Saviour alone that "the glorious coming" is attributed in SS. Scripture. Hence, an argument for the Divinity of Christ. "The blessed hope," regards the beautitude of our souls at death—"the coming," &c., the glorification of our bodies.

14. He not only was born for us, and appeared to us, and instructed us, but he also died for us. "A people acceptable." St. Jerome has translated it, "an especial, eminent people." It is allusive to the passage in Exodus (xix. 5), when God says of the Jews, "you shall be my peculiar possession," &c. The Hebrew for peculiar posses-

Text.	**Paraphrase.**
15. These things speak, and exhort, and rebuke, with all authority. Let no man despise thee.	15. Teach all these things to the ignorant, and exhort all those who already know them, to reduce them to practice. But rebuke the refractory and disobedient with full power, as minister of God, and by acting thus, no one will dare to contemn thee.

Commentary.

sion," *Segullah,* according to St. Jerome, signifies "a most precious treasure." St. Paul here followed the Septuagint version, which means, "acceptable people," an excellent possession, &c.

15. So act in the exercise of authority, that no one will despise thee.

CHAPTER III.

Analysis.

In this chapter, the Apostle inculcates certain duties that were obligatory on the faithful in general, viz., subjection to the existing civil authorities, mildness towards all men, not excepting unbelievers. This feeling they will the more readily cultivate even towards unbelievers, by reflecting that they themselves were formerly like them, and also by reflecting that it was solely owing to the mercy of God that they were rescued from their former state. He shows the greatness of this mercy and its admirable results (3–7); and he exhorts Titus to point out this mercy to the faithful (8). He prohibits useless questions, etc., and he instructs him to avoid a heretic, who, after being twice admonished, contumaciously persists in error (10, 11). He invites Titus to come to him, etc.

Text.	**Paraphrase.**
1. ADMONISH them to be subject to princes, and powers, to obey at a word, to be ready to every good work.	1. Admonish the Cretans to be subject to princes and to all who possess power over them, promptly to obey their orders, and to be prepared to perform every good work enjoined by them.

Commentary.

1. "Powers," *i.e.*, all those who possess authority in the government of the State. The Apostle inculcates: first, submission to their authority, "to be subject to them;" secondly, obedience to their orders, "to obey at a word;" and thirdly, preparation and disposition of mind to obey them in everything good and obligatory, "every good work." If they outstep the limits of their authority, they need not *necessarily* be obeyed; should their mandate have good for object, they *may* be obeyed; should they command evil, they *must* be resisted; as, we should obey God rather than man. The Apostle does not here determine the species of power to which obedience is due, whether kingly, aristocratic, republican, &c. For, although all power comes from God, it is still the most probable opinion, that he makes the people the channel through which he confers power on individuals. How this is done is not quite agreed upon. According to some, this power is placed as a deposit in the hands of the people; according to others, the election of the people is a mere necessary condition, consequent on which God immediately confers power on the object of the people's choice. This latter seems a very probable opinion.—(*See* Romans, xii.; 1 Peter, ii. 13). We

Text.

2. To speak evil of no man, not to be litigious, but gentle : shewing all mildness towards all men.

3. For we ourselves also were some time unwise, incredulous, erring, slaves to divers desires and pleasures, living in malice and envy, hateful, hating one another.

4. But when the goodness and kindness of God our Saviour appeared,

5. Not by the works of justice, which we have done, but according to his mercy he saved us, by the laver of regeneration, and renovation of the Holy Ghost.

Paraphrase.

2. To refrain from unbecoming language regarding their neighbour, especially language of a reproachful, insulting nature, not to be contentious and fond of quarrelling, but to be mild and kind, manifesting the most perfect meekness towards all men.

3. For, we too were, in former times, corrupted in mind and heart : in mind, we were insensible to, and deprived of true wisdom—rebels to the light of faith, straying from the path of truth ; in heart, we were the slaves of different corrupt desires and pleasures which domineered over us, full of secret malice and envy towards others, deserving of being universally hated, and hating others in turn.

4. But when the goodness and singular love for men of God our Saviour shone forth (by the preaching of the Gospel),

5. Not in consideration of the good works which we performed (for, there were no such works in existence), but out of his pure gratuitous mercy, he saved us by baptism, wherein we are regenerated into sons of God and were made new men, through the grace of the Holy Ghost.

Commentary.

are informed by St. Jerome, that the object of the Apostle in inculcating the duty of obedience to temporal authority, both here and in his Epistle to the Romans (xiii.), was to show, that the faithful of Christ had no sympathy with the disciples of Judas of Galilee, to whom reference is made (Acts, v. 37). Probably, among the many Jews who were at Crete, might be found some belonging to the followers of this Judas.

2. "To speak evil of no one." (In Greek, μηδενα βλασφημειν, *to blaspheme no one*). Under "evil (or blaspheming) language" are included all descriptions of language injurious to our neighbour, such as calumny, detraction, contumely, &c. "Showing mildness to all men," not excepting unbelievers.

3. He shows why they should be mild and compassionate towards unbelievers, because they were themselves formerly in the same deplorable condition, out of which the gratuitous mercy of God rescued them. Mindful, therefore, of their own previous state, they should take compassion on others. The Apostle includes himself, although a Jew, as well as Titus, who was a Gentile, by saying "we ourselves." He does not recount the great leading crimes of Paganism, the external commission of which a moral Pagan, or Jew, would avoid, but he speaks of these latent sins, the indulgence of which would be perfectly consistent with external legal justice, for which he claims credit to himself.—(Phil. iii.)

4. Another motive to induce them to act compassionately, &c., is the example of God himself—"The kindness." The Greek is, φιλαντρωπια, *philantrophy*. Some refer this to the Incarnation, but erroneously ; for, there is question of God the Father, as he is distinguished from Jesus Christ (verse 6).

5. It was not in consideration of our just works that he saved us ; for, before his grace there were no good works, or "works of justice," entitled to a reward ; but it was out of his purely gratuitous mercy, he "saved us," *i.e.*, bestowed on us justification, which places us in the way of finally arriving at perfect eternal salvation, and is itself initial salvation. The means by which he has bestowed on us this justification is through the waters of baptism externally poured on us, and by the grace of the Holy Ghost, which is attached to the rite of baptism, interiorly giving us a new birth, a new spiritual essence, making us sons of God, perfectly renewing us, so that we become invested with the virtues of wisdom, faith, &c., opposed to the former vices to which we were slaves. The external instrumental cause of this renovation is baptism ; the efficient invisible cause, which the external operates, is, the grace of the Holy Ghost. This passage manifestly shows that justification does not consist in the

Text.

6. Whom he hath poured forth upon us abundantly through JESUS CHRIST our Saviour:

7. That, being justified by his grace, we may be heirs, according to hope of life everlasting.

8. It is a faithful saying; and these things I will have thee affirm constantly: that they who believe in God, may be careful to excel in good works. These things are good and profitable unto men.

9. But avoid foolish questions, and genealogies, and contentions, and strivings about the law. For they are unprofitable and vain.

10. A man that is a heretic, after the first and second admonition, avoid:

11. Knowing that he, that is such an one, is subverted, and

Paraphrase.

6. Whom God the Father has copiously and abundantly poured forth on us, through Jesus Christ our Saviour.

7. So that, cleansed from sin and gifted with justice through his grace, we are constituted heirs of eternal life, which we have at present, only in the certain hope of one day obtaining it.

8. All the things which I have said regarding justification and its effects, are undoubtedly true; and I wish that regarding them you would confirm your brethren, so that those who believe and trust in God would take care to excel others, and distinguish themselves in the performance of good works; for, these alone are, properly speaking, good and profitable to man.

9. But vain idle questions and genealogies, and futile contentions and strifes of words regarding the Law, reject and spurn, as idle and useless.

10. Shun the heretical man, who, after the first and second admonition, continues pertinacious.

11. Knowing that a heretic of this sort is subverted, the foundation of faith being destroyed; hence he is

Commentary.

mere imputation of the justice of Christ; but that it is the inherent principle of this new life, so long as it perseveres.

6. "Whom," *i.e.*, the Holy Ghost, "he hath poured forth upon us," *i.e.*, God the Father (verse 4) hath poured forth upon us abundantly, "through Jesus Christ our Saviour," in the sacraments of baptism and confirmation, which, immediately after baptism, was given by the imposition of hands. The entire Trinity is referred to in this verse, distinctly contributing by an operation peculiar to each person to our new spiritual existence. The Eternal Father, the Principle of the Divinity itself, is the Father of the baptized, and the Principle of his divine existence; the Eternal Son is, with the Father, the Principle of the effusion of the Holy Ghost; and the Holy Ghost, the Spirit of the Father and Son, becomes the spirit of the baptized, his heart and soul, his supernatural and divine life.

7. Justification implies the remission of sin and the infusion of justice by sanctifying grace, and this holy state constitutes us the rightful heirs of eternal life, which we do not yet actually possess, but which, like the youthful heir, during his minority, we hope one day to attain, and actually enjoy.

8. He tells him to propound these truths regarding justification, the inheritance of eternal life, &c., as certain, undoubted doctrines to his brethren, so that bearing them in mind, they would strive to distinguish themselves and surpass others, not merely in word, but in good works and example. They should strive to become holy, like God the Father, whose sons and heirs they are; holy, like the Son, whose members they are; and holy, like the Holy Ghost, by whom they live. This holiness can be acquired and preserved by good works; and good works alone are "profitable," they alone will constitute a treasure of merit beyond the grave.

9. But as to foolish questions regarding genealogies, in recounting which the Jews felt such pride and boasted so much (1 Tim. i.), and idle questions regarding the Law; these he should spurn. This may also mean, that if objections from these sources are proposed, they should be spurned, as undeserving of reply.

10. The heretic ought to be admonished, corrected, and instructed, once or twice, in order to know if he be really pertinacious and obstinate, and, after that, he is to be shunned.

11. Because such a man, like an edifice whose foundation is overturned, is incurable and undone irreparably; for, he has lost the foundation of faith. Moreover, such a

Text.

sinneth, being condemned by his own judgment.

12. When I shall send to thee Artemas or Tychicus, make haste to come unto me to Nicopolis. For there I have determined to winter.

13. Send forward Zenas the lawyer and Apollo with care, that nothing be wanting to them.

14. And let our men also learn to excel in good works for necessary uses; that they be not unfruitful.

15. All that are with me, salute thee; salute them that love us in the faith. The grace of God be with you all. Amen.

Paraphrase.

incurable, and he sins with full knowledge and voluntarily, condemning himself by his own judgment.

12. After I shall have sent Artemas or Tychicus to supply your place, hasten to come to me to Nicopolis, for I have resolved on spending the winter there.

13. Take care to send forward Zenas, the doctor of the Jewish Law, and Apollo, furnished with all things necessary for their journey, so that they may be in want of nothing.

14. Let our brethren in the faith learn from both your instruction and example, to excel in good works, on all necessary occasions (particularly when the wants of the labourers for the Gospel are concerned), that they may not be unfruitful and sterile in the field of the Lord.

15. All the faithful who are with me salute you. Salute thou those who love us for the faith and according to faith, *i.e.*, with true Christian charity. The grace of God be with you all. Amen.

Commentary.

person sins knowingly and willingly, and with malicious obstinacy perseveres in his error. Such a person, by receding from the Church, in following his own judgment, is deservedly forsaken by her, and suffers no injury in having that sentence of separation passed on him, which he has passed on himself, by the very act of receding. "Condemned by his own judgment." A man always recedes invisibly, whenever he holds doctrine opposed to that of the Church, which, of course, the heretic, by the very fact of being such, is always supposed voluntarily to do. For, a man becomes a heretic by either denying some revealed truth, defined by the Church, or by asserting some error, the contradictory of which the Church has defined to be a revealed truth and of faith. The Apostle here instructs Timothy how, in capacity of Bishop, he is to treat such a person.

12. Nicopolis, of Thrace, according to St. Chrysostom; of Epirus, according to St. Jerome.

13. Zenas and Apollo were to pass by Crete, and he tells Titus to furnish them with a sufficient viatic, so that they may want nothing.

14. "And let our men," *i.e.*, those of our faith, the Christians, seek every occasion of excelling in good works according as circumstances may demand, unless they wish that their faith be barren and sterile, so that they would be like unfruitful plants, in the field of the Lord. "For necessary uses;" he particularly refers to necessities like the present, in which the ministers of the Gospel are concerned.

15. "That love us in the faith," in which he shows that the love of Christians for each other should be founded on faith, *i.e.*, purely Christian and holy.

The Greek subscriptions have the following :—"*It was written to Titus, ordained the first Bishop of the Church of the Cretans, from Nicopolis of Macedonia.*"

The *Codex Vaticanus* simply has :—"*To Titus.*"

THE EPISTLE

OF

ST. PAUL TO PHILEMON.

Introduction.

PHILEMON, a native of Colossæ, in Phrygia, was converted to the faith, either by St. Paul himself, or by his disciple, Epaphras. He was of noble birth, and possessed of much riches. So great was the progress made by him in virtue, that, in a short time, his dwelling resembled a church, owing to the piety of his household, and the religious exercises unceasingly performed therein. He was distinguished for acts of generosity and charity towards the persecuted and distressed members of the Christian faith (5, 6, 7).

The occasion of this brief Epistle was the following :—Onesimus, one of Philemon's slaves, after having robbed him, fled to Rome, where he found out St. Paul, then in his first imprisonment, about the year 62. The Apostle treated him with the utmost tenderness, proportioned to the magnitude of his guilt and the inveteracy of his disorders. And after having instructed him in the faith, converted and baptized him, sent him back to his master, with this commendatory Epistle, wherein he beseeches Philemon to receive him again into favour. This Epistle, though very brief, is regarded by Critics and Commentators, as a masterpiece of eloquence and pleading. In it, the Apostle brings forward, in the most engaging manner, all the motives which should induce Philemon to comply with his request. And, though he merely sought for the pardon of Onesimus; still, it is evident, that he expects from Philemon to grant him his liberty (21) ; a request, however, which the Apostle forbears from making, lest it might appear to be asking too much. Moreover, it might seem opposed to his instructions to slaves (1 Cor. vii. 21). The Epistle consists of an exordium, which, after the usual salutation, commences at verse 4—of the proposition, verse 8—and the conclusion, verse 17.

It was written at Rome, at the same time, as the Epistle to the Colossians—viz., about the year 62.

THE EPISTLE

OF

ST. PAUL TO PHILEMON.

Text.	Paraphrase.
1. PAUL, a prisoner of CHRIST JESUS, and Timothy a brother; to Philemon our beloved and fellow-labourer.	1. Paul, a prisoner in the cause of Christ Jesus, and Timothy our brother in Christ (write) to Philemon, our dearly beloved and our co-operator.
2. And to Appia our dearest sister, and to Archippus our fellow-soldier, and to the church which is in thy house.	2. And to Appia, our dearest sister in Christ, and to Archippus, our fellow-soldier in the struggles for the faith, and to the congregation of the faithful, which is in thy house.
3. Grace to you and peace from God our Father, and from the Lord JESUS CHRIST.	3. Grace and peace to you, from God our Father, and from the Lord Jesus Christ.
4. I give thanks to my God, always making a remembrance of thee in my prayers.	4. Always mindful of thee in my prayers, I give thanks to God (for the blessings bestowed on thee).
5. Hearing of thy charity and faith which thou hast in the Lord Jesus, and towards all the saints.	5. Because I hear of thy faith in the Lord Jesus, and of thy charity to all Christians.

Commentary.

1. "A prisoner of Jesus Christ," and, therefore, meriting that any request made by him should be attended to. It is remarked by Commentators, that from the beginning to the end of this Epistle, there is hardly a word which does not tend to enforce its object, viz., the pardon of Onesimus. For this end, the Apostle commences by referring to his chains, as if preparing Philemon to show mercy to his slave, in consideration of these chains. "And Timothy," he adds him, in order that their joint intercession would prove more powerful. "And fellow-labourer." In Greek, συνεργῷ, *our co-operator;* because, he contributed much both by his temporal wealth and example, to advance the cause of the Gospel.

2. "Appia;" most probably, the wife of Philemon. "Our dearest sister" "Sister," is not in the Greek. "Archippus, our fellow-soldier," in the Apostolic warfare. He was, according to some, a deacon; according to others, a priest or bishop—(*Vide* Colos. iv. 17). "And the church which is in thy house," *i.e.,* his entire family, which was Christian. He enlists all these, so dear to Philemon, viz., his wife and entire family, in his cause. What an example is here given to those charged with the care of the poor and unfortunate! See, what exertions St. Paul, the Apostle of nations, makes in behalf of a fugitive slave, because he viewed him according to God, and in God!

3. These verses include the salutation.

4. In this verse, he commences the *exordium,* praising God for his gifts bestowed on Philemon, which is the same as tacitly praising Philemon himself for his good works, which must be the fruit of God's grace. He also expresses his affection for him, which is best evinced by remembering him in his prayers.

5. His "faith," was in Christ Jesus, and his "charity" towards all Christians shown in deeds of beneficence. This is the clearest and most probable construction, connecting "faith" with the words "in the Lord Jesus," and "charity" with the words

Text.

6. That the communication of thy faith may be made evident in the acknowledgment of every good work, that is in you in CHRIST JESUS.

7. For I have had great joy and consolation in thy charity, because the bowels of the saints have been refreshed by thee, brother.

8. Wherefore though I have much confidence in CHRIST JESUS, to command thee that which is to the purpose:

9. For charity sake I rather beseech, whereas thou art such an one, as Paul an old man, and now a prisoner also of JESUS CHRIST:

10. I beseech thee for my son, whom I have begotten in my bands, Onesimus.

Paraphrase.

6. So that the beneficent results of thy faith are become evident to all, by the knowledge and rumour of the good works, performed by thee, through the grace of Christ Jesus.

7. For, I have derived great joy and consolation from thy charity, my brother, because the Christians in distress have received the most cheering comfort and consolation at thy hands, (and hence my grounds for hoping for the pardon of thy Christian slave).

8. Wherefore, although in quality of Apostle of Jesus Christ, I might use perfect freedom in commanding thee, in reference to a matter of duty;

9. Still, I prefer entreating it as a favour, to be conferred in consideration of friendship; since thou art an old man, like myself, who am now also in chains, for the cause of Jesus Christ.

10. I entreat thee, then, in behalf of my son, Onesimus, begotten by me in chains,

Commentary.

"towards all the saints." Similar is the expression in the Epistle to the Colossians, written at the same time (i. 4). Before praising him for these acts, he refers the glory of these to God, in the preceding verse—"I give thanks to God, whose gifts they are."

6. "That the communication of thy faith," *i.e.*, the beneficent effects or fruits of your faith "is made evident to the acknowledgment of every good work," in the public knowledge of the good works, which you and your entire family perform. For "evident," SS. Jerome and Chrysostom, read, *efficacious*, the rendering of the Greek, ενεργης. According to this reading, the words of the Apostle contain an exhortation to Philemon, to render his faith an active, operative faith. The Vulgate is, however, more in accordance with the context; for, he had already praised his faith, as operative (5). The Vulgate interpreter probably read, εναργης. And the Greek word for "that," όπως, means rather a consequence than a cause; hence, it means, "*so that,* the communication," &c.

7. It is with reason he gives God thanks, because he felt great joy and consolation in hearing of the great comfort and refreshment which the Christians who were in want and distress received from Philemon. "The bowels of the saints," express the great inward consolation they received; and if he was so good to all Christians, he will be equally kind to this Christian slave.

8. Here the Apostle enters on the *proposition.* He might, as Apostle, use perfect liberty, in commanding Philemon in a matter of duty, without feeling any apprehension of meeting with any opposition.

9. Still, he preferred following another course, that of entreating him to do it in consideration of the friendship that subsisted between them, a course, which better suited Philemon, who was an old man, like the Apostle himself; and hence, issuing a command to him would be inconvenient. St. Chrysostom, St. Jerome, &c., make tne words "an old man," refer to St. Paul himself, and this is one of the reasons why his request should not be refused; the fact also of his being an Apostle (" Paul"), and being "a prisoner," &c., should strengthen his request.

10. Before introducing the name of Onesimus, he expresses the most endearing relations. "In bands." The Greek is, εν τοις δεσμοις μου, *in my bands.*

Text.

11. Who hath been heretofore unprofitable to thee, but now is profitable both to me and thee,

12. Whom I have sent back to thee. And do thou receive him as my own bowels:

13. Whom I would have retained with me, that in thy stead he might have ministered to me in the bands of the gospel:

14. But without thy counsel I would do nothing: that thy good deed might not be as it were of necessity, but voluntary.

15. For perhaps he therefore departed for a season from thee, that thou mightest receive him again for ever.

16. Not now as a servant, but instead of a servant, a most dear brother, especially to me: but how much more to thee both in the flesh and in the Lord?

Paraphrase.

11. Who hath been heretofore unprofitable to thee, but now is profitable both to me and to thee,

12. Whom I have sent back to thee, do thou, therefore, receive him as my own bowels.

13. I was desirous of retaining him with myself, in order that he might perform for me, who am in chains, for the cause of the Gospel, those services, which thou thyself wouldst cheerfully have performed wert thou here with me.

14. However, I was unwilling to do anything of the kind, without first consulting you, so that your benefit towards me would not appear the result of necessity, but perfectly voluntary.

15. Perhaps also God permitted him to leave you for a time, in order that you would receive him back, never again to leave you.

16. And that you might receive him, not merely as a slave, but as a most beloved brother, particularly beloved by me; how much more beloved ought he be by you both on account of the bodily servitude he owes you, and on account of spiritual fraternity?

Commentary.

11. While admitting his fault, he extenuates it by merely saying that he was "unprofitable," although, in point of fact, *injurious;* for, he robbed his master, when leaving him. "But now he is profitable to me," by the services which he has rendered me. "And to you," by rendering the services you would have rendered, and he will be profitable to you, in future. In the word "profitable," allusion is made to the etymology of "Onesimus," as much as to say, he will be, in reality, what his *name* imports, viz., "profitable." The Greek adjective, ὀνησιμος, signifies, *advantageous.* In this verse, is contained an additional reason for taking him back, grounded on his usefulness.

12. "Do thou receive him as my own bowels," treat him with some degree of respect. What a reproach to many masters who treat their servants with more severity than they would treat the brute beasts! "I have sent back to thee." The words "to thee" are not in the Greek. They are found in the copy used by St. Chrysostom.

13. Another reason for treating him with indulgence, was the regard the Apostle had for him, and also the fact, that he has discharged those offices towards the Apostle, which his master would have discharged, had he been at Rome. The reference to his chains, and to the vicarious services of Onesimus, all tend to obtain pardon.

14. The defence of the Apostle towards Philemon, tends to the same: he might retain this slave on account of the wants of the Church; but he would not, lest the kindness of his master would appear to be the result of compulsion, instead of seeming to be perfectly voluntary.

15. Another motive for pardoning him is, that his flight was, in the ways of God's Providence, the occasion of his conversion. "That thou mightest receive him for ever," may mean, that he would never again desert his service; or, "for ever" may mean, that as a Christian brother, he would never be separated from him, even in eternal glory. He uses the mildest terms to express the guilt of his flight, "departed for a season." Then, as it was perhaps the will of God that he should depart; surely, Philemon would not oppose this will, nor refuse pardon to a man already reconciled and at peace with God.

16. Again, can he refuse pardon to one who was most dear to St. Paul as his spiritual son, who was his own slave, over whose person he had perfect control? "Both in the flesh," and who from a slave had become a brother in Christ, a fellow-member of his mystical body. "And in the Lord."

Text.

17. If therefore thou count me a partner; receive him as myself.

18. And if he hath wronged thee in anything, or is in thy debt, put that to my account.

19. I Paul have written it with my own hand : I will repay it : not to say to thee, that thou owest me thy ownself also.

20. Yea, brother. May I enjoy thee in the Lord. Refresh my bowels in the Lord.

21. Trusting in thy obedience, I have written to thee : knowing that thou wilt also do more than I say.

22. But withal prepare me also a lodging. For I hope that through your prayers I shall be given unto you.

Paraphrase.

17. If, then, you regard me as partaker of the faith, and value my friendship in Christ, receive him as you would myself, *i.e.*, I shall value the kindness shown him, as if paid to myself.

18. But whatever loss he may have inflicted on you at his departure, or whatever he may owe you, charge to my account (I shall be answerable for it).

19. And as security, that I will fully satisfy your claims, you have this Epistle, written and signed by my own hand. I shall make no mention of a debt of greater value, and of longer standing, which you owe me for your conversion to the faith—you owe me your entire person, your entire salvation.

20. Come, therefore, brother, I shall obtain from you the joy in the Lord resulting from your kindness ; by this act of kindness, refresh my heart in the Lord.

21. I have thus written to you from the firmest reliance on your obedience, knowing well you will do more than I ask.

22. I also entreat of you to prepare for me a lodging ; for, I hope through your prayers, to be delivered from prison and restored to you.

Commentary.

17. He recommences the *conclusion.* He then concludes by conjuring Philemon, if he regards himself as strictly united with him in faith, if he values his friendship, to treat this slave with kindness. " Receive him as myself ; " not that he meant the same degree of respect to be shown Onesimus that was due to himself; but that any kindness shown, he might look on as shown to himself..

18. Lest his having robbed his master should cause any obstacle to his being received back without making reparation, the Apostle undertakes to make restitution himself to the necessary amount, if required.

19. And he gives as a security for the payment, this Epistle written with his own hand, promising it. Some say the entire Epistle was written by the Apostle himself; others say, only this verse. He, at the same time, reminds Philemon of a heavier debt due by the latter to himself—he owed him his conversion, his eternal salvation. He was either converted by St. Paul himself, some say, at Ephesus ; or, by Epaphras, his disciple.

20. He, finally, resorts to the language of blandishment, to gain the same end. " Yea," *i.e.*, come on. " May I enjoy thee in the Lord," *i.e.*, obtain this favour from thee, which will be a source of real spiritual joy. " Refresh my bowels," may refer to Onesimus, as if he said, refresh Onesimus, whom you should receive as my bowels ; any injury shown him would be the same as if my entrails were torn, and the greatest torture inflicted on me.

21. " Do more than I say." In this is implied the giving him his freedom.

22. The very determination of St. Paul to lodge with him, tends to obtain this request. Philemon, on the recommendation of St. Paul, granted Onesimus his liberty, and sent him back to the Apostle to serve him at Rome ; but the Apostle did not require his corporal services, and so he made him a fellow-labourer in the gospel. St. Jerome (*Epistola* 62, c. 2), and other Fathers say, he made him a Bishop. According to Baronius, he was made Bishop of Ephesus ; but this is denied by many, who say, that the St. Onesimus, who was third Bishop of Ephesus, after Timothy, was quite a different person.

This Epistle, though very brief, contains, as St. Chrysostom remarks, most excellent lessons. Among the rest, that we should not despair of the salvation of any one, however abandoned. Again, the example of the Apostle, taking such interest in the concerns

Text.

23. There salute thee Epaphras my fellow-prisoner in Christ Jesus.

24. Mark, Aristarchus, Demas, and Luke, my fellow-labourers.

25. The grace of our Lord JESUS CHRIST be with your spirit. Amen.

Paraphrase.

23. Epaphras, my fellow-prisoner in Christ Jesus, salutes you.

24. So do my fellow-labourers in the cause of the gospel, Mark, Aristarchus, Demas, and Luke.

25. The grace of our Lord Jesus Christ be with your spirit. Amen.

Commentary.

of a fugitive slave, who robbed his master, teaches us that every attention should be paid to the unfortunate; that servants should be treated with the utmost consideration, as being our brethren in Christ Jesus, as also destined for the same glory. "Masters do to your servants," &c., "knowing that you too have a master in heaven." (Colos. iv. 1).

The Greek subscription has the following: "*Written from Rome to Philemon by Onesimus, a servant.*" The *Codex Vaticanus* merely has "*To Philemon.*"

It is needless to remark, that this subscription does not belong to the text, although it correctly states the fact, in the present instance: generally speaking, however, these subscriptions, as has been mentioned already, are of rather doubtful authority, and, in some instances, by no means correct.

THE EPISTLE

OF

ST. PAUL TO THE HEBREWS.

Introduction.

THIS Epistle was, most likely, intended as a circular for all the converted Jews throughout the entire earth. But it was addressed specially to those of Palestine, to whom alone some passages in it could be strictly applicable.—Chap. x. 32, 33, 34; xiii. 19-23.

CANONICITY OF.—The Canonicity or Divine authority of this Epistle was never called in question in the *Greek* Church. The Arians were the first to contest its Divine authority in consequence of the strong arguments it contains in favour of the Divinity of Christ.

The belief of the *Latin* Church was not so constant from the beginning. Until undoubted evidence in its favour was adduced, the Latin Church was slow in admitting its Divine authority, in consequence of the perverse use made by the Novations of certain passages of it, particularly, chapter vi., in support of their erroneous teachings regarding the admission to penance of those who had fallen away from the faith. It was not read publicly in the Church in the days of St. Jerome. But, the earliest among the Latin Fathers, quote from it as inspired Scripture : St. Clement, of Rome, does so, in his Epistle to the Corinthians; the principal Latin Fathers, before St. Jerome, viz., Hilary, Optatus, Ambrose, as also his contemporaries, Augustine, &c., and those who came after him, quote from it, as Scripture. And St. Jerome himself, in his Epistle to Dardanus, speaking of this Epistle and of the Apocalypse of St. John, says :—" *We, altogether dissenting from the usage of the present age, and supported by the authority of ancient writers, admit both.*"

Besides the foregoing Fathers, we have the authority of Innocent I. (*Epistola 3ª ad Exuperium*), St. Athanasius (*in Synopsi*), Gregory Nazianzen (*in Carmine de SS. Scripturis*), all of whom place it on their catalogue of inspired Scripture. We have, moreover, the authority of Councils, in which the catalogues of inspired books were framed, viz.: the Council of Laodicea (last Canon) ; the Third Council of Carthage (Canon 47), presided over by Aurelius, Primate of Africa, and subscribed to by St. Augustine; the Council of Rome, consisting of seventy Bishops, under Pope Gelasius I. ; the Council of Florence, in the Decree for the instruction of the Armenians; and, finally, the Council of Trent, SS. the 4th. The Canonicity of this book is, therefore, now a point of Catholic faith, which no orthodox believer can question for a moment, without incurring the guilt of heresy.

Luther, and most of his followers, deny the Divine authority of this Epistle, while the Calvinists and the Church of England admit it.

In referring to the foregoing authorities, it should have been observed, that the authority of St. Athanasius is of great weight on this subject. For, it is asserted by many, among the rest by St. Jerome, in his Preface to the Books of Judith, that a Canon of SS. Scriptures was framed in the first General Council of Nice ; and, as St. Athanasius assisted at this Council, it is to be fairly presumed, that in placing the " Epistles to the Hebrews," on the Catalogue of inspired Scripture, which he afterwards framed, he had the authority of the great Council of Nice for so doing.

This Epistle was not universally admitted in the *Latin* Church before the fifth century ; although it was quoted from by many of the Fathers of the preceding ages, as we have already seen. Hence, it is reckoned amongst those books of SS. Scripture which are termed, *Deutero-Canonical.* The books of this latter class are so called, because they were not, *at first*, admitted on the Canon of SS. Scripture, nor were they recognised for some time, as inspired, by the universal Church. Owing to the imperfect means of communication, and the distractions consequent on the terrors of persecution during the early ages, it became impossible to ascertain fully, the traditions of particular churches, regarding the Divine authority of these books. On peace, however, being restored to the Church, and the means of communication facilitated, and opportunities of comparing the traditions of the different churches afforded, these Books were found to form a portion of the deposit of faith ; and, so, universally admitted. Their non-admission sooner is no argument against their inspired authority. On the contrary, the circumstance of their non-admission, for some time, on the Canon, shows the care and vigilance observed by the Church, in proposing them to the faithful.

AUTHENTICITY OF.—The authenticity or authorship of this Epistle had been disputed, even by many who admitted its claims to inspiration. By some, the authorship of it was ascribed to St. Clement of Rome. This opinion, however, is satisfactorily refuted from the Epistle itself ; for, the writer of it supposes the Jewish sacrifices to be still offered ; and Jerusalem, the destruction of which occurred before the time of St. Clement, still in being. Others, among them, Tertullian, ascribed the authorship of it to St. Barnabas ; and others, to St. Luke. But all these hypotheses are refuted by the universal voice of tradition, attributing the authorship of it, to the Apostle. In favour of this opinion, which almost obtains the certainty of faith, we have the same authorities that have been adduced in proof of its canonicity. St. Peter, in his second Epistle directed to the converted Jews, tells them (chap iii., verse 16), that St. Paul has written to them an Epistle, which could have reference to no other than the present. The Lutherans, of course, deny the authenticity of this Epistle ; for, as has been already remarked, they deny its canonicity. Luther, it should be observed, attributed the authorship of this Epistle to Apollo, on account of its superior eloquence. The Calvinists, who admit it to be inspired SS., assert that the author of it is uncertain. Erasmus and Cajetan deny that St. Paul is the author of it. The different objections proposed by them, derived from the Epistle itself, against our proposition, will be seen fully answered and refuted in the Commentary.

LANGUAGE OF.—This also has been a subject of much controversy. Most of the ancient Fathers, and almost all the early Commentators assert, that it was written in Hebrew ; and they reply to the objection against its authenticity, grounded on the diversity of style, by saying : this (if there really be any such diversity) may be readily accounted for on the ground, that in his other Epistles, the Apostle wrote in Greek, of which he was not so perfect a master as he was of the Hebrew, the language employed by him, in this Epistle. The supporters of this opinion account for the fact of all the quotations from the Old Testament being taken from the Greek Septuagint version, by saying, that the Apostle did quote from the Hebrew ; but that the translator, whom many assert to be St. Luke, or St. Clement, substituted for these, quotations from the Septuagint, for the sake of uniformity, and also because the Septuagint was then the version most in use. This solution is not quite satisfactory, if we bear in mind, that in some passages, the reasoning of the Apostle would appear by no means conclusive, in the use of any other, than the Septuagint version.—(*See* chap. ix., verse 16). Others maintain, that it was written in Greek ; these deny that there is any diversity of style observable between this and his other Epistles, which one and the same author might not employ, when treating of different subjects. Such diversity, if it exist, is, according to them, wholly attributable to the nature and diversity of subject. Many even of these maintain, that the thoughts were St. Paul's, and the language, that of his amanuensis, St. Luke, who being perfect master of the Greek language, clothed the thoughts dictated to him by the Apostle, in his own words. One of the strongest grounds in favour of this opinion is derived from the argument which the Apostle founds on the signification of certain words, in the Greek, which would not hold, had he written in Hebrew. They cite as an instance, the Greek word for testament διαθηκη (verse ix. 16), the Hebrew word for which, *Berith*, means any ordinary pact or covenant.

OBJECT AND OCCASION OF.—The object and design which the Apostle had in view in this Epistle was two-fold : first, to confirm the converted Jews in the faith ; and secondly, to offer them consolation, under the persecutions and afflictions they were enduring. We learn from the Acts of the Apostles, that the converted Jews of Palestine were persecuted, in divers ways by their countrymen, who pertinaciously adhered to the religion of their fathers. These persecutions had the effect of weakening their faith ; and served as so many temptations, to fall into the hateful crime of apostacy. They had, moreover, to encounter the false teachers, who taught the neces- sity and the sufficiency of the Law of Moses, particularly the portion of it, that regarded the Levitical sacrifices. The principal error refuted by the Apostle in this Epistle differs from those combated by him in his Epistles to the Romans and Galatians, in this respect : that, in his Epistle to the Romans, he refutes the error of those, who maintained the sufficiency of the *moral* portion of the Mosaic law ; in the Epistle to the Galatians, of those who maintained the necessity for Christians of the *ceremonial* part ; and in this Epistle, the errors regarding the *sacrifices* of the same law. These teachers also maintained that the Jewish religion was a sufficiently secure means, for attaining salvation. This latter assertion they founded on the excellence of the promulgators of the Mosaic Law—the Angels—"*ordinata per Angelos*" (Gal. iii.) ; the authority of Moses ; the Pontificate of Aaron ; the perpetual succession of the Levitical Priesthood ; the sanctity of the Tabernacle and its contents ; the intrinsic dignity of the Law ; but principally, the efficacy and perpetuity of the Sacrifices ; the promises of the ancient Testament ; the miracles, wrought in its favour.—(*Vide* Mauduit's Preface to this Epistle). In reply to all these, the Apostle places Christ above the Angels ; above Moses and Levi ; his Priesthood according to the order of Melchisedech, above that of Aaron ; his sacrifice, above the legal victims ; the New Taber- nacle, above the Old ; the miracles of the New Law, above those of Moses. In fine, he establishes the necessity of faith ; and consoles the Jews in their afflictions, by pointing out the advantages of suffering, even to the just of old.

WHEN AND WHERE WRITTEN.—It was written from Italy. According to some, towards the close of the Apostle's first imprisonment at Rome. It is, however, generally supposed to have been written about the year 62 or 63 of our era.

THE EPISTLE

OF

ST. PAUL TO THE HEBREWS.

CHAPTER I.

𝔄nalysis.

The chief object which the Apostle expressly proposes to himself in this chapter, as is clear from verse 4, is to point out the superior excellence of Christ, the promulgator of the New Law—above the Angels, the promulgators of the Old. He thus refutes one of the grounds upon which the false teachers founded the superior excellence of the Law of Moses, with the view of inducing the converted Hebrews to apostatize to Judaism, and leaves it to be inferred that if the excellence of a Law is to be estimated by the excellence of its promulgators, the Gospel must far exceed the Law of Moses. It is remarked however, by Commentators, that before expressly instituting a comparison between Christ and the Angels, the Apostle institutes an implied comparison between him and the most exalted personages in the Old Law, and raises him above them: above the Prophets, who were mere men, mere servants; whereas, Jesus Christ was the Eternal Son of God, himself, true God: above the Patriarchs, who were merely the fathers of the Jewish people, and the heirs of a merely earthly inheritance; whereas, Jesus Christ was the Creator of all things, and the heir of the universe: above Moses, the brightness of whose countenance could bear no comparison with the eternal effulgence of the Father's glory: above Aaron, whom he far excelled in the expiation he made for sin (1, 2, 3).

The Apostle then expressly compares Christ with the Angels, and shows how far he is above them, in his name and origin (4, 5), in the honours paid him, by the Angels themselves; (6) in their respective offices; the duty of one party being to minister, the glorious prerogative of the other, to reign (7, 8); in power and immutability (10-12); in dignity of place; it being the privilege of one, to sit at the right hand of God, the duty of the other, to serve (13, 14).

𝔗ext.	𝔓araphrase.
1. GOD, who at sundry times and in divers manners spoke, in times past to the fathers by the prophets, last of all,	1. God, who formerly revealed himself, in the Old Testament, to our fathers by the Prophets, on different occasions—disclosing one portion of his divine mysteries to one Prophet, and a different portion to another—and in different ways—employing various modes of revelation; such as dreams, ecstasies, visions, corporeal appearances and the rest,

Commentary.

1. The Apostle, contrary to his usual custom, without any mention of his name or office, and without commencing with the usual Apostolical salutation, introduces, at once, the subject of the Epistle. The omission of his name is easily accounted for, on

Text.

2. In these days hath spoken to us by his Son, whom he hath appointed heir of all things, by whom also he made the world.

3. Who being the brightness of his glory, and the figure of his substance, and upholding all things by the word of his power, making purgation of sins, sitteth on the right hand of the majesty on high ;

Paraphrase.

2. Has in these our days, the last period of time, revealed himself to us, not by his servants, but by his only Son Jesus Christ, whom, in his assumed human nature, he has constituted the heir of all things ; by whom, as his eternal Word, he has created the universe, and all that it contains.

3. Who, as the Son of God, being the eternal effulgence of the Father's glory, emanating from him, light of light ; and the express image of his substance (being possessed of the very same divine substance with the Father, which was communicated to him by an eternal generation), by his Providence sustains in existence and rules all creatures ; and after having fully atoned for sin, now holds the highest place, as man, next the glorious Majesty of God, in heaven.

Commentary.

the ground, that it was odious to the Jews, owing to the great zeal displayed by him in proclaiming the abolition of the Mosaic Law, of which he was regarded by many of them, as the enemy. The omission of his name accounts for the omission of the usual Apostolical salutation. He omits referring to his Apostleship, because he was, in a special way, the Apostle of the Gentiles.

"At sundry times," πολυμερως. *in many parts.* To one prophet, he revealed one portion of his mysteries ; and a different portion to another : (*v.g.*) to Isaias. Christ's birth of a Virgin, and his passion ; to Daniel, the period of his coming ; to Jonas, his sepulture, and so of the rest. The word will also mean, he communicated one part, at one time ; and a different part, at another.

"In divers manners." He employed dreams, ecstasies, visions, corporeal appearances, figures, and similitudes.

2. "Last of all in these days ; " the Greek puts it more clearly, ἐπ᾽ ἐσχάτων τῶν ἡμερῶν τούτων, *in these last days,* referring to the period of the New Law, which is often in Scripture termed " the last hour," because it is the last form of religion, that shall be established on earth.

"Hath spoken to us by his Son," as if he said ; no longer by his servants, the Prophets, has he spoken to us and revealed the truths of his Gospel ; but, by his Eternal Son, Jesus Christ, who being infinite and essential truth, has imparted to us the knowledge of his saving mysteries ; not in mere parts, or at different times, but fully, and all at once ; not in obscure figures, but openly, in the full dawn of day, when "the day star" of faith "has arisen in our hearts."—(2 Peter, i. 19).

Of course, the superiority of Christ over all creatures, both Angels and Prophets, Moses included, is clearly implied in the words "his Son." It is however, with the view of showing his superiority above the Angels in particular, in the first instance, as appears from the entire chapter, that he now assigns some of the most glorious attributes of his divine and human natures.

"Whom he hath appointed heir of all things." As man, Christ is the natural Son of God ; the Father conferred on him, as man, at his Incarnation, the heirship of all things created.

" By whom he made the world." (In Greek, τους αιωνας, *sæcula, i.e.,* all created beings). In this, the Apostle refers to his divine nature. Creation being an act of wisdom, is, by appropriation, attributed to the Son. "All things were made by him " (John, i. 3). So here, "the world " (the Greek has *the worlds*) refers to the universe, or, to all creatures ; for, everything created was made by him.

3. "Who being the brightness of his glory." The Greek for "brightness," απαυγασμα, means the refulgence or beam of his glory ; since, from eternity he possessed the same glorious divine nature with the Father. The illustration is borrowed from the emanation of the radiant beams of light from the sun. The Eternal Father is compared to the sun ; the Word, to its rays. The rays emanate from the sun, necessarily, purely,

Text.

4. Being made so much better than the Angels, as he hath inherited a more excellent name than they.

5. For to which of the Angels hath he said at any time: *Thou art my son, to-day have I begotten thee?* And again *I will be to him a father, and he shall be to me a son?*

Paraphrase.

4. He has been rendered as far superior to the angels as the name of natural Son of God, which he inherited, exceeds theirs.

5. For, to which, even of the highest Angels, has God ever addressed these words, spoken to Jesus Christ from eternity, and again repeated at his incarnation and resurrection : " Thou art my Son, this day have I begotten thee ;" and again, speaking of him in another place : " I shall be to him a father and he shall be to me a Son " ?

Commentary.

unceasingly, without any separation. All ideas, however, of inequality between the rays and the sun, all notions of imperfection which may occur in the latter emanation, are by no means to be applied to the eternal generation of the Word, who possesses the same identical nature, and is, in every respect, equal to the Father.

" And the figure of his substance." In Greek, χαράκτηρ της ὑποστασεως. Another illustration of the same eternal generation, derived from the comparison of a seal and figure. The Word is the impression, the image of the Father, the substantial, living, eternal image of his substance, communicated to him, in his eternal generation. The Greek word for " substance," ὑποστάσεως, may be rendered, *subsistence*, or *personality ;* and, then, the words will mean ; that he is the image of the Father's subsistence ; because, the personality or subsistence of the Son is perfectly similar to that of the Father ; although, of course, distinct from it. In the words, " brightness of his glory," there is an implied comparison between Christ and Moses, whose face was beaming with glory, after his long converse with God.

" And upholding all things by the word of his power." This expresses another of the divine attributes of Christ, by his omnipotent " word " or will, " upholding," (*i.e.*), exerting a Providence in sustaining and positively preserving creatures in existence.

" Making purgation of sins." The Greek is, δι᾽ ἑαυτοῦ καθαρισμον ποιησαμενος, *having made by himself a purgation of our sins ;* but neither the Alexandrian nor Vatican MSS., nor the Armenian version have, *by himself.* This he did, as Man God. There is allusion here to the human nature of Christ, which he assumed, in order, as God and Man, to become the Saviour of the world, by making full and adequate reparation for sin, to his offended Father. There is an implied comparison here between Christ and Aaron, and it is tacitly insinuated, that the expiation made by the former infinitely surpasses that made by the latter.

" Sitteth on the right hand of majesty on high." As man, Christ occupies the most honourable place, next to God in heaven.

4. " Being made," &c. The words " being made" do not imply that Christ is a creature. The corresponding Greek word, γενομενος, might be rendered simply " *being*, so much better than the Angels," &c. They merely express that by the union of his human nature with the divine, under the personality of the Word, the Man, Christ Jesus, became the natural Son of God, and so, was as superior to the angels, as the honoured and adorable name of Son of God exceeds, in dignity, that of servant.

5. Another argument, in favour of the superiority of Christ over the angels, is derived from the SS. Scriptures ; and, therefore, a most powerful one in the minds of the Jews. It is founded on the singular use of the words of God the Father addressing his Son (Psalm ii. 7) : " *Thou art my Son, this day have I begotten thee.*" The angels and men are often called " Sons of God," but never " the Son of God."

But, since according to many, these words literally refer to David ; how, then, from the use of them, infer their incommunicability to the angels ?

RESP.—Even supposing the correctness of that opinion, these words refer to David, only inasmuch as he was a type of Christ.

But, since it is far more probable that they refer primarily and literally to Christ ; as is clear from the promise contained, verse 8—*dabo tibi gentes in hereditatem et possessionem tuam terminos terræ.* And then they mean, according to St. Augustine, " I have

Text.

6. And again, when he bringeth in the first begotten into the world he saith: *And let all the Angels of God adore him.*

7. And to the angels indeed he saith: *He that maketh his angels, spirits; and his ministers a flame of fire.*

8. But to the Son: *Thy throne O God, is for ever and ever: a sceptre of justice is the sceptre of thy kingdom.*

Paraphrase.

6. And when the majesty of his second coming to judgment is described, God the Father commands all the angels to pay him adoration, as Lord and God.

7. And speaking of the angels indeed (Psalm, ciii.). he saith: He that maketh his angels, as fleet as the winds, and his ministers as efficient, as a flame of fire.

8. Whereas, when speaking of his Son, he employs quite a different style of language: Thy throne, O God, shall last for ever; the sceptre of thy kingdom is a sceptre of equity or rectitude.

Commentary.

begotten thee *to-day*," *i.e.*, from eternity, which is an everlasting, indivisible, permanent instant. They may also refer to the Incarnation of Christ, when he assumed flesh, and also to his third birth in the glory of his Resurrection, in which latter sense they are used by St. Paul himself.—(Acts, chap. xiii.)

" I will be to him a father," &c. (2nd Book of Kings, chap. xiv.) These words literally refer to Solomon ; but, in their mystical meaning—the meaning principally intended by the Holy Ghost in the present instance—they refer to Christ ; and it is upon their mystical meaning, which the converted Jews themselves admitted (for they were aware that Solomon, in this respect, was a type of Christ), the Apostle builds his argument, a thing by no means unusual with the sacred writers, as appears from several parts of the Epistles (*v.g.*), 1 Cor. chap. ix. ; 1 Tim. chap. v. ; Galatians, chap. v. ; St. Matthew, chap. ii. 15 ; St. John xix. 36. The Jews themselves admitted this mystical meaning ; and though Solomon was a sinner, he was not in his sins a type of Christ, any more than was Cyrus in his misdeeds, although, in other respects, the latter was a type of Christ (*v.g.*) in his rescuing the Jews from the Babylonish captivity.

6. Another argument of his superiority is founded on the adoration which the Heavenly Father commanded all his angels to pay him (Psalm xcvi. 7). This quotation is from the Septuagint version of the Psalms, and the words refer, most probably, to the second coming of Christ to judgment. The construction of the Greek favours this view, *and when he bringeth in the first begotten again in the world.* According to which "*again*" refers to his second coming. Moreover, the entire 29th Psalm clearly refers to the second coming of Christ, and then, all the angels, good and bad, and all creatures, will adore his Majesty—the good, willingly, and with joy, the bad, unwillingly, and with terror. No doubt, the good angels adored him at his first introduction also, in his Nativity. "*Adore*" προσκυνησατωσαν· this word means always, in the New Testament, the supreme worship due to God alone.

7. Another argument is derived from the difference of manner in which the SS. Scriptures speak of the angels and the Son of God. When there is question of the angels (Psalm ciii.), they are spoken of as servants and messengers, executing the commands of God. According to the Paraphrase, the word "*angels*," of whom the Apostle understands these words of the Psalm, and also the word "*ministers*," who refer to the same, are made the subjects of the proposition, which the article prefixed to each in the Greek shows them to be: τους αγγελους αυτου πνευματα, τους λειτουργους αυτου πυρος φλογα. Moreover, the reasoning of the Apostle requires that they should be the subjects, of which "*spirits*," or, winds, and "*flame of fire*" would be predicated.

8. Whereas, speaking of his Son, the employment assigned him is, not to serve, like the angels, but to reign. "*Thy throne O God.*" &c. (Psalm xliv.), which entirely regards the Messiah, and is the marriage song, in which are celebrated his future nuptials with his Church. "*A sceptre of justice.*" In Greek, *a sceptre of rectitude* or *uprightness.* The Socinians, in order to do away with the clear argument which this passage furnishes in favour of our Lord's divinity, endeavour to make it appear that, "*O God,*" is to be read in the nominative case, thus, "*thy throne is God*"—an un-

Text.

9. *Thou hast loved justice, and hated iniquity, therefore God, thy God, hath annointed thee with the oil of gladness above thy fellows.*

10. And: *Thou in the beginning, O Lord, didst found the earth: and the works of thy hands are the heavens.*

11. *They shall perish, but thou shalt continue: and they shall all grow old as a garment.*

12. *And as a vesture shalt thou change them, and they shall be changed: but thou art the self-same, and thy years shall not fail.*

Paraphrase.

9. Because thou hast loved justice and hated iniquity, therefore, O God, Christ, has thy God annointed thee with the oil of gladness beyond all thy fellows, all the co-heirs and sharers in thy kingdom.

10. And in another Psalm (ci.), referring to his Omnipotence, he says: Thou in the beginning, O Lord, didst found the earth, and the heavens are the works of thy power.

11. They shall perish, but thou shalt continue (hence his immutability), and by the continual revolutions, they shall grow old and become like unto a garment, worn by constant friction.

12. And as a garment thou shalt change them, and they shall be changed; but thou art always the self-same, immutable in thy nature; eternal in thy duration. (Of which of the angels was any such thing ever said?)

Commentary.

meaning construction, for, although we often find heaven, earth, angels, and just men, called the throne of God, we never find that God is called a throne. Again, the Attic vocative is like the nominative, and the versions of Aquila and Symmachus make it, " O God," in the vocative. Add to this, the unanimous interpretation of the Fathers of the Church, who argued from this text in favour of the divinity of Christ, In order to elude the strong argument in favour of the divinity of Christ, which the application of the Psalm, regarding the creation of heaven and earth to Christ, supplies, the Socinians deny the authenticity of verses 10, 11, 12. But these verses are found in all the Greek copies of this Epistle, and in all the ancient versions. Others among them understand heaven and earth of the new heavens and earth, foretold by the prophets, viz., the gospel economy of the New Law. But, were these the heavens, &c., made *" in the beginning?"* Was it the new heavens, in their sense of the words, that were *" to perish," " to wax old as a garment,"* and *" to be folded up as a vesture?"*

9. Thou hast loved justice, &c., "therefore, God, thy God," &c. These words may mean, that he has loved justice and hated iniquity, "therefore," *i.e., because* God has bestowed on him the plenitude of grace at his Incarnation; in which case, "therefore," refers to the cause and not to the effect of his "loving justice and hating iniquity;" or, they may mean, that in reward for his having loved justice, &c., God has bestowed the plenitude of heavenly glory and delights. The latter interpretation is more conformable to the Greek, διὰ τοῦτο ἔχρισε σε ὁ Θεὸς, and is the more probable meaning; for, the "oil of gladness" appears to refer to the exalted degree of glory conferred on the Messiah in his resurrection and ascension, after the labours of his mission, in recompense for his heroic actions, characterized by his " loving justice and hating iniquity "—a degree of glory and happiness far surpassing that of any of his saints, who, as fellow-members and co-heirs, were to share in his kingdom. "God, thy God," &c. The first term is used vocatively, according to some, according to others it is a nominative case, and is repeated for the sake of emphasis. The former is more probable; there is no reason for the repetition; but there is every reason why the Psalmist should, in a transport of exultation at the great glory conferred on Christ, cry out : "O God, thy God has annointed thee," &c.

10. The words of this verse refer to the attribute of Omnipotence.

11. This proves his immutability. When the Psalmist says, " *they shall perish*," he only means as to external form; for (verse 12) he declares " *they shall be changed*," " but thou shalt continue." In Greek, *thou dost continue*. The original Hebrew word is in the future tense.

12. " *Thou shalt change them*." In the ordinary Greek reading, it is, ἐλίξεις, thou shalt fold them, as the leaves of a book are folded, when closed. This will have a good meaning. However, that αλλαξεις, " *thou shalt change*," the reading followed by the Vulgate, is the true one, appears clear from the following words—" *and they shall*

Text.	Paraphrase.
13. But to which of the angels said he at any time : *Sit on my right hand, until I make thy enemies thy footstool?*	13. But to which of the angels were the words ever spoken, addressed by the Eternal Father to his Son (Psalm cix.) : Sit on my right hand and reign with me, until I shall have subjected thine enemies so completely, as to make them thy footstool ?
14. Are they not all ministering spirits, sent to minister for them, who shall receive the inheritance of salvation.	14. So far are the angels from enjoying any such dignity, that, we know, they are but ministering spirits whom God sends to take charge of men, especially of such as are to enjoy the inheritance of salvation and eternal glory.

Commentary.

be changed," with which the Vulgate reading accords better than the others. The same appears from the Hebrew, where the original word answers to αλλαξεις, not ελιξεις. Moreover, the Ethiopic version, although made from the Septuagint, has here a word signifying " thou shalt change." " *But thou art the self-same,"* proves his Immutability ; and " *thy years shall not fail,"* his Eternity."

13. This Psalm (cix.) the Jews themselves admit to refer to Christ (Matt. xxii. 43). Moreover, to Christ alone could the characteristic marks there referred to apply (*v.g.*) " Thou art a priest for ever according to the order of Melchisedech."

14. He asks the question, " Are they not all ministering spirits ?" as a thing well known among the faithful. Far from sitting at God's right hand, their duty is to minister ; but, their ministry, like all creation, is ancillary to the good of the elect. The reprobates all have their angels, ; however, they ultimately profit not by their ministry. This verse proves against St. Thomas, that out of every order of angels some are sent on missions to earth, "are they not ALL...sent to minister ?" &c. Besides, SS. Scripture furnishes instances of the mission of the highest angels.

CHAPTER II.

Analysis.

In this chapter, the Apostle infers, from the superior excellence of Christ above the angels, which he demonstrated in the preceding, that the New Law, of which he was the promulgator, was to be observed with greater diligence than was required in the observance of the Old (1–4). Then, reverting to the question of the superiority of Christ over the angels, he shows, that to him, and not to them, was subjected the world to come ; and although we do not see all things subjected to him ; still, the prophecy of David regarding him, a part of which is already fulfilled, shall ultimately receive its full accomplishment (4–9).

As the passion of Christ was a source of scandal to the Jews, on this account, the Apostle points out from several reasons, the congruity of his suffering, and vindicates the economy of redemption (10–15). Finally, he shows how perfectly our blessed Saviour possessed the qualities required in one, who was to undertake the redemption of mankind (17, 18).

Text.	Paraphrase.
1. THEREFORE ought we more diligently to observe the things which we have heard, lest perhaps we should let them slip.	1. Such, therefore, being the dignity and superior excellence of Christ, it is our duty to attend more carefully to what we have heard, and to be more diligent in observing his precepts, lest, perhaps, we may be irrecoverably lost, like water, which flows through a leaky vessel, and forfeit by our sins the great blessings of the new law.
2. For if the word, spoken by angels, became steadfast, and every transgression and disobedience received a just recompense of reward:	2. For, if the law promulgated by the ministry of, angels was firmly ratified and sanctioned in such a way, that every violation of it, great or small, was visited with condign punishment :

Commentary.

1. "Therefore," as Christ possesses such superior excellence above the angels.— "Lest perhaps we let them slip." The Greek for "slip," παραρρυωμεν, conveys the idea of water slipping through a vessel full of chinks. Some understand by it : lest we suffer them to slip from our memories, as water through a leaky vessel; others, lest we be irrecoverably lost and involved in the common rejection of our countrymen, like water, &c. This latter is the more probable meaning, because the word refers to their suffering punishment, as is clear from the comparison (verse 2) instituted between the menaced punishment, and the punishment annexed to the violation of the Mosaic law. "More diligently" than hitherto, or more diligently than we should attend to the law of Moses. The Greek for "diligently," περισσοτερως, literally means, *more abundantly.*

2. "And every transgression," *i.e.,* grievous violation. "and disobedience," lighter violation. "Received a just recompense," a penalty decreed by law. "The word spoken by angels," evidently refers to the law given to Moses on Sinai. This the Apostle more clearly expresses (Gal. iii.), "ordained by angels in the hand of a mediator," *i.e.,* Moses. But, was not the law, although promulgated by angels, on Sinai, still the law of God ? Yes. But the Lord has shown how much the new law exceeds it, by reason of trusting its promulgation to no other than his own Son, its author and promulgator at the same time. Again, the violation of the new law, besides the guilt of the violation of God's law in general, common to it with the old, involved

Text.

3. How shall we escape if we neglect so great salvation? which having begun to be declared by the Lord, was confirmed unto us by them that heard *him*.

4. God also bearing them witness by signs, and wonders, and divers miracles and distributions of the Holy Ghost according to his own will.

5. For God hath not subjected unto angels the world to come, whereof we speak.

Paraphrase.

3. How can we escape punishment, if we neglect a law infinitely more dignified, because it confers on us salvation, which the old law could lay no claim to—a law which was originally promulgated and announced by the Lord himself, and not announced by his ministers, and was, besides, confirmed to our times, or, unto us, Hebrews, by the testimony of those who saw him in the flesh, and heard his teachings?

4. And to their testimony God himself has set his seal by repeated miracles—which were so many proofs of his interposition—so many stupendous works—so many exhibitions of his omnipotent power—and by the copious and abundant effusion of the gifts of the Holy Ghost, according to his will and pleasure.

5. It is not, however, to be supposed, because the angels were the promulgators of the Mosaic law, and were intrusted, in a subordinate capacity, with the government of this world, that they are the rulers of the future world, of which we speak ; for, not to them, but to Christ, as father of the world to come, and pontiff of future blessings, had God confided the future world.

Commentary.

a specific contempt of its promulgator, Christ, in which respect its violation is more sinful than was that of the old. But, is not he who gave the law to Moses (Exodus. xix. 20), styled "Dominus," "the Lord?" Moreover, is it not the common opinion of the Holy Fathers, that the Son of God repeatedly appeared to the patriarchs, and that it was he also, who gave the law to Moses on Sinai ? From this verse, and also from the above cited passage to the Galatians, it is quite clear, that the old law was given to Moses by angels. And the opinion of the ancients can mean nothing more, than that the angel promulgating the law on Sinai represented the Son of God ; and in the instances, in which particular worship was paid to one angel beyond the others, as happened, when Abraham adored one of the three angels on their way to destroy Sodom, the angel in question is supposed to have exhibited the same external form which the Son of God afterwards exhibited, in human flesh, and so on *this*, as on *other* similar occasions, he represented the Son of God ; and as such termed, *Dominus*.

3. In this verse is shown the excellence of the Christian above the Mosaic law. "Confirmed unto us," *i.e.*, unto our times ; or, according to others, unto us, Hebrews, with whom the Apostle identifies himself, by speaking in the first person. "How shall we escape if *we* neglect?" &c.

4. "Signs, wonders, miracles," refer to the same thing, but considered under different respects (as in Paraphrase). "And distributions of the Holy Ghost," &c., refer to the *gratiæ gratis datæ*, such as, tongues, prophecy, &c. He leaves us to infer that the old law was characterized by no such favours ; but, by terrors and chastisements. The miracles referred to in this verse served to *confirm* the truth of the gospel, though not absolutely required for that purpose.

5. Some Expositors include all from the words, "which have begun," &c. (verse 3), inclusively, to this verse, within a parenthesis, and connect this with verse 3, thus :— "How will we escape if we neglect so great a salvation ?"......which salvation does not take its rise from the angels, who are not appointed the rulers of the future world, wherein salvation is obtained. Others (as in Paraphrase), say, that in this verse, the Apostle answers, by anticipation, an objection which might arise in the minds of the Jews, in consequence of the power assigned to angels in many parts of Scripture, of ruling this world (*v.g.*), Daniel, x. 13–20. And he says, that although the angels may have been entrusted with the government of this present world, it is not so with "the

Text.

6. But one in a certain place hath testified, saying: *What is man, that thou art mindful of him: or the son of man, that thou visitest him?*

7. *Thou hast made him a little lower than the angels: thou hast crowned him with glory and honour, and hast set him over the works of thy hands.*

Paraphrase.

6. That it was to Christ he subjected the future world, of which we speak, we have the authority of David (Psalm viii.), when addressing God in words, the mystical, if not the literal, sense of which refers to Christ, he says: "What is man, that thou art mindful of him, or the son of man, that thou visitest him," by assuming him to a union with the Divine Person at his Incarnation?

7. Thou hast made him, for a short time, during his passion, appear lower than the angels; but thou hast, after his passion, crowned him with honour and glory, and placed him over all the works of thy power.

Commentary.

future world," by which some understand the Church, wherein alone salvation is found. But others, more probably, understand by it, the world after the resurrection, when the words adduced next verse in proof, that it is on Christ the government of the future world is conferred, "thou hast subjected all," &c., will be fully verified.

6, 7. He proves that it was to Christ this future world, of which he speaks, (i. 6-12), is to be subjected. "But one in a certain place," &c.—(David, Psalm viii.) The Apostle omits mentioning the passage from which the words are taken, because addressing the Jews, so accurately versed in the Scriptures. Some Commentators understand Psalm viii. to refer, in its *literal* sense, to the benefits conferred on Adam and his posterity. The Psalmist is supposed by them, while in his youth tending his flocks at night, "*oves et boves universas,*" &c., and gazing on the heavens, "*the moon and the stars which thou hast founded,*" (Psalm viii. 4), resplendently reflecting the attributes of the Creator, to have burst forth into the praises of God—"*Domine, dominus noster,*" &c., admiring, at the same time, his concern for man, to whose use and benefit all creation was made subservient. He was specially "*mindful*" of frail, weak man, and "*visited*" him by conferring on him so many signal favours. He set him over the rest of creation, and made him "*a little lower than the angels.*" The Hebrew for "*little*" (*meat*), as also the Greek, βραχυ τι, may signify, either *for a short time*, during his mortal life—for, in heaven all "shall be as the angels of God,"—or, a little, *in dignity*, below the angels, the angelic being superior to human nature. The Hebrew for "*angels*" (*elohim*), is frequently applied to creatures, and is rendered "angels" by the Septuagint, both here and in other places, (*v.g.*) *adorent eum angeli* (elohim) *Dei* (chap. i. verse 6). He "*subjected all things under his feet,*" by giving him dominion over all earthly creatures. Therefore, it is added in the Psalm, "*all sheep and oxen,*" &c. Taken in their *mystical* sense, on which the reasoning of the Apostle, applying them to Christ is founded, the words mean, what is human nature ("*man and the son of man,*") that God should specially visit it by becoming personally united to it at his incarnation. "*For a little,*" during his mortal life, and especially his passion, Christ in his human nature appeared lower than the angels ; or, *in dignity*, the human nature of Christ was lower than the angels (for many hold that of itself the angelic nature is superior to the human nature of Christ). "*Thou hast subjected,*" &c. These words are taken in their widest extent, and from his saying that he "subjected *all things*," the Apostle infers that nothing, not excepting the angels, was left unsubjected. It is not unusual with the Apostle to ground an argument quite conclusively on the mystical meaning of the Scriptures of the Old Testament (*see* chap. i. verse 5).

Others maintain that Psalm viii. *literally* and directly refers to Christ. He frequently styles himself in the Gospel, "*filius hominis,*" to which the words of the Psalmist are, most likely, prophetically allusive. The Psalm is quoted from in three other places of the New Testament (Matthew, xxi. 16 ; 1 Cor. xv. 27 ; Ephes. i. 22), and in all these it is applied to Christ. To this it might be said in reply, that the Psalm is quoted in its *mystical* sense, in the passages referred to. The advocates of this opinion also say, that, although some passages of the Psalm may literally apply to Adam and mankind

Text.

8. *Thou hast subjected all things under his feet.* For in that he hath subjected all things to him, he left nothing not subject to him. But now we see not as yet all things subject to him. .

9. But we see JESUS, who was made a little lower than the angels, for the suffering of death, crowned with glory and honour ; that through the grace of God he might taste death for all.

10. For it became him, for whom are all things, and by whom are all things, who had brought many children into glory, to perfect the author of their salvation, by *his* passion.

Paraphrase.

8. Thou hast subjected all creatures whatsoever under the feet of thy Christ ; and by saying, he subjected *all*, without exception, the Psalmist leaves it to be inferred, that there is nothing left unsubjected. But this part of the prophecy, regarding the universal subjection of all things to Christ, is not yet fully accomplished ; for, we do not yet see all things actually subjected to him.

9. But the other part is fulfilled. We see that Jesus, who was made a little lower than the angels in his passion, now crowned with honour and glory, in reward for this passion, which he submitted to, so as to die for all, owing to the gratuitous love and bounty of God, sincerely wishing for the redemption of all men.

10. (But as the ignominious death and sufferings of Christ might prove to you a subject of scandal, I shall point out to you the congruity, on the part of God, of fixing on suffering as the means of redeeming man, and glorifying his own Son). For, it became the wisdom of God the Father, the end and author of all things, after having decreed to bring many adopted sons to glory (by means of suffering), to fix also upon suffering, as the means of bringing to perfect glory, the author of their salvation, *i.e.*, to adopt unity and identity of means, in glorifying all his children, both natural and adopted.

Commentary.

in general ; still, it is only to Christ the entire Psalm could refer, as there are other passages which could not apply to man (*v.g.*), that after being lowered beneath the angels, he was crowned with honour and glory, that he was set over the works of God and that "all things," except God, as the Apostle interprets it (1 Cor. xv.), were "subjected under his feet." It might, however, be said, in reply, that after being lowered, *in dignity*, below the angels, man was crowned with honour and glory in the high destiny in store for him hereafter, and the lofty dominion over creatures given to him and continued after his fall ; and that, after a *short time*, he shall be equal to the angels in the fruition of heavenly bliss ; with regard to the subjection of all things, it might be said, that the Apostle, in their *mystical* application, gives the words a greater extension, so that in their *mystical* sense, as applying to Christ, they are more fully and more perfectly verified.

8. "Thou hast subjected all things under his feet ;" from the·Psalmist's universal assertion that "he subjected *all*," the Apostle infers that nothing, of course, not even the angels, was left unsubjected. ." But now we do not see," &c. The Apostle admits that the portion of the divine oracle, which regards the universal subjection of all things to Christ, is not yet actually fulfilled in execution. But he says, that from the fulfilment of the *other* part of the promise, which regards the "crowning of Christ with honour," &c., after his passion, we can calculate on the fulfilment of *this* also, in due time ; and that the other part is fulfilled, is clear from verse 9.

9. "But we see Jesus," &c. Hence, one part of the promise is fulfilled. "For the suffering of death," may be also connected with the words, "made a little lower than the angels," as if he said, "he was made a little lower than the angels, on account of the suffering of death." "That through the grace of God" is an explanation of the words, "suffering of death," as if he said, when I refer to the suffering of death, I must explain it, as being the result of the gratuitous love of God by which he sincerely wished for the redemption of the entire human race. "For all." In Greek, ὑπὲρ παντὸς, *for every man*.

10. The ignominious death of Christ was to the Jews a subject of scandal. Hence,

Text.

11. For both he that sanctifieth, and they who are sanctified, *are* all of one. For which cause he is not ashamed to call them brethren, saying:

12. *I will declare thy name to my brethren: in the midst of the church will I praise thee.*

13. And again: *I will put my trust in him.* And again: *Behold I and my children, whom God hath given me.*

14. Therefore because the children are partakers of flesh and blood, he also himself in like manner hath been partaker of the same,

Paraphrase.

11. For the pontiff, who sanctifies (such as Christ), and they who are sanctified, should be of the same stock, of the same nature. Therefore, it is, that Christ having adopted our nature, is not ashamed to call us brethren, saying—

12. "I will announce thy name to my brethren, in the midst of the church will I praise thee."

13. And again (Isaias, viii. 17): "I will put my trust in him." And again :.*"* Behold I and my children whom God hath given me."—(Isaias, viii. 18).

14. Since, then, the children of Christ have partaken of a passible nature, he also assumed the same, in order that, by his death, he might destroy the power of the devil, by depriving him of that empire

Commentary.

the Apostle here sets about vindicating the economy of redemption. "Who had brought many children unto glory." The words, *by suffering*, are understood. Some understand the words, "who had brought," to mean, "who had *decreed* to bring," because no one was brought to heavenly glory, before Christ's Passion and Ascension. Others, who by "glory," also understand *heavenly glory*, take the word "brought," literally to mean, *actually brought*, because the patriarchs, and just of old, were sure of heavenly glory, and were immediately to enter on it; or rather these say, that "glory" means not heavenly glory, but renown, celebrity; and God had rendered many of his sons of old, Abraham, Joseph, Moses, &c., renowned and celebrated, through the ordeal of suffering. Hence, God brought them to glory by suffering, because they performed the works of suffering, to which this glory or renown was attached. "The author of their salvation." In Greek, αρχηγον, *the chief, or captain of their salvation*.

11. "He that sanctifieth," &c. The Apostle more fully explains the preceding verse. The Pontiff who sanctifies, and they who are sanctified, should be of the same nature, or from the same stock. The Pontiffs among the Jews were taken from the Jewish people. Hence, as Christ is constituted by God (verse 19) a Pontiff to redeem men, he ought to be of the same nature, a nature passible and liable to suffering. The reason why Christ, as Pontiff, should assume a passible nature is assigned (verse 17), between which verse and this (verse 11) the closest connexion is clearly traceable. "For which cause he is not ashamed," &c. Hence, to observe this congruity of being of the same nature with the redeemed, Christ assumed our nature, in virtue of which he is not ashamed to call us brethren, as appears from (verse 12).

12. Psalm xxi. from which these words are quoted, evidently refers to the Passion of Christ, and the words quoted from it in this verse have reference to the time after his Resurrection, when he frequently calls his Apostles "brethren" (Mat. xxviii.; John, xx.); he then announced to them the name of God during forty days, and afterwards announced it through them to the world, and it was after the promulgation of his law, that the praises of God the Father, and his own, were solemnly proclaimed in the churches.

13. "*I will put my trust in him.*" These words are found in the Greek version of the Septuagint, from which the quotations in this Epistle are taken (chap. viii. 17, of Isaias). They convey the "*trust*" of a man in distress, and, as in their mystical sense they applied to Christ, they prove that he must have assumed a passible nature; otherwise, he could not be in distress, as the word "*trust*" supposes. "*Behold I and my children*," &c. The words are found in verse 18 of the same chapter, and though, like the preceding, literally applying to Isaias himself, they refer mystically to Christ, and are applied to him by the Apostle, in the next verse.

14. Since the children of Christ have a passible nature (which is meant by "flesh" and "blood"), so, in like manner, he assumed the nature of "these children, whom God gave him" (John, xvii. 15), for the purpose of destroying the power of the devil

Text.

that through death he might destroy him who had the empire of
death, that is to say, the devil :

15. And might deliver them,
who through the fear of death were
all their life-time subject to servitude.

16. For no where doth he take
hold of the angels: but of the seed
of Abraham he taketh hold.

17. Wherefore it behoved him in
all things to be made like unto his
brethren, that he might become a
merciful and faithful high priest
before God, that he might be a
propitiation for the sins of the
people.

18. For in that, wherein he him-

Paraphrase.

of death, which he had abused, by inflicting it on
Christ himself, who was undeserving of it, being wholly
innocent.

15. And might ransom and emancipate those who,
owing to the great dread and terror they had of death,
were, during their lifetime, kept in servitude, or the
servile fear of its approach.

16. For, in truth, it was not the angels, who were
by nature immortal, that he came to rescue, but mortal
men of the seed of Abraham, the spiritual Father of
the redeemed generation.

17. Hence, as Christ came to redeem, not angels,
but mankind, and came to sanctify them, as high
priest, it was meet he should become like them, who
in his assumed nature, were his brethren, in all their
infirmities not unbecoming his dignity, infirm, mortal,
and passible, in order that he might become a merciful
and faithful high priest in the affairs appertaining to
God, his fidelity as a high priest consisting in expiating
for our sins, and propitiating God for them.

18. And his mercy in this, that by suffering and

Commentary.

(*see* Paraphrase), according to which interpretation, the words have the same meaning
as chap. viii. 3, to the Romans. They may also mean, that he destroyed the power
of the devil, by obtaining for men, through his passion and death, the means of
escaping that second and eternal death, in which the empire of the devil principally
consisted.

15. According to the meaning in the Paraphrase, the Apostle says, that by his
death and subsequent resurrection, Christ showed men, that death was a mere sleep,
and not so formidable, owing to his grace, as they were apt to imagine ; for, the terror
of its approach kept them in servile fear, during the entire course of their lives. The
words may also mean, that he rescued men from the servitude of the Mosaic law, which
restrained them within the bounds of duty only by the fear of death, which it proposed
in cases of weightier transgressions.

16. According to the interpretation in Paraphrase, this verse is connected with
verse 15 : he rescued "those who were through fear of death all their lifetime," &c. ;
for, it was not the angels, who, being immortal, were not afraid of death, and required
not to be ransomed, that he grasped and dragged forth from their servitude, and
asserted into liberty. The Greek word for "take hold of," επιλαμβανεται, means,
to seize hold of, and drag back, one flying from us. This is the interpretation of the
verse that accords best with the following. Others connect this verse with verse 14,
thus : "he also in like manner hath been partaker of the same "......for it was not the
angelic nature he assumed to an hypostatic union, but human nature of the seed of
Abraham. This is the interpretation more commonly given of this verse. The
interpretation adopted in the Paraphrase seems, however, preferable ; both because it
is the natural meaning of the verb, "take hold of," and because it accords better with
the following verse ; moreover, the latter interpretation would appear a useless repetition
of the words—verse 15—"he also in like manner hath been partaker of the same,"
which clearly express that he assumed human nature, the nature of his "children."

17. As Christ, then, came to redeem and sanctify mankind ; it was meet that he
should become like them in all their infirmities, not unsuited to his dignity and infinite
sanctity, *i.e.*, become weak, passible, mortal ; this assimilation in these respects being
necessary, in order that he might he adorned with the two great qualities of a high
priest, viz., fidelity, consisting in his satisfying for sin, of which he would be incapable,
if he had not a passible nature ;

18. And mercy, which he is the better fitted to exercise, by having suffered himself ;
for, the circumstance of his own passibility, and of his experimentally becoming

Text.	**Paraphrase.**
self hath suffered and been tempted he is able to succour them also that are tempted.	being tempted himself, he becomes more fit and inclined to carry aid, and show compassion to those who are themselves tempted and afflicted.

Commentary.

acquainted with the miseries of his people, and of his participation in them, will serve to render the pontiff who sanctifies, more apt to compassionate, and will add energy and force ("he is able") to his exertions for their relief.

CHAPTER III.

Analysis.

Although from the superior excellence above the Angels, and from the divine attributes which the Apostle claimed for Christ in the two preceding chapters, would evidently follow his superiority over Moses ; still, such was the high opinion which the Hebrews entertained regarding the latter, that the Apostle finds it necessary to institute a comparison between him individually and Christ. This he does in the first six verses of this chapter In thus establishing the superiority of Christ, he destroys one of the grounds on which the false teachers founded the superior excellence of the Mosaic Law (7).

In the next place, he deters the Hebrews from the crime of apostasy, by proposing to them the example of their incredulous fathers, excluded from the Land of Promise in punishment of their incredulity, and dwells, in the remainder of the chapter, on the explanation and application of the prophetic menace contained in Psalm xciv.

Text.	**Paraphrase.**
1. WHEREFORE, holy brethren, partakers of the heavenly vocation, consider the apostle and high priest of our confession JESUS:	1. Wherefore, brethren, being sanctified by baptism and called to a state of sanctity, shares in the heavenly vocation to which Christ has invited us, cease to regard Moses any longer, and look up to Jesus Christ ; consider how great he is, the Apostle, by whom was announced the faith which you profess, and the Pontiff by whom it was consecrated, and rendered efficacious ;
2. Who is faithful to him that made him, as was also Moses in all his house.	2. Who is as faithful in discharging the duties of this twofold office of Apostle and Pontiff according to the will of God, by whom he was constituted one and the other, as was Moses, whom the Scripture commends for his fidelity (Numbers, xii. 7), in dispensing the concerns of the entire house of God, i.e., of the synagogue.

Commentary.

1. "Wherefore," *i.e.*, owing to all I have said of Christ, in the preceding chapters, "brethren" both by nature and Christian profession. "Consider," *i.e.*, worship with due reverence him, who has united, in his own person, the two-fold office of Apostle or Legate and Pontiff, filled by Moses and Aaron.

2. In point of fidelity the Apostle points out no disparity between Moses and

Text.

3. For this man was counted worthy of greater glory than Moses, by so much as he that hath built the house, hath greater honour than the house.

4. For every house is built by some man : but he that created all things is God.

5. And Moses indeed was faithful in all his house as a servant, for a testimony of those things which were to be said :

6. But Christ as the Son in his own house : which house are we, if we hold fast the confidence and glory of hope unto the end.

7. Wherefore, as the Holy Ghost

Paraphrase.

3. In instituting a comparison between Jesus Christ and Moses, it is not meant to insinuate that between both there was an equality ; for, in point of glory due to him, Jesus is as far above Moses, as the architect who builds a house, is above the house itself, in regard to the relative degree of honour due to each.

4. For, every house has some founder ; Jesus Christ, therefore, the Eternal Son of God, being the Architect of the world, and of all things it contains, is the founder of the synagogue, and consequently infinitely superior to Moses.

5. Moses, it is true, governed the entire house of God with great prudence and fidelity, but it was only in the capacity of servant, in testifying and announcing to the people the divine ordinances.

6. But Christ acted as Son and governed as Master, not in the house of another, but in his own ; which house or family, we Christians aggregated to his Church by faith, constitute ; this, however, will ultimately avail us only on condition of our persevering, and firmly retaining to the end, the intrepid profession of our faith, and of that hope in which we glory.

7. Wherefore, since in order to profit ultimately by

Commentary.

Christ, "that made him," *i.e.*, that constituted him his divine Legate and Pontiff, "as was also Moses in all his house," *i.e.*, the synagogue. In Numbers, xii. 7, it is said of Moses, "My servant, who is most faithful in all my house."

3. This verse is connected with verse 1, thus :—"Consider the Apostle...Jesus,"— (1) for, he has been reputed (by God who judges justly) by so much the more deserving of glory beyond Moses, as the architect deserves to be honoured beyond the house which he built. Of course, while speaking in direct terms of a material house, the Apostle refers more especially to the mystic house of the Jewish synagogue, of which Moses, although he was its principal ruler, formed only a part ; hence, as being only a part of it, he was created by Christ.

4. In this verse, is urged the point of disparity referred to in the preceding, so as to annihilate Moses in the comparison with Christ, the one being God, as was proved in chap. i. verse 10—the other, a mere creature

5. Another point of disparity—Moses, indeed, acted faithfully in explaining to the people the ordinances of God, and bearing witness to the future Messiah (Deut. xviii. 15). This, however, was only in capacity of "servant." The Greek word, θεραπων, is opposed to υιος, *son*, next verse, for this latter word is equivalent to κυριος, *master*.—. (Numbers, xiv. 7).

6. Whereas, Christ acted as son and master—and this not in another's house or family, like Moses, but "in his own," (in Greek, επι τον οικον αυτου, *over his own house*), which house (in Greek, ου οικος, *whose house*) we and all the members of the Church constitute "if we hold fast," *i.e.*, the advantages resulting from our forming the spiritual house, which Christ governs, will ultimately serve us only on condition of our retaining firmly to the end "the confidence." The Greek word, παρρησιαν, means, *the intrepid freedom of speech*, or profession of our faith ; and "glory of hope," in Greek, καυχημα, *glorying* of hope, or the hope in which we glory. The Hebrews, it appears, were faltering in their faith, and, owing to the pressure of present evils, were losing sight of future blessings, which form the object of Christian hope ; hence, the Apostle devotes the remainder of this chapter, and the next, in deterring them from the crime of apostasy.

7, 8. Some Commentators suspend the sense from, "wherefore," to "take heed" (verse 12), enclosing the prophetic oracle within a parenthesis. The connexion in the Paraphrase seems more simple and natural. "*To-day, if you hear his voice*," &c. ;

Text.

saith : *To-day if you shall hear his voice,*

8. *Harden not your hearts, as in the provocation ; in the day of temptation in the desert,*

9. *Where your fathers tempted me, proved and saw my works*

10. *Forty years : For which cause I was offended with this generation, and said : They always err in heart. And they have not known my ways,*

Paraphrase.

your present privileges in belonging to the family of God, you must persevere in the faith ; let me address you in the moving words, addressed by the Holy Ghost through the mouth of David, to your fathers : " To-day if you shall hear his voice," either through the preaching of the prophets, or by interior inspiration.

8. Render not your hearts hard, insensible, and callous to the impressions of divine grace, as happened your fathers in the place called "*provocation* or *contradiction*," on the day of temptation in the desert ; therefore, called, *temptation.*

9. In which desert, says the Lord, they tempted me, proved and saw my wonderful works.

10. Wherefore, in consequence of these and other similar instances of incredulity and distrust, I was for the space of forty years offended with this generation, and I said within myself, these are always erring in heart, madly following the bent of their passions, and blind in intellect, not knowing or attending to the ways of my commandments, or of my miracles :

Commentary.

these words are taken from Psalm xciv. and are the words of David (chap. iv. 7). This Psalm was composed by David, in all likelihood, on the occasion of some great festival in Jerusalem ; it was recited during divine worship, and written for all times ; hence, it is employed in the canonical hours at the commencement of the divine office, as an Invitatory, calling on us to adore God and sing his praises with greater fervour of soul. "*If you shall hear his voice,*" through what medium soever, be it internal, by inspiration, or external, by preaching, "*harden not,*" &c. "*As in the provocation,*" &c. These words are commonly supposed to refer to the occasion recorded (Exodus xvii.), when the people at Raphidim murmured against Moses for want of water, the place was, therefore, called " Meriba," *i.e.*, *contention* or *contradiction*, and " Massa," "*temptation,*" two words, which are repeated in the Hebrew of this Psalm. Others say, there is reference to the 14th chapter of Exodus, when, on the return of the spies, the people having rebelled against Moses, God swore the oath referred to in the Psalm.

9. " *Where,*" (in Greek, οὖ, *when*), viz., in the desert, "*tempted me.*" The Psalmist adds greater force to his words by abruptly introducing God as speaking. One tempts God, when he unlawfully wishes for an extraordinary manifestation of his attributes, either in the order of nature or grace (*v.g.*), when he expects God to perform a miracle in the order of nature or grace, to save him corporally or spiritually from the imminent peril to soul or body, to which he *voluntarily* and *unnecessarily* exposes himself. "*Proved*" (*me*, is added in the Greek). Some understand this word to mean the same as "*tempted*" so as merely to express a more minute degree of tempting God ;— others refer it to the following, thus : they tempted me, although, after examining my stupendous miracles, ("*proved*") they "*saw,*" that no exception could be taken to them.

10. Some connect "forty years" with the preceding, "*they saw my works forty years.*" "*For which cause I was angry,*" &c. It is better, however, connect it with the following (as in Paraphrase), because at the time of this oath on the part of God, they were not forty years out of Egypt. Moreover, in the 17th verse St. Paul joins it with "offended." "*For which cause,*" *i.e.*, therefore, "*forty years I was offended.*" For "*offended*" we read in the Roman Psaltery, " *I was very near to,*" but it will come to the same with the preceding ; he "*was very near to them,*" to be an eye-witness of their infidelities and to punish them for the same. The Greek word, προσωχθισα, may be rendered in both ways ; it literally means, *to loathe, to be weary of.* There is a difference between the Vulgate and the Roman Psaltery, which arose from this : the Council of Trent left the correction of the Missal and Breviary to the authority of the Sovereign Pontiff ; and

Text.

11. *As I have sworn in' my wrath: If they shall enter into my rest.*

12. Take heed, brethren, lest perhaps there be in any of you an evil heart of unbelief, to depart from the living God.

13. But exhort one another every day, whilst it is called *to-day*, that none of you be hardened through the deceitfulness of sin.

14. For we are made partakers of Christ: yet so if we hold the beginning of his substance firm unto the end.

15. While it is said, *To-day if*

Paraphrase.

11. And, on this account, I have sworn in my wrath that they shall never enter the land in which I promised them rest.

12. Do you, therefore, brethren, take care, lest the heart of any of you be infected with the dreadful evil of infidelity, by which you would renounce, through apostacy, the living God.

13. But rather exhort and encourage one another to perseverance every day, whilst the term of time expressed by "*to-day*," lasts, *i.e.*, during this life (in which alone you can work); so that none of you become obdurate, owing to the false allurements of sin.

14. For, although we have been, by our incorporation with Christ in baptism, made partakers of his grace, and rightful heirs of his glory, having become a part of the mystical body of which he is head, we must still bear in mind, that all these privileges will avail us finally, only on condition of our perseverance to the end in the steady profession of faith, which is the basis and foundation of our new spiritual existence.

15. That is to say, whilst it is said to us: "*To-day*

Commentary.

when the correction of the Breviary took place under Pius V., it was deemed right to retain the reading of the old Roman Psaltery in this Psalm, which was regarded as a hymn of Matins. This correction of the Breviary took place before the corrected edition of the Vulgate by Clement VIII.; therefore, no change was made in the words of the Breviary.

11. "*As I have sworn,*" &c. Some readings have, "*to whom I swore;*" both readings are good; the Hebrew word "asher" means "*as*" and "*to whom*"—"*if they shall enter,*" "*if*" in such cases has often the meaning of "*not*," as in the oath of the people to save Jonathan, "*if* a hair of his head shall fall," *i.e.*, a hair, &c., shall *not* fall. And this, it would seem, was a familiar form of oath among the Jews: should, *if*, however, retain its ordinary meaning, then the imprecation, "*may I not be God, may I be a liar,*" or the like, is understood, and not expressed, through reverence for the person of God. The Apostle applies this Psalm to the faithful of his day; and in his reasoning, it regards the whole term of this life. These words of David are not confined to his own day. The man who at any time hardens his heart and becomes incredulous, will never enter into God's rest. In the Psalm "*my rest*" immediately referred to the land of Chanaan.

12. "Take heed, brethren," &c. From this salutary warning, it appears, that many among the Hebrews, yielding to the force of persecution and the errors of false teachers, were on the point of apostatizing from the faith. "The living God," designates the true God, opposed to false gods, who have no life or existence.

13. "*The deceitfulness,*" *i.e.*, the false allurements of sin, which, by withdrawing you from the true and substantial goods, and promising blessings and pleasures never to be realized, deceive you, and cause you to harden your hearts against the calls and impressions of divine grace. Hence, hardness and insensibility of heart are, oftentimes, the punishment of continuance in sin.

14. Let us encourage each other to perseverance, for our present advantages, our incorporation with Christ, will avail us only on condition of our perseverance. By "the beginning of his substance," or (as the Greek word, υποστασεως, means) *of his subsistence*, is meant, faith; which is *the root and foundation of all justification*—Council of Trent—and the source from which we acquire a new spiritual existence, as it were, a new subsistence and personality, having become "a new creature."—(Gal. vi. 15).

15. This verse is connected with verse 14, and explains "unto the end," by which is meant during our entire lives, signified by the words "*to-day;*" and he quotes the text to show that the same words are as applicable to them, who too may provoke God,

Text.

you shall hear his voice, harden not your hearts as in that provocation.

16. For some who heard did provoke : but not all that came out of Egypt by Moses.

17. And with whom was he offended forty years? Was it not with them that sinned, whose carcasses were overthrown in the desert ?

18. And to whom did he swear that they should not enter into his rest : but to them that were incredulous ?

19. And we see that they could not enter in, because of unbelief.

Paraphrase.

if you hear his voice, harden not your hearts, as in that provocation," in other words, during the course of our lives.

16. For, some of those who heard the voice of God, disobeyed, and by this disobedience provoked his wrath, but not all who left Egypt under the guidance of Moses (and, therefore, God was not angry with all).

17. With whom, then, was he angry for the period of forty years? Was it not with them who by their murmurs, incredulity, and temptation of God had sinned, whose bodies, in punishment thereof, were scattered unburied on the arid plains of the desert ?

18. But to whom did he swear in his wrath, that they should never enter his rest ? Was it not to those, who after witnessing so many prodigies of his power, still refused to believe his promises regarding this rest, and murmuring, wished to return to Egypt?—(Numbers, xiv. verses 1, 2, 3).

19. And from the SS. Scriptures we see the fulfilment of this decree. On account of their unbelief, they could not enter the land promised to them.

Commentary.

as it was to their sinful fathers in the time of David ; and that they should not imitate their fathers in irritating God ; otherwise, they would meet with a similar punishment of exclusion from a land of eternal rest, of which Chanaan was merely a figure.

16. "For some," &c.—"but not all," not Caleb nor Josue, nor the Levites, nor the women, nor those who had not attained their twentieth year at the numbering of the people (Numbers, i.) ; and those, though few compared with the disobedient, were still a great multitude, whose example they should imitate in hope of obtaining a like reward.

Mauduit has laboured, in a long and learned Dissertation, to prove the incorrectness of the Vulgate reading of this verse (16). He says it should be read interrogatively, and composed of two numbers, the first of which would be the answer to the second, as in the following verses, thus : *"quinam enim audientes exacerbaverunt ? Nonne universi qui ex Egypto cum Moyse profecti ?"* " For, who are they, who hearing provoked him ? Were they not all who left Egypt with Moses ?" The reasons of his supposition are these :—First, according to the present Vulgate reading, we cannot see the connexion of this verse with the preceding, nor its utility in reference to the scope of the Apostle, which is to deter the Hebrews from the crime of apostasy, by pointing out to them from this (Psalm xciv.), the punishment inflicted on their fathers, for the same crime. Now, the present Vulgate reading would, according to him, by no means serve this purpose ; it would rather weaken the argument by confining the murmurings and provocations to only some of the Jews of old. Secondly, it appears from the SS. Scripture (Numbers, xiv., and Exodus, xvii.), that all did murmur, in punishment of which, out of six hundred thousand men, only two, viz., Caleb and Josue, entered the land of promise. Now, the exception only of two from so large a number as six hundred thousand, would not warrant the Apostle to make the particular proposition, " for some did provoke." Moreover, he says the proposition, as it now stands in the Vulgate, is quite unmeaning, for after saying " some did provoke," it is idle to add, " not all."

In the next place, he establishes his own reading by showing that the Greek will admit of his view of the case ; for by placing the acute accent on τινες, instead of the grave τινὲς, it will mean "*quinam*," as in his version of the words. Again, he says αλλ᾽ ου, which is interpreted "*sed non*" in the Vulgate, sometimes means " *nonne*," and in proof of this, he adduces quotations from Lucian and Demosthenes. The Greek text, he asserts, is determined to either his meaning or the Vulgate reading by the accents, which were posterior to the translation of the Vulgate ; and hence, the present accentuation of the Greek does not militate against him, as it had been made, merely in accordance with what was generally supposed to be the meaning of the words. He

Commentary.

maintains that the reading of the two following verses favours his view of the case : for, in verses 16, 17, 18, is the passage from David analysed : in the 16th, is pointed out the extent of the "provocation," which, he says, includes all who left Egypt, but this was not imputed to the children under twenty on account of their age ; in the 17th, the meaning of "forty years," &c. ; and in the 19th, "to whom I swore," &c.

The chief defect in the foregoing reasoning would seem to be the absence of sufficient proof that "*all*" did provoke God. Because, if the murmurings of those who had not reached their twentieth year, and who were not included in the six hundred thousand numbered, were not imputable to them, owing to their age, as Mauduit himself admits, how could he say that "*all* who left Egypt did provoke him?" for, though all murmured, according to him, still, he admits that this murmuring was not imputed to all : and hence "*all*" did *not* provoke him. And in truth, those under the age of twenty did enter the Land of Promise ; it may, therefore, be held that all did not provoke him. The authority then of the Vulgate, and its conformity with almost every other version of SS. Scripture, as well as the universal agreement of all the ancients (Theophylact and St. Chrysostom excepted), together with the absence of proof on the part of Mauduit, that the Apostle, in the word "provocation," refers exclusively to the six hundred thousand included in the numbering of the people, render the Vulgate reading the more tenable. Mauduit has not proved that the Apostle regards those only who were numbered after attaining their twentieth year ; and hence, the greater part of his reasoning seems inconclusive. As to the apparent want of meaning, which he discovers in the Vulgate reading of the proposition, it may be said in reply, that the Apostle adds "but not all," to vindicate the divine menace ; for, it might be said, if *all* provoked, why not exclude *all* from his rest, but *all* did not provoke, and such as did not were admitted to his rest. And as to its effect on the Hebrews, they would be as strongly deterred by his saying "some provoked." For, from their knowledge of SS. Scripture, they knew that the word "some" comprised the greater number of those who left Egypt ; and, so, it was fully calculated to terrify them ; he also adds "not all ;" because neither the Levites, nor the women, nor the children were included.

In support of his view, Mauduit refers to (1 Cor. chap. x.) ; now, it would appear that the portion of Scripture referred to, if it prove anything, that is to say, if it refers at all to the occurrence of which there is question in this passage, proves against him ; for, it is said (1 Cor. x. 5), " But with the *most* of them God was not pleased." Whence it follows, that *all* did not provoke him ; for if so, he would be displeased, not merely with " the *most* of them," but with *all*.

CHAPTER IV.

Analysis.

The Apostle having, in the preceding chapter, referred to the exclusion of the incredulous Jews from the rest of God; in this, warns the Hebrews against the like incredulity, lest they too be excluded from God's eternal rest (1). And he points out the reason why the punishment of the Jews of old should inspire them with fear—viz., because the same announcement was made to both (2). There remains a rest to be entered by the faithful; and this rest is no other than that, on which God entered, after he finished the works of creation (3). The second part of this proposition, viz., that this rest is the same as that on which God entered after perfecting the works of creation, he proves (4, 5); the first part, viz., that a rest yet remains to be enjoyed by the faithful, is shown (6–10). He deters them from apostasy, by describing the qualities of him who is to avenge their infidelities (12, 13), and he consoles them for their past sins, by pointing out his great mercy and spirit of compassion (14, 15, 16).

Text.

1. LET us fear therefore lest the promise being left of entering into his rest, any of you should be thought to be wanting.

2. For unto us also it hath been declared, in like manner as unto them. But the word of hearing did not profit them, not being mixed with faith of those things they heard.

Paraphrase.

1. Let us, therefore, to whom the promise of entering into God's rest has been also made, under the influence of salutary fear, which the example of God's vengeance on our incredulous fathers is calculated to inspire, take care, lest by neglecting and disregarding this promise, any one be found excluded from this rest, through negligence or want of proper attention.

2. For unto us, as well as unto them, were the glad tidings of entering God's rest announced—a rest, however, of a higher order, the eternal rest of heaven, typified by theirs. But the promise which they heard proved of no avail to them, not being tempered with faith in the things which they heard.

Commentary.

1. "Let us fear," *i.e.*, under the influence of holy and salutary fear, warned by their example, let us take care, "lest the promise," &c.

2. For we also have been favoured with the glad tidings (in Greek, *evangelized*), as well as they. The Apostle refers to the same glad tidings in general; to the Jews of old was announced the tidings of the promised land; to us, of heaven, of which the promised land was but a figure. "But the word of hearing;" *i.e.*, the tidings heard by them and announced to them, "did not profit them," because it was not tempered with faith, conceived from the things which they heard; in a word, because it was not believed. In the words "mixed with faith," is contained an allusion to draughts, which prove injurious, unless well tempered and properly diluted; or rather to our daily nourishment, which proves of no use, unless properly digested and united with our substance. The word of God will prove of no avail to us, unless properly digested by faith, and by the serious consideration on the awful truths which it proposes—"*In meditatione mea exardescet ignis.*"—(Psalm). It is only by proper meditation on the truths of faith, that they will produce their proper effect, and enkindle within us the holy fire of charity and zeal for our own sanctification and that of others. In the ordinary Greek reading, the words run thus: μὴ συγκεκραμένος τῇ πίστει τοῖς ἀκούσασιν, *not mixed with faith in those who heard.* In this reading "mixed" refers to "word of hearing." The Vulgate follows this reading, "*Sermo......non admixtus fidei,*" &c. According to St. Chrysostom and others, the passage means: the word of hearing did not profit them, as they were not associated in faith, with those who heard or believed, viz, with

Text.

3. For we, who have believed, shall enter into rest: as he said: *As I have sworn in my wrath: If they shall enter into my rest;* and this indeed when the works from the foundation of the world were finished.

4. For in a certain place he spoke of the seventh day thus: *And God rested the seventh day from all his works.*

5. And in this *place* again: *If they shall enter into my rest.*

6. Seeing then it remaineth that some are to enter into it, and they, to whom it was first preached, did not enter because of unbelief:

Paraphrase.

3. For, we who have believed, shall enter into his rest—viz., that referred to in the 94th Psalm, from which, in his wrath, he swore he would exclude the unbelieving Jews; and this rest is no other than that upon which he himself entered, after perfecting the works of creation.

4. The latter part of the assertion—viz., that the rest into which we are to be admitted, is the rest on which God entered after perfecting the works of creation, is proved by comparing the words in Genesis, where it is said of the seventh day—the day on which the works of creation were finished—" *God rested on the seventh day from all his works ;*".

5. With these words spoken by God himself in the first person, " *They shall not enter into my rest.*" Now, what is the "*rest of God,*" spoken by a third person, as in Genesis, but "*my rest,*" when spoken by God in the first person of himself? Hence, the *rest of God,* after perfecting the works of creation, and "*my rest,*" (Psalm xciv.), are the same.

6. The first part of the assertion (verse 3), viz., that we who believe will enter on God's rest, or, that a rest yet remains to be enjoyed by the faithful, referred to in the words "*they shall not enter my rest,*" is proved thus: The fact of God's saying, "*they shall not enter into my rest,*" shows, it was a rest destined to be shared in by some, and enjoyed by creatures (otherwise exclusion from it could not be inflicted as a punishment, on the unbelieving Jews). Hence, as this rest cannot be rendered void, some persons must enter on it; and as those, to whom it was first announced, were excluded on account of their incredulity,

Commentary.

Caleb and Josue. This interpretation accords well with the reading of the *Codex Vaticanus*, μη συνκραομενους, which refers not to "the word of hearing," but to the persons, εκεινους. Hence, the promise may prove of no avail to us either, if, like them, we are incredulous regarding the divine promises.

3. The Jews might regard the reasoning of the Apostle in the second verse, in which is implied the liability, they too were under, of being excluded from God's rest in punishment of incredulity, as no way affecting themselves, now actually in the secure possession of the land of Chanaan, from which their fathers were excluded. Hence, the Apostle undertakes to prove in this verse (3), that there is another rest yet remaining for the faithful, different from the rest of Chanaan—no other than that on which God himself entered, after perfecting the works of creation. The proposition of the Apostle, then, is: there is a rest yet remaining for the faithful to enter, and this rest is that on which God himself entered after completing the works of creation. "And this, indeed, when the works from the foundation of the world were finished." The second part of the proposition is proved first in verses 4 and 5, by comparing what the SS. Scriptures say of God in Genesis—viz., that "*on the seventh day God rested from all his works,*" *i.e.,* he ceased to create any more new species, with the words of verse 5, "*my rest.*" And do they not refer to the same thing? for what do the words "*my rest*" mean, but that "*God rested,*" which, in Genesis, we are told, took place after he perfected the works of creation? "Shall enter," The Greek, εισερχομεθα, is the present tense.

6. He now proves the first part of the proposition viz., that a rest yet remains (*vide* Paraphrase).

Text.	Paraphrase.
7. Again he limiteth a certain day, saying in David, *to-day*, after a long time, so as it is above said : *To-day if you shall hear his voice : harden not your hearts.*	7. He again marks out a certain day. "*To-day*," by the mouth of David, after the lapse of a long interval between the issuing of the foregoing threat and the time of David saying, "*To-day if you shall hear his voice, harden not your hearts,*"
8. For if JESUS had given them rest : he would never have afterwards spoken of another day.	8. Which clearly proves that he does not refer to the rest in the land of Chanaan, for, if he referred to the rest of Chanaan into which Josue introduced their children, the Lord would have never fixed on another determinate future day for meriting this rest, upon which they would, in the supposition made, have long since entered already.
9. There remaineth therefore a day of rest, for the people of God.	9. Therefore, there remains a rest for the people of God, which in allusion to the rest of God, may be justly designated, a *Sabbath rest ;*
10. For he that is entered into his rest, the same also hath rested from his works as God did from his.	10. Being in its effects and results perfectly similar to the rest of God ; for, as God ceased from his labours and enjoyed a Sabbath, so will the just man cease from his labours on entering on the eternal rest of God.
11. Let us hasten therefore to enter into that rest : lest any man	11. As, therefore, this eternal rest remains for us, let us use our utmost exertions to enter on it, so that

Commentary.

7. To prove and notify to us, that this rest remains, it is, that God, after the lapse of four hundred years, since the Jews entered Chanaan, specifies a determinate fixed day by the mouth of David, on which they can merit an admittance to this rest, by not hardening their hearts.

8. The Jews were in possession of Chanaan, in the time of David. Hence, God in the words," *they shall enter into my rest*," regards not principally the rest in Chanaan ; for, if this rest into which the children of the incredulous afterwards entered under the guidance of *Jesus, i.e.,* Josue, were the rest referred to, the Lord would not have fixed on a certain, determinate day, in the time of David, for meriting admittance into this rest, of which they had been securely in possession, and their fathers before them, for four hundred years.

9. "Therefore," that is, from the foregoing it follows, that "there remaineth a day of rest (in Greek, σαββατισμος, *Sabbatism*) for the people of God." This is the conclusion of the above argument from verse 6. This rest he calls, a *Sabbatism*, in allusion to God's rest, after the works of creation.

10. He shows in this verse why the rest on which the just will enter, is properly called a *Sabbatism ;* for, a man who enters on God's eternal rest will cease from all further labour, as God ceased on the seventh day from his works, which is commonly understood to mean his having to create no more new species, the seeds of all future beings being contained in those already created. God even still works in his conservative Providence, which is, however, but a continuation of the first creation.

The interpretation of the passage adopted in the Paraphrase is the one given by Mauduit, and defended in an able dissertation. It makes the "*rest*" into which God promises to introduce the believers (for, the unbelievers were excluded in punishment of their infidelity), the same with the rest which the SS. Scriptures ascribe to God himself after perfecting the works of creation ; which rest of God is not past and gone—as some Commentators erroneously think—but remains, and shall remain permanently for eternity; to it our Redeemer himself appears to allude when inviting his elect to the ' kingdom prepared for them since the foundation of the world." If " *requies mea*," " *my rest*," be supposed different from "*requievit Deus*," " *God rested*" (verse 4), the entire passage will be involved in inextricable difficulties, and the introduction of some texts rendered quite unmeaning. Hence it is that Mauduit, in the able dissertation alluded to, maintains, that, throughout the entire passage, there is reference not to a twofold rest, but to the same rest of God.

11. He in this verse exhorts them to exert themselves, before all things, to merit an

Text.

fall into the same example of unbelief.

12. For the word of God is living and effectual, and more piercing than any two-edged sword : and reaching unto the division of the soul and the spirit, of the joints also and the marrow, and is a discerner of the thoughts and intents of the heart.

13. Neither is there any creature invisible in his sight ; but all things are naked and open to his eyes, to whom our speech is.

14. Having therefore a great high priest that hath passed into the heavens, JESUS the Son of God ; let us hold fast our confession.

Paraphrase.

no one will exhibit in his own person an example of infidelity, the consequences of which would be similar to the puishment of exclusion inflicted on the Jews of old.

12. For our infidelities will meet with the same punishment as theirs, since the eternal Word of God is living, active, and efficient to inflict punishment, no less destructive in execution than a two-edged sword ; able to penetrate and see into our hidden and private actions—to perceive their various shades of difference in point of merit or demerit ; nay, he discerns, and keenly distinguishes the very motives of our most private, hidden thoughts and actions.

13. Nothing, whether in heaven or on earth, is invisible in his sight, or concealed from him ; but all things are palpably open to him, and undisguisedly exposed to view. To whom we are to render an account ; or, concerning whom we are treating in this Epistle.

14. Having, then, a great High Priest, Jesus Christ, the Eternal Son of God, who entered not merely the Holy of Holies, like the Jewish Pontiff, but heaven itself, the true Holy of Holies ; let us firmly persevere in our Christian profession.

Commentary.

admission into this eternal rest, which remains for the faithful people of God to be enjoyed. They should, therefore, avoid the crime of infidelity and its punishment, similar to that of the Jews of old.

12. In this verse is assigned a reason why they should dread the just punishment due to their infidelity ; for, the "Word of God," *i.e.*, the Eternal Son of God, the judge of all, is "living," the source of all life and knowledge, and cannot be deceived. And "effectual ;" powerful and omnipotent. "More piercing than a two-edged sword ;" as destructive in execution as a two-edged sword, and as penetrating into the interior. "Reaching unto the division of the soul and the spirit ;" *i.e.*, able to see into our most hidden actions—these actions which proceed from the soul, either as the seat of sensation (*anima*), or reason (*spiritus*). "Of the joints also and the marrow ;" the minutest shades of difference in the degrees of merit or demerit in these hidden actions. "And is a discerner of the thoughts ;" what is most private of all, the very motives and intentions, &c.

13. "Neither is there any creature invisible in his sight." There is nothing which is not manifest to him. "But all things are naked and open to his eyes." The Apostle shows the omniscient knowledge of the word of God, by proving, first, in a *negative* form, that nothing is concealed ; and again, in an *affirmative* universal proposition, that "all things are naked, and open to his eyes." "Open," implies more than "naked ;" the latter conveys that every covering or veil is removed from the exterior of an object ; whereas, "open," conveys that the very interior is exposed to view. Some Commentators understand by the "word of God," the created revealed word, conveying the divine menaces. The opinion of those who refer it to the Eternal Word, seems the more probable ; for, it is only the Eternal Son of God, it is only a Divine Person, that could be well distinguished by the properties here referred to ; it is only of such a one could be predicated the personal actions, ascribed in these two verses by the Apostle to the "word of God." From the all-seeing knowledge and vigilant penetration of Christ, St. Paul wishes the Hebrews to infer, that their own private sins of infidelity will not escape his notice and future judgment.

14. He here passes to another subject, viz., the Priesthood of Christ ; and having in the foregoing chapters compared Christ with Moses, he now institutes a tacit comparison between him as High Priest, and Aaron, giving Christ the preference ; this

Text.

15. For we have not a high priest, who cannot have compassion on our infirmities : but one tempted in all things like as we are, without sin.

16. Let us go therefore with confidence to the throne of grace : that we may obtain mercy, and find grace in seasonable aid.

Paraphrase.

15. We should not despond on account of our past infirmities ; for, we have not a High Priest, who is insensible to, and incapable of, compassionating our infirmities ; but one who, having experienced all our infirmities, except sin, and having been tried like us, is most suited to have compassion on us.

16. Let us, therefore, approach with confidence the throne of grace, that we may obtain forgiveness of our sins, and find the abundance of divine grace, by which we may be aided in the time of necessity, *i.e.*, during our entire lives.

Commentary.

comparison is more fully and expressly instituted in the seventh chapter. His direct and express object in referring to his Priesthood here, is, after having inspired the Hebrews with the dread of him, as judge, to encourage and console them by the consideration of the confidence which his character as Priest is calculated to inspire.

15. Lest the majesty of so great a Pontiff should awe them, the Apostle says, he is capable of sympathizing in our infirmities, having been himself tried in all things like us, and having suffered all the miseries common to our nature ; He endured hunger, thirst, lassitude, fear, sorrow—nay, even death ; in a word, all the miseries common to our nature (sin excepted). He suffered these evils which are purely penal, and temptations from the world and from the devil, but not from the flesh.

16. Having, therefore, a most powerful High Priest, who is after penetrating the true Holy of Holies, heaven, and a most merciful Pontiff, who has experienced our common infirmities, let us with confidence approach the throne of grace, relying on such an intercessor, that we may obtain the merciful forgiveness of sin, and find the abundance of grace to aid us in the time of necessity, that is to say, while we are in this world ; for, we want the aid of grace during the entire course of our lives. "Seasonable aid." The Greek word for aid, βοηθεια, denotes assistance obtained, as the result of crying aloud for it.

CHAPTER V.

Analpsis.

Having introduced the subject of Christ's priesthood rather abruptly in verse 14 of the preceding chapter, the Apostle undertakes in this to show, from the distinguishing marks and qualities which characterised the Aaronic priesthood (for, it is to the Levitical priests, he refers in instituting this comparison), that Christ too was a priest, as possessing in a more excellent degree the qualities of the Aaronic priests. He first points out what these distinguishing qualities are (1–4), and next applies them to Christ. The first note or quality of a priest, viz., that he be a man, he forbears from applying to Christ, as requiring no application, it was a thing known to all. The second, viz., his offering gifts, &c., he defers for a fuller exposition, in a subsequent part of the Epistle. He treats of the two remaining notes, and applies them to Christ, commencing with the last He shows that Christ had as divine a call to the priesthood, as had Aaron or his sons (5, 6).

He then applies to him the third mark, viz., his capability of compassionating sinners, and referring to his infirmities and sufferings during his mortal life, he shows that he had an experimental knowledge of the arduous nature of obedience, and of the difficulty of avoiding sin (7, 8). And having attained consummate glory by suffering, he became to all his true followers, the cause of eternal glory, by the merits of his passion, which, as High Priest, he offered up in sacrifice for us, having been declared by his Father, a pontiff, according to the order of Melchisedech (9, 10).

Although he has much to say concerning this priesthood of Melchisedech, and its relation to Christ, he defers treating of it, until he first gives them further instruction in the principles of faith, which, notwithstanding the length of time they had been professing Christianity, they very much needed.

Text.

1. FOR every high priest taken from among men, is ordained for men in the things that appertain to God, that he may offer up gifts and sacrifices for sins ;

2. Who can have compassion on them that are ignorant and that err :

Paraphrase.

1. (In order to establish the assertion made— iv. 14, &c.—viz., that Christ is our high priest, whom we should approach with confidence, it is merely required to show that he has the qualities and marks of a high priest, such as we know to be necessary for a high priest of the Levitical order). Every high priest, then (of the Levitical order), is taken from among men, and is also constituted by his office in behalf of men, to manage their affairs with God, and to act as their mediator with him. This duty he principally discharges by offering up in sacrifice the gifts voluntarily presented, as also those prescribed by law.

2. He should also be possessed of a merciful, kind disposition to sympathize with and compassionate sin-

Commentary.

1. The first quality of a priest is to "be taken from among men," *i.e.*, to possess human nature. The second is derived from his office. which is to manage the affairs of men, which regard God. And the duty of this office is principally discharged in offering up sacrifice for men. "Gifts," voluntary oblations, presented by the people. "Sacrifices," those enjoined by law.

2. The third, is to have a merciful, kind disposition to sympathize with sinners.

Text.

because he himself also is compassed with infirmity;

3. And therefore he ought, as for the people, so also for himself, to offer for sins.

4. Neither doth any man take the honour to himself, but he that is called by God, as Aaron was.

5. So Christ also did not glorify himself that he might be made a high priest: but he that said unto him, *Thou art my Son, this day have I begotten thee.*

6. As he saith also in another place: *Thou art a priest for ever, according to the order of Melchisedech.*

Paraphrase.

ners of every description, bearing in mind that he himself is surrounded with the infirmities of our sinful nature.

3. And it is because of this sinful infirmity with which every priest is surrounded, that the Levitical priest is bound by the Law of Moses (Leviticus, iv. 3) to offer up sacrifice for his own sins, as well as for those of the people.

4. Again, no legitimate priest ever arrogates to himself, unauthorized, the honour of the priesthood; he alone is a true and legitimate priest who is called by God, as was Aaron.

5. Hence it was, that Christ did not take to himself the glorious quality of high priest; it was bestowed on him by his heavenly Father; for, it was the same who addressed him (Psalm ii.) as his natural son—"Thou art my son, this day have I begotten thee;"

6. That addressed to him also, as we find in another passage (Psalm cix.), these words—"Thou art a priest for ever, according to the order of Melchisedech;" and thus conferred on him the sacerdotal dignity.

Commentary.

The Greek for "have compassion," μετριοπαθειν, means, to be possessed of a capability of sympathizing with a degree of moderation, which would enable him to observe a dignified mean between harsh severity on the one hand, and misplaced clemency on the other. The latter defect is frequently abused by the perverse, in the further commission of sin. "Ignorant and err," extend to all sinners, even those who commit sins that are not the result of ignorance; for, they too are fit objects of compassion. "Because he himself is surrounded with infirmities." The Apostle refers to the infirmities of sin, as appears from the following verse. This note applies to Christ only as far as the sanctity and perfection of his nature will permit. Hence, it will apply to him, so far as regards the common infirmities and passibility of human nature, which he felt, but not so far as sin is concerned; nor is this required, because the liability to sin is a defect in a priest; and hence, follows the perfection of Christ's priesthood; since, he possesses all the good qualities, without any of the defects of other priests.

3. And it is on account of this sinful infirmity to which every priest is subject, that the Mosaic Law (Leviticus, iv. 3) prescribes, &c.

4. The fourth mark or character is a divine vocation, like that of Aaron and his successors. Aaron was called by God, and ordered to be consecrated (Levit. viii.) with the sacerdotal succession, secured to his family. Hence, the necessity of a vocation for the ecclesiastical state, as well as of ordination in the Church. Hence, schismatics and heretics cannot, without sin, perform ecclesiastical functions, not being deputed by God or his Church. Their call is the rebellious usurpation of Core, Dathan, and Abiron, to whom, as they are likened in ministering, so shall they be also in punishment, rather than the divine call of Aaron and his successors transferred to and perpetuated in the holy, Catholic Church.'

5, 6. He now applies these marks to Christ. He passes over the first altogether, it being evident that Christ was a man, and, therefore, needed no application. The application of the second he reserves for chapters vii., viii., ix., of this Epistle; the other two he here applies, commencing with the fourth. Christ did not arrogate to himself, unauthorized and uncommissioned, the glory of the priesthood. He was called to it by his Father. For, it was the same who said to him, "Thou art my Son," &c., that also said, as we find it in another place, "Thou art a priest," &c., and by the very fact of saying it, constituted him such. Christ, then, had the fourth mark of a true priest, viz., a vocation from God. And instead of saying, *God the Father* said to him, "Thou art a priest, &c., the Apostle says, "He who said to him,

Text.

7. Who in the days of his flesh with a strong cry and tears offering up prayers and supplications to him that was able to save him from death, was heard for his reverence.

8. And whereas indeed he was the Son of God, he learned obedience by the things which he suffered:

9. And being consummated, he became, to all that obey him, the cause of eternal salvation.

10. Called by God a high priest according to the order of Melchisedech.

11. Of whom we have much to say, and hard to be intelligibly uttered: because you are become weak to hear.

Paraphrase.

7. Who, when living here on earth, clad in weak, mortal flesh, but more especially while suspended on the cross, having offered up earnest prayers and suppliant entreaties to his Father with a strong cry and tears, to rescue him from the corruption of the tomb, was heard on account of the great reverence he had for his Father; or, on account of the great reverence in which the Father held this venerable high priest, his own beloved Son.

8. Nay, although he was the Son of God, he still vouchsafed to learn experimentally the difficulty of obedience from the sufferings which he underwent, in compliance with the will of his heavenly Father.

9. And having attained consummate glory by sufferings, he is become to all those who obey his precepts, the cause of eternal glory;

10. Being declared by God, a high priest according to the order of Melchisedech,

11. Concerning whom, and the relation of similitude which he bears to Christ, we have much to say, which is not suited to your capacity, and hard to be understood by you, owing to your slowness and indifference in learning the principles of the Christian faith.

Commentary.

thou art my son," &c., also said, "Thou art a priest," &c., to insinuate the superiority of Christ, as priest and Son of God at the same time, over Aaron or any other.

7. He now applies the third mark, viz., his capability of compassionating sinners. "Who in the days," &c........"with strong cry and tears," &c. This most probably refers to his prayers on the cross, and his cry, "My God, my God, why hast thou forsaken me," *i.e.*, do not forsake me. "To save him from death," *i.e.*, from remaining in death. It means, that he begged to be rescued from the grave; and so he was, three days after. "For his reverence." In Greek, απο της ευλαβειας, may be taken either actively, to denote the reverence which Christ had for the Father; or passively, to denote the Father's reverence for him. Calvin understands by the Greek word, ευλαβειας, not reverence, but fear of damnation. Christ had fallen into despair, according to the shocking blasphemous notions of this Arch Heretic.

8. "And whereas he was the Son of God." The Greek omits the words, "of God." "Whereas," in Greek, καιπερ, *although*. Having experienced the miseries of sinners (except sin), and knowing from experience the sacrifice of obedience, and the difficulty of avoiding sin, Christ is, then, perfectly capable of sympathizing with sinners.

9. "And being consummated" by suffering (ii. 10). "He became to all who obey him, *i.e.*, who observe his precepts, among which faith in him is reckoned "the cause of eternal salvation." And to show us how this was effected, viz. :—by his death on the cross—the Apostle refers to his sacerdotal character, in the following verse.

10. The sacrifice of the cross was not offered after the rite of Melchisedech; but the Apostle refers to his priesthood, merely for the purpose of showing that it was as priest he redeemed us, or became for us "the cause of eternal salvation." The sacrifice of the cross was offered after a new and extraordinary rite, different from that of Aaron and Melchisedech, holding a middle place between the cessation of the one, and the succession of the other.

11. "Of whom" may be also rendered "*concerning which*" priesthood of Melchisedech. "Because you are become weak." In Greek, νωθροι, *because you are slow or dull*. Perhaps, this slowness was occasioned by their faltering in faith. This was the place for the Apostle to treat of the priesthood of Melchisedech and its relation

Text.

12. For whereas for the time you ought to be masters; you have need to be taught again what are the first elements of the words of God : and you are become such as have need of milk, and not of strong meat.

13. For every one, that is a partaker of milk, is unskilful in the word of justice : for he is a little child.

14. But strong meat is for the perfect; for them who by custom have their senses exercised to the discerning of good from evil.

Paraphrase.

12. For, although, looking to the length of time you have been Christians, and had the gospel preached to you, you should be able to become teachers of Christianity, you yourselves still stand in need of being taught its first elementary principles, far from being able to profit by its abstruse and difficult truths, like children, who are to be nourished with milk, and not with solid food.

13. For the person requiring to be nourished with the milk of the plain truths of faith, is unable to profit by the doctrine of high perfection ; he is a mere infant in the faith.

14. But the perfect, *i.e.*, those who are practised in the principles of faith, and, by long habit, have their intellectual faculties improved and cultivated, so as to be able to understand more abstruse doctrines, and distinguish one point of faith from the other, are the only persons to be nourished with the solid food of such doctrines.

Commentary.

to Christ ; he defers doing so, however, until he first proposes further instruction ; and while reproaching them for their slowness, he excites their attention. Although he afterwards treats of the priesthood of Melchesidech, he does so only as far as it was necessary for his purpose, and omits many points regarding his sacrifice, which the Hebrews were not prepared to hear.

12. "The first elements ;" the idea is borrowed from children taught the alphabet. "Need of milk ;" another elucidation borrowed from babes, who require to be nourished with milk.

13. He explains what he means by the "perfect"—those who "by custom," &c., *i.e.*, the practice of learning, meditating, and submitting to the truths of faith, " have their senses exercised." " Senses " mean the external organs of the body, through which sensations are transmitted to the soul ; here, the idea is transferred to the soul, which the Apostle invests, as it were, with *internal* senses. The words refer to those who have their intellect cultivated and exercised to distinguish good from bad, Catholic truth from heresy. The idea is precisely the same as that conveyed—1st Epistle to Corinthians, chap. ii. 14, 15—where the subject is fully explained.

CHAPTER VI.

Analysis.

Having said, in the preceding chapter, that the Hebrews, considering the length of time they had professed the faith, should be teachers of Christianity, the Apostle expresses his resolve in this, to pass over, in consequence, these points of Christian doctrine, which formed the subject of instruction for adults, before their admission to baptism. The baptism, to which these matters subserve as a preparation, cannot be again repeated ; and hence, the inutility of treating of them (1–6).

He endeavours to terrify the Hebrews, against apostatizing from the faith, by the example of the accursed land (7, 8). He disclaims, however, the idea of applying to them the example, in its full extent (9\, and he assigns a reason of congruity for hoping, in their behalf, for the gift of perseverance (10).

He introduces the example referred to, solely with the view of animating them to fervent faith and to patient endurance, by which means alone, they could arrive at the inheritance, promised to the faithful and patient Abraham. He shows, that faith and patient endurance are necessary, in order to gain the promises of eternal life ; for, it was by means of these, Abraham, the model of true believers, obtained them (15). And, from the absolute, unconditional nature of the promises made to Abraham, confirmed by the solemn sanction of an oath, on the part of God, he shows that these promises cannot be rescinded, and are to extend to his faithful followers (13, 14).

He next assigns a reason why God swore by himself, and why he swore at all, in the case of Abraham ; he swore by himself, because he had no greater to swear by ; and the reason of his swearing at all was, to mark more strongly the absolute, unchangeable nature of his decree, regarding the transmission of Abraham's inheritance to his children and thus to confirm our hope—to which we fly in our afflictions—of entering the true Holy of Holies in heaven, whither our great Hight Priest, according to the order of Melchisedech, has preceded us.

Text.	Paraphrase.
1. WHEREFORE leaving the word of the beginning of Christ, let us go on to things more perfect, not laying again the foundation of penance from dead works, and of faith towards God,	1. Wherefore (since you ought to be now teachers of Christianity, looking to the length of time you have professed the faith, and the repeated instructions you have received—chap. v. 12), passing over the elementary principles of Christian doctrine, let us proceed to points of higher perfection and of a more abstruse nature, not again laying the foundation of the (baptismal) penance which purifies you from your disorderly habits, and disposes you for the remission of your sins in baptism and of faith in God—the first disposition for baptism ;

Commentary.

1. "Wherefore." Commentators are at a loss to trace the connexion of this word with the foregoing ; because the circumstance of the Hebrews being ignorant of the elementary truths of the Christian religion would seem to be no reason for omitting to treat of these, but the very reverse. Hence, it is usually connected with verse 12 of the preceding chapter (as in Paraphrase). Others connect it with the following verse 4, thus: "therefore...as it is impossible for those who were once enlightened," &c., verse 4, "leaving

Text.

2. Of the doctrine of baptisms, and imposition of hands, and of the resurrection of the dead, and of eternal judgment.

3. And this will we do, if God permit.

4. For it is impossible for those, who were once illuminated, have tasted also the heavenly gift, and were made partakers of the Holy Ghost,

5. Have moreover tasted the good word of God, and the powers of the world to come,

6. And are fallen away; to be renewed again to penance, crucify-

Paraphrase.

2. And of the doctrine regarding the threefold baptism (viz., of *water*, *blood*, and the *spirit*), and of the imposition of hands (in confirmation, conferred immediately after baptism), and of the general judgment, in which the dead arise and the eternal sentence is passed—

3. Omitting, I say, all instruction on these preliminary subjects, we shall, God willing, proceed to the more abstruse points of doctrine.

4. I shall pass over these preliminary points of instruction, because the *baptism* for which they serve, as a preparation, cannot be repeated ; for, it is impossible for those who are once enlightened by the sacramental grace of *baptism*, who have also tasted the heavenly gift (either in the Holy Eucharist, or, in the joy and peace of conscience, usually accompanying the grace of justification), and have been made partakers of the gifts of the Holy Ghost (either in confirmation, or in the infusion of sanctifying grace, which his gifts always accompany) ;

5. And have also enjoyed the consolations which the promises conveyed by God's holy word carry with them, and have received a foretaste of these joys, which the power of God is employed in bestowing in the life to come ;

6. And have fallen away from justice—it is, I say, impossible for them to receive, a second time, perfect

Commentary.

the word of the beginning of Christ," &c. (verse 1). "Let us go on to things more perfect ; " in these words is contained an allusion to the race course, to which it is quite usual with the Apostle, to compare our advancement in the way of Christian perfection, *v.g.*, (Philippians, iii. 14, &c.) "Not laying again the foundation," &c., *i.e.*, omitting a course of instruction, regarding baptismal penance and faith—both necessary preparatory conditions for adult baptism.

2. "The doctrine of baptisms," *i.e.*, regarding the threefold baptism, "*fluminis, flaminis, et sanguinis*," in which the catechumens were most likely instructed, in order to avail themselves of this knowledge, in case of necessity—or, the words may refer to the distinction between the Jewish purification and Christian baptism. "Imposition of hands," *i.e.*, the sacrament of confirmation, which, in ancient times, was conferred immediately after baptism. "And of the resurrection," &c., *i.e.*, the General Judgment, the two great leading features of which were the resurrection of the dead, and the solemn passing of the eternal sentence, "the eternal judgment."

3. He expresses his resolve to pass over these preliminary points, and proceed to the more abstruse and difficult. Any person who will take the trouble of comparing the conditions and preparation, required by the Council of Trent (SS. vi. cap. 6), for adult baptism, with the two first verses of this chapter, can have very little difficulty in concluding that the Apostle treats, in these two verses, of the dispositions required, at all times, in the Church for the baptism of adults.

4. He omits treating of these points, on account of their inutility, since the baptism to which they subserve cannot be repeated ; for, it is impossible for those who were once enlightened by the sacramental grace of baptism, which baptism is frequently called, *illuminatio*, by the Holy Fathers, "and tasted the heavenly gift," probably the Eucharist, to which, the Apostle, for well understood reasons, does not wish to refer in clearer terms.

6. "To be again renewed to penance," *i.e.*, by penance; the preposition "*to*" has often the meaning of "*by*." He speaks of that penance preparatory for baptism, referred to verse 1. The preposition "*to*" must have this meaning here, even in the opinion of those

Text.

ing again to themselves the Son of God, and making him a mockery.

7. For the earth that drinketh in the rain which cometh often upon it, and bringeth forth herbs meet for them by whom it is tilled: receiveth blessing from God.

8. But that which bringeth forth thorns and briars, is reprobate, and very near unto a curse, whose end is to be burnt.

Paraphrase.

renovation through that preparatory course of penance, by which they were before disposed for *baptism;* since, for this they should, a second time, crucify the Son of God (in order that his crucifixion would correspond with its reiterated type), and thus expose him to mockery.

7. (Far from hoping for baptismal renovation, such persons should rather dread the divine malediction), for, while the land which, after frequently drinking in the rain of heaven and bringing forth herbs useful for its cultivators, receives the benediction of full maturity from God;

8. That, on the other hand, which, after repeated culture and irrigation, only produces thorns and briars, is reprobate, very near to a curse, whose end is the fire. This is true of the Christian soul, according as it profits by, or neglects the grace of God.

Commentary.

who say the Apostle refers to renovation by the *sacrament* of penance, because it is *by* penance, even according to them, this renovation is effected. "Crucifying again," &c., for, *baptism* is a type of Christ's crucifixion (Rom. vi.) The Apostle may be referring to the sin of apostasy, in which case, "crucifying," &c., would literally refer to the crucifixion of Christ; for, by apostatizing, they would concur with the Jews who crucified him, again ratifying their act and approving of the mockery, to which the Son of God was exposed—or the words "crucifying," &c., may have been meant for no other purpose by the Apostle than merely to express the enormity of the sin of those, who abused the blessings bestowed on them. In the present Greek reading, instead of "to be renewed to penance," it is, παλιν ανακαινιζειν, *to renew again.* The Vulgate reading, however, is that of St. Chrysostom and of the best copies.

From the interpretation in the Paraphrase, it is clear, the words, "renewed again to penance," are made to refer to renovation by *baptism* and not by the *sacrament* of penance. The chief reason for preferring this opinion, before that which understands the passage of renovation by the *sacrament* of penance, is founded on the scope and reasoning of the Apostle, with which the interpretation now adopted perfectly accords. He omits instructing them in the points of doctrine, mentioned in verses 1, 2 (and these evidently refer to the dispositions required for *baptism*). Why? Because the baptism to which they subserve, as preparatory dispositions, cannot be iterated. Hence, their inutility, as *means,* their *end* being unattainable. The ordinary grounds commonly adduced for preferring the interpretation now adopted, such as the literal meaning of "impossible," the meaning of "renewed," although the word "again" gives it considerable force, are not conclusive on the subject; because, these could be easily explained away in the other interpretation. It is the scope of the Apostle, and the context, that seem quite conclusive in determining the probability of this opinion beyond that which understands the words of renovation by the sacrament of penance—an opinion also which has this advantage over the other, that it leaves not even the shadow of ground for the Novatian errors. The reasoning of the Apostle would not at all hold in the opinion of those who make "renewed to penance," refer to the *sacrament* of penance. What *vis consequentiæ* would there be in saying: I omit treating of these points of doctrine (1, 2), because, it is *very difficult* for those who have abused the many gifts of God to be reconciled by the *sacrament* of penance? It cannot, however, be concealed, that the subjoined example of the accursed land (verse 8), is greatly in favour of the interpretation of those who maintain that the Apostle refers, in verse 6, to the sacrament of penance. It runs very smoothly to say: it is extremely difficult for such persons to be reconciled by the *sacrament of penance;* for, instead of being fit subjects for reconciliation, they are like the barren and ungrateful earth, fitted only for the fire. Whereas, in the interpretation adopted in the Paraphrase, the impossibility of the reiteration for them of *baptism* is no reason why they should be accursed; since penance, the second

Text.

9. But, my dearly beloved, we trust better things of you, and nearer to salvation; though we speak thus.

10. For God is not unjust, that he should forget your work and the love which you have shewn in his name, you who have ministered, and do minister to the saints.

Paraphrase.

9. But far from intending to apply to you this example of the accursed land, dearly beloved brethren, we, from the firmest persuasion, hope better things regarding you, and things which promise salvation, although we refer to these terrible examples to deter you from ever becoming such.

10. This hope and confidence is grounded on the justice of God. For, God is not unjust that he should forget your good works, and especially the charity which you have shown in his name to the saints, to whose wants you have heretofore ministered, and do minister even to the present day.

Commentary.

plank on which to grasp, was still remaining for them. The scope of the Apostle is, however, a far stronger argument in favour of our interpretation, than this is in favour of the opposite. We have, therefore, only to accommodate the example of the accursed land (verse 8), to our interpretation, which can be done in this way : why speak of the impossibility of repeating baptism, since every, even available, means of reconciliation is become almost unavailing for men who, in punishment of their signal ingratitude, and their repeated resistance to grace, are become cast-aways of heaven—delivered over, as it were, to a reprobate sense—like the barren and unprofitable earth, only fitted for the fire. Or, it may be said, that the example is introduced for the mere purpose of inspiring the Hebrews with a salutary terror against the sin of apostasy, without intending it as a rigorous proof of anything that preceded ; for, the Apostle, in verse 9, disclaims any intention of applying it to the Hebrews.

9. He disclaims the intention of applying to the great body of the Hebrews, the frightful example of the accursed earth. He hopes better things, &c.

10. This confidence he grounds on the divine justice, which requires that God would reward their works of merit. He particularizes that of charity, towards the faithful poor in distress.

OBJECTION.—According to the Catholic doctrine of merit (Council of Trent, SS. vi. Can. 32), there are only three things which fall under strict merit, or, which a man can merit, as they say, *de condigno*, viz., an increase of sanctifying grace, eternal life, and the attainment of eternal life, if he die in grace : and although eternal life may, *hic et nunc*, be merited, it may still be lost, for want of final perseverance—for, although Catholics hold that if a man were to die instantly after performing a work meritorious of eternal life, he would have a right to eternal life, in virtue of the gracious promise and goodness of God ; still, they admit, that it is no way against the justice of God, that a man, *hic et nunc*, meriting eternal life, would afterwards fall away and not obtain it is the end ; because without any injustice whatever on his part, God can withhold the great and singular gift of final perseverance, which, strictly speaking, cannot be merited. Since, therefore, a man, who merited eternal life at some particular moment, can afterwards fall away, and be damned for want of final perseverance, which no man can *strictly merit*, and which, without injustice, God can withhold ; how can the Apostle say that, in the present instance, God would be unjust, if the Hebrews were not partakers of salvation ?

ANSWER.—In reply to the foregoing objection, it may be said, that St. Paul does not assert that God would be unjust if the Hebrews were not saved. He only expresses a firm hope and confidence (verse 9) that the case of the Hebrews is unlike that of the accursed land ; and this hope he grounds on the rewards which God, in his justice, is bound to bestow on their charity (verse 10). Now, among the things which God, in justice, is bound to give, is an increase of sanctifying grace, by which they can the more easily persevere, and thus obtain *de congruo*, *i.e.*, by persevering prayer, the great gift of final perseverance ; hence, the ground of the Apostle's confidence (verse 9) ; which is founded ultimately (verse 1), on God's justice, in bestowing an increase of sanctifying grace. If the Apostle were to argue directly (verse 10), from the strict justice of God,

Text.

11. And we desire that every one of you shew forth the same carefulness to the accomplishing of hope unto the end :

12. That you become not slothful, but followers of them, who through faith and patience shall inherit the promises.

13. For God making promise to Abraham, because he had no one greater by whom he might swear, swore by himself,

14. Saying : *Unless blessing I shall bless thee, and multiplying I shall multiply thee.*

15. And so patiently enduring he obtained the promise.

Paraphrase.

11. But, in order that you may securely avoid the fate of the accursed land, we anxiously desire that you exhibit the same fervour of charity unto the end of your lives, until hope is filled up and is succeeded by its term, fruition.

12. And that you become not remiss nor indolent, but imitators of those who, by faith and patient long-suffering, and endurance, inherit the promises of eternal life.

13–15. And as a proof that it is by faith and patience the promises are to be obtained, I will instance the case of Abraham, the father of all believers who had faith, as all know, and who by patience obtained the promise.

13, 14. And that this promise made to Abraham was *absolute* and *unconditional*, is clear, from the fact of God swearing by himself—he had no greater by whom to swear—

14. That he would surely bestow on him the abundance of his benediction, and would multiply his seed exceedingly.

Commentary.

he would not only say, "we trust better," &c., but *we are altogether certain* (verse 9). "And the love," the Greek has, καὶ τοῦ κόπου τῆς ἀγάπης, *and the la our of love ;* but the word, *labour,* is now generally rejected by critics ; it was probably introduced from 1 Thess. i. 3.

11. The Apostle in this verse points out the condition, upon which they may have a claim on the strict justice of God, viz., perseverance to the end, in the performance of the same good works of charity.

12. He anxiously desires and wishes that they would not become remiss, but rather, by faith in the promises of God, and the patient endurance of adversity (the Greek for "patience," μακροθυμίας, means, *long suffering*), become faithful imitators of the saints of old—as well as of those to whose wants they were ministering—who, by these very same means, *i.e.,* faith and patience, were heirs of the promises of eternal life.

13. He adduces the example of Abraham, to prove that it is by faith and patience, the promises of God regarding eternal life, to which he refers, were to be obtained. That Abraham had faith, was a matter so well known to the Hebrews, that the Apostle supposes it here, and merely asserts (verse 15), that he obtained the promises by patient endurance and long suffering. Hence, as Abraham is our model, we must obtain the promises on the same conditions on which he obtained them, viz , by faith and patience. The Apostle, in this reasoning, supposes that the promises to which he refers were of such an *absolute* nature, as that they were to be transmitted to us, and not merely *conditional,* liable to be rescinded. Hence it is that he refers to the mode in which God made this promise, viz., by interposing the solemn sanction of an oath, swearing by himself for want of a greater by whom to swear.

14. Saying (Genesis, xxii. 16) : " By myself have I sworn…I will bless and multiply thy seed—and in thy seed shall all the nations of the earth be blessed." " *Unless blessing I will bless thee.*" *i.e.,* certainly, ' *blessing I will bless thee ;* ' he repeats the words " *blessing*" and " *multiplying* " to express the abundance of his benedictions—or, " unless I bless thee," &c., *may I not be God,* or the like, and then the imprecation is suppressed from reverence for the name of God. However, the former meaning of " *unless* " is more conformable to the Greek, ἦ μήν, and to the Septuagint version of Genesis ; an l it is from the Septuagint version of the Old Testament that St. Paul takes his quotations in this Epistle.

15. The sense of the passage may, perhaps, be more clearly conveyed by transposing this verse and placing it a little in advance, in immediate connexion with the first words of verse 13 (as in Paraphrase). The Apostle adduces the example of

Text.

16. For men swear by one greater tha themselves : and an oath for confirmation is the end of all their controversy.

17. Wherein God, meaning more abundantly to shew to the heirs of the promise the immutability of his counsel, interposed an oath :

18. That by two immutable things, in which it is impossible for God to lie, we may have the strongest comfort, who have fled for refuge to hold fast the hope set before us.

19. Which we have as an anchor of the soul, sure and firm, and which entereth in even within the veil :

Paraphrase.

16. God swore by himself, because he had no greater to swear by, as men have, when they invoke God as a witness, and the reason why he swore at all, was to accommodate himself to the ways of men, among whom an oath is used to confirm the truth and terminate every controversy.

17. Therefore, wishing to mark more strongly the *absolute* and unchangeable nature of the decree in question, regarding the transmission of the promise to the sons of Abraham, who were to be its inheritors, God interposed, and added to the promise the solemn sanction of an oath.

18. This he did in order that by two immovable things, viz., his absolute promise and oath, neither of which is it possible for God to belie, neither one nor the other of which he can fail to fulfil, we would feel the greatest consolation and encouragement when (knowing that the promise is not rescinded) we fly from the difficulties and crosses of life, to grasp and lay hold on the hope of future blessings, in store for us.

19. Which hope is the sure anchor of the soul to keep it fixed and firm amidst the adversities of life ; nor will it part with us until it leads us to fruition, in the kingdom of heaven,

Commentary.

Abraham to prove that it is by faith and patience we are to inherit the promises ; and before he asserted that it was by faith and patience (v. 15), Abraham obtained them, he anticipates a difficulty which might at once be started, viz. :—What has the promise made to Abraham, or his mode of obtaining it, to do with us ? The Apostle refers to the oath of God to prove that it has reference to us. For, the promise itself regards the multiplication of his posterity (Gen. xxii.), and the benediction of all the tribes of the earth in his seed, which the Apostle interprets (Gal. iii.), to refer to Christ. It, therefore, regards us, and the oath on the part of God proves it to be *absolute* and not liable to be rescinded.

"And so patiently enduring he obtained the promise ;" he obtained it in himself and in his carnal descendants, but especially the spiritual part of it is fulfilled now in the blessings bestowed on his spiritual children ; and, in order to obtain this blessing, Abraham had to endure patiently many hardships.

16. The Apostle, in this verse, assigns a reason why God swore by himself, and secondly, why he swore at all. Properly speaking, it could not be called an oath on the part of God. For, an oath supposes the calling to witness of a greater, and God having no greater to call to witness, could not, therefore, strictly speaking, be said to swear.

17. Some decrees of God have a conditional object ; and may, therefore, be rescinded and may never come to pass. But the promise in the present case is *absolute*, which the Apostle is showing all along from verse 13, by pointing to the solemn sanction of an oath on the part of God confirming it, and therefore, it will be fulfilled and obtained by those in whose favour it was made, *i.e.*, by "the heirs of the promise."

18. To his promise God added the sanction of an oath, which proves it to be of a nature absolute and unconditional, "that by two immovable things," &c. (*vide* Paraphrase). If the promise were only conditional and not absolute, it might be rescinded for want of compliance with the required conditions on the part of men ; and we would, therefore, have no such consolation in our hope.

19. "Hope is the sure and firm anchor of the soul," because it keeps the soul firm and unmoved, and preserves her from being tossed about or sunk into despair, by the storms and tempests of adversity.

"And which entereth in even within the veil ;" hope, though retaining the soul

Text.

20. Where the fore-runner JESUS is entered for us, made a high priest for ever according to the order of Melchisedech.

Paraphrase.

20. Whither Christ has gone before us as precursor ; and this, in quality of eternal High Priest, according to the order of Melchisedech.

Commentary.

unmoved against the influence of adversity, still retards not her progress towards her destined haven of rest, the true Holy of Holies of heaven, of which the Jewish Holy of Holies, divided from the *sanctum*, or *Holy*, by a veil, was a mere figure. And the Apostle alludes to this veil of the Holy of Holies, to show us in what capacity Christ entered heaven, viz., as high priest, for the high priest alone could enter the *sanctum sanctorum.*

OBJECTION.—If hope be a certain anchor, may not all be certain of salvation? Hope is certain, in regard to God, uncertain, in regard to us, because no one, short of a revelation, can be absolutely certain, that he will comply with the required conditions; and this is conformable to the providence of God in the present order of things, according to which, "no one can know whether he is deserving of love or hatred," and all are commanded to "work out their salvation with fear and trembling."

Besides, supposing, that hope carried with it the certainty of perseverance, who can be certain that he has that hope?—and, without this certainty, a man is always uncertain of salvation.

CHAPTER VII.

Analysis.

The mention of Melchisedech in the last verse of the preceding chapter, affords the Apostle an opportunity of reverting to the subject of his priesthood, from which, after merely alluding to it (chap. v.), he digressed with a view of inspiring the Hebrews with a salutary fear of relapsing into sin, particularly into the hateful crime of apostasy (chap. vi.) In the first three verses of this chapter, he points out the mystic relation which Melchisedech bore to Christ, in his name, place of residence, office, and genealogy (1–3).

In the next place, he proves the superiority of the priesthood of Christ over that of Aaron, and grounds this superiority on two circumstances: 1st, on the circumstance of Abraham giving Melchisedech, who was a mere type of Christ, tithes out of all his spoils, both for himself and all his descendants, and consequently, for Levi, who was then in Abraham's loins, thus acknowledging the superiority of Melchisedech, as priest, over Aaron. The Apostle notes one feature of this decimation on the part of Abraham, as still more expressive of his inferiority; viz., its perfect voluntariety, without the requirement of any law to enforce payment, as in the case of the Levitical tithes. 2ndly, he founds the superiority on the circumstance of Melchisedech blessing Abraham, which the Apostle regards as an undoubted proof of this superiority of the former, as as priest, over the latter (4–10).

The Apostle proves, in the next place, the translation and total abrogation of the priesthood of Aaron. His first argument is founded on the difference of tribe to which he belonged, to whom God promised an eternal priesthood (11–14). His next argument in proof of the translation of the Aaronic priesthood is founded on the difference of the chiefs of both orders (15). His next argument is founded on the difference of the ordination and fundamental rules of both orders (16, 17). The Apostle then assigns the causes of the abrogation of the Levitical priesthood, as also of the entire Mosaic Law (18, 19). He adduces another proof of the superiority of Christ's priesthood over that of Aaron, grounded on the difference of ceremonies employed by God in the institution of both (21, 22). A further proof of the superiority of Christ's priesthood is derived from its eternal duration, and its incommunicability, by way of succession, to any other (23, 24). Another proof of the same is derived from the superior qualities of Christ, as Pontiff, over the Jewish High Priests.

Text.

1. FOR this Melchisedech *was* king of Salem, priest of the most

Paraphrase.

1. This Melchisedech then (according to whose order Christ was High Priest), was king of the city

Commentary.

1. One of the chief grounds on which the false teachers mainly relied, and one of the principal motives artfully advanced by them, for seducing the Hebrew converts from the faith, under the pressure of persecution, was the consideration of the efficacy and permanency of the priesthood of Aaron. Faith, it was alleged, might be an easier mode of obtaining justification; but, it was not indispensable; since, the Patriarchs and just of old had been justified without it, through the aids administered by the different parts of the Mosaic law, and among the rest, by the ministrations of

Text.

high God, who met Abraham returning from the slaughter of the
kings, and blessed him :

2. To whom also Abraham
divided the tithes of all : who first
indeed by interpretation, is king of
Justice : and then also king of Salem,
that is, king of peace,

3. Without father, without mother,
without genealogy, having neither
beginning of days nor end of life,
but likened unto the Son of God,
continueth a priest for ever.

4. Now consider how great this
man is, to whom also Abraham the
patriarch gave tithes out of the
principal things.

Paraphrase.

of Salem, and priest of the Most High God, the same
who went out to meet Abraham after the slaughter of
the hostile kings (Genesis, xiv. 17, &c.), and, as Priest,
blessed him :

2. To whom Abraham also paid tithes out of all his
spoils ; this same Melchisedech, looking to the etymology of the term, signifies "king of justice " (a title
admirably suited to Christ, his antitype) ; the words
"king of Salem," also signify "king of peace " (a title
equally applicable to Christ).

3. Without father, without mother, *i.e*, neither his
father, nor his mother, nor genealogy, is mentioned
in SS. Scripture. (Christ has neither a father on
earth, nor mother in heaven, and his "genealogy
who shall declare ?") Neither have we any account of
his birth, nor of his death ; hence, he is said to have
neither beginning of days nor end of life. Our Lord
neither had a beginning nor will he have an end. In
all these things, Melchisedech has been a type of the
Son of God ; but his resemblance to Christ is particularly marked in the eternal duration of his priesthood—
respecting the beginning and end of which the Scriptures are equally silent.

4. Consider, then, how great a man this Melchisedech must have been, from the fact that Abraham, though
a patriarch and the father of nations, gave him, in
tithes, the most valuable part of his spoils, which is an
acknowledgement of superiority.

Commentary.

the Aaronic priesthood. The Apostle, therefore, employs the four following chapters
in showing the inefficacy, the inferiority, the total abrogation of the Aaronic priesthood
and its sacrifices, together with the eternal duration and absolute superiority of the
priesthood of Christ and his sacrifice. He devotes the 11th chapter to proving, that it
was by faith, and not by the Sacrifices of the Old Law, the Patriarchs and just of old
were sanctified.

"For this Melchisedech ;" as if he said, I now revert to the subject of Melchisedech's
priesthood, to which I have briefly adverted already (chap v.) "Salem" most probably
refers to Jerusalem, of which Melchisedech was king. "Priest of the most high God,"
and not of the idols of the Chanaanites. "Who met Abraham," &c. The Apostle
refers to the history recorded, Genesis, xiv. 17, 18, &c. He dwells on these two
circumstances, viz., the giving of tithes, and the receiving a blessing, as expressive of
Abraham's inferiority.

2. "Melchisedech" is compounded of *Malak*, a king, and *Sadek*, justice. "Salem,"
signifies "peace."

3. It is not difficult to see how, in the etymology of his name, and of the place over
which he ruled ; in the omission of his genealogy, which was passed over in Scripture for mystical reasons ; in the omission of all mention of his birth and death,
designed by the Holy Ghost for the purpose of typifying eternity, as well as in the
omission of the beginning and end of the exercise of his priesthood, Melchisedech was
a figure of Christ ; and, as such, assimilated to him. He bore as near a resemblance to
Christ, as the type could bear to the thing typified. But it is in the eternal duration
of his priesthood, regarding the beginning and end of which the Scripture is silent, that
this resemblance is particularly marked.

4. From the superiority of Melchisedech, as priest, over Abraham, which the
Apostle proves here, he wishes to establish the superiority of the priesthood of Christ,
according to the order of Melchisedech, over the priesthood of Aaron. The Apostle

Text.

5. And indeed they that are of the sons of Levi, who receive the priesthood, have a commandment to take tithes of the people according to the law, that is to say, of their brethren : though they themselves also came out of the loins of Abraham.

6. But he whose pedigree is not numbered among them, received tithes of Abraham, and blessed him that had the promises.

7. And without all contradiction, that which is less, is blessed by the better.

8. And here indeed, men that

Paraphrase.

5. And the very circumstances of this decimation on the part of Abraham, render it still more expressive of his inferiority. For, how do such of the sons of Levi as enjoy the priesthood, that is to say, the family and descendants of Aaron, receive the tithes ? Is it as voluntary offerings? No—but, they must have recourse to the law to enforce their rights. From *whom?* Is it from strangers? No—but from their own brethren, over whom their claims to superiority are derived solely from the payment of tithes and the exercise of the priesthood ; for, in point of descent, they are their equals, having been, as well as they, descended from Abraham.

6. But Melchisedech, a mere stranger, who had no tie of consanguinity with Abraham, received tithes from him, as quite a voluntary matter, without any legal claim whatever ; and besides, he blessed this great man to whom were made so many splendid and magnificent promises.

7. Is not this an undoubted proof of his superiority over Abraham ? for, beyond all question, the man who solemnly and, *ex officio*, blesses another is, so far, his superior.

8. Another great point of difference between the

Commentary.

dwells upon two points, the payment of tithes by Abraham to Melchisedech, and the receiving his benediction, as a priest, to prove Abraham's inferiority.

5. The Apostle puts forward the mode in which Abraham paid tithes, that is to say, voluntarily, and also the fact of Melchisedech being to him a perfect stranger, as adding still greater weight to this acknowledgement of inferiority to Melchisedech, as priest, and contrasts it with the mode in which the Aaronic priests received tithes ; they had the law to enforce their rights ; and they received tithes, not from strangers, but from their own brethren, over whom, although in point of birth their equals, having been in common with them descended from Abraham, the very payment of tithes and the exercise of the priesthood established their superiority. (This is the meaning adopted in the Paraphrase). Others, among whom is A'Lapide, say, that this verse is intended by the Apostle to prove, that the very fact of Melchisedech receiving tithes from Abraham is a proof of his superiority, as a priest, just as the legal enactment enforcing the payment of tithes to the Aaronic priests by their brethren, was a proof of the superiority of the former, though in other respects, the latter are perfectly their equals, having come forth from the loins of Abraham, as well as they.

6. But the very fact of Melchisedech being a perfect stranger, and having no legal claims for tithes on Abraham, proves still more his superiority over the latter, since Abraham would not have paid a stranger tithes, if he did not acknowledge his eminent superiority in this respect.

7 At least in the time of the Apostle, it was regarded as an undoubted mark of superiority, in one man to bless another. Upon this circumstance, he lays great stress, as a proof of the superiority of Melchisedech over Abraham.

8 There is another circumstance in the payment of tithes by Abraham, worthy of notice. According to the disposition of the Mosaic law, the Levitical priest was entitled to tithes, only during the term of his natural life ; and, therefore, only from his contemporaries ; whereas, in the case of Melchisedech, the very omission of his death in sacred Scripture, tacitly represents him as perpetually living ; and contains also a silent mystery, in which it is intended to teach us, that he is in a condition for receiving tithes, not only on the occasion referred to, not merely from Abraham himself ; but also from all included in the person of Abraham, even in after generations. From

Text.	Paraphrase.

Text.

die, receive tithes : but there he hath witness, that he liveth.

9. And (as it may be said) even Levi who received tithes, paid tithes in Abraham :

10. For he was yet in the loins of his father, when Melchisedech met him.

11. If then perfection was by the Levitical priesthood (for under it

Paraphrase.

payment of tithes on the part of Abraham and that made to the Levitical priesthood is this : that in the case of the Levitical priest, the term for paying him tithes is confined to his natural life, and therefore, his contemporaries alone are bound to him ; whereas, in the case of Melchisedech, the very silence of Scripture respecting his death represents him, as perpetually living ; and therefore, in a condition to receive tithes from all succeeding generations.

9. So that we may say, that Levi himself, though entitled to receive tithes from his brethren, paid tithes to Melchisedech, on this occasion.

10. For he was in the loins of his father Abraham, and consequently, destined to be one of his carnal descendants, at the time Melchisedech met him.

11. If, then, true sanctification, the reconciliation of man with God, were effected by the Levitical

Commentary.

the eternal duration of Melchisedech's priesthood the Apostle infers its superiority over that of Aaron.

9. Levi paid tithes ; for, Abraham on that occasion represented his posterity.

10. And consequently he represented Levi, who was to be descended of him.

OBJECTION.—Was not Christ also in the loins of Abraham and carnally descended from him ? Did he too not pay tithes to Melchisedech, and therefore, as well as Aaron, was he not inferior to him ?

The reply to this is, that although Christ was descended of Abraham ; still, he was born according to a new generation and after a miraculous way, wherein he was exempt from the least stain of sin ; and consequently had no tithes to pay, the payment of which supposed sins to be expiated ; for, he had no connexion with the spiritual disorders of the people, on account of which the priestly order entitled to tithes was established among men. From all this is to be inferred how much Christ must be superior to Levi or Aaron, Melchisedech, a mere type of Christ, being superior as priest to Abraham, who himself was a priest of an inferior order.

But how does the superiority of Christ over Aaron follow from his superiority over Abraham ? Was not the priesthood of Aaron divinely instituted and sanctioned specially by God, in a way superior to anything recorded in Scripture of the priesthood of Abraham ? Hence, although superior to Abraham, as priest, it would by no means seem to follow, that Melchisedech was superior to Aaron.

In reply it is held, that the priesthood of Abraham did not differ from that of Aaron, although the mode of exercising it was different in the time of both. In the time of Abraham, it was exercised by the heads of families, and transmitted successively to the next first-born. In the time of Aaron, the same priesthood transmitted from Abraham was, for the more orderly discharge of the priestly duties, and the better expression of unity, confined to the tribe of Levi. But, the priesthood of both was the same.

The Apostle omits all mention of the sacrifice of Melchisedech and its typical relation to the sacrifice of Christ offered at the last supper, after the ritual of Melchisedech ; because, allusion to it would not serve his purpose in showing the superiority of the priesthood of Melchisedech over that of Aaron ; for, the Levitical victims of choice animals were as dignified as bread and wine, the oblation of Melchisedech. Moreover, until the Hebrews rightly understood the *bloody* offering of Christ upon the cross, they were not in a condition to understand the *unbloody* offering made of him on the altar ; and the Apostle did not wish to expose the sacred mysteries to profanation, by a distinct and express reference to this latter offering here. This same prudence was afterwards observed by the Church, in enforcing the discipline of the Secret.

11. The Apostle, having established the superior excellence of the priesthood of Christ over that of Aaron, now proceeds to refute the error of the Hebrews regarding the efficacy and permanency of the Aaronic priesthood In the supposition, that the

Text.

the people received the law) what further need was there that another priest should rise according to the order of Melchisedech, and not be called according to the order of Aaron.

12. For the priesthood being translated, it is necessary that a translation also be made of the law.

13. For he, of whom these things are spoken, is of another tribe, of which no one attended on the altar.

14. For it is evident that our Lord sprung out of Juda ; in which tribe Moses spoke nothing concerning priests.

15. And it is yet far more evident :

Paraphrase.

priesthood (and what I say of the priesthood, I wish to extend to the Mosaic law also, given to the people in connexion with the priesthood. which it was designed to uphold and regulate), what further necessity would there be for another priesthood according to the order of Melchisedech, and not according to the order of Aaron ?

12. I have connected the law with the priesthood ; because such is their inseparable connexion, that the priesthood being transferred, so must the law also, as it was principally employed in regulating the priestly functions.

13. (The Lord did institute a priesthood of a different order from that of Aaron), for, the person to whom are directed the words regarding the priesthood after the order of Melchisedech (Psalm cix.), is not of the tribe of Levi, but of a tribe, no one belonging to which ministered at the altar.

14. For it is evident—from the genealogical tables extant, as well as from the universal admission of all— that Christ our Lord is of the tribe of Juda, to which none of the precepts regarding the exercise of the priesthood was addressed by Moses.

15. And this translation of the Aaronic priesthood

Commentary.

priesthood of Aaron caused justification, the institution of another order of priesthood would be quite useless ; hence, as God instituted another order of priesthood, after the rite of Melchisedech, this must not be useless ; and consequently the priesthood of Aaron did not confer justice. ("For under it the people received the law"). These words are added by the Apostle, with the view of showing the connexion between the law and the priesthood to be so close, that the abrogation of the one would involve that of the other, as in the following verse.

12. This verse may be connected with the preceding in another way besides that in Paraphrase, by giving "for," the meaning of, *but.* "*But* the priesthood being translated," &c., and, then, the verse will have no other connexion, save merely to express incidentally, the abrogation of the entire ceremonial law, which the translation of the priesthood involves.

13. In the foregoing reasoning, verse 11, the only thing that required proof, or that could for a moment be called in question, was, that God did institute a priesthood of a different order from that of Aaron—and this the Apostle now proved from the fact of the person to whom the words were directed, "Thou art a priest for ever, according to the order of Melchisedech" (Psalm cix.), belonging to quite a different tribe from that of Levi ; to a tribe, out of which no one had hitherto ministered at the altar.

14. "Concerning priests." The Greek is, περὶ ἱερωσύνης, *concerning priesthood.* The genealogical tables extant in the days of the Apostle made it clear, that Christ was of the tribe of Juda, and the Jews themselves admitted, that the 109th Psalm regarded the Messias. Hence, the priesthood of Melchisedech belongs to a different tribe from that of Levi, and is, therefore of a different order.

OBJECTION.—Was not Christ descended of Levi, his mother being cousin of Elizabeth, one of the daughters of Aaron ?

The answer is quite easy. Mary might be cousin to Elizabeth, without a drop of Levi's blood flowing through her veins. Because a Levite might have married the mother of Elizabeth, of the tribe of Juda ; Mary and Elizabeth would thus be cousins. Again, Christ should be paternally descended from Levi, to be qualified for discharging the priestly functions.

15. The Apostle founds another argument in favour of the translation of the Jewish priesthood, on the difference of the chiefs, and the fundamental rules of both orders.

Text.

if according to the similitude of Melchisedech there ariseth another priest,

16. Who is made not according to the law of a carnal commandment, but according to the power of an indissoluble life :

17. For he testifieth : *Thou art a priest for ever, according to the order of Melchisedech.*

18. There is needed a setting aside of the former commandment, because of the weakness and unprofitableness thereof :

19. (For the law brought nothing to perfection) but the bringing in of a better hope, by which we draw nigh to God.

Paraphrase.

will become still more evident, if there arise another priest, after the likeness of Melchisedech,

16. Who is not regulated in his priestly office or power by the rules or law of the carnal mandate, attaching the priesthood to carnal descent and succession ; but who is established in the priestly dignity, by the power or efficacy of an immortal life ; which excludes the idea of succession.

17. Now, that there was to arise another priest, or rather the chief of another priesthood different from Aaron, also admitting of no succession, is clear from Psalm cix., wherein he is said to be "a priest according to the *order of Melchisedech*," therefore, distinct from *Aaron*, and "a priest *for ever ;*" therefore, having no successor.

18. The Levitical priesthood, together with the entire ceremonial law, was abrogated, because of their infirmity and inutility for the purpose of justifying man.

19. For, the law brought nothing to the perfection of justifying man ; it served, however, for another end—it served as an introduction to a covenant, which holds out better hopes, in pledge of which hope, it abundantly ministers grace, which brings us nearer to God.

Commentary.

(The preceding argument is founded on the difference of tribe, from that of Levi). "If, according to the similitude of Melchisedech." The Apostle uses "similitude," in preference to "order" of Melchisedech, to show us, that, although according to the Psalmist, Melchisedech was a type of Christ, and Christ a priest, according to *his* order ; still, this consisted merely in the likeness of Melchisedech's priesthood to that of Christ, the priesthood of Christ being in reality of a more exalted character.

16. "Carnal commandment," according to which the sons of Aaron, by their descent from him, are made priests, one succeeding the other. "According to the power of an indissoluble life," *i.e.*, by the divine power, which grants him immortal life, excluding all grounds for succession. In these words, is contained an allusion to Melchisedech's apparent perpetuity (verse 8).

17. That the chief of this order is different from Aaron, and that there is no succession of chiefs, one to another—one of the fundamental rules of the order of Aaron being, that one high priest was to succeed another when defunct—are both proved from Psalm cix. (*vide* Paraphrase). This is all true of Christ. He is a priest according to the order of Melchisedech, in the sense already assigned. Melchisedech's priesthood was a type of his. Secondly, he has no successor, all other priests are only his vicars and the dispensers of his mysteries.

18. The Apostle, having proved the institution of a priesthood, altogether different from that of Aaron, proceeds to account for the abrogation of the Levitical priesthood ; under it, he includes the entire law, on which account he (verses 11 and 12) shows the inseparable connexion of both. They were abrogated, not because they were evil, but because they were weak and incapable of justifying man.

19. "The law brought nothing to the perfection," of justifying man—a matter which the Apostle abundantly proves in his Epistles to the Romans, Galatians, &c. But it may be said, if the law be thus infirm and useless, why did God institute it? The Apostle replies, that though useless for the purpose referred to—a purpose for which it was never intended—it served another end, it served as an introduction to a covenant or law, &c. (*vide* Paraphrase).

Text.

20. And inasmuch as it is not without an oath, (for the others indeed were made priests without an oath;

21. But this with an oath, by him that said unto him: *The Lord hath sworn, and he will not repent thou art a priest for ever) :*

22. By so much, is JESUS made a surety of a better testament :

23. And the others indeed were made many priests, because by reason of death they were not suffered to continue :

24. But this, for that he continueth for ever, hath an everlasting priesthood,

25. Whereby he is able also to

Paraphrase.

20. And inasmuch as Jesus was not made a priest without an oath (the Levitical priests were constituted without an oath) ;

21. But Christ was constituted priest with an oath on the part of God the Father, who, as the Psalmist tells us, swore by an oath of which he shall never repent, "Thou art a priest for ever according to the order of Melchisedech "),

22. By so much, *i.e.,* in proportion to the excellence shown by the use of an oath on the part of God beyond the omission of the same, does the testament of which Jesus is sponsor, and to which an oath was annexed, excel the other, regarding which it was omitted.

23. And the Levitical priests are advanced to the priesthood in a long line of succession—one succeeding to the other, because, owing to death, they cannot always exercise the priestly functions ;

24. But Jesus, on account of being constituted a priest "for ever," by his Father, has an eternal priesthood, not transmissible, by way of succession, to any other,

25. Whence, he can convey perfect salvation, of

Commentary.

20. Another proof of the superiority of the priesthood of Christ over that of Aaron, and of the consequent abrogation of the latter, is derived from the difference of ceremonies used by God in the institution of both one and the other. "And inasmuch as" Jesus was not made priest "without an oath," which oath is a proof of the exceeding importance of the thing to which it is attached, beyond a similar thing in regard to which it is omitted. This difference is not without foundation ; because, the Levitical priesthood was constituted without an oath.

21. "But this," *i.e.,* Christ, "*with an oath.*" The words, "*the Lord hath sworn and he will not repent,*" are the words of the Psalmist, and not of God, as their collocation in this verse would imply, "*Thou art a priest for ever.*" In some Greek copies are added the words, *according to the order of Melchisedech.* Griesbach doubts their authenticity.

22. "By so much," *i.e.,* in proportion to the difference of excellence proved by the omission, on the one hand, and the adoption, on the other, of an oath by God, does the testament of which Jesus is sponsor—for the fulfilment of whose promises he is surety—exceed the other.

23. Another argument of the superiority of the priesthood of Christ, is derived from the number of Aaron's successors, who succeeded one another in due course, owing to their mortality.

24. But Christ, on account of his eternity, has a priesthood eternal, and incommunicable to any one by way of succession. Christ's priests are only his vicars, not his successors. The Apostle, in these verses, explains the words of the Psalm, "*for ever,*" to which he briefly alluded, verse 16. "Everlasting," in Greek, ἀπαράβατον, not transmissible. The difference here pointed out between the Christian and Levitical priesthood does not exclude the succession of *inferior* priests to each other in the New Law. The comparison is only instituted between the *High Priests* of both Laws. The argument of the Apostle requires no further extension.

25. "Whereby," *i.e.,* because, "he continueth for ever, and hath an everlasting priesthood " (verse 24), he can save those who have recourse to his intercession, bestowing on them the life of grace here, to be consummated and perfected by a life of glory hereafter. "Always living to make intercession for us." In Greek, *for them.* Of course, this intercession is quite different from the intercession of the saints, to which

Text.

save for ever them that come to God by him : always living to make intercession for us.

26. For it was fitting that we should have such a high priest, holy, innocent, undefiled, separated from sinners, and made higher than the heavens :

27. Who needed not daily (as the *other* priests) to offer sacrifices first for his own sins, and then for the people's : for this he did once, in offering himself.

Paraphrase.

grace here, and of eternal glory hereafter, on those who, through him, approach to God, because always living and exercising an eternal priesthood, he can always make intercession for us, in quality of high priest.

26. For, Christ alone is gifted with the qualities and attributes with which it is meet and necessary that the Pontiff who undertakes to make full and adequate reparation for the sins of man, should be gifted, viz., endowed with sanctity, free from malice, exempt from the stain of sin, segregated from sinners, and placed beyond the reach of moral contamination, more exalted than the highest creatures in heaven.

27. Who is not bound by the Law (like the Levitical high priests) to offer up daily sacrifice of expiation, in the first place, for his own sins, and in the next place, for those of the people ; for, he offered himself once as a sacrifice of expiation, not for his own sins, but for the sins of the world—the value of which bloody oblation of himself being such, as to render any repetition thereof, as a *Redemptory* sacrifice, and in a *bloody* manner, quite useless.

Commentary.

it is no ways opposed. Christ intercedes, as high priest ; whereas, the intercession of the saints has no reference to the priestly character, which some of them may have borne on earth.—(*See* 1 John, ii. 2). The Apostle, for reasons already stated (verse 10), forbears referring to the principal exercise of Christ's priesthood, in the sacrifice of the Mass. In this verse, the Apostle merely refers incidentally to one of the effects, or results of his priesthood, viz., his interceding for us.

26. Another argument of the superiority of Christ's priesthood over that of Aaron is derived from the superior qualities and attributes, which Christ, as high priest, possesses over the Jewish high priests. Christ alone has the attributes required in every high priest who can make reparation for sin, being, "*holy, innocent,*" &c. "And made higher than the heavens," which means, that he has penetrated the highest heavens, and is more exalted than the highest creature therein ; for, no creature, however exalted, could redeem us. The implied contrast supposes that the Jewish high priest was not possessed of such qualities.

27. Another point in which Christ was superior to the Levitical priest. First, he had no sins to expiate, and therefore, was not bound by the law to offer a sacrifice of expiation for his own sins ; this first point is proved next verse, 28 ; secondly, he was not bound by the law prescribing the offering of daily sacrifice of expiation for the sins of the people ; this second point he proves in this verse ; for, the meritorious value of 'the *bloody* oblation of himself, which he " once " offered, as a *redemptory* sacrifice for others, on the altar of the cross, are such as to render its repetition useless. It is to be observed, that although Christ once offered himself, in a *bloody* manner on the cross, he still continues to offer himself, in an *unbloody* manner. This he does in heaven by presenting his humanity continually to his Father (ix. 24) ; but it is on earth, he chiefly performs this function, by offering himself daily, being *really, truly, and substantially present* under the appearance of bread and wine, in the adorable Sacrifice of the Mass, which is the same with the Sacrifice of the Cross—the victim the same, the principal offerer the same ; differing only in manner ; the one, *bloody*, the other, *unbloody*. This latter part is abundantly proved in the several treatises on Theology. The Eucharistic Sacrifice is, then, a commemoration and continuation of the Sacrifice of the Cross. The principal parts or actions of a sacrifice are, the *immolation* of the victim, and the *oblation* of the same, once immolated. Now, the Sacrifice of the Cross ended only as to the *bloody* immolation ; the same victim is immolated *mystically* by the separate consecra-

Text.

28. For the law maketh men priests, who have infirmity : but the word of the oath, which was since the law, the Son who is perfected for evermore.

Paraphrase.

28. The law very properly enacted that the priests should offer up sacrifice for their own sins ; because it instituted as high priests men liable to sin, which required a sacrifice of expiation. But the oath referred to by David, long after the promulgation of the law and the institution of the Levitical priesthood, has constituted as High Priest, the Son of God, not for a time but for ever, not subject to sin, but wholly perfect; and free from it.

Commentary.

tion of the bread and wine, and continues, as to the *oblation*. It is also to be borne in mind, that the oneness of Christ's sacrifice no more excludes sacrifices *applicatory* of this one Redemptory Sacrifice, than it excludes the sacraments, which are merely the channels for applying the merits purchased on the Sacrifice of the Cross. The Apostle makes two assertions in this verse, viz., that our High Priest was not under the necessity of offering up sacrifices daily, first, for his own sins, and secondly, for those of his people. In proving these points, he inverts the order, proving the second point in the first place.

28. The Apostle explains the words "as the *other* priests," or as the Greek has it ἀρχιερεῖς, *high priests* (verse 27), and proves the first assertion made by him in preceding verse, viz., that our High Priest did not offer up daily sacrifice for *his own* sins, because he was sinless ; the enactment was necessary as regarded the Levitical priests ; because, they themselves were subject to sin ; but Christ, whom God constituted priest by oath, which was expressed by David long after the law, was the Son of God, free from all sin ; in all things perfect and constituted, *for evermore.*

CHAPTER VIII·

Analysis.

In this chapter, the Apostle, raises Christ above Aaron, and thus evidently raises his Priesthood above that of Aaron, and his successors. The superior excellence of Christ, as Priest, is shown from the exalted place he holds in heaven (1), and from the superior excellence of the heavenly tabernacle, of which he is the ministering Pontiff (2). From the very nature of his Priestly office is shown that he is a ministering Pontiff (3), and the superior excellence of the victim which he offers, clearly proves his exalted dignity (4). His superiority over Aaron is also shown from the superior excellence of the Testament, of which he is Mediator (6).

The Apostle, finally, proves the translation not only of the Jewish Priesthood, but of the entire ancient Testament. For, this Testament was not faultless ; there was room, therefore, for a better. The translation of the ancient Testament, on this ground, he proves from the Prophet Jeremias (8–12). The Apostle grounds another argument in proof of the translation and abrogation of the Old Testament, on the word " new "—the epithet, with which Jeremias designates the Second Testament—and from the meaning of this word, he infers that the Old Testament must now have ceased.

Text.	Paraphrase.
1. NOW of the things which we have spoken, this is the sum : We have such an high priest, who is set on the right hand of the throne of majesty in the heavens,	1. The summary abridgment of all we have said concerning the priesthood of Christ is this : that in him we have a Pontiff, who sits at the right hand of the throne of majesty in heaven,
2. A minister of the Holies, and of the true tabernacle, which the Lord hath pitched, and not man.	2. The ministering pontiff of the celestial Holy of Holies, that is to say, of the true tabernacle (to which the Jewish bore the relation of type), which the Lord hath framed, and not man.

Commentary.

1. St. Chrysostom understands by "sum," κεφάλαιον, the chief, the greatest of all the qualities yet enumerated ; others, the recapitulation of the foregoing ; but, the interpretation in the Paraphrase is preferable.

2. He was minister of the true tabernacle, of which the Jewish tabernacle—built after the model proposed to Moses on the Mount, verse 5—was a mere type. The Greek for "minister," λειτουργος, means one who performs publicly religious services ; it is a term, which applies to all priests ; but particularly to a high priest. "Holies and true tabernacle," probably refer to the same thing—viz., the Church triumphant in heaven and militant on earth ; then, "and" means, *that is.* He is "minister of the holies and *(that is)* of the true tabernacle "—or, if they refer to different things ; then, "the holies" refer to heaven, and "the true tabernacle," as distinguished from it (although, in reality, "the holies," formed a part of the Jewish tabernacle), means the Church militant ; and Jesus is minister in both ; for, he exercises his priesthood in heaven and on earth. "True" is said, not in opposition to false, it means *real,* opposed to type and figure.

By an allusion to the duties of the high priest in the old law, the Apostle points out the superior excellence of Christ. The great duty of the Jewish high priest was to enter yearly and minister in the earthly "Holy of Holies," which might be termed a "throne of majesty" (verse 1), but not "in the heavens." He did not "*sit*" there ;

Text.

3. For every high priest is appointed to offer gifts and sacrifices : wherefore it is necessary that he also should have something to offer.

4. If then he were on earth, he would not be a priest : seeing that there would be *others* to offer gifts according to the law,

5. Who serve unto the example and shadow of heavenly things. As it was answered to Moses, when he was to finish the tabernacle : See (says he) that thou make all things according to the pattern which was shewn thee on the mount.

Paraphrase.

3. (Although sitting at the right hand of God, he still acts as ministering pontiff of the true tabernacle), because every high priest, by the very nature of his office, is constituted to offer gifts and victims in sacrifice to God. Hence, as Christ is priest even in heaven, he must have something to offer.

4. If, then, he were a priest of an earthly tabernacle, and belonged to that department which is opposed to the celestial, or rather, if this "something," or victim, which, as priest, he must offer, were terrestrial, he would be no priest at all ; because, not belonging to the tribe of Levi, he would be disqualified by the law for such offerings, or, rather, because his priesthood would be quite useless, since the established ministry of the Aaronic priests would suffice for that purpose :

5. Who minister in the tabernacle, which is but the obscure delineation, and mere shadowing representation of the heavenly (of which Christ is ministering pontiff—verse 2), according to the divine response given to Moses, when about to make the tabernacle : —"See (he says), that thou do all things according to the model shown thee on the mount."

Commentary.

he rather trembled before it. Our High Priest sits down in the real Holy of Holies, "in the heavens," next the majesty of God himself.

3. Christ exercises the office of priest by presenting his humanity and passion to God the Father (ix. 24) ; but especially by the ministry of his vicars on earth, in the sacrifice of the Mass. It is the former mode of ministering that the Apostle here principally regards. The question of the Eucharist did not fall within his scope, and he omitted direct reference to it, for reasons already assigned. However, the universal proposition employed by the Apostle, together with the word "gifts," which refers to unbloody oblations, as well as his frequent allusions to the order of Melchisedech, which is fulfilled only in the Eucharistic sacrifice, renders it very probable, that reference is here made to that sacrifice, at least in such a way, as to be perceived and understood by the faithful.

4. "If then." In the ordinary Greek copies, εἰ μὲν γὰρ, *for if.* The Vulgate is supported by the Alexandrian and other manuscripts, and is generally preferred by critics.

"On earth," may refer to the priest, if Christ were priest of an earthly tabernacle, or, more probably, it refers to the victim, "should have something to offer" (verse 3), as if he said, *If then this "something," or victim, were earthly,* Christ would not be priest at all ; since "there would be others to offer gifts according to the law," which law would disqualify him, not being of the tribe of Levi. Moreover, his priesthood would be, in that case, quite useless ; as the Aaronic priests would suffice. And since, according to the Psalmist, he is a priest ; he is, therefore, a priest of the heavenly tabernacle, of which the Jewish is a mere type. He is, of course, as superior to the Levitical priests, as heaven is to earth ; as the reality, to its type and figure.

5. The Aaronic priests "serve." The Greek word, λατρευουσι, implies worship, in a tabernacle, which is but "the example." In Greek, ὑποδείγματι, a mere obscure delineation ; "and shadow of heavenly things," *i.e.,* of the heavenly sanctuary and true tabernacle of the Church, militant and triumphant (verse 2). The word "example" is not taken here in its ordinary signification, which is, that of model or pattern, as in the words, "according to the pattern," κατὰ τὸν τύπον. The Greek word already quoted, shows the meaning given in the Paraphrase to be correct. "As it was answered to Moses," &c. The tabernacle of Moses was, according to the Apostle, only a figure and obscure representation of things done by Christ in the Church

Text.

6. But now he hath obtained a better ministry, by how much also he is mediator of a better testament, which is established on better promises.

7. For if that former had been faultless, there should not indeed a place have been sought for a second.

8. For finding fault with them, he saith: *Behold, the days shall come, saith the Lord: and I will perfect unto the house of Israel, and unto the house of Juda, a new testament.*

9. *Not according to the testament, which I made to their fathers on the day when I took them by the hand to lead them out of the land of Egypt: because they continued not in my testament: and I regarded them not saith the Lord:*

Paraphrase.

6. But now, in his heavenly sanctuary, Christ has obtained a priestly ministry as far exceeding in superior excellence the priesthood of Aaron, as the covenant, of which he is mediator, surpasses the covenant of Moses, and as the promises, with which this new testament is promulgated, exceed the promises of the old.

7. But if the former covenant were free from imperfection, so that nothing were wanting to it, there would be no room for a second, nor would a second and better covenant have been sought for.

8. (Now, there was room and necessity for a second), for, finding fault with the Jews themselves, and indirectly with their testament, God says—(Jeremias, xxxi. 31)—"Behold the days shall come, saith the Lord, and I will perfect unto the house of Israel and unto the house of Juda, a new testament.

9. "Not like the testament which I made to their fathers, the time I took them by the hand to lead them out of Egypt. Because they violated my covenant, I in turn, slighted and neglected them, saith the Lord.

Commentary.

militant and triumphant. And this, Moses clearly perceived, from the divine oracle commanding him, when about to frame the tabernacle, to make it according to the pattern, sensibly presented to him on the Mount. He saw that this pattern had a typical relation to the future things to be done by Christ in his Church and in heaven. "See thou make all things," &c. The words, "*all things*," are not found in the text (Exodus, xxv. 40), they have been added by the Apostle.

6. The Apostle having already clearly proved the translation of the Aaronic priesthood, is preparing, in this verse, while adducing a further argument in favour of the superior excellence of Christ's priesthood, to show us, that the entire Mosaic law or covenant is to make way for, and to be abolished by, a more excellent one introduced by Christ.

7. "If that former had been faultless," *i.e.*, free from all imperfection—it contained nothing positively bad, being "holy, just, and good" (Rom. vii. 12); but, it was imperfect, for remitting sin and imparting justification. "There should not, indeed, a place have been sought for a second;" *i.e.*, a second and better covenant would have no place, as there would have been no use or occasion for it; and consequently, it would not have been sought for.

8. "For, finding fault with them;" as if he said : but, a place for another and better testament was to be found, "for, finding fault with them he saith," or, "finding fault" (*with the covenant*), he saith to them, *i.e.*, the Jews. The Greek, μεμφόμενος γὰρ αὐτοῖς λέγει, will admit either construction ; the former is, however, the more probable. "Finding fault" with the Jews, implies, finding fault with the old testament, which did not of itself supply them with the means of observing its laws, in a manner pleasing to God and meritorious of eternal life ; for, all the graces attached to the old testament, and justifying its children, were, properly speaking, derived from the new. The words are taken from the 31st chapter of the Prophet Jeremias, and are quoted by the Apostle from the Septuagint version ; the Jews themselves admit that, in its literal sense, this passage refers to the Messiah. The Prophet is speaking of a new testament, which the Lord promises to make "*with the house of Israel and the house of Juda,*" *i.e.*, with the faithful of the Christian Church.

9. And he says, it will not be like the covenant or testament which he made with their fathers, the Israelites, on the fiftieth day after their deliverance from the Egyptian

Text.

10. *For this is the testament which I will make to the house of Israel after those days saith the Lord: I will give my laws into their mind, and in their heart will I write them: and I will be their God, and they shall be my people.*

11. *And they shall not teach every man his neighbour, and every man his brother, saying, Know the Lord: for all shall know me from the least to the greatest of them.*

Paraphrase.

10. "But this is the testament which I shall make with the house of Israel after those days, saith the Lord. I shall give my laws into their minds, and in their hearts will I write them ; and I will be their God, and they shall be my people."

11. Nor will there be any further necessity for each one to teach his neighbour, or his brother, to know the Lord (by a practical knowledge consisting in loving him and keeping his commandments); because all, who, properly speaking, belong to this new testament, will have this knowledge impressed on their minds and written on their hearts by grace.

Commentary.

bondage. They violated his covenant, and on this account, he in turn forsook them, withdrawing his special care and protection from them.

10. And then he declares what this testament shall be, as contrasted with the old :— "*I will give my laws unto their minds, and in their hearts will I write them,*" which is evidently allusive to the manner in which the Old Law was given ; for, God gave his laws (the decalogue) to the Jews, written on the tables of stone. The same laws he gives to the Christians of the new testament, written on their hearts and minds, by grace and love.

11. Another thing peculiar to the new testament, and an effect of the laws being written on their hearts is, that "*they shall not teach every man his neighbour,......know the Lord,*" &c. It is by no means easy to see how these words are verified in the new testament ; hence, the variety of interpretations given, all of which render the passage difficult and perplexing. Whatever may be the true meaning of the words, it can be clearly shown from several passages of the Gospel and the Epistles, particularly Ephesians (chap. iv.) that they cannot exclude the external ministry of teaching, in the Church. The same clearly follows from the Apostle's writing this Epistle. If the external ministry of teaching were excluded, why should the Apostle write this Epistle to instruct the Hebrews? Some Expositors say the Prophet refers to the crime of idolatry, to which the Jews were particularly prone, and against which they required to be constantly cautioned, by proposing the knowledge of the true God. "*Know the Lord:*" but amongst Christians, no such danger was to be apprehended ; and therefore, no necessity for reminding them of the true God. The words are, most probably, to be understood of instruction, not in mere speculative knowledge ; but, in the practical knowledge and love of God. In the old testament, each one was obliged to put his neighbour in mind of God, and instruct him in that practical knowledge which consisted in knowing the Jewish law and observing it, not merely externally, so as to avoid the penalties of its infraction, but in observing it through grace, and in a manner, meritorious of eternal life. The reason why this was required in the Old Law arose from its being necessarily imperfect. To the Old Law, as *such,* the grace referred to here had not been attached, nor could it beget that practical love and knowledge, of which there is question in the words of the Prophet. God had promised the Jewish people temporal blessings—under the figure of which he promised eternal blessings also—and as a condition for securing these, he required the observance of his law ; but the greater part of the Jews did not observe the law in a proper way, "*they continued not in my testament*" (9). In the New Law spiritual blessings, viz., the inheritance of God's kingdom, are promised to such as observe the gospel.

Another great difference is, that in the Old Law, God left the Jews in a great measure to themselves, to observe the conditions necessary for arriving at the promised goods. Whereas, in the New Law, he not only promises the kingdom of heaven, but as a part of the testament, he gives the graces necessary for fulfilling his law, and for observing the conditions, necessary for arriving at this kingdom. · That Jeremias or St. Paul speaks

Text.

12. *Because I will be merciful to their iniquities, and their sins I will remember no more.*

13. Now in saying a new, he hath made the former old. And that, which decayeth and groweth old, is near its end.

Paraphrase.

12. Because I will be merciful to their iniquities, and I will no longer remember their sins (and consequently will give them grace to fulfil my law).

13. Now, in promising a *new* testament by the mouth of Jeremias, God has represented the former as *old* and *antiquated.* But what is grown old and antiquated, is approaching dissolution : consequently, the testament grown old in the days of Jeremias, must, by this time, have perished.

Commentary.

of this practical knowledge or love of God, which consists in fulfilling his law, is confirmed by the following verse.

12. Here the prophet assigns the reason why it will not be necessary for every man to be teaching his neighbour; because God will *"no longer remember their sins,"* he will fully pardon them, and give the grace necessary to fulfil his law—a grace peculiar to the new testament ; it did not belong to the old testament, as *such.* But how is it, that in the new testament *"all from the least to the greatest of them,"* will have this knowledge ; surely, all do not love God? The Apostle here refers to such as were, properly speaking, children of the new testament—viz., the just of the Church ; for, these have received a portion of the inheritance here below, in the remission of their sins, grace, &c. ; and, by persevering, they will obtain the whole hereafter. There are, doubtless, many sinners under the *New* Law, who might be called children of the *Old ;* as, on the other hand, there were many just under the *old,* who were sanctified by the graces belonging to the *new* testament, and could, therefore, be justly called children of the *new* testament. Such appears to be a probable interpretation of the passage so perplexing to Commentators, and presenting under every view, very grave difficulties.

13. The Apostle, having proved from the prophetic testimony, that the first testament was not faultless, and that there was room for a second and better (7) ; now, grounds a new argument in proof of the abrogation of the Mosaic law, and of the old testament, on the word "new," by which the prophet designates this second testament. By calling it "new," he represents the former testament, as antiquated. Now, whatever is grown old and antiquated, and consequently weak and useless (as in the ordinary affairs of nature), is approaching dissolution; and hence, the testament, grown old in the days of Jeremias, must now have altogether ceased.

CHAPTER IX.

Analysis.

Having proved, in the preceding chapter, the abrogation of the Old Testament, and the substitution of a better one in its stead, the Apostle commences this, by enumerating the several ordinances of the Mosaic worship. This he does with a view to show that its abrogation was not owing to its being really bad, since it contained so many pledges of the divine protection. He first describes the tabernacle, its several parts and their contents, as well as the different functions performed in them (1–8). From the mystical signification of these parts of the tabernacle, and the functions performed in them, he argues in favour of the necessity of another form of worship to sanctify men, and open to them the gates of heaven (8–11).

He contrasts Christ with the Aaronic high priests, and shows how far he excelled them, both as to the tabernacle through which he passed, the blood he carried with him, and the redemption he accomplished (11, 12). He shows how much greater efficacy the blood of Christ possessed for cleansing from the guilt of sin, than the blood of the legal victims had for the removal of legal defilement (13, 14).

He next adduces several reasons to show the moral necessity of the death of Christ, which are explained in the Commentary. This point was a subject of scandal to the Jews, and the Apostle merely touched on it, in the second chapter of this Epistle (15–23).

Finally, he contrasts Christ with the Jewish high priest, as well in the unity of his death, as in the unity of his bloody oblation, which, as a redemptory sacrifice, could not bear repetition, one such offering having amply sufficed to atone for the sins of the entire world.

Text.

1. THE former indeed had also justifications of *divine* service, and a worldly sanctuary.

2. For there was a tabernacle made the first, wherein were the candlesticks, and the table, and the setting forth of loaves, which is called the Holy.

Paraphrase.

1. Now, indeed, the former (testament) had its ordinances regulating the decent observance of divine worship, and its sanctuary of earthly materials (unlike that of the New Testament, whose origin and materials are celestial).

2. For, a tabernacle was constructed (divided into two parts)—the first part of which was called the *sanctum* or *holy place*, containing the seven-branched candlestick, and the table of the loaves of *proposition* or *show bread ;*

Commentary.

1. "The former, indeed." Some Greek copies have *the former (tabernacle, σκηνη).* The more probable opinion, however, is, that "former" refers to "testament," of which mention was made in the foregoing chapter, and between which and the entire New Testament the comparison is instituted.

"And a worldly sanctuary" (το τε άγιον κοσμικον), that is, of earthly materials. The words mean the same as, "made with hands," in verse 11, opposed to the sanctuary of heavenly origin and tendency.

2. He now describes the different parts of the material tabernacle. The tabernacle measured thirty cubits, two-thirds of which was taken up with the *Sanctum*, and the remainder, with the *Sanctum Sanctorum.* "For there was a tabernacle made the first ;" that is, the first part of the tabernacle (for it was composed of two compartments), or, the part into which one first entered, was simply called the "holy." "Wherein were the candlesticks," or the one candlestick with seven branches, equivalent to seven

Text.

3. And after the second veil, the tabernacle, which is called the Holy of Holies :

4. Having a golden censer, and the ark of the testament covered about on every part with gold, in which was a golden pot that had manna, and the rod of Aaron that had blossomed, and the tables of the testament,

5. And over it were the Cherubims of glory overshadowing the propitiatory: of which it is not needful to speak now particularly.

Paraphrase.

3. And behind the second veil was the other part of the tabernacle, called the *Holy of Holies*, or *most holy place*,

4. Having a golden censer, and the ark of the covenant, covered about on every side with gold, alongside of which was a golden urn, that had manna, and the rod of Aaron that blossomed ; in it were also the tables of the testament ;

5. And over the ark were two cherubim reflecting the glory and majesty of God, covering with their wings the propitiatory, which served as a lid for the ark. Of the mystical meaning of all and each of these parts, it is not our intention at present to treat.

Commentary.

candlesticks. Hence, the word is used in the plural number (λυχνια), "candlesticks," as being virtually many. "And the table, and the setting forth of loaves ;" that is the table on which were laid the loaves of proposition, twelve in number, representing the twelve tribes of Israel. They were called, "*the bread of the face ;*" because they were always-placed before the face of the Lord, or, the throne of the Lord which was in the Holy of Holies—(Leviticus, xxiv. 6).

3. "And after the second veil," which divided the *sanctum* from the *sanctum sanctorum*—for a first veil, of which the Apostle makes no mention, divided the *sanctum* from the rest of the temple—lay the part of the tabernacle in which was the *Holy of Holies*, in the Hebrew idiom, signifying, *most holy*.

4. "Having a golden censer." In the construction of the *Holy of Holies*, there is no mention of any such censer. Hence, it is commonly supposed to refer to the altar of incense, which was concave, in the form of a large thurible or censer, so as to receive coals. In reality placed in the *sanctum*, it only opened into the *sanctum sanctorum*, so as to emit incense into it.

OBJECTION.—How could the Apostle say of the "golden censer," or altar of incense, that it was in the *sanctum sanctorum ?*

RESP.—The Apostle does not say the "golden censer" in question was *in* the *sanctum sanctorum*. He only says of it, "*having* a golden censer," just as, of a town it may be said, that it *has* fortifications, without their being in it. The altar of incense was placed at the entrance of the *sanctum sanctorum*, so that it might be said to belong to it. It may also be said, that the Apostle speaks of the tabernacle, not as it was in the days of Solomon, but in the time of Moses.

"And the ark of the testament." The ark was an oblong chest, two and a half cubits long, and a cubit and a half, in width and height, in which were contained "the (*second*) tables" of the law (for the *first* were broken to pieces by Moses), "of the testament," because it contained the law, the conditions of the covenant. This ark, though made of setim wood, was overlaid with gold, both inside and outside. It was brought from the tabernacle to the temple of Solomon, and remained there until the Babylonish captivity. What became of it ultimately, cannot be fully ascertained ; it was not in the temple of Jerusalem, in the time of Christ, as we are assured by Josephus. "In which was a golden pot," &c.—(Numbers, xvii.)

In the 3rd Book of Kings (chap. xiii.), is it not said that there was nothing in the ark, except the tables of law ?

Yes.—But the words of the Apostle do not contradict this ; they may, and do really, mean, that *alongside* the ark, the things mentioned here were placed, and attached to it. The word "in," according to scriptural usage, frequently bears the meaning of, *near* or, *close by*. The tables of the law alone were inside the ark.

5. What the form of these cherubim was, is quite uncertain ; probably, they represented winged young men—the form of representing angels, approved of by the seventh General Council. With their outspread wings, they covered the propitiatory, or lid of

Text.

6. Now these things being thus ordered, into the first tabernacle the priests indeed always entered, accomplishing the offices of sacrifices.

7. But into the second, the high priest alone, once a year : not without blood, which he offered for his own, and the people's ignorance :

8. The Holy Ghost signifying this, that the way into the Holies was not yet made manifest, whilst the former tabernacle was yet standing.

9. Which is a parable of the time present ; according to which gifts and sacrifices are offered, which cannot, as to the conscience, make him perfect that serveth, only in meats and in drinks.

Paraphrase.

6. These things being thus ordered and arranged ; into the first part of the tabernacle, the priests entered daily, accomplishing in turn the offices of sacrifices :

7. But into the latter part, or, the *Holy of Holies*, the high priest alone entered ; and that, but once a year ; carrying with him blood which he offered for his owns sins, and those of the people.

8. By confining to the high priest only the entrance into the *Holy of Holies*, and that so seldom, the Holy Ghost most plainly intimated ; that whilst the Jewish economy, which the first portion of the tabernacle, viz., the *sanctum* or *holy*, represented, remained in vigour—heaven, which the *Holy of Holies* represented, was closed against mankind. This was clearly signified by the exclusion of all other men, except the high priest, from the *Holy of Holies*.

9. The allegorical instruction conveyed to us, in the exclusion of every one else, but the high priest, from the *sanctum sanctorum* is well suited to the entire term of the Mosaic law, up to the present time, when it has been abrogated ; during which time, gifts and sacrifices were offered, which had not the effect of purifying interiorly the server or minister, who offered them, his service being confined to the choice of food and drink ;

Commentary.

the ark. By their wings stretched over the propitiatory, their faces turned to each other they formed a seat, which was the throne, on which God sat. Hence, the words, *qui sedet supra cherubim ;* and from that seat, *i.e.*, from over the propitiatory, God delivered his oracles. The Apostle is describing the furniture and constituent parts of the Mosaic tabernacle.

6. He explains one or two of the functions performed in both parts of the tabernacle. "The offices of sacrifices." Not that sacrifices were offered in the *sanctum*, but the function of burning incense in the *sanctum* closed the sacrifices of the day. Moreover, the Greek word for "offices," &c., λατρειας, only expresses priestly functions of what kind soever. "The priests always entered." In Greek, εισιασιν δια παντος "always *enter*," in the present tense.

7. "Ignorance" (in Greek, αγνοηματων, *ignorances*), is put for all kinds of sin, every sin being the effect of speculative or practical ignorance. The high priest sacrificed for his own sins, and those of his house, a calf, and for those of his people, a buck goat ; he brought with him the blood of both, into the *sanctum sanctorum*, on the great day of expiation.—(Leviticus, xvi. 11).

From the functions performed in the *sanctum sanctorum*, for the more perfect explanation of which, the Apostle contrasts them with those daily performed in the *sanctum*, is derived an allegorical instruction (*vide* Paraphrase . The *sanctum*, with the functions performed therein, represented the Jewish religion ; the *sanctum sanctorum*, heaven. The allegorical instruction, then, is, that as long as the *sanctum*, *i.e.*, the Jewish religion, remained in vigour, so long would the true *sactum sanctorum* of heaven, be closed against men. This was well represented by the exclusion of all others, except the high priest, from the Jewish *sanctum sanctorum*.

9. The Greek reading of the *Codex Vaticanus* is, ἥτις παραβολη εις τον καιρον τον ενεστηκοτα καθ' ἥν, *which is a parable unto the present time, according to which (parable) gifts,* &c. He says, the allegorical instruction conveyed in the exclusion of all others, except the high priest, from the *sanctum sanctorum*, is well suited to the entire term of the Jewish religion, from the time of Moses (when it commenced), to the present time (when it has

Text.

10. And divers washings, and justices of the flesh laid on them until the time of correction.

11. But Christ, being come an high priest of the good things to come, by a greater and more perfect tabernacle not made with hand, that is, not of this creation:

12. Neither by the blood of goats,

Paraphrase.

10. And to several legal ablutions and justifications of the flesh—conferring no real internal sanctification —imposed only for a time, until Christ would have corrected them by the institution of better rites. This service, therefore, did not qualify him for entering the true holy of holies of heaven).

11. But Christ having come, or, having been constituted from his very birth, a high priest (not of present, as were the Jewish high priests, but) of future blessings, to be enjoyed in the life to come, by the better and more perfect tabernacle, not reared by human hands, that is to say, not of this earthly, but of heavenly construction ;

12. Not carrying with him the the blood of goats or

Commentary.

been abrogated), because, during this entire time, the expiatory gifts offered had not the effect of purifying in conscience "the server," *i.e.*, the priest who offered them ; nor by consequence, the people for whom they were offered ; they did not, therefore, qualify men for heaven, into which nothing defiled can enter ; this service, by which they prepared for the offering of these gifts, being as carnal as the gifts themselves, consisting merely in the choice of food and drinks. From all intoxicating drinks the ministering priest was obliged to abstain, when officiating in the temple.—(Leviticus, x. 9). Estius, *in hunc locum.*

10. Several corporal ablutions and justices of the flesh, *i.e.*, legal justifications, which conferred no real sanctity (for, interior sanctity was not required as a necessary qualification for the ministrations of the Jewish religion), but only legal sanctity. "Laid on them," *i.e.*, imposed for a time, until Christ corrected them by the institution of better rites, substituted by him in their stead, conferring real, internal sanctity. The Jewish religion conferred no real sanctity, worked no true remission of sin, without which no one could enter heaven ; hence, the necessity of another priesthood to justify man.

How, then, could the Jews be justified? By true repentance, joined to hope and faith, in the future or promised Messiah. The difference of reading in the Greek renders this passage rather complicated. The interpretation, which seems most probable, has been adopted in the Paraphrase. The ordinary Greek reading has been adopted in the first part of verse 9 ; and the words, "only in meats," &c., have been connected with the words, "that serveth," immediately preceding.

11. The Apostle now shows the superior excellence of Christ's priesthood, by contrasting with the typical ministrations of the Jewish tabernacle, the great benefits which he procures for us, in the more perfect tabernacle into which he has entered. "But Christ being come," παραγενομενὸς, *i.e.*, having been by his very coming, and from his birth, constituted "an high priest of good things to come," to be fully enjoyed only in the life to come. "Entered" (verse 12) "by a greater and more perfect tabernacle not made with hand," &c. What this "more perfect tabernacle" refers to, is much disputed. Some, with St. Chrysostom, say, it refers to the body and flesh of Christ, in which the plenitude of the divinity dwelt corporally. This, however, would not perfectly correspond with many things in the Jewish and less perfect tabernacle ; for, the high priest entering the *sanctum sanctorum*, did not carry with him the *sanctum*, as Christ has carried his body into the *sanctum sanctorum* of heaven ; the type, therefore, and its antitype, would not well correspond in this interpretation. It, then, more probably refers to the Church militant, through which, for forty days after his resurrection, he passed into the Church triumphant, after having offered on the altar of the cross the sacrifice of expiation, which the Jewish high priest used to offer on the altar of holocausts.—A'Lapide. Others say, it refers to the visible portion of the heavens, through which Christ entered the empyrean heavens. It is hard, however, to see in this latter interpretation, how it could be said to be "not of this creation."

12. "Neither by the blood of goats,"&c., unlike the Jewish high priest, he has entered the *true* Holy of Holies, not *yearly*, but "once ; " not after obtaining a remission requir-

Text.	Paraphrase.
or of calves, but by his own blood, entered once into the Holies, having obtained eternal redemption.	of calves, but his own most precious blood shed on the altar of the cross, has entered once for all, and not annually, into the true celestial sanctuary, after having obtained a redemption which is everlasting.
13. For if the blood of goats and of oxen, and the ashes of an heifer being sprinkled, sanctify such as are defiled, to the cleansing of the flesh :	13. (Surely the blood of Christ ought to contain greater efficacy for purifying our souls, than that of animals for the purification of the body). Now, if the blood of goats and of oxen, and the ashes of a heifer, or the red cow, mixed with water, and sprinkled on those legally defiled, had the effect of legally purifying the body :
14. How much more shall the blood of Christ, who by the Holy Ghost offered himself unspotted unto God, cleanse our conscience from dead works, to serve the living God?	14. How much more shall the divine blood of Christ —who, at the impulse of the Holy Ghost, offered himself to his Father, a victim without spot—have the effect of purifying our consciences from all sins, which cause spiritual death, and of thus enabling us to serve the living God, in a proper and becoming manner ?
15. And therefore he is the mediator of the new testament : that by means of his death, for the redemption of those transgressions, which were under the former testament, they that are called may receive the promise of eternal inheritance.	15. And it is on account of the efficacy of his blood in washing away sin, that he is constituted the mediator of the new testament, in order that by his death, having made atonement for those sins, committed under the old testament (and which were remitted solely in consideration of the retrospective moral efficacy of his future passion), those who are called would receive the promise of eternal inheritance ; in other words, redeemed mankind would receive the eternal inheritance, to which they are called.

Commentary.

ing *annual* repetition, but, after having brought about a redemption, which is everlasting, the value of his atonement being of such enduring infinite merit, as to render its repetition quite useless. Hence, the difference of effects between Christ's entering the celestial *sanctum sanctorum*, " to appear in the presence of God for us " (verse 24), and the entrance of the Jewish high priest, into the earthly *sanctum sanctorum*.

13. The Apostle proves, that Christ has purchased for us an eternal redemption, by an argument, *a fortiori*. " The blood of goats and of oxen." In some Greek copies, the order is inverted—it is, *the blood of oxen and of goats*. But the Vulgate is supported by the most ancient manuscripts, and the Syriac interpreters; "and the ashes of a heifer," or the red cow (Numbers, xix. 2, &c.), when mixed with water and sprinkled on the legally defiled, had the effect of producing legal purification of the body.

14. Therefore, *a fortiori*, the divine blood of Christ should purify the soul. "Who by the Holy Ghost." In Greek, δια πνευματος αιωνιου, *by the eternal spirit*, which is more probably understood of the "Holy Ghost," at whose impulse, Christ offered himself a victim without spot, to give satisfaction to God the Father. "Our conscience." In Greek, συνειδησιν υμων, *your conscience*. "From dead works," *i.e.*, from sins, which being, as it were, fetid before God, pollute the soul, as contact with a dead carcase pollutes the body ; moreover, they deprive the soul of spiritual life, and have for stipend, death. *Stipendium peccati, mors.*—(Rom. xi. 23).

15. The Apostle, having made allusion to the bloody offering of Christ, proceeds to point out the necessity of his death—a subject of great scandal to the Jews. The first reason is grounded on the nature of the character which he had assumed, viz., that of mediator. He is mediator of the New Testament, the middle person between God and man, promising on the part of God the blessings marked out for man, together with the aids of divine grace, necessary for complying with the part required of him ; and, on the part of man, a faithful correspondence aided by divine grace, with the beneficent designs of God, in the observance of the commandments. "That by means of his

Text.

16. For where there is a testament; the death of the testator must of necessity come in.

17. For a testament is of force, after men are dead : otherwise it is as yet of no strength, whilst the testator liveth.

18. Whereupon neither was the first indeed dedicated without blood.

19. For when every commandment of the law had been read by Moses to all the people, he took the blood of calves and goats with water and scarlet wool and hyssop, and sprinkled both the book itself and all the people,

Paraphrase.

16. For, Christ was not only a *mediator*, but a *testator*, making a will. And for the firmness and ratification of a will the death of a testator is required ;

17. Since, during the testator's life he may change or annul it ; and hence, while he lives, it is of no weight.

18. Wherefore, the old testament was not dedicated without blood.

19. For, after Moses had read every commandment of the law to all the people, he took and mixed the blood of goats and of calves with water, and having immersed therein scarlet wool with hyssop, he sprinkled both the book and the entire people,

Commentary.

death," &c., according to the decree of God, the sins of those who lived formerly under the old testament were remitted, solely in consideration of Christ's future death ; hence, to redeem this moral pledge, and to secure a continuance of this remission, and the consequent enjoyment of the promise by future ages, it was fit he should die. "Called," may affect either the men called, or the inheritance to which they are invited (as in Paraphrase).

16. A second reason, why Christ should die, is founded on the nature of the new alliance, which is that of a testament, Christ being *testator ;* hence, for the ratification of the new testament, he should die. It may be asked, how can the reasoning of the Apostle, grounded on the nature of a testament, be of any weight ; for the Hebrew word, *Berith*, the word used to express the *new covenant*, does not mean a *testamentary* more than any other description of covenant. Hence, the Apostle could not argue from the word *Berith*, regarding the peculiar requirements of a testament? The answer to this is, that the seventy-two, or, Septuagint Interpreters translated, *Berith* by διαθηκη, which commonly means, *a testament*. Moreover, St. Paul, as an inspired writer, gives the word in reference to the new alliance, a particular meaning, which serves as an authentic interpretation of it ; for, it is the same Holy Ghost that dictates in both cases. And St. Paul, addressing the Jews, might argue from their own admissions ; for, they admitted that the new alliance was a testament—an argument, though, humanly speaking, a mere *argumentum suasorium*, when used by an inspired penman, quite certain.

18. The next reason is founded on the dedication of the old testament, in which blood was shed, and death, intervened. It may be objected, that in the case of the old testament, God, the testator, did not die. Therefore, for a testament, the death of the testator is not always required. The reply to which is, that the old testament was only a typical testament ; hence, the blood shed should be blood of a typical character, figurative of the blood of Christ, who should, therefore, die, to correspond with his type.

19. The Greek reading is, λαληθεισης γαρ πασης εντολης κατα τον νομον, *for, when the entire law, according to command, was spoken*, &c. The meaning is, however, more probably that conveyed in the Vulgate reading, viz., when all the commandments which were contained in the law were read or recited by Moses. "He took the blood of calves and goats, with water," mixing it with water in a vessel ; he also took some scarlet wool, and attaching it to a bunch of hyssop, which served as an *aspersory*, dipping it in the vessel of blood and water, he sprinkled "*the book*," *i.e.*, the commandment shaped in the form of a book. In the account given in the 24th chapter of Exodus, Moses omits all mention of "the blood of goats," "of water," "of scarlet wool," "of the hyssop," "and of the sprinkling the book of the law." These circumstances the Apostle most probably had learned from ancient tradition, or, perhaps, from revelation ; and he refers to these, as things well known to his readers. As on similar occasions, the same

Text.

20. Saying : *This is the blood of the testament, which God hath enjoined unto you.*

21. The tabernacle also and all the vessels of the ministry, in like manner, he sprinkled with blood :

22. And almost all things, according to the law, are cleansed with blood : and without shedding of blood there is no remission,

23. It is necessary therefore that the patterns of heavenly things should be cleansed with these : but the heavenly things themselves with better sacrifices than these.

24. For Jesus is not entered into the Holies made with hands, the patterns of the true; but into heaven

Paraphrase.

20. Saying, this is the blood whereby the testament is solemnly dedicated, which God had enjoined unto you, and confirmed by my ministry.

21. The tabernacle also, and all the vessels of the ministry, he sprinkled with blood.—(Exodus, xl. ; Leviticus viii.)

22. And almost all the legal defilements were, by the disposition of the Mosaic law, removed by bloody oblations ; and without the shedding of blood there is no remission of sin.

23. It was, therefore, necessary, according to the commands of God, that the mere types of heavenly things should be cleansed and purified by blood offerings, such as we have mentioned ; and hence it is fit, that the heavenly things typified, viz. : the Church militant and triumphant, should be cleansed with blood also, but blood of a more precious kind.

24. For, it is not into the earthly Holy of Holies, reared by mortal hands, after the fashion or form of the true original exhibited to Moses on the mount

Commentary.

ceremonies were used (Leviticus, xiv.), there can be little doubt, that they were not omitted in the present instance. The water and hyssop were necessary for sprinkling the blood ; it was usual to have water mixed with blood (Leviticus, xiv. 49, 51), and as for the sprinkling of the book, it is very likely that it was sprinkled, together with the altar on which it was placed.

20. This is the blood in which is solemnly ratified the testament, &c.

21. The dedication of the tabernacle here referred to, did not occur at the time of the dedication of the new testament ; for, the tabernacle was not then made ; the same is to be said of "all the vessels of the ministry," though, no doubt, such of them as were made at the time of the reading of the law, were sprinkled, together with the sacerdotal vestments. The dedication of the tabernacle referred to in this verse, is narrated (Exod., xl. 8, &c. ; Leviticus, viii. 10, &c.)—the sprinkling of it, "with blood " is omitted by Moses ; mention is, however, made of it by Josephus (lib. 3 *de Antiq.*, cap. 9), who, as a Levitical priest, must have had it from ancient tradition, the source from which the Apostle could have received it. The knowledge of it might have also been received by the Apostle, from revelation.

22. An additional reason, why Christ, in purifying and remitting our sins, should shed his blood. All these bloody oblations were types and figures of Christ's death remitting sin, and of redemption by him ; hence he should die, in order that the object typified should correspond with its type. He says, "and *almost* all things," because some things were purified by water only ; others, by fire (Exodus, xix. 10 ; Leviticus, xvi. 28 ; Numbers, xxxi. 23).

"And without," &c. The legal remission of sins among the Jews, as explained, verse 10, was effected by the blood of victims.

23. From the forgoing, the Apostle draws this inference, "therefore it is necessary ;" according to the command of God, it was necessary "that the patterns" (in Greek, ὑποδείγματα, *the figures* or "*types*,") "of heavenly things" should be purified by blood offerings, such as have been mentioned ; "but the heavenly things themselves," the things typified, should be cleansed by blood of a more excellent kind ; for, the types were cleansed with blood, for the purpose of shadowing forth the others. But what "the heavenly things themselves" refer to, is not so easy to be seen. From the following verse, they would appear to refer to heaven itself ; for, the Apostle proves that as *the sanctum sanctorum*, into which the Jewish high priest entered, was purified, so should the sanctuary into which Christ entered.

24. "For Jesus is not entered," &c. The Greek is, "*Christ* is not entered," &c. In these words, the Apostle explains what he means by "heavenly things," in the

<table>
<tr><td>

Text.

itself, that he may appear now in the presence of God for us.

25. Nor yet that he should offer himself often, as the high priest entereth into the Holies, every year with the blood of others:

26. For then he ought to have suffered often from the beginning of the world : but now once at the end of ages, he hath appeared for the destruction of sin, by the sacrifice of himself.

</td><td>

Paraphrase.

(chap. viii. 5), that Jesus entered ; but into heaven itself, that he may appear now in the presence of God as our advocate.

25. Nor yet was it for the purpose of offering himself frequently, like the Jewish high priest, who entered the Holy of Holies, every year with the blood of others.

26. For, if this one oblation of Christ were not of infinite value, he should have frequently suffered death even from the beginning of the world ; because the repetition of his bloody oblation would be no less necessary than that annually offered by the Jews is as present, to which reference is made. But, now, at the last period of time, he has made his appearance with his victim of propitiation, for the destruction of sin.

</td></tr>
</table>

Commentary.

preceding verse. The *sanctum sanctorum*, into which Christ has entered, is heaven itself. The question then, is, how could heaven be "cleansed?" The supporters of this opinion say, it is "cleansed" in a manner analogous to the way in which its type, the Mosaic tabernacle, was purified ; now, the Mosaic tabernacle, was not really cleansed or purified ; but it was said to be purified in this sense, that certain legal defilements or irregularities, on the part of men, excluding them from it, were removed ; so, in like manner, heaven is cleansed ; because, the way or access to it is free and open for men, by the removal from men, through the merits of Christ's bloody oblation, of the guilt of sin, which kept heaven closed, and prevented them from entering. Others say, that "heavenly things" (verse 23) refer to the Church militant, which can be easily understood to be cleansed by more excellent victims, than those offered in the Old Law ; and the Church is called "heavenly," on account of its founder, doctrine, sacrifice, and the end of its institution on earth ; finally, because heaven is its term and final resting-place. The advocates of this interpretation say, that the words of this verse 24, are adduced merely for the purpose of proving that the Church should be properly designated by the appellation "heavenly," as it is the *sanctum*, through which Christ passed into the *sanctum sanctorum* of heaven ; and the *sanctum* and *sanctum sanctorum* should both be of the same nature, both belonging to the same tabernacle. Those who understand the words, "heavenly things," of heaven, also say, that heaven was purified from the sins of the angels, who sinned there. "That he may appear now in the presence of God for us." The Greek word for "appear," εμφανισθηναι, is a legal term, applied to a witness or advocate ; in the latter sense, it is applied here to Christ. "Patterns of the true," as appears from the Greek, αντιτυπα, convey the idea, that the Jewish Holy of Holies was a representation of the model, to which "true" refers, pointed out to Moses on the Mount. Hence, "true," does not mean Heaven, of which the Jewish Holy of Holies was a mere type ; but, the true model shown to Moses, according to which the Tabernacle was framed. With it, as well as with the Tabernacle of Moses, Heaven is here contrasted. Hence, although the Tabernacle built by Moses may be called the *antitype* (αντιτυπα) of the model shown on the Mount ; still, both may be regarded, as being themselves mere *types* of the celestial Tabernacle, in which Christ ministers.

25. He points out the dissimilarity between the entrance of Christ into heaven and that of the high priest into the Holy of Holies. The high priest entered with the "blood of others," *i.e.*, of the victims slain ; Christ with his own. The high priest entered not *once*, but repeated, each successive year, his ingress and egress ; Christ but *once* entered heaven ; not to leave it, or repeat again the same bloody oblation of himself, his one offering being of infinite value ; and hence, its repetition as a *redemptory* sacrifice, would be quite useless.

26. If the one bloodly oblation of himself by Christ were not of infinite value, and did not suffice for the remission of all sin, an absurdity would follow, viz., that Christ should suffer frequently, and for every generation from the beginning of the world ;

Text.

27. And as it is appointed unto men once to die, and after this, the judgment :

28. So also Christ was offered once to exhaust the sins of many ; the scond time he shall appear without sin, to them that expect him, unto salvation.

Paraphrase.

27. And, as by the decree of God it is appointed for men to die only once, and after that, comes judgment :

28. So also Christ, who was once offered up to take away and make atonement for the sins of many, will appear a second time, without bearing the imputability of sin, or the liability of again atoning for it ; not to be judged (like other men) ; but to carry consolation and glory to those, who patiently expect his coming.

Commentary.

because as no sin could be remitted, except by the sacrifice of Christ, which is inseparable from his death, and as sin existed from the beginning of the world, he should, therefore, die to remit the sins of every single generation, in preceding ages.

"But now once at the end of ages, he hath appeared for the destruction of sin, by the sacrifice of himself," *i.e.*, he has died but once, and that "at the end of ages." The period of the Christian religion is frequently called "the end of ages," *the last hour ;* because it is the last system of religion, that will be established on earth. "He hath appeared by the sacrifice of himself." Some make this refer to heaven, as if he appeared there exhibiting his wounds to his heavenly Father. The Greek for "appeared," πεφανερωται, which means, *he has been manifested,* would render it more probable that it refers to his appearance on earth in the bloody oblation he made of himself on the cross ; and the allusion to the expediency of his dying often, which should happen on earth, makes this latter interpretation still more probable. The Apostle here only excludes the repetition of *bloody* and *redemptory* oblations of Christ— he by no means refers to *unbloody* offerings, *applicatory* of the merits and atonement achieved in the one *Redemptory* Sacrifice. Hence, no argument against the Adorable Sacrifice of the Mass. He only says if the *bloody and redemptory* sacrifice of Christ did not suffice for the ransom of the sins of all ages, he should again suffer and pour out his blood for their redemption, which "now," that he "appeared once," &c., or, in the present order of things, would be an absurdity, considering the *infinite* value of his Sacrifice.

27. Another argument in proof of the unity of Christ's death, is derived from the decree of God fixing on one death only, for mankind, to which decree Christ is supposed to conform.

28. "So also Christ was offered once." The word "was" is superfluous ; it is not in the Greek, nor is it necessary for the sense of the passage. Christ will again appear not as before, "bearing the iniquities of us all," as to imputability ; but "without sin," without the liability of being again offered up in Sacrifice to atone for sin. He will appear glorious and immortal, not to be judged like the rest of men, but to judge the world, to carry consolation to those who, submitting to privations for his sake, patiently expect his coming—a very appropriate exhortation for the Hebrews, who were suffering for the faith. Christ died once for the sins of "many" his satisfaction was offered for the sins of *all,* and *all* are "many." The *infinite* value of Christ's death excluded the necessity of its repetition—one death answered all the ends of univesal redemption ; the Jewish oblation had only a limited effect, *toties quoties.*

CHAPTER X.

Analysis.

The Apostle, having shown in the preceding chapter, that one bloody oblation of Christ had amply atoned for sin and answered all the ends of universal redemption, proceeds to show, in this, that Christ alone could redeem us and remit sin For, as to the law and the sacrifices of the Levitical priesthood, in which the Hebrews so much confided, he proves by several arguments, from verse 1 to 19, that they contained no efficacy whatever for the remission of sin. First, the law and the legal sacrifices were only the shadow of the future goods promised us by Christ ; but not the reality promised. Secondly, the repetition of these sacrifices—and reference is directly made to the annual great sacrifice of expiation—for the self-same sins that were before remitted, proves their inefficacy for remitting sin. And thirdly, it was impossible for the blood of animals, of its own nature and intrinsic efficacy, to remit sin, as the Hebrews vainly imagined (1–5).

The Apostle proves from SS. Scripture, the inefficacy of the ancient sacrifices for the remission of sin. He introduces Christ addressing his Father, Psalm xxxix., " Sacrifices and oblations," &c., and from this prophetic quotation, he draws a two-fold conclusion— first, by saying " Sacrifices......thou wouldst not," Christ has shown the abolition of the sacrifices referred to ; and secondly, by saying, " Behold I come," &c., the institution of the second description of sacrifice, which Christ offered according to the will of God (6–10).

Their repetition proved the inefficacy not only of the annual sacrifices, but also the inefficacy of the daily sacrifices, offered morning and evening among the Jews ; whereas Christ, by one bloody oblation of himself, has made full atonement for sin, and purchased a treasure of grace for sanctifying men, at all times (11–14). The Apostle then proves, from the Prophet Jeremias, the inefficacy of the ancient sacrifices for remitting sin (15–19).

Having proved the abrogation of the legal sacrifices, and shown the superior excellence of the priesthood of Christ, and of his sacrifice over the Levitical priesthood and their offerings, he exhorts the Hebrews to constancy in the faith (19–21). He deters them from committing the dreadful crime of apostasy (24–31). He calms the fears which his words were calculated to inspire, by reminding them of their past good works of charity (32–34). Finally, he exhorts them to hold out for a short time, when they shall reap the full fruit of their past labours and sufferings.

Text.

1. FOR the law having a shadow of the good things to come, not the very image of the things : by the self-same sacrifices, which they offer continually every year, can never make the comers thereunto perfect :

Paraphrase.

1. Christ was offered to make atonement for the sins of all (ix. 28), and Christ alone could remit sin ; for, as to the law, it contained only the shadow, or mere representation of the future goods, procured for us by Christ, but not the things promised, in their real form. Hence, it could neither justify nor remit the sins of the priests officiating under it, much less those of the people by the *self-same* annual victims continually offered up, as sacrifices of *expiation*.

Commentary.

1. In verse 28, of the preceding chapter, it is implied, that Christ *alone* could confer justification and remit sin ; and, to prove this implied proposition, the Apostle proceeds

Text.	Paraphrase.
2. For then they would have ceased to be offered : because the worshippers once cleansed should have no conscience of sin any longer :	2. For, if these victims had the effect of remitting sin, there would be no occasion for their renewal (*in commemoration of the self-same sins*, for which they were before offered); because the ministers once purified would require no further expiation, and would have no further consciousness of the sins already remitted.
3. But in them there is made a commemoration of sins every year.	3. But what is the fact? It is, that in the annual sacrifices—namely, of *expiation*—there is made a commemoration and confession of the *self-same sins*, as if actually subsisting and uncancelled.

Commentary.

to point out the utter insufficiency for justification of the Jewish sacrifices, in attributing too much efficacy to which the principal error of the Hebrews consisted.

" For the law." By " the law " is understood the entire law of Moses. The word " shadow," is understood by some to mean, an obscure delineation and outline, opposed to the perfect picture of a thing. The idea is borrowed from the art of painting. Others, more probably, understand it of the shadow as opposed to the body or reality, of which it is a shadow, which opinion better accords with the words of the Apostle (Colossians, ii. 7).

" Of the good things to come," *i.e.*, to be given us by Christ—viz., grace, remission of sin, justification, &c., of which the legal remission was a mere figure.

" Not the very image of things." " Image," (εἰκόνα) signifies the things themselves appearing in their most perfect representation—viz., in their own real form, in which sense, the word is employed, when it is said of Christ, that " he is the image of God." (2 Cor. iv. 4 ; Col. i. 5).

" Which they offer every year," refers to the great sacrifice of expiation offered once a year, by the high priest.

" Cannot make the servers perfect ;" and the Apostle leaves it to be implied, that if they cannot sanctify the ministering priest, nor remit his sins, much less, can they remit the sins of the people.

2. " For then they would have ceased to be offered." The ordinary Greek reading is, οὐκ ἄν επαυσαντο, *they would* NOT *have ceased.* The negative, *not*, is omitted in the Syriac and other copies ; it is inserted by Griesbach, on the authority of manuscripts, and will make no difference in the meaning of the passage. The words mean, that if these victims had the effect of remitting the sins for which they were offered, they would not have been repeated, for *the self-same sins.*

3. Now, they are repeated for *the self-same sins.* In these annual sacrifices of expiation there is made a remembrance and confession of the *same* sins commemorated in preceding years ; for, in the sacrifice of the emissary goat (Leviticus, xvi. 21), the pontiff is enjoined to confess over him " all the iniquities, offences, and sins of the children of Israel," without exception or distinction. Therefore, the very law itself supposes the inefficacy of preceding annual sacrifices of expiation ; since, if once expiated, what necessity would there be for offering up sacrifices for the *same sins* continually ?

OBJECTION.—Catholics have the sacrifice of the Mass daily offered up ; they also recur daily to the sacrament of Penance, and maintain, still, that the repetition of either does not prove its inefficacy. Does not this manifestly contradict the doctrine of the Apostle ?

ANSWER.—In reply, it is merely necessary to say, that if the reasoning of the Apostle be closely examined, it will be easily discovered, that the Catholic practice does not furnish the slightest ground for the foregoing objection. The Apostle is proving the inefficacy of the sacrifices of expiation annually presented for sin, from the fact of these sacrifices being offered up each year for the *self-same sins*, for which they were offered up in preceding years. " In them there is made a *commemoration* of sins every year " (verse 3). He does not suppose that they were offered up for the sins of the current year merely ; for, the law commands the high priest to offer up the

Text.

4. For it is impossible that with the blood of oxen and goats sins should be taken away.

5. Wherefore, when he cometh into the world, he saith : *Sacrifice and oblation thou wouldest not : but a body thou hast fitted to me:*

Paraphrase.

4. (These sacrifices, then, did not remove the guilt of sin—in them was only made a remembrance of sin) ; for, it is absolutely impossible that the blood of animals, of oxen and of goats, could, of its own intrinsic efficacy, remit the guilt of sin. (This was reserved for the precious blood of Jesus Christ).

5. Hence it is, that entering into the world at his Incarnation, he says to his heavenly Father (Psalm xxxix.), sacrifice and oblation thou hast rejected and abolished, as no longer grateful to thee ; but, a body fit for immolation thou hast given to me.

Commentary.

sacrifice of expiation annually for his sins, whether he sinned that year, or not ; from this, the law abstracts. It is on the circumstance of the repetition of the sacrifices *for the self-same sins*, that the Apostle grounds his argument, which may be reduced to this form :—*If the sacrifices of the Old Law had the effect of justifying and remitting the sins of the servers, they would not be offered repeatedly for the self-same sins* (verse 2). Which proposition he proves thus :—*Because if they remitted sins, then, the worshippers would have no further consciousness of the sins remitted* (verse 2). *But, we find there is a confession of the* SAME *sins made in them every year* (verse 3). *Therefore, they do not remit sin.* That such is the reasoning of the Apostle will appear quite clear, if it be borne in mind that the proposition, though apparently affirmative, "they would cease to be offered," is equivalent to the negative proposition, *they would not be offered*, contradictory of the proposition, verse 3 : "*But in them there is made a commemoration*," &c. These contradictory propositions must, therefore, have the same subject and attribute ; and to the former proposition, "they would cease to be offered," must be added the words, "in commemoration of sins," which is the same as, *for the self-same sins*, "every year ;" otherwise, the reasoning of the Apostle would be inconclusive. Where, then, is the parity between the cases of repetition referred to by the Apostle and the Catholic practice ? Is Mass offered up for sins already remitted ? —or, is penance resorted to, as a *matter of precept*, for sins already forgiven ? Certainly not. Hence, there is no parity. Besides, the reasoning of the Apostle would not prevent the repetition of the Mass, as a *holocaust*, as a *peace-offering*, &c. ; his argument, even supposing it to apply to the Mass, would only prove against its repetition, as an *expiatory* sacrifice ; for, it is of such he is speaking.

Nor is it true, that the repetition of the Mass is, even in this latter respect, that is to say, as a sacrifice of *expiation*, in the slightest degree affected by the reasoning of the Apostle ; for, he is treating of *redemptory* sacrifices. Now, one *redemptory* sacrifice, if efficacious, should not be repeated ; for, it is only an Infinite Being could offer it. Its value, therefore, would be *infinite*, and its repetition, useless. Whereas, the Mass, being only an *applicatory* sacrifice, subordinate to, and in substance, the same as, the sacrifice of the cross, of which it is a real commemoration and unbloody continuation, deriving from it all its efficacy, should be no more abolished than the other channels of divine grace, to say nothing of its repetition, as an *holocaust* or *peace-offering*, &c.

4. This is confirmatory of the preceding. "It is impossible," &c., in the sense of the Hebrews, who imagined it could remit sin, of its own *intrinsic* efficacy. No doubt, the blood of animals could remit sins, if there were a connexion divinely instituted, as in the case of the water, in baptism ; but no such connexion had been instituted in the Old Law. If sin had been ever remitted, it was, *ex opere operantis*. The Apostle, by saying, "it is impossible," &c., shows, that he is speaking of our *redemption*, which was to be effected by the substitution and vicarious offering of Him, "on whom the Lord laid the iniquity of us all."—(Isaias liii.)

5. He proves the inefficacy of the ancient sacrifices, from the SS. Scriptures. It was on this account, that in Psalm, xxxiv. (which, some say, regards Christ ; at least, if it regard David directly, it refers to Christ mystically) Christ is introduced as addressing his Father in these words—" *Sacrifice*," &c. These words show the little regard in which every species of ancient sacrifices was held by God the Father. " *Sacrifice*," *i.e.*,

Text.

6. *Holocausts for sin did not please thee.*

7. *Then said I: Behold I come: in the head of the book it is written of me: that I should do thy will, O God.*

8. *In saying before, Sacrifices, and oblations, and holocausts, for sin thou wouldest not, neither are they pleasing to thee, which are offered according to the law.*

9. *Then said I, Behold, I come to do thy will, O God: he taketh away the first, that he may establish that which followeth.*

10. *In the which will, we are sanctified by the oblation of the body of JESUS CHRIST once.*

Paraphrase.

6. *Holocausts for sin did not please thee.*

7. Then, said I : Behold, I am present, prepared (according to what has been foretold of me in the entire of the Scriptures) to do thy will.

8. In this quotation from Psalm xxxix., spoken by Christ, two things are to be specially noted: first, he says, sacrifices, and oblations, and holocausts for sin thou hast held in no regard, nor have any of the offerings prescribed, by the Old Law, been pleasing to thee :

9. Secondly, he says :—Behold, I am ready, O God, to do thy will. In the first words, "*sacrifices,*" &c., he shows the abolition of the ancient oblations there referred to ; and by saying, *Behold I come,* &c., he has established the second kind of sacrifices, which Christ offered, according to the will of God.

10. Conformably to which will of God (whereby he wished that Christ would be offered as a victim), we are sanctified by the bloody oblation of the body of Christ, once.

Commentary.

offering of *bloody* victims. "*Oblation,*" of, *unbloody.* "*Thou wouldst not.*" He did not wish for them permanently ; because they did not possess the effect of remitting sin ; moreover, as they were but types, he did not wish for their continuance, after the reality had come. "*But a body thou hast fitted to me.*" These words are quoted by St. Paul from the Septuagint version, as, indeed, are all his quotations in this Epistle. In the Hebrew version, followed by St. Jerome in our Vulgate on the Psalms, the words are, " But thou hast bored ears for me," expressive of his servile condition and obedience, in allusion to the boring of the ears of perpetual servants, among the Jews.—(Exodus, xxi. 6). The meaning of both readings is not different, as the "boring of his ears," and "fitting a body to him," both denote the obedience of Christ. The reading of the Septuagint better suits the scope of the Apostle : God gave him a passible body, otherwise he could not offer sacrifice to God, nor "take away the first, by establishing that which followeth " (verse 9).

6. "Holocausts for sin did not please thee," not because they were bad ; but, imperfect. In the Greek of this place, and in the Psalm, it is, ὁλοκαυτωματα καιπερι αμαρτιας, *holocausts and for sin, i.e.,* holocausts and sin offerings. The "*holocausts for sin,*" according to our version, probably regard the great sacrifice of expiation, which was both a holocaust and sin offering ; but, generally speaking, holocausts and sin offerings were quite distinct.

7. "*Then said I.*" The word "*then,*" according to some, refers to the time when the ancient sacrifices ceased to please God the Father ; or, more probably, it has the force of, *therefore,* "*I come,*" I am ready "*to do thy will (it is written of me in the head of the book.*)" It will make the reading more clear, if these words, "*in the head of the book, &c.,*" be enclosed within a parenthesis. In the Hebrew, the reading is, "*in the volume, or, roll of the book,*" in which allusion is made to the mode, in which the books of the law among the Jews were folded up on rollers. The words, most probably, mean, that the sum or contents of the SS. Scriptures, placed at the beginning of the book, regarded the obedience of Christ to his Father.

9. From the quotation, the Apostle draws this two-fold conclusion, by saying—"*Sacrifice thou wouldest not,*" Christ has shown the removal or abolition of the first kind of sacrifices referred to ; and, by saying, "*Behold I come,*" &c., the institution of the second description of sacrifice, which he offered according to the will of God.

10. The Apostle shows what this will of God, which Christ was ready to do, is : it

Text.

11. And every priest indeed standeth daily ministering, and often offering the same sacrifices which can never take away sins.

12. But this man offering one sacrifice for sins, for ever sitteth on the right hand of God,

13. From henceforth expecting, until his enemies be made his footstool.

14. For by one oblation he hath perfected for ever them that are sanctified.

Paraphrase.

11. And not only does the high priest annually repeat the sacrifice of expiation (making a commemoration of the *same sins*), but in the daily sacrifices, at which the priests minister in turn, the same victims are offered, the same repetition made—hence, they too, for a like reason, cannot take away sins.

12. But Christ, after having offered one sacrifice, which satisfies for all sins, sitteth glorious at the right hand of God,

13. Awaiting the time, when his enemies shall be made his footstool.

14. For, by one bloody oblation of himself—an oblation of infinite value, extending to all generations—he perfected those who are sanctified at all times ; in other words, by this one bloody oblation of himself, he made atonement for all sin, and purchased the treasures of grace, whereby men are sanctified at all times.

Commentary.

is this—viz., that in the body which his Father had given him, he would make one bloody offering of himself, which would be a source of redemption and sanctification to the entire world.

11. In this verse he proceeds to show, that the circumstance of their repetition did not prove the inefficacy of the annual sacrifices of expiation only ; that it also proved the same, for a like reason, in regard to the daily sacrifices, offered morning and evening, by the priests in their turn. "And every priest standeth," in fear and awe ; "daily ministering," morning and evening (Numbers, xxviii.) "Often offering the same sacrifices, which can never take away sin," any more than could the annual sacrifice of expiation, offered by the high priest alone.

12. "But this man offering one sacrifice," *i.e.*, after having offered one sacrifice. The Greek for "offering," προσενέγκας, means, *having offered.* "Sitteth" in glory and triumph. The Jewish priest "stood" with fear and awe ; he "sitteth" in glory and majesty.

13. Nor will he leave this seat of glory until his enemies are prostrated, according to the promise of the Royal Prophet (Psalm cix.)—"Sit at my right hand, until I make thine enemies thy footstool." This subjection of all things to Christ will be manifested at the end of the world."

14. He need not leave heaven to repeat, like the Jewish priest, the *bloody* oblation of himself ; for, by one such oblation, he has compassed all the ends of Redemption, he has made perfect atonement for sin, and merited the graces, whereby men are, at all times, sanctified.

OBJECTION.—Against the sacrifice of the Mass. In these two chapters, the Apostle allows only one oblation of Christ, therefore, he excludes the repeated oblation of him in the Mass, as opposed to the unity of his offering.

ANSWER.—The oblation of Christ referred to by the Apostle in these chapters, and the repetition of which he rejects, is the *bloody* oblation on the cross ; for, there is question of the oblation, by which "he perfected" (or sanctified) "all ;" *i.e.*, redeemed mankind, and atoned for sin ; the oblation wherein, if repeated, he should suffer death (ix. 26). But, from the fact that he cannot be offered up again, in a *bloody* manner, can it be inferred, that he cannot be offered, in an *unbloody* manner ? As well might it be inferred from the fact of God having promised, that the world would not be again destroyed by *water*, that therefore, it is not to be destroyed in any other way, whether by water or by fire, which would be contrary to faith. Christ is offered up, in an *unbloody* manner, in the sacrifice of the Mass ; and the Apostle, for reasons already assigned, does not refer to that oblation ; it does not fall within his scope ; nor, perhaps, would it be expedient at the time, to do so.

Text.

15. And the Holy Ghost also doth testify *this* to us. For after that he said :

16. *And this is the testament which I will make unto them after those days, saith the Lord. I will give my laws in their hearts, and on their minds will I write them :*

17. *And their sins and iniquities I will remember no more.*

Paraphrase.

15. The testimony of the Holy Ghost is corroborative of the same, viz., that the remission of sin was not attached to the Old Law, this being a distinguishing characteristic of the New; for, having said, (Jeremias, xxxi) :—

16. This is the testament, which I will make unto them, after those days, saith the Lord, I will engrave my laws on the their hearts, and on their minds will I write them.

17. And their sins and iniquities I will remember no more.

Commentary.

But, by saying, he can be offered, *only once*, does he not exclude a *second* oblation or more ; and hence, the oblation made of him, in the Mass ?

ANSWER.—He excludes a second oblation of the *same kind*, and presented in *the same way.* The unity of Christ's oblation is insisted on, in opposition to other reiterated oblations. Now, to any person attentively examining the reasoning of the Apostle, in these two chapters, it must appear quite clear, that the opposition instituted is, between the bloody oblation of Christ on the cross, and the *annual* and *daily* sacrifices of the Jews, the efficacious and fruitful unity of the former being contrasted with the useless multiplicity of the latter. The objection, therefore, is quite inconclusive ; *Christ will not be offered up a second time*—which, to be true, must mean—*in a bloody manner. Therefore, he will not be offered up, in an unbloody manner.* Just as conclusive would it be to say—*The world will not be destroyed again by the waters of deluge. Therefore, it will be destroyed in no other way, and it shall be eternal.* The Apostle excludes the repetition of the sacrifice of Christ in the Mass, as a *redemptory* sacrifice, as making atonement and offering satisfaction for sin ; in which respect only, the sacrifice of Christ is contrasted with the annual and daily sacrifices among the Jews ; he never contemplates rejecting the repetition, or rather the continuation of the same, in an *unbloody* manner, as *applicatory* of the merits purchased on the cross. On the cross, an infinite treasure of merit was purchased ; a satisfaction offered, adequate to make reparation for the sins of ten thousand worlds. But, no Christian can deny that by the institution of God himself, there are certain channels required for the application to our souls, in a limited degree, of this treasure of grace, in itself infinite. What else is the end of the sacrament of baptism, to which all Christians have recourse for the remission of original sin ?—and Catholics regard the sacrifice of the Mass, as a channel through which are applied to us the merits and graces purchased on the cross. Surely, it cannot be alleged that the sins of the elect are directly remitted by the merits of Christ, the instant they are committed. Would this not be plainly opposed to the precept, inculcated in several passages of SS. Scripture, of recurring to baptism for the remission of sin ? Would not be opposed to the words of our redeemer :—" He that believeth and is baptized, shall be saved ; but he that believeth not, shall be condemned ?"—(Mark, xvi. 16). It is opposed to the manner in which the Jews converted after St. Peter's first sermon were justified. They were told, " to do penance, and to be baptized, every one of them, for the remission of their sins " (Acts, ii. 28). Now, on their justification was to be modelled that of all the Gentiles, who at the preaching of the Apostles did penance, believed, were baptized, and their sins thus remitted.

, 15. The Apostle adduces the testimony of the Holy Ghost, to prove that the remission of sin was not effected by the sacrifices of the Old Law, but only by those of the New. He quotes from chapter xxxi. of Jeremias, referred to in chapter viii. of this Epistle. The proof is taken from verse 17. By saying that in the new testament which he was to make with his people, " he would no longer remember their sins," *i.e.,* that he would remit them, he implies, that in the old testament there was no such efficacy, this being a distinguishing characteristic of the new. The reading from verse 15, in our version, is suspensive and imperfect. There is nothing corresponding with the words, " after that he said " (verse 15) ; nor does it appear, that there are any words

Text.

18. Now where there *is* a remission of these, there is no more an oblation for sin.

19. Having therefore, brethren a confidence in the entering into the Holies by the blood of Christ :

20. A new and living way which he hath dedicated for us through the veil, that is to say, his flesh,

21. And a high priest over the house of God :

Paraphrase.

18. Now, where these are remitted, and a ransom adequate to make atonement for them offered, there is no further need for any such oblation for sin.

19. Having, therefore, brethren (from what has been already shown regarding the efficacy of the blood of Christ, his entering heaven in quality of our high priest, to open it for us, &c.), a well grounded confidence of entering the Holy of Holies of heaven, through the efficacy of the same blood.

20. And having a new way hitherto untrodden, and a living way which Christ dedicated, and first entered on through the veil of his own flesh.

21. And a great meditating Pontiff, placed over the entire Church militant and triumphant, to guard the concerns of both.

Commentary.

expressing the result which they would seem to imply or denote. Hence, some Expositors endeavour to remedy this, by making the words, "*saith the Lord*," the beginning of the second member of the sentence, as if they ran thus :—"After that he said" (verse 15), "THEN *saith the Lord, I will give my laws*, &c." (verse 16). The words, "*saith the Lord*," however, regard the preceding, and are a part of the prophetic quotation. Others supply, at verse 17, such words as these :—"THEN, HE SAID, *and their sins*," &c. It may be, that the sense is suspended from verse 15 to 18 ; as if, the Apostle made the conclusion drawn from the prophetic quotation, the second member of the sentence, thus :—" For, after that he said," &c. (verses 15, 16, 17), then, the only conclusion to be arrived at is, that where sins are remitted, there is no need for any further such oblation (verse 18).

18. "Now where there is remission of sin," &c. There is no necessity for repeating oblations for sins already remitted. This is quite clear, if there be question of *actual* remission. Nor can there be any difficulty about it either, if there be a question of *potential* remission, in the sense that there has been a ransom paid, and a *redemptory* sacrifice offered for them ; because, one *redemptory* sacrifice, if efficacious, must be a sacrifice of infinite value ; and hence, its repetition as such, would be useless ; but neither signification of the words is opposed to the repeated offering of *applicatory* sacrifices for sins, not yet actually remitted ; the Mass, therefore, as an *applicatory* sacrifice, is not excluded ; if so, the other means of grace, faith, hope, contrition, sacraments, should be excluded as well, on the same principle.

19. Some Expositors say, that the second, or *moral* part of this Epistle commences at this verse. It is more likely, that one of the principal dogmatic parts of the Epistle, regarding the necessity of divine faith, concerning which, it would appear, the Hebrews entertained rather serious doubts, yet remains to be treated of ; but before engaging them in this point, he wishes to deter them from the crime of apostasy, by a strong denunciation of its heinous enormity. "In the entering into the Holies," of entering heaven, the true Holy of Holics.

20. "And a new and living way," "New," because untrodden by any before Christ ; "living," because it leads to life eternal, or, "living," *i.e.*, permanent, and not to be destroyed, like the Jewish tabernacle. "Which he hath dedicated for us." The Greek, ενεκαινισεν, literally means, *which he initiated, or, first opened for us*. "Through the veil, that is to say, his flesh." The allusion to the Jewish tabernacle is kept up, the veil of which was a type of Christ's flesh ; because, as the veil was to be removed for the entrance of the high priest into the Holy of Holies, and he should pass through it ; so was Christ to pass through our assumed nature, and through its division on the cross, into the sanctuary of heaven, and open it for us. His flesh may be also called the "veil," because, it concealed his Divinity, as the veil of the tabernacle concealed the sanctuary from the gaze of the people ; the former reason is the more probable.

Text.

22. Let us draw near with a true heart in fulness of faith, having our hearts sprinkled from an evil conscience, and our bodies washed with clean water.

23. Let us hold fast the confession of our hope without wavering (for he is faithful that hath promised),

24. And let us consider one another to provoke unto charity and to good works :

25. Not forsaking our assembly, as some are accustomed, but comforting *one another*, and so much the more as you see the day approaching.

26. For if we sin wilfully after having the knowledge of the truth, there is now left no sacrifice for sins,

Paraphrase.

22. Let us approach with sincere minds, in the fullest conviction which faith carries with it, having our hearts cleansed from the defilements of sin, and our bodies washed with the cleansing waters of baptism.

23. Let us hold firm and unwavering, the confession of faith and hope which we professed in baptism (for he is infinitely veracious, on whose promises, our faith and hope are grounded) ;

24. And let us observe each other attentively, so as to be excited to emulation, in the exercise of charity and good works ;

25. Not imitating the perverse example of a certain class of persons, in forsaking our public meetings, and the Church itself, but rather consoling each other, and by charitable admonitions, exhorting each other to perseverance, and this with greater zeal, as we know that the day of retribution is drawing near.

26. For, to us, who, after receiving a knowledge of the truth, and becoming members of the Church, wilfully commit the sin of receding from her, there is left, in that state, no redeeming victim for sin.

Commentary.

22. " Having our hearts sprinkled from an evil conscience ; " *i.e.*, purified from sin, which generates an evil conscience, "and our bodies washed with clean water," *i.e.*, having our bodies washed with the cleansing waters of baptism. In the words, "sprinkled" and "washed," is contained an allusion to the legal ablutions and aspersions, required for entering the Jewish sanctuary. These had mystical reference to the purity of conscience, required for Christians to enter heaven.

How could the Apostle, in the sense assigned to them, address the words, "*and our bodies washed*," &c., to those already baptized, since baptism cannot be repeated ?

ANSWER.—Some say, that the words merely regard catechumens ; others, that, even in regard to the baptized, they mean, having that purity of soul, which is like your baptismal renovation.

23. "The confession of our hope ; " because subjects of hope form a part of the profession of our faith, and hope is founded on faith, in the promises of God, hence he adds ("for he is faithful," &c.)

24. The circumstance of viewing each other's actions was calculated to create a rivalry, and this should be in the right way, in exercising charity, by being blind to the faults, and alive to succour the wants of one another.

25. "The day approaching," by which some understand the destruction of Jerusalem, when, by the total extirpation of their present persecutors, they will obtain a respite from persecution ; it more probably, however, refers to the day of retribution in the life to come ; for, this is the balm of consolation, which the Apostle usually proposes to those who are suffering for justice sake. "Forsaking not our assembly ; " by which some understand the common assemblies of the faithful, convened for the purposes of mutual instruction and edification. Others say, it refers to the Church, which they were deserting by apostasy, to which allusion would appear to be made in the following verses. The passage will admit of both interpretations, the one subordinate to the other—the desertion of the places of divine worship, and of the meetings, in which the Christians consoled and encouraged each other under persecution, would serve as a preparation for desertion of the Church, or the society of Christians altogether, by the sin of apostasy.

26. The sin, to which he refers in the words, "sins wilfully," and from the commission of which, or exposure to it, he wishes to deter them, is the sin of apostasy. This is clear from the strong language, which the Apostle applies to it (verse 29). It is true to say of such, that "no sacrifice for sin" is left them, not in Judaism, into which they

Text.

27. But a certain dreadful expectation of judgment, and the rage of a fire which shall consume the adversaries.

28. A man making void the law of Moses, dieth without any mercy under two or three witnesses :

29. How much more, do you think, he deserveth worse punishments, who hath trodden under foot the Son of God, and hath esteemed the blood of the testament unclean, by which he was sanctified, and hath offered an affront to the Spirit of grace?

30. For we know him that hath said : *Vengeance belongeth to me, and I will repay.* And again : *The Lord shall judge his people.*

Paraphrase.

27. We have only to expect the terrible and dread judgment of God, and the raging vehemence of the fire of hell, which is destined to devour God's enemies.

28. A man apostatizing from the law of Moses, is inexorably put to death, on the testimony of two or three witnesses.

29. How much heavier punishment, think you, does he not deserve who, by his apostasy, has trodden under foot and treated with the greatest ignominy the Son of God—approving of this conduct in the Jews—has esteemed the blood of the testament, in which he was sanctified, common and unclean, and offers an affront to the Holy Ghost, the fountain of grace?

30. And we know, he shall suffer all the punishment he deserves ; for, the Lord has declared, that the fulness of revenge is his, and that he will inflict it, and also, that he will take judgment for his people, and punish their enemies.

Commentary.

relapse—the Jewish sacrifices being incapable of remitting sin, and, therefore, abolished for their inefficacy—nor in Christianity, which they are supposed to have abandoned.

OBJECTION.—In the interpretation now given, the words, "after having the knowledge of the truth," will have no meaning, since it is true of those who had never received the truth, but remained in Judaism, that no sacrifice was left for them either.

ANSWER.—It is perfectly true of them also ; but, the Apostle mentions this circumstance, as peculiarly affecting those whom he addresses, and aggravating their sin ; while their conversion would be more difficult than would be the conversion of those who never embraced the faith.

27. Hell fire is personified and represented, as zealously exerting itself to punish God's enemies.

28. The Apostle, by an argument, *a minore ad majus*, shows the enormous guilt of the Christian apostate, and the heavy anger which he provokes. "Making void the law of Moses," refers to apostasy from the law—the punishment inflicted is that marked out for apostates.—(Deuternomy, xvii.) The word "making void," involves more than violating a single precept ; it involves the throwing away the entire law. The comparison shows that the Apostle, in the preceding verse, is referring to the crime of apostasy.

29. The apostate from Christianity, by the one act, perpetrates three crimes of the blackest enormity : "He treads under foot the Son of God," by approving of the act of the Jews, trampling on him and maltreating him. "He esteems the blood of Christ unclean." (The Greek for "unclean" is κοινον). By deserting to Judaism, he looks upon the blood of Christ, in which he was before sanctified, of no more efficacy than the common blood of oxen or of goats—nay, of less, since deserting the latter, he recurs to the former ; "and hath offered an affront to the spirit of grace," or the Holy Ghost, by despising and undervaluing the several gifts of the Holy Ghost, received in the faith, which he now deserts. These words could be strictly true of a sinner relapsing into any mortal sin from a state of grace ; but, they are more particularly so of the apostate.

30. "For we know that he saith ;" *i.e.*, so surely as the apostate from Christianity deserves more severe punishment than the apostate from the law of Moses, so surely shall he be visited with this merited punishment. "*Vengeance belongeth to me,*" &c. These words, taken from Deuternomy (chap. xxxii.), were originally applied to the idolatrous Gentiles, the enemies of God. "And again : *the Lord shall judge his people.*" These are the words of Moses. The word "*judge,*" is generally understood, *will*

Text.	**Paraphrase.**
31. It is a fearful thing to fall into the hands of the living God.	31. It is a dreadful thing for the impenitent to fall into the hands of the living God, who, therefore, will never cease to inflict punishment.
32. But call to mind the former days, wherein, being illuminated, you endured a great fight of afflictions.	32. Call to mind the days of your first fervour, in which, having been enlightened in baptism, you endured a great struggle with afflictions ;
33. And on the one hand indeed by reproaches and tribulation were made a gazing stock ; and on the other, became companions of them that were used in such sort.	33. Partly by being yourselves exposed to public insult and suffering, and partly by being made partakers by sympathy, in the sufferings of the others similarly maltreated.
34. For you both had compassion on them that were in bands, and took with joy the being stripped of your own goods, knowing that you have a better and a lasting substance.	34. You were made partakers in the sufferings of others, when you sympathized with the Christians cast into chains, and were personally exposed to injury in the plunder of your property, knowing from faith, that a better and more lasting substance was in store for you in heaven.
35. Do not therefore lose your confidence, which hath a great reward.	35. Do not, therefore, abandon that confident hope which has sustained you in misfortune, and which has annexed to it a great remuneration.
36. For patience is necessary for you : that, doing the will of God, you may receive the promise.	36. For, the patient expectation of future goods and liberation from present evils is necessarny for you that, after having complied with the will of God (wishing you to submit to sufferings), you may obtain the promised inheritance.

Commentary.

avenge, or *take punishment for his people.* Some understand it, *will punish his (apostatizing) people.*

31. "It is a fearful thing to fall into the hands," *i.e.*, to fall into the power, for revenge or punishment, "of the living God," who being eternal and omnipotent, will allow his enemies no escape from punishment. The words of David, "it is better fall into the hands of God than of man," are not opposed to this, because David speaks of the penitent ; St. Paul, of the impenitent.

32. To the foregoing threats of punishment, the Apostle now joins the allurements of the rewards to which their past fervour and fortitude will entit le them, provided they persevere with patience, for a short time. "You endured a great fight of afflictions," *i.e.*, with afflictions : the metaphor is borrowed from the public contests for prizes.

33, 34. He explains what their sufferings were :—They consisted partly, in their being publicly and openly exposed to insult and tribulations ; and partly, in their being made partakers of the sufferings of others similarly treated, by mental sympathy and by contributing to their support. He further explains the two members of the preceding sentence, both as to how they suffered personally, and how they suffered by mental sympathy ; he inverts the order and illustrates the second member first. "They became companions of them" that suffered ; for, they sympathized with the Christians cast into chains, and administered to their wants, and they were made "a gazing stock" (verse 36), by tribulation, in the confiscation and plunder of their entire property, to which they submitted with joy, calling to mind, that a better and more permanent substance awaited them in heaven. "You had compassion on them that were in bands," is read by some, τοις δεσμοις μου, "you had compassion on my bands.' The other reading τοις δεσμοῖς, followed by the Vulgate, *vinctis*, is more common, and best supported by the authority of manuscripts and critics generally. The Greek adds, εν ουρανοις, *in heaven.* These words are wanting in the Alexandrian and Cambridge MSS.

35. Hence, suffering for justice sake, has a reward annexed to it, and is a subject of merit. By "confidence," some understand the object of confidence, "which hath a great reward."

36. "(Patience," υπομονη) means not only the enduring of present evils, but also the

Text.

37. For yet a little and a very little while, and he that is to come, will come, and will not delay.

38. But my just man liveth by faith : but if he withdraw himself, he shall not please my soul.

39. But we are not the children of withdrawing unto perdition, but of faith to the saving of the soul.

Paraphrase.

37. For, yet a very short time, and he who is to come will come, and will not delay, and will render to each one the reward of his merits.

38. But, in the mean time, until he come, the just man will live through faith (in which his spiritual life is begun and strengthened) ; but, if he withdraw himself from faith, he shall not please me.

39. But I trust we shall not be children of withdrawal from the faith, *i.e.*, of unbelief, unto our destruction, but of perseverance in faith, in order to obtain life everlasting.

Commentary.

enduring of them in hope of liberation from them, and is the reward to which they conduct, as means.

37. The shortness of the time of their suffering is an encouragement to them " For, yet a little, and a very little while." These words are supposed by many to be the Apostle's own, and not to form a part of the following prophetic quotation ; others say, they are a part of the quotation. "He that is to come, will come," &c. These words, with the following verse, are taken from the prophet Habacuc (chap. ii.), and are quoted by the Apostle, from the Septuagint version. They literally refer to the vision which the prophet saw, and recounted, regarding the liberation of the Jews by Cyrus, from the Babylonian captivity. But, in their mystical and principal sense, they regard the first and second coming of Christ ; here, they are applied to the time of his second coming to judgment, which time, though distant and long in itself, is, still, very short, a mere point compared to eternity.

38. "But my just man liveth by faith, but if he withdraw himself," &c. This is according to the Septuagint, with this difference only, that the Apostle transposes the reading, making the last member of the sentence in the prophet, first, and *vice versa*, in order to render the assertion next verse, 39, more connected. " My just man lives by faith." In the Hebrew version, it is " *the just man liveth by his faith.*" Faith is the life of the just man ; by it, he receives first and second justification, kept alive by charity and good works. The Apostle evidently includes good works ; for, he refers to the patient endurance of the crosses of life, in the midst of which faith sustains the just man—good works are, therefore, included—so does the prophet also ; for he supposes the faithful Jew suffering in captivity, to continue in good works and patient endurance, supported by faith until the coming of the deliverer, Cyrus, promised by God. It is to the faithful Hebrew, suffering for the faith from his countrymen, the Apostle proposes the second coming to judgment of him, whom Cyrus typified.—(*See* Romans. i. 17—Commentary on.)

CHAPTER XI.

Analysis.

The Hebrews, it would appear, were not sufficiently impressed with the importance and necessity of faith ; and were, therefore, in danger of losing it by apostasy. They were taught to look upon it as a mode of justifying wholly unknown to the saints of the Old Testament ; and to these false notions, with which they were imbued, might be traced their fatal facility, in deserting it under the pressure of persecution. The Apostle (x. 38) takes occasion from the words of the Prophet Habacuc, to confute this pernicious error. Before making the application of it, in this chapter, to the sainted heroes of old, he first gives a description of faith, describing it by two of its qualities, best accommodated to the circumstances of those, whom he addresses (verse 1).

In the next place, applying this faith to the saints of old, he shows that it was owing to it, the most distinguished among them obtained justification (2–39).

He, finally shows the great advantage which we, in the New Law, possess over the ancients. We can, at once, enter on the possession of the promised blessings, while they were obliged to wait for our time to enjoy them in common with us ; and, surely, we should display no less heroism in the cause of faith, of which the blessings and promise are present, than they did, for whom the fulfilment of the promise was distant.

Text.

1. NOW faith is the substance of things to be hoped for, the evidence of things that appear not.

Paraphrase.

1. (As, then, the just man lives by faith, [x. 38] it is of importance for us to know the nature of this virtue, which is the spiritual life of our souls). Faith is the foundation of the blessings we hope for ; or, the subsistence in our intellect of the things we hope for ; it is the fullest convincing argument of the existence of these things, which are neither the immediate object of our sight nor perceived by reason, but which we still more firmly believe than if we saw them.

Commentary.

1. " Now faith is the substance of things to be hoped for." In order to render more clear the application of faith to the examples he is about adducing, the Apostle commences with a description of faith, and he describes it, by two of its leading qualities, First—"It is the substance of things to be hoped for," to which words, some, with St. Augustine give this construction, "*it is the substance of those who hope.*" These attach an active signification to the middle verb in the Greek, ἐλπιζομένων ὑπόστασις, corresponding to the words in our version, "to be hoped for." Ours is the more probable construction. "The substance," *i.e.*, the basis and foundation, on which rest the blessings of salvation we hope for. For, it is, "*the root and foundation of all justification.*" (Council of Trent, SS. 6, c. viii.) Without faith we could no more obtain justification than we could build a house without a foundation, or have an *accident*, ordinarily speaking, without a *substance*. Or, the word "substance " (in Greek, ὑπόστασις) more probably means, *subsistence*, of the things to be hoped for ; inasmuch as, faith makes the future goods of the life to come, so to exist in our apprehension, as if we actually possessed them. It gives these things, we hope for, a new and anticipated existence in our minds.

Secondly—It is "the evidence of things that appear not "(οὐ βλεπομένων), *i.e.*, of things

Text.

2. For by this the ancients obtained a testimony.

3. By faith we understand that the world was framed by the word of God; that from invisible things visible things might be made.

Paraphrase.

2. For, it was by this faith in God's promises, holding out distant and, humanly speaking, unattainable goods, that the ancient fathers were distinguished, and obtained from God an illustrious testimony of their sanctity.

3. Such a faith is as necessary for us, as for them, for understanding the very first principles of revealed religion; for, by faith we learn that creation was moulded into its present harmonious and perfect form, by the command of God, so that from being an invisible shapeless mass or chaos, it assumed its present visible perfect appearance.

Commentary.

that are neither visible to the senses, nor perceived by reason. This by no means appears to be an adequate or reciprocal definition of faith; for, things to *be dreaded* form subjects of faith no less than "things to be hoped for" (*v.g.*) hell's torments; so did Noe's deluge (verse 7). Neither does it appear that obscurity essentially belongs to subjects of faith; for, if so, how could the Blessed Virgin Mary or the Apostles have faith in many of the miraculous works of our Divine Redeemer, which they witnessed? Do we not believe in death, although sensibly taking place, and its universality confirmed by experience? Do we not believe in God, *as Creator of heaven and earth*, an evident natural truth? This definition cannot exclude the application of faith to things clear; because, although such things be naturally evident, we can abstract from their natural evidence, and believe them like every point of faith, on the authority of God, whose revelation is necessary in order that they should become subjects of faith. Moreover, in the present obscured state of the human intellect, there are but few things so evident as not to be susceptible of confirmation, and of greater subjective certainty, from the authority of God, upon which all faith must be based. The opinion, therefore, of the Thomists requiring obscurity in an object to be necessary, in order to become a point of faith, appears improbable; because, the principal ground of this opinion, viz., that the Apostle here gives a reciprocal definition of faith, is unfounded. The Apostle only describes faith by two of its qualities, the most praiseworthy, viz., its giving the things to be hoped for, an anticipated existence in our minds; and its making certain for us, things that are obscure and inevident—two qualities best accommodated to the circumstances of those whom he addresses, who possessed not, and could, therefore, only " hope for " the invisible blessings of the life to come; neither did they clearly see them, because they "appear not." These men were to be animated to patient suffering, with the prospect of the same blessings in hope.

2. Some interpreters connect this verse immediately with verse 38 of last chapter, "the just man liveth by faith,......for by this the ancients obtained," &c. Others, with preceding verse, as in the Paraphrase.

It is not undeserving of remark, that the faith commended by the Apostle in this chapter, is not the *special faith* of Protestants, in reference to each man's justification and salvation; but, as is clear from the entire chapter, a firm belief in the things revealed by God, which all the examples quoted clearly demonstrate.

3. The Apostle, before applying the faith now described to the saints of old, shows that even in reference to the Hebrews whom he addresses, it is " the evidence of things that appear not;" because, creation, the first truth proposed to the Jews in Genesis, was not known from any other source than faith; for, the ancient philosophers, one of whose favourite axioms was, *ex nihilo nihil fit*, derided it. " That the world was framed by the word of God," this some understand of the first creation or eduction out of nothing; others, more probably of the arrangement into its present form, of the matter of creation already educed from nothing into existence; "that from invisible things," *i.e.*, from the pre-existent dark, confused or shapeless mass of matter, this the word " invisible" means in Genesis; (for, instead of the words, "the earth was void and empty"—Genesis i. 2.—the Septuagint version, followed all through, by St. Paul in

Text.

4. By faith Abel offered to God a sacrifice exceeding that of Cain, by which he obtained a testimony that he was just, God giving testimony to his gifts, and by it he being dead yet speaketh.

5. By faith Henoch was translated, that he should not see death, and he was not found because God had translated him : For before his translation he had testimony that he pleased God.

6. But without faith it is impossible to please God. For he that cometh to God, must believe that he is, and is a rewarder to them that seek him.

Paraphrase.

4. It was owing to his being animated with a lively faith that Abel offered a more choice and more excellent sacrifice than did Cain (who made no selection in the gifts offered), by means of which sacrifice offered through faith he obtained the testimony of being just, God himself testifying the acceptance of his gifts by some external sign ; and even after his death, he sends forth a cry for redress, which God listened to in consideration of his faith and justice.

5. It was by faith Henoch was translated into some place of rest, to escape death, and he was not found, because God had translated him (Genesis, v. 24). That his translation was owing to his faith is clear ; for, before his translation, the Scripture bears testimony, that he pleased God.

6. Now, without faith it is impossible to please God ; for, in order to come to God, *i.e.*, to worship and please him, one must believe that he exists, and that he is a rewarder of those who seek and serve him (in which it is implied that he punishes those who offend, and disobey him).

Commentary.

this Epistle, has, 'Η δὲ γῆ ἦν αορατος και ακατασκευαστος, *the earth was invisible and confused*) it would become visible in its present perfect form Of course, the creation of matter from nothing is supposed in this arrangement or last finish given to it, referred to here by the Apostle.

4. It was his faith that made Abel select the choicest portions of his flock to offer them in sacrifice, while Cain heeded not to make any selection : he is not commended in Genesis for making any choice in the fruits of the earth which he offered—" by which " faith or sacrifice, or perhaps both ; that is to say, his sacrifice offered through faith, " God giving testimony to his gifts " by some sensible sign, commonly said to be his sending fire from heaven to consume them, while no such sign was exhibited in the case of Cain. " And by it being dead he still speaketh," which some understand of his blood crying to God (*vide* Paraphrase). Others say, he speaks by the force of his good example.

5. " Was translated " into some seat of rest, or, as in Ecclesiasticus (chap. xl. 4), " into paradise," in order to escape death. The common opinion of the Holy Fathers is, that he still lives in some place of rest expressed by the general term of " paradise," whence he and Elias will come at the end of the world to war with Antichrist, " and he was not found, because God had translated him." These are the words of Genesis (chap. v. 24), according to the Septuagint, from which the Apostle proves Henoch's translation. In the Vulgate version of Genesis, by St. Jerome, the words are, " he was seen no more, because God took him." And that it was owing to faith he was translated, the Apostle proves thus—for, before his translation, the Scriptures testify that he pleased God, " he walked with God," (Gen. v. 22), and, therefore, pleased Him.

6. But, without faith no one can please God ; it was, therefore, through the merits of faith, Henoch pleased him. The Apostle proves that without faith no one can please God ; for, in order to please God, a man must approach him, " must come to him," but no one can approach or come to him, without first believing " that he exists, and that he is a rewarder to them that seek him." In these latter words, it is implied, that he punishes those who disobey him ; the words, " come to God," mean, to pay him due worship. The Greek for " rewarder," μισθαποδοτης, means, that God gives a reward due to merit ; hence, an argument in favour of the Catholic doctrine of merit, it is a point of faith, that a reward is strictly due to merit. The two articles now referred to were of indispensable necessity for salvation at all times and under every

Text.

7. By faith Noe having received an answer concerning those things which as yet were not seen, moved with fear framed the ark for the saving of his house, by the which he condemned the world: and was instituted heir of the justice which is by faith.

8. By faith he that is called Abraham, obeyed to go out into a place which he was to receive for an inheritance : and he went out, not knowing whither he went.

9. By faith he abode in the land,

Paraphrase.

7. It was by faith, that is to say, by his firm reliance on the divine veracity, holding out threats and promises, that Noe, seized with religious awe, after having been admonished by the divine oracle respecting the things still hidden in the womb of futurity, built with great labour, for his own salvation and that of his family, the ark, by which ark built through faith, he sealed the condemnation of an incredulous world, who scoffingly disregarded his preparation against the coming deluge, and was made the abundant participator and inheritor of the justice of faith.

8. It was by faith that he who, from *Abram* or *high father*, was called *Abraham*, or *father of a multitude*, went forth in obedience to the divine call into the inheritance he was about to receive, not knowing in what particular part of the promised land he was to fix his abode.

9. It was by faith that he lived in the land of

Commentary.

dispensation, the *explicit* faith in them being a *necessary means* of salvation. This is clear, from the universal assertion made regarding them by the Apostle without limitation either as to *time* or *place*—" it is impossible ; " and also from his asserting it in reference to Henoch, who lived long before the written law was given to Moses. In addition to these two articles, the *explicit* faith in the Trinity and Incarnation, also, is now commonly considered by Divines to be necessary, as they term it, *necessitate medii*, that is to say, necessary as a *means of salvation*, after the promulgation of the gospel, so that be the ignorance of them vincible, or invincible, there can be no justification for the sinner ; and consequently, no salvation without them ; they are necessary *means* for the justification of a sinner ; without them, the *end* of salvation can, in no case, be secured by adults, requiring justification. From the very creation, God communicated his supernatural knowledge to man by revelation, without which, in the present order of things, the supernatural end cannot be attained. The Gentiles could have the necessary faith, through the primitive revelations made to Adam, which were transmitted among them from father to son. In the above, there is question of responsible beings, attaining the use of reason.

7. " Concerning those things which as yet were not seen." This shows that faith is " the evidence of things that appear not," (verse 1). " Moved with fear," shows that besides " things to be hoped for," things to be *dreaded* also form subjects of faith. " Framed the ark," &c. ; the building of the ark, in consequence of its magnitude and the number of its compartments, must have been very laborious ; and hence, a great proof of his faith. " By which," some refer to " faith," others to " the ark ; " it may refer to both ; by which *ark*, built through *faith*, he condemned by word and work an incredulous world (1 Peter, iii.), " and was instituted heir," *i.e.*, the abundant participator in " the justice of faith," or, the inheritor of the justice of his fathers, Henoch, Seth, &c., " which is by faith." This latter interpretation is grounded on the strict signification of the word " heir," which implies the possession of an inheritance transmitted from father to son. On the last day, those who, with simplicity and with unhesitating faith in God's promises, work out their salvation in the practice of good works, will condemn the world which scoffs and derides their simplicity. *Nos insensati, vitam illorum estimabamus insaniam*," &c.—(Wisdom, v. 4).

" He that is called." The Greek copy, followed by the Vulgate, had, *ὁ καλουμενος*. This is also the reading of the Alexandrian Manuscript. In this reading, allusion is made to the change of name in Abraham (Genesis, xvii. 3). The article (*ὁ*) is omitted in the ordinary Greek copies, and the words are rendered, *Abraham, when called, obeyed to go*, &c., in which rendering the participle "called," which in the Greek, is the present tense, receives a past signification. Our reading is, however, the better sustained.

9. He dwelt as a pilgrim in the land of promise where he did not occupy a foot of

Text.

dwelling in cottages, with Isaac and Jacob, the co-heirs of the same promise.

10. For he looked for a city that hath foundations : whose builder and maker is God.

11. By faith Sara also herself, being barren, received strength to conceive seed, even past the time of age : because she believed that he was faithful who had promised.

12. For which cause there sprung even from one (and him as good as dead) as the stars of heaven in multitude, and as the sand which is by the sea-shore innumerable.

13. All these died according to faith, not having received the promises, but beholding them afar off, and saluting them, and confessing that they are pilgrims and strangers on the earth.

Paraphrase.

promise, as in a strange land, dwelling in moveable tents ; the co-heirs of his promise, Isaac and Jacob, did the same.

10. It was by faith he did so ; for, assured of the divine promises, he firmly expected and anxiously longed for a city immoveably fixed and founded (not like the tents), the artificer of which was God himself.

11. It was through faith that Sara herself, notwithstanding the twofold obstacle of barrenness and old age, received strength to conceive a son, believing him to be faithful, who promised.

12. Wherefore there sprung from one man only (and he was dead as to the powers of propagation), a posterity, countless as the stars of heaven, or the sand on the sea shore.

13. In faith, these Patriarchs died, without receiving the promises, only beholding them from afar, and saluting them, and confessing themselves to be strangers and pilgrims on earth.

Commentary.

ground, as his fixed habitation, "with Isaac and Jacob :" "with " has the meaning of *as well as*, it denotes parity of circumstances. Though it might be said that he dwelt in tents *with* Isaac and Jacob ; for, Jacob was fifteen years old at Abraham's death, the former meaning, viz. : they, *as well as* Abraham, dwelt successively in tents ; is the more probable.

10. "For, he looked for a city," &c. In this verse, the Apostle proves that it was owing to faith that Abraham dwelt as a stranger in moveable tents in the land of promise, because he looked forward to the heavenly city of eternal stability, firmly fixed and founded by God himself. What an idea of the condition of man here below is conveyed to us, in the faith of the Patriarch !—like him, we are here but strangers in this foreign land ; heaven is our true home, our eternal dwelling-place, on which our thoughts and affections should be fixed. Our conversation should be in heaven, whither we are tending.

11. "Being barren." These words are omitted in the ordinary Greek copies, but they are found in the Alexandrian and other Manuscripts.

OBJECTION.—Was not Sara rebuked by the angel for laughing from incredulity ?— (Genesis, xxiii. 15).

ANSWER.—Although Sara smiled at first, still, on discovering the dignity of him who made the promise, she believed. Some, among whom is Estius, by "faith " understand the faith of Abraham himself, which the Apostle would appear to be specially commending, and in consideration of which, Sara conceived ; in the same way, the walls of Jericho are said to have fallen by faith, *i.e.*, the faith of the Jews, and the following verse in some measure favours this opinion. However, the following words, "She believed," are in favour of the other interpretation. "To conceive seed ;" to which the Greek adds, *and brought forth*.

12. "As the stars….as the sand," &c. These are hyperboles easily understood, signifying a very numerous progeny. They may refer to carnal Israel, in the first place, and to spiritual Israel, or to all Christians, in the second.

13. "All these," *i.e.*, the three last mentioned Patriarchs, to whom were made the promises, "died according to faith," *i.e.*, persevered till death in faith, believing in God's promises, although they did not receive the promises, nor did they enjoy them

Text.

14. For they that say these things, do signify that they seek a country.

15. And truly if they had been mindful of that from whence they came out, they had doubtless time to return.

16. But now they desire a better, that is to say, a heavenly country. Therefore God is not ashamed to be called their God; for he hath prepared for them a city.

17. By faith Abraham, when he was tried, offered Isaac; and he that had received the promises, offered up his only begotten Son :

18. (To whom it was said : *In Isaac shall thy seed be called*).

Paraphrase.

14. For, by professing themselves to be strangers, they showed they were anxiously in search of some country different from that of Chanaan, in which they were sojourning, as pilgrims and strangers.

15. It cannot be Chaldea, their native land, from whence they came ; for, if so, they had leisure to return to it, and an opportunity of doing so, its distance from Chanaan—where they sojourned—being so short.

16. It is, therefore, evident that the object of their longing desires was a better, that is to say, a heavenly country ; and because they sought God and heaven ; hence, God was not ashamed to be called, in a particular way, the God of Abraham, Isaac, and Jacob, since he prepared for these as his chosen friends a fixed abode in the heavenly Jerusalem, where they shall reign with him for ever.

17. It was by faith that Abraham determined to offer up his son Isaac. when, to test him, God commanded him to do so, and he who received the promises, offered up his only begotten son :

18. To whom it was said : In Isaac, shall thy seed be reckoned.

Commentary.

immediately themselves. This is true, whether the promises be referred to the occupation of Chanaan by their innumerable offspring, or to heaven, which was closed until after the ascension of Christ ; they confessed themselves, on all occasions, to be foreigners and sojourners on earth ; "but beholding them from afar, and saluting them," like sailors, who, after a dangerous and distant voyage, on descrying land for the first time. joyously salute it. After the words, "beholding them afar off," are added in some Greek copies, *being persuaded of them.* But, this addition is generally rejected by critics, as unsupported by the authority of the chief Manuscripts. The Apostle refers to the promises, which the Patriarchs themselves did not obtain during life, in order to show the firmness of their faith, and thus to animate the Hebrews, of his own day, to perseverance under affliction, although the promised goods of heaven in store for them, were distant and invisible ; for, they had been still more so, for the Patriarchs.

14. Having observed in the preceding verse, that the Patriarchs died without obtaining the promises, the Apostle shows what the promises regarded, at least, so far as they themselves were to enjoy them ; surely, not the possession by them of the land of Chanaan ; for, by saying they saluted them from afar, there could not be question of the place where they actually dwelt. Moreover, by calling themselves pilgrims, they showed that they were in search of some permanent country, and Chanaan was not their country.

15. Nor was there question of Chaldea ; for, if so, they might have returned, as it was not more than fifty leagues distant from Chanaan.

16. Then, it follows, they were in search of a better, that is to say, their heavenly country ; hence it is, that God, though God of all mankind, calls himself their God in particular, as if rendering them equal value with the rest of creation.

17. Some interpreters make the words, "he who had received the promises," refer to Isaac, thus : he offered up his only begotten son, who had received the promises. The former construction, which refers it to Abraham's receiving the promises, is more probable, as appears from the following verse. "Offered Isaac," *i.e.*, was about offering him, and would have done so if he were not prevented ; he did so in heart and will.

18. The seed promised him was to come only through Isaac. Hence, the heroic firmness of Abraham's faith in sacrificing him.

Text.

19. Accounting that God is able to raise up even from the dead. Whereupon also he received him for a parable.

20. By faith also of things to come Isaac blessed Jacob and Esau.

21. By faith Jacob dying blessed each of the sons of Joseph, and adored the top of his rod.

22. By faith Joseph, when he was dying, made mention of the going out of the children of Israel: and gave commandment concerning his bones.

Paraphrase.

19. It was through faith he did so ; firmly believing that God could, if he wished, raise up Isaac from the dead (and would do so, if necessary, for the realization of his promises), whence it came to pass that he received him back in figure or type of some future great mystery, *i.e.*, of the resurrection of Christ, as well as of the general resurrection of all men, from the tomb.

20. It was through faith, that Isaac blessed Jacob and Esau, promising the future blessings which he could not see, but which were known to him from revelation.

21. It was through faith that Jacob, on his death-bed, blessed each of the sons of Joseph—preferring the younger Ephraim to the elder Manasses—and worshipped the top of his rod.

22. It was through faith in God's promises, regarding the deliverance of his people, that Joseph, on his death-bed, made mention of the future egress of the children of Israel out of Egypt ; and gave orders to have his bones transferred to the land of promise.

Commentary.

19. Abraham was firmly persuaded through faith, that if the resuscitation of Isaac from the dead were necessary for the realization of God's promise of giving him seed in Isaac, God would raise him. "Whereupon also he received him for a parable," *i.e.*, according to some, as a memorable example and prodigy of faith, worthy of being celebrated by future ages.

20. This blessing is remarkable for the circumstances of his conferring on Jacob, the younger, the fulness of the paternal benediction.

21. "Blessed each of the sons of Joseph," preferring Ephraim, the younger, to Manasses, the older, "and adored the top of his rod," και προσεκυνησε επι τον ακρον της ραβδου αυτου. After having obtained from Joseph a promise that his bones would be carried out of Egypt, and deposited in the grave of his fathers, he "adored the top of his (Joseph's) rod." In the Protestant versions of the Bible, these latter words are read differently from our Vulgate. In one version (1562–1579), they run thus, *leaning on the end of his staff, he worshipped God:* the words, *leaning,* and *God,* are unwarrantable additions, not found in the original text ; in a later edition (A.D. 1683), *and worshipped, leaning on the end of his staff* (*vide* Ward's Errata). The Protestants reject the Vulgate reading ; because, it furnishes some grounds for the relative worship of sacred images. The only grounds they have for their version of the words is, the interpretation of St. Augustine, peculiar to him alone ; they substitute a mere interpretation—man's word —for God's own inspired word in the sacred Scripture ; and thus, unwarrantably, make additions to the sacred text, contrary to the common interpretation of the Holy Fathers. They also lay some stress on the Greek word, "επι," which they translate, *upon.* The Catholic and Vulgate version has the sanction of the ancient Fathers, St. Augustine excepted. And as for the particle, "επι," it frequently has the meaning of, *ad,* it has no force except to show the case of the following word, as, "o avit *ad* Dominum" (Kings, i. 10), *i.e.*, *oravit Dominum.* It also signifies *against* or *opposite* (Psalm v. 8), *adorabo ad templum, i.e., versus templum;* and, so little importance did the Holy Fathers attach to "επι," that they inferred from the passage not only adoration *towards* the rod ; but, *of* the rod itself ; ought not the Greek Holy Fathers be better judges of the meaning of a Greek particle, than our modern reformers could be ? The Vulgate version of St. Jerome, translated from the Hebrew, has it (Genesis, xlvii. 31), "Israel adored God turning to the bed's head." The Hebrew word, according to the difference of vowel points, signifies either *a rod* or *a bed.* St. Jerome gave it the latter meaning ; the seventy-two interpreters, from whose version St.

Text.

23. By faith Moses, when he was born, was hid three months by his parents : because they saw he was a comely babe, and they feared not the king's edict.

24. By faith Moses, when he was grown up, denied himself to be the son of Pharao's daughter ;

25. Rather choosing to be afflicted with the people of God, than to have the pleasure of sin for a time.

26. Esteeming the reproach of Christ, greater riches than the treasure of the Egyptians. For he looked unto the reward.

27. By faith he left Egypt, not fearing the fierceness of the king ; for he endured as seeing him that is invisible.

Paraphrase.

23. It was through faith that the parents of Moses, struck with the more than natural comeliness of the infant, disregarding the king's edict, concealed him for three months.

24. It was under the influence of the same faith (grounded probably on the revelation made to his parents, or some inspiration imparted to himself), that Moses, when he grew up, disdained to be reputed the son of Pharaoh's daughter ;

25. Preferring a share in the afflictions of God's people, before the transitory enjoyments of temporal and sinful gratification ;

26. Setting greater value on the reproachful sufferings, which, as a Hebrew, he was to undergo for his people, in type of the future sufferings of Christ, than on all the riches of the Egyptians ; for, with the eye of faith, he kept in view the future remuneration of his labours in heaven.

27. By faith, he left Egypt as the leader of God's people, not fearing the fierceness of the king ; for, beholding the invisible God, as if visible, he bore the crosses and dangers attendant on his ministry.

Commentary.

Paul quotes in this Epistle, have given it the former meaning of, *rod*. Both versions are canonical ; it is likely that Israel did both, that is, "turning to the bed's head," he adored the royal staff of Joseph, referring it, in a spirit of prophecy, to the future Messiah, whom Joseph—called by Pharaoh, *the Saviour of the world* (Genesis, xli. 45)—represented, and of whose kingly power, the staff given to Joseph was a figure The Greek for "his," αὐτου, not aspirated, in the words, "his rod," shows that it refers not to Jacob's staff, but to Joseph's sceptre or rod.

23. Where was the revelation upon which the parents of Moses acted in concealing him, without which there could be no faith ?

It may refer to the faith in the general promise of God to liberate the Hebrews, towards the fulfilment of which promise they concurred, as far as they could, by preserving Moses. Moreover, Josephus expressly states, that a revelation was made to Amram, the father of Moses, regarding his future ministry (lib. 2, *Antiq.*, c. 10), and the supernatural "comeliness," by which it was shown that "he was acceptable to God" (Acts, vii. 20), confirmed this revelation.

24. Pharaoh's daughter, called, according to Josephus (*ut supra*), *Thermutis*, was his sole heiress ; being herself without issue, she adopted Moses. Philo says she feigned pregnancy, and pretended that Moses was her son.

25. "The pleasure of sin for a time." The enjoyment of the opulence and pleasures of a most wealthy and magnificent court (such as Pharaoh's was at that time) is almost always attended with sin, and in the present instance, it would be particularly sinful in Moses, who knew the designs of God on him, as the future liberator of his people, which he would resist by remaining in Pharaoh's court ; he should, moreover, take a share in the execution of the king's cruel edicts.

26. "The reproach of Christ" may also mean the sufferings he was to undergo in conformity and union with the future sufferings of Christ. "For he looked unto the reward" in store for him in heaven. "The treasure of the Egyptians ;" in Greek, των εν Αιγυπτω θησαυρων, *the treasures in Egypt*.

27. "He endured," the fierce animosity of Pharaoh, and the crosses he had to encounter in the ministry of leading forth God's people. "Seeing him that is invisible." Keeping the mandates of the invisible God always in view. Oh ! what a stimulus to deeds of heroic virtue, to walk always in God's holy presence and keep him before our eyes !

Text.

28. By faith he celebrated the pasch, and the shedding of the blood : that he, who destroyed the first-born, might not touch them.

29. By faith they passed through the Red Sea, as by dry land: which the Egyptians attempting were swallowed up.

30. By faith the walls of Jericho fell down, by the going round them seven days.

31. By faith Rahab the harlot perished not with the unbelievers, receiving the spies with peace.

32. And what shall I yet say? For the time would fail me to tell of Gedeon, Barac, Samson, Jephthe, David, Samuel, and the prophets :

33. Who by faith conquered kingdoms, wrought justice, obtained promises, stopped the mouths of lions :

34. Quenched the violence of fire,

Paraphrase.

28. It was by faith, he celebrated the Pasch, performed the ceremony of sprinkling with blood the door-posts of the Israelites, that the destroying angel, who slew the Egyptian first-born, might not touch any of his people (Exodus, xii.)

29. By faith, the Israelites entered the Red Sea, and passed through it as if through dry land, whilst the unbelieving Egyptians were swallowed up in the waters in attempting to follow them (Exodus, xxiv.)

30. It was owing to the faith of Josue and the Jews, that the walls of Jericho fell down on the seventh day after Josue and his army had gone round them seven times, once a-day, for seven days, relying on the divine promises (Josue, vi.)

31. It was by her faith, that Rahab, the harlot, was saved from the common ruin of the incredulous Chanaanites in the destruction of Jericho, having treated the Hebrew spies, in a friendly and peaceful manner (Josue, ii.)

32. What need I adduce any further examples on this subject? In truth, time would fail me, were I fully to detail the prodigies of faith performed by Gedeon, Barac, Samson, Jephthe, David, Samuel, and the Prophets :

33. Who, through faith, overcame kingdoms, performed good works, that conferred justice and increased it; obtained the promises, in the belief of which their faith was exercised; closed the mouths of lions ;

34. Passed unhurt through the raging flames ;

Commentary.

30. It was owing to the faith of Josue and of the army in the assurances of the Lord, that at the end of seven days, the period foretold by God, the walls of Jericho fell down.

31. " Rahab," being formerly a " harlot," went by this name, even after her conversion. In her, the future chosen of God were typified.

But how could she have faith?—what revelation was made to her?

The revelation made, and the faith conceived, must regard the giving up of the promised land to the Jews, which revelation was publicly spread through the Chanaanite nations—hence, their fears ; and this revelation confirmed by miracles, Rahab believed.—(Josue, chap. ii.)

32. "Gedeon," believing in God's promises, with a few of his entire army, routed and entirely destroyed the Madianites.—(Judges, vii.) "Barac," who lived before Gedeon, was distinguished for his victory over the Chanaanites under Sisara. He firmly believed in the promises of God, made known to him by Debora, the prophetess.—(Judges, iv.) "Samson's" stupendous exploits against the Philistines are recorded (Judges, xv., xv., &c.) In all his encounters with the Philistines it is said that "he invoked the Lord," also, that "the Spirit of God rushed upon him." "Jephthe" who, in point of time, was anterior to Samson, was distinguished for his victory over the Ammonites—(Judges, xi.) The histories of Samuel and David, recorded in the first book of Kings are known to all. The Apostle, in his enumeration of the heroes of faith, two by two, sets the more distinguished first, though posterior in point of time.

33. "Who by faith conquered kingdoms." This relates to the victories of the heroes of faith : " obtained promises," (*v.g.*) Isaac's birth, also the promised victories referred to. This does not regard the promise (verse 39) ; for, there, reference is made to the promise of heaven ; here, to particular promises. "Closed the mouths of lions," (*v.g.*) as was done by David, Samson, and Daniel.

34. Quenched the violence of fire," regards three children, Sidrach, Misaac, and

Text.

escaped the edge of the sword, recovered strength from weakness, became valiant in battle, put to flight the armies of foreigners :

l 35. Women received their dead raised to life again. But others were racked not accepting deliverance, that they might find a better resurrection.

36. And others had trial of mockeries and stripes, moreover also of bands and prisons :

37. They were stoned, they were cut asunder, they were tempted, they were put to death by the sword, they wandered about in sheepskins, in goat-skins, being in want, distressed, afflicted :

38. Of whom the world was not worthy ; wandering in deserts, in mountains, and in dens, and in caves of the earth.

39. And all these being approved

Paraphrase.

escaped the edge of the sword ; recovered from their maladies ; became valiant in war ; put to flight the armies of foreigners.

35. Owing to whose faith, women received back their sons raised from the dead. Supported by faith, they endured the greatest tortures and sufferings. Some were racked, and would not accept of a liberation on the infamous terms proposed to them, having in view a better life, a more glorious resurrection.

36. Others were exposed to mockery, and subjected to the lash ; others cast into chains, and thrust into prison.

37. They were stoned ; cut asunder ; tempted ; put to death by the sword ; wandered about in sheep skins, in goat skins, being in want, distressed, afflicted ;

38. Of whom the world was not worthy, wandering in deserts, in mountains, in dens, and in caves of the earth.

39. And all these died without receiving the

Commentary.

Abdenago, in the Babylonian furnace ; "escaped the edge of the sword," David, persecuted by Saul ; Elias, by Jezebel ; "recovered from their infirmity," Ezechias, Tobias, Job ; "became valiant in war," refers to the leaders of the people, and particularly to Samson, Judith, and the Machabees ; "put to flight the armies of foreigners," refers to Gedeon, Jonathan, with his armour bearer.

35. "Women received their dead," &c. The woman of Serephta received back her son, owing to the faith of Elias ; and the woman of Sunam received her's, owing to the faith of Elizeus.—(3 Kings, xvii. ; 4 Kings, iv.)

"But others were racked, not accepting deliverance," &c., (*v.g.*) the Machabees, the aged Eleazar. "Racked ; " what the nature of this rack or torture is, cannot be well determined. The Greek word, ετυμπανισθησαν, means that they were tortured with the instrument called, the *tympanon*, commonly supposed to be a kind of *knout* or flogging instrument. There is allusion here, very probably, to the punishment of Eleazar.—2 Machabees, vi. 30.

36. Samson was mocked by the Philistines ; Elizeus, by wicked boys. The Israelites were scourged by the Egyptians (Exodus, v.) Joseph, Micheas, and Jeremias, were cast into chains, and into prison.—(3 Kings ; Jeremias, xx., xxxvii.)

37. Naboth, and Zacharias, son of Joida, "were stoned" (3 Kings, xxi. ; 2 Paral. xxiv.) ; and so was the Prophet Jeremias, according to a Hebrew tradition, as we are informed by Tertullian (*adversus Gnosticos*, cap. 8) ; by St. Jerome, (lib. 2, *contra Jovinianum*). Isaias was cut "asunder," he was sawn in two. Job was "tempted ; " the prophets persecuted by Jezebel, and a great many innocent persons, persecuted by the impious Manasses, "were put to death by the sword." "Wandered about in sheep skins and goat skins," Elias and the prophets of his day.

38. "Of whom the world was not worthy," *i.e.*, the world was not worth, or of equal value with them ; or, was not worthy of possessing holy men like these who would ward off the merited anger of God. For, no doubt, the prayers and merits of the just avert the anger and heavy vengeance of God from the guilty ; in proof of this we have only to refer to the destruction of Sodom, which the possession of a certain number of just souls would have averted.—(Genesis, xviii. 32).

39. "And all these being approved by the testimony of faith," *i.e.*, testimony being

Text.	Paraphrase.
by the testimony of faith, received not the promise,	promised inheritance of eternal life; although they were proved to be just men by the splendid testimony which their works and sufferings rendered to their faith,
40. God providing some better thing for us, that they should not be perfected w thout us.	40. God in the exercise of his Providence in the present order of things, so favouring us, that *they* could not enjoy perfect happiness of soul or body till the time had arrived, when they should enjoy it in common with us.

Commentary.

borne to the heroic firmness of their faith, owing to the works they performed and the sufferings they endured for it, "received not the promise" of eternal life. If they held out, though the promises were distant, why should not Christians, who immediately after death, may be admitted to the enjoyment of the merited happiness of heaven? This is the conclusion drawn by the Apostle, in the next chapter (verse 1).

40. From which arrangement of Providence, is clearly seen, the special advantage which we enjoy under the New Law over them, who could not enjoy these blessings till our time, when they shall be enjoyed by them in common with us; for, they were not admitted to the beatific vision of God; nor could they finally receive consummate felicity of soul and body in the general resurrection, except in common with us.

CHAPTER XII.

Analysis.

In this chapter, the Apostle points out the practical instruction which the Hebrews should derive from the examples of the illustrious heroes of faith, who served at the same time as witnesses of its great efficacy. It is this ; that they should, like them, enter on the spiritual struggle, with patience and alacrity (1). He also animates them by the prospect of the rewards, which Jesus holds out for them (2), and by the example of suffering which he set them (3). He adduces the testimony of the Holy Ghost, wherein is set forth the advantage of affliction, in order to console them under persecution and suffering (5–8). He institutes a comparison between the correction administered to us by our earthly parents, and that administered by God, and the effects of both (8–10). He shows that the effect of our present affliction, although bitter at present, shall be, in the end, most sweet and agreeable (11).

From the foregoing, he exhorts them to advance straightforward with courage and vigour in the path of Christian perfection (12, 13), to cultivate peace and purity of heart (14), to correspond with God's grace, and by prudent vigilance and circumspection, to see that there be found amongst them neither impure nor impious men, who may, like Esau, be reprobated and lose their eternal inheritance (15–17).

He institutes a comparison between the New and the Old Testaments, with a view of exhorting them to purity of life and morals, corresponding with the dignity of the better and more perfect covenant to which they belonged ; or, perhaps, as appears from verse, 25, with a view of deterring them from apostasy, by showing the grievousness of that crime, and the heavy punishment in store for such transgressions (18–25). He points out, with the same view, the rigours of future judgment (29).

Text.

1. AND therefore we also having so great a cloud of witnesses over our head, laying aside every weight and sin which surrounds us, let us run by patience to the fight proposed to us :

Paraphrase.

1. Having, therefore, so great a multitude of illustrious witnesses, bearing testimony to the excellence and efficacy of faith, surrounding and enveloping us in every direction, like a cloud ; let us, casting away all weight of sensual, terrene affections, all grossness of ideas respecting faith and sin entangling us in our inward course, by patient endurance, enter on the path marked out for us.

Commentary.

1. "A cloud of witnesses," for, in what direction soever we look, some of these illustrious heroes meet us, bearing testimony to the excellence and efficacy of faith. "And the sin that surroundeth us," probably refers to the disposition to commit the sin of apostasy, to which so many temptations were impelling them ; or, it might refer to the external provocations and seductive examples, which were urging them on to sin. To these, he opposes the examples of the saints of old. "That surrounds us ;" in the Greek, ευπεριστατον *that easily besets us*, as flowing garments impede men in their onward course. It is needless to remark, that there is an agonistic allusion, contained in this verse. "By patience, run to the fight," &c. In Greek, *run the contest, i.e.*, race, *proposed to us.* The Apostle frequently represents the Christian's progress, as in a race-course, in which men are striving for the prize of eternal life. The innumerable multitude of the saints of old are, like the spectators of the agonistic exercises in the amphitheatre, placed over our heads, and encouraging us in the combat. And Jesus

Text.

2. Looking on JESUS the author and finisher of faith, who having joy set before him, endured the cross, despising the shame, and now sitteth on the right hand of the throne of God.

3. For think diligently upon him that endured such opposition from sinners against himself: that you be not wearied, fainting in your minds.

4. For you have not yet resisted unto blood, striving against sin :

5. And you have forgotten the

Paraphrase.

2. Keeping a steady eye on the master of the race, Jesus himself, who is both the author of our faith—having by his merit secured the graces necessary for it ; and its finisher—because he will reward and bring it to a happy issue ; who instead of the joy, upon which, in a different order of things, he might have entered, freely and voluntarily bore the cross ; and having despised the ignominy attached thereto, now sits at the right hand of the throne of majesty in heaven.

3. For, reflect diligently on the example he has given you, who, although Son of God, has borne such persecution in the way of bodily suffering, contempt, and reproaches against himself from sinners, so that by the contrast you will feel ashamed to yield or despond in mind, under the trifling privations which you are doomed to endure.

4. For, while he has poured out the last drop of his sacred blood, you have not yet shed a single drop in the spiritual contest, in which you have been engaged against sin.

5. Have you forgotten the consolatory exhortation,

Commentary.

himself is the distributor of the prizes to such as comply with the prescribed conditions of the race. In this race, two things are to be removed, viz., all unnecessary weight, and all obstacles that lie in the way.

2. Jesus is the distributor of the prizes to such as win according to the prescribed laws of the contest. "Who having joy set before him," which is interpreted by some, who, in consideration of the joy set before him, as the reward of his sufferings. The interpretation in the Paraphrase is more in accordance with the Greek, $\alpha\nu\tau\iota$ $\tau\eta\varsigma$ $\chi\alpha\rho\alpha\varsigma$, "who," *instead of the joy*, which, in a different order of Providence, it was free for him to select, "endured the cross," &c. Of course, there is question of the joy which he might enjoy, as *man ;* for, as *God,* he necessarily enjoyed the glory of the Divinity.

3. They are not to look upon Jesus, merely in the light of one holding the prize of eternal life for the victor (verse 2), but they should also regard him as their model in suffering. "Think diligently upon him," *i.e.,* upon the exalted dignity of him who "endured such opposition," *i.e.,* torments. persecution, reproaches, &c. He is the eternal Son of God. From *whom* did he endure it ? "From sinners," in whose behalf he suffers. All our present sufferings will appear trifling, if compared with the sufferings of the Son of God, and in meditating on his sacred passion, we should never lose sight of these two thoughts. *Who,* is it that suffers ? and *why,* is it he suffers? The sufferer is the Eternal God, the Creator of the universe. He suffers torments, which he could not merit, to save us from the eternal excruciating torments we justly merited, and to which we should be otherwise infallibly subjected without hope of alleviation ; nay, with the certain knowledge, every moment we suffered, that these tortures should be for eternity, as long as God would be God. *Ut servum redimeres, filium tradidisti.* How the consideration of Christ's Passion, with all its circumstances, should humble his sinful creatures, and challenge their everlasting love and gratitude !

4. The confiscation of property and the ignominious treatment which they had hitherto endured, were comparatively light trials. They did not yet pour out their blood, in their resistance to sin. By "sin," some understand, *sinners,* the abstract, for the concrete. Others, more probably, think that the word "sin," is personified as an adversary, with whom they are contending (for, the agonistic metaphor referred to, verse 1, is here again introduced) ; and, then, this adversary, "sin," refers to the temptation and allurements, held out to them by the false doctrines and pernicious examples of apostates.

5. "And you have forgotten," &c. This is read interrogatively by some, and with

Text.

consolation, which speaketh to you, as unto children, saying : *My son, neglect not the discipline of the Lord : neither be thou wearied whilst thou art rebuked by him :*

6. *For whom the Lord loveth he chastiseth : and he scourgeth every son whom he receiveth.*

7. Persevere under discipline, God dealeth with you as with *his* sons : for what son is *there*, whom the father doth not correct ?

8. But if you be without chastisement, whereof all are made partakers : then are you bastards, and not sons.

9. Moreover we have had fathers of our flesh, for instructors, and we reverenced them : shall we not much more obey the Father of spirits, and live ?

10. And they indeed for a few days according to their own pleasure instructed us : but he, for our profit, that we might receive his sanctification.

Paraphrase.

which, in the sacred Scriptures, God holds forth to you as to his own children, saying : My son. disregard not the disciplinary chastisement of the Lord, and be not disheartened, when corrected by him ? (This is a sign of his fatherly benevolence towards thee).

6. For, whom the Lord loveth, him does he chastise by temporal afflictions, with a view of trying, instructing, and amending him ; and he scourges every one whom he has received into the adoption of sons.—Proverbs, iii. 11.

7. Persevere under chastisement, since, by inflicting it, God shows himself as a father, and treats you as children ; for, what son is there, whom his father does not correct and chastise ?

8. But if you are left without chastisement or correction, in which all true sons of God are made to share ; then, you are regarded by him not as legitimate sons, but as bastards, of whose education and morals the father takes no care.

9. Moreover, our earthly fathers according to the flesh, corrected us, and we reverenced them ; with how much greater reverence ought we not receive the paternal correction of the heavenly father of our souls, and thereby receive eternal life for recompense ?

10. And (mark the difference of correction in both instances) the fathers of our flesh instructed us in reference to the regulating of this short life ; and that, following their own capricious wills ; but, our heavenly Father instructs and chastises us in reference to what is useful for us, not for a merely temporal end, but for the end of our sanctification.

Commentary.

great force, *and have you forgotten ?* &c. The meaning is the same in both readings. These words are quoted from the Book of Proverbs (chap. iii.) according to the Septuagint version. They are introduced by the Apostle to encourage the Hebrews in their afflictions ; since they show that crosses and afflictions, far from being evils, are, on the contrary, a mark of God's special love and adoption. "Consolation." The Greek, παρακλησεως, also means, *exhortation.* "Neglect not the discipline," &c. "Discipline," in the Greek, παιδειας, means, *the chastisement of children.*

7. "Persevere under discipline," &c In Greek, ει παιδειαν υπομενετε, *if you patiently endure discipline.* "God dealeth with you as with his sons." "For what son is there whom the father does not correct ?" and hence, as sons of God, they should not expect to be exempted from the common lot of all true children. The Greek reading derives great probability from the antithesis, next verse. If you persevere under discipline, God, by sending it, treats you as children ; "for, what son is there whom the father does not correct ?"

8. But if he does not send you chastisements, he treats you as bastards are treated by their fathers, who neglect their education and moral culture.

9. This contains a new motive for patiently receiving correction from the hands of God. God is said to be "the father of spirits," *i.e.,* of our souls, because, although he is the father of our bodies also, still he creates our souls without any instrumentality on the part of man, and he regenerates them in a new way, by his holy Spirit.

10. The Apostle points out the different effects of the chastisement and paternal correction in both cases. "According to their own pleasure," *i.e.,* according to their capricious and changeable wills, proposing as end, in many instances, not so much our amendment, as the gratification of their own whims and caprice. "That we might receive his sanctification." The end of his castigation and correction is to purge and

Text.

11. Now all chastisement for the present indeed seemeth not to bring with it joy, but sorrow: but afterwards it will yield, to them that are exercised by it, the most peaceable fruit of justice.

12. Wherefore lift up the hands which hang down, and the feeble knees;

13. And make straight steps with your feet: that no one, halting, may go out of the way; but rather be healed.

14. Follow peace with all men, and holiness: without which no man shall see God:

15. Looking diligently lest any man be wanting to the grace of God: lest any root of bitterness springing up do hinder, and by it may be defiled.

Paraphrase.

11. And if we look to the immediate effect of God's chastisement, this would seem to be, while we are suffering under it, not joy, but sorrow; but those exercised in it will reap in abundance, hereafter the fruit of justice, which justice carries with it peace and consolation of soul.

12. Wherefore, such being the good effects of suffering, shaking off all sloth, brace your nerves for further exertion, lift up the hands which hang down, and the tottering knees.

13. And instead of staggering, from the effects of persecution, between Christianity and Judaism, walk straightforward in the way of the gospel, that no one halting in the right path, may turn aside from it, but rather may be healed.

14. Cultivate peace as far as possible, with all men, and that general purity of heart, without which no one shall see God.

15. Exercising also a prudent and charitable vigilance over others, seeing that no one amongst you be wanting to the great grace of faith and of his Christian calling, lest any root of bitterness (either in the shape of depraved example or false doctrine) springing up, should impede your onward straight course and prove the cause of spiritual defilement to many.

Commentary.

prepare us to become "partakers of the divine nature," (2 Peter, i. 4), *i.e.,* of his sanctity here, and of his glory hereafter.

11. The present effect of correction and suffering would appear to be, not joy, but sorrow, during the time we are enduring it.   He says, "seemeth not to bring with it joy, but sorrow," because it is commonly regarded in that light; however, in its effects, it is *really* "all joy."—(St. James, i. 2).   "The most peaceable fruit of justice," According to the interpretation in the Paraphrase, by the "fruit of justice," is meant, justice itself: thus we say, *the virtue of humility, i.e.,* humility itself, &c., and "justice." or, "the fruit of justice," has the same meaning as "sanctification,"—verse, 10. Others understand the words to mean, that the patient endurance of affliction will give the fruit of eternal peace, due to it as a matter of justice, or as the reward of strict merit.   The former interpretation is the more probable; because the Apostle is not treating of the fruit which justice produces, but of the fruit which patience under affliction begets, and that is, *justice.*

12. He continues the allusion to the agonistic exercises, from which he borrows many illustrations of a Christian life.   He exhorts them, leaving aside all indolence and remissness, to prepare themselves for the patient endurance of evil, in their struggles with adversity.

13. And also to prepare themselves for the performance of good works, signified by "straight steps," instead of "halting" in the path of Christian faith, and of inclining to turn aside and not persevere; they should "rather be healed," *i.e.,* be restored to Christian integrity, in case of departure from it.   "The figure is taken from a rough, uneven road, on which, if a man who is somewhat lame walk, his lameness is increased; while, by moderate exercise on a smooth road, an incipient lameness from paralysis might gradually disappear by the strengthening of the foot.—Kenrick, *in hunc locum.*

14. "Follow peace," &c.   The Greek word for "follow," ἐιωκετε contains an allusion to the eager pursuit of battle or the chase.   It shows how earnestly the Apostle recommends them to cultivate peace.

15. "Looking diligently," &c., ἐπισκοπουντες, *i.e.,* not merely confining your attention, each one to his own spiritual concerns, but also exercising a charitable superintendence and vigilance, over the spiritual good of his neighbour.   "The grace

Text.	Paraphrase.
16. Lest there be any fornicator, or profane person as Esau: who for one mess sold his first birth-right.	16. Lest there be any fornicator among you, any sacrilegious person, like Esau, who, for one mess of pottage, sold his birth-right.
17. For know ye that afterwards when he desired to inherit the benediction, he was rejected: for he found no place of repentance, although with tears he had sought it.	17. For, you should remember, that when afterwards anxiously endeavouring to obtain his father's blessing, he was rejected; for, he could find no means of inducing his father to change his act, although he sought it with tears.
18. For you are not come to a mountain that might be touched, and a burning fire, and a whirlwind, and darkness, and storm.	18. (Your sanctity should be greater, as the religion which you profess is the more holy and exalted); for, you have not approached the material tangible mountain (Sinai), nor the fire kindled on its summit, nor the impetuous winds, nor the dense clouds, nor the storm of rain, thunder, and lightning;
19. And the sound of a trumpet,	19. Nor the sound of a trumpet through which were

Commentary.

of God," *i.e.*, the grace of faith and of Christian vocation. "Lest any root of bitterness springing up." This is the just designation which the Apostle gives the sin of apostasy and of bad example.

16. "Or profane person, as Esau," &c. By "profane" βηβηλος is meant a sacrilegious person, who having no sense of religion, treats sacred things with contempt. The chief point of profaneness in the conduct of Esau consisted in his having so far undervalued the right of primogeniture—then considered a singular gift of God, particularly on account of the right to his father's blessing—as to sell it for a mere mess of pottage. It is said of him in Genesis, chap. xxv.. "that he made little account of having sold his first birthright." This is the more tenable opinion, because, if the profaneness be made to consist in his *selling* a spiritual thing, it will be hard to excuse Jacob from sin in *buying* it. Nor will it mend the matter much to say, that he knew God had transferred it from Esau to himself; for, still it would be true to say, that he *bought* a *spiritual* thing.

17. "No place of repentance," *i.e.*, on the part of his father Isaac. Others understand it of Esau's own inefficacious sorrow for having sold his birthright, in neither of which interpretations, is there left the slightest ground of objection to the Novatians. And even should it be referred to penance for sin, no objection still exists; since, Esau had not true sorrow, being intent on killing his brother, as appears from the book of Genesis, xxvii. 41. The Apostle wishes to teach them, by the example of Esau, not to barter heavenly and spiritual things for the earthly, nor to sell the precious inheritance of faith for any human consideration.

18. Some Commentators say, that the object of the Apostle, in contrasting here the New with the Old Testament, was, to anticipate or answer an objection which the Hebrews might make against the New Law, on the ground, that its promulgation was not attended with the splendid phenomena, which ushered in the Old. The Apostle, according to their view, admits the many distinguished marks of divine sanction which characterised the Old Testament; but still, he shows the New was marked by still greater (verse 22). Others, more probably, maintain. that the comparison between both laws was instituted for the purpose of showing the heinousness of desertion from the New Law; for, if the violators of a less perfect law were punished so severely, how much more so will be the apostates from Christianity? which is the conclusion drawn (verse 25). "Approached the mountain which could be touched." "Approach," is a term signifying religious worship generally (*v.g.* xi. 6); here, it signifies embracing a religion. The two laws are designated by two mountains, Sinai and Sion. "Which could be touched," *i.e.*, the material and corporeal. or tangible mountain, as opposed to the incorporeal and spiritual one (verse 22). All the solemnities which accompanied the promulgation of the Old Law are mentioned (Exodus, chap. xix.) "And a burning fire." Sinai "appeared like a furnace" (Exodus, xix.) "To a whirlwind, and darkness, and storm" (Exodus, xix., and Deut. iv.)

19. "And the sound of a trumpet, and (*i.e.*), the voice of words," since it was by a

Text.

and the voice of words, which they that heard excused themselves, that the word might not be spoken to them.

20. For they did not endure that which was said : *And if so much as a beast shall touch the mount, it shall be stoned.*

21. And so terrible was that which was seen, Moses said : *I am frighted and tremble.*

22. But you are come to mount Sion, and to the city of the living God, the heavenly Jerusalem, and to the company of many thousands of angels,

23. And to the church of the first-born, who are written in the heavens, and to God the judge of all, and to the spirits of the just made perfect,

Paraphrase.

uttered the words of the angel, which the Jews hearing, exclaimed : "Let not the Lord speak to us, but Moses, lest we die."—(Exodus, xx. 19).

20. For they could not bear the dreadful edict, that should even a beast approach the mount, it should be stoned.

21. And so terrible was the entire appearance, that Moses himself, though accustomed to long and familiar converse with God, said, I am seized with fright and trembling.

22. But you have approached the spiritual Mount Sion, or the Church of Christ founded on Sion, and the city of the living God, the heavenly Jerusalem, and the joyous assemblage of many thousands of angels, not arrayed in terror, like the angels of Sinai, but celebrating an eternal festival of joy ;

23. And to the Church of the first-born, *i.e.*, of the Apostles, Martyrs, and primitive faithful, who, having been first regenerated in Christ, and having received the first fruits and abundance of the spirit, are now enrolled as citizens of heaven, in which they reign with Christ, and to God the Judge of all, who will reward your fidelity and punish your persecutors ; and to the spirits of the just of the Old Testament, who now, after performing prodigies of faith, are possessed of consummate felicity, in the enjoyment of the beatific vision of God ;

Commentary.

trumpet the angel spoke. "Which they that heard excused themselves," saying, "speak thou to us......let not the Lord speak to us, lest we die."—(Exodus, xx. 19).

20. They could not endure the dreadful edict menacing them, "*if so much as a beast....it shall be stoned,*" to which is added in some Greek readings, *or thrust through with a dart.* But these words are commonly rejected, because wanting in many ancient manuscripts.

21. And so terrible was the entire scene, all that was seen and heard, that Moses himself, though accustomed to long converse with God, said, "*I am frighted and tremble.*" In the narration of Genesis, we have no record that Moses uttered these words ; but the Apostle must have learned them from tradition or inspiration, the same way in which he learned the names of the Egyptian magicians.—(2 Timothy, iii.)

22. "They are come to Mount Sion," *i.e.*, they embraced the religion or Church of Christ, founded on Mount Sion. This refers to the Church militant. "And to the city of the living God, the heavenly Jerusalem," which refers to the Church triumphant, whereof the earthly Jerusalem was a figure. The Apostle, then, alludes, in this verse, to the entire Church, militant and triumphant, regarded here, as one by him ; the Church militant here below, is the entrance to the Church militant in heaven, which it continually peoples with blessed spirits, between whom and us here on earth, there is a constant, unceasing communion. They communicate their merits to us, and present our petitions to God, and act as our intercessors with him in heaven.

23. He here, more fully and in detail, points out the inhabitants of the heavenly Jerusalem, with whom we are associated. "To the Church of the first-born," who are enrolled as citizens of heaven, (*vide* Paraphrase). In the Greek πανηγυρει και εκκλησια, *to the general assembly and church of the first-born.* Others, by "first-born," understand all the elect, selected out of the mass of creation ; and chosen, as the sons of God, to the inheritance of the first-born. "God the Judge of all." This is said to console them, because God will reward them, and, as is just, will punish their persecutors (2 Thess. 1. 6).

Text.	Paraphrase.
24. And to JESUS the mediator of the new testament, and to the sprinkling of blood which speaketh better than that of Abel.	24. And to Jesus, the Mediator of the New Testament (on the part of God promising eternal rewards to such as observe the conditions of the testament, and on the part of men, enabling them, by the grace which he has merited, to observe the law), and to the sprinkling of the blood of Christ (typified by the sprinkling of the blood of the legal victims), speaking better things than that of Abel (the blood of Abel cried aloud for vengeance, that of Christ, for peace and mercy).
25. See that you refuse him not that speaketh. For if they escaped not who refused him that spoke upon earth, much more *shall not* we, that turn away from him that speaketh to us from heaven.	25. See, then, lest you refuse attending to the voice of him who thus speaks to you. For, if your fathers were dealt with so severely, for refusing to listen to him (*i.e.*, Moses), who spoke on earth; how much more severely will we be punished, if we refuse to listen to Christ speaking to us from heaven (and enforcing, through his Apostles and ministers, that law, promulgated by himself, while here on earth).
26. Whose voice then moved the earth: but now he promiseth, saying: *Yet once more, and I will move not only the earth, but heaven also.*	26. Whose voice, as God, then moved the earth when the law was given on Sinai: but which now again will, according to the prophecy of Aggeus, yet once more move not only the earth, but heaven also.

Commentary.

"And to the spirits of the just made perfect." This is, more commonly understood of the just of old, who, having performed glorious works, were still not perfected until now, when Christ opened the gates of heaven—(chap. xi. 40).

24. Jesus is the Mediator of the New Testament, because he holds out promises on the part of God; and on the part of man, merits the graces necessary for fulfilling the conditions of the promises, that is to say, the proper observance of the law. The Apostle makes a similar allusion to the mystical signification of Sinai and Jerusalem, in his Epistle to the Galatians (iv. 24).

25. From this verse appears the scope of the comparison between the Old Testament and the New. He wishes them to understand, that, if the Jews of old, though not favoured with so many advantages, though not permitted to approach him, as we are, nor even to touch the mountain from which he spoke, were visited with such chastisements, for the violation of a law, which had a mere man of earth for its promulgator; how much greater rigour will be exercised against the apostates from the Christian law, which, though, in promulgation, not equal to the Old Law in terror, yet was far beyond it, in majesty and grandeur, its promulgator being God himself, who, by the mouths of his vicars, ceases not to enforce it from heaven! The idea is the same as that conveyed, chap. ii. 2, 3. of this Epistle.

But when did the rejection of Moses by their fathers, or refusal to hear him, referred to here by the Apostle, take place?

It more probably refers to their repeated violations of the law promulgated by him, so that the rejection of him here refers to the violation of his law.

26. "I will move." In the Greek, σειω, *I shake.* The future is used in the Septuagint version, from which this passage is taken. That Sinai was moved at the giving of the law, we know from Psalm lxvii. : "The earth was moved, and the heavens dropped at the presence of the God of Sinai," which refers to the giving of the law. The words of the Prophet Aggeus, "*yet once,*" &c., are quoted from the Septuagint version. In the Vulgate by St. Jerome, they are "yet a little while, and I will move," &c. (chap. ii.) There is, however, but very slight variation in sense ; for by, *yet a little,* he refers to some permanent change not far off. The words of the prophet were first used in reference to Christ's coming. And the star appearing at his birth, the darkening of the sun, the earthquake, &c., at his death, all show the change which the heavens and the earth underwent. It is, however, far more probable, that the Apostle here applies

Text.

27. And in that he saith, *Yet once more*, he signifieth the translation of the moveable things as made, that those things may remain which are immoveable.

28. Therefore, receiving an immoveable kingdom, we have grace : whereby let us serve pleasing God, with fear and reverence.

29. For our God is a consuming fire.

Paraphrase.

27. And by saying, *yet once*, &c., he implies the translation of the changeable and moveable things, as of merely temporary institution, to make room for the immoveable.

28. Therefore, receiving an immoveable kingdom, which is prepared for us, let us firmly possess the grace of Christianity, whereby alone we can please God, serving him with fear, which will prevent our offending him by sin, and with reverence, by rendering unto him the worship due to him.

29. For, our God is like a most destructive fire in consuming his enemies, in torturing and taking vengeance on them.

Commentary.

the words, in an extended sense, and in accommodation to his present purpose, to Christ's second coming, when, in the language of the Church, *cæli movendi sunt et terra*. Some Expositors say, that the words of Aggeus refer to Christ's first coming, and embrace the entire period from his birth, to the end of the world, when this movement and change of the heavens and the earth shall be completed.

27. " Moveable things." Those who refer the foregoing words of the prophet, in the meaning given them by the Apostle, to the general judgment, understand by these words, the present heavens and the earth, which are to be changed into " new heavens and a new earth " (2 Peter, iii. 13) ; this is the more probable meaning ; since, the Apostle would appear to introduce the future judgment of Christ, as a motive to secure their steadfastness in the faith. Those who confine them to his first coming (an improbable interpretation), refer the words " moveable things " to the Jewish tabernacle with its contents.

28. In this verse, he appears to show what the " immoveable things " are, viz., the new heavens and kingdom of Christ.

29. " Fire," the most active of the four elements aptly represents the avenging wrath of God. These words are taken from Deuteronomy (chap. ix. 4), where Moses threatens the people with the heavy anger of God, should they violate his precepts, particularly by falling into idolatry. They are introduced here by the Apostle to show that we should " please God with fear and reverence," and also, that we shall be visited with more rigorous punishments, than were the Jews of old, if we violate his precept (verse 25).

CHAPTER XIII.

Analysis.

In this concluding chapter, the Apostle inculcates certain duties of morality, and exhorts the Hebrews to the practice of several virtues, both as regards their neighbour and themselves. With regard to the virtues to be exercised towards their neighbour, the Apostle exhorts them to persevere in fraternal charity, to exercise hospitality, and manifest a practical sympathy for those who were suffering for the faith (1–3). He exhorts them to guard strictly conjugal chastity, and shunning avarice, to exhibit their confidence in God (4–6).

He exhorts them to be mindful of their deceased prelates, the consideration of whose edifying lives and holy death should be an encouragement to persevere in the same faith which they professed—a faith as unchangeable as Jesus Christ himself (7, 8). Hence, they should not be led away by fluctuating and contrary doctrines, particularly in reference to the useless distinction of food, and the legal victims. The Christians, although deprived of Jewish victims, have a still more excellent one, whereof those cannot partake who adhere to Judaism ; for, in order to be able to partake of it, they must relinquish the synagogue, and the profession of the Jewish religion (9–13).

He recommends liberality towards the poor, and obedience to their prelates (16, 17). He begs the assistance of their prayers, and finally concludes with a prayer and salutation.

Text.

1. LET the charity of the brotherhood abide in you.

2. And hospitality do not forget, for by this, some being not aware of it, have entertained angels.

3. Remember them that are in bands, as if you were bound with

Paraphrase.

1. Persevere in the exercise of mutual love towards each other, as Christians.

2. And forget not to continue the usual practice of the kind offices of hospitality, *i.e.*, receiving the harbourless, supporting the stranger and the needy ; for, it was in reward for the exercise of this virtue, that some persons, not knowing who their guests were, entertained angels, whom they supposed to be mere men.

3. Sympathize with your brethren imprisoned for the faith, as if you were yourselves partners in their

Commentary.

1. " Let the charity of the brotherhood abide in you." The words " in you " are not in the Greek. The meaning, however, is not much affected, whether they be expressed or not, because they are understood.

2. The exercise of hospitality, which, in the proper sense of the word, consisted in affording lodging and shelter to distressed strangers, was particularly obligatory in the early ages of the Church, when accommodation was so imperfect, and the Christian converts incurred great risk, both as to faith and morals, by associating and lodging with the infidels. Hence, the exercise of this branch of charity is particularly required of bishops and ecclesiastical widows.—(1 Tim. iii. 2 ; v. 10).

" For, by this," *i.e.*, in reward of this virtue, " some, not being aware of it, have entertained angels." God had thus shown, how acceptable and agreeable to him, this virtue of hospitality must be. He alludes to the cases of Abraham and Lot (Genesis, xviii., xix.) On the day of judgment, eternal life will be given, as the reward of this virtue. " I was a stranger and you took me in."—(St. Matthew, xxv. 35).

3. They should not only exercise charity towards their distressed brethren, who were

Text.

them; and them that labour, as being yourselves also in the body.

4. Marriage honourable in all, and the bed undefiled. For fornicators and adulterers God will judge.

5. Let your manners be without covetousness, contented with such things as you have. For he hath said: *I will not leave thee, neither will I forsake thee.*

6. So that we may confidently say: *The Lord is my helper: I will not fear what man shall do to me.*

7. Remember your prelates who have spoken the word of God to you; whose faith follow, considering the end of their conversation;

Paraphrase.

chains; compassionate those who are oppressed, bearing in mind, that you yourselves are liable and exposed to the like distress, during the time you live in frail, mortal bodies.

4. Let due honour be paid to the marriage state in all things appertaining thereto, and let the marriage bed be free from all defilement. For, God will judge and punish, with the utmost severity, fornicators and adulterers.

5. (Be not deaf to the cry of affliction). Let your morals be free from all disposition to indulge in the sordid vice of avarice; be content with a sufficiency at present, and as regards the future, cast yourselves with confidence on God's bountiful providence; for, his promise pledged to Josue also extends to all who confide in him: "*I will not leave thee, neither will I forsake thee.*"—(Josue, i. 5).

6. So, that we may even confidently expect to vanquish our enemies, as did David under the like circumstances, when he exclaimed: *The Lord is my helper; I will not fear what man shall do unto me.*"—(Psalm cxvii.)

7. Remember your former deceased prelates, who preached to you the word of God, and confirmed you in the faith; looking to their edifying lives and holy death, imitate their faith—the source of their sanctity in life, and happiness in death.

Commentary.

at large, by receiving them into their houses; but they should also sympathize with and succour their brethren, who were prisoners for the faith, bearing in mind, that they themselves, as long as they were in the body, were liable and exposed to similar distress. "Them that labour;" των κακουχουμενων, *maltreated.* It is implied, that it was *on account of the Faith*, they were so treated.

4. "Marriage honourable in all." This is clearly *hortatory;* hence, it means, "let marriage be," &c. "In all." Some make, *in all persons;* and then, it only refers to such as can lawfully engage in the marriage state; but, it could by no means convey a precept to marry on the part of *all;* nor could it commend marriage in all *persons,* without exception; because, St. Paul himself would have violated the precept (1 Cor. vii. 8), the widows who married, after their vows of chastity, incurred damnation. (1 Tim. v. 12). The meaning which makes it, *in all things,* connected with marriage, is the true one, as appears from the words immediately subjoined, "for God will judge fornicators," &c., by which is shown that in the preceding words is inculcated the avoidance of the sin to which damnation is attached in these. Instead of "for fornicators," the Greek is, πορνους δε, *but fornicators.* The Alexandrian manuscript has "for."

5. It is likely that some among them, under the pretext of want, brought on by the confiscation of their property, were indulging in the vice of avarice; hence, his exhortation to avoid it; moreover, they should shun it as being "the root of all evils" (1 Tim. vi.) "*I will not leave thee,*" &c. In these words, the Lord promises Josue not to desert him, but to give him all necessary assistance in the government of the people. This the Apostle extends to the aid which God will grant the just in all their wants; and, thus, he accommodates them to his present purpose.

6. So that we may confidently say, "*The Lord is my helper,*" &c. These words, quoted from Psalm cxvii., express the interposition of God to save David from the persecution of his enemies; and are very applicable to the condition of the Hebrews, persecuted, on account of their faith, by their fellow-countrymen.

7. "The end of their conversation" means their death, in justice and sanctity. The words of this verse clearly show that the Apostle refers to their deceased prelates and

Text.

8. Jesus Christ yesterday, and to-day; and the same for ever.

9. Be not led away with various and strange doctrines. For it is best that the heart be established with grace, not with meats : which have not profited those that walk in them.

10. We have an altar, whereof they have no power to eat who serve the tabernacle.

Paraphrase.

8. (Their faith and yours must be the same), since Jesus Christ—the principal object of their faith and yours—is the same, yesterday, to-day, and for ever.

9. Be not carried about by the varying and strange doctrines (of heretics), an example of which is found in the choice of legal, or, rather, in the effects attributed to, sacrificial meats ; it is much better to strengthen your hearts by the grace of the New Law, which faith in Christ brings with it, than trust in the efficacy of the observances referred to, which never had the effect of sanctifying those who followed them, and spent their lives in them.

10. (Let it not, however, be supposed, that by giving up the legal offerings, we are without victims, or sacrifice); for, in Christianity, we have on our altars, a victim, that supplies us with the grace which strengthens the heart, whereof they cannot partake who serve the tabernacle and still adhere to the Jewish religion.

Commentary.

religious guides, viz., James, Stephen, &c., who trampled under foot, and undervalued all earthly things : the example of these they should follow, and to their faith they should firmly adhere ; for, this faith was the source of their sanctity in life, and of their happiness in death.

From this passage we can clearly perceive the advantage of perusing the lives of the saints, who have gone before us. Their lives are to us a practical illustration of the gospel ; they point out the means, and serve as an incentive, to labour for heaven, *Nonne potes tu, quod isti et istæ.*—St. Augustine. It is to the pious reading of the lives of the saints, that the Church is, to a certain degree, indebted for the illustrious Society of Jesus, whose equals the world has never seen ; the first, whom the enemies of God and man are sure to assail, as being the leading and the most powerful defenders of religion and social order ; their persecution, in any particular country, as the annals of modern rebellions against the altar and the throne too clearly attest, is a sure sign of national reprobation ; the certain forerunner of terrible religious and social disasters. '

8. As Jesus Christ—the principal object of faith—is always the same ; therefore, the faith in him must always be the same ; and hence, the faith of the Hebrews, and of their predecessors in the faith, must be identical. These words, most probably, refer to Jesus Christ, as God-man. "Yesterday" refers to the time of his Incarnation. This verse connects the preceding with the following verses. The words, "the same," are, according to the Greek punctuation, joined to " to-day."

9. As faith must be, therefore, always one and indivisible, be not carried about by doctrines "various," *i.e.,* varying in themselves, and from the truth ; "and strange," foreign to the deposit left by God to his Church. " For, it is best to establish the heart with grace." He gives a particular instance of the false doctrines, to which he has been referring in a general way, in the words, "various...doctrines." He, most likely, refers to the doctrine regarding the distinction of meats, some of which were forbidden, and others allowed by the law ; or rather to the doctrine regarding the effects of meats offered in sacrifice, to which the Judaizers attributed the power and efficacy of sanctifying men. This latter interpretation is rendered probable by the following verse. The Apostle says, it is better to establish and render the heart firm by the grace of Christianity, than by recurring to the use of such meats, which never conferred true sanctity on the worshippers (ix. 10).

"To walk in," is a Hebraism for principles of action followed out in practice.— Kenrick, *in hunc locum.*

10. "We have an altar," &c. This *altar*, which is understood of the victim offered

Text.

11. For the bodies of those beasts, whose blood is brought into the Holies by the high-priest for sin, are burned without the camp.

12. Wherefore JESUS also, that he might sanctify the people by his own blood, suffered without the gate.

13. Let us go forth therefore to him without the camp; bearing his reproach.

Paraphrase.

11. This exclusion of the ministers and followers of the Jewish tabernacle, from a participation of the victim of our "*altar*," was typified by the ordinance of the law respecting the great sacrifice of expiation. For, the bodies of the animals, viz., the goat and the heifer, whose blood was carried by the high priest into the *sanctum sanctorum*, in the great sacrifice of expiation, were burnt outside the camp (wherein dwelt the Jews, at this time, sojourning in the desert).

12. For which cause, Jesus also, the reality typified, in order to fulfil this figure, suffered outside the gate of Jerusalem, sanctifying the people, with his blood.

13. We, therefore, and all who wish to be partakers of the Christian sacrifice, must go forth to him, outside the camp of the synagogue. In other words, we must desert the synagogue, and join the Church; bearing the reproach attached to the name of Christian.

Commentary.

on it, refers, according to some, to the adorable Eucharist, the first step to obtain which must be, to go forth from the synagogue; and, that in order to partake of it, they must first leave the synagogue, or Jewish religion, he proves (verse 11), from the rite observed in the great sacrifice of expiation, a type of the sacrifice of Christ on the cross, of which the Eucharistic sacrifice is a continuation, and a real unbloody commemoration. The word "eat," greatly serves to confirm this opinion. "Serve" (λατευοντες) has reference directly to the priests; it also embraces, in a general way, all who approach the Jewish altar, as *worshippers*.

11. "Are burned without the camp." The Jews, at the time of this ordinance dwelt in the desert, in a moveable camp, outside which were burned the bodies of the heifer and the goat, whereof neither the priests nor the people could partake.

12. On this account it was that Jesus, in order to correspond with his type (for, of his sacrifice, the great sacrifice of expiation was a mere type and figure) suffered outside the gates of Jerusalem.

13. Hence, we should go forth to him outside the camp, and leaving the synagogue, submit to the reproach of Christ, before we can be partakers of the victim of the Christian "*altar*," that is to say, of Christ in the Holy Eucharist, where he is offered up daily, in an unbloody manner, and partaken of by the faithful. Whether the opinion which refers "*altar*" to the Eucharist, be true or false, matters but little in regard to the faith of the Church, on the subject of the Eucharist, which is clearly demonstrated from other passages; and such of the Fathers as understand this passage of it, show their faith regarding the Eucharist to have been the same as ours. Others make "*altar*" refer directly to the altar of the cross; because it was of the sacrifice of the cross that the sacrifice of expiation, to which he alludes (verse 11), was typical. The Hebrews were attaching great importance to the sacrifices of the Mosaic law. Now, he says, it would be far better for them to have recourse to grace (verse 9), which they cannot receive, since it is purchased by a sacrifice wherein they can have no share, without first going forth from the synagogue (verse 10); for, the bodies of the victims, &c., were burned outside the camp (verse 11). Hence, Jesus suffered outside the gate of Jerusalem (verse 12); and hence, to become partakers of the merits of his sacrifice, "*to eat of the altar*," according to these interpreters, we must go forth from the synagogue, and join the Church, "*bearing his reproach*;" for, the name of Christian was counted a reproach. Should this passage refer *directly* to the sacrifice of the cross, in it must be *indirectly* included the sacrifice of the Eucharist; inasmuch as it is the same sacrifice with that of the cross, from which it differs, only as to the *mode* of offering.

Some Expositors say, that in this verse is conveyed an exhortation to bear our cross patiently, after the example of Christ. "Bearing his reproach" will then mean: bearing his cross after him, which is a reproach and folly.

Text.	Paraphrase.
14. For we have not here a lasting city; but we seek one that is to come.	14. And this voluntary exile, and departure from the synagogue and Jerusalem, should not disturb or frighten us, for we, Christians, have not on this earth any permanent city; as exiles and pilgrims, we are in search of one to come, that is, the heavenly Jerusalem.
15. By him therefore let us offer the sacrifice of praise always to God, that is to say, the fruit of lips confessing to his name.	15. Having, therefore, been united to Christ, let us continually present through him to God a sacrifice of praise, that is to say, the fruit of lips confessing his name.
16. And do not forget to do good and to impart: for by such sacrifices God's favour is obtained.	16. And to this piety towards God, neglect not to add charity towards your neighbour. Forget not liberality, nor omit to impart your goods to the poor, by relieving them according to your ability; for, by such sacrifices the favour of God is obtained, with them he is well pleased.
17. Obey your prelates, and be subject to them. For they watch	17. Obey your prelates, and reverence them; for, you are to regard them as watching over your souls

Commentary.

14. In this verse is contained a reason why we should not hesitate to leave the synagogue; because, we are in search of our heavenly Jerusalem; according to others, in it is contained a reason why we should be prepared to suffer for Christ's sake; because, no matter what may befall us, whether exile, death, &c., it will not deprive us of our country, but rather hasten our approach to it.

Commentators remark that the Apostle explains, in the foregoing passage, the sacrifice of expiation, according to the four-fold sense attached to SS. Scripture—viz., the *literal*, the *allegorical*, the *tropological* (or *moral*), and the *anagogical*. (*Litera gesta docet; quid credas, Allegoria; Moralis, quid agas; quo tendas, Anagogia*). According to the *literal* sense, the victim in the sacrifice of expiation was carried out of the camp and burned, and the blood was carried by the high priest into the sanctuary, as an expiation for sin—*litera gesta docet*—verse 11. According to the *allegorical* sense, this victim was a figure of Christ ignominiously driven outside the city, to suffer death, as an atonement for sin—quid credas, *Allegoria*—verse 12. According to the *tropological* or *moral* sense, those who wish to partake of the sacrifice of Christ, must go outside the precincts of the synagogue, and abandon the Jewish religion; thus bearing their share in the ignominy which he was pleased to undergo—*Moralis*, quid agas—verse 13. And according to the *anagogical* meaning of the ceremony, they are not to regret this temporary exile, since neither Jerusalem nor the synagogue is our true country or lasting home; we are in search of our heavenly and everlasting dwelling-place above—quo tendas, *anagogia*—verse 14. Rutter, *in hunc locum.*

15. Having given up the legal sacrifices prescribed by law, let us offer up to God, through Christ, to whom we are united, after deserting the synagogue, "a sacrifice of praise," according to some, the sacrifice of the Eucharist. This is the opinion of those who refer "*altar*" (verse 10) to the Eucharist. The explanation, however, given by the Apostle himself, of what this sacrifice is, "that is the fruit of lips," &c., shows that it refers to the spiritual offering of thanksgiving to God, in every shape and form. These acts of thanksgiving are called "the fruit of lips, confessing his name;" because, it is by the lips his praises are sounded, and his benefits deserving thanks, together with his eternal attributes, proclaimed. No doubt, among the most acceptable channels of thanksgiving and praise, the sacrifice of the Eucharist holds the first place; but, it is only in this general respect, as a means of thanksgiving, that the Apostle seems to make any reference to it in this verse.

16. In this verse is prescribed another offering most pleasing to God, the offering of charity and beneficence to our neighbour; "for by such sacrifices," viz., praise of God, and charity towards our neighbour, "God's favour is obtained." The Greek, ευαρεστειται ὁ Θεος, means, *God receives delight; or, in them he is well pleased;* unlike the sacrifices of the Old Law, which were unpleasing to him.

17. To the two-fold sacrifice of praise (verse 15), and of charity (verse 16), he wishes

Text.

as being to render an account of your souls: that they may do this with joy, and not with grief. For this is not expedient for you.

18. Pray for us. For we trust we have a good conscience, being willing to behave ourselves well in all things.

19. And I beseech you the more to do this, that I may be restored to you the sooner.

20. And may the God of peace, who brought again from the dead the great pastor of the sheep, our Lord JESUS CHRIST, in the blood of the everlasting testament.

Paraphrase.

(as they are bound to do in virtue of their office), since, in the day of judgment they must render an account of you. Obey them, therefore, from the heart, that they may discharge this responsible duty of watching over you with joy and not with pain. This would not be expedient for you; for, the groans of the pastor would provoke against you the heavy vengeance of God.

18. Pray for us, and this favour we beg with the greater confidence of obtaining it, since our conscience bears testimony, that in all things connected with the gospel ministry, we have acted with truth and sincerity, and not from any hostility to the law of Moses, or from motives of self-interest.

19. And I beseech you still more to pray for me with the greater earnestness, that I may be restored to you the sooner.

20. Now may God, the author of peace, who raised from the dead our Lord Jesus Christ, the supreme pastor of the sheep, which he has redeemed by his blood, wherein is sanctioned the new and eternal testament—

Commentary.

them to add, the sacrifice of their own will, by obedience to their prelates and pastors. "For they watch" (*for your souls*, ὑπὲρ τῶν ψυχῶν ὑμῶν, is added here in the Greek; the Vulgate construction, which places these words not here but after the words "render an account"—*rationem pro animabus vestris reddituri*—is preferable)—this merely expresses the duty of the pastors; and the light in which the faithful are bound to regard them. What a heavy responsibility, those charged with the care of souls have incurred! they must account for each and every one of them, at God's judgment-seat; for each and every one, Jesus Christ shed his blood, with the dispensation of which the pastor is charged. Woe to him if it shall have flowed in vain for immortal souls, through any fault of his! "That they may do this," *i.e.*, watch over your souls, "with joy, and not with grief," seeing your disobedience, and the absence of progress made by you, "for this is not expedient for you." The groans of the prelates, whose words you slight, will provoke God's wrath, which he shall manifest in his own time. He who shall disobey or despise ecclesiastical authority shall be overtaken, sooner or later, by the justice of God, whom he despises.

18. If the Apostle did not derogate from the intercession of Christ, in begging the prayers of the Hebrews, how can it be said we derogate from it in supplicating the saints reigning in heaven?—(*See* 1 John, ii. 2).

"For, we trust that we have a good conscience;" he adds this, to remove the false impressions which his enemies were anxious to create regarding him, charging him with being the enemy of the Mosaic Law, and an apostate from Judaism. He says he has the testimony of conscience assuring him that he had been no such thing, and that "in all things" appertaining to the gospel ministry, "he behaved well," injuring no one; and also, labouring without any regard to filthy lucre, or selfish emolument. The words, "in all things," are rendered by some, "towards all persons," Jew and Gentile, without distinction, giving no cause of offence to any man, either by word or deed.

20. "The great pastor of the sheep," to whom all other pastors bear merely the relation of vicars. "In the blood of the everlasting testament." Some join these words with "pastor," as if they expressed how he was the pastor of the sheep—viz., by redeeming them, and feeding them with the blood in which the New Testament was sanctioned, "everlasting," in opposition to the Old, which was temporary; and because its promises have for object an eternal inheritance; moreover, it will be succeeded by no other covenant. Others connect them with, "who brought again from the dead," in the blood, *i.e.*, through the merits of his blood, since by his passion (says St. Thomas) he merited for himself and for us the glory of the resurrection.

Text.

21. Fit you in all goodness, that you may do his will : doing in you that which is well pleasing in his sight, through JESUS CHRIST : to whom is glory for ever and ever. Amen.

22. And I beseech you, brethren, that you suffer *this* word of consolation. For I have written to you in a few words.

23. Know ye that our brother Timothy is set at liberty : with whom (if he comes shortly) I will see you.

24. Salute all your prelates, and all the saints. The brethren from Italy salute you.

25. Grace be with you all. Amen.

Paraphrase.

21. May he, I say, perfect you in every good work, so that you may do his will, working in you that which is well pleasing in his sight, through the merits of Jesus Christ, to whom be glory for ever and ever.— Amen.

22. I beseech you brethren, to take in good part this Epistle, designed to console and exhort you ; for, considering the vast and comprehensive nature of the subject, I have written to you very briefly.

23. Know ye that our brother Timothy is at large after his imprisonment; should he come to me without delay, I will visit you, accompanied by him.

24. Salute in my name all your prelates, and all the faithful who serve Jesus. The brethren of Italy salute you.

25. The grace of God be with you all. Amen.

Commentary.

21. " Doing in you," by his inspiration and co-operation, " that which is well pleasing in his sight," he is said to work or perform that which he gives us by his grace, the power to perform, " through Jesus Christ," *i.e.*, through the merits of Jesus Christ.

22. " In a few words," considering the importance and comprehensive nature of the subject, and the sublime mysteries of which the Epistle treats.

23. " Is set at liberty." From these words some Expositors infer that Timothy had been in chains, not at Rome, as the words " with whom (if he come shortly, &c.,") show ; he announces his enlargement as agreeable to the Hebrews, with whom Timothy was in great favour. Others say the words " set at liberty," only mean, that he was disengaged from any urgent duty which could prevent him from accompanying the Apostle. The former is more probable. (" If he come shortly ") shows the Apostle's anxiety to visit them. Some say, he did not visit them ; however, he only expresses here his present resolution to do so.

The Greek subscription is to the following effect : " *Written to the Hebrews from Italy, by Timothy.*"

CATHOLIC EPISTLE OF ST. JAMES.

Introduction.

AUTHOR OF.—Who is the St. James to whom this Epistle is attributed? There were two, who bore the name of James, mentioned among the Apostles—one, the son of Zebedee, and brother of St. John; he was put to death by Herod (Acts, xii.) He is called James the Greater. The other frequently styled in Scripture the brother of our Lord, was the son of Alpheus, also called Cleophas, and of Mary, the cousin, although in SS. Scripture, frequently called the sister, of the Blessed Virgin. He was the brother of St. Jude and of Joseph, called the Just. To distinguish him from the other James, he is called James the *Less*, a title bestowed upon him, either on account of his age, or the lowness of his stature, or, from being called later to the Apostleship. He is also styled James, the *Just*, a title which it is universally agreed, he merited, owing to his eminent sanctity, so generally recognised, that it procured for him the singular veneration of the Jews themselves, by whom he was called "the just man." To his death Josephus attributes the final destruction of Jerusalem and the total dispersion of the Jews. The true cause, Josephus appeared, or at least affected, not to understand, viz., the murder of the Son of God, whose blood they invoked on themselves and on their children. Saints Jerome and Epiphanius relate, that our Lord, at his ascension, recommended to St. James the Church of Jerusalem, of which city he was, in consequence, constituted first Bishop, by the other Apostles. He was a Nazarite, never drank wine, and was particularly distinguished for his love of prayer. Ananias the son of Annas, of whom mention is made in the Gospels, being High Priest about the year 60, when St. Paul had appealed to Cæsar, having assembled the Sanhedrim, summoned St. James before them. Josephus narrates, that he was accused of violating the laws, and handed over to the people to be stoned to death. Hegesippus adds, that they compelled him to be carried to the battlements of the temple, and would fain have compelled him to make a public renunciation of his faith in Christ; but St. James took this public opportunity of proclaiming the Divinity of Jesus Christ. He was, in consequence, hurled from the battlements, and after his fall, dispatched by a blow from a fuller's club. This occurred in the year 62. This latter St. James, and not James the Greater, is the author of this Epistle, the best proof of which is, that in it, the inspired writer undertakes the refutation of errors which did not exist at the time St. James the Greater was put to death by Herod about the year 42, full fifteen years before St. Paul had written his Epistle to the Romans. The error referred to, which this Epistle is principally employed in refuting, was occasioned by the false interpretation of certain passages of St. Paul to the Romans. From these passages some persons inferred the absolute inutility of good works, without which St. James here clearly points out that faith is dead, and salvation, unattainable; he delivers also many other precepts of a holy life.

CANONICAL.—This, together with the following Epistles of Saints Peter, John, and Jude, are termed "CANONICAL," either because they belong to the catalogue or canon of inspired Scripture; or, because they contain rules and precepts for the regulation of a Christian life.

CATHOLIC.—They are commonly styled "CATHOLIC," either on account of the doctrine which they contain; or, more probably, because addressed, not to any particular church or person, as were the Epistles of St. Paul, (*v.g.*) to the Romans, Corinthians, Timothy, Titus, &c., but, to the whole body of the converted Jews, and intended for the instruction of the rest of the faithful throughout the entire earth.

CANONICITY OF.—The Canonicity or Divine authority of this Epistle has been called in question by Luther only, who designates it "*An Epistle of straw, and unworthy of an Apostle.*" The unanswerable arguments which it furnishes in proof of the Catholic doctrine of good works, sufficiently account for Luther's antipathy to it. Its Canonicity has been admitted by Calvin. The Church of England also admits it to be Divine Scripture. It is, indeed, difficult to conceive how she can do so, consistently with the sixth of the Thirty-nine Articles, which runs thus : "*In, i.e., By, the name of the Holy Scripture, we understand the Canonical Books of the Old and New Testament, of whose authority was never any doubt in the Church.*" Now, the authority of this Epistle of St. James was, for some time, *doubted*, and not always admitted in the Church. For, it is classed among the books of Sacred Scripture termed by Catholics, *Deutero-Canonical, i.e.,* whose Canonicity had not been *always*, nor *everywhere*, received· Hence, the utter inconsistency in Protestants to receive it as Divine Scripture. But, as regards Catholics, every Catholic must believe its Canonicity, or Divine authority, as firmly as that of the Four Gospels, after the formal definition of the Council of Trent on the subject.—*SS. 4ta de Canonicis Scripturis.* We have the same undoubted authority for its Divine inspiration, that we have for the rest of the Scriptures—the only certain means we can have for knowing the Divine inspiration of any writing—viz., the unerring authority of the Catholic Church. The same arguments adduced in proof of the Epistle to the Hebrews, are also in favour of this. It is mentioned in all the Councils in which a catalogue of inspired books was drawn up : in the Councils of Laodicea (60th Canon), Third of Carthage (Canon 47), Council of Rome, under Gelasius, Florence, Trent. It is mentioned by Origen (*Hom. 7, in Josue*), Athanasius (*in Synopsi*), Epiphanius (*Heresi,* 76), St. Jerome (*ad Paulinum Epistola*), St. Augustine (*Libro 2do de doctrina Christiana,* c. 8), Gregory Nazianzen (tom. 2, page 94), Innocent I. (*Epistola ad Decentium*), &c.

LANGUAGE OF.—It is commonly agreed, that it was written in the Greek, the language spoken everywhere at the time, and commonly used by the Jews. Hence, we find the Greek, or Septuagint Version, indiscriminately used by the dispersed Jews, and our Redeemer and the Apostles quote from the same. St. James quotes from the Scriptures according to it (chap. iv. verse 6).

OCCASION OF.—It has been already remarked, that the object of St. James in this, as well as of the other Apostles in their Catholic Epistles, was, to refute the error of Simon Magus, of the Nicolaites, and others, regarding the sufficiency of faith alone—an error which they founded on the false interpretation of St. Paul to the Romans (St. Augustine *de Fide et Operibus,* c. 16). It devolved, in a particular manner, on St. James to arrest the progress of this error, having been charged with the Church of Jerusalem, which bordered on Samaria, where Simon Magus had been disseminating his pernicious doctrines:

DATE OF.—There can be nothing determined for certain respecting the particular year in which this Epistle has been written. All we know is, that it must have been written some time between the year 58—the date of the Epistle to the Romans—and the year 63, when St. James was put to death.

CATHOLIC EPISTLE OF ST. JAMES.

CHAPTER I.

Analysis.

St. James commences this chapter, with the Apostolical salutation (1). He, next, exhorts the converted Jews, to whom this Epistle is directly addressed, to receive with joy, the different afflictions with which they were visited (2, 3). He encourages them to practise the virtue of patience in all its perfection (4), and points out the source from which the true wisdom to understand, and practically conform to these admonitions, is to be derived, and the means of obtaining it, viz., Prayer; one of the conditions of which he mentions (4–7). He next alludes specially to the temptations peculiar to the rich and to the poor, and points out the remedies to be adopted both by one and the other (9–11). He points out the reward, in store for patient and persevering suffering (12).

He, next, obviates a difficulty which might arise from a false conception of his doctrine, owing to the different respects under which "temptations" might be considered. He says that, viewed in the light of seductions to sin, God is not their cause, but rather man's own corrupt passions, which, when indulged, end in death (13–16).

Having pointed out the cause of moral evil, he next proceeds to point out the source of all good (17), and refers particularly to one great blessing for which we are indebted to God's pure bounty, viz.—our regeneration and call to the faith (18).

He next delivers wholesome instructions regarding the government of the tongue, particularly in reference to religious teaching, and assails the fundamental error, then prevalent, probably deduced from a false conception of the words of St. Paul to the Romans, respecting the sufficiency of faith alone—an error, the refutation of which was one of the principal objects of this Epistle (22). He shows by an example the inutility of faith without good works (23, 24), and points out certain works as necessary (26, 27).

Text.	Paraphrase.
1. JAMES the servant of God and of our Lord JESUS CHRIST, to	1. James, a servant of God (the Father) and of our Lord Jesus Christ, who has a special dominion

Commentary.

1. "A servant of God," which is commonly understood to refer to God the Father, "and of our Lord Jesus Christ," who, by purchase, has a special dominion over us. St. James might be called the servant of God on the several grounds of Creation, Redemption, Call to the Faith, &c.; but in this passage, the word, "servant," most probably, designates the special engagement to exercise the functions of Apostle. He selects this title of "servant," for many reasons, but principally from motives of humility. It is at the same time a most honourable designation; since, *to serve God is to reign.* From this heading, some interpreters infer that the author of this Epistle was not an Apostle. Hence, besides the two Apostles who bore the name of James, they assert there was a third of the name, not an Apostle—who was the author of this Epistle. But the grounds of this argument are quite weak and futile; for, in some of his Epistles, St. Paul does not assume the title of Apostle, (*ex. gr.*) to the Thessalonians, Philippians, Philemon. Neither does St. John nor St. Jude, assume the title of Apostle, in their respective Epistles; and yet, no one has denied these to be the productions of Apostles. Besides, the Council of Trent, expressly states that this Epistle was written by "James the Apostle."—(SS. 4th *Decreto de Canonicis SS. &c.*; SS. 14 *de Extrem. Unct.* ch. 1).

Text.	Paraphrase.
the twelve tribes which are scattered abroad, greeting.	over us by right of redemption (writes), to the faithful Jews converted to Christianity out of the Twelve Tribes of Israel, scattered all over the earth, wishing them the abundance of spiritual joy and of all blessings conducive to salvation.
2. My brethren, count it all joy, when you shall fall into divers temptations :	2. My brethren, it is not without cause I wish you the abundance of joy, notwithstanding the many temporal afflictions under which you labour ; for, I would have you regard it as a subject of pure, unalloyed joy, when you are visited with tribulations and afflictions, in various shapes and forms.
3. Knowing that the trying of your faith worketh patience.	3. For, you should feel perfectly assured, that these afflictions by which your faith is tried and tested, are the cause of producing and increasing the virtue of patience.

Commentary.

" To the twelve tribes which are dispersed." In the Greek, εν τη διασπορα, *which are in the dispersion*. It is disputed which "dispersion" of the Jews is referred to here. Some make it refer to that which occurred after the death of St. Stephen (Acts, viii. 1). It probably refers to the Jews converted to the faith from among those, who were dispersed throughout the different countries of the earth, after the captivity under Salmanazar (4 Kings, xvii.), and afterwards, to whom reference is made (Acts, ii. 5). "To the twelve tribes." He directly addresses the Jews converted from the twelve tribes, into which the Jewish people were divided, having been specially charged with the Apostleship of the Jews. The Epistle is, however, indirectly addressed to the converted Gentiles also. Its title, "Catholic," forbids us to confine it to the converted Jews exclusively. Hence, we can say that the " Twelve Tribes," embrace all spiritual Israel, who are numbered in a manner analogous to the division of carnal Israel ; and this is borne out by the numbering of the thousands of saints, out of the different tribes, the *duodecim millia signati*, out of each tribe—(Apocalypse, vii. 5-9). "Greeting." The Greek, χαιρειν, to *rejoice*, expresses the abundance of spiritual joy, and all blessings conducing to salvation (as in Paraphrase).

2. In the preceding verse, St. James wished the converted Jews, the abundance of all spiritual joy ; but, as they might naturally say, what joy could they have, who were, the victims of sufferings and afflictions ; he now tells them that they are in the very circumstances wherein they should most rejoice. " All joy," may mean, perfect joy, unmixed and unalloyed by sorrow ; or, "all," as embracing every subject of joy in this life, so that whatever matter for joy there is in all the goods of this life, is included in this one universal good of tribulation and sufferings ; and thus we should rejoice more in tribulation alone, than if we were the sole possessors of all the honours, riches, and pleasures of this earth.

" When you shall fall into divers temptations." By "temptations," are meant the crosses, afflictions and persecutions of this life. With these the early Christians were, in a special manner, visited. They are called " temptations," because sent by God to try and exercise our virtue. " Divers," by confiscation and plunder of property, incarceration, scourging, death, &c. This doctrine of St. James, though to the philosopher and worldly wise a paradox (as which of the gospel maxims is not ?) is perfectly in accordance with the uniform teaching of Sacred Scripture, wherein we are taught, that afflictions are a proof of the divine regard (Hebrews, xii.) ; that they serve to render us conformable to Jesus Christ, the predestined model of God's elect (Rom. viii.) ; that they serve to wean us from all inordinate attachment to the world and the things of this life. They are the bitter medicine, which our heavenly physician administers, to cure the corrupt inclinations of our fallen nature, and to serve as an antidote against future relapses. They help to remind us that this is not our final resting-place, that our happiness is to be found in heaven. The most perfect stage of Christian patience is that recommended here, viz., the bearing of tribulation not only willingly, but with "joy."

3. The reason of this apparently strange assertion is now assigned by St. James.

Text.

4. And patience hath a perfect work : that you may be perfect and entire, failing in nothing.

5. But if any of you want wisdom, let him ask of God, who giveth to all men abundantly, and upbraideth not; and it shall be given him.

Paraphrase.

4. But let this patience be perfected by the indispensable quality of perseverance, so that you may be perfect by having reached the end, to which patience conducts, viz., eternal life, and be not found wanting in anything required for the crowning and consummation of patience. Or, let your patience be so perfected in its kind, that you may possess all the virtues required for its fulness and integrity ; wanting none of the necessary qualities that usually accompany it.

5. But if anyone require the true wisdom (and who does not ?) by which to understand the designs of God's providence in visiting us with afflictions, and to conform to it in practice, let him beg it of God, who liberally dispenses his gifts to all, without exception, who pray for them as they ought, and unlike men, upbraids us not with the gifts received already at his hands ; and it shall be given to such a person.

Commentary.

"Knowing," *i.e.*, being fully convinced, "that the trying (το δοκιμιον) of your faith" (which he supposes to be effected by tribulation), "worketh patience," by supplying matter for its continual exercise and increase; since, without suffering, you could suppose no patience.

Is not the reverse stated by St. Paul to the Romans (verse 4)—"Patience worketh trial ?" δοκιμην.

There is no contradiction whatever ; for, the word "trial," bears a different meaning in both cases. In this passage, by "trying of your faith," are meant tribulations, which work patience, by being its object and occasional cause. Hence, "trying," is here regarded as the *act* of trying by tribulations, which are the cause or occasion of the virtue of patience ; whereas, in St. Paul, "trial," is regarded as the proof or demonstrated test, the *result* of patience. The difference in the Greek words in both cases shows the correctness of this answer—(*see* Romans, verse 4).

4. "And patience hath," &c. In the Greek, it is, *Let patience have*, εχετω, *a perfect work*. And this reading seems preferable ; for, the words are plainly *hortatory ;* as appears from the following, "that you may be," &c., and even in the Vulgate reading there is very little difference as to sense ; for, an exhortation is implied. "Perfect work," may regard the necessity of perseverance in patience ; or, the perfect fulness of patience accompanied by charity especially, and by the other virtues necessary to constitute its full integrity. Both interpretations are given in the Paraphrase.

5. As the doctrine of the Apostle regarding our rejoicing in tribulation is folly with the world, while it is the true wisdom of God ; from God, then, it is to come and to be obtained, by prayer. "If any of you want wisdom." The word "if," implies no doubt or hesitation, since all want wisdom ; the words mean, *whereas*, you all want wisdom. By "wisdom," is understood not only a speculative, intellectual knowledge of the economy and gracious designs of God in sending us afflictions ; but also, a practical conformity of will to the same ; and this is to come from the grace, which is to be obtained by earnest prayer. "Abundantly." The Greek word, απλως, literally means, *with simplicity* or *candour*, as opposed to private ends or selfish motives ; the word is more commonly used to imply, abundant liberality, as here ; the other meaning is also included. "And upbraideth not," *i.e.*, unlike men, who grow tired of always giving, and expect a return, and when importuned for new favours, upbraid us with those already received ; God, the liberal and bountiful dispenser of good gifts, is never tired of giving, and never upbraids us, whenever we turn his gifts to a good account. God, it is true, sometimes puts sinners in mind of their ingratitude, as well as of their other sins ; but this he does either for their conversion, or, in vindication of his own adorable Providence.

Text.

6. But let him ask in faith, nothing wavering. For he that wavereth is like a wave of the sea, which is moved and carried about by the wind.

7. Therefore let not that man think that he shall receive any thing of the Lord.

8. A double minded man is inconstant in all his ways.

9. But let the brother of low condition glory in his exaltation :

Paraphrase.

6. But as an indispensable condition for the efficacy of his prayer, he should ask with a firm, undoubted confidence, founded on the principles of faith, of being heard, no way wavering or doubting. For, he who doubts or wavers, is like unto the troubled waves of the sea, when it is raised into billows and tossed up and down by the wind.

7. Let not, then, a person, of this wavering, hesitating character, now hoping, again despairing,—now trusting, again distrusting, in the goodness and power of God—imagine that he will obtain from God the fruit of his faint petition.

8. The man who entertains in his mind different and conflicting thoughts, fluctuating and unsettled opinions, is, on this account, inconstant in all his actions and does nothing ; nor will such a person, when approaching the throne of God, now doubting, again confiding, obtain anything for want of the necessary disposition of a firm confidence.

9. Let the poor Christian who is placed in a lowly, humble position, instead of repining at his lot, or, feeling ashamed, rather glory in the exalted state of divine filiation to which he is raised, and in the crown to which it gives him a claim and title.

Commentary.

6. " In faith." One of the conditions for the efficacy of our prayers is, that they should be presented in a spirit of "faith," by which is commonly understood, the belief in God's power and willingness to hear us, as far as shall be expedient for us ; from this belief follows a firm and undoubting confidence of our being heard, so far as God is concerned. Of course, this confidence must always be accompanied with uncertainty, grounded upon our own unworthiness. " Nothing wavering." The Greek word, διακρινομενος, means, *expending the reasons on both sides*. Hence, it means to waver in belief and confidence. " For he that wavereth (in the sense already assigned), is like the wave of the sea, &c.," *i.e.*, is agitated by various reasons and doubts between hesitation on one side, and confidence on the other ; now sees reasons for hoping ; again, for desponding. The figure employed by the Apostle, is often used to designate the opposite of calm confidence. When such a man should immoveably adhere to God by faith in his unerring promises, he is tossed here and there by opposite doubts and reasonings.

7. " Let him not think," for, he will be disappointed in his hopes, "that he shall receive anything," *i.e.*, the object of his wavering, hesitating petition "from the Lord;" for such diffidence and hesitation is a direct insult to God's sovereign goodness and liberality.

8. " A double-minded man." The Greek word, διψυχος, means, *a man having two souls*. By it is meant here, not the hypocrite, who thinks one thing in his heart, and expresses another with his lips—an acceptation in which the word is oftentimes employed—but the man who entertains at the same time in his mind different and conflicting sentiments. Such a person never does anything ; he is always hesitating in irresolution. The inference, which St. James wishes to deduce, is implied in the general proposition of this verse, viz., that he cannot approach the throne of God with firm confidence, so as to obtain the fruit of his prayer. "In all his ways," *i.e.*, his actions and purposes. Most likely, allusion is here made to those vacillating and fainthearted Jewish converts, who, from the pressure of persecution, and for want of due confidence in God, were on the point of abandoning the Christian religion. It is to these the Apostle addresses his Epistle to the Hebrews.

9. St. James passes from general temptations (verses 2, 3) to particular ones, and

Text.

10. And the rich, in his being low, because as the flower of the grass shall he pass away.

11. For the sun rose with a burning heat, and parched the grass, and the flower thereof fell off, and the beauty of the shape thereof perished: so also shall the rich man fade away in his ways.

12. Blessed is the man that endureth temptation: for when he hath been proved, he shall receive the crown of life, which God hath promised to them that love him.

Paraphrase.

10. And on the other hand, let the rich and haughty, instead of priding in his riches and despising his poorer brethren, rather feel *shame* and *confusion* in the lowly condition to which he will soon be reduced, owing to the fleeting and uncertain nature of riches; for, neither they nor he shall be of greater durability than the flower of the grass.

11. For, no sooner has the sun fully risen with its burning heat, and parched the grass, than the flower thereof falls off, and all the beauty of its appearance is gone; in the same way, will the rich man fade and wither away, in all his pursuits and purposes.

12. Happy is the man, who with persevering patience endures the afflictions and crosses of this life; because, after having passed through the ordeal, by which his virtue had been tried and tested, he shall receive the crown of eternal life, which God has promised those who love him; without which love, no man could, through life, patiently endure tribulation.

Commentary.

here refers to the temptations peculiar to poverty and riches; discontent in the former case, pride and arrogance in the latter. It would appear from chap. ix. 1 Ep. to Cor. that some among the richer Christians haughtily looked down upon their poorer brethren, many of whom were reduced in circumstances, owing to the generous cession which they made of all their property, At this state of things, the poor man naturally repined; and hence, to remedy this growing evil, St. James tells the poor man to glory in his "exaltation" to the state of divine filiation.—(*Vide* Paraphrase).

10. "But the rich, in his being low." Some verb is understood to complete the sense. By some Expositors the word "*glory*," is inserted, bearing an ironical meaning. "Let the rich (*glory*) in his being," &c. Others, with greater probability, insert the words (" *be confounded or feel shame*") "in his being," &c. It is not at all unusual in Scripture, to supply a verb of contrary signification, to that expressed in the sentence (*v.g.* St. Paul, 1 Ep. to Tim. chap. iv.) "Forbidding to marry, to abstain from food," *i.e.*, *commanding*, "to abstain from food." The rich man should feel humbled were he to consider the lowly, fleeting, and inconstant nature of these riches, in which he places his confidence. "Because as the flower of the grass," which is its frailest and tenderest part, he shall pass away.

11. By a very striking illustration, he now shows how frail and fleeting is a man's tenure of riches. "For the sun rose with a burning heat." This regards the time of day, when the sun is fully risen and its heat most intense. Others understand the Greek word for "burning heat," τω καυτωνι, to mean the burning wind, called in Arabia, the Simoom, which blows at sun-rise, as is asserted by Oriental travellers. "And the beauty of the shape thereof." In Greek, προσωπον, *of the face thereof*, which, by a Hebrew idiom, refers to the external appearance of a thing. "So shall the rich man fade away in all his ways." "By ways," are meant his actions, his purposes, his designs of enjoyment, and of aggrandizement. In these latter words is contained the application of the foregoing illustration.

12. The Apostle pronounces the man happy, who patiently and perseveringly endures, with a prospect of future rewards (for, this is the meaning of the Greek verb, υπομενει), the tribulations of this life. "For when he hath been proved," *i.e.*, shall have tested in the ordeal of tribulation ("gold and silver are tried in the fire, but acceptable men in the furnace of humiliation"), and his virtue proved to be solid and genuine, he shall then receive the crown of eternal life, "which God (in some Greek

Text.

13. Let no man, when he is tempted, say that he is tempted by God. For God is not a tempter of evils, and he tempteth no man.

14. But every man is tempted by his own concupiscence, being drawn away and allured.

15. Then when concupiscence hath conceived, it bringeth forth

Paraphrase.

13. Let no one presume to say, whenever he is tempted to the commision of sin, that this seductive temptation comes from God; for, although God sends us temptation, in order to try us, he never tempts to the commission of evil. He tempts no one in this way.

14. But every man is tempted to the commission of evil by his own concupiscence, *i.e.*, by the corrupt desires of his own heart; by the inordinate desire of indulging in illicit pleasures, at variance with God's laws, being drawn away by it from the line of duty, and captivated and ensnared by it.

15. Afterwards, when the seductive blandishments of concupiscence are fully consented to, and it

Commentary.

copies, "*which the Lord*," in the *Codex Vaticanus, which he*) has promised to those that love him." He says, "love him;" because, without the love of God, no man could patiently endure the trials of a long life; and this patience, to be genuine, must be, what Divines call, an *actus imperatus*, of charity: for, "charity is patient," *i.e.*, dictates acts of patience, and without charity the greatest sufferings, even the giving of our bodies to the flames, is worth nothing.—(1 Cor. xiii.)

13. In this verse, the Apostle considers temptation in a different light from that in which he viewed it, verses 2, 3. There, it was considered as the temptation of trial or *probation*; in this verse, as the temptation of *seduction*. It appears that in the time of St. James many dangerous errors were propagated regarding the origin of good and evil. Simon Magus and others had been industriously circulating among the people, that temptations, even when viewed under the light of seductions to evil, come from God; and, not unlikely, they grounded these erroneous doctrines on the mistaken interpretation of the words of the Apostle to the Romans (chap. i.), where God is said to have *delivered* men to a reprobate sense, &c. St. James here corrects this growing error, and says, that "God is not a tempter of evils," *i.e.*, by no means tempts us to commit sin; since he tempts no one. Some interpreters give the Greek word, απειραστος, which is rendered into our Version, "a tempter of evils," a passive signification, of which it is certainly susceptible. "God is *incapable of being tempted to evil*, and he tempts no one, *i.e.*, he cannot be tempted himself, nor can he tempt others; just as we say of his veracity, *he cannot be deceived nor can he deceive*. In order to understand this verse clearly, and reconcile it with the foregoing, it is to be remarked, that in Scripture language, temptation is two-fold; of *probation*, or trial; of *seduction*, or deceit. Of the former, which has for object to try our virtue, and show us what we are, God is frequently said to be the author and direct cause (*v.g.* Genesis, xxii. regarding Abraham, also regarding Job, *see* also Deut. xiii. 3). Of the latter kind of temptation, which has for object to entice us, by the promises of enjoyment, or impel us by the threats of punishment to commit sin, God cannot be the author; and to it there is reference in this verse and also in the words of the Lord's Prayer, "and lead us not into temptation," *i.e.*, permit us not by the subtraction of thy grace, to fall into temptation.

14. Here he points out the source of temptation viewed under this latter respect, viz., concupiscence, *i.e.*, the strange proneness to evil and to the gratification of illicit pleasures, at variance with the laws of God, implanted in human nature, in its present fallen state. "Drawn away." Turned aside from God, and the straight path of duty. "Allured," the Greek word, δελεαζομενος, means, *ensnared* and *caught* as *fishes with a bait*.

15. The Apostle now describes the different stages in the commission of sin. First, concupiscence tempts us, (verse 14), by working on our weakness, and proposing to us gratification, whether coming interiorly or exteriorly. Next, "then, when concupiscence hath conceived," (verse 15), which, most probably, means by a full internal consent,

Text.	Paraphrase.
sin. But sin, when it is completed, begetteth death.	conceives, after the full consent of the will is given, it brings forth sin. But when sin is fully accomplished and consummated, by the external commission of the act, to which concupiscence impels us, it generates, and brings forth as its fruit, spiritual and eternal death.
16. Do not err therefore, my dearest brethren.	16. Do not then, my dearest brethren, be led astray by the erroneous and dangerous doctrines, in which it is asserted, that God is the author of evil.
17. Every best gift, and every perfect gift is from above, coming down from the Father of lights, with whom there is no change, nor shadow of alteration.	17. Far from being the author of evil, it is from Him—the source of all light, physical or moral, natural or supernatural—every good and excellent gift, whether of nature or grace, alone proceeds, descending from his heavenly throne; and, unlike the great luminary, by which light is diffused throughout this earth, and in which there is daily change of position, in his apparent course through the heavens, and alternating vicissitudinous change of shadow, in his annual passage from tropic to tropic, in God there is no change in the distribution of his gifts; now dispensing good, again, evil. He, the ever unchangeable author of all good, dispenses to all who pray to him, with a liberal and plentiful hand.

Commentary.

"it bringeth forth (mortal) sin." If resisted, instead of being a sin, it is a source of merit. Again, "When sin is completed," *i.e.*, externally commited, "it begetteth," or, gives birth to "death," *i.e.*, the spiritual death of the soul here, entailing a liability to eternal death, hereafter. This interpretation, which is adopted by Estius, appears to be the most probable among the many given of this passage.

But it may be objected:—Might it not be said in this interpretation, that concupiscence, when it conceives, *begetteth death*, since we understand "conceive," to mean, full internal consent, which constitutes a mortal sin?

Yes, so it might; but, it is only of the external consummation of the deed, which manifests a proneness to sin and fulness of consent difficult to be remedied, and moreover, aggravates the internal consent, and is attended with the injury of a third person, that we can say beyond all exception, "it begetteth death." And the very absence of time and place, the want of opportunity to commit the external act, although the thought was fully consented to, is, to a certain extent, a favour from God, whom St. Augustine (*Homil.* 22, chap. 6), thus introduces, as addressing the sinner—"*Ut adulterium non committeres, suasor defuit ; ut suasor deesset, ego feci ; locus et tempus defuit, ut hæc deessent, ego feci.*"

OBJECTION.—Does not God concur in actions intrinsically bad (*v.g.*), the hatred of God, from which act, even materially considered, malice can, in no order of things, be conceived to be separated?

RESP.—The concurrence of God in such actions is only what is termed a "*concursus generalis*," whereby man receives the power to love or hate God. But, that in the exercise of this power, he selects the hating of God, is the act of his own free will.

16. From this verse, it would appear there were some erroneous opinions circulated respecting the origin of good and evil. "Therefore," is not in the Greek.

17. Having shown the source and true cause of evil, St. James now points out the origin of all good. This comes "from above," from heaven, where God in a special manner dwells, from whom "every best gift," (in Greek, πασα δοσις αγαθη, *every good giving*), "and perfect gift" proceeds, by which it is implied, that not alone every good gift, but the very giving thereof, comes from God. Some interpreters say, that "every best gift," and "perfect gift," refer to the same thing, and are repeated for the sake of greater emphasis. Others make the former refer to all natural gifts, and the latter,

Text.

18. For of his own will hath he begotten us by the word of truth that we· might be some beginning of his creature.

19. You know, my dearest breth·

Paraphrase.

18. And in confirmation and illustration of his being the unchangeable author of every good and perfect gift, we may adduce the fact, that of his free and gratuitous will, without any claim or title of justice on our part, he has given us a new spiritual birth in baptism, whereof faith, conceived from his revealed word of truth, is an indispensable condition ; so that by our vocation to the faith we are become, in a certain sense, the choicest and first fruits of creation.

19. This is a gift of the excellence of which you

Commentary.

which is called "perfect," or superexcellent, to the supernatural gifts of grace. In this verse, two things are asserted, viz., that everything coming from God is good and excellent, which refutes the impious assertion of Simon Magus, afterwards more fully evolved by the Manichees ; and secondly, that God alone is the source of all good, which refutes the errors of Pagan philosophy, afterwards revived by the Pelagians. "The father of lights ;" he is called "father," because the first source and author "of lights," which may regard the natural lights of the sun, moon, and stars. Light is emblematic of good, as darkness is, of evil, or "*lights*" may be understood of the intellectual, spiritual lights, whether of nature, grace, or glory ; and from God, as their great source, proceed all the good gifts, represented by the light of the heavenly bodies, and the gifts of intellectual knowledge, whether natural or supernatural, actual or habitual. To him, then, we should have recourse, in order perfectly to understand these sublime paradoxes put forward by St. James, regarding the blessings of tribulation, and the joy they should cause in us (verses 2, 3), &c., and as father of all light and knowledge, he will enlighten our understanding to perceive them.

"With whom there is no change," &c. The Apostle represents God, as a great luminous sun or body of light, diffusing his radiance and blessings throughout all creation ; but, he removes from him all the imperfections of our present sun. He need not change from place to place, as our sun, who in his apparent daily motion, makes his place different at morning, noon, and night. To this, the word "*change*" most probably refers, which, in reference to God, means that there is no change in him, in reference to the distribution of his gifts, now dispensing good ; again, evil. "Nor shadow of vicissitude," which, in reference to the natural sun, refers to his annual motion, when he apparently moves towards the tropics, and from them ; and according to his proximity or distance are the shadows cast by him, shortened or lengthened. It is to this alternate lengthening and lessening of the different shadows, that the Greek words for "shadow of alteration," τροπης αποσκιασμα, refer. In reference to God, it means, that God is the constant and ever liberal source of good, not dealing it out at one time with a sparing, at another, with a liberal hand.

18. As an illustration of the good gifts conferred on us by God, the Apostle adduces that most excellent of good gifts, our spiritual regeneration in baptism. "Of his own will," *i.e.*, without any merits of ours ; and hence, this was on his part a perfectly gratuitous gift. "Hath he begotten us," which, most probably, refers to our spiritual birth in baptism, whereby a new spiritual existence was conferred on us. "By the word of truth," may refer to the form of baptism ; or, more probably, to the word of God, conceived through faith, which in adults is an indispensable condition, for receiving a new spiritual regeneration in baptism. The same idea is, very likely, conveyed here, as in chapter v. 26, to the Ephesians : "By the laver of water, in the word of life." "That we might be some beginning," in Greek, απαρχην, *first fruits*, "of his creature," may refer to the members of the Church, who are selected by God, in preference to all other men, as his choice portion out of the rest of the mass of mankind. Others understand the words, of those who were first called to the Church and the faith ; they were taken from the Jews, and they were the first fruits of such, as were, through their instrumentality in all future ages, to be associated to the Christian Church.

19. "You know, my dearest," &c. "You know ;" in some Greek copies, it is ὥστε *wherefore ;* in the *Codex Vaticanus,* ἴστε, "you know."

S

Text.

ren. And let every man be swift to hear, but slow to speak, and slow to anger.

20. For the anger of man worketh not the justice of God.

21. Wherefore, casting away all uncleanness, and abundance of naughtiness, with meekness receive the ingrafted word, which is able to save your souls.

Paraphrase.

are yourselves fully conscious, and for which, my dearest brethren, you must feel duty grateful. And let every person amongst you be ready and prepared to listen with docility to the word of truth already referred to, and be tardy in acting the part of teacher in giving utterance to it. And let each one control all feelings, and every expression of anger, into which those who have an inordinate pruriency for speaking and disputing with others are apt to fall.

20. And first, regarding anger. The man who acts under the influence of anger, far from performing works consistent with real justice, by which we are justified before God, will, on the contrary, perform bad works, by which true justice is lost.

21. Wherefore, in order to live up to the new spiritual birth you have received (verse 18), and more effectually to repress anger, laying aside all uncleanness and defilement of sin, all impure and unclean affections, which defile the soul, but particularly the redundant affections of malevolence and malice, in the spirit of meekness, receive and foster the doctrines of truth already implanted among you, which alone can save you.

Commentary.

"And let every man be swift to hear, &c." St. James now proceeds to deliver wholesome instructions regarding the proper government of the tongue, and the repressing of all feelings of anger. It is commonly supposed by Commentators, that St. James here refers to the abuse of the gift of tongues, accorded to many in the infancy of the Church, to which reference is made (1 Cor. xiv.) The Jewish converts had an inordinate wish, after their conversion, to display the same power of speaking, which they exercised in the synagogue, to the confusion and disorder of the Christian assemblies. St. James cautions them against this abuse. "And slow to anger," which a spirit of disputation is apt to engender. No doubt, the admonition of St. James here applies to Christians at all times, and recommends a due regard to silence on all occasions, together with a proper regulation of the tongue, and a restraint on the impulse of anger. The admonition conveyed in this verse, together with that subjoined in verse 22, forms a theme whereon St. James dilates, up to chapter iv. 12, with the exception of a brief digression, at chapter ii. 1–13.

20. Inverting the order of treating the admonitions of the preceding verse, he first refers to anger. In the words of this verse more is conveyed than is expressed; by it is meant, that not only an angry man does not perform good works whereby "the justice of God," i.e., true justice, is acquired and preserved, but that he performs wicked, evil works.

21. He now recommends them to live up to their new spiritual existence (verse 18); and in order thereto, they should avoid evil, by laying aside their vicious affections; and do good, by receiving the word of God with meekness, &c. (verse 21). "All uncleanness." The Greek word, ῥυπαρίαν, literally regards the filth adhering to the body. Hence, some understand it of the sordid vice of avarice; others, of impurity. It more probably refers to sinfulness of all kinds, whereby the soul is defiled. "And abundance of malice." In this is specified the viciousness in general, referred to in the preceding words. It probably regards feelings of malevolence towards our neighbour. This is a source of anger. In the word "abundance," is conveyed an idea borrowed from agriculture. The husbandman carefully prunes away all superfluous and redundant weeds, whereby the earth is exhausted, and the good seed choked up; so they, too, should carefully cut away all the noxious affections, of which human nature, in its present fallen state, is so prolific; which, like tares, choke and prevent the growth of the good seed of God's word and grace in their hearts. "With meekness, receive the

Text.

22. But be ye doers of the word, and not hearers only, deceiving your own selves.

23. For if a man be a hearer of the word and not a doer : he shall be compared to a man beholding his own countenance in a glass.

24. For he beheld himself, and went his way, and presently forgot what manner of man he was.

25. But he that hath looked into the perfect law of liberty, and hath continued therein, not becoming a forgetful hearer, but a doer of the work ; this man shall be blessed in his deed.

Paraphrase.

22. But you should guard against contenting yourselves with merely receiving and hearing those doctrines of truth, without reducing them to practice by good works, deluding yourself by false and sophistical reasonings on this most important subject.

23. For the man that contents himself with merely hearing the word of God, without reducing to practice the precepts which it inculcates, may be justly likened to a person who views in a looking-glass his natural countenance.

24. And who, after a merely cursory and careless view, goes his way, presently forgets what manner of man he was—what were the faults and blemishes he beheld—and pays no attention to wiping them off, thus deriving no profit from looking into the glass, and unprofitably squandering his time.

25. Whereas, on the other hand, the man who shall have diligently and carefully looked into the law of the gospel, which, unlike the Old Law, perfects and justifies us, making us free sons of God, exempting us from servitude and from the yoke, "*which neither we nor our fathers could bear,*" and shall continue meditating and reflecting on it, and, instead of hearing its precepts, merely to forget them again, shall faithfully reduce them to practice by good works ; such a man shall be happy in following a course of this kind ; that is, he shall receive the happiness of justification here, and of glory hereafter.

Commentary.

ingrafted word." In the place of vindictive, revengeful desires, they should substitute a spirit of meekness, and in this spirit receive, or rather foster, the doctrines of truth, which, to distinguish them from those truths known by the light of reason, are termed "ingrafted." In these latter words the Apostle inculcates the admonition given in the first part of verse 19, "be swift to hear," &c.

22. The Apostle here enters on one of the principal subjects of this Epistle—viz. the refutation of the erroneous doctrine of the sufficiency of faith alone, a doctrine broached, even at this early period. "Deceiving yourselves." The Greek word for " deceiving," παραλογιζομενος, means, *adopting sophistical reasoning.* The sophism by which the heretics, in the days of St James, as well as in modern times, deceive themselves, is founded on the difference of meaning between the "works of the law," without which St. Paul says (Rom. iii.), we are justified by faith, and the "works" performed by grace and faith, which Catholics require for justification.

23, 24. From this example, and from its applications (verse 25), the necessity of good works is clearly inferred. Such a man, carelessly and hurriedly looking into the mirror (εσοπτρῳ), sees his countenance, but afterwards forgets to wipe off and remove the blemishes which the looking into the mirror may have disclosed to him. To such a person, the looking into the glass proves to be quite useless, of no service whatever ; so it is with the man, who merely hears the word of God, without reducing it to practice. In the application of this comparison, the mirror is the word of God, which represents to us what we are, and what we ought to be. "The countenance of a man" is the state of his conscience ; the defects in his visage, are the sins whereby the purity of his soul is sullied ; to see one's self in the mirror is to hear the word of God, and remark the difference there is between what we are and what we ought to be, according to the gospel ; to forget the state of one's countenance, is to forget the truths preached ; and to neglect removing the blemishes, is to neglect wiping off by tears of repentance, the uncleanness caused by sin, in the soul. How many are there to whom the example of the mirror is perfectly applicable.

25. This is an application by contraries of the example already adduced—" hath

Text.

26. And if any man think himself to be religious, not bridling his tongue, but deceiving his own heart, this man's religion is vain.

27. Religion clean and undefiled before God and the Father, is this : to visit the fatherless and widows in their tribulation : and to keep one's self unspotted from this world.

Paraphrase.

26. Now, among the works necessary for this happiness is the government of the tongue ; for, if any person looks upon himself as really religious, without bridling his tongue, thus deceiving his own heart, while persuading himself that piety is compatible with giving free reins to his tongue, such a man's Christian faith and profession is vain, and of no use to him.

27. The religion which is pure and free from spot, not merely in the sight of men, who often imagine religion and piety to exist where it does not ; but in the sight of God and our heavenly Father, dictates these acts of mercy ; viz., to visit the widows and orphans, so as to relieve their wants and offer them consolation, and to preserve one's self, as to body and soul, pure and immaculate from the vices of this wicked world.

Commentary.

looked into." The Greek word, παρακυψας, means to look into narrowly and closely as is done by those who stoop down to obtain a closer view. "The perfect law," i.e., the gospel law, which, unlike the old, "that brought nothing to perfection." (Heb. vii. 19), perfects us by grace and justification ; "of liberty," exempting us from servitude and the fear of punishment, so that we can set all the menaces of the law at defiance, it makes us free sons of God, and not slaves of the synagogue ; "and hath continued therein," by making it the subject of meditation, day and night ; "this man will be blessed, &c." Hence, according to St. James, it is only on condition of not forgetting the precepts of the law, and of performing the works which it enjoins, a man will obtain the happiness of justice here and of glory hereafter. Can a stronger argument be adduced in proof of the necessity of good works for justification and eternal life ?

26. "If any man think himself," &c. In some Greek copies, if any man (among you) think, &c. ; "among you," is omitted in the Codex Vaticanus. The Apostle, among the works required, reckons governing the tongue, and restraining it from detraction, rash judgments, self-praise, and other faults, to which persons, who have the character of piety, are liable. "Deceiving his own heart," while endeavouring to reconcile two things perfectly incompatible, viz. : true religion and the unrestrained indulgence in the vices of the tongue—"this man's religion," i.e., his religious practices and profession, are of no avail to him. St. James, then, refers to those vices of the tongue, such as boastful, slanderous, polluting language, which are mortal and deadly sins. Is there any vice more common, than this shocking vice of the tongue, and withal, so little attended to, or scrupled ?

27. Lest it might be imagined that the mere act of bridling the tongue, and not injuring our neighbour, would suffice ; he now mentions some of the principal works in which pure religion is exercised. "Religion, clean," in opposition to the vain and empty religion of the Jews, who regarded all its purity as consisting in certain ceremonies and legal purifications, "and undefiled," in opposition to the impious and impure rites of the Pagans and Heretics—consists in "this," or rather dictates the following acts ; for, the following are the, actus eliciti, (as they are called) of the virtue of mercy, and only the, actus imperati, of religion, "to visit the fatherless," &c., or, what comes to the same, to administer to their wants, and this is "pure religion," since there can be no other than a pure motive in relieving such, there being no hope of temporal retribution in the case, "and to keep one's self unspotted from this world," i.e., from the vices of this wicked world, principally luxury, avarice, and ambition ; for, the great leading maxims of this world are, the concupiscence of the flesh, the concupiscence of the eyes, &c. ; the preserving of one's self from these is "undefiled religion." This proves the necessity of good works, since it is in the performance of them, "clean," or pure religion consists.

CHAPTER II.

Analysis.

St. James commences this chapter, by exhorting the Christian converts to avoid the crime of "respect of persons," of which he adduces an example (1, 2). *The example in question, although, apparently at first sight, not quite in point, however, as explained in the Commentary, will be seen to be perfectly so* (3, 4). *As it had reference to the undue preference shown the rich before the poor, St. James points out how unbecoming such conduct is, being opposed to the economy of God, in reference to the poor* (5), *and unmerited on the part of the rich, whose vices he enumerates* (6, 7). *This, however, should not interfere with the respect, which the order of charity inculcates in regard to the rich, and those to whom respect and honour are due,* (8). *But this honour should not be carried to the extent of " respect of persons," which the law of God condemns* (9), *and which, like every grievous violation of any other single precept, involves us, to a certain extent, in the guilt of violating the entire Law* (10, 11).

As a remedy against all sin, he proposes the constant consideration of future judgment (12). *He inculcates the necessity of showing mercy to all those, who may be involved in miseries of any kind* (13).

In the next place, he treats of the principal subject of the Epistle, viz., the necessity of good works, for justification and salvation (14), *and the inutility of faith alone, which he shows—firstly, by the example of the inutility of a mere speculative knowledge of our neighbour's want, without actually relieving it* (15-17); *secondly, by showing the necessity of good works, for the discharge of the duty of externally professing and manifesting our faith* (18) ; *thirdly, by comparing dead faith, in a certain sense, with the faith of demons* (19); *fourthly, by the example of Abraham, justified through works* (20-24); *fifthly, by the example of Rahab* (25) ; *finally, he compares dead faith to a dead body* (26).

Text.	Paraphrase.
1. MY brethren have not the faith of our Lord JESUS CHRIST of glory with respect of persons.	1. My brethren, do not, while professing the faith of our Lord Jesus Christ, who is the Lord of glory, be guilty of the crime of exception of persons ; that is to say, do not attempt to unite two things which are incompatible, and which mutually exclude each other, viz., the faith of our Lord Jesus Christ and the crime of exception of persons.

Commentary.

1. "Have not the faith of our Lord Jesus Christ of glory." The word "*glory*" is, by some Commentators, connected with "*faith*," *i.e.*, the glorious faith of our Lord, &c. the connexion in the Paraphrase, joining it with " our Lord," is the more probable. Our Lord Jesus Christ is called " the Lord of glory " (1 Cor. ii.) " With respect of persons," *i.e.*, do not attempt to unite two things so incompatible. " Respect, or exception, of persons " takes place, whenever an unjust preference is shown to one party beyond another ; (*v.g.*) a judge would incur the guilt of "respect of persons," by pronouncing sentence, on account of the appearance and external circumstances of a person, without any regard to the merits of the case. Others, among whom is A'Lapide, interpret the words thus : do not believe that the glory of our Lord Jesus Christ consists in an exception of persons, so that he is honoured when to your Agapes

Text.

2. For if there shall come into your assembly a man having a golden ring, in fine apparel, and there shall come in also a poor man in mean attire,

3. And you have respect to him that is clothed with the fine apparel, and shall say to him: Sit thou here well: but say to the poor man: Stand thou here, or sit under my footstool:

4. Do you not judge within yourselves, and are become judges of unjust thoughts?

Paraphrase.

2. In illustration of the crime to which I refer; suppose two men come into your place of public worship, one of them a rich man, in showy apparel, and wearing on his finger a gold ring; the other, a poor man, in mean and squalid dress,

3. And that you assign to the rich man some commodious honourable seat, while the poor man is contemptuously made either to stand up, or sit down in some lowly place.

4. Do you not, by treatment so different in both cases, come to a very unfair and partial decision, and do you not found your judgment, on false estimates and erroneous reasonings.

Commentary.

and meetings you admit the rich only and the noble, to the exclusion and contempt of the poor and squalid, as if the glory of Christianity consisted in external pomp and show.

2. He illustrates by an example, what this "respect of persons" is, against which he has been cautioning them. Suppose "there shall come into your assembly," in Greek, συναγωγην, *synagogue*, which, most probably, refers to their place of public assemblage for religious worship, like the Jewish synagogue; or, perhaps, to one of the old synagogues, converted into a place of worship for the converted Jews; "a man having a gold ring," which, as appears from the Greek, χρυσοδακτυλιος, was worn on his finger, a thing generally done by the rich; "in fine apparel;" in Greek, εσθητι λαμπρα, *shining apparel*. "Your assembly" is understood by some to refer to judicial assemblies, such having been, as they say, according to Jewish custom, held in places of worship.

3. And you assign an honourable commodious seat to the rich man, on account of his riches, while the poor man, because he is poor, is treated contemptuously, and made either to stand up or sit down in some humble, lowly place.

4. "Do not judge within yourselves." In Greek, διεκριθητε εν εαυτοις, *are you not judged within yourselves*, your conscience reproaching you, and stinging you with remorse for your unjust conduct. The Vulgate reading is the more probable, as appears from the following words, "and are become judges," &c., which are explanatory of the former. In some Greek copies, και is prefixed to this verse, "*and*, do you not judge," &c., but it is omitted in the chief MSS. "And are become judges of unjust thoughts." In the Greek, διαλογισμων, *reasonings*, i.e., unjustly reasoning, and concluding from false estimates, that the rich man, as such, is to be preferred before the poor. It is not easy to see what St. James means by this example. Hence it is, that Commentators are perplexed about the meaning of the passage. They cannot discover anything like great guilt, in the preference shown to the rich man in the case alluded to, nor do they see any reason for ranking it with the crime of "respect to persons," which (verse 6) is called, "dishonouring the poor;" since, there is no great dishonour shown a poor man in having a rich man accommodated with a seat in any assembly, whether sacred or profane, before him: or of classing it (verse 11) with adultery or murder. It is on account of this difficulty, that St. Augustine and others assign to the example in question an enigmatical meaning; and say, that, it is not so much the giving of a place of honour to the rich man and refusing it to the poor, St. James here condemns, as the crime signified by this preference, viz., the preference given to the rich on account of their worldly connexions in ecclesiastical dignities and offices, before the poor, who may be better qualified for such dignities. "*Quis enim ferat eligi, divitem ad sedem honoris Ecclesiæ, contempto paupere instructiore ac sanctiore?*"—St. Augustine (Ep. 29), referring to this passage. The same interpretation is adopted by Mauduit. Hence, according to them, St. James is treating of the odious crime of simony. This interpretation derives probability from verse, 5, where the Apostle would appear to allude

Text.

5. Hearken, my dearest brethren: hath not God chosen the poor in this world, rich in faith, and heirs of the kingdom which God hath promised to them that love him?

6. But you have dishonoured the poor man. Do not the rich oppress you by might; and do not they draw you before the judgment seats:

7. Do not they blaspheme the good name that is invoked upon you?

Paraphrase.

5. See, my dearest brethren, how different from your conduct is the example set us by Almighty God in his treatment of the poor. Has he not given them a preference and selected them before the rich and powerful according to the world, to enrich them with the gift of faith and other spiritual blessings, and make them heirs of his heavenly kingdom, which he has promised to such as love him, and evince this love by their actions.

6. And those very persons, whom God himself has thus honoured and preferred, you dishonour. Moreover, do not the rich, by committing crimes against you never perpetrated by the poor, forfeit all claim to peculiar respect? Do they not violently oppress you and drag you before the tribunals of unbelieving judges?

7. Do they not, by their wicked conduct and perverse morals, bring odium on, and cause to be blasphemed, the sacred name of Christ, from which you are termed Christians?

Commentary.

to the selection, which God made of poor fishermen, preferably to the great ones of the earth, for exercising the exalted and sublime functions of the Apostleship. Others understand the example of the preference shown to the rich before the poor in courts of justice, which unjust sentence is signified by the preference in seats alluded to. Others understand it to refer to the crime denounced by St. Paul in the first Epistle to Cor., chap. xi., viz., the contempt shown to the poor in the *Agapes* or love feasts, which in the infancy of the Church were celebrated immediately before receiving the Holy Eucharist (*vide* 1 Cor. xi.) The neglect shown the poor, on such occasions, was highly scandalous and injurious to religion, on which account, St. Paul denounces it in the strongest language. This opinion has this advantage, that it solves the difficulty without departing from the literal meaning of the text. If we understand the passage to refer to the ordinary meetings in the church, we must suppose the neglect, referred to by St. James, to be greatly aggravated by the contempt, with which the poor must have been treated. This, in the infancy of the Church, must have proved very detrimental to religion.

5. He shows how opposed their conduct is to the example set us by God himself in the work of man's redemption; "the poor in this world," whether we regard the preachers of the Gospel, or those to whom it was first preached (*vide* 1 Cor. i. 26); "rich in faith," *i.e., to be* rich in faith, this being the end for which he had chosen them; for, before their call, they were not rich in faith; "and heirs," to inherit his heavenly kingdom. "That love him," shows, that an idle, merely speculative faith, is of no avail.

6. You have dishonoured the poor, to whom God has shown such preference. From this verse, it is clear, that the example adduced cannot be understood of a mere preference in seats in any assembly, since a poor man could not look upon himself as dishonoured by such a preference, unless there were great contempt accompanying it. The example may, besides the meaning already assigned (4), be understood of a preference shown the rich before the poor, in the administration of the sacraments of the Church, the souls of the poor being as valuable in the sight of their common Father, as those of the rich and powerful. "Do they not draw you before the judgment seats" of infidels?—a vice denounced in the strongest language by St. Paul (1 Cor. vi.)

7. "Do they not blaspheme?" or cause to be blasphemed by the infidels (for they are themselves supposed to be Christians), the sacred name of Christ, which you bear, from him being called Christians.

Text.	**Paraphrase.**
8. If then you fulfil the royal law, according to the scriptures, *Thou shalt love thy neighbour as thyself;* you do well.	**8.** If, however, in the preference shown to the rich and powerful before the poor and humble man, you follow and depart not from the order prescribed by that most excellent of precepts, in which is summed up all the rest, laid down in the sacred Scriptures, "*Thou shalt love thy neighbour as thyself;*" you do well.
9. But if you have respect to persons, you commit sin, being reproved by the law as transgressors.	**9.** But if this preference be of such a nature as to constitute the crime of exception of persons; then, you commit sin, being reproved as transgressors, by the law, which, in a general way, prohibits every act of injustice.
10. And whosoever shall keep the whole law, but offend in one *point,* is become guilty of all.	**10.** For, whosoever observes the entire law, except in one point, in which he mortally violates it, is become guilty, and is adjudged to eternal punishment, just as much (though not, of course, to the same extent), as if he violated all its precepts.

Commentary.

8. Lest it might be inferred, from the charges which are alleged by St. James, against the rich, that he was encouraging the poor to entertain positive hatred for them, he, with a view of removing any such misconception, inculcates the virtue of fraternal charity towards all ; and says, that if their preference for the rich man does not exceed the limits which the precept of fraternal charity sanctions, they sin not. In other words, if their respect for the rich be only such as they would reasonably expect to be paid themselves in like circumstances, giving honour to whom honour is due, and paying that respect which the order of charity marks out, as due to each one, according to his rank and station, they commit no sin—they act well. By others, the connexion of this verse with the preceding is made thus :—If in the distribution of ecclesiastical places of dignity and importance, you select a man who has equal qualifications and merit with a poor man, you in such a case commit no sin in preferring him.

9. But, if their preference be so unjust and unfair, as to constitute the crime of " respect of persons," that is, treating the rich man with marked distinction and preference where he has no right, and treating others with contempt and injustice; then, they " commit sin," and are " reproved by the law," the law of God in general, or the law of charity, to which belongs the precept just referred to. If, in the preceding, St. James were referring to the exception of persons in courts of justice, then, " the law " would refer to special prohibition contained in Leviticus (xix. 15), and Deuteronomy (x. 17), " respect not the person of the poor, nor honour the countenance of the mighty, but judge thy neighbour according to justice."

10. By violating this single point they are reproved by the law as transgressors ; for, " he who keeps the entire law, but offends in one point, is become guilty of all." How this can be, has caused Commentators much perplexity, and so difficult did this passage appear to St. Augustine that he consulted St. Jerome about its meaning (in Epistle 29). " Offends in one point," refers to a grievous offence, which constitutes a mortal sin ; " is become guilty of all," because he incurs the wrath of God, and loses his sanctifying grace and friendship, as if he violated all the commandments, and is as liable to eternal flames, as if he violated the entire law, though, of course, not to the same degree of intensity, since the pains of hell will be proportioned to the number and grievousness of our sins ; or, " is guilty of all," because he violates charity, the sum or abridgment of all the commandments—this is St. Augustine's interpretation ; or, as all the commandments constitute one perfect whole, and the entire law is made up of a chain of precepts, by breaking one link or precept, the integrity of the whole chain is broken ; or, because the violation of one precept involves the contempt of the Legislator, by whom all the rest are also enjoined. This latter interpretation is rendered probable by the following verse. If we unite the two last interpretations, and say that he " is guilty of all," by violating grievously one point ; because, he violates

Text.

11. For he that said, Thou shalt not commit adultery, said also, Thou shalt not kill. Now if thou do not commit adultery, but shalt kill : thou art become a transgressor of the law.

12. So speak ye, and so do, as being to be judged by the law of liberty.

13. For judgment without mercy to him that hath not done mercy. And mercy exalteth itself above judgment.

Paraphrase.

11. (All the precepts constitute one perfect law, emanating from the divine Legislator), for, it is the same Legislator who, for instance, prohibited adultery, that also prohibited murder. If then, thou committest not adultery, but committest murder, thou art become a transgressor of the law, of which this latter precept forms an integral part.

12. As a sovereign remedy against violating any of God's commandments, so compose and regulate all your words and actions, as if you always kept in view that you are one day to be judged by the Gospel law, which has freed us from the yoke of the Mosaic precepts, and which requires greater perfection from us.

13. And you should particularly keep in view the future judgment of God, whenever there is question of showing or refusing mercy to our neighbour; in such a case, our own conduct will determine the nature of the judgment to be passed on ourselves. For, he shall experience a judgment without mercy, and, therefore, of condemnation, who refuses to show mercy to his neighbour; on the other hand, the mercy which we show others will have a great effect, by disarming God's wrath, in vanquishing his just judgment, and exalting itself above his justice.

Commentary.

the integrity of the law, all the precepts, or parts of which were enacted by the same Legislator, we will adopt the more probable interpretation—an interpretation, which is also most in accordance with the words of the context, for, "guilty of all," in this verse, means the same as, "transgressor of the law" (verse 11). Some interpreters say, the words of this verse were intended by St. James as a refutation of an error of the Pharisees, viz., that by violating a few of God's commandments, a man does not cease to be just before God, provided he observe the greater portion of them.

11. All the commandments form one whole, emanating from the same Legislator; therefore by violating any one, you break the integrity of this whole, and contemn the Legislator, from whom they have all equally emanated.

12. This is the remedy against sin, "as being to be judged," the Greek, μελλοντες κρινεσθαι, means, *being about to be judged.* What a salutary restraint the consideration of God's future judgment should impose upon us. Were we to consider, that for every word we utter, every action we perform, we are one day to render an account to God, with what cautious circumspection, would we not act on all occasions. "*Quid sum miser tunc dicturus. Quem patronum rogaturus.. Cum vix justus sit securus ?*"

13. "For judgment," &c. It is not easy to see the connexion between this verse and the preceding. The more probable is that adopted in the Paraphrase, according to which, the particle "*for,*" has reference to some clause omitted, and the Apostle takes advantage of the mention made of God's judgment in the preceding verse, to treat of the necessity of showing mercy to those who require it. He makes the announcement of this general truth, the connecting link between his teaching, regarding the injury done the poor in the religious assemblies, to which the preceding part of this chapter has been devoted, and the dissertation regarding the refusal to relieve their corporal wants, whereof he treats in the remainder of it. "Judgment without mercy" —which is a judgment of condemnation—"to him that hath not done mercy." This is a general proposition, extending to all kinds of miseries, whether corporal or spiritual, which are the objects of the virtue of mercy. "And mercy exalteth," &c. Some Expositors understand this of the mercy of God, so as to mean, that the mercy of God exceeds all his attributes. The interpretation in the Paraphrase, which refers it to the mercy that one man shows another, seems the more probable ; for, this pro-

14. What shall it profit, my brethren, if a man say he hath faith, but hath not works? Shall faith be able to save him?

14. But of what avail will it be for a man, my brethren, to have faith, and to place reliance on his faith, if he have not works corresponding with it? Will his faith, without works, be sufficient for salvation? By no means.

Commentary.

position would appear to announce the converse of the preceding, In the preceding, is stated, what the lot of the *unmerciful* man will be ; a just judgment of God, without that mercy, always exhibited in his generous and merciful treatment of his elect ; whereas, in this, the Apostle points to the reward of the *merciful* man, viz., a judgment, wherein mercy will predominate over justice ; this predominance of mercy over justice, is a feature that always characterizes the judgments of God upon his elect. The Greek for exalteth itself, καταϰαυχαται, means, *glories against*, as happens, when a conqueror triumphs over his vanquished foes.

14. The Apostle now enters on one of the principal subjects of this Epistle, viz., the refutation of the errors of the followers of Simon Magus, regarding the sufficiency of faith alone for justification. As this erroneous doctrine, so ably and clearly refuted here by St. James, is one of the fundamental errors revived by modern Reformers, it may not be amiss to explain, in a few words, the doctrine of the Catholic Church on this subject ; this doctrine has been so clearly laid down by the Council of Trent (SS. vi., *de justificatione*).

Every Catholic admits the absolute, indispensable necessity of faith for justification. " Without faith it is impossible to please God " (Hebrews, xi.) ; without it, no man was ever justified, *sine qua (fide) nulli unquam contigit justificatio* (Council of Trent, SS. vi., 7). Although, not absolutely the first grace (the proposition, *fides est prima gratia*, put forward in the Schismatical Council of Pistoia, was condemned in the Bull, *Auctorem fidei*) ; still, it is the first grace in the order of justification, of which it is " the root and foundation," in the language of the Council of Trent (SS. vi., 8). But every Catholic denies the *sufficiency* of this faith, for justification or salvation. It is *necessary*, not *sufficient*. Besides faith, Catholics require other dispositions, viz., hope, fear, penance, initial charity. All these are required, as previous *dispositions, before* God infuses the grace of justification. These may all exist in the soul ; but they do not, by any means, constitute this grace, nor do they establish any *claim* to it, that either on the grounds of justice or fidelity, God might not refuse. It is quite certain, however, that whenever they exist in the soul, God will, of his own goodness, gratuitously infuse the grace of justification, which is a grace inhering in the soul—this is a point of faith—and it is theologically certain, that it inheres, *permanently, by way of habit*. It cleanses the soul from the stains of sin whereby it is defiled, in a manner analogous to the defilement caused the body by leprosy ; and according as this grace is increased, the soul becomes brighter and fairer in the sight of God ; in the language of the Psalmist, " whiter than snow." This grace of justification is accompanied with the virtues of faith, hope, and charity, and the several gifts of the Holy Ghost. The same good works, the same acts, which, performed under the influence of divine grace and faith by a sinner *before* he is justified, serve only as *dispositions* for justification, will, when performed by the same man, *after* he is justified, and in a state of sanctifying grace, give him a *claim*, and a *strict right*, grounded on God's gratuitous and liberal promise, to an increase of sanctifying grace, to eternal life, and its attainment, if he die in grace, and to an increase of glory. This is what Catholics call *merit*, grounded, however, on God's grace, and his gratuitous promise, through the merits of Christ (Council of Trent, SS., ver. ; Can. xxxii.)

Modern sectaries, on the other hand, maintain, that in order to be justified and saved, faith alone is sufficient ; this justifying faith, according to them, consists in a firm and undoubted confidence, which each one has, that, although in sin, God does not impute to him his sins, in consideration of the merits of Christ. As for good works, they deny them a share in justifying man, they require them merely as the fruits of faith, signs of its presence ; since without them, true faith, according to their notions, cannot exist.

Text.

15. And if a brother or sister be naked, and want daily food :

16. And one of you say to them : Go in peace, be you warmed and filled : yet give them not those things that are necessary for the body : what shall it profit ?

17. So faith also, if it have not works, is dead in itself.

Paraphrase.

15. Suppose a Christian of either sex to be naked or hungry, and in want of the common necessaries of life,

16. And that any of you, aware of this want, dismiss them with the cold expression of your sympathy and good wishes for their relief, without, at the same time administering to their wants, of what avail will your knowledge of their wants be to them ?

17. As, then, fine professions of regard will nowise profit the distressed, with whose wants we are acquainted, unless we administer relief ; so neither will the knowledge we have from faith avail us without works, without complying with what it points out. Unaccompanied with works, it is dead in itself ; for, it is destitute of the vivifying principle of sanctifying grace, whereby, we are perfectly connected with the head of which we are members, and his grace and mercy communicated to us.

Commentary.

Now, that their idea of justifying faith is wholly erroneous, will appear quite evident to any person who reads the 11th chapter of St. Paul to the Hebrews, wherein he describes this justifying faith to be the "evidence of things that appear not," and in applying it to the several examples, he always supposes it to consist in a firm belief in the truth of God's revelation.

Again, that, besides faith, good works are required for justification and salvation, is so evident from the following part of this chapter, that it only requires to be read over attentively, to be convinced of it. In truth, the words bear no other meaning, and on this account it was, that some of the early Reformers rejected the Epistle altogether. Finally, that true faith may exist without good works or charity, is clear from several passages of Sacred Scripture. St. John says (chap. xii. 42), "many of the chief men *believed* in him,......but did not *confess* him, for they loved the glory of man more than of God." The word, "*believe*," here has reference to real, true faith, as is evident from the use of the word, in the entire chapter. St. Paul tells us, that "if he had faith strong enough to remove mountains, &c.," *and had not charity*, it would profit him nothing (1 Cor. xiii), and that this faith can be separated from charity, is clear from chapter vii. of St. Matthew, wherein, we are told, that many will say, "Lord have we not performed many wonders in thy name," and shall receive for answer—"I never knew you."

OBJECTION.—St. James does not deny the sufficiency of *real* faith, because he is referring to mere putative faith, "*if a man say*, he has faith."

ANSWER.—He speaks of real faith ; for, he adds, "shall *faith* be able to save him?" He therefore, supposes the person in question to have *real, genuine* faith.

15. The Apostle illustrates the inutility of faith and the knowledge it gives us, unless accompanied with good works, by an example of the inutility, to a distressed neighbour, of our knowledge of his wants, and of our sterile sympathy, unless it be accompanied by acts of benevolence administering to his wants. "If a brother or sister," *i.e.*, a Christian of either sex, "be naked," &c., *i.e.*, in want of the common necessaries of life.

16. "And one of you," without relieving them, merely wishes them well, "be you warmed," &c., "what will it profit ?" which is equivalent to saying—it shall be of no profit whatever to them.

17. "So faith also, if it have not works, is dead in itself." In the Greek, καθ᾽ ἑαυτήν, *by itself.* This is the application of the foregoing example. As kind words, and fine professions of regard, even accompanied by good wishes, will prove of no avail to the distressed ; so, neither will faith profit the believer ; "it is dead in itself ;" because, the person who only has faith, although he be a member, is still but a dead member of the body of Christ ; his faith is altogether dead, as to justification. The Apostle explains this more fully in verse 26, "as the body without the spirit is dead," &c.

18. But some man will say: Thou hast faith, and I have works: shew me thy faith without works; and I will shew thee, by works, my faith.

18. (Another argument of the inutility of faith without works, grounded on the impossibility of externally professing our faith otherwise than by good works). Suppose two Christians, one having works and faith. the other having no works; and that the former calls upon the latter to profess his faith, can he do this? By no means. Since it is by works alone it can be manifested; whereas, the other can, from his works, give a proof of his faith, from which his works have emanated.

19. Thou believest that there is one God. Thou dost well: the devils also believe and tremble.

19. You may say that you have other means of manifesting your faith besides works, viz., the symbols and external profession of faith, the first article of which is the faith in one God, in which, you say, you believe; no doubt, in doing so, you act well, but, of what avail will this be to you? Do not the devils, forced by the conviction of evidence, assent to the same truths, and express this belief by trembling; and still, this faith is of no avail to them.

Commentary.

From this, it by no means follows, that faith without good works is not *real* faith. St. James looks upon faith in this verse, as destitute of the vivifying principle of charity, or good works, by which it is enlivened or roused to action (Gal. v. 6); he compares it to a human body, destitute of the soul that animates it, which, although dead, is still a *real* body. So, charity is the soul or form of faith, which, although proceeding from the principle of divine grace, is, still, dead as to justification without charity, which alone *perfectly* unites us with Christ, our head. "*Faith*," says the Council of Trent (SS. vi. c. 7), "*unless hope and charity be added to it, does not perfectly unite one with Christ, nor render him a living member of his body.*" Faith, even without charity, *really* subsists in its subject, viz., the soul of man; in its object, God and eternal glory,; in its motive, revelation; but, it is dead as to justification. From this very example, it is clear, that faith can be without good works; because, as we can have a knowledge of our neighbour's wants without actually relieving them; so, also, can we have the knowledge imparted by faith, without acting up to it by good works.

18. This is a new argument of the inutility of faith alone, without good works.—Faith cannot be manifested without them; now, this external profession is obligatory on all, both for the sake of example, and for holding that communion of saints, in which we all believe.

QUERY.—How can a man show his faith from his works, since an unbeliever can perform many good works?

ANSWER.—St. James, in the present instance, supposes both the persons in question to have faith, and that the man having works, recurs to them as a proof and manifestation of his faith. Hence, he does not infer faith from works; for, he supposes faith to have existed previously. Moreover, from works we can infer the existence of faith; because, there are certain good works, or a continued performance of them, which only a person having faith could accomplish. For, although an unbeliever may, aided by actual divine grace, perform certain good works; still, he could not persevere in performing a continued series of good works, without sin; and there are certain heroic deeds of virtue, which he could not perform at all.

19. These may be the words of the Christian having faith and works, in continuation of his appeal to the other, whom he is supposed to be addressing in the preceding verse; you may, possibly, say; you have the symbols of faith, as a means of externally professing your faith, the first article of which is to believe "that there is one God," which is also a distinguishing point of true faith from the false belief of Paganism; or, they may be the words of St. James, adducing a new argument of the inutility of faith unaccompanied by good works, since it resembles the faith of demons, who, compelled

Text.	Paraphrase.
20. But wilt thou know, O vain man, that faith without works is dead?	20. But, O vain man, who dost foolishly glory in thy faith without works, dost thou wish for a convincing argument to see that faith, without works is dead and useless for justification?
21. Was not Abraham our father justified by works, offering up Isaac his son upon the altar?	21. Was it not by works that Abraham our father, and the father of all the faithful, whose justification is the model of ours (Rom. iv. 23), was justified, having in heart and will offered up his son Isaac, in sacrifice, from the consummation of which, he was arrested by the hand of the Angel?
22. Seest thou that faith did co-operate with his works : and by works faith was made perfect.	22. You see, then, that faith is co-operated with the works of Abraham, it being the principle from which they emanated, and by which they were directed and regulated; while, on the other hand, his works perfected his faith, by bringing it to its destined end of justification, and by animating and increasing it in the soul.

Commentary.

by evidence in favour of our creed, viz., miracles, prophecies, &c., are constrained to believe the same things which we believe, and by their "trembling," externally profess this interior conviction, without any advantage. "Thou believest there is one God." This article being the first and most important distinguishing feature of true faith, is probably put for all the points of faith. "Thou dost well ;" this act of faith is a good act, but it does not, alone, suffice as a disposition for justification, or for obtaining salvation. "The devils also believe and tremble." The word, "*tremble*," is used metaphorically to express the dread, horror, and despair, with which the devils are inspired, in considering their eternal punishment and the just judgment of God.

OBJECTION.—From this verse is it not evident that St. James looks upon faith without works, or as Catholics term it, *fides informis*, as no faith at all ; since he compares it with the faith of demons, who surely cannot elicit an act of the theological virtue of faith ; for, they are not susceptible of grace, without which faith cannot exist ?

ANSWER.—St. James, by no means, intends to compare the faith of devils, and that of wicked Christians, in every respect. He only compares them as to the utter inutility of both for salvation ; his object in introducing the comparison does not warrant us in urging it further ; and the only criterion by which we are to be guided, in judging of the extent to which a comparison can be urged, is, the scope and object of him who introduces it. There is another point, in which the faith of both is compared ; viz., in their objects. The same thing is believed by the demons *involuntarily*, and forced by the conviction of evidence, which the sinner believes *voluntarily*, and freely, aided by divine grace. So far the comparison is made, and no further ; no comparison can be urged, as they say, *ad vivum*.

20. St. James now introduces a new argument, and undertakes to prove, from the example of Abraham, whose justification is the model of ours, the necessity of good works for justification. This argument is the more convincing, and better suited for the refutation of the error he is combating, as it was on the very same example, urged at full length by the Apostle, in his Epistle to the Romans, (chap. iv.), and erroneously interpreted, the Simonians grounded their doctrine of the sufficiency of faith alone for justification. "O vain man !" *i.e.*, foolish man, who art blind in a matter of such evidence.

21. "Offering up." In Greek, ανενεγκας, *having offered*. The determined resolution to offer up Isaac, from the execution of which the voice of the angel from heaven prevented him, was accepted by God as a perfect offering.

22. "Faith did co-operate with his works." This shows that the faith of Abraham was not an idle, inoperative faith, a mere act of belief, unaccompanied by works ; that it was an active, operative faith ; it was the principle of the works which Abraham performed, and it was it that regulated, how they were to be performed : and hence, in saying that Abraham was justified by works, St. James refers to works grounded on, and accompanied by faith. The words, "and by works faith was made perfect," show

Text.

23. And the Scripture was fulfilled, saying : *Abraham believed God, and it was reputed to him to justice, and he was called the friend of God.*

24. Do you see that by works a man is justified ; and not by faith only ?

Paraphrase.

23. And the words of Scripture, *Abraham believed God, and it was reputed to him unto justice* (Gen. xv. 6), *and he was called the friend of God*, were fully completed, in the full enumeration of all the causes of justification.

24. From this you see that faith is not the only ingredient in man's justificatication, that he is justified no less by works than by faith.

Commentary.

that it was works which brought faith to its destined end of justification. Both one and the other mutually concurred in Abraham's justification.

23. *"And he was called the friend of God."* These words are not found in Genesis (xv. 6), from which the preceding words of Scripture are quoted. They are the words of St. James himself.

QUERY.—How can St. James say, "the Scripture was fulfilled, saying, Abraham believed," &c. (Genesis, xv. 6), since we find no prophecy contained in these words to be afterwards fulfilled ? All that is recorded of Moses in this passage is simply historical. Again, had not these words, *"Abraham believed, &c.,"* reference to his believing in God's promise regarding his son Isaac (Genesis, xv.) ; which was prior to his sacrifice, (Genesis, xxii.), the matter in question here ? How then say, a Scripture was now "fulfilled," which was long before accomplished ?

ANSWER.—The Scripture is said, by St. James, to be fulfilled in this sense, that when Moses (Genesis, xv. 6), said, *"Abraham believed, and it was reputed to him unto justice,"* he omitted all mention of another ingredient and disposition for justification, viz., works. These are referred to here by St. James ; *all* the disposition for justification are therefore enumerated, and the cause of the justification referred to (Genesis, xv.), fully expressed ; and so, the Scripture account of the causes of justification is "fulfilled" or *complete*—which is more clearly expressed in the Vulgate version, "Et scriptura *suppleta* est," scilicet, *quoad enumerationem dispositionum justificationis.* Secondly, Although the words of Genesis, *"Abraham believed,"* &c., were referred by Moses to an occasion prior to that of which St. James now speaks ; still, we may apply them to every subsequent act by which Abraham afterwards was justified ; and hence, they were verified in the present instance also.

24. Can there be a clearer refutation of the doctrine of modern innovators on the subject of justification by faith only ? St. James expressly states, that faith is not the only disposition or cause of justification ; that in whatever way faith produces or concurs in justification, works concur in the same way, "a man is justified *by works and not by faith only."* The word, *by*—(εξ)—shows that faith and works concur in the same way.

OBJECTION.—Does not St. Paul (Rom. iii. iv.), say, that works have no share in justification ? How, then are the two Apostles reconciled ?

ANSWER.—There is no contradiction whatever between them ; there is question of different works in both cases. What description of works does St. Paul exclude from a share in justification ? The works performed by the sole aid of our natural faculties, or of the law of Moses, without grace or faith. These, alone, are the works which the scope of the Apostle, in his Epistle to the Romans, required of him to exclude. These, alone, are the works on which the Jews and Gentile converts respectively grounded their claims to the gospel, viz., the works they performed, *before* they received the gospel, or embraced the faith.

Does St. James here assert the necessity of the *same* works? By no means. He speaks of works performed, *after* they received the gospel, under the influence of grace and faith. For, he addresses men who had embraced the faith, but denied the necessity of works performed in this state. And it was to refute their error that St. James, as well as St. Peter, St. John, and St. Jude, wrote their Catholic Epistles, as we are assured by St. Augustine (*Libro de Fide et Operibus*, c. 14). If the doctrine of St. Paul, in his Epistle to the Romans, be joined to that delivered by St. James in

Text.

25. And in like manner also Rahab the harlot, was not she justified by works, receiving the messengers, and sending them out another way?

26. For even as the body without

Paraphrase.

25. In like manner, was it not by works that Rahab, the harlot, was justified, by the exercise of humanity in saving the messengers sent by Josue to explore the land of Chanaan and city of Jericho?—(Josue, ii.)

26. For, as the body without the soul to animate it

Commentary.

this, we have a *full* and perfect account of *all* the causes and dispositions of justification, viz., faith and works conjointly. No other interpretation, save that warranted by Catholic doctrine, can reconcile the apparent discrepancy that exists between both Apostles. In the Catholic interpretation, there is no difficulty whatever; although the same example of Abraham would seem to be employed for opposite conclusions. The matter is thus explained. Abraham was justified even *before*, Moses said of him, that "*he believed*," &c. (Genesis, xv. 6), as is clear from chapter xi. verse 8, of Epistle to the Hebrews, where it is stated, that he was justified by faith going forth from his native country—an event which took place long before the promise of a son was made to him. The words, therefore, "*it was reputed to him unto justice*," must be understood of *second* justification, or increase of justice; and St. Paul (Rom. iv.), adduces the mode in which Abraham's *second* justification, or increase in justice took place, viz., by faith, as an argument *a fortiori* to prove, that to faith, independently of the works which he performed *without the influence of grace or faith*, his *first* justification, or, his translation from a state of sin to that of grace was owing (*vide* Rom. iv.); whereas St. James employs the same example to prove the necessity of good works *done in faith*, for preserving, and progressing in the justification once acquired; and, of course, it is implied that they are still more necessary for acquiring *first* justification. Were St. Paul, in the passage referred to, to insist on the necessity of good works also, and describe *all* the concurring dispositions for justification, it would only embarass him, and more or less obscure his arguments against the Romans, and render them less forcible; for they might imagine, that he coincided with them in their error, respecting the efficacy of works performed *before* faith, for obtaining justification. St. James supplies what St. Paul, for good reasons, omitted, and removes any misconception to which the words of the latter might have given occasion. There is no other mode of reconciling the two Apostles, save that furnished by the Catholic doctrine, as above.

25. "In like manner also," *i.e.*, by faith, which works consummated, and by works, which co-operated with faith, as in the case of Abraham. "Rahab, the harlot;" her history is given (Josue, ii.) Some persons understand this to refer to *second* justification. They suppose that Rahab had, already, before the arrival of the spies, conceived divine faith, and having believed in the God of the Hebrews (of whose power she already had heard, Josue, ii. 11), had been justified; and that, by the act of humanity in concealing the spies, she obtained *second*, that is to say, merited an increase of justification. Others maintain, that although Rahab may have had faith before the arrival of the spies—in which they had, probably, more fully instructed her—still, she had been in sin; for, she is called "a harlot," and that this act of humanity only disposed her for *first* justification. It might be said in reply to this reason, that Rahab was called "a harlot," even after she ceased to commit acts of sin; because she had been previously such, and that her former appellation had been retained; just as Simon is called "the leper," and Matthew "the publican." To this it might also be added, that the Hebrew word for "harlot" also signifies a *hostess*. The former signification is, however, the more probable meaning. In this latter interpretation, we will have the necessity of works both in *first* and *second* justification; in the one case, as *dispositions* ; in the other, as *concurring* and *meritorious causes*. It is worthy of remark, that all through, St. James supposes that, without works, no man can be justified; for, in all the examples adduced, he leaves us to infer, that if the *just* man did not perform good works, he would lose justice, and the *sinner* could not otherwise acquire it.

26. OBJECTION.—Does not this verse show that *dead* faith, or, as Catholics term it, *fides informis*, is no faith at all, as a dead man, properly speaking, is no man?

Text.	Paraphrase.
the spirit is dead: so also faith without works is dead.	is dead and devoid of all motion, incapable of any action good or evil ; so, faith also, unaccompanied by good works, is dead.

Commentary.

ANSWER.—Faith is compared not with a dead *man*, but with a dead *body*, which, although dead, and not animated by the soul, is still a *real body*. Hence, *dead* faith is real, genuine faith, in the sense already given in this chapter.

CHAPTER III.

Analysis.

St. James resumes, in this chapter, the subject briefly glanced at (chap. i. 19 & 26) regarding the government of the tongue : and after showing the danger caused by the tongue in teaching, others (1), he proceeds to treat, in a general way, of the faults committed by means of that member. He says, that by governing the tongue, we show that we can keep all our passions under control (2). He compares the tongue to the bits of horses and the helms of vessels, also to a small spark of fire, which can set a large quantity of timber in a blaze (3-6).

He next points out the difficulty, and, consequently, the great care to be employed, in subduing the tongue (7, 8) ; the monstrous and incompatible uses, to which it is applied (9, 10) ; and from the analogy of nature, from what is impossible in the natural order, he argues against what is inconsistent and opposed in morals.

After a lengthened digression regarding the vices of the tongue, he returns to the subject with which he commenced the chapter, regarding those who wish to act in the capacity of teachers, and shows the qualities with which a teacher of others should be gifted, (13, 14). He notes the characters of true and false wisdom (15-18).

Text.	Paraphrase.
1. BE ye not many masters, my brethren, knowing that you receive the greater judgment.	1. Let not too many of you, my brethren, ambition and take upon yourselves the office of teaching others ; knowing that the higher and more exalted your office, the weightier your responsibility, and condemnation, should you be found wanting,

Commentary.

1. "Be not many teachers." St. James here enlarges upon, and fully developes, the subject referred to (i. 19), regarding the proper management of the tongue. In this verse, he refers to its abuse in taking upon one's self the office of religious teacher. In the remainder of the chapter, although some interpreters understand him to refer to the abuse of the tongue, in religious teachers exclusively, it is still more probable, that he refers to the evils of the tongue, in general. "Many teachers." By these St. Augustine (in *Prologo Retrac.*) understands teachers propounding opposite and conflicting doctrines; because, although many were to propose the same doctrine of Christ, they could, still, according to him, be said to be only one teacher. It is more likely, that St. James censures the inordinate desire of being esteemed and respected as teachers in religion, for which the Jews were particularly remarkable (Matth. xxiii. ; Rom ii.) "That you receive." In Greek, λεμψομεθα, *that we shall receive*, &c., or entail upon ourselves greater responsibility.

Text.

2. For in many things we all offend. If any man offend not in word: the same is a perfect man. He is able also with a bridle to lead about the whole body.

3. For if we put bits into the mouths of horses that they may obey us, and we turn about their whole body.

4. Behold also ships, whereas they are great, and are driven by strong winds, yet are they turned about with a small helm, whithersoever the force of the governor willeth.

5. So the tongue also is indeed a little member, and boasteth great things. Behold how small a fire what a great wood it kindleth?

Paraphrase.

2. You will incur the greater judgment; for, we all offend in many things, without entailing upon ourselves the responsibility of teachers. If any man offend not in word, and completely master his tongue, the same is a perfect man, and shows what perfect control he can have over all his passions. Such a person, by bridling his tongue, can govern all his other members, and regulate the whole body of his actions.

3. For, behold, we put bits into horses' mouths, to make them obedient to our will, and by this means we can govern and turn about their whole body.

4. Behold also how great ships, although driven forward by strong violent winds, are still turned about by a small helm, wherever the will of the steersman chooses to steer them.

5. As, then, horses are managed by a bit, and ships turned about by a small helm ; so also is the tongue, though a small member, compared with the entire body, capable of great things, whether for the purposes of good or evil. Behold how large a wood, a small spark of fire can set in a blaze.

Commentary.

2. "In many things," &c. As if to say, we needed not the additional responsibility of teachers, to have to render a heavy account already. St. James manifestly makes the tongue the principal instrument in the commission of those daily faults into which we all fall ; to this fault of the tongue the teacher is, of all others, the most liable. This is one of the texts which are adduced in proof of a point of faith defined in the Council of Trent (SS. vi., Canon 23), viz. :—"*That no man can, during his entire life, avoid all, even venial sins, except by a special privilege, on the part of God, such as the Church holds was conferred on the Blessed Virgin.*" "A perfect man," inasmuch as he shows how perfectly he can master all his other passions, having mastered his tongue, which it is most difficult to restrain. "The whole body," *i.e.*, the other members of the body—this interpretation is rendered probable by the following comparisons—or, it may mean the whole moral body of his actions.

3. By two comparisons, the Apostle illustrates the importance of governing the tongue, and the influence it exercises over all the other members, and the entire body of our actions. From the same examples, we may easily infer the evil of not bridling it. "For, if we put," &c. In some Greek copies it is, ιδε, βαλλομεν, behold, we put, &c., according to which reading the sentence is complete. In our Vulgate, the sense is suspended, and the proposition, conditional. The proposition can, however, be made absolute, by throwing out "and" in the words "and we turn," &c. We find the word "and" oftentimes to be superfluous ; or, we may give it the meaning of "also." Some suppose, by comparing this with verse 4, that the true reading is, ιδε, behold, to which ει δε, "but if," followed by the Vulgate, is so like in the Greek. The reading in the *Codex Vaticanus* is ειδε, "but if."

4. Another comparison, "the force," ορμη, *impetus*, the will which the "governor," or steersman, forcibly exerts in turning round the vessel in a storm.

5. "So the tongue also is indeed a little member." This is the application of the two foregoing examples—the bit and helm are comparatively small, so is the tongue. "And boasteth great things." "Boasteth" (μεγαλαυχει, *magna exaltat*), operates, stirs up, great things—sets whole communities, cities, nay, even kingdoms, in a blaze. According to its proper use, or, abuse, it is a powerful instrument for accomplishing good or evil. "Behold how small a fire, what a great wood it kindleth." Another

Text.

6. And the tongue is a fire, a world of iniquity. The tongue is placed among our members, which defileth the whole body, and inflameth the wheel of our nativity, being set on fire by hell.

7. For every nature of beasts, and of birds, and of serpents, and of the rest, is tamed and hath been tamed by the nature of man :

8. But the tongue no man can tame, an unquiet evil, full of deadly poison.

Paraphrase.

6. And the tongue is a fire ; nay, an universal instrument for effecting iniquity of all kinds ; it is placed among our members, and corrupts the entire body of our actions during the whole course of our lives, being itself set on fire by the powers of hell, and the agency of the infernal spirits.

7. And wild beasts of every description, all sorts of birds and of crawling things and of marine monsters are capable of being tamed, and have been actually tamed, or at least, forcibly mastered and subdued by the skill, power, and industry of man.

8. But the tongue no human power or industry can bring under subjection ; it is a restless evil, which cannot be stopped, full of deadly poison, which oftentimes causes ruin to both soul and body.

Commentary.

illustration of the evil effects which the tongue, although a small instrument, is capable of producing.

6. "The tongue is a fire," capable of setting the world in a blaze. Nay, it is "a world of iniquity," *i.e.*, a general, universal instrument for effecting every sort of evil ; this general universal power of the tongue, as the instrument of all sorts of evil, is aptly represented by "the world," composed of so many different elements, and species of creatures of every description ; for this reason, it is called "a world," a general instrument of "iniquity," *i.e.*, evil of all kinds. In the construction preferred by A'Lapide, the words are interpreted thus :—"The tongue is a fire, the world of iniquity —that is to say, this wicked world—is the wood, which the tongue sets in a blaze." So that, according to him, the example adduced in the preceding is fully explained in this verse ; as the tongue is the small fire, so the "world of iniquity" is the great wood, which it enkindles and sets in a blaze. The construction adopted in the Paraphrase is, however, far the more probable, as appears from the following words, in which, according to the ordinary Greek reading, the preceding illustration is applied and explained :—"The tongue is placed," &c. According to the ordinary Greek, ουτω και η γλωσσα, it is "*so the tongue is placed*," &c. the meaning of which is, as the fire kindles up a great burning ; so, is the tongue, though with a very different intention, placed among the members of man, having become, instead of being the instrument of good, according to the original design of God, the corrupter of the entire body, owing to the malice of man. "So," is wanting in the principal manuscripts and chief versions, and rejected by critics generally. "It sets on fire," *i.e.*, it inflames with the fire of lust, anger, and all the passions, "the wheel of our nativity," *i.e.*, the entire course of life, consisting of a revolving succession of days, and seasons, and years. Certain vices are peculiar to certain seasons and periods of life ; but the vices of the tongue pervade every season of human existence ; "being set on fire by hell," *i.e.*, it is an instrument of evil prepared for mischief, by the powers of hell, the devil, and his infernal associates.

7. Here, St. James points out the great difficulty o. curbing and subduing the tongue, and consequently, the great vigilance and care that should be employed with regard to it. "And of the rest ;" in Latin, "*cæterorum*." The present Greek reading is, εναλιων, *of whales*, or the whole tribe of marine monsters—των αλλων, "of the rest," or, εναλλων, *of various kinds*, was the reading followed by our Vulgate interpreter. "Is tamed," *i.e.*, capable of being tamed, "and hath been tamed." The Greek word for "tamed," δεδαμασται, means, *subdued*, and reduced by force, so as to be deprived of the power of inflicting injury.

8. "But the tongue no man," *i.e.*, no human skill or industry, "can tame," or render innocuous. Man cannot do so, of himself, without God's grace ; or, the words, more probably, mean, that the evils arising from tongue are more difficult to be checked, than those produced by the most savage beasts. "An unquiet evil." (In some Greek copies, ακατασχετον κακον, *an unruly evil*. The Vatican and Alexandrian

Text.

9. By it we bless God and the Father: and by it we curse men, who are made after the likeness of God.

10. Out of the same mouth proceedeth blessing and cursing. My brethren, these things ought not so to be.

11. Doth a fountain send forth, out of the same hole, sweet and bitter water?

12. Can the fig-tree, my brethren, bear grapes; or the vine, figs? So neither can the salt water yield sweet.

13. Who is a wise man and endued with knowledge among you?

Paraphrase.

9. It is made the monstrous instrument of opposite and conflicting results. By it, we praise and glorify God, who is also our Father, and, strange inconsistency! by the same tongue, we curse man, made after the image and likeness of God.

10. Out of the same mouth proceed two things, both contrary and perfectly incompatible, benediction and malediction. My brethren, it is quite incongruous, that such opposite effects should exist.

11. The analogy of nature itself shows the inconsistency of such conduct. Will a fountain discharge, through the same passage, sweet and bitter water? Certainly not. Why then should man send forth from the same mouth, the sweet water of benediction, and the bitter water of malediction?

12. Will the fig-tree produce grapes, or the vine, figs? By no means. So neither can the salt water yield sweet.

13. But who amongst you is gifted with the wisdom and knowledge, indispensable qualifications of a

Commentary.

MSS. have ακαταστατον, "unquiet.") The idea is borrowed from a virulent disease, the progress of which cannot be stopped. "Full of deadly poison." The idea here, probably, is borrowed from the incurable bite of a venomous reptile.

9. He here shows the monstrous and incompatible uses for which the tongue is employed. It is employed to "bless God," *i.e.*, to praise and glorify the Adorable Trinity, who is also our "Father," both by creation and redemption, "and curse men," *i.e.*, wish all kinds of evil for them; by it, we calumniate, detract, and treat them contumeliously, although made to the image of God, his most perfect work; and hence, we curse God himself in those creatures by whom his attributes are most clearly reflected.

10. "Out of the same mouth proceeds blessing" of God, "and cursing" of him in his creatures. "My brethren, these things ought not to be." This is the mild language of rebuke, wherein is conveyed more than is expressed, and even the asperity of the rebuke is softened down by the words, "my brethren."

11. By a reference to the analogy of nature, he shows the justice of his rebuke, and the incongruity of employing the tongue for such opposite purposes, for, producing such opposite effects. From what is impossible in nature, he argues against what is inconsistent and opposed in morals.

12. "Bear grapes." The Greek for *grapes* is, ελαιας, *olive berries.* "So neither can the salt water yield sweet." In some Greek readings it is—*so no fountain can yield salt and sweet water,* as if it were a repetition of the idea conveyed in the words (verse 11), "doth a fountain send forth...sweet and bitter water?" The Vulgate reading is that of the chief manuscripts, of all the Latin copies, and of the Syriac. Hence, it was probably the ancient Greek reading followed by the Syriac. Reason itself would seem to favour the Vulgate; for, what necessity is there for repeating a thing so clear and incontrovertible as the sentence in verse 11? In our reading, then, a fourth illustration is derived from the salt water of the sea. The reasoning of St. James, in these verses, is this:—The same fountain will not produce sweet and bitter water, nor will the same tree produce fruits different from those of its own kind; such, then, being the order of nature, it is monstrous, that in the order of morals, the same instrument should produce not only different, but contrary effects—viz., good and evil.

13. After a rather lengthy digression regarding the vices of the tongue, the Apostle now returns to the subject with which he commenced this chapter, regarding the inordinate desire of acting in capacity of teachers, wherein men are most liable to fall into serious faults of the tongue. He now explains the qualities with which a teacher

Text.

Let him shew, by a good conversation, his work in the meekness of wisdom.

14. But if you have bitter zeal, and there be contentions in your hearts; glory not, and be not liars against the truth.

15. For this is not wisdom, descending from above; but earthly, sensual, devilish.

Paraphrase.

teacher? If there be any such person amongst you, let him, in addition to the foregoing qualifications, by the example of an edifying life, exhibit his good works, which will be seasoned by meekness in teaching true wisdom; or, which will be accompanied by meek wisdom in teaching.

14. But if you indulge, and give way to, corroding envy, and an inordinate internal disposition for contention, you should not vainly glory and be liars against the truth by claiming what you have not, viz., true wisdom.

15. For, the wisdom exhibited by the envious and contentious is not the true wisdom, which only comes from above, from the throne of God, the unchangeable author of every good gift (i. 17). But the wisdom of such persons is "*earthly*," having for its object the attainment of mere earthly goods, the gratification of avarice. "*Sensual*," having for object the gratification of beastly lusts and animal pleasures. "*Devilish*," seeking for the gratification of pride, and for self-advancement, by the base means of intrigue, low cunning, and deceit. .

Commentary.

of others should be gifted. " A wise man and endued with knowledge." Wisdom and knowledge are two indispensable qualifications for a religious teacher. By " wisdom," which is the same as the *sermo sapientiæ* (1 Cor. xii. 8), is meant the power or faculty of explaining the truths of faith, on the principles of faith (*v.g.*), showing the congruity of the Incarnation, on the grounds pointed out by faith ; by " knowledge," the faculty of explaining moral precepts, or of explaining the truths of faith, by examples derived from human things. St. James, by asking the question, " who is gifted with knowledge and wisdom ?" supposes that no one can undertake the office of teacher without these qualifications. "His word." (In Greek, τα εργα αυτου, *his works*). " In the meekness of wisdom ;" without showing good example, teaching will avail but very little. The example of a teacher will be a stronger incentive to virtue than his words can be. " Meekness " is a quality of all others the most necessary; a supercilious moroseness in the exercise of teaching or correction, will only serve to disgust the hearers, instead of promoting edification.

14. " Bitter zeal ;" feelings of envy, which imbitter the mind, and are " bitter " in their effects to others. " And there be contentions in your heart." The Greek has not "there be," it simply is, και εριθειαν, *and contention in your heart, i.e.*, an inward disposition to indulge in contentions and strife, the constant attendants of bitter zeal or envy; and this bitter zeal results from an inordinate desire to exercise unduly the functions of teacher. " Glory not and be not liars against the truth," by laying claim to what they have not, viz., true wisdom ; for, this they could not possess, together with a spirit of envy in their hearts. " And be not liars," &c. " Not," is omitted in the Greek. It is, however, clearly understood.

15. He assigns in this verse reasons for saying, that the envious, contentious men of whom he spoke, would glory against the truth by laying claim to true wisdom ; because, the wisdom of such person is not the wisdom " descending from above," whence alone true wisdom can come (i. 17). He describes this wisdom by three characters wholly incompatible with true wisdom—" earthly," " sensual," " devilish."— *Vide* Paraphrase. It is *diabolical* or *devilish*, because the devil is a spirit of pride, the author of lies, of cunning and deceit ; and this false wisdom, seeking only for the gratification of pride, urges us on, by means of cunning and intrigue, to self-advancement and self-exaltation. How perfectly similar to the description of the spirit of the world given by St. John (1 Ep. ii.) (" Concupiscence of the flesh "), " sensual." (" Concupiscence of the eyes "), " earthly." (" Pride of life "), " diabolical." (" Which is not from the father.") "This is not wisdom descending from above."

Text.

16. For where envying and contention is, there is inconstancy, and every evil work.

17. But the wisdom, that is from above, first indeed is chaste, then peaceable, modest, easy to be persuaded, consenting to the good, full of mercy and good fruits, without judging, without dissimulation.

18. And the fruit of justice is sown in peace, to them that make peace.

Paraphrase.

16. For, bitter envy and contention are the parents of confusion and disorderly conduct of every kind, and of all sorts of wicked works.

17. But true wisdom, which descends from above, from the throne of God, is distinguished by opposite qualities and characteristics. First, it inculcates, and disposes to, purity both of soul and body; next, it inculcates, and disposes us to cultivate, as far as possible, peace with all men; it is opposed to all vain display and ostentation, or, it is urbane and affable to all; it is not obstinately wedded to self-opinion and judgment; but, easily persuades us to adopt the good measures and advice proposed by good men; it inclines us interiorly, to take compassion on the wretched and miserable; and prompts us to works of beneficence and charity to the poor, which are the good fruits, springing from the virtue of mercy; it is not precipitate in judging of our neighbour's actions and intentions; or, it has no respect for persons and parties; it is opposed to all hypocrisy, all intriguing, all affectation of superior sanctity.

18. And the fruit of increasing merits here, and eternal life hereafter, to be reaped from justice, are sown, not in contention, envy, or strive; but in peace, to be possessed by those only, who cultivate peace both with themselves and with others.

Commentary.

16. "Inconstancy," *i.e.*, disquietude, tumults, and seditions. St. James proves that the wisdom of the envious is *"earthly, sensual, &c.,"* because it is inconstant and turbulent, creating tumults and seditions, clearly observable in the conduct of the heretics, in all ages, but particularly true of modern reformers, as may be seen from the history of their times. The conclusion which St. James wishes us to derive from this verse is, that men acting under the influence of such a spirit cannot be possessed of true wisdom.

17. Having, in the preceding, described true wisdom *negatively*, the Apostle now gives its peculiar distinguishing characteristics, quite the opposite of those, by which false wisdom is distinguished. First, it is "chaste," opposed to "sensual" (verse 15). "It is peaceable, modest, easy to be persuaded," three qualities opposed to "devilish," "easy to be persuaded," not obstinately inflexible in its own judgment, but "consenting to the good." There is no word corresponding with this, in the Greek. It is, most probably, inserted in the Vulgate, as a fuller explanation of the words, "easy to be persuaded," as if to say; by "easily persuaded" is not meant, easily persuaded to either good or bad measures, by either good or bad men; but consenting and easily persuaded to good measures, proposed by good men. It is not unusual for the Vulgate translator, wherever the Greek word is susceptible of a two-fold meaning (as the Greek word here, ευπειθης, is), to give both; hence, for one word in the Greek, we have sometimes two, in the Vulgate.—*Vide* Epistle to Galatians, v. 21, 22, 23, &c. "Full of mercy," &c., opposed to "earthly," to that selfish spirit of avarice, which makes us close our ears to the wants of the poor, and the relief of the necessitous. "Mercy," refers to the inward feelings of compassion, "and good fruits," to the external manifestation of these feelings by good works, which spring from it, as fruits from their root. "Without judging."—(*See* Paraphrase). "Without dissimulation," ανυποκριτος.

18. "The fruit of justice," may refer to justice itself, so that the words may mean, that justice itself, as a fruit always increasing, is reaped by those who cultivate peace, or (as in Paraphrase) "the fruit of justice," may mean the fruit, which the *seed* of justice produces; viz., eternal life, which proceeds from, and is produced by peace, for such as practise and cultivate it.

CHAPTER IV.

Analysis.

In this chapter, St. James points out the source of the dispositions which he censures, as opposed to that peace recommended by him in the foregoing chapter—viz., the corrupt passions of the human heart (verse 1). He shows, in the next place, the utter folly of seeking for true happiness in the gratification of these passions, instead of having recourse by prayer to God, from whom alone true happiness can come (2). And although they have recourse to God, still their prayer is of no effect, for want of the proper dispositions, either as regards the object of petition, or its motive (3). He then points out how utterly incompatible are the friendship of God and the opposite friendship of the world, enticing us to commit sin, and desert from God (4). This he illustrates by a reference to the testimony of Sacred Scriptures (5), and he mentions the claims God has on our undivided service and love (6).

He next exhorts them to range themselves under the banners of God, and fight manfully against the devil (7); and in order to battle in the service of God, as they should, he recommends them to enter on a new life of virtue, to do penance for the past, and practise the virtue of true, unaffected humility (8-10).

He then cautions them against another vice, springing also from pride—viz., the vice of detraction, and all the other vices of the tongue, whereby our neighbour's character is unjustly injured. He shows the enormity of detraction; because, the man guilty of it constitutes himself a judge of the law (11), and intrudes into the province of the Supreme Lawgiver (12).

He censures another fault of the tongue, common among worldly-minded men, consisting in this: that in giving expression to their future resolves, they speak, as if they reposed their entire reliance on their own strength, without any dependence on the will and adorable Providence of God (13-17).

Text.	Paraphrase.
1. FROM whence are wars and contentions among you; are they not hence, from your concupiscences, which war in your members?	1. From whence, think you, spring these strifes and contests that exist amongst you? Is it not from the corrupt passions and irregular desires of your hearts, which employ the different members of your bodies, as the instruments of the warfare, which they constantly endeavour to sustain in the soul?

Commentary.

1. "Wars and contentions" (in the Greek, for "contentions" we have, μαχαι, *fights*), probably refer to the same thing—viz., quarrels and disputes, which may be either of a civil or religious nature, to which latter kind the Jews were particularly prone. Some Commentators refer this also to the teachers—it is better, however, extend it to all Christians; and as these words are written for all times, probably the word "wars" may refer to those which St. James foresaw would take place at a future day, even between Christian states. They all originate in their "concupiscences," *i.e.*, their unsubdued lusts, "which war in your members," *i.e.*, which employ the members of the body, viz., the eyes, the ears, the tongue, the hands, &c., as instruments of that warfare, which the unsubdued passions of pride, selfishness, avarice, &c., endeavour eternally to carry on in the soul of man.

Text.

2. You covet and have not; you kill and envy, and cannot obtain. You contend and war, and you have not, because you ask not.

3. You ask, and receive not; because you ask amiss : that you may consume it on your concupiscences.

4. Adulterers, know you not that the friendship of this world is the enemy of God? Whosoever therefore, will be a friend of this world, becometh an enemy of God.

Paraphrase.

2. (Behold both the utter folly of seeking true happiness in the gratification of your corrupt passions, and the total disappointment in which this gratification ends) : for, although you obey the dictates of these corrupt passions, still you cannot secure their object ; although you indulge in mortal hatred and envy towards whomsoever you think to obstruct your designs ; still, you cannot possess that which you seek. You strive and labour hard in pursuit of happiness, and you cannot find it ; because, you have not recourse to the proper means of obtaining from God, from whom alone they can proceed (i. 17), these real and substantial goods, alone capable of satisfying the cravings of the heart ; that means is, fervent and humble prayer.

3. And although you may have recourse to prayer, it is of no use to you, from a want of the proper dispositions ; you ask for what you may waste on the guilty gratification of your corrupt passions, instead of seeking for what will advance your spiritual interests, the concerns of your eternal salvation.

4. Know you not, who, in the criminal indulgence of your passions, violate the vows pledged to God in baptism, and are, therefore, guilty of a spiritual adultery, that the inordinate love and friendship of this world, in obedience to which you gratify your corrupt passions, are the enemies of God. Whosoever, therefore, wishes to become the friend of this world, must become the enemy of God, who cannot bear a divided heart or allegiance.

Commentary.

2. In this verse, he shows the utter folly of seeking for pleasure and real happiness in the gratification of these concupiscences, since this gratification ends in total disappointment. " You covet," *i.e.*, indulge these passions, " and have not," and still you cannot secure the object of their gratification. " You kill and envy and cannot obtain." For " kill," the reading in some Greek copies is, φθονειτε, και ζηλουτε, *you envy and are jealous*. And this reading Estius thinks would make better sense. The reading followed by the Vulgate, φονευετε, *you kill*, has, however, the authority of the best manuscripts, in its favour ; and the word " kill," most likely refers to the will and disposition to commit murder, the guilt of which it entails ; rather than to the act, although, even amongst the early Christians, some might possibly be found to commit the deed ; and what wonder, was not a Judas found among the twelve Apostles to do worse?

" You contend and war, and you have not, because you ask not," *i.e.*, you strive and labour hard to gratify your desires ; and still, you possess not the happiness, of which you are in search, " because you ask not," because you have not recourse to God by prayer, to obtain these solid and substantial goods, alone capable of satisfying the cravings of the heart, which come only from Him, who is the source of every good gift (i. 17).

3. The words of this verse are an answer to an objection which the converted Jews are supposed to make to St. James ; *we do ask, and this is of no use for us.* St. James answers, that their prayers are fruitless, for want of the proper dispositions, either because the *object* of their petition is bad, and the required feelings of humility, confidence, and perseverance, are wanting, both of which, as to the object and dispositions of their prayer, are included in the word " amiss ;" or, because the *motive* of their prayer may be bad—their object in begging for temporal goods is, " to consume," to squander them in gratifying their corrupt passions ; to such prayers, God will never lend an ear.

4. " By adulterers," some understand those guilty of carnal adultery. In the *Codex*

Text.

5. Or do you think that the Scripture saith in vain: *To envy doth the spirit covet which dwelleth in you?*"

Paraphrase.

5. Or, can you imagine, that the Scripture speaks in vain, when in many passages, referring to the holy jealousy which God entertains for our souls, so as not to endure a rival, it says, at least in terms equivalent to the following: "the holy spirit of God, that permanently dwelleth in you, covets you to such a degree, as to be jealous of any rival in your affections?"

Commentary.

Vaticanus, the reading is, μοιχαλιδες, *adulteresses*, as if addressing those carnally guilty of this grievous crime. It is, however, more commonly understood to refer to spiritual adultery, of which the sinner is guilty, when he deserts and proves unfaithful to God, to whom he was betrothed, and to whom he pledged his faith in baptism. This latter interpretation is rendered probable by the following words : "know you not that the friendship of this world is the enemy of God," as if he said ; in the desertion of God for the friendship of his enemy and rival, this "adultery" consists. St. James here exhibits God and the world as two rivals, both of whom cannot be served at the same time, as God will not admit of a divided heart, of a divided service or allegiance. St. James, of course, here speaks of that "friendship" and love "of this world," which implies a conflict with, and a violation of, the law of God. It is, as considered and viewed in this latter respect, that we always find the "world" reckoned in Scripture as the enemy of God and of man's eternal welfare ; because it demands a service inconsistent with the undivided service we owe God. The Commentators who, with Œcumenius, understand the preceding verses of this chapter to refer to the teachers, have very little difficulty in tracing the connection of this verse with the preceding, thus : Know you not, who in the exercise of your ministry, seek only your own elevation, and the praises of men, before the glory of God, and are, therefore, guilty of spiritual adultery, that the friendship and inordinate love, which you have for this world, for its riches, honours, and praises, is opposed to the love you owe God ; and that by becoming the friends of this world, you become the enemies of God ? In the interpretation adopted in the Paraphrase, it is not at all necessary to trace any connexion with the preceding. It may be said, that the Apostle enters here on a new topic altogether, a thing quite in accordance with his style in this Epistle.

5. This passage has been variously interpreted by different Commentators. Some understand by "spirit," the corrupt spirit of man. This opinion is preferred by Estius. Others—and, it would seem, with greater probability—refer it to the spirit of God, received in baptism. Of this spirit we find it frequently said, *that it dwells* in the souls of man ; and of the same only could the words of the following verse be verified. "But he giveth greater grace." The meaning of the passage, then, appears to be (as in Paraphrase), that the Holy Ghost, dwelling in a Christian, so loves him, as to entertain feelings, analogous to envy, at his being possessed by any other. The connexion of this interpretation with the context is quite evident ; it goes to show, that the man who gives the world a place in his heart, is become the enemy of God, who cannot peaceably dwell in a soul that has an affection for his rival.

But the question may be asked : What does the word "Scripture" refer to, and in what part of Scripture is the text here quoted to be found ?

Answer.—Whenever the Scripture is quoted by any of the writers of the New Testament, reference is made to some part of the Old Testament ; to the law and the prophets.

It is not clearly ascertained in what part of the Old Testament the text referred to is found. Most likely, reference is made to the passage in which God is described as a "jealous God" (Exodus, xx. 6, and elsewhere) ; and St. James quotes not the language but the sense of these passages, which he develops and explains in his own words. Others make the word, "Scripture," allude to the foregoing; and these place a note of interrogation after the words "in vain," thus : "Do you think that the Scripture saith in vain?" when, in several passages, it represents the friendship of this world as the enemy of God. And then, again, they ask, "*Does the spirit that dwells in you covet*

Text.

6. But he giveth greater grace. Wherefore he saith : *God resisteth the proud, and giveth grace to the humble.*

7. Be subject, therefore, to God, but resist the devil, and he will fly from you.

8. Draw nigh to God, and he will draw nigh to you. Cleanse your hands, ye sinners; and purify your hearts, ye double-minded.

Paraphrase.

6. But, if he be jealous of every other, what wonder, since he bestows benefits incomparably greater than those bestowed by any other, which therefore, entitle him exclusively to our love and, undivided affection. But in order to be partakers of this abundant grace which the spirit of God bestows, we must be humble ; hence it is, that in referring to the dispensation of this abundant grace, he saith : "*God resists the proud and gives his grace to the humble.*"

7. In a spirit, then, of humble submission and obedience, place yourselves under the banners of the Almighty, and manfully resist the devil, and you shall put him to flight.

8. With true humility of heart, aided and assisted by his preventing grace, approach unto God, and he will draw nigh to you, by a greater effusion of his graces ; aided by the same grace, cleanse your actions and reform your conduct in future, you sinners ; and purify your thoughts and motives, you who have been wavering between pleasing God and gratifying your passions.

Commentary.

unto envy ?" (The Greek for " in you," is, *εν ημιν, in us*). By no means ; since the Holy Spirit of God, rather prompts to acts of benevolence and virtue. According to this latter construction, there is no scriptural allusion or quotation whatever, contained in the words, "*to envy doth the spirit,*" &c. The interpretation adopted in the Paraphrase seems preferable, and more in accordance with the context.

6. " But he giveth greater grace," &c., *i.e.*, it is no wonder that he should be jealous of every other rival in our affections ; since every other, that may claim our affections, can bestow, at best, but fleeting, unsubstantial goods, which end in bitterness and remorse, and bear no proportion with "the greater grace," the eternal blessings, he has in store for us, of which he gives us a sure earnest in this life. In the other interpretation, the words of this verse may be connected with the preceding, thus : " Does the Holy Spirit of God prompt us to acts of envy ?" (verse 5). By no means ; since, on the contrary, he bestows abundant grace to overcome these vicious dispositions of our nature, and to incite us to acts of benevolence.

"Wherefore he saith : *God resisteth the proud,*" &c., *i.e.*, in order to be partakers of this abundant grace of God, the first and most necessary disposition on our part is humility, to the absence of which we may trace the vices we have been denouncing in the preceding part of the chapter. This quotation would appear very much to favour the interpretation and construction just referred to ; since, far from promoting us to envy, the spirit of God bestows great grace, but only on those who have dispositions of humility so opposed to the spirit of envy. The words, "*God resists the proud,*" &c., are quoted here by St. James according to the Septuagint version. In the Vulgate of St. Jerome, they run thus : "He shall scorn the scorners, and to the meek, he shall give grace."—(Proverbs, iii. 34).

7. "Therefore," whereas, it is only to the humble he will give grace, "be subject to God." In Greek, *υποταγητε*, *i.e.*, with true humility of heart, and a ready disposition to obedience, *range yourselves under the banner of God*. "And resist." The corresponding Greek word, *αντιστητε*, means, *stand against the devil*, in which, as in the preceding word, "be subject," a military metaphor would appear to be implied.

8. "Draw nigh unto God." Of course, this is to be effected by the aid of divine grace ; but, as in the performance of a salutary action, the human will and divine grace concur, the entire effect is sometimes in SS. Scripture wholly ascribed to the will of man, as here, and at other times, to the more principal cause, viz., divine grace. "Cleanse your hands, ye sinners." The most effectual means to be adopted by those who have been enrolled under the sacred banners of God only of late—"ye

Text.

9. Be afflicted, and mourn and weep: let your laughter be turned into mourning, and your joy into sorrow.

10. Be humbled in the sight of the Lord; and he will exalt you.

11. Detract not one another, my brethren. He that detracteth his brother, or he that judgeth his brother, detracteth the law and judgeth the law. But if thou judge the law, thou art not a doer of the law but a judge.

Paraphrase.

9. In order to correct your vicious habits, and make atonement for the past, devote yourselves to the salutary rigours of holy penance; weep and mourn over your past infidelities. Let the laughter, to which you gave expression, and the joy, which you inwardly felt during the enjoyment of the passing and fleeting pleasures of sin, be now exchanged for mourning and inward sorrow of heart.

10. Humble yourselves sincerely and profoundly not alone before men, who only see the exterior, but also in the sight of God, who sees the very thoughts of the heart; and he, who raises up the humble, will exalt you also, with the gifts of grace here, and eternal glory hereafter.

11. My brethren, refrain from the odious and common vice of detraction (and all the cognate vices of the tongue, whereby our neighbour's character is damaged), for, he that detracteth his brother in any of the different ways in which this crime is committed, or he that judges his brother, detracts, judges, and condemns the law itself, as unjustly prohibiting detraction, and thereby depriving him of the full right, which nature gave him over his tongue. But if thou constitutest thyself a judge of the law, thou dost not acknowledge thyself any longer a doer of the law, bound by its precepts; but, rather its superior and judge, quite exempt from its obligation.

Commentary.

sinners"—for resisting the devil is, "by cleansing their hands," in other words, by ceasing from wicked actions, and by performing good works, of which the "hands" are the chief instruments. As to those, who have been wavering between pleasing God and gratifying their passions, or between their inveterate habits of sin, and their weak purposes of good—"ye double minded" (δίψυχοι, *having two souls*)—their duty, aided and assisted by divine grace, is "to purify their hearts," *i.e.*, their thoughts, motives, and intentions. "If thine eye be simple, thy whole body will be lightsome; but if thy eye (*i.e.*, the intention or motive) be evil, thy whole body (*i.e.*, the body of thy actions) will be darksome" (St. Matthew, vi. 22). For the full meaning of "double minded," *see* chapter i. verse 8.

9. In order to make atonement for the past, and dispose themselves for reconciliation, they should have recourse to the salutary exercises of holy penance; they should "afflict" themselves, "mourn and weep;" the laughter in which they indulged during the temporary and transient enjoyment of sinful pleasures, should now be exchanged for "mourning," and the passing "joy" which they then felt should be exchanged for the opposite and contrary feeling of penitential "sorrow." Similar is the exhortation of the Prophet Joel (ii. 12): "Be converted to me with all your hearts, in fasting, and in weeping and mourning." From this passage it is clear, that external works of satisfaction form a part of the penance, which is necessary for our reconciliation with God.

10. "Be humble," &c. The chief disposition for our reconciliation with God, is true humility, "in the sight of the Lord," *i.e.*, truly humbled; for things are seen by God, as they really are; the words also suggest the most effectual means of acquiring true humility, which is the consideration of God's infinite greatness, and of our own nothingness. "*Quis tu Domine? quis ego?*" exclaims St. Francis. *Tu abyssus omnis boni, et ego abyssus omnis mali et nihili. Noverim te Domine, noverim me,* was the favourite exclamation of St. Augustine. O God! grant us this all-necessary virtue of humility.

11. St. James now cautions them against a vice which, like the other vices denounced

Text.	Paraphrase.
12. There is one lawgiver and judge, that is able to destroy and to deliver.	12. (Thou dost, therefore, usurp a function, which does not belong to thee) for, there is (only) one lawgiver and judge, who can alone affix a proper sanction to his law, who can save those who obey his law, and can destroy the refractory.

Commentary.

by him in the preceding part of the chapter, springs from pride, viz., that of detraction, under which are included calumny, contumely, and all the other vices of the tongue, whereby the reputation of our neighbour is unlawfully injured. This vice has its origin in pride, in the inordinate desire to raise ourselves by lowering the character of our neighbour. "He that detracteth his brother, or judgeth," &c. In some Greek copies, in place of "or," we have, *and* ; but the disjunctive particle is found in the chief MSS. "Detracteth the law and judgeth the law," because by detracting and judging his brother, he practically declares and, by a virtual and implicit judgment, pronounces the law prohibiting detraction to be unjust, as interfering with his natural right over the full use and exercise of his tongue. No doubt, the same is true of the violation of every other precept of the law ; the man who violates it practically condemns the law, as in the case of theft, murder, &c. But this in a more special manner applies to the rash judgment regarding our neighbour, in which an act of judgment is expressly contained ; and that, in opposition to the law prohibiting it ; St. James appropriates to the violation of the law, as regards the rash judgment in question, the inconvenient consequence of condemning the law itself—although a consequence in some measure common to it, with the violation of every other precept—because the crime is committed by *judging*, which is expressly forbidden by the law.

St. Thomas and others understand by the law "which is judged," the law of fraternal charity. It is "judged" by being contemned by him who rashly judges his neighbour ; this opinion is preferred by Estius, who thinks the words have a peculiar application to teachers, who, with supercilious haughtiness, despise others and wish that their own *dicta* should pass for law. The words are particularly true, in the case where detraction is employed in vilifying our neighbour's character, on account of his more exact observance of the duties and counsels of Christian perfection.

There is no vice more common in the world than this dreadful vice of detraction. "*Tanta libido hujus mali mentes hominum invasit, ut etiam qui procul ab aliis vitiis recesserunt in istud, quasi in extremum diaboli laqueum, incidant.*"—St. Jerome (*Ep. ad Celantium*). How few are there to be found, even among those who appear to lead a regular Christian life, to scruple this matter, as they ought ! How few who bear in mind that, while judging their neighbour, they are only adding to the weight of their own judgment, before a just judge whose prerogatives they usurp ! How little do men think of setting up a tribunal and anticipating the judgment of God ! "*Tu quis es qui judicas alienum servum ?*"—(Rom. xiv. 4). Truly, "*si quis verbo non offendit, hic perfectus est vir.*" "Place, O Lord ! a guard on my mouth, and a gate of prudence on my lips."

"But if thou judge the law, thou art no longer a doer of the law but a judge." Thou settest thyself above the law, as its superior, instead of regarding thyself, as bound by it.

12. "And judge," και κριτης. This word is omitted in some Greek copies ; however, it is in the chief manuscripts and versions. By thus sitting in judgment on thy neighbour thou dost usurp a function, and dost intrude on a province that does not belong to thee. To the Supreme Judge and Legislator alone does it belong to judge his creatures. He alone can affix a proper sanction to his law by rewarding those who obey it, and punishing the refractory. From Him is all legislative and judicial authority among men, derived, "*per me, reges regnant, et legum conditores justa decernunt,*" and for Him, are we to obey all legitimate authority, whether temporal or spiritual. "*Omnis anima subdita sit sublimioribus potestatibus ; Qui vos audit, me audit.*" The man, then, who rashly judges his neighbour, is guilty of judging the law (verse 11), and of presumptuously usurping the prerogative of the Almighty (verse 12).

Text.

13. But who art thou that judgest thy neighbour? Behold now you that say: to-day or to-morrow we will go into such a city, and there we will spend a year, and will traffic and make our gain.

14. Whereas you know not what shall be on the morrow.

15. For what is your life? It is a vapour which appeareth for a little while, and afterwards shall vanish away. For that you should say: if the Lord will, and, if we shall live, we will do this or that.

Paraphrase.

13. But who art thou, what right, or authority or control hast thou over any other, thus to presume to sit in judgment on him? Come on, now, and see how foolish and irreligious is your conduct, in another matter, viz., when relying on your own strength, and without a proper acknowledgment of your dependence on God's holy will and Providence, you say: to-day or to-morrow we shall go into such a city, and remain there, for a year, in traffic and in pursuit of gain.

14. (Although you are wholly ignorant of what may happen on the morrow.

15. For what is human life on which you thus confidently calculate? What is it but a thin vapour, which appears for a short time, and afterwards is dissipated and vanishes from our sight)? Instead of such irreligious conduct and language, you should always express, or, at least, imply the following conditions before proposing to yourselves the execution of any purpose: "if the Lord will," and, "if we shall live."

Commentary.

13. "But who art thou?" &c. "But," is not in some Greek copies. It is found in the Vatican MS. "Thy neighbour;" in some Greek copies, *another:* πλησιον, neighbour, is the reading of the Vatican and Alexandrian MSS. As if he said, wretched worm of the earth, who art thyself one day to be judged, what right or control hast thou over thy fellow-creatures?—who is it authorized thee, thus to sit in judgment on him? "For his own master will he stand or fall."—Rom. xvi. 14.

"Behold now you that say," &c. For "behold" it is the Greek, αγε, *go to*, or *come on*, as in chap. v. verse 1. It is merely a form soliciting attention. Some Commentators endeavour to trace a connexion between these words and the foregoing, thus:—Who art thou to judge thy neighbour? you who are so foolish, in the ordinary language of life, as altogether to renounce practically your dependence on divine providence, although your weakness and frail dependence be such as not to be able to promise yourselves a moment's continuance in existence. This connexion is warranted, in a certain sense, by the division of the verses in the Vulgate. The more probable opinion, however, appears to be (as in Paraphrase), that St. James is censuring another vice of the tongue, then so common among worldly-minded persons, who relied too confidently on their own strength, in the execution of their designs and purposes, and seemed altogether to forget their dependence on God's adorable providence. Such persons propose to themselves to traffic for years, and to execute other purposes at some future time with a degree of certainty and security, that would imply their independence of God's providence. It is the irreligious sentiments expressed by such language that St. James here condemns, as appears from verse 1, their "rejoicing in their arrogancies." In some Greek copies, instead of "we will go, will spend," &c., it is, *let us go, let us spend,* &c. But the Vulgate translator has better expressed the sense of St. James, by employing the future Indicative, which more clearly conveys their foolish resolves in regard to the future. Moreover, the future is the reading of the *Codex Vaticanus.*

14. Such foolish men may experience the fate of the rich glutton in the Gospel, who gave up his soul, in the very execution of his projects of self-aggrandizement.— (Luke, xii. 20).

15. The words of the preceding verse (14) and of this, as far as "For that you should say," are to be read parenthetically. "What is your life?" "It is a vapour," &c. The Greek has, "γαρ," *for,* it is a vapour, &c. It is like the morning dew, which ascends in thin vapour, and immediately after disappears altogether from our eyes. We frequently meet in sacred Scripture with beautiful comparisons of the same kind

Text.	**Paraphrase.**
16. But now you rejoice in your arrogancies, all such rejoicing is wicked.	16. But now, while employing the language I have censured, you boast and glory in the expression of your arrogant and proud rejection of God's adorable Providence ; all boasting of this sort is wicked and sinful.
17. To him, therefore, who knoweth to do good, and doth it not, to him it is sin.	17. Of course, as Christians, you must be fully aware of your dependence on God's Providence ; this knowledge, however, only serves to aggravate the sinfulness of your conduct ; since the man who knows good and does it not, or acts against it, sins the more, by reason of his knowledge.

Commentary.

" Remember," (says Job. vii. 7), " that my life is but wind......as a cloud is consumed and passeth away," &c. (Psalm cxliii.) The conclusion is, that as human life is thus fleeting, precarious, and uncertain, it is the excess of folly, and the height of presumption in them, thus to calculate for certain, on the success and enjoyment of their future projects. " For that you should say." These words are to be immediately connected with the words, verse 13 : " You say, to-day or to-morrow, we shall go into such a city," &c. "For that you should say," *i.e.*, instead of which mode of speaking, you should say, "if the Lord wills," and "if we shall live." These two conditions should be always expressed, or at least implied, whenever we propose to ourselves the accomplishment of any future project. The example of St. Paul alone shows us how much these forms of expression, recommended by St. James, were at the time in use.— Acts, xviii. ; 1. Cor. iv. and xvi. ; Hebrews, vi. ; Rom. i. ; Philipp. ii. Even among the Pagans, viz., Socrates, Cicero, Cato, &c., such forms were in use.

16. In this verse, the Apostle shows that he is condemning dispositions of mind, the opposite of the Christian and religious forms of speech, which he is recommending. He is censuring such persons as attributed the merit of their success to themselves, without a due regard to God's Providence and assistance. Such conduct on their part is "*arrogance*," or pride, since, of themselves, they can do nothing. "All such rejoicing is wicked," such haughty, presumptuous reliance on our powers is, in every case, evil, because it is a practical lie, and a lie, too, injurious to God's supreme dominion over his creatures. St. James by no means condemns a prudent provision for futurity, dependent on God's will and Providence.

17. The connexion adopted in Paraphrase is : You know, as Christians, all that I am saying : you know your dependence on Providence and the uncertainty of life ; now, this knowledge will only aggravate the sinfulness of your impious and unchristian mode of expressing your future resolves. Or, the words of this verse may be only a conclusion drawn from the two foregoing chapters, wherein St. James instructs them in several points of Christian morality ; and now, he tells them, that if they hereafter sin in any of the particular points in which he instructed them, the instruction and knowledge imparted will only aggravate their sin ; for, sins committed with knowledge are more grievous, than if they were committed in ignorance.

CHAPTER V.

Analysis.

In this chapter, St. James denounces against the hard-hearted rich, the heaviest punishments in the life to come, on account of their crimes and cruelties towards the poor (1). These cruelties he enumerates. First—Their hard-heartedness was such, as to suffer their wealth to rot, sooner than give it to the poor (2), and their money to rust, sooner than dispense it: the consequence of which is, that they will suffer the severest punishments (3). The next crime he charges them with is, defrauding the labouring poor of their hire, one of the most iniquitous means of amassing riches (4). He then charges them with leading luxurious and debauched lives, pampering themselves in delicacies, like cattle destined for slaughter (5). And finally, he charges them with committing the most heinous crime, of persecuting unto death, innocent just men; and, as an aggravating circumstance of their injustice, he states, that these were unable to make resistance (6).

Turning to the poor and persecuted, he exhorts them to patience by several considerations such as the near approach of the Lord—the example of the husbandman, who patiently endures hardships in hopes of the distant harvest (7–8). He cautions them against murmurings (9), and consoles them by the examples of the prophets of old, and especially by the example of Job. He prohibits rash swearing.

He promulgates the Sacrament of Extreme Unction (14, 15). He exhorts them to the confession of their sins, and to prayer for one another, and he adduces the example of Elias, as an instance of efficacious prayer (16–19). Finally, he points out the great merit of converting sinners from their evil ways.

Text.	Paraphrase.
1. GO to now, ye rich men, weep and howl in your miseries, which shall come upon you.	1. Come on, now, ye (hard-hearted and haughty) rich men, weep and howl on account of the miseries in which you shall be eternally involved (unless you expiate your crimes by a true repentance).

Commentary.

1. "Go to," ἄγε, an interjection, having for object, to excite attention (as in chapter iv. 13). "Ye rich;" some interpreters understand these words to refer to the hard-hearted rich among the Pagans. But it is most probable (as in chapter ii.) that he is addressing the rich, who, contrary to their Christian profession, were guilty of the crimes here enumerated. Of course, there is question of such among the rich, as "were not poor in spirit," and were guilty of inhumanity towards the poor. "Weep and howl" in anticipation of the miseries, in which you shall be eternally involved hereafter, unless you repent for your crimes; it is to induce them to do penance that St. James menaces them with the rigorous judgments of God. Some Commentators understand the woes here denounced by St. James to have reference to the coming destruction of Jerusalem by the Romans, and the injuries which the rich were to sustain from the party of the zealots, the dominent party at Jerusalem, before its total destruction. It is more probable, however, that the words are to be understood in a more general sense, as extending to the punishments with which the abuse of riches, and the crimes consequent thereon, are visited at all times.

Text.	Paraphrase.
2. Your riches are corrupted, and your garments are moth-eaten.	2. (As a proof of your inhumanity and hard-heartedness towards the poor, who are perishing for want of food and raiment), you permit your substance to rot, and your garments to be eaten by moths, sooner than feed or clothe your famishing brethren.
3. Your gold and silver is cankered: and the rust of them shall be for a testimony against you, and shall eat your flesh like fire. You have stored up to yourselves wrath against the last days.	3. Your gold and silver (which you should have expended on the suffering poor) is idly laid by; and the rust of this money, hoarded up, shall serve to accuse your barbarous inhumanity, and be a witness against you on the day of judgment, and shall serve as the moral cause of your tortures in inextinguishable flames; you have laid up for yourselves a treasure of wrath and heavy punishment, against the day of final judgment.
4. Behold the hire of the labourers who have reaped down your fields, which by fraud has been kept back by you, crieth: and the cry of them hath entered into the ears of the Lord of sabaoth.	4. You have resorted to the most iniquitous practices for amassing wealth. Behold the hire of the labourers, who have reaped down your fields, which you have unjustifiably withheld from them, cries for vengeance against you; and the cry of those whom you have thus injured, has been attended to by Him who is able to inflict summary vengeance on you—the Lord God of armies.

Commentary.

2. St. James now recounts the crimes of the rich which draw down such heavy chastisements. The first charge against them is, their inhumanity to the poor, the proof of which is, that they suffer "their riches," *i.e.*, the abundance of food of all kind sored up in their granaries, to rot, and their superfluous garments to become "moth-eaten," sooner than feed and clothe the hungry and famishing poor. There cannot be a greater proof of their inhumanity and hard-heartedness—crimes so strongly denounced in every part of sacred Scripture.

3. "Your gold and your silver is cankered." Another instance or proof of their inhumanity to the poor, against whose cries, their hearts are steeled and their bowels closed. Their gold and silver utensils, probably, had a greater proportion of alloy than in modern times; and hence, were liable to rust. "And the rust of them shall be for a testimony against you," inasmuch as it will be a witness of their inhumanity, in having these riches uselessly laid by—contrary to all laws natural and divine, while the wretched poor were starving. "And shall eat your flesh as fire," because it shall be the moral cause of their tortures in the avenging flames of hell; or, because the recollection of this rusting of their wealth, which they might have meritoriously expended on God's poor, will supply fresh food to the eternal gnawing of the never-dying worm of conscience, one of the bitterest torments of the damned. Some even add, that there is allusion here made to the painful effects of rust rubbed into raw flesh, which gives us a vivid idea of the dreadful punishment, that is sure to overtake either the abuse, or the unjust acquisition of riches.

"You have stored up to yourselves (wrath) against the last days," this is referred by some to the days then immediately preceding the approaching destruction of Jerusalem. Others, more probably, understand the words of the day of general judgment, when both body and soul shall be tormented. "Wrath" is not found in the Greek, which runs thus, *you have treasured up for yourselves*, &c. Hence, the word was, most likely, added to the passage from (Rom. chap. ii. 5), where the phrase is very like the present, and refers to the punishments of the life to come. The Greek reading is understood by others to mean: You have been so eager for sordid gain as not to cease from amassing it even in your last days, in extreme old age, when you can have but very little time for enjoying it.

4. The crime with which he charges them, and which is calculated to draw down upon them the heavy vengeance of God is, defrauding the labourer of his hire. This is said "to cry against them," a form of expression which strongly points out its

Text.	Paraphrase.
5. You have feasted upon earth; and in riotousness you have nourished your hearts in the day of slaughter.	5. You have lived in delicacies and debaucheries upon earth, and you have feasted your hearts, preparing yourselves for vengeance, like the animals fattened for slaughter.
6. You have condemned and put to death the just one, and he resisted you not.	6. You have procured the condemnation and death of just and unoffending men, whenever they stood in your way, and what adds to, and aggravates your guilt—you did this, when the victims of your unjust persecution were quite helpless, and unable to resist you.

Commentary.

enormity. Hence, it is reckoned among the sins, *which cry to heaven for vengeance.* "Which by fraud has been kept back by you." The Greek word, αφυστερημενος means, *to keep back by any unjustifiable means.* "And the cry of them," *i.e. of those who have reaped* (for, this latter is expressed in the Greek, των θερισαντων), "hath entered the ears of the Lord of sabaoth," which shows the prompt vengeance to be inflicted in punishment of this crime. "Lord of sabaoth," *i.e.,* the Lord of armies, who, therefore sets at nought all human power and greatness. In him the poor and the orphan, although here apparently helpless, have a powerful defender. "*Tibi derelictus est pauper, orphano tu eris adjutor.*—Psalm ix.) "Sabaoth," this Hebrew word is retained by St. James, because it sounds better in the ears of the Jews, as expressing God's power and majesty. The same has been done by the Septuagint translators who always retain the Hebrew word "Sabaoth." If such heavy punishments are here denounced by the Apostle against individual cases of the unjust detention of the labourers' hire, what must the grievous enormity of their crimes, who, after ruthlessly exterminating entire districts, unjustly appropriate to themselves, against the clearest dictates of every law, natural and divine, the accumulated and permanent fruits of the labour, sweat, time, and money of the defenceless occupier of the soil? If this be not detaining and defrauding, on a gigantic scale, the hire of labourers, it is hard to say what else is. Will not this National sin, in many instances aggravated by heartless cruelty, and committed against the defenceless poor, out of hatred of their religion, cry to heaven for vengeance?

5. "You have feasted upon earth," *i.e.,* like the rich glutton in the Gospel (Luke xvi. 20, &c.), you indulged in unbounded and sumptuous gratification in eating and drinking and the enjoyment of good cheer. "And in riotousness you have nourished your hearts." In Greek it is, και εσπαταλησατε, εθρεψατε κας καρδιας, *and you have rioted; you have nourished your hearts.* "You have rioted," refers to the crime of voluptuousness and the indulgence of impure pleasures—an inseparable attendant of excess in eating and drinking—"*in vino luxuria*" (Eph. v. 18), "*venter æstuans mero spumit in libidinem*" (St Jerome). "You have nourished your hearts," *i.e.,* indulged in good cheer unto satiety." "In the days of slaughter." In some Greek copies, *as in a day of slaughter;* the Vulgate follows the Vatican MS., which, besides the meaning in the Paraphrase, may also mean, that their daily banquets were like festival days, on which the victims were slain, and great feasting indulged. The meaning in the Paraphrase, however, seems preferable.

6. The next crime with which he charges them is of a still blacker character. "You have condemned," *i.e.,* caused to be condemned, contrary to all justice—or, the word may mean, that, while by a mockery of justice, instituting a trial, in which might was the only rule of justice, they condemned and put to death the just man. "And he resisted you not," which shows the helplessness of their victim, and the consequent aggravation of their cruelty and injustice towards him. Of the injustice referred to by St. James, the murder of Naboth by Achab (3 Kings, xxi.), is adduced by Commentators, as a most striking exemplification. By "the just one," some interpreters understand Him, who was JUST by excellence—our Blessed Redeemer, whom the Jews put to death. It more probably, however, refers to just men in general, who might stand in the way of the aggrandizement or further enrichment of those unjust rich men, whom

Text.

7. Be patient, therefore, brethren, until the coming of the Lord. Behold, the husbandman waiteth for the precious food of the earth : patiently bearing till he receive the early and the latter *rain.*

8. Be you, therefore, also patient and strengthen your hearts ; for the coming of the Lord is at hand.

9. Grudge not, brethren, one against another, that you may not be judged. Behold the Judge standeth before the door.

Paraphrase.

7. Do you, on the other hand, afflicted poor, who are the objects of this unjust treatment, bear it with enduring patience, until the coming of the Lord to judgment, when you will receive an unfading crown. With the prospect of this reward before you, follow the example of the husbandman, who waits for the fruits of the earth, from which he is to derive sustenance ; in expectation of it, he patiently continues his labours, awaiting the early rain, which irrigates the earth after the seed is committed to it, and the latter, which ripens the crop.

8. You should, therefore, after his example, amidst the trials of this life, patiently expect the fruit of eternal life and the consoling effusion of divine grace, and strengthen your hearts against all temptation to impatience or despair ; for, the coming of the Lord is not far distant.

9. Do not fretfully indulge in murmurings and rash judgments against one another, lest you should be, in turn, condemned. For, the judge is near at hand, to pass sentence of condemnation upon you.

Commentary.

St. James is here addressing, and the singular number, " the just one," is employed, for emphasis sake, to show the helplessness of each victim of oppression, which is more clearly seen, by considering each case individually.

7. St. James now points out the duty of the oppressed, and offers them consolation under affliction. The first consoling consideration which he proposes is, " the coming of the Lord," which is understood by some to refer to his coming at the destruction of Jerusalem ; others, more probably, refer it to his coming at the general judgment, when both soul and body shall be glorified. The last day is frequently proposed in sacred Scripture, as a subject of consolation to the just, when under persecution. Both interpretations may be united ; for, both events were associated in the minds of the Jews, as appears from the mode, in which our Redeemer details the circumstances of one and the other, in the gospel. The straits to which the Jews were reduced at the capture of Jerusalem, might be regarded as a fair type of the anguish, in which the reprobate shall be involved, on the dreadful day of judgment. " Behold, the husbandman," &c. The next consideration which St. James proposes to console them is the example of the husbandman, who patiently waits for " the fruit of the earth ;" " precious," because procured by great labour ; and also because it supplies him with bread, the most necessary part of human food. " Patiently bearing." In Greek, μακροθυμων επ' αυτου, *long suffering for it,* viz., the expected fruit. " Till he receive the early and latter *rain."* The word, *rain,* is not in the Vulgate, nor in the Vatican MS. ; it is found in some Greek copies. And the words " early " and " latter " refer to the rain ; the early to that which irrigated the earth, after the sowing of the seed ; this fell in Palestine towards the end of October—and the " latter," to the harvest rain, by which the crops were ripened ; this fell about the middle of April. St. James calls them, " early and latter," looking upon the interval that elapsed between the sowing of the seed in October (the morning), and the gathering of the harvest about the middle of April (the evening), as one day, the end of which the husbandman was, with care and toil, anxiously looking for.

8. St. James exhorts them to persevere, after the example of the husbandman, in patiently enduring evils and miseries, until they receive the never-fading crown of eternal life, for which the abundant effusion of divine grace (" the early and latter rain,") will dispose them. " Strengthen your hearts " against all temptations to impatience or despair ; " for the coming of the Lord is at hand," because the day of judgment virtually takes place for each one, at death.

9. " Grudge not, brethren, one against another." St. James cautions them, while

Text.

10. Take, my brethren, for an example of suffering evil, of labour, and patience, the prophets who spoke in the name of the Lord.

11. Behold we account them blessed who have endured. You have heard of the patience of Job, and you have seen the end of the Lord, that the Lord is merciful and compassionate.

Paraphrase.

10. Take, my brethren, for examples to stimulate you to the patient and persevering suffering of evils and afflictions, the prophets, who have gone before you into bliss, who have not been freed from suffering, notwithstanding their high commission, of reclaiming sinners in the name and authority of the Lord, or of predicting future events.

11. Behold, we account those blessed, we have regarded their lot as happy, who have suffered for the cause of righteousness. You have all been acquainted with the patience of Job; and you have seen the happy end, to which the Lord brought his sufferings, rewarding him, even in this life, an hundred fold. The Lord will bring your sufferings also, to a happy issue; for, of his own nature, he is full of the tenderest compassion, and inclined to exercise acts of mercy, at all times.

Commentary.

under afflictions and persecution, against murmuring in regard to one another, or fretfully misjudging, or envying one another, a state of feeling apt to spring from the pressure of persecution and misery. As a motive for avoiding this, and for practising the opposite virtue of patience, he proposes the fear of being condemned by God. "Behold the judge standeth before the door," a form of expression frequently emplyed in Sacred Scripture, to intimate the near approach, or immediate presence of a person. Here, it is used with a view of cautioning them against incurring judgment and condemnation, on account of their murmurings and impatience; for, the judge is near to condemn them; or, perhaps, by it is meant to encourage them to overcome impatience, at the prospect of the rewards which the Judge, who is near, will render them. The phrase has the same meaning as the words in verse, 8, " for the coming of the Lord is nigh." Some understand the words, of the approaching destruction of Jerusalem and the total dispersion of the Jews by the Romans. The former interpretation, which extends to all times, appears, however, far the more probable.

10. St. James stimulates them to the patient endurance of evil by the example of the prophets, who preceded them; they could not reach heaven, without first passing through the ordeal of suffering, notwithstanding the high and exalted commission they received from God. "An example of suffering evil, of labour, and patience." In the Greek there are only two words, *της κακοπαθειας και της μακροθυμιας, of suffering evil and patience,* or, rather, *long suffering.* Hence, the word, "labour," must have been inserted by some scribe, who, perhaps, finding in some copies, the Greek word translated, *labour,* in others, *evil suffering,* united both. This does not much affect the meaning of the passage. By "the prophets," are meant the prophets of old, of whose sufferings mention is made in the Old Testament, and (Ep. ad Hebrews xi.) "Who spoke in the name of the Lord," which may either mean, that they spoke to reclaim sinners, or, to predict future events; in the name of the Lord," *i.e*, by divine commission and authority. Hence, as the prophets, whose lot they envy, did not reach heaven, except in passing through the ordeal of suffering, they are not to expect happiness on easier terms.

11. He proposes the example of Job, as a memorable instance of patience for the instruction of all ages. "The end of the Lord," which is understood by some to refer to the death and sufferings of our Saviour—the most perfect pattern of patience. The same example is proposed by St. Paul (Hebrews, xii.), after having counted up the heroic exploits of the saints of old (chap. xi.) It is more likely that the words refer to the end to which the Lord happily brought the sufferings of Job, rewarding him an hundred-fold even in this life; and this interpretation is rendered probable by the following words: "that the Lord is merciful and compassionate," as if he said, you have seen the happy end to which the Lord has brought the sufferings of Job, which is an effect of his merciful disposition to exercise acts of mercy at all times, and the same

Text.

12. But, above all things, my brethren, swear not, neither by heaven, nor by the earth, nor by any other oath. But let your speech be yea, yea ; no, no ; that you fall not under judgment.

13. Is any of you sad ? Let him

Paraphrase.

12. But above all vices of the tongue. you should avoid, with special care, the common vice of swearing, or invoking either the name of God, or heaven, earth or any other creatures, or employing any other form of oath, without sufficient cause, and without due conditions in swearing. All your assertions should be simple asseverations of truth, or "*yes*," and all your denials, simple and bare negations, or "*no*," without the interposition of an oath, lest, otherwise, you may incur condemnation on account of your profane irreverence towards God's holy and adorable name.

13. Should any one among you be in a sad mood,

Commentary.

mercy, you have good grounds to hope, will one day be extended to you also. The word "merciful," in Greek, πολυσπλαγχνος, means, *full of interior, visceral mercy*, and refers to the divine nature, of itself merciful. The other word "compassionate," in Greek, οικτειρμων, refers to acts of this mercy.

12. St. James here proceeds to caution the converted Jews against a vice resulting from impatience, which vice being prevalent among the Jews of old, was. most likely, not wholly eradicated after their conversion ; this was the abusive practice of indiscriminate swearing in common conversation. It appears from the Gospel, that there were erroneous doctrines taught by the Jewish doctors, and consequent abuses on two points, connected with the taking of an oath. The first was, that no matter how trivial or unnecessary the occasion of an oath might be, it was not sinful to invoke the name of God, provided it was done in truth ; and hence, in the prohibition (Exodus, xx. 7), "thou shalt not take the name of the Lord thy God in vain," they understood the words "in vain," to mean, *falsely*, or *in a lie*—a signification which the original Hebrew word bears, but not exclusively, as they interpret it. Secondly, they held, that an oath by creatures, except in the cases favourable to their own avarice, "by the gold of the temple" (Matthew xxiii. 17), was not binding. These erroneous and abusive teachings our divine Redeemer corrects in his Gospel (Matt. v. 34), and tells men "not to swear at all," *i.e.*, indiscriminately and in common conversation—even though their assertions should be true, in the sense, in which swearing was permitted by the Jewish teachers ; and he also declares that swearing by heaven, or earth, was equally binding with the direct invocation of the name of God, since his attributes were reflected both in one and the other. Now, as St. James, the disciple, is to be supposed to have in view the same prohibition, which he heard from the lips of his Divine Master, his words ; in this passage, are to be understood in the same meaning.

St. James, any more than our divine Redeemer, does not prohibit our resorting to an oath, when accompanied with the necessary dispositions of "judgment, justice, and truth" (Jeremias, iv. 2) ; for, then, it is an act of homage in recognition of the supreme veracity of God, who knows all truth, and is incapable of sanctioning falsehood of any kind. But to be invoking God's name on every occasion, is only insulting him, and profanely irreverencing his holy name. That it is sometimes lawful for Christians to swear, is a point of faith defined against the Anabaptists and Wicliffe, and clearly proved, from the example of God himself, "*juravit Dominus et non pœnitebit eum*," from the examples of Moses, Abraham, St. Paul, &c. "Nor by any other oath," *i.e.*, by any other mode of invoking God's veracity, as witness of truth. "But let your speech be, yea, yea ; no, no ;" in Greek, the word "speech" is not found, it is, ήτω δε υμων το ναι, ναι, και το ου, ου ; *but let your yea be yea ; and your no be no ;* the word, "speech" was, most likely, introduced here from (Matthew, v. 37), as both passages referred, in the mind of the interpreter, to the same thing. "That you fall not under judgment." In some Greek readings it is, *that you fall not into hypocrisy*. The reading adopted in our Vulgate is, however, the most probable. They would fall under judgment or condemnation. by swearing in violation of God's law and prohibition.

13. St. James here prescribes a rule for the guidance of such as are in sadness ; he had prohibited them already from uttering complaints against one another (9). He

Text.	Paraphrase.
pray. Is he cheerful in mind? Let him sing.	owing to his afflictions and adversity, let him seek consolation from God in prayer. Should he be in a joyous mood, let him nourish this feeling by singing spiritual songs, and by offering to God in thanksgiving a sacrifice of praise.
14. Is any man sick among you? Let him bring in the priests of the church, and let them pray over him, anointing him with oil in the name of the Lord.	14. Is any one among you labouring under grievous and dangerous bodily infirmity? Let him send for, and have called in, some one of the priests ordained and consecrated to minister in the church, and let the priest pray over him, anointing him, at the same time, with oil, in the name and person, or by the authority and command of the Lord.
15. And the prayer of faith shall save the sick man; and the Lord shall raise him up: and if he be in sins, they shall be forgiven him.	15. And the form of prayer which is based upon the faith of the Church, and which the Church has marked out, will effect the salvation of the sick man, both in this life (if it be expedient), and in the life to come ; and the Lord will assuage his bodily pains, and lighten his mental anxiety, and remove his spiritual torpor. And should there remain any sins not yet remitted, they will be forgiven him.

Commentary.

now tells them to have recourse to God for consolation and to commune with him in prayer. "Is he cheerful," *i.e.*, in a happy and joyous mood of mind, "let him sing," *i.e.*, sing spiritual canticles, a befitting way of nourishing this happy mood of mind, and of rendering God thanks—*See* Epistle to the Ephesians, v. 19.

14. "Is any man sick among you?" By "sick," is meant, as appears from the Greek, ασθενει, *labouring under grievous bodily infirmity*, or in danger of death from sickness. "Let him bring in (in Greek, προσκαλεσασθω *call in*,) the priests of the Church," *i.e.*, "either bishops or priests duly ordained by them by the imposition of hands."—(Council of Trent, xiv. c. 3)—to officiate in the Church. "And let him pray over him ;" the words "over him" show there was a ceremony or rite to be observed in this prayer. "Anointing him with oil." Of course the oil of olives, which, pro-perly speaking, is alone to be termed, "oil." "In the name of the Lord," *i.e.*, in the person of the Lord, or by his commission and authority. The words, "in the name of the Lord," most probably affect the entire action of praying over the sick man, and anointing him with oil.

15. "And the prayer of faith," *i.e.*, the form of prayer which the priest will pronounce over him, called "of faith," because proceeding from faith and grounded on the faith of the Church, which prescribes one particular form, "will save the sick man." "Save," *i.e.*, restore him to health, should it be expedient for his salvation, or save his soul in the life to come, should he die. "And the Lord shall raise him up," *i.e.*, shall alleviate his bodily pains, and fortify him against the terrors of death, and remove all the langour, and anxiety, and sadness with which the dying are afflicted, and which prevent the application of their minds to God. "And if he be in sins," most likely, includes all kinds of sin, mortal or venial ; for, owing to some cause, his mortal sins may not have been remitted by penance, and the sacrament may have been invalidly administered : in that case, this prayer of faith, joined to the anointing with oil, will remit them, "they shall be forgiven him."

PROOF OF THE SACRAMENT OF EXTREME UNCTION.—From this passage is derived a most satisfactory proof, in favour of the Sacrament of Extreme Unction. We have all the conditions necessary to constitute a Sacrament of the New Law, viz., *a sensible external* rite—"anointing with oil,"—coupled with the prayer of faith, pronounced over the sick man. A *permanent* rite—St. James places no limitation as to time, nor are we to affix any limitation to the continuance of the precept, given here by the Apostle, any more than to the other precepts, laid down by him in this Epistle. Besides, the rite has been permanently continued in the Church. A rite, *collative of sanctifying grace*, as appears from the words, "if he be in sins, they will be forgiven," which can be done

Commentary.

only by the infusion of sanctifying grace. The same follows from the words, "the prayer of faith will save the sick man," which most probably, mean—saving him in the life to come, wherein is implied the conferring of sanctifying grace or its increase. A rite also, *instituted by Christ ;* since St. James could not have instituted a means of grace ; he only promulgated this sacred rite instituted by his Divine Master, "*in nomine Domini.*" The rite, therefore, here promulgated by St. James, and to which he makes it imperative on Christians to resort, in dangerous illness, has all the conditions requisite to constitute a Sacrament of the New Law.

The Council of Trent treating on this subject (SS. xiv. c. 1, &c.) teaches—"that the Sacrament of Extreme Unction has been *insinuated* by Mark, and *promulgated* by James, the Apostle. From the words of this verse, 'is any man sick,' &c., as handed down to us, and interpreted from apostolical tradition, the Church teaches us the matter, form, minister, effect of this sacrament. The matter is oil, consecrated by the bishop ; ...the form is the words, '*per istam unctionem,*' &c. ; 'the prayer of faith ;' the effect is conveyed in the words, 'the prayer of faith will save the sick man ; the Lord shall raise him up, and his sins shall be forgiven,' which means, that the grace and unction of the Holy Ghost wipes away his sins (or faults), if there be any remaining to be expiated, and also the relics of sin ; and alleviates and strengthens the soul of the sick man, by exciting in him a great confidence in God's mercy, owing to which he bears more patiently the inconveniences and labours of his sickness, and resists more easily the temptations of the devil, 'and sometimes obtains health of body, when it will be expedient for the salvation of his soul.'"—(SS. xiv. c. 2).

The ministers are either bishops or priests, duly ordained by the imposition of hands. "Let him call in the priests of the Church." That by the word "priests," are meant those who have received holy orders in the Church—"Priests ordained by the bishop" —and not the elders of the people, is clear from the fact, that in the New Testament the word, *presbyter*, is employed to designate an office of some kind ; and when there is question of Ecclesiastical functions, it refers to those who are ordained, as is seen in the Acts, Epistles of St. Paul, 1 Epistle of St. Peter, chap. iii., and St. John, Epistles 2 and 3 ; and here, they are called, *Presbyteri Ecclesiæ.* The tradition of the Church has placed beyond all doubt the interpretation given of "*presbyter*," which the Council of Trent (*ibidem*, canon iv.) has defined, as a matter of faith, to be the true meaning. St. James says, "Let him call in the priests," *i.e.*, some one of the priests. This change of number is often to be met with in SS. Scripture. Thus, it is said (Mark, chap. xv. 32). "*They* that were crucified with him reviled him," although only *one* of them did so. Thus. Hebrews, xi., it is said, "*they* closed the mouths of lions," although we read only of *one*, viz., Daniel, having done so ; also, "they were cut asunder," although, it happened only to Isaias.

The objections raised by heretics against the Catholic doctrine and interpretation of this passage, hardly deserve refutation. The false interpretation of those who say that St. James prescribes anointing with the generous oil of Palestine, as a means of natural cure, cannot stand for a moment ; for, in that case, why call in the "*priests* of the Church ?" Would not *physicians* or *nurses* answer better ? . Moreover, why prescribe the anointing with oil. in every case ? In some cases of disease, the use of oil is decidedly noxious and injurious. Again, St. James is not merely addressing the Jews of Palestine, but "the twelve tribes" scattered all over the earth, even in cold regions, where such oil could not be had.

The false interpretation of Calvin, who understands the passage to refer to the grace of healing miraculously. accorded in the infant Church, and which has long since ceased, is equally unfounded ; for. the grace of healing, and, in general, the grace of miracles, only extended to corporal and not to spiritual effects. Moreover, in the distribution of these *gratiæ gratis data*, which continued only for a time in the Church, St. Paul tells us, that the Spirit distributed them to each one at will.—1 Cor. xii. Hence, most likely, priests were not the *only* persons endowed with the gift of healing, nor was it probably conferred on *all* priests. Why, then, should St. James tell them, "call in the priests ?" He should rather have told them, call in such as had the gift of healing miraculously. Again, we do not find those who were endowed with the gift of healing, commanded or advised to make use of it for *all* the sick, nor were the sick

Text.

16. Confess therefore your sins one to another: and pray one for another, that you may be saved. For the continual prayer of a just man availeth much.

Paraphrase.

16. Confess, then, your faults to one another, both for the purposes of mutual counsel, and the assistance of your prayers ; or, confess your sins to such as are empowered to absolve from them, that is, the priests of the Church, and pray for each other, particularly the just for sinners, that freed from their sins, they may come to God and be saved ; for, the fervent and earnest prayer of the just man has great efficacy with God.

Commentary.

ordered to seek for a cure from those who had this gift. Thus, St. Paul, who had this gift, did not cure Timothy (1 Tim. v. 23), nor Trophimus (2 Tim. iv. 20), nor Epaphroditus (Phil. ii. 27) ; whereas, here is issued a general precept, *to all the sick*, when dangerously ill, "*to bring in the priests of the Church*." Again, Christ promised his disciples, after his resurrection, that by imposing hands on the sick, they would cure them (St. Mark, last chapter). And in the different cures performed by Christ's disciples, in virtue of this promise after his resurrection, we find no instance of the application of oil. Why, then, should St. James restrict the exercise of this power to the ceremony of anointing with oil? It is, therefore, clear that St. James does not here refer to the exercise of any such power ; but that he promulgates one of the sacraments of the New Law, instituted by our Lord Jesus Christ as a means of grace, of strengthening the dying Christian against the horrors of despair, and the violence of the approaching combat, when the enemy of his salvation shall strain every nerve to effect his destruction.

From this, we see the great and tremendous responsibility of those who are charged with the care of the dying sick to have the Sacrament of Extreme Unction administered —a sacrament which saves the patient, at least in the life to come, and in this life too, if administered in time, should it be expedient for his salvation ; *alleviates and strengthens the soul of the sick man*, by assuaging his pains, invigorating his spirit, pouring into his soul the balm of consolation and hope, and enabling him to direct his mind to God ; finally, "*remits his sins, if there be any to be remitted.*" How many are the souls saved by this sacrament, which deprived of it, would be damned? Surely those who are negligent to have the priests called in, will render "soul for soul, blood for blood." The different questions raised about the mode in which this sacrament operates the remission of sins, and the quality of the sins which it remits, &c., more properly belong to Treatises of Theology, where these and other such questions are fully and professedly explained.

16. "Confess, therefore, your sins one to another." "Therefore," is omitted in some Greek readings. It is found in the Vatican MS. The words may mean, acknowledge your offences against one another, and mutually beg pardon of each other. Similar is the precept in the Gospel (Matt. v.), "if your brother shall sin against thee," &c. Others understand the words to have reference to the confession of our faults to our brethren, for the purpose of seeking counsel, or of obtaining the assistance of their prayers ; and this latter reason is suggested by St. James, "pray one for another," &c. This practice or acknowledging their faults within due limits is observed in religious communities, with great spiritual advantage. The practice of mutually confessing their sins is followed by the priest and the people at the beginning of Mass. "*Confiteor Deo......et tibi, pater...... et vobis fratres.*" By others, the passage is understood of the confession of sins to a priest, in the sacrament of penance; and then, "one to another" is to be understood (as the Greek corresponding word, αλληλοις. frequently is), in accommodation to the subject matter of the precept, of such as are empowered to hear confession and bestow absolution. These are alone the priests and bishops, "whose sins you shall forgive, shall be forgiven, and whose sins you shall retain," &c. "One to another," has the restricted meaning assigned to it here in several passages of Scripture, thus : (Romans, xv. 7), "receive one another," though it only refers to the strong supporting the weak ; (1 Thes. v. 11), "comfort one another"; (Ephes. v.), "be subject to one another." And St. James says, "confess to one another," in order to remove the shame of confessing

Text.

17. Elias was a man passible like unto us : and with prayer he prayed that it might not rain upon the earth, and it rained not for three years and six months.

18. And he prayed again : and the heaven gave rain, and the earth brought forth her fruit.

19. My brethren, if any of you err from the truth, and one convert him ;

20. He must know that he who causeth a sinner to be converted from the error of his way, shall save

Paraphrase.

17. Of the truth of this latter assertion, we have a striking proof in the case of the Prophet Elias, who, though a mortal man, subject to the same passions of soul, and bodily wants with ourselves, still obtained by fervent prayer, that rain would not descend on the earth, for three years and six months.

18. And having again fervently prayed for rain, the heaven gave its rain, and the earth produced its fruit.

19. My brethren, should any among you stray from the path of truth, either in the order of faith or morality ; and if any one convert him to the right path from his evil ways,

20. Let him know, that whosover shall effect the conversion of a sinner, from the error of his way, will save his soul from spiritual death here, and eternal

Commentary.

our sins, by showing that it is not to angels or beings of a higher nature we are confessing ; but to weak mortal men like ourselves, and perhaps also to show that the priests too are bound by this precept. At all events, whether this latter interpretation be the true one or not matters but very little, as far as the warrant for absolving from sins, on the part of the priests is concerned. It is from the words of Christ to his Apostles, " receive you the Holy Ghost, whose sins you shall forgive," &c., and from the constant tradition of the Church, that the existence of this power is clearly demonstrated. " And pray one for another." This is specially to be understood of the just praying for sinners. " That you may be saved," i.e. obtain conversion to God, and the great gift of final perseverance. " For the continual prayer of the just," &c. The Greek word for "continual," ἐνεργουμένη, means, fervent, earnest. " Availeth much " with God ; because, he is his favourite and friend.

17. He shows, by the example of Elias, the truth of the assertion, that the fervent prayer of the just man avails much. " He was a passible man, like unto us," subject to the same passions of soul—but of course kept under control—and wants of body ; hence, he was hungry, thirsty, subject to the other common wants and miseries of this mortal life. " And with prayer he prayed," a Hebrew form for, he fervently prayed, " that it might not rain," &c. (3 Kings, chap. xvii.) There is a slight difference in the Greek, from our Vulgate. In the Greek, the words "upon the earth" are joined to the latter part of the verse, thus : " And it rained not upon the earth, for three years and six months." The sense is the same in both.

18. " And he prayed again." After Achab and his people did penance, Elias prayed fervently for rain ; casting himself upon the earth, he placed his face between his knees."—(3 Kings, xviii. 42). From the efficacious and fervent prayers of Elias, for the opening and shutting of the heavens, St. James wishes us to infer, that we should employ more earnestness, to obtain by our joint prayers, a matter of far greater consequence—viz., the salvation of our brethren.

19. But prayer is not the only means to be employed for their conversion. " Err from the truth," whether practical or speculative—as regards faith or morals.

20 " Shall save his soul from death," i.e., spiritual death here, and eternal death and torments hereafter. In most Greek copies, " his," is wanting ; shall save a soul, which is more valuable than all material creation put together. It is found in the Vatican MS. αὐτοῦ. In the Greek copies in which it is used, " his " may also mean, according to the breathing, whether smooth or rough, placed over it, his own. It is better, however, understand it of the soul of our neighbour, which is supposed to have been in danger. And the same is conformable to the words, " if your brother shall hear you ......you shall have gained your brother," (Matthew, xviii.) " And shall cover a multitude of sins," by being instrumental in their remission ; for, the covering of sins with God supposes their total remission (vide Ep. ad Rom. ch. iv.) It is disputed whose sins are referred to here, whether those of the man who is converted, or of the

Text.	Paraphrase.
his soul from death, and shall cover a multitude of sins.	death hereafter, and shall cover—by being the instrument in effecting their total remission before God—th: multitude of his transgressions.

Commentary.

person who converts him. It more likely refers to the former; the idea is the same as that conveyed (1 Peter, iv. 8), "charity covereth a multitude of sins," *i.e.*, of our neighbour's defects. And there as well as here, allusion is made to (Proverbs, x. 2), "hatred begets disputes—charity covers all faults." Hence, the meaning of the passage is, that the man who is instrumental in the conversion of a sinner, performs the meritorious work of saving a soul, and covering the multitude of the sins of the person thus converted. No doubt, indirectly reference is made to the sins of the man who exercises the good work of converting his neighbour; for by this act of charity, he will obtain from God the remission of his own sins, or an increase of grace to persevere in justice, and the remission oɪ the temporal penalties, due to his sins already remitted.

From this passage we can see the great merit of labouring for the salvation of souls. By the Prophet Abdais (verse 21), such persons are called "saviours"; and justly, for, they are continuing the great work in which our Redeemer and Saviour had been engaged during his mortal life, and in which he shed the last drop of his most precious blood. They are "the coadjutors of God" (1 Cor. iii. 8). They resemble the angels, whose ministry is employed about such, as are to be saved—(Hebrews, i. 14). The merit of this sublime occupation can be estimated from the priceless value of immortal souls, one of which is prized more highly in the sight of God than all the riches of creation put together. It is the most sublime exercise of charity, and one of the surest proofs we can give that we sincerely love God, who is so deserving of the love of our entire hearts.—"*Si amas me, pasce oves meas.*" To this faithful discharge of this exalted function of saving souls is attached a special crown, a bright *aureola* in heaven. "*Qui erudierint multos ad justitiam, fulgebunt quasi stellæ in perpetuas eternitates*"—Daniel. "*Qui fecerit et docuerit, hic magnus vocabitur in regno cœlorum.*"—St. Matthew, v.

FIRST EPISTLE OF ST. PETER.

——◆——

Introduction.

CANONICITY OF.—The Canonicity or Divine authority of this Epistle has never been questioned in the Church. From this follows the admission of its authenticity, or the certainty of its having for author, St. Peter, the Prince of the Apostles, who prefixes his name to it, in the usual form of apostolical salutation (chap, i. 1).

SUBJECT OF.—This Epistle, like almost all the inspired Epistles of the other Apostles, embraces subjects of a twofold nature, partly of a doctrinal, and partly of a moral, character. The doctrinal portion of it is confined to the first twelve verses of the first chapter. In it, are proposed to the consideration of the faithful, the eternal decrees of God predestining them to grace and glory—the sublime excellence of the great mystery of the Incarnation—and the exalted nature of the incorruptible and heavenly inheritance, to which they are called; to obtain which they must pass through an ordeal of suffering and trial, from which the first-born of God, our Divine Redeemer himself, had not been exempted. The Apostle also employs in many parts of the Epistle, reasons, grounded on the principles of faith, to inculcate certain precepts of morality. In the moral part, he enjoins on all Christians, in a general way, to preserve that innocence of soul, which they acquired in baptism—to mortify their passions —to defy the unbelievers by their holy and exemplary lives—to be subject to temporal powers, &c. Descending to particular precepts, he enjoins on wives, slaves, and the faithful in general, the duty of obedience and subjection to masters, husbands, and the pastors of the Church; on the other hand, to masters, husbands, and pastors, he prescribes their reciprocal duties. But, in a special manner, he prescribes the exercise of patience, under the afflictions the early converts were exposed to for the faith. In short, the subject matter of this Epistle is very much the same with that of the Epistle of St. James.

WHERE WRITTEN ?—It was written from "Babylon" (chap. v. 13). What the place designated by "Babylon" is, has been a subject of much controversy between Protestants and Catholics. Protestants maintain that it refers to "*Babylon*" of Assyria, on the Euphrates, whether to the New Babylon (Seleucia), or to the old, is a matter not agreed on amongst themselves. The more common opinion among Protestants, however, makes it refer to old Babylon, there being no evidence that Seleucia was, at this early period, called by the name of Babylon.

By Catholics, it is made to refer to the city of Rome, an appellation which Rome richly deserved, in consequence of being, at that time, the centre of idolatry and vice. It was usual with the Jews to call such cities by the figurative name of Babylon; as to cities, infamous for debaucheries, they gave the name of Sodom; an idolatrous country, they called Egypt; and to a race cursed by heaven, they gave the name of Chanaan. It s very probable, therefore, that the early Christians called Rome by the name of Babylon. In support of the Catholic opinion, we have the early Fathers and Ecclesiastical writers. Papias, the disciple of St. John (*Apud Eusebium, libro 2do Histor.* c. 14, *alias* 15), St. Jerome (*in Isaiam* c. 24–27, *et libro 2do contra Jovin.*), Tertullian (*libro 3tio contra Marcion,* c. 13), Bede, Œcumenius, &c. That the Babylon from which this Epistle is dated, was not the Babylon of Assyria, on the Euphrates, appears extremely probable (leaving the authorities, in favour of the Catholic opinion, altogether aside), from the fact that, at this time, Babylon was in ruins, as we learn from Strabo (*libro* 17) and Pliny; we are, moreover, assured by Josephus (*libro* 18 *de Antiq.* c. *ultimo*), that the Jews were expelled from Babylon and Assyria by Caius Claudius; and as for Babylon in Egypt, it was no more than a castle. It is, then, extremely probable, that it was written from Rome, called "*Babylon*," (Apocalypse, xvii. xviii.) The reason why St. Peter, in inditing this letter from Rome, calls it "*Babylon*," was, according to the conjecture of Baronius, to keep his place of abode a secret, and elude Herod, who, in all probability, would inform Cæsar of his being at Rome, and would thus draw down fresh persecutions on the faithful.

WHEN WRITTEN ?—There is a diversity of opinion also respecting the date of this Epistle. By some it is maintained, that it was written some time about the year 45 of our era; for, in it the Apostle conveys the salutations of St. Mark, who, according to Ecclesiastical authority, left St. Peter about the year 45, after having written his Gospel at Rome, and proceeded to found the Church of Alexandria in Egypt, in the third year of the Emperor Claudius. According to these, this Epistle was written prior to any of the Epistles of St. Paul; for, that to the Thessalonians—the first written by him—was written about the tenth year of Claudius, and the fiftieth or fifty-second of Christ. Others maintain that it could not have been written earlier than the year 64 of our era. This they infer from the allusion which the Apostle makes to certain disturbances in Judea, that must have occurred shortly before his death, which, we are informed by all the Holy Fathers and Ecclesiastical historians, took place at Rome (whither St. Peter had transferred his see from Antioch), about the year 67 of Christ, towards the close of the reign of Nero. Hence, they fix the date of the Epistle about the year 64. Nothing definite, however, can be known on this point.

To WHOM WRITTEN ?—This also has been much controverted. Some maintain that it was addressed to the converted Jews only, dispersed throughout the provinces of Asia, mentioned (i. 1), whom St. Peter, as Apostle of the circumcision, takes under his special care. These assert that the "dispersion" referred to (i. 1) regards the Jews dispersed at different periods, no matter how remote and far asunder, from that under Salmanazar, to the last dispersion, which happened after the death of St. Stephen; and they are called "strangers dispersed" (verse 1), because, although centuries might have elapsed since the abduction of their fathers into these countries, and although they might have been perfectly naturalized, and have enjoyed all the rights and privileges of citizens in these regions, still, Judea alone could properly be called their country, "the land flowing with milk and honey," originally marked by God for his chosen people, where alone was the temple, wherein they could practise all the rites, and offer up the sacrifices of the Jewish religion. Hence, although they might be inhabitants of these countries for any term, be it ever so long, they still could be called "strangers." These admit that the precepts given in the Epistle apply equally to the converted Gentiles also; that they were, however, primarily addressed to the converted Jews.

Others maintain that it was equally addressed to the Gentiles and Jewish converts ; and in support of this view of the case, they adduce certain passages in the Epistle which would appear to apply to the Gentiles in a special way (i. 14 ; ii. 10 ; iv. 3, 4). In reply to the reasons of the former opinion, they say, that the word " dispersed," or dispersion (i. 1), does not apply in Sacred Scripture exclusively to the Jews, it is applied also to the Gentiles (*v.g.*), it is said : "*nunquid ibit in dispersionem gentium*" (John vii. 35 ; xi. 52), in which passages " dispersed " only means, scattered or extended over these countries. They say also, that the word "*strangers*" could not have reference to the countries in which they were located—(for, from the periods of the forcible abduction under Salmanazar, Nebuchodonzor, and Antiochus, seven hundred and sixty-three, six hundred and eleven, and two hundred and thirty-nine years, respectively, elapsed)—but that it refers to the Church, into which both Jews and Gentiles had lately entered. In support of this opinion—which was adopted by St. Augustine—Mauduit has written an able dissertation. It is, however, probable that the Apostle primarily addresses the converted Jews, and includes, at the same time, the converted Gentiles.

FIRST EPISTLE OF ST. PETER.

CHAPTER I.

Analysis.

In the first two verses of this chapter, the Apostle addresses his apostolical salutation to the faithful who are elected to grace here, and to glory hereafter, and shows that the Three Persons of the Adorable Trinity concur in the work of redemption. He next bursts forth into the praises of God, for the great gift of spiritual regeneration bestowed on the faithful, which carried with it a lively hope (verse 3); and this regeneration was bestowed on them in order to qualify them, as sons of God, to enter on the possession of his priceless and undying inheritance, securely laid up in heaven for them, who are protected by the strong fortress of faith, until they enjoy this consummate salvation, which shall be manifested on the last day (4, 5). And on account of the blessings in store for them, they now rejoice under the afflictions which it may please Providence to send them, with a view of testing their faith, and bringing it to a happy issue (6, 7). He points out the greatness of the blessings bestowed on them, by referring to the anxiety of the prophets of old to become fully acquainted with them, and of the angels themselves to view these mysteries of grace with awe and wonder (10–12). Here closes the dogmatical part of the Epistle.

He next enters on the moral part, and exhorts them to remove every obstacle, arising from their unsubdued passsions, to the attainment of the bliss prepared for them (19), and to obey, as children of God, his precepts, and perform good works (14). He exhorts them to sanctity of life, after the example of God (15, 16), and to have reverential fear of him as just judge (17). He reminds them of the value God attaches to their souls, owing to the price paid for them (19); not only did Christ shed his blood for them in due time, but this was pre-ordained from eternity; hence, a new motive for sanctity of life (21). He exhorts them to practise fraternal charity (22), and points out the excellence of their new spiritual birth (23–25).

Text.	Paraphrase.
1. PETER, an Apostle of Jesus Christ, to the strangers dispersed through Pontus, Galatia, Cappadocia, Asia, and Bithynia, elect,	1. Peter, an Apostle of Jesus Christ, (addresses) the Christian converts, dispersed throughout the districts of Pontus, Galatia, Cappadocia, Ionia, and Bithynia, called and elected,

Commentary.

1. "Peter." With the history of this name all are acquainted. He was originally called "Simon," the son of Jonas. This name was changed by our Redeemer into "*Cephas*" in Greek, Πετρος, or *rock*, expressive of the high pastoral jurisdiction and authority over the entire Church, "lambs and sheep," *i.e.*, people and pastors, promised him (Matt. xvi.), and conferred on him (John xxi.)

"An Apostle," he might add, "*Prince of the Apostles*," but from this title he abstains through humility. "Strangers" (*see* Introduction). The word refers in a special

Text.

2. According to the foreknowledge of God the Father, unto the sanctification of the Spirit, unto obedience and sprinkling of the blood of Jesus Christ; grace unto you and peace be multiplied.

3. Blessed be the God and Father of our Lord JESUS CHRIST, who according to his great mercy hath regenerated us unto a lively hope, by the resurrection of JESUS CHRIST from the dead,

Paraphrase.

2. According to the predestinating decrees and foreknowledge of God, the Father, to become sanctified by the grace of the Holy Ghost, to obey Jesus Christ, by performing the good works which he has marked out, and thus become partakers, both in this life and the next, of the merits which he has purchased by the effusion of his sacred blood. May you enjoy the abundance of all spiritual blessings, and the quiet, undisturbed possession of the same.

3. Eternal praise and thanksgiving be rendered to God, the Father of our Lord Jesus Christ, who, regardless of any merits of ours, whether actual or foreseen, and influenced solely by his copious and abundant mercy, has given us a new spiritual birth, which carries with it a firm and undying hope of life everlasting; and this new birth of grace has resulted from the resurrection of Christ from the dead, by which our justification has been completed.—(Rom. iv. 25).

Commentary.

manner to the converts from Judaism, under whom are also included the Gentile converts. "Pontus, Galatia," &c., districts in Asia Minor. "Asia" designates "*Ionia*" of which Ephesus was the capital; but not Asia, Major or Minor, since the other provinces here mentioned are in them; and Asia is sometimes taken in this sense in Scripture (*ex. gr.* Acts, ii. 9, and xix. 22). St. Peter addressed these provinces in particular, in consequence of the grievous persecution to which the converted Jews, residing therein, were subjected; and, as "Apostle of circumcision," he wishes to exhort them to patience and perseverance in the faith. "Elect," to the grace of Christianity, which, in regard to many of them, doubtless, implies election to glory; to this latter election, however, the Apostle does not immediately refer, nor does he wish to tell those to whom he wrote, that they were all elected to glory.

2. "According to the foreknowledge of God the Father." This foreknowledge includes predestination, or the decrees of God's providence, to give grace and the means of salvation. By the predestination, then, of God the Father, they were elected. To what? "Unto the sanctification of the spirit," *i.e.*, to be sanctified by the grace of the Holy Ghost in this life, and to receive its consummation in glory, in the next; for, grace is the seed of glory. For "unto the sanctification," we have in some Greek copies, "*by* or *in* the sanctification;" but, *in*, frequently means, *unto*, in the Greek. The meanings supplied by the Greek reading referred to, and by Vulgate, are united in the Paraphrase. The idea intended by St. Peter is the same as that expressed by St. Paul (Ephes. i. 4), "he chose us in that we should be holy," &c. "Unto obedience," *i.e.*, the performance of good works (similar is the idea, Ephes. ii. 10) and the observance of God's commandments, which is obeying the gospel, a necessary condition for their attaining the end of their predestination. "And sprinkling of the blood of Jesus Christ," *i.e.*, they were elected to be partakers of the merits of Christ, purchased by his blood, and applied to them in baptism and the other means of grace in the New Law; and it is only through the merits of Christ that our good works or obedience can be of any value whatever. In these words, the Apostle probably refers to the remission of our sins, effected by the application of the blood of Christ; and then he fully describes our justification, consisting in the remission of sin through the infusion of sanctifying grace, and the performance of good works, expressed by the word "obedience." In the word "sprinkling," St. Peter makes allusion to the sprinkling of the blood of the legal victims, the effects of which are far beneath that of the blood of Christ (Hebrews, ix. 13). St. Peter in this passage shows that the Three Persons of the Adorable Trinity, the Father, Son, and Holy Ghost, concur in the work of our salvation. "Grace and peace," &c. The usual form of apostolical salutation.

3. The Apostle commences the subject of the Epistle with the praises of God— "blessed be the God," &c. Our blessing of God is different from his blessing of us.

Text.

4. Unto an inheritance incorruptible and undefiled, and that cannot fade, reserved in heaven for you.

5. Who by the power of God, are kept by faith unto salvation ready to be revealed in the last time.

Paraphrase.

4. He has given us this new birth of grace, in order to qualify us, as sons, for the enjoyment of an inheritance, which, unlike earthly heritages, is neither subject to coruption nor decay; and, unlike the voluptuous and impure pleasures proposed to themselves by the impious, shall be free from all stain and defilement— an inheritance also which will not only remain incorruptible in substance, but will also retain its original lustre and never-fading beauty ; it is, moreover, securely laid up in heaven, "*where thieves cannot break through nor steal,*" and securely reserved there for you.

5. Who, by the powerful grace and protection of God, are guarded by faith, as by a strong fortress, for that perfect salvation both of soul and of body, which only awaits the last period of time for its full and open manifestation.

Commentary.

His blessing of us consists in bestowing benefits ; whereas, our blessing of him consists in benevolence towards him, in acts of praise, thanksgiving, and gratitude. "The God and Father of our Lord," &c. This refers to God the Father, the First Person of the Adorable Trinity. The words bear the same meaning as in Rom. xv. 6 ; Ephes. i. 3. He begot the Son by an eternal generation. "Regenerated us," *i.e.,* has given us a new and second birth of grace, in the laver of baptism, thus bestowing on us a new spiritual essence by grace. "Unto a lively hope," this new spiritual birth carries with it a "lively hope," *i.e.,* a hope of life everlasting. "Hope," may be also put for the *object* of hope, which is an object ever living, viz., life eternal ; and unto this life and the hope of it has he regenerated us, "by the resurrection of Jesus Christ from the dead." The resurrection of Christ is the *exemplary* cause or model of our justification, and it completed our justification by carrying with it, the graces necessary for our spiritual life. "*Resurrexit propter justificationem nostram.*"—(Rom. iv. 25). Or, if we join the words "by the resurrection," &c., not with the word "regenerated," as in the preceding, but with "living hope," then, they will mean—this lively hope is confirmed by the resurrection of Christ, which is a sure pledge and earnest of our spiritual and immortal life (1 Cor. xv. 12-14). The hope of the faithful is called "lively," because animated with charity and good works, which give a foretaste of eternal life, a foretaste never enjoyed by the impious, who "have no hope."—(1 Thes. iv. 12).

4. "Unto an inheritance," &c. This is the object of the living hope into which we are regenerated. Even though we were to connect this verse with "living hope," it still must be connected with "regenerated." He gave us this new existence, in order to qualify us to enter, as sons, on his inheritance. Such is God's goodness that he wishes to grant eternal life and never ending happiness on the most exalted titles as a "kingdom," as an "inheritance," &c. The Apostle shows the exceeding great excellence of this inheritance—"incorruptible," never to crumble away, or be ruined or dissipated, like an earthly inheritance ; "undefiled" ("nothing defiled can enter it,' Apocalypse, xxi. 27), unlike the voluptuous enjoyment which many unbelievers and heretics propose to themselves ; such, for, instance, was the carnal elysium of Mahomet : "and that cannot fade ;" it will never grow old ; it will retain for ever its original freshness and beauty, not only incorruptible in substance, but unfading in its form and appearance. And finally, he says, it is "reserved in heaven." This shows its excellence as being a heavenly inheritance, and its certainty, as being safely laid up, "where thieves cannot break through nor steal." "For you—." In some Greek copies, *for us.* The Vatican and Alexandrian MSS. have εἰς ὑμᾶς, "for you," the Vulgate reading. It is reserved in heaven for the sons of God ; an inheritance is destined for children ; and they, whom the Apostle addresses, have become sons of God in their spiritual regeneration, which is for them a new and second birth.

5. "By the power of God," *i.e.,* the powerful grace and succour of God. "Are kept

Text.

6. Wherein you shall greatly rejoice, if now you must be for a little time made sorrowful in divers temptations:

7. That the trial of your faith (much more precious than gold which is tried by the fire) may be found unto praise and glory and honour at the appearing of JESUS CHRIST:

Paraphrase.

6. On account of this hope of future blessings in store for you, and of which you even at present enjoy a foretaste, you now rejoice in the very midst of the painful trials wherewith it may please God's providence to visit you.

7. The object God has in view in sending these sufferings is, that your faith, well tried and tested by afflictions (a faith, more precious than gold, which men try in the furnace), may be found to terminate in the praise, honour, and glory, that sha'l be bestowed on you on the last day, when the majesty of Jesus Christ will be fully revealed.

Commentary.

by faith." The Greek word for "kept," φρουρουμένους, conveys the idea of being protected as by a strong military fortress ; faith is the medium through which the justifying grace of God protects us, being *the root and foundation of all justification* (Council of Trent), and they are guarded " unto salvation "—that perfect salvation of soul and body—" ready to be revealed in the last time," that is, which requires only the last period of time, or the day of judgment to arrive, in order to be fully revealed and manifested. What motives have we not in this passage to aspire, with all the ardour of our souls, after the possession of our heavenly heritage, to disregard and undervalue everything else in comparison with it ; to omit nothing, in order to secure this inheritance stored up for us by the boundless goodness of our heavenly Father. " *Filii hominum, usquequo gravi corde, ut quid diligitis vanitatem et quæritis mendacium?*" And, in truth, what are all things else, all pleasures, all enjoyments, not conducing to the possession of our heavenly inheritance, but delusive, cheating vanities and lies ? Of this alone can it be said, that it is, " *incorruptible*," " *undefiled*," and " *never fading*." It alone is our true end, our only rest—" *fecisti nos ad te, et inquietum est cor nostrum, donec requiescat in te.*"—St. Augustine. O God ! grant us true wisdom ever to keep in view our heavenly inheritance ; never to barter it for any temporal emolument or gratification, whatever. Mary, " gate of heaven," pray for us.

6. " Wherein you shall greatly rejoice." If the word " wherein " be connected with those immediately preceding, " in the last time," then the words, " you shall greatly rejoice," retain their future signification, as in our Vulgate (although in the Greek they are read in the present tense, αγαλλιασθε, *you rejoice*), and mean, that in the last day they will rejoice, although they may have been afflicted with several trials and temptations for a short time in the present life, should it be the will of God to send them. If the word " wherein " refer not to " the last time," but to the preceding benefits (as in Paraphrase), then, the Greek reading is to be strictly adhered to in the present tense ; and the words mean : on account of which hope of future inheritance and salvation prepared for you, you now rejoice in the very midst of the trials which it may fall to your lot to suffer for a short time here below ; for, although the inferior part may feel pain, the spirit will rejoice.

7. " That the trial of your faith," &c. This is connected with the foregoing, " if you must now be made sorrowful," &c. The end of these afflictions is, " that the trial of your faith," whereby is meant their faith, tried and tested by afflictions (" much more precious than gold, which is tried in the fire "), and hence, it is left to be inferred, that it is no wonder, that their faith, also, which is more precious, should be tried in the furnace of tribulation—" may be found unto praise," that is, may be found to eventuate in the praise and commendation, which will be bestowed by God on his faithful servants, " well done, thou good and faithful servant," &c. ; " and glory," the celebrity and good fame consequent on their virtuous actions—and " honour," the exalted dignity which will be conferred on them " at the appearing " (in Greek, αποκαλυψει, *the revelation*), " of Jesus Christ, on the last day, when his glory will be revealed. To the words, " more precious than gold," are added, in the Greek, the words, *which perisheth*. " Glory and honour." This order is sustained

Text.

8. Whom having not seen, you love : in whom also now, though you see him not, you believe : and believing shall rejoice with joy unspeakable and glorified,

9. Receiving the end of your faith even the salvation of your souls.

10. Of which salvation the prophets have inquired and diligently searched, who prophesied of the grace to come in you.

11. Searching what or what

Paraphrase.

8. Whom, although never seen by you who have lived so remote from Judea, you still love, in whom also, although invisible to you, now that he has ascended into heaven, you still believe, and while believing, you enjoy, by anticipation, a foretaste of that inconceivable joy, which is the portion of God's glorified elect in heaven.

9. Receiving as the fruit and end of your faith the salvation of your souls, by grace and justification here, and by glory hereafter.

10. After which salvation, now enjoyed by you, the prophets of old, who had prophesied concerning the gracious benefits to be conferred in time upon you, ardently sighed and inquired, and anxiously examined its nature and multifarious details (Ephes., chap. iii.)

11. Searching and investigating at what particular

Commentary.

by the Alexandrian and Vatican MSS. The ordinary Greek has, " honour and glory."

8. "Whom having not seen," because, when on earth, he had not gone amongst them, who lived so far remote from Judea, and, although some amongst them might have seen him at Jerusalem on the occasion of the great festivals (Acts, ii. 9), still, the greater portion of those, to whom the Apostle writes, had not. For, "seen," the ordinary Greek is, *ειδοτες, known,* but the Vatican MS. has, *ιδοντες.* "You love," as your God and Redeemer. "Though you see him not, you believe ;" the words, "you believe," are not in the Greek. They are implied, however, in the following words, "believing you shall rejoice," &c. For, "you shall rejoice," we have in the Greek, *αγαλλιατε, you rejoice,* in the present tense, "with joy unspeakable," *which neither eye hath seen, nor ear heard,* &c. ; "and glorified," such as is enjoyed by the saints of God in glory. Of course, if the words be read in the present tense, as in the Greek, they mean, as in the Paraphrase, that even now they enjoy a foretaste of the unspeakable and glorified joys of heaven.

9. "Receiving the end of your faith," the end for which faith is given and to which it conducts us. "The salvation of your souls." If the preceding words be read, as in the Greek, then these words regard the present salvation of their souls by grace and justification, which is the seed of future glory. If the Vulgate reading be followed, the words regard the consummate salvation of their souls in glory, which carries with it the glory and salvation of their bodies. The following verses are in favour of the opinion which makes "salvation," immediately and directly refer to salvation by justification and grace in this life.

10. The Apostle shows the exalted nature and great value of the salvation, the faithful now enjoy, which is as a foretaste of future glory, by pointing to the eager longings of the prophets of old after it, and their anxiety to obtain a full knowledge of its nature. By referring to the prophets of old, he also shows that it was not a novel system, but such as the Jews themselves should expect. "Of which salvation," viz., of justification and grace, and the whole economy of redemption. The words are very like the passage (Eph. iii. 5–10, &c.), "have inquired and diligently searched." The prophets of old anxiously inquired and sighed after the accomplishment of redemption. How often, from the gloomy prison of Limbo, did they send forth their sighs and entreaties, "*rorate cæli desuper et nubes pluant justum, aperiatur terra et germinet salvatorem*" (Isaias, xiv. 8), "*Oh, that thou wouldst rend the heavens and wouldst come down*" (Isaias, lxiv.) ; similar is the allusion (Luke, x. 24) : "*Many prophets and kings have desired to see the things that you see, and have not seen them.*" "And searched diligently." The prophets were ignorant of many circumstances of man's redemption, afterwards fully developed, and made known in the Church (Ephes. iii. 5–10).

11. "Searching what, or what manner of time," that is, after how many years, or, at

Text.

manner of time the Spirit of Christ in them did signify; when it foretold those sufferings that are in Christ, and the glories that should follow;

12. To whom it was revealed, that not to themselves but to you they ministered those things which are now declared to you by them that have preached the gospel to you, the Holy Ghost being sent down from heaven on whom the angels desire to look.

Paraphrase.

period, or at what description of times, whether prosperous or otherwise, the Spirit of Christ, or the Holy Ghost, which dwelt in them, would point out, as the term of the accomplishment of these great events, while it inspired them to foretell the sufferings which Christ was to undergo, and the glories which were to be consequent on them.

12. To whom, in remuneration for their anxious search and eager longings, it was revealed, that it was not for themselves, but for you, they were made instrumental in predicting these wonderful mysteries of grace, now clearly announced to you, by those who have preached the gospel to you as already fulfilled, after the Holy Ghost was sent down from heaven to descend upon them, and teach them all truth; upon whom the angels themselves are anxious to gaze, and with mingled feelings of awe and astonishment, to contemplate in him those mysteries of grace, by appropriation, ascribed to him.

Commentary.

what kind of times, whether of national prosperity or adversity, "the spirit of Christ," the Holy Ghost, who proceeds from the Father and Son, "in them," (the Greek has, *which was in them*), "did signify;" or, referred to, when, treating of the accomplishment of this event; "when it foretold," *i.e.*, previously inspired them with a knowledge to foretell. "The sufferings that are in Christ," *i.e.*, the sufferings which Christ was to undergo, "and the glories, which should follow." He says, "glories," owing to the many instances in which Christ, after his passion, received glory, (*v. g.*) in his Resurrection, Ascension, &c. As his glory was consequent on his sufferings, so must we too suffer with Christ, before we can enter with him on his glory.

12. "To whom (the prophets of old) it was revealed, that not to themselves, but to you, they ministered these things;" that it was not to confirm or strengthen their own faith, or that of their contemporaries, but to confirm your faith in after ages (for, the the things that happened in figure, were written for our admonition—1 Cor. x. 6), they were employed in the ministry of predicting beforehand, "those things," those mysteries of redemption and grace, "which are now declared to you," announced to you as already accomplished "by them that preached the gospel to you," by the Apostles, who preached in Pontus, Galatia, &c. "The Holy Ghost being sent down from heaven;" after the Holy Ghost descended upon them from heaven, on the day of Pentecost, teaching them all truth. The ordinary Greek has "*in* the Holy Ghost," but the preposition, *in*, is not found in either the Alexandrian or Vatican MS. "On whom the angels desire to look;"—"on whom" is referred by Venerable Bede, and others, to "Christ," of whom mention is made in the preceding verse. Others refer it to the Holy Ghost, the word immediately preceding. In the Greek, instead of "on whom," we have, εἰς ἅ, *into which*, referring to the mysteries of redemption and grace, which the angels are anxious to examine into most closely, in order to know them fully. And this will have the same signification with chap. iii. 10, Epistle to Ephesians. It will, moreover, contain a further commendation of the exalted benefits, conferred on the faithful, when we know that the angels themselves, with mingled feelings of admiration and awe, are anxious to search narrowly into them. The present Greek reading is preferred by Estius and others. The Greek word for "look," παρακυψαι, which means, *to stoop down*, for the purpose of examining a thing more narrowly, also favours this reading. The meaning will not be very different, even though we adhere to the Vulgate reading, and understand it of the Holy Ghost; for, in him they would see the wonderful mysteries of grace, by appropriation, ascribed to the Third Person of the Adorable Trinity.—A'Lapide. From all this, we, who, as well as the faithful in the time of St. Peter, are sharers in the benefits of redemption, can clearly see the debt of gratitude we owe Almighty God, for having favoured us, in preference to mil-

Text.

13. Wherefore, having the loins of your mind girt up, being sober, trust perfectly in the grace which is offered to you in the revelation of Jesus Christ,

14. As children of obedience, not fashioned according to the former desires of your ignorance :

15. But according to him that hath called you, who is Holy, be you also in all manner of conversation holy :

16. Because it is written: *You shall be holy, for I am holy.*

Paraphrase.

13. Such, therefore, being the exceeding great value of the blessings and inheritance in store for you, you should, by the perfect subjugation of your passions, remove every obstacle to your onward march towards your heavenly country, and with vigilance and sobriety, constantly and perseveringly hope for that grace of perfect happiness, which is to be brought to you at the coming of Jesus Christ to judgment.

14. As obedient children of God, you should also comply with all the precepts of his law, and not live any longer following the dictates of your carnal desires, or in exhibiting this in your external demeanour, as you did heretofore, while you lived in ignorance of Christ.

15. But, following the example of the Holy One, who called you to faith and salvation, be you holy in all the actions of your life.

16. For, it is not a new, but an old precept, that commands you to imitate, as far as the weakness of human nature will permit, the sanctity of God : " *Be you holy,*" &c.—(Leviticus, xi. 44, &c. ; xix. 2 ; xx. 7 ; xxi. 8).

Commentary.

lions of his creatures, upon whom, both in past and present generations, never has beamed a single ray of his revelation. It is the effect of his great mercy, "*secundum magnam misericordiam regeneravit nos.*" "*Misericordias Domini in eternum cantabo.*"

13. The Apostle, in this verse, commences the moral part of the Epistle. "Wherefore," since the inheritance and the blessings reserved for you in heaven, of which you have here a foretaste and sure earnest, are so great, that the prophets sighed after them, and the very angels regard them with astonishment. " Having the loins of your mind girt up." These words contain an allusion to the custom among the ancients of girding their flowing robes, when preparing for any active feat, and "the loins of the mind " are taken metaphorically, to denote the passions of the soul ; hence, the words mean, subjugating all their passions, and removing every obstacle, arising from the concupiscible and irascible appetites, to the onward march towards their heavenly country. " Being sober ;" the Greek word, νηφοντες, means also, *being vigilant*, as in 1 Timothy, iii. 2 ; both meanings are given in the Paraphrase. "Trust perfectly in the grace, &c." " Perfectly" may mean, *perseveringly unto the end*, or, trust with a hope, animated with charity and good works. " In the grace," the perfect salvation of soul and body, " which is offered." The Greek, φερομενην, means, which is *to be brought you* "in the revelation," &c., on the day of general judgment.

14. In order to gain the inheritance, they should not only repress the passions of the soul, but as obedient sons of their Father, who has this inheritance in store for them, they should obey all his precepts, and "not be fashioned." The Greek word, συσχηματιζομενοι, means, *putting on the external form and dress* of a thing ; similar is the idea conveyed (Ephes. iv. 22). Hence, it means here, not to exhibit in their external actions and conduct, the workings of their corrupt passions and carnal desires ; "former," according to which they formerly lived ; "of your ignorance," before they were gifted with the true knowledge of Christ. These latter words apply to the Jewish, as well as to the Gentile converts. Hence, they furnish no argument that this Epistle was addressed principally to the latter.

15. He encourages them to sanctity of life after the example of God, "him that called you, who is Holy." God is such, by his very nature and essence. "In all manner of conversation ;" they should exhibit sanctity of life in all their actions, in all places, and in all circumstances of life.

16. " Because it is written : *you shall be holy,*" &c.—(Leviticus, xi. 44, and xix. and xx.) Hence, the precept of being holy after the example of God—who is holy by essence—as far as our infirmity will permit, is not a new precept, having been enjoined

Text.

17. And if you invoke as Father him who, without respect of persons judgeth according to every one's work : converse in fear during the time of your sojourning here.

18. Knowing that you were not redeemed with corruptible things as gold or silver, from your vain conversation of the tradition of your fathers :

19. But, with the precious blood of Christ, as of a lamb, unspotted and undefiled,

Paraphrase.

17. And although, in your daily prayers, you address God, and invoke him as your Father ; still, you must bear in mind, that he holds in your regard another relation, viz., that of a most just and impartial judge, who judges without favour, or exception of persons, according to every one's works; hence, you should spend the short period of your passing sojourn here below in a reverential awe and fear of offending him.

18. And you can form an idea of the great rigours of his justice, should you not lead holy lives, from the great price paid to ransom you, and to enable you to become saints. For, you have been redeemed, not with corruptible gold or silver—the most valuable of earthly possessions—from the vain and useless ceremonial observances, handed down to you by your fathers ;

19. But, with the precious blood of Christ, of whom the Paschal lamb, which should be free from all spot and defilement, offered up among the Jews, was an exact type and figure.

Commentary.

of old, on the Jewish people. It is promulgated in the New Law, "be you perfect as your heavenly Father," &c.—Matthew, v. 48. The ordinary Greek, instead of, "*you shall be holy*," has, γενεσθε, "*be ye* holy ;" but, the Vulgate is the reading of the chief MSS.

17. Another motive to stimulate them to sanctity of life, "and if you invoke as Father," as you daily do in the Lord's prayer, "*Our Father who art in heaven.*" "Without respect of persons," for the meaning, and application of these words (*see* Rom., ii. 11). "Converse in fear ;" similar is the exhortation (Philip. iv. 12). "During the time of your sojourning here." The word, "sojourning," conveys the idea of strangers or pilgrims travelling through a strange land, and such is truly our condition, while travelling through this vale of tears towards our heavenly country. Hence, though God be a father, whom we should love, he is also a just judge, of whom we should have a reverential fear.

18. "Knowing that you were redeemed," &c. This is an additional motive for sanctity of life. They were "redeemed," and their ransom effected, "not with corruptible gold and silver," which are the most valuable of earthly possessions ; "from your vain conversation of the tradition, &c.," that is, from the observances of the legal and ceremonial law, handed down to them from their fathers, but which were "vain," of no effect, for really cleansing their consciences from sin and justifying them. The legal ceremonies were useless for conferring justice, while the Scribes and Pharisees added many mandates, even opposed to God's law (*v.g.*), the tradition referred to Matthew (xv. 6), about giving to the temple, what was necessary for the support of their parents. The Apostle wishes, in those verses, to show, that as God has so valued our souls, as to give for their ransom the blood of his Son, he will exercise, as a just judge, the utmost rigour, if we undervalue this great gift, and ruin these souls so dearly purchased, by not following a course of sanctity.

19. "But, with the precious blood of Christ ;" it is called "precious," being the blood of God, a person of infinite dignity. "As of a lamb ;" "as," means, that he was like a lamb, both in innocence of life and patience in suffering. "Unspotted and undefiled," is allusive to the Paschal lamb among the Jews, which should be without blemish, (Exodus, xii. 5), and was an exact type of Christ, who was a victim, which was "*holy, innocent, &c.,*" (Hebrews, vii. 26). Can anything give us so exalted an idea of the value of immortal souls in the eyes of God, or stimulate us so strongly to co-operate in their salvation, as these words of the Apostle, "*Redempti pretioso sanguine Christi !*" Woe to us, if either through neglect and indifference in regard to

Text.	**Paraphrase.**
20. Foreknown, indeed, before the foundation of the world, but manifested in the last times for you,	20. Who was predestined from eternity to ransom us; however, it was only in the last stage of the world, upon which you have fallen, that he has been fully manifested, and all the circumstances of redemption fully made known, for your peculiar advantage.
21. Who, through him, are faithful in God, who raised him up from the dead, and hath given him glory, that your faith and hope might be in God.	21. Who. through his grace and merits, have faith in God, who raised him from the dead, and conferred glory on him, that your faith and hope might be firmly founded on God.
22. Purifying your souls in the obedience of charity, with a brotherly love from a sincere heart love one another earnestly :	22. Having, by obedience to the precepts of the law, of which charity is the plenitude, purified your hearts, through the grace of God's holy spirit, love each other ardently and perseveringly, as brothers, with a sincere brotherly love, and from a pure heart.

Commentary.

those under our care, or, through positive scandal, we cause the blood of a God to have flown in vain, for immortal souls! "Better for us that a mill-stone were tied about our neck and we were drowned in the depth of the sea."

20. "Fore-known," that is predestined, "before the foundation." In Greek, προ καταβολης, "*before casting the foundation* of the world," that is to say, from eternity. "But manifested in the last times." Christ made his appearance on this earth, and displayed the mysteries of his redemption, in the last stage of the world; "for you," Jews, to whom the kingdom of God was first announced, or "for you," who live in this last age, who are partakers of redemption, and are in a special manner bound to make a return of love; each one can appreciate to himself the passion of. Christ.—"*dilexit me* et tradidit semetipsum pro *me.*"—(Galatians, ii. 20).

21. "Who, through him," through his grace and merits, "are faithful in God." In the ordinary Greek, *believe in God;* the Vatican MS. supports the Vulgate; from God's grace alone faith can come. "Who raised him from the dead;" the raising of Christ from the dead, although common to the three Persons of the adorable Trinity, being an act of power, is, by appropriation, ascribed to God the Father. "And hath given him glory;" the glory of Christ commenced in his Resurrection, and was continued in his Ascension, in the mission of the Holy Ghost, in the preaching of his gospel, &c., so that he was declared the Lord of angels and of men, of heaven and earth, and received that renown which he had before the world was— (John, xvii. 5). "That your faith" (which would be vain, if Christ had not risen, 1 Cor. xv. 5)— "and hope, might be in God;" for, by rising from the dead, has given us a sure hope and earnest of being one day raised with him, our glorified head, to a glorious and immortal life.

22. From verse 17, to this, may be included in a parenthesis, in which the Apostle turns aside from the moral exhortation commenced verse 13 to enlarge on the blessings of man's redemption, "purifying your souls in the obedience of charity." In the Greek, *in the obedience of truth,* the meaning of which will be, having purified your hearts through faith in God's truths. Similar is the passage (Acts xv.), "*fide purificans corda eorum.*" In the ordinary Greek are added here the words *through the spirit ;* they are not, however, found in our Vulgate, nor in the Vatican MS. "With a brotherly love." In Greek, εις φιλαδελφιαν ανυποκριτον, *unto a brotherly love without hypocrisy.* According to which the meaning would be: having purified your hearts by obedience to faith, through God's spirit, so as to promote and advance a sincere brotherly love. "From a sincere heart." In the ordinary Greek, εκ καθαρας καρδιας, *from a pure heart.* The word "pure" is not found in the Alexandrian or Vatican MMS. From the Greek words above quoted, it is clear, the word "sincere" or *without hypocrisy,* ανυποκριτον, should be joined not with "heart," as in our English version, but with "brotherly love." The meaning of the entire verse comes to this : that having purified their souls and affections, by the observance of the entire law, and having particularly in view to advance in brotherly love, they should continue to entertain

Text.	**Paraphrase.**
23. Being born again, not of corruptible seed, but incorruptible by the word of God who liveth and remaineth for ever.	23. This brotherly love, which you should have for one another, is grounded on the spiritual regeneration you have all received in common ; for, you have been born again, and received a new spiritual existence, not from a principle, or seed of corruption, but from the seed of incorruption, and that is the word of God, who liveth and endureth for ever.
24. For *all flesh is as grass : and all the glory thereof as the flower of grass. The grass is withered and the flower thereof is fallen away.*	24. In your *first* birth, you were begotten of a corruptible seed ; for, according to the prophet Isaias, (chap. xl. 6), every man is as frail and corruptible as grass, and all his glory as transient and fleeting as the flower of grass; the grass withers and its flower falls away. Hence, as man viewed according to his earthly origin, with all his glory passes away, the seed from which he springs must be corruptible.
25. But the word of the Lord	25. But the seed from which you derive your *second*

Commentary.

a pure and ardent love for one another. Alas! where is there any other precept of our blessed Redeemer so shamefully violated as this peculiar one, which he emphatically calls his own—" This is *my* precept, that you love one another " ?

23. " Being born again not of corruptible seed." In these words, he shows the chief grounds on which their pure and persevering brotherly love is founded. They are brethren, by a new spiritual generation, having received a new essence and existence, not from any human principle or corruptible seed (*qui non ex sanguinibus, neque ex voluntate carnis, neque ex voluntate viri*—John, i.), " but from an incorruptible seed "— (*Sed ex Deo nati sunt*), this seed is " the word of the living and ever enduring God." What is meant by this "word" is a matter of dispute with Commentators ; some understanding by it, the word of revelation, the gospel preached to them ; or, rather, the faith and preventing graces of God, consequent on hearing the preaching of the gospel. All these dispositions of faith, joined with hope and penance, being placed in the soul, serving as the seed of the new life, God infuses sanctifying grace, and thereby bestows a new spiritual existence of which the word of God was the seed. Others understand by it the form of the sacrament of Baptism—" *I baptize thee in the name of the Father, &c.*"—which, being added to the matter or element, constitutes the sacrament of regeneration, *accedit verbum ad elementum et fit sacramentum*—St. Augustine. The former opinion, referring it to the word of revelation, which is the seed of faith, and the other dispositions, that precede the infusion of sanctifying grace, appears the more probable.

" The word of God who liveth and remaineth for ever," may be also rendered from the Greek, λογου ζωντος Θεου και μενοντος, *which* (word) *liveth and remaineth for ever.* The latter signification is, however, included in the former ; for, if God remains for ever, so shall his word, which is his seed.

24. He proves the first part of the assertion implied in verse 23, that in their *first*, or carnal birth, they were born of a corruptible seed ("being born *again* not of corruptible seed.") This he shows from the prophet Isaias (chap. xl. 6), " *all flesh is as grass ;*" by "*flesh*" is meant human nature, or, man viewed according to his earthly or carnal generation ; then, every man, viewed in this respect, is as frail and corruptible "*as grass,*" and, consequently, the seed from which he was begotten, or, the principle of his human generation, was corruptible. " *And all the glory thereof as the flower of grass,*" that is, all the celebrity, fame, and honours, which dazzle and attract the eyes of men, are as nought, passing away, like smoke and vapour. " *The grass is withered and the flower thereof,*" its frailest part, thus, an apt image of all earthly and human grandeur, " *is fallen away.*" Oh ! what an idea is here conveyed to us of the uncertainty and instability of all human honours and enjoyment. They are likened by the Spirit of God to " *the flower of the grass,*" the frailest thing that exists—" *homo, sicut fœnum dies ejus, sicut flos agri sic efflorebit, tanquam spiritus transibit in illo et non subsistet, et non cognoscet amplius locum suum.*"—(Psalm cii. 15).

25. From the same passage of Isaias, he proves, that the seed from which we have

Text.

endureth for ever, and this is the word which by the gospel hath been preached unto you.

Paraphrase.

generation is incorruptible ; for, according to the same prophet, "the word of the Lord remains for ever." Now, the word referred to by Isaias, is the same that was preached to you, and the same that has been the seed of your spiritual regeneration.

Commentary.

derived our *second*, or spiritual generation, is incorruptible ; for, in Isaias it is said "that the word of the Lord endureth for ever."—(Chap. xl. 8). Now, the word which, according to Isaias, endureth fer ever, is that, "which by the gospel has been preached to you ;" and this same is the word or seed of which you have been spiritually begotten, and have derived your new spiritual existence by sanctifying grace. The "word," of which we are spiritually begotten, most likely refers to the word of God's revelation, from which we conceive faith—the first grace in the order of justification, and the first of the dispositions consequent on which, as a seed, God infuses the form of a new spiritual existence, viz., sanctifying grace. The conclusion which the Apostle wishes us to draw from this incorruptibility of the principle of our new birth is, that our charity and love for our brethren (verse 22) should correspond with the qualities of this principle, that it should be constant, enduring, persevering, pure, and holy.

CHAPTER II.

Analysis.

In this chapter, the Apostle, alluding to the spiritual regeneration (1–23), by which the faithful contracted towards one another the relation of spiritual brotherhood, calls upon them to lay aside the vices opposed to the exercise of fraternal charity (1), and as they had lately received a new spiritual existence, to continue to covet the milk of the divine word (2), the sweets of which they already experienced (3).

He, in the next place, views them under a different respect, as living stones of the spiritual edifice, of which Christ was the chief corner-stone ; and that he was the corner-stone of his Church, the Apostle proves from Isaias (4–7). He shows, that while to the believers Christ is a source of glory and honour, by their incorporation with him, to the unbelievers, he is the occasion of ruin (7, 8).

He applies to the Christian converts, the exalted titles bestowed by God on his chosen people of old (9), and shows the magnitude of the blessings bestowed on them, by contrasting their present benefits, with their former deplorable condition (10). He encourages them to subdue their passions, and to edify, by their good works, the unconverted Gentiles (11, 12).

He inculcates the duty of subjection to temporal rulers, whether exercising supreme or subordinate authority, as both derive it from God (13, 14), and he enjoins this duty on the ground, that God wills it so. He also tells them not to make the liberty, into which Christ asserted them, the pretext of insubordination, and of unrestrained licentiousness, (15, 16).

He, then, descending to domestic obedience, enjoins on servants, the duty of obedience to their masters, even to such as are unkind (11). He encourages them, to suffer wrongs patiently after the example of Christ, he shows the great merit of such patience (19–24), and points out the great blessing of redemption through Christ (25).

Text.

1. WHEREFORE laying away all malice, and all guile, and dissimulations and envies and all detractions.

Paraphrase.

1. As, then, you have received a new spiritual regeneration (i. 23), having divested yourselves of the vices and evil inclinations, opposed to fraternal charity, that is to say, the deliberate desire of injuring one another, every deceitful design of inflicting on your neighbour a private injury, all feelings of dissimulation and hypocrisy, all feelings of envy at our neighbour's prosperity, all attempts at slandering his reputation.

Commentary.

1. "Wherefore," has reference to chap. i. 23, where it is said, the converted Jews and Gentiles received a new spiritual birth, whereby they contracted the relation of a spiritual brotherhood towards each other. The Apostle now exhorts them to lay aside the vices and wicked passions, opposed to the exercise of fraternal charity.

" Laying away ;" these words probably contain an allusion to their laying aside their clothes at baptism, which was an emblem of their putting away the sinfulness of their corrupt nature.

Text.

2. As new born babes, desire the rational milk without guile, that whereby you may grow unto salvation.

3. If so be you have tasted that the Lord is sweet.

4. Unto whom coming, as to a

Paraphrase.

2. Like newly born babes, on whom has been lately conferred the new birth of grace, eagerly long for, and imbibe the spiritual and intellectual milk of divine truth, free from every corrupt admixture of error, so that it may strengthen and nourish you, until you shall have arrived at the full vigour and maturity of spiritual manhood, in the life to come.

3. Continue to imbibe this spiritual milk, since, indeed, you have already tasted in baptism the sweetness of those graces and consolations, which the Lord Jesus has benignly bestowed upon you.

4. Unto whom approaching by a conformity of life,

Commentary.

"Guile," a deceitful design of circumventing and injuring our neighbour. "Dissimulations," showing in our actions, the opposite feelings of those which we actually entertain. The vices here enumerated are quite opposed to the simplicity of that spiritual infancy, upon which they have just entered.

2. "As new born babes," *i.e.*, as persons, who have just received the spiritual life of grace, "desire the rational milk." By "milk," is commonly understood the doctrine of Christ whether it regard faith or moral duties, and this he calls "rational," that is, *spiritual* or *intellectual*, to show that he is not referring to material milk. The word "rational," (in Greek, το λογικον), is employed in this sense by St. Paul (Rom. xii.), "*rationabile obsequium vestrum*," which the Greek, αἐολον γάλα, shows to be connected with the word "milk." It is also termed "without guile," unadulterated by the admixture of false and erroneous doctrine. The Jewish converts, in particular, were anxious to add to the Gospel truth certain false tenets respecting the necessity of the ceremonial law of Moses. "That thereby you may grow unto salvation," that, owing to the vigour imparted to you by this spiritual milk of God's holy word, you may arrive at the consummation of spiritual manhood, which is accomplished in the life to come.

QUERY.—How reconcile this with St. Paul (1 Epistle to Cor. chap. iii.), where he says that not milk but solid food is the nourishment of those who are well instructed in the faith?

ANSWER.—There is no opposition between both Apostles. The word "milk," in this passage, is contrasted with their former carnal mode of living, and not with the solid food, referred to by St. Paul. It may be, also, said in reply, that, during our term here below, we are in a kind of spiritual infancy; in a certain sense, all the doctrines of Christ are milk, accommodated to our present condition, contrasted with the life to come. The words, "unto salvation," are wanting in many Greek copies. They are, however, admitted to be genuine by critics, on the authority of the chief manuscripts.

3. "If so be you have tasted," &c. The word "*if*" may be taken conditionally, thus: If, however, you have tasted, &c. (as I know you have). It is better, however, understand it to mean, *since*, a meaning warranted by the Greek, εἰπερ, as if he said, since, indeed, you have tasted, how sweet the Lord is. In the Vatican MS it is εἰ not, εἰπερ. The Apostle here alludes to Psalm xxxiii. : "*gustate et videte, quoniam suavis est Dominus.*" For "sweet," the Hebrew word in the Psalm is, *good*, and in the Greek, as here, *benign*, χρηστος. By some, this verse is understood of the participation of the Holy Eucharist, which in the early ages was received after baptism. The words are employed by the Apostle to imply, that as children, after tasting of their mother's milk, become fonder of it, so ought the Christian converts desire more and more, that wholesome milk of God's holy word, the sweets and consolations of which they have already experienced.

4. After having regarded the Christian converts under the relation of spiritual children, who should continue to partake, during life, of the pure and nutritious food of Christian doctrine, the Apostle views them under a different respect viz., as living stones of the spiritual edifice of the Church, the great foundation and corner-stone of which was

Text.	Paraphrase.
living stone, rejected indeed by men, but chosen and made honourable by God :	as unto a living stone, whereon is built the sacred edifice of the Church, and whereby is also communicated a spiritual life to the parts that form the superstructure ; a stone, rejected as valueless, by men ; but, chosen by God as the foundation of his Church, and honoured by him in his Resurrection, Ascension, and the other mysteries of his glory.
5. Be you also as living stones built up, a spiritual house, a holy priesthood, to offer up spiritual sacrifices acceptable to God by JESUS CHRIST.	5. You, also, as living stones, to whom he imparted the life of grace, are built up to form the spiritual edifice of his Church. You are, likewise, in a certain sense, an assemblage of holy priests ; inasmuch, as you are constituted to offer up the spiritual sacrifices of good works, rendered acceptable to God through the merits of Jesus Christ.

Commentary.

Christ. He it is, that continually imparts life and animation to the different parts of this spiritual edifice ; and they should continue to approach him by good works and charity, after having been incorporated with him in baptism. " Unto whom coming," by good works and charity, " as to a living stone "—"*living,*" because he imparts life to all the other parts of the spiritual edifice. These words, "living stone," show that the Apostle is here employing metaphorical language—"rejected by men,"—"*his own received him not.*"—(John i. 11). They would not have "*this man to reign over them.*" (Luke xix. 14). There is an allusion in the Text to (Psalm cxvii. 22), "*the stone which the builders rejected,*" &c. "But chosen by God," as select and excellent, to become the foundation of his Church, "and honourable by God." Honoured in his Resurrection, Ascension, in the glorious and adorable name of Jesus, &c. The Apostle, addressing the Jewish Christians, borrows his images from the temple and its service ; hence, he represents Christ as the corner-stone of the edifice, and the faithful were to lead the life of grace, as its living, component parts.

5. "Be you also as living stones ;" "living," through the life of grace, which Christ has imparted to you ; the word "living" is also employed to show more clearly the metaphor, and to admonish them to promote, by good works, the advancement of the mystic edifice. "Be you built up ;" the Greek word, οικοδομεισθε, admits of being rendered in the indicative mood also, *you are built up :* and, this latter is the more probable construction ; for the Apostle, has principally in view here, to point out the dignity to which Christians are raised by their connection with Christ ; "a spiritual house," the faithful are built up, and from the superstructure of the spiritual and mystical edifice of the Church.

OBJECTION.—Is not the Church, then, invisible ?

ANSWER.—By no means. The word "spiritual," is not opposed to *visible,* but to a *material* house, such as the temple of Solomon. Hence, it means mystical, as typified in the Old Testament, by the material temple of Solomon and the Tabernacle ; but, this, by no means, implies, that the thing typified is invisible ; for, the men who constitute the living stones of this edifice surely are visible, and so must the house which they compose. "A holy priesthood."

OBJECTION.—Is not the Christian, therefore, a priestly state, and are not all Christians priests ?

ANSWER.—By no means. It is clear that the words are taken metaphorically, for the entire passage is nothing more than a series of metaphors, contained in the words, "infants," "milk," "living stone," "living stones," "spiritual house ;" hence, the words mean, you are a collection of priests in a general, figurative sense, inasmuch as you are constituted to offer up "spiritual sacrifices," that is, good works, called "sacrifices" in a general sense, as offered to the Supreme Being, and "spiritual," as opposed to the offerings of bulls and goats, presented by the Jews. "Acceptable to God by Jesus Christ," since it is in consideration of the merits of Christ applied to them, that our works are acceptable with God. From the entire context, it is quite evident, that the word " priesthood " is taken metaphorically, as are the functions of

Text.

6. Wherefore it is said in the Scripture : *Behold I lay in Sion a chief corner-stone, elect, precious. And he that shall believe in him, shall not be confounded.*

7. To you, therefore, that believe, he is honour ; but to them

Paraphrase.

6. It is to point out to us, that Christ is the living foundation of his Church, that the following words are contained in the sacred Scripture (Isaias, xxviii.) : Behold I place in Sion—in which was contained the palace of David, and, was a type of the Church, wherein Christ reigns—a chief corner-stone, whereby the entire edifice is bound together, propped up and supported ; chosen for this, in preference to every other, and "precious," owing to the infinite dignity of his person, in which are united the divine and human natures. Whosoever shall believe, and place his trust in him, will not be confounded in his expectation.

7. To you, therefore, that believe in him, will belong the special privileges of not being confounded in

Commentary.

these priests, consisting in offering to God spiritual sacrifices, since a *sacrifice*, properly so called, must always contain an external object, &c. But, what puts the matter beyond all doubt, is the expression in verse 9, "a kingly priesthood." These words refer to the same priesthood, of which mention is made here, "a holy priesthood." Now, in verse, 9, the word "priesthood" is used figuratively ; for it is one of the glorious titles which God confers on his chosen people, the Jews, whom he calls "a priestly kingdom" (Exodus, xix. 6) ; and this glorious title, St. Peter here tells us, is typically verified in the Christian Church. Now, will any one say, that all the Jews were priests in the strict sense of the word ? If so, why confine the priesthood to the tribe of Levi and family of Aaron ? Why should Core, Dathan, and Abiron, be punished for attempting to discharge the priestly functions ? The word, then, is taken figuratively in its typical meaning, when referred to carnal Israel (Exodus, xix.), as it is also in its typified application to the spiritual Israel of the Christian Church in this passage. Moreover, the word "priests" is to be applied in the same sense to Christians, as the word "kingdom," that is to say, *kings* (Apocalypse, i. 6), where there is question of all Christians, and, where it is manifest the word must be employed figuratively. Should, however, any one insist in giving the word its literal meaning, then it is to be confined to such as God has called in his Church to the office of priests, as he called Aaron.

6. "Wherefore, it is said in the Scripture." In Greek, περιεχει εν γραφη, "*is it contained in Scripture.*"—(Isaias, xxviii. 16). The Apostle quotes the passage, with some transposition of the words. He expresses the sense, however, both of the Hebrew and Septuagint. He proves, from the prophet, that Christ was made the living foundation of his Church. "*Behold I will place in (Mount) Sion*"—a type of the Christian Church—"*a chief corner stone,*" because, he supports the edifice ; and, by a Hebrew idiom, the *rulers* and *governors* are called the corners or angles of the people, as being their chief props of support.—(Judges, xxi. 1 ; 1 Kings, xiv. ; Isaias, xix.) Christ might be called the "*corner-stone,*" because he connects and unites in one, the two walls of Jews and Gentiles (Ephes. ii. 14–21) ; "*elect,*" for, in no other name can salvation be found ; "*and precious,*" and most highly honoured, since, "in His name every knee in heaven, &c., must bow." (Philip, ii. 10). "*And he that shall believe in him shall not be confounded.*" The Apostle quotes from the Septuagint version. In the Hebrew, instead of "*shall not be confounded,*" we have "*let him not hasten.*" The sense, however, is the same, for, the word "*hasten,*" expresses the hurry and trepidation, consequent on confusion or disappointment in one's expectation ; hence, the words mean, he need not be in that hurried anxiety into which those are thrown, who dread disappointment in any important concern (*see* Rom. ix. 33).

7. "To you, therefore, that believe, he is honour." The word "honour" may refer either to the last part of the preceding verse, "*shall not be confounded,*" or, to "*precious,*" that is, honourable. This "*corner-stone*" is honourable and precious. To you, therefore, who as living stones, are constructed as a part of the spiritual edifice on him, and incorporated with Him, shall be given a share in the honour and preciousness, which belongs to him.—(*See* Paraphrase). The Apostle wishes to show the glory of the

Text.

that believe not, *the stone which the builders rejected, the same is made the head of the corner:*

8. And a stone of stumbling, and a rock of scandal, to them who stumble at the word, neither do believe whereunto also they are set.

9. But you are a chosen generation, a kingly priesthood, a holy nation, a purchased people; that you may declare his virtues, who hath called you out of darkness, into his marvellous light,

Paraphrase.

your hopes; or, to you, who by faith are incorporated with him, will belong, a share and participation in the honour conferred on him; but to those who refuse to believe in him, this same stone, which the builders rejected, shall, in despite of their efforts and machinations against him, become "*the head of the corner*," by being vested with supreme, legal, and judicial authority, so as to punish and destroy them.

8. And he shall become a stone of offence, which shall cause them to fall, and a rock of scandal, against which they shall be dashed, who stumble against his word, and refuse to obey; into this blindness and incredulity, they are permitted by God to fall, in punishment of their sins, and their resistance to divine grace.

9. But you are, in a still more exalted sense than were the Jewish people of old, a chosen generation, peculiarly selected by God as his chosen people—a kingly priesthood, in whom are united the exalted dignities of kings and priests at the same time—a holy nation called to interior sanctity, and rendered such, by the plentiful effusion of heavenly and sanctifying grace—a purchased people, whom your Lord has rescued and redeemed by the effusion of his blood, and asserted into liberty, thereby making you his own peculiar possession, in order that you may announce, and loudly proclaim the wonderful attributes and perfections of him who called you forth from the darkness of vice and ignorance, in which you were involved, into the light of faith, which reveals to you the admirable truths and mysteries of his gospel.

Commentary.

believers, and the greatness of the benefits conferred on them, by being incorporated with Christ, and this he does the more clearly, by contrasting their advantages with the evils, in which the unbelievers are involved." But to them, that believe not;" "*the stone which the builders rejected ;*" by "*builders*" are meant the Scribes and Pharisees, who under pretext of zeal for their religion, rejected Christ, and persecuted him unto death, this stone is "*made for them, the head of the corner*," that is, He who is represented by this stone, is vested with supreme authority, to punish and destroy them. The words are taken from Psalm cxvii. 21.

8. In the first words of this verse, there is an allusion to Isaias (viii. 14). The words "stone of stumbling, and rock of scandal," probably mean the same thing, which is repeated, for the sake of emphasis, in two different forms of expression ; "who stumble at the word," that is, who make it the occasion of sin and unbelief; "neither do believe," they stumble against his word, by their positive incredulity and unbelief. "Whereunto also they are set." Some Commentators understand these words to mean, that they were set, and appointed by God to believe this word, which, through incredulity, they rejected. Looking, however, to the construction in the Greek, where, for "neither do believe," we have but one word, απειθουντες, *disbelieving ;* the most probable construction seems to be that given in the Paraphrase. "Whereunto," *i.e.*, into which unbelief they are permitted by God to fall in punishment of their sins. There is nothing in this, which is not perfectly warranted by the sacred Scripture. "God *delivered* them up to a reprobate sense."—(Rom. i. 28 ; 1 Thessal. ; 2 Thessal. ii. 10). On which passages, (*see* Commentary.)

9. The Apostle now reckons up the glorious titles and prerogatives conferred by God on the faithful. These several titles were originally bestowed on his chosen people, the Jews, but, as "all things happened unto them in figure" (Cor. x.), hence,

Text.

10. *Who in time past were not a people: but are now the people of God. Who had not obtained mercy; but now have obtained mercy.*

Paraphrase.

10. You can estimate the magnitude of God's favors to you, by considering your former wretched condition, and comparing it with the present. You, who were not his people, while following the bent of your passions, are now become the people of God, by the obedience of faith and love, and you who had not obtained mercy, while involved in the darkness of ignorance and servitude of sin, have now obtained mercy, by being called to the bosom of his Church.

Commentary.

the Apostle applies, in a still more exalted sense, the same glorious titles to spiritual Israel, the children of the promise called in Isaac. "You are a chosen generation," which according to some, is taken from Isaias (xliii. 20), "my people, my chosen," also from Deuteronomy (chap. iv., viii., x., xiv.), and elsewhere; "a kingly priesthood," from Exodus (xix. 6), where it is written, "a priestly kingdom." The Apostle, however, here quotes, according to the Septuagint version. The words mean that they are priests and kings at the same time. This meaning is also conveyed (Apocalypse, i. 6). Hence, it appears, that as the word "kings" is employed figuratively, so is the word *priesthood*, or *priests*, in like manner.

"A holy nation," from Deuteronomy (vii. 6), "because thou art a holy people to the Lord thy God." Also (Exodus, xix. 6). They are called a "holy nation" in the same sense, in which the Church is termed *holy*, viz., in her doctrine, sacraments, founder, and many members, in the abundant means of sanctity, and the plentiful effusion of sanctifying grace; all Christians are called to the state and practice of sanctity; "a purchased people," that is, a people asserted into liberty, and fully ransomed, so as to become peculiarly his (Exodus, xix. 6), "*you shall be my peculiar possession above all people;*" also, Deuteronomy (vii. 6). "That you may declare his virtues;" by "virtues," as appears from the Greek, ταϛ αρετας, are meant, his attributes and perfections, his power, his goodness, mercy, &c. There is allusion made to the canticle, which the Jewish people sang, proclaiming God's perfections after their deliverance from the Egyptian bondage, when they crossed the Red Sea. "Who hath called you out of darkness," that is, the darkness of sin and ignorance, in which the Jews, as well as the Gentiles, were involved (Isaias, lx.), "*surge, illuminare Jerusalem*" (Matthew, iv.), "*populus qui sedebat in tenebris, vidit lucem magnam.*" "Into his marvellous light," the light of faith, which proposed to their view, the marvellous mysteries of God's designs upon man, and the whole economy of man's redemption.

10. The Apostle places in a clear light the magnitude of God's benefits towards them, by reminding them of their former wretched condition—"*Who in time past, were not a people,*" &c. This quotation is taken from the Prophet Osee (chap. ii. 23, 24), and it is quoted by St. Paul (ix. *ad Rom.*) to prove the vocation of the Gentiles to the faith. This, he shows, by taking the text in its *mystical* sense; for, in its *literal* signification, it refers to the deliverance of the Jews from the kings of Syria, after they turned aside, to the worship of the false gods. From this passage, some Expositors derive an argument in favour of the opinion, that this Epistle was addressed to the Gentile converts. All, however, that would follow at most from this and other such passages is, that the Epistle was addressed to Jews and Gentiles indiscriminately, and that some parts of it primarily regard the Gentile converts; and others, the Jews. Nor, would that necessarily follow, because, passages, like that from Osee might refer to both Jews and Gentiles; to the former, in its *literal*, and to the latter, in its *mystical* sense, and St. Peter here applies it in a far more exalted meaning to the Jews, to whom it was originally addressed. (In v. 12. He addresses the Jews directly.) This is the opinion of St. Jerome on Osee, or, we might say, that "the children of Juda, and the children of Israel, who were to be gathered together," (Osee, i. 11), represented, respectively—the former, the Jewish converts; the latter, the Gentiles; and that the text here taken from Osee (ii. 23), includes both; St. Paul applies it to the Gentiles, and St. Peter here applies it to the Jews converted to the faith. Hence, no proof that this Epistle was addressed to the Gentile converts.

Text.

11. Dearly beloved, I beseech you as strangers and pilgrims, to refrain yourselves from carnal desires which war against the soul,

12. Having your conversation good among the Gentiles ; that whereas they speak against you as evil doers, they may by the good works which they shall behold in you, glorify God in the day of visitation.

13. Be ye subject therefore to every human creature for God's sake : whether it be to the king as excelling :

Paraphrase.

11. Dearly beloved, I earnestly exhort and implore of you, as strangers here below, and pilgrims travelling on through this vale of tears towards your heavenly country, to refrain from, and have no communication with, these carnal desires so much valued by this world, and which war against the soul, and ruin its eternal interests.

12. Leading an edifying and praiseworthy life, among the unconverted Gentiles, so that instead of reproaching you, and speaking against you as malefactors, as they do at present, they may, upon a closer inspection of your good works, give glory to God in the day on which he may be pleased to visit them in his mercy, and give them his grace and faith.

13. Be subject, therefore, and obedient to every human being, whether Jew or Gentile, faithful or unbeliever, placed in authority over you, for the sake of God whom they represent, and by whose ordinance they rule, whether to the king or emperor, as exercising supreme *temporal* authority in the state.

Commentary.

11. "I beseech you," may also bear, as appears from the Greek, παρακαλω, the signification of, *I exhort you*, as "strangers and pilgrims." Reference is made to the condition of Christians here below, whose country is heaven, and who are here living in a foreign land. The idea may have been suggested by the condition of the Jews scattered in foreign regions, far away from Judea. "To refrain yourselves from carnal desires." As travellers should not busy themselves with the concerns of the countries through which they pass, so neither should Christians, travelling on through this strange land, towards their heavenly country, take any part in these carnal, noxious desires of pleasures, honours, and riches, so much prized by this world. "Which war against the soul ;" these desires, if indulged into an illicit extent, and for bad ends, ruin the life of the soul, and involve it in spiritual and eternal death.

12. "Having your conversation," that is, the whole course of your conduct and actions, "good," or praiseworthy and edifying. "Among the Gentiles," the unconverted Gentiles, among whom they live in Pontus, Galatia, &c. "That whereas they speak of you as evil doers." The Greek for "whereas," ἐν ᾧ, means, *instead of*. "Speaking ill of you as evil doers," probably refers to the charges of infanticide and other obscenities, which the early Christians were accused of having committed at their meetings by the Pagans. This we learn from St. Justin Martyr, Eusebius (*libro* 5, *Hist. Eccles.* 1). The frightful crimes committed by the Gnostic heretics, in their conventicles, might have given some grounds for charging Christians in general with the perpetration of impure actions at their meetings (Epiphanius *in Heresi Gnosticorum*). The principal accusation, however, to which St. Peter here refers, would appear to be, as the context warrants us in thinking, that of refusing to obey the temporal magistrates and governors. "In the day of visitation," most probably regards the gracious visitation of God, when he will visit them in his mercy, and call them to his holy faith.

13. It appears that at this time the Jews were imbued with a spirit of disaffection towards the Roman emperors, as we learn from Josephus and Suetonius ; they considered it degrading to the chosen people of God, the descendants of Abraham, to whom were made so many and such magnificent promises, to obey or pay tribute to foreigners and unbelievers. This spirit they carried with them into the very bosom of Christianity. The foolish rebellion of Judas of Galilee (Acts, v. 37), would serve to fasten more closely this imputation of insubordination, so injurious to the spread of the Gospel, on the Christians, whose teachers were Galileans. Hence, the zeal displayed by St. Peter and by St. Paul (Rom. xiii., and Titus, iii.) in instructing the Christians of their own day, and at all future times, regarding their obligations in this respect. "Be ye subject, therefore, to every human creature." The word

Text.

14. Or to governors as sent by him for the punishment of evil doers, and for the praise of the good:

15. For so is the will of God, that by doing well you may put to silence the ignorance of foolish men:

16. As free, and not as making liberty a cloak for malice, but as the servants of God.

Paraphrase.

14. Or to governors or other inferior magistrates as sent by the same God, for the purpose of upholding order, by rewarding those who do good, and punishing such as do evil.

15. For the will of God is this, that by your good actions you close, or rather muzzle, the mouths of foolish, ignorant men, who wrongfully bring charges against our holy religion, of the teachings and principles of which they are utterly ignorant.

16. (Be subject to every human being placed in authority over you—verse 13—from a free spirit of generosity, and a love of justice), and make not the liberty into which Christ asserted you the pretext for insubordination and other wicked deeds, but serve temporal rulers, as if you were serving God himself, from whom they derive their power.

Commentary.

"therefore" shows that the chief point in which they were reproached, "as evil doers" (verse 12), was on the subject of insubordination and disaffection towards temporal authority. " For God's sake." In Greek, δια τον κυριον, *for the Lord's sake.* "Whether to the king." The word "king" refers to the Roman emperor, called by the Greeks, βασιλευς, or *king.* Claudius, or according to others, Nero, was the reigning emperor at this time. " As excelling," *i.e.*, exercising *supreme secular* authority ; for, the state, or secular authority is *supreme* in its own sphere, that is to say, in regard to merely *temporal* matters, or *temporal* government ; and the Church is, by divine appointment *supreme*, in its own sphere also, in regard to all that spiritual and ecclesiastical government involves. It is of faith that *spiritual* authority, which resides in the Church, comes *immediately* from God. *Secular* authority also comes from him ; " for, there is no power but from God " (Rom. xiii. 1) ; but in what sense these words, as far as they regard *secular* authority are to be understood, that is to say, in what way *secular* authority comes from God whether *mediately* or *immediately*, is still an open question very much disputed. Some maintain that secular authority comes, *immediately*, from God. Others maintain, that it comes only, *mediately*, from him ; that by him it has been placed, as a deposit, in the hands of the community ; and by them transmitted to the objects of their choice, be the form of government instituted by them what it may, whether *kingly, republican, &c.* This seems a very probable opinion (*see* Rom. xiii. 2). Others maintain, that the election of the people does not immediately confer power—that it is a mere necessary condition, consequent on which, God himself *immediately*, confers power on the object of the people's choice. This also seems a very probable opinion (*see* Epistle to Titus, iii. 1).

14. " Or to governors as sent by him." Under the word "governors " are included all those in a subordinate capacity, entrusted with authority ; " as sent by him ; " by God. The opinion referring " him " to God, is preferred by Estius ; because, he says, the Roman emperors did not always send out governors. This was often done by the senate. Again, they did not always send them for the object here specified, viz., " for the punishment of evil doers," &c. Others understand the words to mean, " as sent " by the emperor or king ; for, he ordinarily did so, and the general end for which they were and should be sent was, for the punishment of those who did ill, and the praise or reward of such as acted well. Similar are the words (Romans, xiii.)—" for he is God's minister to thee for good ; he is God's minister, an avenger to execute wrath upon him that doeth evil." For the nature and extent of the duty of obedience, (*see* Commentary on chapter xiii. to the Romans.)

15. " For so is the will of God." These words, as appears from the Greek, refer not to the preceding, but the following. " That by doing well, you may put to silence." The Greek word for " put to silence," φιμουν, means, *to muzzle.* " The ignorance of foolish men," who attempt to revile a religion, of which they are wholly ignorant. The " doing well," regards good works in general, but especially subordination to temporal authority.

16. " As free." These words, as appears from the Greek, ως ελευθεροι, are to be

Text.

17. Honour all men. Love the brotherhood. Fear God. Honour the king.

18. Servants be subject to your masters with all fear, not only to the good and gentle, but also to the froward.

19. For this is thanksworthy, if for conscience towards God, a man endure sorrows, suffering wrongfully.

20. For what glory is it, if com-

Paraphrase.

17. Treat all men with the honour and respect due to them; but in a special manner, cherish and love the brethren of the faith. As a safe check against carrying your obedience too far, so as to extend to things evil as well as good, have a filial fear of God; and hold in special honour the supreme ruler on earth, the king or emperor.

18. Servants, be subject to your masters with great reverence and respect; not only to such as are kind and gentle, but also to such are froward and morose.

19. For, this is the work of God's grace, exceedingly pleasing to him; if from a consciousness of God's will and pleasure that he should do so, or from a pure motive of religion, a person submit to troubles and sorrows, and suffer unjustly.

20. I say, suffer *unjustly;* for, what subject for

Commentary.

connected with verse 13, and not with "doing well," αγαθοποιουντας, which is in a different case (verse 14). "And not as making liberty," the liberty into which Christ asserted you by his grace; a liberty and freedom from the dominion of sin and of the passions; "a cloak for malice," a pretext for insubordination and other crimes. It appears that the Gnostics, Nicholaites, and other heretics in the Apostolic age construed the liberty into which Christ asserted them, as implying a total independence of all temporal authority, and even a freedom from moral restraint. Hence, they thought themselves justified in indulging in the most unbounded licentiousness. This is what the Apostle here alludes to in saying, "not making liberty a cloak for malice," *i.e.,* licentiousness of all sorts. "But as the servants of God," serving our temporal rulers in all things lawful, as if we were serving God, whose vicegerents they are, and from whom they hold the reigns of government.

17. "Honour all men, *i.e.,* pay all men the degree of honour and respect due to each one. Similar is the injunction (Rom. xiii.), "honour to whom honour." "Love the brotherhood." The members of the household of the faith should be, in a special manner, the objects of our affection. "We should do good to all, but especially to those who are of the household of the faith."—(Gal. v. 10). "Fear God" with a reverential fear, which should serve as a check upon us against carrying our compliance with the mandates of authority too far, to evil and unlawful things, as well as to the lawful subjects of obedience. "Honour the king," is probably added, because the reigning prince, whether Claudius or Nero, were not the most deserving objects of respect or reverence.

18. The Apostle passes from inculcating obedience to public authority, to treat of domestic obedience, which servants and slaves owe their masters. It appears that, on this subject also, false notions were afloat, and that many were of opinion, that the duties of servitude were inconsistent with the liberty of the gospel, and that slaves, after their conversion, were exempted from obedience to their temporal masters. One of the charges against Christianity was, that it subverted the relations between masters and slaves. "Servants." The Greek word, οἱ οικεται, means, *domestics.* The word, *slaves,* might be offensive to the Jews, whom St. Peter addresses. "With all fear," that is, great reverence and respect. "To the froward," such as may be rough and unkind in their treatment of them.

19. "Thanksworthy," χαρις, *grace,* that is the effect of God's grace, or a thing exceedingly pleasing to him. "If for conscience towards God," that is, from a conscientious knowledge that God wills it so; in other words, from pure religious motives, "a man endure sorrows," anguish of mind, and miseries. "Suffering wrongfully," suffering unmerited punishment.

20. "For what glory is it, if committing sin and being buffeted." The word "buffeted" expresses the contumelious treatment of offending slaves—"you endure?" The Apostle does not deny that a man may have glory and merit, even while suffering

Text.

mitting sin and being buffeted *for it* you endure? But if doing well you suffer patiently, this is thanksworthy before God.

21. For unto this are you called: because Christ also suffered for us, leaving you an example that you should follow his steps.

22. *Who did no sin, neither was guile found in his mouth.*

23. Who, when he was reviled, did not revile: when he suffered, he threatened not: but delivered himself to him that judged him unjustly.

24. Who his ownself bore our sins in his body upon the tree: that

Paraphrase.

special glory or distinguished praise can you have, if you merely endure the punishment and buffetings *justly* due to your transgressions? But if for your good actions, you patiently suffer wrong, this is exceedingly pleasing and acceptable with God.

21. For, it is a condition of your Christian vocation to suffer patiently, and endure evil for your good actions; since Christ, the predestined model of God's elect, suffered thus for us, leaving you an example to follow by walking in his footsteps.

22. He suffered *unjustly;* for, he did nothing to merit it; he committed no offence either by deed or word.

23. He suffered *patiently;* for, when he was reproached and reviled, he did not recriminate or retort; when suffering, he did not threaten his enemies with the divine vengeance; but he delivered himself to Pontius Pilate, by whom he was judged and condemned unjustly.

24. He bore our sins as to their imputability and the punishment due to them, in his body, extended

Commentary.

the penalty due to his crimes; but, he denies that this is a subject of any peculiar merit o: singular praise, which is the meaning of "glory" (in Greek, ελεος), in this passage. " But if doing well, you suffer patiently." The Greek is, αγαθοποιουντες και πασχοντες υπομιενειτε, *but if doing well, and suffering, you endure.* The meaning is the same as that conveyed in our reading. "But if doing well......this is thanksworthy," *i.e.*, grateful and acceptable "before God."

21. "For, unto this are you called," viz., to suffer unjust persecutions and wrongs patiently, even when doing good. This is a condition of our call to Christianity. "By many tribulations we must enter the kingdom of God." All who wish to live piously in Christ Jesus will suffer persecution." "Because Christ also suffered for us." In Greek, υπερ υμων, *for you.* He is the predestined model of God's elect: and we must tread in his footsteps, and follow the example he left us, if we wish to share in his glory.

22. He committed not sin either by word or deed. The quotation, "*who did no sin,*" &c., is taken from Isaias, liii. 9. He did no sin; he was incapable of sin, whether original or actual; "*neither was guile,*" that is, lying or deceit, "*found in his mouth,*" a Hebrew form of saying, there was no guile or deceit in him. Hence, he suffered, *unjustly.*

23. "He also suffered *patiently*"; for, "when reviled," charged with being a "drinker of wine," a Samaritan, possessed by a devil, &c., "he did not revile," or recriminate. And although he occasionally reproached his enemies (*v.g.* John, viii. 44), he did not do so, in a spirit of recrimination. "When he suffered, he threatened not;" for, although, at times, he threatened sinners with eternal death, (Matt. x. 15; Luke, x. 5, and elsewhere); still, he did not do so when suffering, lest it might savour of impatience or vindictiveness. "But delivered himself to him, that judged him unjustly." According to which reading the meaning is, that he patiently and silently submitted to the unjust judgment of Pontius Pilate. In the Greek the reading is, τω κρινοντι δικαιως, *to him that judged him justly:* the meaning of which is, that he committed his cause to the just judgment of his heavenly Father, by whom he was charged with the full imputability of our sins, and *justly* punished as the victim of atonement for them.

24. "Who, his ownself, bore our sins." He had no sins of his own to bear. He bore ours as to their imputability, and the punishment due to them, "in his body upon the tree." "The tree" of the cross, was his altar of sacrifice. In this verse there is allusion to Isaias, liii., "*vere languores nostros ipse tulit.........ipse peccata multorum tulit.*" "That we being dead to sins," holding no more commerce with them than the

Text.	**Paraphrase.**
we being dead to sins, should live to justice : by whose stripes you were healed.	on the wood of the cross, to the end, that we, being dead to sins, having no more commerce with them than the living have with the dead, should lead a life of justice ; by the stripes and marks inflicted on his body, you have been healed.
25. For you were as sheep going astray : but you are now converted to the shepherd and bishop of your souls.	25. And you required healing ; for, like sheep wandering abroad without a shepherd, you were wandering astray from God, from virtue, from heaven, rushing headlong to vice and eternal ruin ; but now, through the bountiful grace of God, you are brought back to your good Pastor, who will feed you with the wholesome pastures of eternal life, and to the Bishop of your souls, who will watch over you, and guard you from straying away from him in future.

Commentary.

living hold with the dead, "should live to justice." The end of his suffering was, to effect our spiritual death to sin, and our resuscitation to a perpetual and undying life of grace. Hence, St. Paul says (Rom. vi., "let not sin reign in your mortal body," &c. "Let us live to God through our Lord Jesus Christ." "Let us exhibit our members as arms of justice to God." "By whose stripes you were healed." The Apostle changes the person, and says, "you." The word "stripes" is allusive to the bad treatment slaves sometimes receive from their masters, when scourged by them. In such cases, they should remember and derive consolation from reflecting, that the Son of God was scourged and treated unjustly and harshly, to atone for their sins, while he was wholly innocent. Oh ! how it would alleviate the miseries in which we may often chance to be involved, owing to the injustice of men, were we, after seriously reflecting that the Son of God suffered still more for us, to unite our sufferings with his, and to bear in mind, that, unlike him, we, at some time, deserved punishment—"*quoniam ego in flagella paratus sum, peccatumme um contra me est semper ?*"—(Psalm.)

25. "For, you were as sheep going astray," owing to your spiritual disorders, and, therefore, required to be healed ; but now you are brought back, as it were, to your original condition. You were converted to the good Pastor, who will lead you into wholesome pastures, and support your souls with his heavenly word, his sacraments, and especially with his own most precious body and blood. "And bishop of your souls ;" he will *watch* over you, as the word "bishop," επισκοπος, signifies, and guard you unless it be your own fault, from straying away any more from him. Can anything so strikingly demonstrate to us the greatness of the benefits of our redemption, as the forlorn and wretched condition of those, from whom a participation in this blessing has been withheld. This state of wretchedness is most clearly exhibited in the affecting idea which the Apostle gives us of it, when comparing it to the condition of sheep wandering and scattered abroad without a shepherd, to tend or protect them from the incursions of ravenous wolves. Oh ! what gratitude do we not owe to the infinite bounty and gratuitous mercy of our good shepherd, who has rescued us, at the price of such excruciating tortures, in preference to millions of his creatures, from this deplorable condition ? Who can enumerate the countless advantages we enjoy in the bosom of his holy Church, within the precincts of his saving fold ? What return then should we make him ? "*Quid retribuam Domino, pro omnibus quæ retribuit mihi ?*" From our mother's womb he was our God—(Psalm xxi. 11). And who can sufficiently comprehend *all* that he has done for us ? "*In loco pascuæ, ibi me collocavit.*" In this place of pasture has he placed us from our mother's womb, without any claim on him, on the grounds of merit, actual or foreseen ; for, before we were born, or capable of good or evil, has he loved us with a love of predilection ; while others he has left outside his saving fold. See what immense sacrifice of feeling, of friends, of worldly position, of all that the world values or esteems, it costs the few, at one time placed outside his fold, whom his grace enables to return to the bosom of his church, while it costs us nothing. We should, by sanctity of life, endeavour to correspond with his goodness, and seek by all means to promote the salvation of our brethren. "*Si diligis me, pasce oves meas.*" This is the return he demands from each one, in his proper sphere and capacity.

CHAPTER III.

Analysis.

In the preceding chapter, the Apostle had been inculcating the duty of political subjection, on the part of the governed, to their rulers, and the domestic subjection of servants to their masters, from which he digressed at verse 18, to treat of the benefits of redemption. In this, he resumes the subject with reference to another species of subjection, somewhat different from the preceding, viz., that which is due by wives to their husbands ; and he inculcates this duty, by pointing out the advantages its observance might confer on the husbands, in case they should have continued to be unbelievers (verses 1, 2). He next shows, in what manner women should adorn themselves, viz., by attending more to the decoration of their souls than of their persons (3, 4). He inculcates the same duty of subjection, by the examples of the wives of the patriarchs of old, and particularly by that of Sara (5, 6).

He then enjoins on husbands the faithful observance of the reciprocal duties of more abundant attention and respect, which they owe their wives, whom they will thus relieve from a consciousness of their inferiority (7).

He briefly and summarily enjoins on all, the exercise of charity and compassion for one another (8). He prohibits retaliation for injuries, whether in word or deed (9) ; and proves from the Psalms, that in order to be heirs to their destined benediction, they must return blessing for cursing, avoid evil, and do good (10-12). He shows that if they are zealous in the practice of good works, unjust persecutions will not only be ultimately harmless (13), but will procure a special benediction for them (14). He exhorts them to fear God only, and to be prepared with some satisfactory answer when questioned, in due circumstances, respecting their faith. He encourages them to suffer patiently for justice sake ; since, in doing so, they conform to God's will (17) ; and moreover, by so doing, they perfectly conform to the example of Christ, who also suffered unjustly, even death, for our sins ; he shows, for their consolation, the efficacy and good effects of the unjust suffering of Christ, both in reference to himself, who was raised to a glorious and immortal life, "enlivened in the spirit" (18), and with reference to his creatures, whether we regard past generations—and among them the most signal instance of the great efficacy of his merits was the salvation of the Ante-deluvians ; to whom he went and preached during the interval between his death and resurrection, in the prison of Limbo, the glad tidings of their approaching admittance unto glory (19, 20)—or, whether we regard present or future generations during the entire term of the law of grace, during which, men are saved by the waters of baptism, received with due dispositions, of which waters those of the deluge were a type and figure (21, 22).

Text.

1. IN like manner also let wives be subject to their husbands : that if

Paraphrase.

1. Let wives also be subject to their husbands, and exhibit towards them that liberal and free obedience

Commentary.

1. "In like manner." In these words the Apostle by no means conveys that the wife should exhibit the same kind of servile subjection to her husband that the slave owes to his master (iii. 18), for, she is only subject to her husband, as her head ; as the Church is to Christ, who treats her as his spouse.—Ephes. v. The Apostle only intends

Text.

any believe not the word, they may be won without the word, by the conversation of the wives.

2. Considering your chaste conversation with fear.

3. Whose adorning let it not be the outward plaiting of the hair, or the wearing of gold, or the putting on of apparel :

Paraphrase.

which the marriage contract implies, in order that, should there be any husbands who have resisted the preaching of God's holy word, and his invitations to embrace the faith, these may be gained over to Christ by the pious conduct and exemplary obedience of their wives, without any further necessity for a formal preaching of the word to them.

2. When they consider and examine into the chaste and holy conduct of their wives, together with their respectful and reverential deportment towards themselves.

3. Whose decoration should not consist so much in the external embellishment and decking out of their persons, either in braidings or toppings of the hair, or in the use of golden ornaments, or excessive costliness of dress :

Commentary.

to inculcate the duty of obedience in one case as well as the other; an obedience, however, in both cases, differing in kind. " Be subject ; " the Greek is, ὑποτασσομεναι, *being subject.*

"That if any believe not the word." The Greek word for "believe not," απειθουσι, conveys the idea of *positive* unbelief, or *positively* rejecting the word. "May be won without the word," *i.e.*, without the necessity of any formal preaching of the word, a second time. Of course, this is not opposed to St. Paul to the Romans (x.), "faith comes from hearing," for, the Greek word for "believe not," already quoted, supposes them to have heard the word already. It is only meant that a second preaching of the word to them would be unnecessary.

2. "With fear," may also refer to the husbands, when with feelings of reverential respect they consider and examine into your chaste conversation and holy life. In the Paraphrase it refers to the wives. "Your chaste conversation." Chastity and fidelity to her marriage engagement should be the first and chiefest ornament of a Christian wife ; and this, not only with regard to others, but also with reference to her own husband, and the obligations of conjugal chastity.

3. The decoration of women should not consist so much in excessive fineries and decking-out of their persons, as in embellishing their souls—verse 4. In the interpretation now given, the words, "whose adorning let it not be the outward," &c., are employed in a *comparative* sense to mean, that the ornaments of females should not consist *so much* in external decoration of their persons, *as* in the embellishment of their souls—verse 4. The injunction given here by St. Peter is perfectly similar to that given by St. Paul, (1 Ep. to Tim. ii. 9). An excessive regard for the fineries of dress, and an undue attention to the decoration of their persons, are faults at all times, peculiar to females. It is likely, that in the luxurious cities of Greece and Asia Minor, even the converted females carried with them into the church their former faulty habits in this respect, to the scandal of the Pagans, and the injury of the faith. Hence, the severe strictures of St. Paul (Ep. 1 ad Cor. xi.), on the same subject. " The wearing of gold " refers to the extravagant golden ornaments, such as armlets, bracelets, headbands, &c., of gold. "Or the putting on of apparel " refers to the excessive costliness of cloaks, &c., worn by females. From the fact of two Apostles delivering wholesome instructions on this subject, we can estimate the importance of the precept regarding it ; for, although custom be variable, there can be no doubt that the precept given here by the Apostle is binding at all times, and is violated, whenever, females deck themselves out in dresses beyond their means, or when their dresses, either in shape or form, are not conformable to the laws of modesty or of Christian propriety. The Apostle by no means censures the use of costly ornaments suited to one's rank and station, for "the valiant woman" is commended for wearing "*purple and fine linen,*" but, these were suited to her rank ; for "her husband *is honourable* in the gates, when he sitteth among the *senators* of the land."—Proverbs, xxxi. 23.

Text.

4. But the hidden man of the heart in the incorruptibility of a quiet and meek spirit, which is rich in the sight of God.

5. For after this manner hereto-ore the holy women also, who trusted in God, adorned themselves being in subjection to their own husbands.

6. As Sara obeyed Abraham, calling him Lord : whose daughters you are doing well, and not fearing any disturbance.

7. Ye husbands, likewise dwelling with them according to knowledge, giving honour to the female as to the weaker vessel, and as to the coheirs of the grace of life : that your prayers be not hindered.

Paraphrase.

4. As in the embellishment of their interior, that is, of their souls, with the incorruptible and imperishable virtues of meekness, and of a peaceful, unruffled serenity of mind, which interior, thus ornamented, is rich and valuable in the sight of God.

5. For, it was by interior embellishment of this sort that the holy women of old, of whom you are begotten, and to whom you are to look up as models, putting their trust in God, adorned themselves; but particularly by exhibiting obedience and due subjection to their husbands.

6. Among these holy women, Sara shone conspicuous, and afforded a signal instance of subjection to her husband, Abraham ; obeying him, and reverentially calling him her lord—whose daughters you are when doing good, and not deterred from the discharge of your Christian duties by the nervous fears and timidity inherent in the female character.

7. Husbands, do you in like manner, attend to the duties of respect and love which you owe your wives ; in cohabiting with them, treat them according to the dictates of your superior reason, and the principles of religion, bestowing on them more abundant respect and attention as the weaker parties, (thus relieving them from the consciousness of their inferiority) you should also treat them as equally destined with you to share the heavenly inheritance which Christ has purchased for us, and thus you will be enabled to attend to the duty of prayer, to which family broils and domestic discord are a great hindrance.

Commentary.

4. Their chief care should be to purify their affections, of which the "heart" is the seat, and to ornament "the hidden man," that is, their souls, which are imperishable, with the virtues "of a quiet," an unruffled, peaceful, "and meek spirit," that are incorruptible, unlike the ornaments of dress, which, like the external person, they are applied to, are fading and perishable, "which is rich," &c., which spirit thus decorated is precious in the sight of God.

5. It is by interior ornaments of a quiet and meek spirit, that the "holy women," of whom they were descended, the wives of the Patriarchs and others, Rebecca, Rachael, &c., Abigail, Esther, Judith, &c., "who trusted in God," and loved and served him faithfully and devoutly (for, under "trusted in God," are included the other virtues of faith, love, devotion, &c., by which they pleased God), "adorned themselves, being in subjection," &c. (_see_ Paraphrase).

6. Among these holy women whom the Apostle proposes as models for their imitation, he particularizes Sara, the wife of the Patriarch Abraham, whom she obeyed reverentially calling him "her lord," as appears from many passages of Genesis (her own name implied, that she was mistress, _Sarai_, that is, _domina mea_). She obeyed him, going with him wherever he went, whether to Canaan, Egypt, Gerara, &c.

"Whose daughters you are, doing well." These words furnish no argument in favour of the opinion that this Epistle was addressed to the converted Jews ; because, as all the faithful of the male sex, whether from among the Jews or Gentiles, might be termed the spiritual sons of Abraham, so might all of the female sex be termed the spiritual daughters of Sara ; in this sense it would appear from the words, "doing well," the word is taken here—when doing well, they were the spiritual daughters of Sara. "And not fear any disturbance," that is, not to be deterred from the faithful discharge of their Christian duties by the nervous fears and timidity which are the characteristics of the female character.

7. The Apostle in this verse addresses himself to the husbands on whom he enjoins

Text.

8. And in fine be ye all of one mind, having compassion one of another, being lovers of the brotherhood, merciful, modest, humble:

9. Not rendering evil for evil, nor railing for railing, but contrariwise, blessing: for unto this are you called, that you may inherit a blessing.

Paraphrase.

8. In a word, or to sum up all briefly, be of one way of thinking and willing, of one heart and one soul; sympathize with one another; love one another as brethren, rendered such by a new generation (i. 23): have feelings of real inward compassion for one another; become affable and benign, lowly and humble in your own eyes and your own estimation:

9. Not returning evil for evil, nor abusive language for reproachful, abusive language; in other words, not retaliating either by word or action, but on the contrary, returning benediction for malediction; for, you have been called to enter on the possession of your heavenly inheritance, which is the effect of God's benediction conferred on you, and prepared for you even when his enemies by sin; hence, like him, you should bless your enemies.

Commentary.

the reciprocal duties they owe their wives. "Dwelling with them." The Greek συνοικουντες, means, *cohabiting with them.* "According to knowledge." "Knowledge" refers both to the superior intellectual faculty with which man is gifted beyond the woman; hence, it means the superior knowledge of reason; it also refers to the knowledge of religion. The two meanings are united in the Paraphrase. "Giving honour to the female as to the weaker vessel;" as we should clothe our weaker or less honourable members with more abundant honour (1 Cor. xii. 23, &c.), so ought the man bestow greater honour on the woman, as "the weaker vessel," or person, in order that by this more abundant honour and more careful attention on the part of her husband, she might be relieved from the consciousness of her inferiority. "The weaker vessel." The word "vessel" is frequently used to signify a body (*v.g.*, 1 Thes. iv. 4). It is frequently used to signify anything created. Hence, it is applied to the female person. "And as to the co-heirs of the grace of life." The husband should treat his wife with the care and attention due to an equal; for, the female is made equally sharer in the inheritance of salvation with the man. "That your prayers be not hindered." This is another reason why the husband should treat his wife with due respect.—*Vide* Paraphrase. Some interpreters understand the injunction here given by the Apostle to regard the legitimate exercise of marriage, and to prohibit the sins committed in this way, sins most common in the Gentile world, and perhaps, not regarded by many of the newly converted, with due feelings of horror. The similarity between the words, "that your prayers be not hindered," and the passage of St. Paul (1 Cor. vii.), "that you may give yourselves to prayer"—where he counsels abstinence at times from marriage intercourse—confirms this interpretation. It is better, however, give the words a general import, as affecting the whole conduct of husbands, in regard to their wives, the lawful exercise of marriage specially included.

8. "And, in fine," which means, briefly to sum up all, "having compassion one of another." The Greek word, συμπαθεις, means, *sympathizing with one another.* "Merciful;" the Greek word, ευσπλαγχνοι, signifies, that their bowels should be moved with tender compassion for one another. "Modest," "humble." For these two words we have but one in the Greek, ταπεινοφρονες, the reading of the three chief MSS. For it, in some copies, we have φιλοφρονες, which means, *affable* or *humane.* The former Greek word was most likely rendered differently in different versions; and probably, to reconcile all, the Vulgate gives both translations—a thing by no means unusual. "Modest" means "benign," "kind." "Humble," entertaining a low opinion of one's self, a virtue very much recommended in sacred Scripture.

9. "Not rendering evil for evil, nor railing for railing," in other words, not retaliating by word or action, "but contrariwise blessing." "*Bless them that curse you,*" says our divine Redeemer. "*Bless them that persecute you, bless and curse not*" (Rom. xii. 12). "For unto this are you called," viz., "that you may inherit a blessing." In his construction, also adopted in the Paraphrase, "unto this," regards the following

Text.

10. *For he that will love life, and see good days, let him refrain his tongue from evil, and his lips that they speak no guile.*

11. *Let him decline from evil, and do good: let him seek after peace, and pursue it:*

12. *Because the eyes of the Lord are upon the just, and his ears unto their prayers: but the countenance of the Lord upon them that do evil things.*

Paraphrase.

10. For, whosoever anxiously desires to enjoy eternal life, and see happy days in the land of the living, must refrain his tongue from speaking ill of the neighbour, and must guard his lips against giving utterance to the language of fraud or circumvention for the purpose of injuring him.

11. He must avoid evil, not only of the tongue, but of all kinds, and also do good; he must diligently search after and find peace, with his neighbour, and after having found it, even though it should attempt to fly from him, he must vigorously grasp it, and retain it.

12. For the merciful and benevolent regard of the Lord is upon the just, to them all the decrees of his Providence subserve, to their entreaties he is always ready to lend a willing ear; but upon the doers of evil frowneth the ire of his angry countenance.

Commentary.

words: "that you may inherit," &c. Reference is made by St. Peter to the final sentence which is to take place on the last day: "*Come, you blessed of my Father, possess the kingdom prepared,*" &c. And hence, as persons called to the possession of an inheritance, which may be called "a blessing," as being its effect—a blessing also which God prepared for us even while his enemies—we should, like him, bless our enemies, and wish for them the possession of the greatest good. The construction may be so arranged, that the words "unto this," be referred to the foregoing, thus: You are called to render benediction for malediction, as being a necessary condition for your obtaining the heavenly inheritance of bliss which is in store for you. And this the Apostle proves from the following passage of the Psalms, where eternal life is promised. "*For he that will love life,* &c." Some Greek copies have, *Knowing that to this you are called.* The words, *Knowing that,* are wanting in the chief manuscripts.

10. These words are adduced, by the Apostle, from Psalm xxxiii., to prove that in order to inherit the heavenly benediction in store for us, we must guard our tongues from evil, under which is included, "*malediction,*" we should, therefore, not return malediction for malediction, but on the contrary, benediction; for, it is not sufficient to avoid evil, we must also "*do good.*" In the Psalm, the words are read interrogatively, "*Who is the man that desireth life?*" &c. But there is no difference in sense from the reading of the Apostle. "*He that will love life and see good days.*" These words were spoken in their literal sense by David, of temporal happiness and longevity, but in their mystical meaning—the one principally intended by the Holy Ghost, and in which they are quoted here by St. Peter—they refer to life eternal. "*Let him refrain his tongue from evil,*" from speaking ill of his neighbour either by detraction or calumny, or by contumeliously affronting him, when present, "*and his lips that they speak no guile,*" from uttering words of fraud to deceive and injure him.

11. Let him avoid not only all evils committed by the tongue, but all evils whatsoever; it is not sufficient merely to avoid evil, he must do positive good: "*Let him do good.*" "*Let him seek after peace,*" with his neighbour; by some it is also understood, of peace with himself too and with God. "*And pursue it.*" The Greek, διωξάτω, means to follow after it constantly. Then, the words mean, after having sought and found peace, let him follow after it, to secure it fast, even should it attempt to fly from him.

12. "*The eyes,*" i.e., the gracious, benign regard of the Lord is upon the just. All the decrees of his Providence have them in view. "*And his ears unto their prayers.*" God is always ready to listen favourably to the petitions of his friends and chosen servants. "*Countenance,*" means the frowning, wrathful countenance of one in anger, "*upon them that do evil things,*" so as to punish and destroy them, even here. For, in the Psalm, the words are added, "*to cut off the remembrance of them from the earth.*"

Text.

13. And who is he that can hurt you, if you be zealous of good?

14. But if also you suffer any thing for justice sake, blessed are ye. And be not afraid of their fear, and be not troubled.

15. But sanctify the Lord Christ in your hearts, being ready always to satisfy every one that asketh you a reason of that hope which is in you.

Paraphrase.

13. And who is it that can ultimately harm you, if you be zealous followers of good, really anxious to conform your life, all your words and actions in the standard of goodness?

14. But if you suffer anything for justice sake, you will not only be really free from harm, but blessed. And fear not the evils with which they menace you, and show no apprehension of them.

15. But reverence in your hearts the Lord Christ, and manifest this reverence in the edifying practice of all Christian virtues; and be always prepared to give some satisfactory answer or apology to every one that asks, in due circumstances, for some reason of the hope that is in you.

Commentary.

13. Since, then, "*the eyes of the Lord are upon the just,*" who can in reality harm you in the end, if you be zealous imitators of good, if you take care to conform all your words and actions to the standard of goodness, for, "if the Lord be with us, who is against us?" "All things work together unto good for them that love God." (Rom. viii.) Others interpret this verse differently. According to them, the Apostle, in it adduces an argument derived from ordinary experience to confirm what he had already said with reference to God's Providence regarding his elect. If a man "be zealous of good," if he take care to govern his tongue and refrain from retaliation either by word or deed, very few will have any disposition to injure him in his temporal prospects. And in reply to the objection against this interpretation derived from the words of St. Paul, "all that will live godly in Christ Jesus shall suffer persecution" (2 Tim. iii. 12), they say that the words of St. Paul regard times of persecution for the faith, or at least that the just shall always carry the cross in some shape or other, if not from external persecution, at least from temptations on the part of the leagued enemies of man's salvation. The first interpretation seems the more probable.—(*Vide* Paraphrase). "Zealous of good." In some Greek copies, *followers of good*. The chief manuscripts and versions are in favour of the Vulgate, τοῦ ἀγαθοῦ ζηλωταί.

14. And by suffering in the cause of justice and Christian virtue, while they continue "zealous of good," they shall not only be free from real harm, but they shall positively gain a blessedness by this very circumstance; for, "blessed are they who suffer persecution for justice sake."—(Matt. v.) According to the other interpretation of the preceding verse, the connexion of this is: But should there be found men perverse enough to persecute you for your faith and virtues (and there shall be found such in every age, perhaps in the very bosom of Christianity, whose cry it shall be, "*opprimamus justum, contrarius est operibus nostris,*" let us not put up with his conduct, which is a direct censure on our corrupt principles and immoral practices), and that you are doomed to suffer for justice sake, "you are blessed." "And be not afraid of their fear." The word "fear" is put for the object or evil menaced, and the punishment feared. The words mean, be not afraid of the evils with which they menace you when they endeavour to inspire you with fear, "and be not troubled," or seized with confusion or apprehension, on that account.

15. "But sanctify the Lord Christ in your hearts." The word "sanctify" means to proclaim him "holy," and endeavour to show him forth as such to the world. The Apostle adds this to show that, if the fear of the Lord reign in their souls, they will be proof against every other base fear which would prompt to acts opposed to his holy will. These words, as well as the words in the preceding verse, "and be not afraid of their fear, and be not troubled," are taken from Isaias, chap. viii. 13, with this difference, that in the latter the words are, "Sanctify the Lord of Hosts himself," whereas here it is "the Lord Christ;" and St. Peter adds "Christ," probably to show that Christ is "the Lord of Hosts" referred to by Isaias. In some Greek copies the reading is, *Sanctify the Lord God.* But the Vulgate reading is supported by the Syriac, and found in the chief manuscripts. "Being always ready to satisfy every

Text.

16. But with modesty and fear, having a good conscience: that whereas they speak evil of you, they may be ashamed who falsely accuse your good conversation in Christ.

17. For it is better doing well (if

Paraphrase.

16. But your answer should be always marked by gentleness and due reverence for those who interrogate you, having a good conscience and leading lives conformable to the principles of your holy faith, so that instead of speaking evil of you, those may be confounded and put to shame, who now falsely accuse and calumniate your virtuous edifying life and Christian conversation.

17. For, it is much better and far more meritorious

Commentary.

one," which, in the Greek, runs thus: ετοιμοι αει προς απολογιαν, "*being always ready for an apology to every one*," &c., that is to say, being always furnished with, and having ready at hand, some satisfactory reply to give to those who, in due and proper circumstances, interrogate you about the grounds of that hope which you entertain, and which supports you against the pressure of evil and persecution. In this the Apostle does not require that every person among the faithful should be a Theologian, able to account for *all* the truths of faith, and to dispute regarding them; neither does he require that under all circumstances, whether interrogated from idle, impertinent curiosity, without any regard for instruction, or, from motives of embarrassing us, we should enter on a defence of our holy faith or give answer: all he requires is, that when interrogated at proper times, and in due circumstances, every Christian should be instructed in some general satisfactory reasons for embracing and adhering to the Catholic faith (*v.g.*), if the question were proposed by *infidels*, he might ground his hopes in Christ on the fact, that He was proved to be the God predicted of old by the Prophets, from the circumstances of the prophecies being all fulfilled in Him and Him only; from his having confirmed by miracles his declaration that He was the Son of God; and finally, as he had foretold, from his having raised himself from the dead; that this infinitely veracious God promised us eternal life, provided we adhered to his true faith and kept his commandments; and that the enduring of crosses here below, far from showing that he did not exercise a paternal care over us, was, on the contrary, a necessary condition for obtaining the heavenly inheritance marked out by him beforehand for his followers; he himself having first given us the example, by taking up the cross, and despising the ignominy attached thereto, even when joy had been proposed to him.—(Hebrews, xii.) To *heretics*, one general answer should be:—That we believe all the truths which the Catholic Church proposes, because that Church is infallible, being "the pillar and ground of truth"—having been vested unto the end of time with power and knowledge, "*to preserve us from being carried away and tossed about by every wind of doctrine*" (Ephes. iv.)—having the plentitude of truth deposited with HER by the Holy Ghost, in teaching which he promised to abide with her for ever — having Christ himself remaining with her "*all days even to the end of the world.*"

16. Our answer should be wholly exempt from harshness or contentious arrogance of any kind. In truth, no man was ever converted by abuse; and it is to be feared that the practice of abusing such as differ from us in religion, under ordinary circumstances, proceeds from another spirit than the spirit of God, from passion and caprice rather than from zeal. The ample benedictions poured on the labours of a De Sales and a Xavier are the clearest evidence of the will of God in this repect. "Having a good conscience," otherwise our reasonings will prove prejudicial; for, it may fairly be said, if we believe what we say, why not live up to this belief? Hence, in order that our disputations or instructions may prove of any avail, we should lead lives conformable to our faith; and then, by this readiness to account, with meekness, for the hope which is in us, and by our exemplary lives, we will confound such as now calumniate us and our holy faith. In some Greek copies, after the words, "who speak evil of you," are added the words, ὡς κακοποιων, *as malefactors*. It is likely, however, that they were added from verse 12, of the preceding chapter. In the Syriac version, the words run thus—*that your enemies may be confounded as calumniators of your good conversation in Christ.*

17. To such as are suffering for justice sake, the Apostle proposes motives of consola-

Text.

such be the will of God) to suffer than doing ill.

18. Because Christ also died once for our sins, the just for the unjust : that he might offer us to God, being put to death indeed in the flesh, but enlivened in the spirit.

Paraphrase.

to suffer for our good actions (if such be the will of God, without whose will nothing happens, except sin), than to be forced to undergo punishment for our misdeeds.

18. (And by thus suffering unjustly you will more perfectly conform to Christ). For, he also suffered, nay, even died once, not for his own, but for our sins ; the just suffered for the unjust ; that he might offer us to God; and, by breaking down the enmities that existed between him and us, bring us nearer to him, by a conformity of our virtues, by our faith and belief in his gospel, "being indeed put to death in the flesh," when his mortal life was put an end to, but again resuscitated in the reunion of his soul—now become the principle of a glorious and immortal life—with his body, on which were conferred the properties of glorification.

Commentary.

tion founded on the advantages and merit of such suffering, and also on the consideration of God's holy will, that they should thus suffer. "For, it is better," &c. These words would appear to be immediately connected with verse 14. "It is better," that is, more meritorious for you ("if such be the will of God.") This he adds to show, that in thus suffering, they are only conforming to God's holy will ; for, everything happens by his positive will, sin excepted. "Than to suffer doing ill," because, then you would be only paying the just penalty due to your misdeeds. No doubt the very act of submitting to merited punishment may be rendered a just and meritorious thing ; but, still not so meritorious as suffering for justice sake. This latter is "better" than the former, which may sometimes be good.

18. In this verse, the Apostle adduces another motive for consolation under the unjust sufferings for justice sake, to which the faithful, whom he is addressing, may have been exposed. This is, the example of Christ, to whom in such circumstances they most perfectly conform. "Because Christ also died once for our sins." "Also," shows that the Apostle is exhorting them to suffer for justice sake even unto death ; which can happen only once, "and Christ also died once for our sins," for, he was himself incapable of sinning ; "the just for the unjust ;" hence, he could not himself merit the tortures and death to which he was subjected. "That he might offer us to God," for which we have in the Greek, προσαγαγῃ, "that he might *bring* us to God." The meaning furnished by both readings is given in the Paraphrase. We were afar off from God owing to our sins. Christ "broke down the wall of separation," "the enmities in his flesh" (Ephes. ii. 14), and by paying an adequate and sufficient ransom, of which a Man-God alone was capable, purchased the grace by which we were enabled to draw near and approach to God. "Being put to death indeed in the flesh," that is, his mortal and animal life, requiring the aid of earthly aliments, for its continuance—which life Christ voluntarily led, and preferred up to the time of his death, although he might, if he pleased, have enjoyed, from his Incarnation, a life independent of all the requirements of animal existence—was put an end to by the separation of his soul from his body on the cross. "But enlivened in the spirit." By "the spirit," some interpreters understand, the *Holy Ghost*, or Spirit of Christ, by whom Christ was raised from the dead ; this resuscitation was an act of the Divinity, of the three Adorable Persons of the Trinity, to whom all acts, *ad extra* are common. Others, and it would seem with greater probability, understand it of the Soul of Christ, in which Christ "was enlivened," just as it is said (1 Cor. xv. 45), "the last Adam was made into a quickening spirit," inasmuch as his soul, after his Resurrection, imparted to his glorified body the gift of *spirituality*, in virtue of which it subsists without the aid of earthly aliments, such as food, clothing, &c.—required for the continuance of an animal life,—and will also be the principle of similar spiritual life, at a future day, to others. Of course, from his very Incarnation, Christ could have led such a life,

Text.

19. In which also coming he preached to those spirits that were in prison ;

20. Which had been some time incredulous, when they waited for the patience of God in the days of Noe, when the ark was a building : wherein a few, that is, eight souls, were saved by water.

Paraphrase.

19. In which soul he came, during the interval between his death and resurrection, and preached to the departed souls of the ancient just who died in the Lord, and were confined in the prison of Limbo, the glad tidings of their near deliverance, when they were to accompany Him on high, while he "*led captivity, captive.*"

20. And among those to whom Christ then preached, should be reckoned, and especially noted by us, those who for some time, had been great sinners and incredulous in the days of Noe, for whose conversion the patience of God had been waiting during the term of years that Noe had been employed in constructing the ark, wherein only eight persons were saved from death, by the water on which, borne aloft, it floated in security amidst the surrounding desolation.

Commentary.

exempt from all the necessities of animal existence ; but it was only after his glorious birth at his Resurrection, that he actually entered on that glorified spiritual state.— *Vide* 1 Cor. xv. 45, Commentary.

19, 20. "In which also coming he preached to those spirits that were in prison." There is a great diversity of opinion respecting the meaning of this obscure passage. Dismissing the improbable and heretical interpretations, the probable opinions regarding it may be reduced to two : the one, that of St. Augustine (*Epistola* 99), who, at first, understood the word "spirits in prison," to refer to the souls of men departed out of life ; but when he came to interpret the words, verse 6, of next chapter, "for this cause, was the *Gospel preached also to the dead*," he made the word "dead" refer to the same person with "*spirits*" in this verse. Seeing the difficulties involved in the interpretation of verse 6, of next chapter, should it be understood of the preaching of the Gospel to the departed souls of men ; and still holding, that in both passages there was reference made to the same persons, he adopted a different interpretation of the words of this verse, and understood "spirits in prison," to refer to those who were detained, while in the body, in the prison of vice and infidelity. According to St. Augustine's interpretation, the meaning of the passage is this : "Christ was vivified in the spirit," that is, by the Holy Ghost (verse 18) ; and to prove that Christ always lived in the spirit, he says it was in the same spirit that he came and preached to the unbelievers, who were detained in the prison of vice and infidelity, through the ministry of his prophets and chosen servants (verse 19), and he particularizes one signal instance, viz., that of the great sinners, to whom he preached through the ministry of Noe, during the one hundred and twenty years employed by him in building the ark, in which only eight persons were saved from the waters of the deluge (verse 20). Instead of the Vulgate reading, "when they waited for the patience of God," the Greek reading preferred by St. Jerome and St. Augustine, and preserved in the Roman Missal, corrected by Clement VIII., in the Epistle of Friday in Easter week is ὅτε ἀπεδέξετο ἡ τοῦ Θεοῦ μακροθυμια, *When the patience of God was waiting in the days of Noe ;* and this seems the more natural reading of the passage ; since, of the incredulous, who mocked and derided Noe, it could hardly be said, that "*they waited* for the patience of God ;" this is true only of such as, sincerely anxious for a reconciliation with him, expect, that in his patience he will avert the scourges of his wrath, which their sins deserve ; whereas, it is quite fair to say, that the patience of God *was waiting* for the conversion of these sinful, incredulous men, whom he graciously forewarned of their impending destruction, during the one hundred and twenty years that Noe had been employed in building the ark.

The interpretation of St. Augustine appears open to insuperable difficulties. In the first place, it makes the word "spirits" refer, not to the disembodied souls of men, but to the very persons, souls and bodies, of the antediluvians, to whom he supposes Christ, in his Divine Spirit, to have preached through Noe ; now, this is clearly opposed to the

Commentary.

general usage of sacred Scripture, designating men by the flesh—their visible part, rather than by the spirit, which is invisible. Besides, it might suit prophetic style, to call men, while in this life, "spirits in prison," such a form of expression is, however, clearly unsuited to the plain, historical style here employed by the Apostle. In the next place, the form of expression used here, far from supposing the preaching attributed here to Christ, to have been the same with the preaching, for which the ministry of Noe was employed (as St. Augustine has it), supposes the very reverse ; it supposes that the preaching made by Christ (verse 19), to which the antediluvians were incredulous (verse 20) was posterior to that made by Noe : τοῖς πνευμασιν εκηριξεν απει-θησασιν ποτε. *He preached to those spirits which had been some time incredulous in the days of Noe.* Is it not plain, then, that the preaching of Noe must have preceded his ? His could be no other (since they all perished in the waters of the deluge) than that made to their departed souls, in the prison of Limbo. In truth, in order to be warranted in making the preaching of Christ referred to (verse 19) identical with that which, in the opinion of St. Augustine, he is supposed to have made (verse 20) by the ministry of Noe, we should change the entire structure of the sentence, and make it run thus : "In which coming formerly, in the days of Noe, when the patience of God was waiting for them, he preached to spirits that had been incredulous to himself ;" but, this is, obviously, quite different from the real construction of the sacred text.

But what particularly militates against this opinion is the context of the Apostle. For, in the preceding passage (verse 18), he is encouraging the faithful to endure unjust persecutions, nay, even martyrdom, for the faith, by the example of the unjust sufferings of Christ ; and, as a further inducement, he proposes the salutary effects of these unjust sufferings with regard to Christ himself, who "was enlivened in the spirit," and underwent these sufferings "to offer us," (or, *to bring us nearer*) "to God," doubtless by our faith and belief in the gospel. He next adds (verse 19), that Christ went and preached to the incredulous men, who had been mocking the preaching of Noe ; now, what connexion can there be between our reconciliation (verse 18), and the incredulity of the antediluvians, who perished in the waters of the deluge, and were eternally lost, according to the interpretation of St. Augustine ? What object could the Apostle have in view, in introducing the example of the inefficacious preaching of Noe in a passage, where, from the context, it is evident, he is recommending the efficacy of the death and resurrection of Christ ? Hence, it is, that the common interpretation seems by far the more probable, as being more in accordance with the obvious meaning of the words of the text, as also with the context. The Apostle is encouraging the faithful to endure persecution, nay, even death itself for the faith, and, as a most consoling motive, he adduces the example of Christ, who died for the unjust (verse 18), and for the purpose of *bringing us nearer to God.* (This is the Greek reading for, "that he might offer us to God.") As a further motive, he proposes the efficacy of the death of Christ, both with reference to himself, who was raised to a glorious and immortal life, "enlivened in the spirit ;" and with reference to his creatures, whether we regard those who in ages past, preceded him, to whom his future merits were applied ; or, those of the present and future generations (verse 21). As an example of the efficacy of the merits of Christ, with reference to past ages, he adduces one of the most signal manifestations of his great mercy, in the salvation of those giant sinners who perished in the deluge, whose crimes are described (Genesis, chap. v.) ; and, in order to extol still more this great mercy of God, the Apostle mentions the aggravating circumstances of their obstinacy. God had through Noe, preached to them their coming destruction ; they continued in their obstinate unbelief ; and it was only when they saw the waters of the deluge overflow the earth, that, touched with repentance amid the wreck of all nature, they felt concern for the salvation of their souls, while their bodies were submerged in the desolating waters. It was to announce to these souls confined in the Prison of Limbo, expiating the temporal punishment due to their sins, that the soul of Christ, after his death on the cross, descended, announcing the joyous tidings of their near deliverance, the termination of their pains, and the throwing open of the gates of heaven, for so many ages closed against them.

Text.	**Paraphrase.**
21. Whereunto baptism being of the like form, now saveth you also :	21. To this diluvian water, baptism corresponding, as the antitype, or thing typified, to its type and figure,

Commentary.

The chief difficulties against this opinion are :—First, What grounds are there for saying that the incredulous, to whom Noe preached, on seeing the waters of the deluge overflow the earth, were converted, and died in sentiments of penance? Secondly, why should St. Peter, in this passage, confine to those who perished in the flood, whose conversion and salvation is supposed in this opinion, the preaching which Christ addressed to all the souls of the just, detained in the prison of Limbo, including patriarchs and prophets?

In answer to the first difficulty, to which great weight has been attached by some writers, as being the chief reason, which induced St. Augustine to desert the common opinion, it is to be said, that the words, "*some time* incredulous," would imply, that they did not always continue such ; and, even though we should have no positive or demonstrative reasons, in favour of this supposition, there are none against it ; the silence of sacred Scripture on this subject, is no more a reason against it, than it is against other points, on which it is equally silent, and which we still know to be incontrovertible facts. It is perfectly conformable to our ideas of the mercy and goodness of God to suppose that, while in his justice he submerged the bodies of those sinful men, in the waters of the deluge, in his mercy he poured into their souls a deluge of graces. And, it is not very likely, that those men, who mocked and derided Noe, as a senseless visionary, on witnessing this universal shipwreck, on seeing the waters rushing from the heavens, the earth, and the sea, and his predictions and menaces fully verified by the event, turned to God with their whole hearts (a thing not unusual in *ordinary* shipwrecks), and offered up that inevitable death which menaced them as a sacrifice of expiation for their crimes? At all events, this supposition enables us to interpret this difficult passage, which, in any other interpretation, would be open to insuperable difficulties. The probable opinion then is, that they were all saved ; there is no reason for limiting the application of the words of the Apostle ; on the contrary, the salvation of *all* would be a greater argument of the mercy of God, and of the retrospective efficacy of Christ's merits, which the Apostle is commending in this passage.

In answer to the second point of objection it may be said, that although Christ had preached to all the souls shut up in the prison of Limbo, and while announcing to them their near deliverance, had, most probably, remitted what remained to be discharged of the *temporal* debt due to their sins, thereby consecrated, by being the first himself to exercise it, the power of granting indulgences, to be afterwards exercised by his Church ; still, the Apostle specially refers to those, who were converted in the waters of the deluge, as the most signal instance he could adduce of the divine mercy, whether the number or the enormity of their crimes be considered, by which "*all flesh corrupted its way on the earth,*" and which provoked an immutable God to cry out, "it repenteth me that I have made them" (Genesis, chap. vi.) ; and he, thereby supplies the firmest grounds of confidence in the merits of Christ, for such as died for righteousness sake ; seeing that his future merits were so efficacious in saving the souls of those sinful men, whose crimes provoked the divine justice to sweep them off the face of the earth. Another reason why St. Peter particularizes those who perished in the deluge is, that the deluge, in which they were drowned, was typical of the baptismal waters, in which those whom he addresses received their spiritual regeneration, and the surest earnest of the efficacy of Christ's merits with reference to themselves.

Who, after considering the consoling teaching of the Apostle in this passage, can, for an instant, distrust the boundless mercy of God? The salvation of those giant sinners of old, whose crimes drew down the deluge or universal shipwreck of the first creation, and provoked an immutable God to exclaim, that he was "*sorry for creating man,*" furnishes the most striking and the most consoling exemplification, that could be adduced, of his boundless mercies. Well therefore, may we all, whom God has spared in our sins, cry out with the Psalmist ; "*The mercies of the Lord I shall sing for ever.*" "*His mercy is above all his works.*"

21. In this verse the Apostle points out the efficacy of Christ's merits, in regard to

Text.	Paraphrase.
not the putting away of the filth of the flesh, but the examination of a good conscience towards God, by the resurrection of JESUS CHRIST.	now, in the New Law, saves you too from the death of your souls by the graces and right to life eternal, which it confers ; and these effects it produces, not inasmuch as it is a mere external rite, washing away bodily uncleanness ; but, inasmuch as this external rite is accompanied by the internal dispositions which the subject of baptism, when interrogated sincerely, and before God, declares that he possesses ; these effects baptism produces owing to the resurrection from the dead of our Lord Jesus Christ ; for " he rose for our justification."—(Rom. chap. xiv.)
22. Who is on the right hand of God, swallowing down death, that	22. Who, in his *divine* nature, being equal to God in his *human* nature, sits at His right hand, and holds,

Commentary.

the present and future generations, during the time of the New Law. "Whereunto, baptism being of the like form." In our English version the Greek reading is followed, and the same has been adopted in the Paraphrase. The Vulgate reading runs thus : *quod et vos nunc similis formæ salvos facit Baptisma ;* and this accords with the Vatican reading :—" *Which* (water), *the antitype of that in the deluge, and which is Baptism, now saves you.*" According to others, there is a Hebraism in the Vulgate readings wherein the relative precedes the antecedent, and is thus explained : "and now baptism, saves you, which baptism of like form," &c. " *Whereunto,*" that is, to which water of the deluge, "baptism being of like form." The Greek for "like form," αντιτυπον, means, *being the antitype,* corresponding with it, as the antitype to the type, the truth to the shadow. "Now," that is, in the New Law, "saveth you," (in Greek, *saveth us,* the *Codex Vaticanus,* has ὑμας, *you*), from the death of the soul ; as the waters, on which the ark was borne aloft, saved Noe and his family from temporal drowning. The points of correspondence between the diluvian water and baptism are many. In the former, while the inmates of the ark were saved, the wicked, were drowned and buried ; in the latter, our sins are buried, and we are become dead to sin. In the former, the ark was borne aloft, and salvation secured to its inmates ; in the latter, we are raised to a new life and saved from the consequences of our sins, viz., spiritual and eternal death. "Not the putting away of the filth of the flesh," that is ; it is not inasmuch as it is an external rite cleansing our bodies, that baptism produces these salutary effects of grace and spiritual regeneration : " but the examination of a good conscience ;" but, inasmuch as this rite is accompanied by the internal conditions and dispositions ("a good conscience"), which the subject of baptism, when interrogated, sincerely, and in the presence of God, declares he possesses. There is allusion in this to the questions usually put to the person to be baptized, whether "*he believes in God ?*" &c., "*renounces Satan and all his pomps ?*" The word "examination," or interrogation, is put for the aforesaid dispositions, regarding which the subject of baptism is usually interrogated before receiving the sacrament, and "a good conscience towards God," regards the sincerity of his conviction that he possesses the necessary dispositions. These salutary effects are ascribed to baptism in consequence of " the resurrection of Jesus Christ ; " either, because this resurrection is the exemplary cause or model of our spiritual resurrection and justification ; " *resurrexit propter justificationem nostram,*" or its supplemental cause ; since, "if Christ had not risen, our faith would be vain," and proved to be unfounded, as resting on the promises of one who would have deceived us, and proved himself to be an impostor.

22. "Who is on the right hand of God ;" this refers to his human nature ; considered according to this nature, he holds the highest place in heaven next to the Divinity. and before all other creatures. In these words, the Apostle conveys a tacit exhortation to us to suffer with Christ for justice sake, in order to become partakers in his glory. "Swallowing down death, that we might be made heirs of life everlasting." These words are not found in the Greek ; they are, however, read in all Latin copies, and cited by the Latin Fathers. They contain an allusion to the words of the Prophet Osee (13, 14), *O death ! I will be thy death ; O hell ! I will be thy bite.*" This will be

Text.

we might be made heirs of life everlasting : being gone into heaven, the angels and powers and virtues being made subject to him.

Paraphrase.

next him, the most honourable place in heaven, by his own death and resurrection he destroyed death, and deprived it of its sting, in order that we might be made heirs of life everlasting ; he has, also, ascended and gone into heaven, the entire heavenly host, of every order and degree, whether from the ranks of angels, powers, virtues, or any other order, having been subjected to him by his heavenly Father.

Commentary.

fully accomplished only on the final day, when the last enemy, death, shall be destroyed.—(1 Corinthians, chapter xv.)

"Being gone into heaven," whither he ascended by the power of his own divinity. These words are immediately connected with the words, "on the right hand of God." "'The angels,'" viz : those belonging to a lower order of blessed spirits ; " and powers and virtues," refer to the higher ranks ; under these are included all the the orders of heavenly spirits, and of all creatures that can be named, or that exist.—(Colos. i. 18, and ii. 10 ; Ephes. i. 22) ; "being made subject to him," as man ; for, his heavenly Father " *has subjected all things under his feet.*"—(Psalm viii. ; 1 Cor., xv. ; Ephes. i. &c.) As man, Christ is the head of the entire Church, militant and triumphant, comprising both angels and men.

CHAPTER IV.

Analysis.

In this chapter, the Apostle, after having digressed from the subject of the death of Christ (iii. 18), now returns to point out the lesson of instruction, which they should all derive from it, viz.: that they should no longer live in sin, but that their whole lives should be employed in performing the will of God (1, 2). For, they had already devoted too much time to the gratification of the corrupt passions, to which the unconverted Gentiles are prone (3), who, on seeing the Christian converts, now refuse to join them in the perpetration of their former crimes, execrate and blaspheme both them and their holy religion, as the enemies of all social and friendly intercourse among men (4). For these blasphemies, they shall one day have to render a most strict account to Christ, the judge of the living and the dead (5).

Against the Epicureans and other sects, who held, that, at death, man ceases to exist, and hence, no judgment or accountability, he proves from the fact of Christ having preached in the prison of Limbo, to those who had been long since dead, that Christ was to be judge of the dead as well as of the living (6). Not only have these been judged; but, in a short time, all things are to come to their final close; and hence, those whom he addresses, as well as all future generations, should be very circumspect and watchful duly to discharge the great duty of prayer (7).

He exhorts them to the practice of uninterrupted charity towards one another, and particularly of that branch of it, which consists in affording lodging and support to poor indigent stangers (8, 9).

He, next, prescribes the proper mode of exercising the spiritual gifts with which they might have been endowed for the good of others (10). These gifts he reduces to two heads, viz.: the gift of speaking, and the gift of action or administration; and both one and the other, should be exercised so as to promote, as indeed all our actions should, the glory of God through Jesus Christ (11).

He then renews his former exhortation to patience, on several grounds: because, by suffering they only submit to what all the elect before them had to undergo (12). Because, patient sufferings cause us to share in the sufferings of Christ, and lead to unalloyed joy and transport (13). Because, these sufferings and reproaches are the source of peculiar blessedness (14). From this peculiar blessedness, he excludes sufferings, undergone for the commission of crime (15, 16). He exhorts them to patience, because they are thus submitting to the general will of God, in saving his elect (17). Finally, he encourages them to commit their souls to God (19).

Text.	Paraphrase.
1. CHRIST therefore having suffered in the flesh, be you also	1. Since, therefore, Christ has suffered for us in his human and passible nature, the just for the unjust, to

Commentary.

1. "Christ, therefore, having suffered in the flesh." In some Greek copies it is, *having suffered for us.* The words "*for us*" are omitted in the *Codex Vaticanus.* The Apostle returns to the subject of the death of Christ, from which he had digressed (iii. 18), and points out the moral lesson, of which it is suggestive, "you should be armed with the same thought," *i.e.*, a thought, which his death suggests, owing to the

Text.

armed with the same thought : for he that hath suffered in the flesh hath ceased from sins.

2. That now he live the rest of his time in the flesh, not after the desires of men, but according to the will of God.

3. For the time past is sufficient to have fulfilled the will of the gentiles, for them who have walked in riotousness, lusts, excess of wine, revellings, banquetings, and unlawful worshipping of idols.

Paraphrase.

atone for, and destroy our sins, you too should be armed with the same, or a similar thought, of which his death is typically suggestive, viz. : that the Christian, who has suffered in his carnal passions, and crucified them, conformably to the lesson mystically taught us, by the crucifixion of Christ, has ceased from sins, and holds no more commerce with them, than the living do with the dead.

2. So as to live no longer according to the sinful desires of men, to which he has died, but to devote the remainder of his life in fulfilling the precepts of God, which are the formal expression of his will.

3. For, the portion of our time that has passed was sufficiently long (nay, too long), for complying with the corrupt will of the unconverted Gentiles, while we habitually indulged in deeds of uncleanness, whether interiorly, by illicit desires, or exteriorly, by drunken debauch and excessive indulgence in wine, in revolting and wanton feastings, in drinking matches, and in the execrable and abominable worshipping of idols.

Commentary.

mystical signification which it bears ; for, his death mystically represents our death to sin ; as his resurrection represents our resurrection to a new life of grace.   This idea is inculcated in many passages of St. Paul (Rom. vi. ; Colos. ii. and iii.)   "For he that hath suffered in the flesh ;" this is the thought with which they should be armed, and which they should be disposed to carry out in practice, viz. : that the man, who, after the example of Christ dying on the cross, "hath suffered in the flesh ;"—"flesh" here is taken in a different signification from that which it bears in the foregoing part of the verse, " Christ suffered in the flesh," which means, in his human or passible nature ; here, it means, having suffered in his carnal passions, and having crucified them—such a person, I say, "hath ceased from sins," holds no more intercourse with them, than the living hold with the dead.

2. "That now he may live the rest of his time in the flesh."   The Greek, literally translated, will run thus, *so as to live the remaining time in the flesh*, which may either refer to the man who has suffered in his carnal passions, as our Vulgate has it, or to the persons whom St. Peter addresses, "that now *you* may live the rest of *your* time," &c., "not after the desires of men," or, following the corrupt passions of men, "but according to the will of God," *i.e.*, in obeying and fulfilling God's commandments.

3. "For the past time is sufficient."   There is here, a *meiosis ;* the phrase implies more than it expresses, viz., that *too much* time was devoted to the corrupt practices to which he refers.   "To have fulfilled the will of the Gentiles."   In some Greek copies, the words, *for us*, are added, but they are not in the Vatican or Alexandrian MSS. " The time past is sufficient (*for us*) to have fulfilled," &c., that is, to have practised these evil deeds, to which the unconverted Gentiles are prone ; "for them who have walked," &c., *i.e.*, habitually lived and indulged "in riotousness, lusts," &c.   The former refers to outward, external deeds of uncleanness ; the latter, to internal desires, and acts of consent ; "excess of wine," drunkenness, arising from drinking wine, under which are included other strong intoxicating drinks ; revellings, feasts or banquets instituted for the purpose of wanton excesses ; "banquetings," drinking matches, which lead to intemperance and debauchery.   To such reference is made (Proverbs, xxii. 30), *"they that pass their time in wine, and study to drink off their cups."* "And unlawful," the Greek, αθεμιτοις, means *execrable*, or, *abominable*.   "Worshipping of idols."   It is not unlikely, that the Jews, to whom this Epistle is addressed, were prevailed upon by the Gentiles, among whom they lived, either from fear or friendship, or poverty, to join, at least in the illicit use of idolothytes, and that they

Text.

4. Wherein they think it strange, that you run not with them into the same confusion of riotousness, speaking evil of *you*.

5. Who shall render account to him, who is ready to judge the living and the dead.

6. For, for this cause was the gospel preached also to the dead; that they might be judged indeed, according to men, in the flesh : but may live according to God in the Spirit.

Paraphrase.

4. At this they are amazed, as at something strange and unaccountable, viz., that you refuse to join any longer with them, in the same evil practices of dissoluteness and luxury, and hence, they blaspheme your holy religion, and curse yourselves, as the enemies of all friendly and social intercourse.

5. For these blasphemies, as well as for all their deeds of dissoluteness, they shall render a rigorous account to him, who is ready soon to exercise the power given him by his Father, of judging both "the living," viz., those who shall be alive immediately before his coming, and "the dead," viz., those who departed this life during all preceding ages.

6. And it was in order that it might be clearly seen, that Christ is to be judge, not only of the living, but also of the dead, that the gospel was preached by him to the dead, shut up in the prison of Limbo, (iii. 18, 19), so that (*although*) these, long since departed, may have been judged by men, who look only to appearances, to be for ever lost, once their life in this world has been extinct, or at least to be fools in restraining their passions in hopes of future bliss, as, indeed, you are regarded now by the unconverted Gentiles (*v.* 4), (*still*) they may be found to enjoy with God—who judges according to truth—a glorious and immortal life in the world to come—("*in the spirit.*")

Commentary.

partook of them in common with the Gentiles ; or, it may be, that in this verse, the Apostle, in a special manner, addresses himself to the converted Gentiles. The corrupt practices of the Gentile world are here reduced, by the Apostle, to two sorts, viz., sins of uncleanness, and excessive intemperance in eating or drinking, the latter crime generally produces the former, "*in vino luxuria ;*" the excessive indulgence in strong drinks is a sure source of uncleanness, "*venter æstuans vino spumit in libidinem*" (St. Jerome). In order to incur the mortal guilt of intemperance, here denounced by the Apostle, it is by no means necessary, that a person should lose the use of reason. The excessive habitual indulgence in strong drinks, even unaccompanied with the loss of reason, would appear to entail mortal guilt, "*væ vobis, qui potentes estis ad bibendum vinum, et viri fortes ad miscendam ebrietatem.*"—(Isaias, v. 22).

4. "Wherein." The Greek, *ἐν ᾧ* means *at which*, but as it has reference to what follows, viz., their refusal to join in the former wicked practices, it is explained in Paraphrase, *at this ;* "they think it strange," or are completely at a loss to know how it could come to pass, viz., "that you run not with them into the same confusion." In Greek, *αναχυσιν, profusion*, or practices of abominable dissoluteness ; "speaking ill of you," and your holy religion, as opposed to friendly feelings and social intercourse.

5. For these blasphemies, and their wicked deeds, they shall one day render an account to Christ, who is ready, and armed with judicial power, to pass sentence on the "living and the dead." By "the living," whom Christ is to judge, are commonly understood, those who shall be alive at the time of his second coming, whose death will be followed by an instantaneous resuscitation, so that they may be regarded as having never died, and as always "living," the interval between their death and resuscitation being so very short. By the "dead," are understood such as have died during all preceding ages.

6. This verse is regarded by the generality of Commentators as exceedingly difficult and perplexing, and, indeed, it is not easy to see what interpretation to adopt, regarding it. It was the evident connexion which he thought he perceived between this, and verse 19 of the preceding chapter, that made St. Augustine interpret the words, "spirits

Commentary.

in prison" (iii. 19), of living men detained, in the days of Noe, in the prison of infidelity and vice; it was this that involved him in the insuperable difficulties attached to that strange interpretation. He thought the only interpretation of the word "dead," in this verse, that could at all accord with the context, is that which makes the word refer to sinners and infidels, "dead" to grace and faith; for, it is of such the Apostle is treating (4) and it is in reference to their blasphemies, he introduces the judgment to be passed by Christ (5), on the living and the dead, and the word "*dead*" (5) clearly refers to the same persons, that it refers to in this verse. Mauduit, who has been followed in the interpretation of verses 19, 20 of preceding chapter, while he rejects the opinion of St. Augustine regarding the passage referred to, and denies that there is reference to the preaching made by Christ, through Noe, to the incredulous antediluvians, follows St. Augustine in his interpretation of this verse, and in a dissertation, in which his reasoning is principally aimed against the interpretation of Estius—reasoning which seems to be more specious than solid—endeavours to show, that in this verse there must be question only of those who are "dead" to grace and faith. These are the dead, of whom it is said in the gospel, "suffer the dead to bury their dead;" and by the " living," in verse 5, he understands those who believe in Christ and are not deaf to his voice, of whom it is said, "*arise ye who sleep, and come forth from the dead, and Christ will enlighten you.*" "*The hour cometh, and now is, when the dead shall hear the voice of the Son of God, and those who shall hear will live.*" Mauduit lays some stress, also, on the difference between the original Greek words for "*preached*," in 19 of iii., and in this verse; in iii. 19 it is εκηρυξεν *proclaimed as herald*, in this, ευηγγελισθη, *evangelized*. The interpretation adopted in the Paraphrase is that given by A'Lapide. It has this advantage, that it retains the common meaning of the words "living and dead," when referring to the judging power of Christ, and it is free from the objections to which the reasoning of Estius is liable, although both agree in giving the same interpretation of the passage, and understand it of the preaching made by Christ, during the brief period of the separation of his soul from his body, to the souls shut up in the prison of Limbo.

"For, for this cause was the gospel preached also to the dead," viz., to show that those who were long dead were to be judged by Christ; this the Apostle is anxious to demonstrate, in opposition to the false tenets of the Pagan sects, particularly the Epicureans, among whom the early converts from Judaism and Paganism lived. With them it was a favourite maxim, that after death the soul had perished with the body, without further accountability; and hence, during life, we should deny ourselves no gratification whatever; their motto being, "let us eat and drink, for to-morrow we shall die," (1 Cor. xv.); against these St. Paul directs chap. xv. of his 1st Epistle to the Corinthians. "That they might be judged, indeed, according to men, in the flesh." If we confine the word "dead," merely to the antediluvians, whose souls were saved in the deluge, then the words mean, so that *although* they may have been judged by men, Noe and his children, as by all future generations, whom the history of the deluge reached, to be for ever lost to God and heaven—as many suppose with St. Augustine—"in the flesh," that is, judging merely according to appearance, as mankind always do: *still*, they "live" in the judgment of God—which is always according to the truth—"in the spirit," that is, a life of immortality and glory in the world to come. If the word "dead" refer to *all* the spirits shut up in Limbo, then, the latter words will have a meaning perfectly in accordance with the context, that *although* all these dead, to whom the gospel was preached, may, during life, have been judged by foolish men, to have perished for ever, "in the flesh," *i.e.*, the moment the dissolution of their souls from their bodies occurred—or, judged by men, who merely look to external things ("in the flesh") to be fools and madmen for mortifying their passions, as they judge of you now (4)—*still*, in the judgment of God, they will be found to have earned for themselves a glorious and happy life. The same judgment you, too, are to expect if you live "according to the will of God" (2). The only objection that can be urged against this interpretation is, that the particles "*although*" and "*still*," expressive of opposition between the two members of the sentence, "that (*although*) they might be judged," "but (*still*) may live according to God," &c., are added to the interpretation. This difficulty will vanish on a close examination of the

Text.	Paraphrase.
7. But the end of all is at hand. Be prudent therefore, and watch in prayers.	7. Christ is ready to judge the living and the dead, to punish the wicked, and reward the patient suffering of the just, and that at no distant time ; for, the final end of all is fast approaching. In order, then, to be fully prepared for his coming, be prudent and circumspect, and be sober and vigilant for the due exercise of the important duty of prayer.
8. But before all things have a constant mutual charity among yourselves : for charity covereth a multitude of sins.	8. Above all things, entertain for each other mutual unceasing feelings of charity, which nothing can interrupt ; for, this charity covers the sins of the neighbour, be they ever so numerous, and obtains or merits the remission of our own.
9. Using hospitality one towards another without murmuring.	9. Practise the virtue of hospitality, by harbouring in your houses and supporting your indigent Christian brethren, without murmuring at the inconvenience or expense which the laudable exercise of this virtue may entail upon you.

Commentary.

text, for, it is clear, there is an opposition between the two members of the sentence—"judged according to men in the flesh "—"live according to God in the spirit ; " and the addition, in the interpretation of the particles in question, serves only to express more clearly this implied opposition.

7. This verse may be connected with the preceding, thus : not only has the end of these men, to whom Christ preached in Limbo, and upon whom judgment has been already passed, come, but the end of us all, and the entire world, is fast approaching. It is, however, more commonly connected, as in Paraphrase. "The end of all is at hand," may refer to the near approach of the death of each individual, at which his judgment takes place, and his eternal doom sealed ; or to the near approach of the day of judgment, the world being now in its last stage, "*hæc est hora novissima*' (1 John, ii. 18) ; "*in quos fines seculorum devenerunt*" (1 Cor. x. ii.) ; and the time that intervenes, be it ever so long, compared with eternity, is but as yesterday, which is past and gone. "Be prudent, therefore," that is, circumspect, in all your actions, observing that prudence of salvation, which is true wisdom with God. "And watch in prayers." The Greek word for "watch," νήψατε, also means, *be sober*, in which signification it is taken (chap. v. 8). Watch and be sober for the exercise of prayer ; for, the prayers of such as are given to intoxication are heavy, drowsy, and unacceptable to God. There is allusion in these words to the words of our Redeemer (Matthew, xxv. 13, and xxvi. 41).

8. "But before all things." These words show the importance of charity, which is justly designated, *the queen of virtues*. "Have a constant mutual charity among yourselves." The word "constant" means, that their charity for one another should be persevering and uninterrupted. "For charity covereth a multitude of sins." These words are commonly understood to refer to the sins of our neighbour, and to the offences committed by him against us. These charity dictates to us to palliate and excuse ; for, "charity is patient, kind, beareth all things, endureth all things " (1 Cor. xiii.) ; and hence, by dissembling and pardoning the sins of our neighbour, we most effectually secure the inestimable blessing of concord and peace. The Apostle appears to allude to the words (Proverbs, x. 12), "hatred stirreth up strifes, and charity covereth all sins," wherein reference is made to the sins of our neighbour. No doubt, the words will, even in this interpretation, indirectly include the sins of the man who exercises charity, by *obtaining* their remission, should there be question of *mortal*, or by *meriting* the remission of *venial* sins, in a man already justified. Some interpreters say, there is direct reference to the sins of the man who exercises charity, and that this is proposed by the Apostle as a motive of reward for the cultivation of charitable feelings. Both interpretations are adopted in the Paraphrase.

9. "Using hospitality one to another," that is, towards such as require it. By "hospitality" is meant, the exercise of Christian charity in affording shelter, lodging

Text.

10. As every man hath received grace, ministering the same one to another: as good stewards of the manifold grace of God.

11. If any man speak, *let him speak* as the words of God. If any man minister, *let him do it* as of the power, which God administereth: that in all things God may be honoured through JESUS CHRIST: to whom is glory and empire for ever and ever. Amen.

Paraphrase.

10. Let each one, who has been endowed with any spiritual gift, employ and minister it with the same liberality with which it was bestowed on him by God, for the service of his neighbour; all persons thus gifted should regard themselves merely as faithful stewards of the manifold grace and gifts of God, and dispense them accordingly.

11 If any one be endowed with the grace of the word; if he speak, whether to explain the mysteries of faith, and instruct in the Christian doctrine, or to console those under affliction, or to exercise the gift of tongues or interpretation, let him employ words perfectly in accordance with the truths of faith, without any admixture of error—if he exercise any spiritual ministration, whether in curing the sick, or administering the sacraments of the Church, let him, in the exercise of such ministry, display that zeal and fervour with which God inspires those engaged in his service; so that by the proper exercise of all these gifts and all your actions, God may be honoured and glorified, through the merits of our Lord Jesus Christ, to whom is due eternal honour and empire for ever and ever. Amen.

Commentary.

and support to destitute Christian strangers. The practice of receiving Christian strangers into their houses was much recommended in the primitive Church, and was a very necessary exercise of Christian charity, owing to the want of accommodation at inns, and on account of the dangers, both to faith and morals, to which the recently converted would be exposed, by associating with infidels. Hence, the usage among the early churches of giving passports or "*tesseræ hospitalitatis*," on showing which, a Christian was sure of a hospitable reception from his brethren of the faith. The Apostle here recommends the exercise of this virtue, "without murmuring," either at the number or condition of the poor Christian strangers, to whom it might become necessary at times to afford accommodation.

10. He now instructs them in the proper exercise of the spiritual gifts and ministrations gratuitously conferred on them by God. "Hath received grace." By "grace," as appears from the Greek word, χαρισμα, is meant, any gratuitous gift. These gifts were bestowed on them liberally and gratuitously for the good of others; and hence, they should be exercised in the same way ("as every man hath received," &c.), gratuitously and liberally. "As good stewards of the manifold grace of God," they should recollect that they are merely dispensers of a deposit placed in their hands; they should, then, administer it according to the will of him from whom they received it, neither allowing it to remain idle, nor employing it for their own interest or selfish advantages. "The manifold grace of God" (*vide* Rom. xii. 6).

11. These gifts are reduced by the Apostle to two great divisions, viz., the gift of the word and of action. This is conformable to the division made by St. Paul (Rom. xii., and 1 Cor. xii.) "If any one speak," by which is meant: if any one is called to exercise in the Church the gift of *wisdom*, or *knowledge*, or *prophecy, doctrine, exhortation, interpretation* (*vide* Rom. xii.), "let him speak as the words of God," that is, let him say nothing that is not perfectly in accordance with the truths of God, and worthy of the minister, through whom God speaks. The phrase, "as the words of God," is perfectly similar to the words, "according to the rule of faith."—(Rom. xii. 6). "If any one minister," that is, be gifted with the grace of action, if he exercise any spiritual ministry, whether in curing the sick; or, as probably the words refer to the duties of the early deacons, in administering the Holy Eucharist, or relieving the corporal wants and necessities. "As of the power which God administereth," that is, let him display that zeal and fortitude in overcoming difficulties which God supplies

Text.

12. Dearly beloved, think not strange the burning heat which is to try you, as if some new thing happened to you:

13. But if you partake of the suffering of Christ, rejoice that when his glory shall be revealed you may also be glad with exceeding joy.

14. If you be reproached for the name of Christ, you shall be blessed: for that which is of the honour, glory and power of God, and that which is his Spirit, resteth upon you.

Paraphrase.

12. Dearly beloved, be not surprised, nor consequently troubled, at the fire of tribulation and persecution which you endure, sent you by God, to test your virtue, and exercise your patience, as if something new had happened you, that is to say, as if your case were a departure from the ordinary providence which God has at all times manifested towards his elect.

13. But since by thus suffering patiently for justice sake, you share and take a part in the sufferings of Christ, you should now rejoice, in order that, at the revelation of his glory hereafter, you may become partakers of unmixed joy and ineffable transport.

14. And if you suffer reproach for bearing the name of Christian, and professing the doctrine of Christ, you are blessed here in firm hope, and shall be blessed, hereafter, in the enjoyment of never ending happiness; for, far from its being dishonourable; inglorious, or cowardly in you to bear silently such reproaches; on the contrary, you alone are possessed of real honour, glory and fortitude abidingly conferred on you by the power of God and of his Holy Spirit, the only source of good gifts.

Commentary.

to those engaged in his service. "That in all things," in all our actions, no matter how apparently indifferent, "God may be honoured." This should be the great end of all our ministrations and actions, "through Jesus Christ," since it is to his merits we are indebted for the grace through which our actions are rendered acceptable with God. "To whom," refers either to Jesus Christ or to God, "is glory and empire," &c.

12. The Apostle again adverts to the subject of patience under afflictions, of which he had been treating already, in several passages of this Epistle. "Think not strange the burning heat." In the Greek are added the words, τῇ ἐν ὑμῖν, *which is in you. i.e.*, feel not surprised at seeing yourselves subjected to the fire of persecution and tribulation, which you have to submit to. "Which is to try you." The object of God in sending these afflictions is to try your virtue, and test your patience ; for, "as gold and silver are tried in the fire, so are acceptable men in the furnace of humiliation."—(Eccles. ii. 5). "As if something new had happened to you," that is, be not surprised at the tribulations which befall you, as if something new or strange had happened you, as if, in your case God had departed from the ordinary treatment which he always exhibits towards his elect. Persecutions have been always the chosen inheritance of God's servants. *"From the protomartyr Abel, to the last of the elect, persecution will never cease to be the portion of God's children."*—Venerable Bede.

13. This is an additional motive to suffer patiently, because, by so doing, they share in the sufferings of Christ, their sufferings are united with his (2 Cor. i. 5), "as the sufferings of Christ abound in us."—(Heb. xiii. 13, xi. 26; 2 Cor. iv. 10; Rom. viii. 17 : Gal. vi. 17). Christ is our head—we his members; we are also incorporated with him by baptism. "Rejoice," then, as you know that these sufferings are united with those of Christ. "That when his glory shall be revealed," on the day of judgment, "you may also be glad with exceeding joy;" and the present joy which you now feel, although embittered by pains and crosses, will then be exchanged for ineffable, unalloyed joy, which will manifest itself in transport and the rapturous joy of your glorified bodies.

14. "And if you be reproached for the name of Christ." The profession of Christianity had been to the first Christians a subject of reproach and disgrace. "You shall be blessed." This is a subject of peculiar blessedness rather than of reproach. "For that which is of honour," &c., that is, far from its being either dishonourable, or inglorious, or cowardly, to profess Christianity, and to bear such reproaches silently, as

Text.

15. But let none of you suffer as a murderer, or a thief, or a railer, or a coveter of other men's things.

16. But if as a Christian, let him not be ashamed, but let him glorify God in this name.

17. For the time is that judgment should begin at the house of God. And if first at us, what shall be the end of them that believe not the gospel of God?

Paraphrase.

15. But in pointing out the merit of patient suffering, I speak not of suffering in a bad cause, on account of outraging the laws of society; for none of you should draw down upon himself merited punishment, due to a homicide, or a thief, or a slanderer, or to such as curiously pry into other persons' affairs, in order to circumvent and rob them.

16. But if any one of you suffer for being a Christian, and for practising Christian virtues, far from feeling ashamed, he should give glory to God on this account.

17. For, the present life is the time during which judgment is to commence with the house of God, with his own chosen elect; but if God be so severe in his remedial punishment which he exercises in the salutary chastisements of his mercy towards us, if the merciful beginning be so severe, what shall be the severity with which his outraged justice shall continue to punish for eternity, those who obstinately disobey and refuse to embrace his gospel?

Commentary.

probably had been charged upon the faithful by their enemies; on the contrary, they alone were possessed of real honour, and glory, and fortitude, which God only can confer, and which comes from his Holy Spirit, the giver of every good gift. In the Greek we have not "honour or power;" it runs thus: ὅτι τὸ τῆς δόξης καὶ τὸ τοῦ Θεοῦ πνεῦμα, *because what is of glory, and the Spirit of God, rests upon you.* But in some Greek copies are added the following words: *indeed in them it* (the Spirit of God) *is blasphemed, but in you it is glorified.* These words are not found in any Latin copies, nor in the Syriac version, nor in the chief manuscripts.

15. The Apostle excludes from all merit suffering in a bad cause; for, to suffer the penalties due to human justice, in consequence of outraging the laws of society, far from being honourable, is a disgrace to religion. Or "railer;" for this the Greek has κακοποιός, *an evil doer*, one who maliciously injures his neighbour in person or property. "Or a coveter of other men's things." The Greek word for this, αλλοτριοεπισκοπος, means, *one who pries into the concerns of others.* The Vulgate has, however, fairly given the meaning, because the words mean, one who pries into other men's concerns, for the purpose of circumventing them, and rapaciously depriving them of their property, taking advantage of the knowledge tuus unwarrantably acquired.

16. But if any one among you be subjected to suffering for bearing the name of Christ and for practising the virtues which Christianity prescribes, far from feeling ashamed, he should glory "in this name," that is, on this account, or, as in some Greek copies, *in this part.* The Alexandrian and Vatican MSS. support the Vulgate, ἐν τῷ ὀνόματι τούτῳ. Such was the conduct of the Apostles, who "went rejoicing from the presence of the council, because they were judged worthy to suffer reproach for Christ."—Acts, v. 41.

17. The Apostle holds out, as an additional motive of consolation for the faithful under affliction, the consideration, that in enduring affliction, they are only submitting to the general will of God in bringing his elect to salvation. "The time is," the present life is the time, "that judgment," the consoling chastisements of God's mercy, "should begin at the house of God," viz., his Church, termed by St. Paul to Timothy, "the house of God." There is allusion to the passage in Ezechiel, ix. 6, where the Lord commands the destroying angels—"begin ye at my sanctuary." "And if first at us," which shows what the Apostle means by "the house of God," in the foregoing, "what shall be the end of them that believe not"—(or, as in the Greek, ἀπειθούντων, *disbelieve*)—"the gospel?" that is, if the storm of God's wrath shall commence with God s elect, whom he shall visit with punishment, as a merciful chastisement for the past, and as a preservative against the future, what shall be its endless continuance on

Text.

18. And if the just man shall scarcely be saved, where shall the ungodly and the sinner appear?

19. Wherefore let them also that suffer according to the will of God, commend their souls in good deeds to the faithful Creator.

Paraphrase.

18. And if the just man shall obtain salvation only at the expense of so much suffering and sacrifice, where shall the impious and sinful man appear on the day of judgment?

19. Wherefore, since it is only on condition of suffering that the just are saved, let those who, according to God's holy will, are doomed to suffer, commend their souls, as a deposit, into the hands of a faithful depositary, their Creator, not failing, however, on their own part, to co-operate by the performance of good works.

Commentary.

the reprobate upon whom it shall exercise its fury for eternity? If God be thus severe in the remedial chastisements of his mercy, what shall he be in the vindictive punishments of inexorable justice? Oh! blessed for ever be his mercy which has spared us from the eternal vengeance which our sins deserved.

18. "And if the just man shall scarcely be saved," *i.e.*, if he shall obtain salvation only at such sacrifices, by sufferings and afflictions in this life, "where shall the ungodly and sinner appear" when called to render an account to God in judgment? Of course, the Apostle wishes us to understand, that the impious and sinners shall be so terrified at the prospect of coming judgment, that, like men certain of condemnation, they will endeavour to shun the presence of the Judge; "they shall call on the mountains, &c., to hide them from the face of him that sitteth on the throne." The first part of the verse by no means regards the day of judgment, as if the Apostle wished to say, that on the day of judgment the just man shall scarcely be saved; for, on that day, "they shall stand in great constancy against those that afflicted them."—Wisdom, chap. v. The word "scarcely" regards the suffering of crosses in this life. This verse is quoted by St. Peter, from Proverbs, chap. ii., according to the Septuagint version. St. Jerome translates it from the Hebrew, thus: " if the just man receive (the punishment of his sins) in the earth, how much more the wicked and the sinner" (shall receive, in the life to come, the punishment of their crimes).—Proverbs, xi. 31.

19. This is the conclusion of the Apostle. "In good deeds" may mean (as in Paraphrase), not relying solely on their Creator, so as to do nothing themselves, but rather, on their own part, co-operating by good works; or, while suffering, commend your souls to God, "in good deeds," doing good for the evil inflicted on you by your persecutors.

"In good deeds." In Greek, *ἐν ἀγαθοποιΐα, in well doing*. The Vulgate is supported by the Syriac interpreter and the Alexandrian manuscript.

"The faithful Creator." In Greek, *as unto a faithful Creator*. The particle " as " is not in the Alexandrian nor in the Vatican manuscripts.

CHAPTER V.

Analysis.

In this chapter, the Apostle addresses himself to the pastors of the Church, and points out the mode in which they should tend the flocks committed to their care, and acquit themselves of their pastoral functions. They should, in tending their flocks, shun three vices directly at variance with their exalted calling ; these are, firstly, the performance of their functions not cheerfully, but with restraint arising from the necessity they were under of procuring thereby the necessary means of support, so opposed to the cheerfulness which springs from viewing their flocks, according to God ; secondly, the base vice of sordid avarice, so opposed to liberal and generous disinterestedness (2) ; and thirdly, domineering pride, so opposed to the example of humility, which every pastor is bound to give (3). By avoiding these vices and practising the opposite virtues, the pastors will merit to obtain, on the day of judgment, from Jesus Christ, the unfading crown of eternal life (4).

He next points out the reciprocal duties of the laity towards their pastors. They should be subject and obedient to them.

All, both pastors and people, should clothe themselves with humility, as their chief ornament (5). He tells them to humble themselves before God, in order that he may exalt them, by the effusion of the heavenly graces which he has in store, only for the humble—and, this humility they should manifest, by laying aside all anxious cares, and casting themselves on the Fatherly Providence of God (6, 7). He, next, recommends them to practise the virtues of sobriety and vigilance—two virtues most necessary for a soldier on guard, in order to defeat the stratagems and assaults of a powerful and subtle foe, such as the devil, the sworn enemy of man, is. They should courageously resist him, by the unshaken firmness of their faith (8, 9). He next promises them the powerful protection of God to guard them, and bring them to a happy end (10).

He closes the Epistle with informing them, that Silas is the bearer of this Epistle to them ; they will thus be secured against the imposition often practised by false teachers, in substituting counterfeit Epistles. He ends with the usual salutation.

Text

1. THE ancients therefore that are among you, I beseech, who am myself also an ancient and a witness of the sufferings of Christ ; as also a partaker of that glory which is to be revealed in time to come :

Paraphrase.

1. Since, therefore, the just man will be saved only with great difficulty, and God's judgment is to commence with his own house (iv. 17, 18), I, who am myself a fellow-bishop and pastor, a witness also of the sufferings of Christ, to be a sharer in that glory to be revealed at a future day, implore and exhort the bishops and pastors who preside over you :

Commentary.

1. "The ancients, therefore, that are among you." "Therefore," is not in some Greek copies. It is found in the Alexandrian and Vatican MSS. It may be connected with the foregoing, as in Paraphrase :—therefore, since judgment commences first with God's house (iv. 17), and in a special manner with the pastors of God's people, it is meet, they should prepare for this responsibility. "The ancients." The Greek word, πρεσβυτερους, viewed according to etymology, means *elderly men*, or men advanced in years but since the word is employed in Scripture to designate

Text.

2. Feed the flock of God which is among you, taking care *of it* not by constraint, but wil ingly according to God ; not for filthy lucre's sake, but voluntarily :

Paraphrase.

2. Feed, with the wholesome pastures of spiritual knowledge, with the heavenly graces imparted through the sacraments, the flock of God, over whom you have charge, superintending and caring it, not from feelings of co-action, as if forced thereunto by the mercenary motive of securing the necessary means of support ; but with cheerfulness, regarding it according to the will of God, which is, to promote its spiritual good, and in view of a spiritual reward—not with the sordid view of acquiring thereby wretched pelf, more enlarged incomes, but with feelings of generous and cheerful disinterestedness.

Commentary.

offices and dignity rather than age (the signification which the word bears here, as is clear from verses 2 and 4), the office has been expressed in the Paraphrase, bishops and pastors, or priests of the first order ; for to them alone, strictly speaking, could be applied the words (verse 2), "feed the flock," &c., in the fullest and most exalted sense. Of course, the admonition contained here applies also to the priests of the second order, charged with the care of souls. That the Greek word for "ancients," includes not only priests of the second order, but of the first order, or bishops also, is clear from Epistle to Titus (chap i. 5, 7). "That are among you," that is, that preside over you. "I beseech." The Greek word, παρακαλῶ, means also, *I exhort.* "Who am myself also an ancient." The Greek word, συμπρεσβυτερος, means, *who am a co-presbyter,* or, fellow-bishop ; the word expresses the Episcopal office. Although, as Prince of the Apostles, he might call himself, *chief of bishops ;* still, from a feeling of humility, he places himself on an equality with them. The same feeling of humility is observable in all the documents addressed by St. Peter's successors, the Sovereign Pontiffs, to the other bishops, during the different ages of the Church : *Servus Servorum Dei,* they take as their ordinary title. "And a witness of the sufferings of Christ," may mean (as in Paraphrase), that he witnessed all that Christ endured, both through life and in his sacred passion—or, a witness or martyr (by my sufferings), to the sufferings of Christ, and to the faith founded thereon. This latter interpretation is grounded on the signification of "witness," in Greek, *martyr.* They were called *martyrs,* who, by their own sufferings, bore the sincerest testimony to the truth of the Christian faith. The antithesis which exists between this and the following member of the sentence, renders this latter interpretation very probable ; the Apostle, by referring to his own sufferings, wishes to animate his brethren to the faithful discharge of their pastoral functions, notwithstanding the violence of persecution. "And also a partner of that glory," &c. This may express merely a strong Christian hope, or it may be the result of some revelation with which God had favoured him.

2. "Feed the flock of God." They are charged with the flock of another, to whom they shall render an account of their stewardship. "Feed," ποιμανατε. This word is employed to signify, *govern, direct,* &c. It expresses a charge analogous to that which shepherds have over their flocks. "Which is among you," or which is given in charge to you ; each one is responsible for that portion of God's flock, confided to his care. "Taking care of it." The Greek word, επισκοπουντες, literally means, *Episcopizing,* or *superintending it ;* it expresses the vigilant care, which a pastor of souls should use, in guarding and tending his flock. "Not by constraint," from the necessity you are under of doing so in order to acquire a livelihood, while you would otherwise neglect them ; "but willingly, according to God." The words "according to God," are not in the Greek. They are found in the Alexandrian MS. They explain more fully what the word, "willingly," means, viz., with that cheerfulness which the consideration of the exalted nature of your functions, viewed according to God and his holy will—and that is, that we should advance the spiritual interests of souls, with a view to a spiritual reward—is apt to engender. "Not for filthy lucre sake," that is, from motives of sordid avarice, a vice so disgraceful in a pastor of souls ; the effect of which is to harden his heart, to inspire him with low, grovelling ideas, to make him prostitute the most exalted

Text.

3. Neither as lording it over the clergy, but being made a pattern of the flock from the heart.

4. And when the prince of pastors shall appear, you shall receive a never-fading crown of glory.

5. In like manner, ye young men, be subject to the ancients. And do ye all insinuate humility one to another, for *God resisteth the proud, but to the humble he giveth grace.*

Paraphrase.

3. Neither acting as persons lording it over the flocks specially intrusted to each ; but exhibiting yourselves as patterns and models to them in all sincerity and truth, and with a view of advancing their spiritual interests.

4. And when the prince of pastors, Jesus Christ, by whom both pastors and people were purchased, shall appear, to pass sentence on all mankind, you shall receive an unfading, ever-blooming crown of glory—or, the glorious crown of eternal life.

5. In like manner, do you, both inferior clergy and laity, fulfil the reciprocal duty of obedience and subjection to your bishops and pastors ; and I enjoin you all, both pastors and people, to manifest feelings of humility towards one another, making this great fundamental virtue your chief exterior ornament ; for, God resists the proud, but to the humble he giveth grace.

Commentary.

mysteries of his sacred calling to the gratification of this wretched and unmeaning passion, and even at the awful moment of death, to blind him against the terrors of approaching judgment. "But voluntarily," from feelings of liberal and generous disinterestedness. Detachment from early treasures should be a distinguishing characteristic of him, who, at his first step into the sanctuary, takes God for his inheritance. "*Dominus pars hereditatis meæ et calicis mei, &c.*," are the words of the Cleric on his first entrance into the sanctuary.

3. "Neither as lording it over the clergy." By "clergy," are meant, according to some, the subordinate ministers of religion, subject to the bishop. The Greek word, however, των κληρων, *lot* or *inheritance*, renders the opinion which understands it of the particular congregations which fell to the *lot* of each pastor to superintend, by far the more probable interpretation. In it is contained an allusion to the usage observed among the Jews of old, of receiving by lot their different inheritances. Hence, the word, *clergy*, is generally applied to the sacred ministers who are especially the inheritance of the Lord. "A pattern" (in Greek τυποι, types or *patterns*) "of the flock ;" these latter words show that it is to the flock, the word "*clergy*" refers here. "From the heart," is not found in the Greek. It means, not by a false, hypocritical show of virtues ; but by an exhibition of real, genuine virtues, or from a sincere regard for their spiritual welfare and the glory of God.

4. "And when the prince of pastors," Jesus Christ, to whom belong pastors and people, purchased by his blood, "shall appear," come in his glory to judge the world, to reward and punish, according to man's deserts, "you shall receive a never fading crown of glory. "A crown," the reward of merit, "never-fading," αμαραντινον, the amaranth, a flower so called, because it never fades, is employed as an image of heavenly bliss, unlike the crown given to the victors in the Grecian games, made of bay, laurel, &c., this shall always remain the same, ever-blooming and unfading. Such is the reward which the Apostle wishes the ministers of the gospel ever to keep in view in the discharge of the arduous and exalted functions of their sacred office. It is disputed whether the "crown of glory" regards the *essential* happiness of the blessed, the "*corona justitiæ*," which St. Paul expected (2 Tim. iv. 8), or, the *aureola*, or *accidental* reward, which in heaven is reserved for the Doctors, who, after instructing many unto justice, "*shall shine as stars for ever.*"—(Daniel). In the preceding passage, can be seen how strongly the Apostle enjoins on pastors the avoidance of three vices, so much at variance with the pastoral state, viz., performing their spiritual functions solely with the view of avoiding poverty ; avarice (verse 2), and pride (verse 3) ; or, it should rather have been said, that he points out the vicious ends and motives that destroy the good effects of the pastoral ministry.

5. He now points out the duty which the people reciprocally owe their pastors ; and

Text.	Paraphrase.
6. Be you humbled therefore under the mighty hand of God, that he may exalt you in the time of visitation :	6. Be ye, therefore, humbled under the powerful hand of God, that he, who gives his grace to the humble, may, after having copiously showered down upon you his graces, exalt you in the day when he shall come to judge the world, to separate the sheep from the goats :
7. Casting all your care upon him, for he hath care of you.	7. Casting aside all anxious care, and placing your trust in him ; for, he has charge of you.

Commentary.

this is subjection and obedience. This is the peculiar virtue of persons placed under authority ; the other virtues the people may learn from the lives and conduct of their pastors, who should be a "pattern to them from the heart" (verse 3). "Ye young men." The laity, who are contrasted with the "ancients," or pastors. He calls them "young men," because generally younger in age than their pastors, who, in the time of St. Peter, were far advanced in life, when vested with the pastoral dignity. Others understand by "young men," young persons in general, who ought to be reverential towards those, who are advanced in life. The former interpretation is more probable ; for, all young men are not bound to be "subject" to the old, as is here required. By the "ancients," are meant the pastors of the Church, especially the bishops, to whom both laity and inferior clergy should be subject and obedient. The word, viewed according to etymology, only means persons advanced in age ; but in almost all languages, men vested with authority, whether in church or state, are designated by words expressive of age ; because, those appointed to such offices were, generally speaking, far advanced in life. For instance, the terms, *Senate, Patricians,* &c., though according to etymology referring to age, are employed, according to present usage, to express office or dignities. In many instances, to adhere strictly to etymology would be silly in the extreme, as is apparent, for example, in the original etymological signification of the word, *Pontiff*, which means "*a bridge maker*" (Pontifex), "*Episcopus*," bishop, which meant originally, "*an inspector*." "Deacon" originally meant, a "*waiter ;*" "Apostle," "*one sent*," &c. "But, do ye all insinuate humility to one another." The Greek is, "*but do ye all (subordinate to one another) put on humility as an exterior garment.*" The Greek word for "insinuate," εγκομβωσασθε, means, *put on as the exterior garment covering all the rest,* or, as the fibula closely knotting together the other virtues ; hence, it means to put on humility, as their chief habit or ornament. This applies to both pastors and people. The word, *subordinate,* or *subject,* is not found in either the Alexandrian or Vatican MS. "For *God resisteth the proud*," &c. This sentence, quoted by St. James also (iv. 6), is taken, as to sense, from the Book of Proverbs (iii. 34). It is translated by St. Jerome from the Hebrew : "he shall scorn the scorners," which is in substance the same as, "he shall resist the proud," for, the "*proud*," scorn and deride others, "and to the meek he will give grace," in substance, the same as "*he shall give grace to the humble ;*" for they are generally meek and forbearing.

6. With all humility, therefore, and fear, walk in the presence of God, whose powerful hand is raised to humble and depress the haughty. "That he may exalt you in the time of visitation ;" that, after having bestowed on you here the gifts of grace in store for the humble, he may bestow on you hereafter the crown of everlasting glory, when he shall come to judge the world. The words, "of visitation," are wanting in the Greek, which run thus : ἱνα ὑμας ὑψωση ἐν καιρῳ, *that he may exalt you in the time,* that is, in his own good time, or at a befitting opportunity. This entire passage is very like the passage of St. James (iv. 6 and 10).

7. These words express the humiliation of ourselves, which the Apostle inculcates (verse 6), "under the mighty hand of God." They involve the full resignation of ourselves and all our concerns into his adorable hands. They are perfectly similar to the words, Psalm liv. 23, "Cast thy care upon the Lord and he will sustain thee," and most probably, the Apostle quotes the words of the Psalmist. Of course, in this the Apostle prohibits neither the exercise of prudent foresight nor the employment of our active faculties, to bring about our ends. He only prescribes to us, after having done

Text.

8. Be sober and watch : because your adversary the devil, as a roaring lion, goeth about seeking whom he may devour.

9. Whom resist ye, strong in faith : knowing that the same affliction befalls your brethren who are in the world.

Paraphrase.

8. Be sober and temperate in the use of meat, drink, sleep, and the other comforts of life, and be also vigilant ; for, the sworn enemy of your race, by whom sin was first introduced into this world, the devil, the calumniator of mankind, is always on the alert, going about, like a roaring, hungry lion, seeking for some object of prey.

9. Whom resist ye courageously, firmly grasping the shield of faith, bearing in mind that the same crosses that befall you are borne by your brethren all over the earth, who join you in filling up what is wanting in you to the sufferings of Christ.

Commentary.

according to the rules of human prudence what in us lies, to leave the result of our undertakings in the hands of God, and to conform ourselves to his adorable will ; for, he will dispose of us better than we could ourselves either divine or anticipate ; even the crosses, trials, and privations, so opposed to our natural inclinations, are, in the gracious designs of his Providence, so many visitations of his mercy, weaning us from things of earth, and fixing our desires on things heavenly and eternal. We should, therefore, cast aside all undue anxiety in the several concerns of life, placing all our undertakings in the hands of God. " *Oculi mei semper ad Dominum, quoniam ipse evellet de laqueo pedes meos.*"—(Psalm xxv.)

8. " Be sober." The Greek word for this, *νηψατε*, is rendered *watch* (iv. 7) ; it means either " to be sober " or " vigilant," but here it must be rendered " be sober," because the following word signifies only " *to watch*," or "be vigilant." " Be sober," that is, temperate in the use of meat," &c., " and watch." Vigilance is an accompaniment of sobriety, as drowsiness and sleep are of intemperance. Similar is the precept given (Luke, xxi. 34):—"Take heed to yourselves lest, perhaps, your hearts be overcharged with surfeiting and drunkenness, and the cares of this life." Sobriety and vigilance are most indispensable for a soldier, while engaged in warfare and on guard, against the attacks of a wily and dangerous enemy. Such is the state of every Christian, during the whole course of his life. " Because your adversary," the sworn enemy of man, by whom sin and death were first introduced into this world (" *Satan*," or *accuser*," is the Hebrew word for " adversary.") " The devil," which means, calumnia·or ; hence called (Apocalypse, xii.) "the accuser of our brethren," for, he always endeavours to make men enemies to God and render them deserving of accusation before him. " As a roaring lion," the strongest and most furious animal in nature, " goeth about," seeking for some weak point of attack, in order to avail himself of the weakness of our nature and of that passion in particular, to the gratification of which we are most prone ; hence, commonly termed, our *predominant passion.* "Seeking whom he may devour." When drowsy and sluggish from the effects of intemperance, we are most exposed to the attacks of this powerful and subtle enemy. Hence, the Church commences the concluding hour of the divine office, Complin, with the words of this verse, in order to remind her ministers of the necessity of temperance and vigilance, at the close of the day, for resisting the temptation of the devil. From this passage we may clearly see the great power of the devil, this prince of the " *principalities and powers and spirits of wickedness in high places,*" with whom we are constantly engaged in deadly conflict.—(Ephes. vi.) Job assures us there is no power on earth *equal* to the devil : " *There is no power on earth that can be compared with him, that was made to fear no one.*"—(Job, xii. 24).

9. "Whom resist ye, strong in faith." In the panoply or full suit of spiritual armour, which St. Paul wishes the Christian warrior to put on, " faith " is marked out as the shield for resisting " all the fiery darts of the most wicked enemy."—(Ephesians, vi. 16). Here, St. Peter wishes the Christian warrior first to " resist " the enemy, and to do so firmly and bravely. " Strong in faith," the Greek word. *στερεοι*, means, *solid and fixed in faith*, it may be allusive to a fortification, wherein they are protected ; or,

Text.

10. But the God of all grace, who hath called us unto his eternal glory in Christ JESUS, after you have suffered a little, will himself perfect you, and confirm you, and establish you.

11. To him be glory and empire for ever and ever. Amen.

12. By Sylvanus, a faithful brother unto you, as I think I have written briefly: beseeching and testifying that this is the true grace of God wherein you stand.

Paraphrase.

10. But God, the source and author of every good gift, who out of his pure and gratuitous mercy, has called us through the merits of Jesus Christ, to a participation in his eternal glory, and has given so many pledges thereof by his grace, will himself bring you to consummate and perfect glory, and confirm and establish you unalterably in its eternal enjoyment, after you shall have borne comparatively light and trivial crosses, for a short time here below.

11. To him is due all glory for his gifts, and all power over creatures, for ever and ever. Amen.

12. Sylvanus, a faithful brother, I have made the bearer of this Epistle, which I have written to you, I should think briefly, considering the interest and pleasure its perusal will afford you, imploring and exhorting you to perseverance, and bearing witness, that the grace of faith, in which you still have faithfully persevered, is the true grace of God leading to eternal life.

Commentary.

more likely, the idea is the same as that conveyed by St. Paul—"taking the shield of faith"—by which is meant the consideration of the truths of faith, the menaces and hopes which they propose to us. Under "faith," is included the great confidence in God, which the consideration of the principles of faith is so calculated to inspire, and which will secure us against all our enemies. "If God be with us, whom shall we fear? "Knowing that the same affliction" (in Greek, τα αυτα των παθηματων, *the same afflictions*) "befalls your brethren," &c. Deriving consolation from the consideration, that in suffering, you are only conforming to the decrees of God's providence, wishing that all his elect should enter heaven by the road of suffering; and hence, nothing peculiarly difficult in their case, all "their brethren who are in the world" are treated similarly.

10. "But the God of all grace," from whom proceed all gratuitous gifts, "who hath called us unto his eternal glory." The Alexandrian and Vatican MSS. have, ὁ καλεσας ὑμας, called *you*. Among his gratuitous gifts is to be reckoned our call to a share in his eternal glory, of which he has given us an earnest in the manifold graces he bestows upon us, "in Christ Jesus." This call, and the graces consequent on it, are all owing to the merits purchased by the blood of Jesus Christ. "After you have suffered a little." "A little," probably refers both to the *duration* of their sufferings, "for that which is at present momentary and light," &c. (2 Cor. iv. 17), and the comparatively *light nature* of them. "The sufferings of this time are not worthy to be compared with the glory to come."—(Rom. viii. 18). "Will himself perfect, confirm, and establish you." In some Greek copies the words are read optatively, thus: "*may he perfect, confirm, strengthen, and establish you ;*" the sentence being thus composed of four members, instead of three, as in our version. But the Alexandrian and Vatican manuscripts, as also the Syriac version support the Vulgate reading. The words are nearly synonymous; and the idea derived from the material building is applied to the spiritual edifice of virtue and grace, which the Apostle here prays that God would perfect in them, unto the unchangeable state of glory.

11. "To him be glory and empire," that is, all the glory of his gifts, and power over all his creatures, for ever and ever. Amen.

12. "By Sylvanus ;" this is, most probably, Silas, the companion of St. Paul in preaching the gospel.—(Acts, xv. 40). "A faithful brother unto you, as I think I have written briefly." "Unto you," according to the Greek, ὑμιν τον πιστον αδελφον, is joined with "faithful," and means, who discharges a faithful ministry for you; but according to the Latin and Syriac copies, it is connected with "I have written." Silas was the bearer of the Epistle from Rome to the East. "As I think," *i.e.*, faithful to you, as I think; or more probably, I have written to you this Epistle, I think, briefly,

Text.	Paraphrase.
13. The church that is in Babylon, elected together with you, saluteth you : and so doth my son Mark.	13. The assemblage of the faithful at Rome, elected to the same grace with you, salute you, and wish you the abundance of all temporal and spiritual blessings, and so does my son, Mark, whom I have spiritually begotten, or who serves me as a son.
14. Salute one another with a holy kiss. Grace be to all you, who are in Christ JESUS. Amen.	14. Salute one another with a holy and chaste kiss. Grace and peace be to you all, who are incorporated with Christ Jesus, by your Christian profession.—Amen.

Commentary.

considering the matter so interesting to you, and your affectionate regard for myself. The Epistles of those we love are always considered brief, and never tiresome. "Beseeching;" the Greek word, παρακαλῶν, means also, *exhorting* you to perseverance in the faith, wherein you hold out, notwithstanding the pressure of persecution ; and "testifying that this is the true grace of God." As Apostle of God, I bear witness that the faith you received from us, and in which you still "stand," is the true grace of God, which leads to eternal life.

13. "The Church that is in Babylon," or the assemblage of the faithful, "elected together with you," called to the same faith and hope in eternal glory, "saluteth you," or wish you all blessings both temporal and spiritual. "In Babylon." Meaning the City of Rome.—(*Vide* Introduction).

"And so doth my son, Mark.' He refers to St. Mark, the Evangelist, whom he afterwards sent to found the Church of Alexandria, A.D. 45. "My son ;" either because he was spiritually begotten by him, and fully instructed in the faith (Baronius *Annal. Anno Christi*, 45) : or because he served him in the work of the Gospel with the fidelity and affection of a son, as St. Paul says of Timothy (Philippians ii.)

14. "With a holy kiss." that is a chaste embrace. "Grace be to you all." In Greek, ειρηνη, "*peace* be to you all." There is scarcely any difference in sense. The Hebrews, by wishing a person *peace*, wished him all spiritual and temporal blessings, which we mean by "grace." "Who are in Christ Jesus," that is, Christians incorporated with him, and forming the body, of which he is the mystic head.

SECOND EPISTLE OF ST. PETER.

Introduction.

CANONICITY OF.—We are informed by Origen (*in Explicatione* 1*mi Psalmi*); by Eusebius (*libro 3tio*, c. 3 and 19, and *libro 6to*, c. 19, *Hist. Eccles.*) ; and by St. Jerome (*in
Catalogo*), that the Canonicity or Divine authority of this Epistle was at first called in
question by some persons. The question of its Divine authority, as well as of its
authenticity, was raised, St. Jerome informs us, in consequence of the difference, or
dissimilarity of style, observable between it, particularly in the second chapter, and the
first Epistle. But this difficulty is answered by St. Jerome himself (*Ep. ad Hedi-
biam, quest.* 11), by attributing the difference of style to the different scribes, whom
the Apostle was obliged to employ in both cases. St. Mark had been employed by
him, as scribe, in penning the first Epistle (chap. v. verse 13) ; Glaucias acted in the
same capacity, in reference to this, as we are assured by St. Clement (*lib.* 7, *Strom.*)
According, then, to the opinion of St. Jerome, the Apostle dictated this Epistle in
Hebrew ; but, his scribes, in penning them in Greek, each followed his own peculiar
mode of writing ; and hence, the diversity of style. It may be, also, said in reply to
the difficulty arising from the difference of style in the two Epistles, that the difference
of the subjects and matter treated of in both, accounts for the diversity of style. One
and the same person, in treating of different subjects, even under the influence of
inspiration, may employ a different style in each. Of this, the diversity of style, which
marks the Epistle of St. Paul to the Hebrews, and his other Epistles, furnishes a clear
illustration. The strong feelings of holy indignation and burning zeal, with which the
heart of the Prince of the Apostles was filled, in denouncing the heretics of the day,
have, doubtless, altered the meekness of his tone, and the usual character of his style in
this Epistle.

Others maintain, that there is no difference of style at all observable in both Epistles.
The subject matter of both is quite different ; but, the style, the same. This latter
opinion is held by the Centuriators of Magdeburg.

It is now a point of Catholic faith, that this Epistle of St. Peter is Canonical or
divinely inspired. This has been defined in the Council of Trent (*SS.* 4 *Decretum de
Canonicis Scripturis*). All the ancient Councils, in which catalogues of the books of
Scripture were drawn up, place this second Epistle of St. Peter amongst them, viz. :—
the Council of Laodicea, the third of Carthage, the Council of Florence, and, finally,
the Council of Trent. The Holy Fathers also, who have drawn up catalogues of
the inspired books, reckon this among the number, viz. : Athanasius (*in Synopsi*) ;
Augustine (*de doctrina Christiana*, c. viii.) ; Innocent I. (*Ep.* 3, *ad Exuperium*) ;
Gelasius I., in the Council of Seventy Bishops ; Origen (*Homilia* 7, *in Jos*) ;

and St. Jerome, in many parts of his writings. The objection against its Canonicity, founded on the circumstance of its not being found in the Syriac edition of the Scriptures, has very little weight. For, the Syriac Fathers, Ephrem and John Damascene, quoted from the Greek version of it, as inspired ; and the latter Father placed it on the catalogue of Sacred Scripture. The objection would militate equally against the Second and Third Epistles, and the Apocalypse of St. John, and the Epistle of St. Jude ; for, they too are wanting in the Syriac version.

OBJECT AND OCCASION OF.—The object, or design, of the Apostle in this Epistle was, to put the faithful on their guard against the errors of false teachers (iii. 17), generally supposed to be the *Gnostics*, who were soon to spring forth, or, more probably against the followers of Simon Magus, or the Simonites, who were the forerunners of the *Gnostics*. The more effectually to attain its object, the Apostle first points out the greatness of the promised blessings which the gratuitous bounty of God had in store for them, of which he had already given them so many pledges in this life and the sure grounds upon which these promises were founded. Such were the unspeakable blessings of which the false teachers wished to deprive them (chap. i.) He, next, employs the strong language of indignant denunciation, as head of Christ's Church, while describing the infamous and depraved morals of these pretended reformers, also permitted and sanctioned by them, in their deluded followers ; he vividly describes the punishment that awaits them (chap. ii.) Finally, he refers to one leading error of these impious scoffers, regarding the coming of CHRIST to judgment, and the end of all things ; this error he refutes, and after explaining the final dissolution of all things, he draws the moral conclusions, of which the subject itself is naturally suggestive (chap. iii.)

WHEN AND WHERE WRITTEN.—It was written, probably, about the year 66, shortly before his martyrdom (chap. i. verse 14), which occurred about the 35th year after our Lord's Ascension. It is his last dying legacy and monument of burning zeal for the faithful, over whom he was constituted by Christ, as chief pastor (i. 12, 13, 14). It was addressed to those to whom he had directed his former Epistle (iii. 1). And, it is generally agreed, that it was written from Rome, where the Apostle suffered under Nero, in the year 68. By some, it is asserted, that a considerable interval—twenty years, or upwards—intervened between it and the first Epistle. This is the opinion of those, who refer the date of the former Epistle to the year 45.

SECOND EPISTLE OF ST. PETER.

CHAPTER I.

Analysis.

The Apostle commences this chapter with the usual form of apostolical salutation (verses 1, 2). *In the next place, he exhorts the faithful, seeing that God has bestowed on them the most exalted gifts (3, 4), to correspond with his gracious designs, by performing, on their part, aided by divine grace, the good works necessary for securing the end of salvation, and by practising, in an exalted degree, the Christian virtues, of which he points out, in a beautiful order, a perfect series or gradation. In this chain of virtues, the first link is the virtue of faith ; the last, charity (5–7). He points out the good effect of cultivating, in a perfect degree, these exalted virtues (8) ; and, on the other hand, he shows the great evils which their absence entails on a Christian, who, without them, is blind and groping in the dark (9).*

He next exhorts them to insure, by good works, the object of their vocation and election (10). And he points out the end and glorious rewards to which perseverance in good will conduct them (11). He declares his determination to instruct them in these truths ; this he considers a matter of duty, during the short time he had to live ; that his continuance in life was to be very brief, he knew from revelation (12–14).

He expresses his anxiety to take some steps, whereby they may be enabled, even after his death, to call these truths to mind, probably, by leaving his written Epistles, or, "by commending these things to faithful men," as did St. Paul (2 Tim. ii.) No wonder, he should be anxious to impart to them his doctrine ; for, he received it not from any false or erroneous source ; he only declared concerning Christ's glory, what he, himself, was an eye-witness of, at the transfiguration, a type of the glory to be displayed at his second coming (16). He refers, also, to the splendid testimony rendered to him by God the Father (17) ; a testimony which St. Peter, together with John and James, heard when they were with him on Mount Thabor (17–18).

He next adduces the testimony of the prophets, which, in the mind of the Jews, carried greater weight with it, than any attestation of the Apostles ; and, he commends them for attending to this testimony, until they are firmly established in the faith (19).

He tells them, in attending to the oracles of sacred Scripture, to bear in mind, that the sacred Scriptures are to be interpreted, not by any private exposition ; but, to be explained by the same spirit, by which they were originally dictated (20, 21).

Text.	Paraphrase.
1. SIMON Peter, servant and apostle of Jesus Christ, to them	1. Simon Peter, a servant, that is to say, an Apostle of Jesus Christ, being specially engaged in the divine

Commentary.

1. "Simon Peter ;" the first, the name given him at circumcision, by his parents ; the second, given him by Christ (Matthew, xvi.), expressive of his office and

Text.

that have obtained equal faith with us in the justice of our God and Saviour JESUS CHRIST.

2. Grace to you and peace be accomplished in the knowledge of God, and of Christ JESUS our Lord:

3. As all things of his divine power, which appertain to life and godliness, are given us, through the knowledge of him who hath called us by his own proper glory and virtue.

Paraphrase.

ministry of preaching the gospel, (writes) to those who, without any merits on their part, have gratuitously received the gift of faith, equally precious and of equal value with ours, together with the grace of justification from God the Father,—its efficient cause,—and from our Saviour Jesus Christ,—its meritorious cause.—

2. May the blessings of grace and peace be increased and multiplied for you, along with, or, through your knowledge of God, and of Christ Jesus our Lord, which knowledge is the source of all spiritual blessings.

3. As God has, by his divine power, conferred on us all the gifts, which contribute to bring us to godliness, or spiritual life here, and eternal life hereafter, through the knowledge and faith of him, who has called us, by his glorious benignity, or merciful humanity.

Commentary.

dignity, as the rock or foundation of Christ's Church—(*see* 1 Ep. i. 1). "Servant and Apostle of Jesus Christ." The word "servant" regards that special engagement to preach his gospel, as is more clearly expressed by the word "Apostle;" for a full exposition of both (*see* Commentary, Gal. i. 1). "To them," the word, *writes, addresses,* or some such is understood; "that have obtained equal faith with us." The Greek for equal, ισοτομον, means, *equally precious;* although, of course, faith is more worthy and more perfect in some persons than in others; for, in Scriptures, some are upbraided with weakness of faith, "*modicæ fidei,*" and others praised for their "*great faith,*" and the disciple asks our divine Redeemer, to "*increase their faith*" (Luke, xvii.); still, it is here said, to be *equally precious,* objectively considered, in all Christians, as it proposes the same truths and promises to all, and is the foundation of the same objective beatitude. "Have obtained;" the Greek word, λαχουσιν, means to obtain as if by lot, and expresses the *gratuitousness* of the gift, as if we obtained it by mere chance in a lottery; but, with regard to God, it was given by the express arrangement of his adorable will —(*vide* Ephes. i. 11). "In the justice of our God," &c., may mean, "*through* the justice (or merits) of our God and Saviour Jesus Christ;" for, all spiritual blessings come to us through the merits of Christ, who is "our God and Saviour." Others make "in the justice," the same as, *with the justice;* for, such often is the meaning of the Hebrew, *Beth,* and they explain it, as in the Paraphrase: who have obtained equal faith, together with the justifying grace, of which faith is the foundation—"of God" the Father, its efficient cause—and justification is called "the justice of God" (Rom. i. 3), and "of our Saviour Jesus Christ," its meritorious cause.

2. "Grace" &c.—the apostolical salutation—"be accomplished." The Greek, πληθυνθειη, means, *be multiplied* or *increased,* "in the knowledge," &c. The particle "in," is interpreted, *with,* here, also (*vide* Paraphrase). Others make "in" the same as *by,* or *through,* so as to give the words this meaning: may peace and grace be multiplied for you, *through* the knowledge you will obtain of God, and of "Jesus Christ" (as man), "our Lord;" for, almost all the fundamental articles of our faith have for object, the divinity and humanity of Christ. "Of Christ Jesus." The word "Christ" is omitted in the Greek. It is, however, found in the Alexandrian MS. and versions generally.

3. Some interpreters connect this verse with the preceding, thus: "may grace and peace be increased for you through the knowledge of God" (verse 2), as it was through the knowledge of him, who called you by his glorious power, that all the gifts of the divine virtue, which conduce to your spiritual and eternal life, were originally conferred on you. According to these, the Apostle prays for an increase of all spiritual blessings, "grace," and their secure possession, "peace," through the same medium or channel, through which they were originally imparted, viz., the knowledge of Jesus Christ, "of him who called you, by his own power and virtue." Others, with greater probability, suspend the sense, until we come to verse 5 (the construction adopted in Paraphrase).

Text.

4. By whom he hath given us most great and precious promises : that by these you may be made partakers of the divine nature : flying the corruption of that concupiscence which is in the world.

5. And you employing all care, minister in your faith, virtue : and in virtue, knowledge :

Paraphrase.

4. Through whom he has bestowed on us the most exhalted and precious gifts, promised in the Scriptures of the Old Testament, so that by these gifts you may become, in a certain sense, partakers of the divine nature by imitation, flying the obstacles to this spiritual existence, viz., the corrupt deeds of concupiscence or lust, which reigns in the world.

5. (As God, then [verse 3], has, on his part, conferred the greatest blessings on you, by thus raising you to a participation in his divine nature, &c.), so do you, on your part, co-operate with him, by employing all diligence and care, for the permanence and perpetuity of these gifts ; *with* faith supply, or join the moral virtues, and performance of good works; with the performance of good works join prudence, or the practical knowledge of the befitting circumstances of each action.

Commentary.

It is to be remarked, that in the Greek, the words, "are given to us," are read in the past participle passive, agreeing in the genitive case with " of his divine power," τηϲ θειαϲ ϲυναμεωϲ ϲεϲωρημενηϲ. But in the next verse, the same is rendered actively (" he hath given us "—verse 4, in Greek, ϲεϲωρηται), and so it should, most probably, in this also ; hence, adhering to the Greek, it ought to run thus : "*as his divine power hath given us all the gifts which appertain to life, &c.*" " By his own proper glory and virtue ; " (" his own " are not in the Greek), "glory and virtue," mean, *glorious power.* " Virtue," however, in this latter case, is different in signification from " power," in the words, " of his divine power " (ϲυναμεωϲ), where it refers to his attribute of omnipotence ; in this (as appears from the Greek, αρετηϲ), "*virtue*" means, his benignity, goodness, or humanity.

4. " By whom ; " in the Greek it is (ϲι ὧν) "*by which*" gifts of his divine power, conducing to spiritual and eternal life ; some, however, of the best copies support our Vulgate, "by whom," viz., Christ ; and this accords best with the sacred Scriptures, which exhibit the Father, as bestowing all blessings on us, through Christ ; " that by these you may be made partakers of the divine nature," refers to sanctifying grace, which is a quality that *permanently* resides in the soul by way of *habit*, gives to it a new spiritual essence, a supernatural subsistence ; makes it the constant abode of the Holy Ghost ; and this spiritual, supernatural subsistence, makes us sharers or partakers of the divine nature by imitation, as nearly as a creature can approach the nature of the Creator in this life, and in the next life, when "we are transformed into him." "Flying the corruption of that concupiscence which is in the world." The Greek is, αποφυγοντεϲ τηϲ εν τω κοσμω εν επιθυμια φθοραϲ,*flying the corruption that is in the world, in, or through, concupiscence.* The Apostle points out the obstacles to the preservation of this spiritual existence, viz., mortal sin, with which sanctifying grace can never co-exist in the soul ; the corrupt deeds of concupiscence or lust, which reigns in the world, are, in a particular way, opposed to the purity of sanctifying grace ; he calls these unclean deeds " corruption," because indulgence in them corrupts and degrades the rational nature of man, blinds his intellect, and perverts his will.

5. Here, the sentence commencing at verse 3 is now completed, as, God, on his part, has conferred the greatest blessings (verse 3) ; *so*, do you, on your part, co-operate with him. The words, αυτο τουτο *for this very reason,* are added in the Greek ; and mean, for the purpose of permanently enjoying those blessings already conferred on you ; "employing all care." The Greek word for "employing," παρισενεγκαντεϲ, expresses the subordinate co-operation of our faculties, aided by God's grace. The Apostle, in a beautiful gradation, now points out the deeds wherein our free will, aided by divine grace, should co-operate, and manifest our gratitude "for the great and precious promises " (4) gratuitously fulfilled for us by God ; for, although our co-operation is the effect of divine grace, he still wishes to remind us of the necessity

Text.

6. And in knowledge, abstinence: and in abstinence, patience: and in patience, godliness:

7. And in godliness, love of brotherhood: and in love of brotherhood, charity.

8. For if these things be with you, and abound, they will make you to be neither empty nor unfruitful in the knowledge of our Lord JESUS CHRIST.

Paraphrase.

6. With prudence, join the government of your passions, and abstinence from illicit indulgence in carnal and sensual pleasures; with abstinence, join patient and persevering endurance of afflictions and mortification; and with patience, join godliness, making the good will and pleasure of God, the pure motive of your virtuous suffering and endurance.

7. And with piety towards God, join a due regard and love for your neighbour, and with this love of your neighbour, join the motive of charity or loving him for God, and not from any purely natural motive.

8 For, if these virtues now enumerated be with you, and abound with you, as with good and perfect Christians, they will render you neither empty nor idle, nor devoid of the fruit or merit of good works, in the faith of our Lord Jesus Christ.

Commentary.

of this co-operation on our part, just as the husbandman should be reminded of the duty of planting and watering, although the increase be the work of God alone. " Minister " (in Greek, επιχορηγησατε, supply) "in your faith, virtue." " In " signifies, with, the meaning of the Hebrew, beth ; with faith supply virtue, that is, to your faith join the moral virtues or good works ; since without them, faith is dead ; " and in virtue, knowledge," to the moral virtues, join the practical knowledge commonly termed prudence, which considers all the circumstances of any moral work to be performed.

6. " And in knowledge, abstinence," to prudence join temperance, or the governing of the passions, together with abstinence from carnal pleasures ; for, nothing so much blinds the mind, or obscures the prudent judgment of the intellect, as the inordinate indulgence in sensual pleasures. " And in abstinence, patience," since, if a man have not patience to bear up against crosses and adversity, he will not long persevere in abstinence ; for, as this very abstinence, this mortification and crucifixion of the carnal man, is itself opposed to our corrupt nature, it will require great patience to hold out ; without such patience, we will give up this state of suffering, and fall back for solace on carnal pleasures and enjoyment. " And in patience, godliness," to patience, join piety. The service and good pleasure of God should be the motive of this self-mortification, and of our sufferings. This will distinguish our virtues from that of the Pagan philosophers, whose motive in suffering was pride and vain glory.

7. " And with godliness (join) a love of brotherhood." Many who are severe on themselves, and apparently pious and exact in regard to the duties which they owe God, are frequently wanting in a due love and consideration for their brethren. The Apostle corrects this mistaken idea or neglect of duty. " And in love of brotherhood, charity ;" their love of the neighbour should not be grounded on mere natural feelingse nor on motives of interest—such would be mere Pagan virtue, "do not even the publicans and heathens this ? "—(Matthew, v. 46, 47) ; he must be loved with the love of " charity," for God's sake. It is worthy of remark, that in this chain of virtues the first link is "faith," without which the moral virtues will rarely or never be practised ; and the last, " charity," the queen of virtues, without which all the rest will not secure our salvation.

8. If you be possessed of the virtues now enumerated, and if they abound with you in an exalted degree, as with good and perfect Christians, they will render you " neither empty," for which in the Greek it is, ουκ αργους, neither idle, nor indolent in the practice of good works, nor without their fruit ; you will be furnished with those virtues, and with the fruit of good works, which the faith of Jesus Christ should produce in all. This the Apostle adds for the purpose of refuting the errors of the Simonites and Gnostics, regarding the sufficiency of faith alone, without good works.

Text.

9. For he that hath not these things with him, is blind, and groping, having forgotten that he was purged from his old sins.

10. Wherefore, brethren, labour the more, that by good works you may make sure your calling and election. For doing these things, you shall not sin at any time.

11. For so an entrance shall be ministered to you abundantly into

Paraphrase.

9. But, on the other hand, the man who is devoid of these virtues, and practises not good works, is blind in heart, and sees not beyond present and earthly things, having forgotten the great benefit of the remission of his former sins, remitted on condition of his not falling into them again, and of his leading a life of virtue.

10. Wherefore, brethren, since your call to the faith requires of you not to be found devoid of good works, nor to fall into your former sins, you should the more diligently and earnestly exert yourselves, by the performance of good works, to render firm your vocation to the faith, and to secure the end of your vocation, which is eternal life ; for, by so doing, you will not fall into sin at any time.

11. For, thus, by your abounding in virtue and good works, you will be abundantly supplied with

Commentary.

9. " Is blind and groping," *blind* in heart ; for, nothing so much blinds the heart as indulgence in vice, and "*groping*," may mean, that although not entirely blind, he can only see things immediately near him, and held up to his sight, and cannot raise himself beyond earthly and sensible objects ; he is blind, in expecting salvation without these virtues which the gospel requires for that end. Others understanding the word, "*groping*" to contain an allusion to moles—a signification warranted by the Greek, μυωπαζων—interpret the passage thus: Such a person, like a man who walks in darkness, and feels his way, knowing not where to direct his steps, knows not practically what course to take, or what actions to perform, in particular instances. " Having forgotten that he was purged from his old sins." This, the Apostle adds, with a view of pointing out more clearly the ingratitude of such persons.

10. " Wherefore," since your vocation to the faith requires of you not to be found devoid of good works (verse 8), nor to fall into your former sins (verse 9), "labour the more;" you should the more diligently exert yourselves, "that by good works"— (these latter words are not found in all the Greek copies, but only in a few ; they are, however, found in all the Latin copies of the Vulgate, and in the Alexandrian manuscript, as also in the Syriac version, and even where they are omitted, they are evidently understood from the context ; the Council of Trent quotes them with this passage (SS. xi. chap. 1)—"you may make sure your calling and election ;" by "calling" is, most probably, meant, their vocation to grace and faith, and this vocation they will render sure, or (as in the Greek, βεβαιαν, *firm*), "by good works,' which will secure their perseverance in the faith ; while, on the other hand, by sinful acts, men fall away, and in punishment thereof, are permitted to make a shipwreck of it. By "election," is most probably, meant, election to glory, and this being only conditionally annexed to their vocation to the faith, viz., on the condition of perseverance in good works, will also be made firmly secure by the same. The words may be simply explained thus : make sure the object or end of your vocation and election, which is, ultimately, life eternal ; "for doing these things," by good works, and by adding virtue to virtue (5–7), to secure the end of your vocation, "you shall not sin at any time." The Greek word for sin, πταισητε, means, *to fall*. Hence, it means here, to fall into grievous sin ; the word might mean, also, to fall away from obtaining the object of their vocation. The former, however, is the meaning attached to the word, by the Vulgate interpretation. The meaning of the Apostle may be expressed in this syllogism ; whosoever shall endeavour to preserve himself from the stain of grievous sin, will secure his eternal salvation ; now, the man who performs good works, will preserve himself from the stain of grievous sin ; and hence, will make sure his salvation.

11. " For so," that is, by persevering in good works, and thus endeavouring to secure your vocation, "an entrance shall be ministered to you abundantly :" the

Text.	Paraphrase.
the everlasting kingdom of our Lord and Saviour, JESUS CHRIST.	their rich rewards, by obtaining a sure entrance into the eternal kingdom of our Lord and Saviour Jesus Christ.
12. For which cause I will begin to put you always in remembrance of these things: though indeed you know them, and are confirmed in the present truth.	12. In order, therefore, to promote your salvation, and the secure possession of Christ's eternal kingdom, I will not cease admonishing you of the necessity of persevering faith and good works, even although you are fully instructed and confirmed in the knowledge of the truths of which there is question at present.
13. But I think it meet as long as I am in this tabernacle, to stir you up by putting you in remembrance.	13. For, as your pastor, I think it a duty attached to my office, as long as I remain in the tabernacle of this body, to resuscitate in your minds the memory of these truths, and thereby excite you to fervour, by reminding you of them.
14. Being assured that the laying away of this my tabernacle, is at hand, according as our Lord JESUS CHRIST also hath signified it to me	14. I shall be the more zealous in the discharge of this duty, being perfectly certain, that I am soon to lay aside the earthly tabernacle of this body, according as the Lord Jesus Christ hath signified it to me.

Commentary.

abundant rewards of these good works and merits shall be furnished to you "abundantly," that is, with a degree of abundant liberality on the part of God, proportioned to the abundance of your merits here on earth.

12. "For which cause," that is, in order to promote your salvation, and your possession of the eternal kingdom of Jesus Christ, "I will begin." In some Greek copies, *I will not neglect*, or *omit*, in which more is conveyed than is expressed; hence, the meaning is well expressed in our Vulgate, "I will begin," (which is supported by the Vatican Codex, ἐω μελλησω) now with fresh ardour, "to put you always in remembrance of these th ngs;" that is, of the necessity of persevering in faith and good works, in order to secure salvation: "though indeed you know them, and are confirmed in the present truth," the truth regarding the necessity of faith and good works. This latter is added by the Apostle, to soften down the offence which they might conceive, from the suspicion contained in his foregoing expressions regarding them. Similar is the prudence of St. Paul (Rom. xv. 14, of St. Jude, chap. i., and of St. John, 1 Ep., chap. ii.) From this verse we can clearly see the great zeal for the salvation of souls which burned in the heart of St. Peter. This aged Apostle, now approaching his end, "begins," as if afresh, to instruct his people in the truths of salvation, although already fully instructed. What a reproach to those idle pastors, who hide the truths of God in injustice, by neglecting to instruct their flocks—even when famishing for want of spiritual knowledge—in the necessary and essential truths of faith. Is not eternal woe to be justly apprehended by those idle, negligent pastors (thank God, but very few), who, unmindful of their covenant with God on the day they were prostrate before his altar, anointed with the "oil of gladness beyond their fellows," either misspend their time, or devote their energies to things not appertaining to their calling, thus allowing the poor, for whom Christ died, to be lost eternally! "His sheep were scattered, because there was no shepherd?"—(Ezechiel, xxxiv.)

13. "Meet," a duty which I am in justice, and in virtue of my office, bound to discharge, "to stir you up, by putting you in remembrance." No matter how well instructed a flock may chance to be, the pastor, still, is not exempt from the important duty of instructing them ; for, he shall always find among them some subjects either for "healing, or strengthening, or binding, or bringing back."—(Ezechiel, chap. xx. xiv. 4). "In this tabernacle," this body, called a "tabernacle," because in its present state, it is only a temporary abode of the soul ; and also, because tabernacles, or tents, are the temporary abodes of soldiers engaged in warfare, such as the life of man here below is. (2 Cor. chap. v.)

14. "Being assured that the laying a way." &c., as if he said, I will the more zealously exert myself during the very brief period I have to live ; for, I am assured that I am soon to lay aside "this tabernacle;" this body, in which the soul dwelt for a time

Text.

15. And I will do my endeavour, that after my decease also, you may often have, whereby you may keep a memory of these things.

16. For we have not followed cunningly-devised fables, when we made known to you the power and presence of our Lord JESUS CHRIST: but having been made eye witness of his majesty

Paraphrase.

15. But I will endeavour that, even after my departure out of this life, you may be enabled often or at all times, to call to mind those precepts and truths which I have inculcated.

16. This doctrine, even now on the point of death, we wish firmly to impress upon your minds; it deserves at all times to be cherished by you; for it was not in following learned and cunningly-devised fables, that we have made known to you the powerful and glorious coming of our Lord Jesus Christ to judge the world; but, we have told you that, of which we ourselves have been immediate eye-witnesses. (The glory of his transfiguration was a type of the glory and power, which he will display when he shall come to judge the world).

Commentary.

as in a tabernacle, "according as our Lord Jesus Christ hath also signified to me." The Apostle refers to some revelation, made to him regarding the near approach of his death; what it is, cannot be well ascertained. Some say, he alludes to the apparition with which he was favoured shortly before his death. We are told by St. Ambrose (Ep. 33), by St. Gregory on Psalm iv., and by Hegesippus (*libro* 3, *de excidio Jerusalem*), that Christ appeared to St. Peter shortly before his martyrdom, as he was leaving the city by the advice of some Christians, in order to avoid death; and St. Peter, having asked the Redeemer, whither was he going, received for answer, *I am going to Rome to be again crucified*, which words the Apostle took for an intimation of the divine will that he should suffer, and accordingly returned to Rome. However, it is said by many, that it was after escaping from prison, St. Peter was favoured with the vision referred to; and hence, in this Epistle, written in prison, there could be no allusion to an event, which occurred subsequent to his leaving it. It is, therefore, likely that he refers to some other revelation, unknown to us, or to that mentioned (John, xxi. 19), regarding his death.

15. "And I will do my endeavour," that even after my departure, or exit hence, you may be enabled, "often," or, at all times, "to keep a memory of those things," of these truths and precepts which I have delivered to you. This St. Peter could do, by leaving after him his Epistles, in which these things would be fully explained, or, by enjoining on the pastors, who were to come after him, zeal in preaching the word, according to the injunction of St. Paul to Timothy (2 Ep. ii. 2). Some interpreters give the words this meaning:—I will endeavour, after my departure, to have you in remembrance, by interceding with God for you. Many Catholic controversialists adduce this text as a proof, that the saints pray for us in heaven. But this latter interpretation is not borne out by the text, as will appear evident to any one who consults the Greek version. Estius well remarks, that it is by no means proper to adduce, in proof of a certain and doctrinal truth, arguments that are quite doubtful, while we have abundance of irrefragable ones, in its favour. Such a course will only have the effect of directing the entire attention of the heretics to these doubtful arguments, leaving the certain ones unheeded. From this verse, we can see the solicitude of the Apostle to have the true doctrine propagated and continued among the faithful. Similar was the solicitude of St. Paul (2 Tim. ii. 2) : " and the things thou hast heard from me by many witnesses, the same commend to faithful men, who shall be fit to teach others."

16. The connexion is given in the Paraphrase. At the very point of death he is not afraid to inculcate these doctrines, of future punishment, and they are so important, that even after death he would wish to impress them on their minds. For, it was not in following "cunningly-devised fables," such as the false teachers, among the Jews and Gentiles, dealt out for truths, and for which they will one day render a most rigorous account, "that we made known to you the power and presence," (in Greek, παρουσιαν, . *coming*) "of our Lord Jesus Christ." Most likely he refers to the second coming of

Text.

17. For, he received from God the Father, honour and glory : this voice coming down to him from the excellent glory, *This is my beloved Son in whom I have pleased myself, hear ye him.*

18. And this voice we heard brought from heaven, when we were with him in the holy mount.

19. And we have the more firm prophetical word : whereunto you

Paraphrase.

17. For he received from God the Father an honourable and a glorious attestation, a voice having been pronounced over him, after issuing from the bright cloud, in which the majesty and glory of the Father shone resplendent, to the following effect: "This is my well beloved Son, the object of my singular and infinite complacency, hear ye him."

18. And this voice of the heavenly Father, I myself, James, and John, heard coming down from the cloud, when we were with him on the holy mountain.

19. And we can adduce a testimony in favour of the same, of greater weight with you, to which

Commentary.

Christ, which is to be in "power," (his first coming was in infirmity); and this second was the coming which was questioned by many, to whom St. Peter refers (chap. iii,) "saying where is he coming?" Of this coming, Christ's transfiguration, to which the Apostle refers immediately after, was a type and figure. "Having been made eye witness of his majesty." The Greek word for "eye-witnesses" ἐπόπται, means *immediate lookers-on.* He refers to the transfiguration, with the sight of which he himself, and James, and John, were favoured. The Apostle selects this from among the other miracles of our divine Redeemer, in order to silence the injurious suspicions of certain persons, who wished to call in question all that the Apostles had taught regarding Christ's glorious coming. This he does most effectually, by referring to a splendid manifestation of the Redeemer's glory, of which he had, himself, been an eye-witness ; and this is further strengthened, by the unequivocal testimony of his heavenly Father, as in the following verse.

17. "He received honour and glory," that is, a glorious and honourable testimony, "from God the Father ;" "this voice," that is, a voice, to the following effect, " *this is my beloved Son,*" &c. "Coming down to him from the excellent glory," that is, from the bright cloud in which the glory of God the Father shone forth resplendent. " *This is my beloved Son,*" eternal and con-substantial with me, singularly beloved, " *in whom I have pleased myself,*" the object of my infinite good will and eternal complacency. Some understand the words to mean : in whom I have pleased myself with man, and have become reconciled to the world ; " *hear ye him.*" The words are not in the Greek of this passage ; they are, however, found invariably in the gospel, whenever allusion is made to the transfiguration, to which St. Peter here refers.

18. As a proof, that I have not followed fables, I can adduce the testimony of the other Apostles, James and John, to confirm my own ; we not only beheld the majesty of our Redeemer, when transfigured before us, but we heard the voice of the heavenly Father, "brought from heaven," that is, from the cloud which overhung the mountain ; "when we were with him in the holy mount." It is disputed what mount is referred to. Some say it was Mount Libanus. The common opinion, however, transmitted by tradition, with the authority of St. Jerome and of almost all sacred writers in its favour, is, that the mountain alluded to, is Mount Thabor, situated in the centre of Galilee, and called " *holy,*" on occount of its having been the theatre of many wonderful manifestations of our divine Redeemer, viz. : his transfiguration, his apparition *after* his resurrection to five hundred brethren, his sermon commencing with the eight Beatitudes (Matthew, v., &c.)

19. "And we have the more firm, prophetical word ;" the common interpretation given of this passage is : If you do not attach due weight to this testimony of the Father, as related by us Apostles, although eye-witnesses of the whole event, I can refer, in favour of Christ's glory and power, to a testimony, which, in your mind, carries with it more weight, than any attestation, furnished by us, viz., the testimony of the ancient prophets. The words, "more firm," do not mean, according to this interpretation, that the testimony of the ancient prophets carried with it, in reality, more weight and certainty, than that rendered by the Apostles ; but it did so relatively to the Jews, with

Text.

do well to attend, as to a light that shineth in a dark place, until the day dawn, and the day-star arise in your hearts :

Paraphrase.

you attach more value than to any whatsoever coming from us Apostles : and this testimony is, that which is borne by the oracles of the ancient prophets, to which you do well to attend, as to a lamp or light, that shineth in a dark place until the more brilliant light of sure and firm faith dawn and illumine you, and Christ, the morning star, arise in your hearts, by the plentiful effusion of the light of perfect and unerring faith. Or (as interpreted by Mauduit) :—We have, therefore, a testimony firmer and more certain than the fables of the heretics (verse 16), viz., the testimony or prophetic oracle of God the Father, to which you do well to attend, as to a lamp shining forth dimly, with the light of faith, in this darksome world, until the day of eternity dawns upon you, and the light of glory, like the morning star, shines in your hearts.

Commentary.

whom St. Peter here identifies himself, "we have," &c. They placed more reliance on the testimony of the prophets, as being of longer date, and more authentic in their minds.

"Whereunto you do well to attend," for, they will lead to Christ. He exhorts them to the perusal of the prophetic Scriptures ; for, they serve to confirm the faith of the believers, and to bring the unbelievers to the faith. Thus, we see that the Bereans are praised "for searching the Scriptures daily with all eagerness" (Acts, xvii.) ; and the Catholic Church recommends to her children the reading of God's word, provided it be expedient, and done with proper dispositions ; otherwise, as is known from melancholy experience, the indiscriminate reading of the SS. Scriptures becomes the fertile source of heresies, fanaticism, and errors of all kinds, alike subversive of religion and society. " As to a light that shineth in a dark place." The oracles of the prophets are compared to the imperfect light, held out by a lamp shining in a dark and misty place, contrasted with the perfect light of faith. " Until the day dawn ;" by " the day," in this interpretation is meant, the light of faith in this life ; " and the day-star arise in your hearts," expresses, in other words, the idea conveyed by the words, " the day dawn." By " the day-star," or lucifer, is understood Christ, pouring forth the light of faith in our hearts. The obscurity of faith in this life, as contrasted with the full light of glory in the life to come, is well expressed by the shining of " the day-star," which precedes the rise of morning ; its light weak and feeble, compared with the full splendour of the meridian sun.

Mauduit dissents from the common interpretation, which, in an able dissertation, he undertakes to refute, and he gives a new one of his own (vide Paraphrase). He says, that the phrase, " the more firm prophetical word," regards not the predictions of the ancient prophets ; that it by no means conveys a comparison regarding the value of the testimony of the prophets, even in itself, or in the minds of the Jews ; but, that it refers to the testimony or prophetic oracle of God the Father, alluded to (verse 17) ; and that it is between this and the fables of the heretics (verse 16), the comparison is instituted, hence called "more firm." Similar is the comparison instituted by Moses (Deuteronomy, xxxiv. 31), "for our God is not as their gods." In this verse is drawn the conclusion, which he announced (verse 16), "that he had not followed fables," he had a stronger testimony. This he proves in verses 17, 18, and then concludes, "and we have," that is, we, therefore, have a firmer testimony to follow than fables, viz., the prophetic oracles of God the Father. Mauduit says, that the words, "prophetical word," refer to the inspired word of God, revealed to men. When utterly orally, as here, it is called " a prophetical word ; " when written, "a prophecy of Scripture," as in next verse. He undertakes to show, that the comparison conveyed in the words, " more firm," cannot be instituted between the Apostle's own testimony and that of the prophets ; for, to give the oracles of the ancient prophets a preponderance, in any

Text.

20. Understanding this first, that no prophecy of Scripture is made by private interpretation.

21. For prophecy came not by the will of man at any time: but the holy men of God spoke, inspired by the Holy Ghost.

Paraphrase.

20. You will do well to attend to the oracles of sacred Scripture, understanding this well beforehand, in order to guard against error, that no exposition of Scriptures should be made by private interpretation; or, no prophetic scripture or scriptural oracle, is effected by the private invention of any one.

21. For, no prophetic oracle was ever produced in the mind of the inspired author, or communicated by him to mankind through any human exertions or power; but the holy men of God, the authors of the inspired writings, uttered and wrote these sacred oracles, from the impulse and inspiration of the Holy Ghost.

Commentary.

sense, over that furnished by the Apostles, is opposed to the usage of the inspired writers, in the New Testament. To do so would be useless, and would be even perilous to the faith of those whom he addresses. The following words, "as to a light that shineth in a dark place," refer in this interpretation, to the light of faith; "until the day dawn," the day of eternity, "and the day-star arise in your hearts," that is, the light of glory be fully communicated to you. The common interpretation is open to one difficulty; it supposes, that the "day," and "day-star," which it understands of faith in this life, had not yet shone for those, whom the Apostle addresses, although he supposes them to have embraced the faith—"that have obtained equal faith with us" (verse 1). The interpretation of Mauduit leaves no room for any such difficulty, and has the advantage, in this respect, over the other.

20. "Understanding this first," that is to say, in attending to the scriptural oracles (verse 19), they should bear this beforehand in mind, in order to secure them against fanaticism or error; "that no prophecy of Scripture," by which some understand, the prophetic oracle found in Scripture; others, more probably, the exposition of Scripture, in which sense, "prophecy" is frequently employed in the sacred writings (Rom. xii; 1 Cor. xii. 12, 13, 14; 1 Thes. v., &c.), "is made by private interpretation." The Greek word for "interpretation," επιλυσεως, which means *unfolding*, or *developing*, favours this latter meaning of "prophecy." No exposition of Scripture is made by private interpretation. The former meaning is: no true prophecy, contained in Scripture, is effected by the private invention of any man.

21. "For, prophecy came not by the will of man at any time," that is to say, it was not owing to any human exertion of intellect or will, that any man, at any time, propounded the hidden truths, revealed in God's word. And this the Apostle adduces, as a reason why the Scripture should be explained, not by private interpretation, but, by the same spirit by which it was originally inspired, viz., the Holy Ghost residing in the Church, with which Christ promised that His Spirit would remain for ever. This passage clearly refutes the fanatical doctrine of modern heretics, regarding the right of private interpretation of SS. Scripture. "But the holy men of God,"—the writers of sacred Scripture, with the exception of Solomon, whose end is uncertain, were all holy men, "spoke," that is, orally delivered their oracles; under this is, also, included *writing* the same; "inspired by the Holy Ghost," they were inspired and impelled to write freely, while in the full enjoyment of their faculties, unlike those, who, in a phrenzied state, and bereft of all consciousness, delivered diabolical oracles.

CHAPTER II.

Analysis.

The Apostle, having referred in the preceding chapter, to the divinely inspired prophets, takes occasion from thence to advert to the false prophets, and enters on the principal subject of the Epistle, which is, to caution the faithful against such. He, in the first place, informs the faithful, that impostors of this sort shall be always in the Church (1). He next describes their corrupt morals and doctrines (2), together with the punishment in store for them (3).

From the rigorous punishment inflicted by God in past times on the fallen angels, on the antediluvian world, on the cities of Sodom and Gomorrha—and from his preserving the just Lot, the Apostle concludes that He will also, in his own good time, rescue the just from their afflictions and trials, and punish eternally the wicked (4–9); this latter point he applies in a special manner, to the heretics in question. He then describes their morals, their impurities, their blasphemies (10).

He contrasts the conduct of these wicked men in uttering blasphemies with the forbearance shown by the good angels to their fallen associates, to whom, although deserving of it, they never apply execratory language; while, on the other hand, these men blaspheme what they understand not (11, 12). He describes their sensuality, wholly engrossed with present earthly pleasures, incessantly indulging in impurities and seeking after gain (13, 14). They are imitators of the avaricious Balaam, whose conduct is described (15, 16).

He points out their utter worthlessness, their pride and hypocrisy, promising things which they have no power to give—promising men true liberty, although themselves the slaves of their corrupt passions (17–19). He shows that far from giving their followers true liberty, they inthral them in a worse description of slavery, than that from which they at first escaped (20), and that the present condition of those whom they succeed in alluring from the way of justice, is worse than their former sinful state (21).

In the case of such relapsing and apostatizing sinners, the old proverbs, of the dog returning to his vomit, and of the sow wallowing in the mire, are fully verified and applicable.

Text.

1. BUT there were also false prophets among the people, even as there shall be among you lying teachers, who shall bring in sects of perdition and deny the Lord who brought them : bringing upon themselves swift destruction.

Paraphrase.

1. (But not only were there true prophets inspired by God, whose writings you may read with profit, among the Jewish people of old) ; but there were false prophets also, as there shall be even amongst you, numerous false teachers (some of whom have already made their appearance), who will secretly and furtively introduce pernicious heresies—even denying, both by word and action, the Lord, who purchased them with the last drop of his blood, bringing upon themselves speedy destruction here and hereafter.

Commentary.

1. There were false prophets among the Jewish people who represented themselves as true prophets (Jeremiah, xxiii. 16), "who spoke visions of their own hearts, and not out of the mouth of the Lord," and constantly had in their mouths, "*hæc dicit Dominus.*" "Even as there shall be among you lying teachers." He speaks of the Christian Church, and says, "there shall be," because, although some appeared in the

Text.

2. And many shall follow their riotousness, through whom the way of truth shall be evil spoken of.

3. And through covetousness shall they with feigned words make merchandise of you. Whose judgment now of a long time lingereth not, and their perdition slumbereth not.

Paraphrase.

2. And they shall have many imitators of their lasciviousness, and followers of their corrupt doctrines, whom they shall involve in the like ruin, on whose account the gospel of truth shall be blasphemously traduced, as if it sanctioned such immoralities in its followers.

3. And through insatiable avarice they will, with words artfully and smoothly framed for the purpose of deceit, drive in you a lucrative trade ; whose judgment of condemnation, long since decreed, is not put off or slow of approach, and whose perdition, far from slumbering, shall overtake them in due time.

Commentary.

days of the Apostle, they were to spring forth in still greater numbers afterwards. Thus, St. Paul says, "there shall be men lovers of themselves," &c. (2 Tim. iii.), although some of them made their appearance, at the very time ; for, he tells Timothy to "shun them" (verse 6) "Lying teachers," in Greek, ψευδοδιδασκαλοι, *false teachers ;* who these were, is disputed. He probably refers to the Simonites, Nicolaites, and Gnostics. "Who shall bring in sects of perdition," in Greek, αἱρεσεις απωλειας, *heresies of perdition,* or pernicious heresies. He adds "of perdition ;" because the word, *heresy,* of itself did not originally express bad doctrine ; "of perdition," fully qualifies it. The words, "and deny the Lord who brought them," may be also construed thus : *denied him who redeemed them, to be Lord ;* for, although they admitted Christ to be the Messiah— otherwise they would not be Christians at all—they still denied him to be supreme Lord. It is, then, likely, that he refers to the errors of the Simonians, who erred regarding the Divinity and Supreme Lordship of Christ. "Bringing upon themselves swift destruction." This is not far off ; as the interval which is to intervene until the hour of their death is very brief. The words may also refer to their sad temporal fate. The history of the Church records several instances of the frightful end of the propagators of heresy.

2. They shall not only err in faith, but they shall be also corrupt in morals, and they shall have many imitators of their dissolute conduct and lasciviousness. In many Greek copies, for ασελγειαις, "riotousnesses," we have, απωλειαις, *destructions.* The Greek reading followed by our Vulgate, is the more probable. Both readings are united in the Paraphrase. "Through whom the way of truth," that is, on account of whom the gospel or Christian religion "shall be spoken evil of." (In Greek, *blasphemed*), and brought into disrepute, as if it sanctioned the immoralities of those who went forth from its bosom. "*Per vos nomen Dei blasphematur inter gentes.*"—(Rom. ii.) It was owing to the immoral lives of the early heretics, that the Christian religion was designated by Tacitus, "*Superstitio exitialis,*" (Annal. 15).

3. "Through covetousness," or the insatiable desire of amassing wealth. "They shall with feigned words," words artfully formed to deceive—the idea is borrowed from the fraudulent language and practices employed by merchants in disposing of their wares— "make merchandize of you," *i.e.,* abuse the confidence which they shall gain by teaching the people for their own selfish and avaricious purposes. Similar is the description given of them by St. Paul (Rom. xvi. 18) : "*By pleasing speeches and good words, they seduce the hearts of the innocent, they serve not Christ but their own belly.*" Such have been the corrupt motives of heretics in all ages. It requires but a very slight knowledge of the unhallowed attempts, that throughout this entire country, have been made of late years, during seasons of dire distress, by many of the Anglican heretical emissaries and heartless proselytizers, to pervert the faith of the poor starving victims of famine, to whom relief was proferred on yon the cruel condition of hypocritically abjuring the faith of their fathers, dearer to them than life itself, to be convinced, that modern heretics also are still true to their lucrative trade, in the souls of men. "Whose judgment," or punishment, "lingereth not," will not be slow in undertaking them, "now a long time," from eternity decreed for them, or long since prefigured in the punishment of the wicked in the Old Testament ; hence St. Jude says (verse 4), "who were written

Text.

4. For if God spared not the angels that sinned : but delivered them, drawn down by infernal ropes to the lower hell, unto torments, to be reserved unto judgment :

5. And spared not the original world, but preserved Noe, the eighth person, the preacher of justice, bringing in the flood upon the world of the ungodly.

6. And reducing the cities of the

Paraphrase.

4. For, if God spared not the exalted spirits, his angels, after having fallen into sin ; but, after having dragged them down by infernal cables to the lower hell, delivered them unto torments, to be confined until the day of judgment.

5. And if he spared not the men who lived of old, before the deluge, having only preserved Noe with seven others as a herald to proclaim His justice to mankind, while the rest of the impious race who inhabited the earth he submerged in the waters of the deluge.

6. And if, after having reduced the cities of the

Commentary.

of long ago unto this judgment." " And their perdition slumbereth not." God keeps in mind their crimes, and will visit them with his destructive vengeance in his own good time.

4. The Apostle adduces in these verses the examples of God's rigour in punishing his angels, in the judgment of the deluge, in the punishment of Sodom and Gomorrha, to prove that he will " not slumber " in punishing the Heresiarchs, which conclusion he draws, (verses 9 and 10). The sense of the passage is kept suspended in this and the following verses ; it is concluded at verses 9 and 10. " If God spared not the angels," although more exalted than man, "greater in strength and power," (verse 11), " that sinned," after they had sinned. He refers to the sin of the rebel angels. What this sin is, has not been known for certain. The most probable opinion is, that it was the sin of pride, for, " pride is the beginning of all sin," (Eccles. x.) " in it all perdition took its rise," (Tobias iv). The sin of Lucifer is commonly supposed to be described mystically by Isaias (xiv. 13,) when, in the person of the haughty king of Babylon, he introduces him saying, *I will ascend...I will become like the Most High.* " But delivered them, drawn down by infernal ropes to the lower hell." There are no corresponding words for " drawn down unto torments " in the Greek, in which the whole sentence runs thus : ἀλλὰ σειροις ζοφου ταρταρωσας, παρεδυκεν εἰς κρισιν τηρουμενους, " *but, after having hurled them into Tartarus, he delivered them unto the ropes or cables of darkness to be kept unto judgment.*" *The infernal ropes,* by which God dragged down the angels, mean, the great power of God hurling them irrecoverably from their seats in heaven ; or if we follow the Greek, *the ropes of darkness,* to which he gave over the fallen angels, mean the barriers of hell within which they are confined, and the punishment to which they are doomed. " Drawn down to the lower hell." The Greek of which is, ταρταρωσας, *hurling them into Tartarus,* by which is meant the infernal regions, the place of confusion (as the word, *Tartarus,* implies), " where no order but everlasting horror dwells.—(Job.) The common opinion of the Fathers is, that God hurled all the apostate angels into hell. Some of them, at the temptation of Adam were permitted to leave it, and St. Jerome (in cap. 6, Ep. ad Ephes.) assures us that it is the common opinion of all the learned, " *that the space which lies between heaven and earth called ' inane,' is filled with these contrary powers,*" who, of course, carry their hell about with them ; and are there to tempt man and to carry on their fiendish war against him. " To be reserved unto judgment." On that day they shall be subjected to the rightful punishment of appearing with the reprobate before the eternal judge, than which there can be nothing more humiliating to their pride.

5. " The eighth person." He was not eighth, but tenth from Adam ; hence, the words mean, he was the eighth of those saved in the ark. " The preacher of justice," " justice," may either mean the vindicative justice of God, which Noe proclaimed to be impending while he was building the ark ; or, his justice, by which we are justified through faith and good works ; and this he preached by his words (most likely he exhorted men to be reconciled with God), and by the deeds of his own life, particularly the building of the ark in which the mystery of our justification was contained ; for, it was figurative of the Church and baptism.—(1 Ep. iii. 21).

6. " And reducing," (in Greek, τεφρωσας, *having reduced*), " the cities of the Sodomites and Gomorrhites ;" two other cities, Adama and Seboim, were also destroyed.

Text.

Sodomites and of the Gomorrhites into ashes, condemned them to be overthrown, making them an example to those that should after act wickedly.

7. And delivered just Lot, oppressed by the injustice and lewd conversation of the wicked.

8. For in sight and hearing he was just; dwelling among them, who from day to day vexed the just soul with unjust works.

9. The Lord knoweth how to deliver the godly from temptation, but to reserve the unjust unto the day of judgment to be tormented:

Paraphrase.

Sodomites and Gomorrhites to ashes (by raining fire and brimstone on them from heaven, Genesis xii.), he executed judgment on them by their utter destruction, making them serve for a typical example of the punishment in reserve hereafter for all who were to live a life of impiety.

7. And if the just Lot, grievously afflicted and wearied out by the unjust treatment and profligate conduct of lawless sinners, was rescued by him from sharing in their punishment.

8. For, neither by sight nor hearing did he offend or contract the contagion of vice and wickedness, although dwelling amongst them, who by their wicked deeds tortured his soul, while witnessing these crimes which he could not put a stop to.

9. If, then, in past ages the Lord neither spared his angels, nor the antediluvian world, nor the cities of Sodom, &c.; and if he rescued the just Lot, he therefore knoweth how, on future occasions also, to rescue the godly and just men out of the dangerous trials to which they shall be exposed; but the wicked he knows how to reserve unto the day of judgment to be tortured.

Commentary.

Segor, the fifth city of Pentapolis, was spared through Lot's intercession. "Making them an example." The Greek word, ὑπόδειγμα, means a *typical example* of the future punishment of the wicked, "who shall be cast into a pool of fire and brimstone," &c. —Apocalypse, xx. 10.

7. "And delivered"—by his grace, he delivered from sin, and by the ministry of his angels, from punishment—"just Lot, oppressed by the injustice," that is by the unjust and violent treatment which the men of Sodom inflicted on him (*v.g.*), when they offered him violence in his house, until the angels came to his rescue.—Gen. xix. 9. There is no word for "injustice" in the Greek. "And lewd conversation of the wicked." The Greek for "wicked," αθεσμων, means, *lawless*. The word "*if*" is all along to be understood in these verses; for, the sense is still suspended.

8. "For in sight and hearing he was just." This verse is to be included in a parenthesis. Neither by the sense of sight or hearing did he offend, or contract the contagion of vice, although (Commentators add) through both he was solicited to crime. "Dwelling among them." This was what rendered his virtue and exemption from crime the more meritorious and wonderful; for, "he that toucheth pitch shall be defiled by it."—Eccles. xiii. 1. "Who from day to day vexed the just soul with unjust works." The Apostle wishes to convey to us, that Lot, on beholding the abominable crimes of the Sodomites, which he could not prevent, and whereby God was so outraged and offended, was tortured thereat in his very soul. Similar were the feelings of David when he exclaimed : "*Vidi prævaricantes et tabescebam.*" The common Greek reading of this verse differs from that adopted by our Vulgate—"*for, the just man dwelling amongst them, by seeing and hearing tormented his just soul with their wicked deeds.*" The meaning of which is, that whilst dwelling amongst them, he tortured his just soul in consequence of seeing and hearing their wicked deeds, which it was out of his power to prevent. The Vulgate is partly sustained by the *Codex Vaticanus.*

9. In this verse the sentence, commenced (verse 4), the sense of which had been suspended in the intervening verses, is concluded. *If God spared not the angels* (verse 4), nor the antediluvians (verse 5), nor the Sodomites (verse 6), and if he rescued Lot (verse 7), the conclusion is, that he knows how to preserve just men, and rescue them out of trials and dangers, in future times, as well as he has done in the past. "But to reserve the unjust unto the day of judgment to be tormented." The devils shall be

Text.

10. And especially them who walk after the flesh in the lust of uncleanliness, and despise government, audacious, self-willed, they fear not to bring in sects, blaspheming.

11. Whereas angels, who are greater in strength and power, bring not against themselves a railing judgment.

Paraphrase.

10. But those in a special manner will he punish, who, following after and obeying the desires of the flesh, live in the enjoyment of all sorts of lustful, impure pleasures, despise divine and human dominion, daring and self-willed, fearing not to introduce sects or heretical doctrines, blaspheming God and his holy angels.

11. Whereas, on the other hand, the angels, who both in natural strength and supernatural power are far superior to man, who is but dust and ashes, do not utter the language of execration or indignant denunciation against the fallen members of their own order, who deserve it.

Commentary.

judged anew on the day of judgment; they shall undergo a new torment in being humiliated before the assembled nations of the earth; and the reprobate shall be more grievously tortured in soul and body, than they had been hitherto in their souls only. Some Greek Commentators supply the conclusion from the preceding verses thus:— "If God punished the angels, &c., and preserved Lot, *he will, therefore, punish those false teachers, and rescue you from your dangers.*" Pope Hyginus (*Epistola 2da*) fills up the sense in the same way. According to the latter connexion, this verse furnishes not a conclusion from the preceding, but a new reason to prove that God will punish the false teachers. For, the Lord is well versed in the exercise of Providence like this.

10. The Apostle now applies the general principle regarding God's Providence referred to in the preceding verse, to the heretics of whom he treats, and resumes the description he was about giving of them, left off (verse 3); in the subsequent part of the chapter, he graphically delineates their corrupt morals. "In the lust of uncleanliness," the Greek, ἐν ἐπιθυμία μιασμου, means, *the lust of pollution* or *defilement.* This refers to their abominable impure practices. "And despise government." Some understand this of the high dominion and exalted Providence of God, which the heretics brought into contempt by their ridiculous, foolish fables; others, of their contempt for Ecclesiastical authorities, to undervalue whom is a never-failing practice with heretics, in all ages; others, of their contempt for temporal or civil authorities. Hence, among the charges made against the first Christians, for which these heretics gave some pretext, was that of insubordination to the governing powers. "Audacious, self-willed," who are pleased only with their own conceited notions, claiming the right to speak and act, as they please. "They fear not to bring in sects," or heretical doctrines, is a great display of hardihood and daring, considering the authority on which the true doctrine rests, "blaspheming" God and his angels. The foregoing is the exposition of the text, according to the Vulgate reading.

The Greek reading of the latter part of the verse is, however, quite different. In the Greek, we have no word for "to bring in." It runs thus: ἐνδξας ου τρεμουσιν βλασφημουντες, *fear not, blaspheming glories,* or, "*fear not to blaspheme glories.*" So that the meaning most probably is that of St. Jude, who closely follows St. Peter in this chapter, "and blaspheme majesty" (verse 8), which some refer to Ecclesiastical authorities; others, more probably, to the heavenly spirits whom the heretics blasphemed by their degrading, disparaging fables, regarding them.—(*See* St. Jude). The Greek word for "sects," or *opinions*, ἐνξας. will bear that meaning as given in the Vulgate; but it more commonly signifies "*majesties* or *glories*," the meaning given the same word by the Vulgate.—(Epistle of St. Jude, verse 8).

"11. Bring not against themselves," that is, against the angels who had fallen. The Greek is, κατ' αὐτῶν, *against them*, *i.e.,* the powers. "A railing judgment," that is, do not employ against them the language of denunciation and execration, expressive of their fate, and their being condemned for ever to hell, as cursed, hideous, rebellious devils. That this is the meaning of the passage becomes clear by comparing it with a similar passage of St. Jude (verse 9), where he refers to the contest which Michael the archangel, and the devil, had for the body of Moses, on which occasion, he says,

Text.

12. But these men, as irrational beasts, naturally tending to the snare and to destruction, blaspheming those things which they know not, shall perish in their corruption,

13. Receiving the reward of *their* injustice, counting for a pleasure the delights of a day: stains and spots, sporting themselves to excess, rioting in their feasts with you,

14. Having eyes full of adultery and of sin that ceaseth not: alluring

Paraphrase.

12. But these men, like senseless beasts formed by nature, to be captured and destroyed for the use and service of man, blaspheming truths which they know not, as placed far beyond their reach, shall perish eternally, owing to their corrupt libidinous practices.

13. They shall have thus received the punishment due to their sins; having placed their entire happiness in the fleeting and passing delights of sensual pleasures, regardless of a future state. They are stains and spots, a disgrace not only to Christianity, but to human nature itself, abounding and sporting themselves in delicacies, and rioting in their feasts which they join in with you;

14. Betraying in their very looks, the adulterous feelings of their hearts; never ceasing to view and

Commentary.

Michael abstained from all language of reproach or execration. The Greek has in this verse, παρα κυριω, *before the Lord*, which means, when the angels and the devil stand before him (Job, chap. i.), or dispute concerning any matter. These words are wanting in the Alexandrian MS. (Jude, verse 9).

12. "As irrational beasts." The same words άλογα ζωα, in the Greek, are rendered in St. Jude (verse 10), "dumb beasts." "Naturally tending to the snare, and to destruction." Instead of "naturally," we have in the Greek φυσικα, *natural*, that is, borne away and guided by the senses and instinct, rather than by reason, and created for the purpose of serving man, to be captured and destroyed by him. "Blaspheming these things which they know not." He probably alludes to their blasphemies regarding the angels, whose nature and qualities they were ignorant of, or to some other mysteries of the Christian faith, which they treated disrespectfully. "Will perish in their corruption." They will corrupt and destroy their rational nature here, by being immersed in deeds of corruption, and will suffer eternally hereafter, in punishment thereof.

13. "Receiving the reward of *their* injustice," that is, while thus perishing eternally (verse 12), they shall receive the puishment due to their sins; "injustice" is put for sins of all kinds. "Counting for a pleasure the delights of a day." Some interpret these words (as in Paraphrase) to mean: they regard the fleeting pleasures of the present time ("of a day") as the only true happiness, without any regard for a future life. Others, adhering to the Greek, την εν ημερα τρυφην, *the delights in the day*, understand the words to express their utter shameless profligacy, while indulging in broad daylight, in those riotous revellings, which should be veiled by the darkness of night. "Stains and spots," the very essence of infamy itself; thus we say of a very impudent person, *he is impudence itself.* So the Apostle says of these that they are not only stained and defiled, but "spots and stains," infamy itself, a disgrace to human nature. We are assured by St. Epiphanius, that the abominable impurities and corruption of the Gnostics, and the first spawn of early heretics, exceeded all conception, and could not decently be described in language.

"Sporting themselves to excess, rioting in their feasts with you." The common Greek reading for "feasts," άπαταις, means, *deceits*, that is, by their deceits and illusions practised on you through their false teaching, they are enabled to live riotously. The Vulgate translator, found in the Greek, άγαπαις, "feasts," as it is read in a like passage of St. Jude (verse 12). The Apostle most probably refers to the love feasts or *Agapæ*, which were usual in the infancy of the Church (*see* 1 Cor. xi.); and he describes the misconduct of the heretics at these assemblies of Christian charity. The Vatican and Alexandrian manuscripts, together with the Syriac and Arabic versions, support the Vulgate reading.

14. "Having eyes full of adultery," betraying in their libidinous looks, the impure

Text.	Paraphrase.
unstable souls, having their heart exercised with covetousness, children of malediction :	think on objects, calculated to excite them to sin; artfully ensnaring weak souls, not firmly grounded in the faith, having their hearts practised in all the arts of amassing wealth; men marked out and destined for eternal malediction ; •
15. Leaving the right way they have gone astray, having followed the way of Balaam of Bosor, who loved the wages of iniquity,	15. Having turned aside from the straight way of the gospel, they have wandered through all the winding mazes of error, imitating the conduct of Balaam, the son of Bosor, who eagerly loved the wages of his unjust conduct, in cursing the Jewish people ;
16. But had a check of his madness, the dumb beast used to the yoke, which speaking with man's voice, forbade the folly of the prophet.	16. But he received a rebuke for his mad transgression of the divine precept, ordering him not to curse the Israelites ; for, the dumb ass, used to the yoke, in whose mouth an angel miraculously formed human articulate words, forbade the prophet to follow up his foolish intention of cursing the people of God, to which course he was stimulated by avarice.

Commentary.

feelings of their corrupt hearts ; for, the eyes are the inlets of sin and spiritual death. "*Averte oculos meos, ne videant vanitatem.*"—(Psalm cxviii.) "*Pepigi fœdus cum oculis meis,*" &c.—(Job. xxxi.) "And of sin that ceaseth not." This refers to the eyes, as appears from the Greek ; ἀκαταπαυστους αμαρτιας, their eyes cease not from viewing objects calculated to beget in them feelings of sin. "Alluring unstable souls," insnaring, by the promises of pleasures, souls not firmly grounded in the Christian faith. "Having their heart exercised with covetousness." The word "covetousness" is read in the plural in the Greek, πλεονεξιαις, hence, it means, all the arts of gaining and accumulating riches. "Children of malediction," a Hebraism to denote men marked out for the eternal malediction, which God will pronounce on the reprobate.

15. "Having followed the way of Balaam." His history is given (Numbers, xxii. xxiii., xxiv.) He was a soothsayer, noted for his avarice ; for a reward, he engaged to curse God's people (Numbers, xxiii.) He likewise councelled Balac, king of Moab, to send the beautiful women of Moab and Madian into the Hebrew camp, in order to entice the Jews to commit fornication, and afterwards worship Beelphegor (Numbers, xxiv. 14, xxv. 2, xxxi. 16 ; Apocalypse, ii. 14). So, in like manner, these corrupt teachers falsify the gospel, and pervert the people for the purposes of avarice and sensuality. "Balaam of Bosor," that is, as the Greek article, τοῦ Βοσὸρ, would appear to imply, *the son of Bosor.* In numbers (xxii. 5) he is called "the son of Beor," which, in being translated into Greek, might, by a slight inflexion or corruption, be made, *Bosor.* In the Vatican MS. it is, τοῦ Βεωρ. Others make it "Balaam from Bosor," where he was born, or lived.

"Who loved the wages of iniquity," that is, the money and presents which he hoped would accrue to him from his malediction of the people whom God blessed : and hence, he repeatedly wished to curse them.—Numbers, xxii. xxiii.

16. But he had a check of his madness. For "madness," the Greek word παρανομιας, means, *wickedness* or *transgression of the law.* "The dumb beast used to the yoke." We have no word in Greek for "beast." It is, however, implied in the Greek word corresponding with, "used to the yoke," ὑποζυγιον, which means *a beast of burden.* "Which speaking with man's voice." By a Hebrew idiom, he calls the articulate words, which the angel had formed in the ass's mouth, "a man's voice." In the *Codex Vaticanus,* the construction is, ὑποζυγιον ἀφωνον ἐν ανθρωποις,φωνῃ φθεγξαμενον, *a dumb beast under the yoke among men, speaking with a voice.* "Forbade the folly of the prophet." In the words uttered by the ass (Numbers, xxii. 28–30), there is no prohibition conveyed to Balaam, or rebuke for his crime ; but from the extraordinary circumstance of his speaking, Balaam could perceive that the course he had in contemplation, of cursing God's people, notwithstanding the divine prohibition, was displeasing to Him. And this also gave him an opportunity of seeing the angel who forbade

Text.	Paraphrase.
17. These are fountains without water, and clouds tossed with whirlwinds, to whom the midst of darkness is reserved.	17. These are fountains, promising to give the refreshing waters of grace and Christian knowledge, of which they are wholly destitute. They are light clouds, scattered and carried about by the whirlwinds; they are men for whom eternal darkness is reserved.
18. For speaking proud words of vanity, they allure by the desires of fleshy riotousness, those who for a little while, escape such as converse in error:	18. For, speaking pompous, high-sounding and empty words, they allure, by the concupiscences of the flesh, prone to lasciviousness, in which they permit their followers to indulge, those converts from Paganism, who had been lately or imperfectly converted:
19. Promising them liberty, whereas they themselves are the slaves of corruption. For by whom a man is overcome, of the same also he is the slave.	19. Promising them a license to do what they please, an exemption from all laws, civil and ecclesiastical, which they dignify with the specious name of Christian liberty; as if they could grant liberty to others, who are themselves the slaves of their corrupt passions; for, according to the principle generally acted upon and admitted, the vanquished party is the slave of him, by whom he is vanquished.

Commentary.

him to curse God's people.—(Numbers, xxii. 35). Balaam is called a "prophet" (although—Numbers, xxii. 5—he is called a soothsayer," *ariolus*,) because he uttered true prophecies (*v.g.*) he predicted, "*orietur stella in Jacob*" (Numbers, xxiv. 17). And in the account given of his communication with Balac, king of Moab, (Numbers, xxii., xxiii., xxiv.), he everywhere says, he will declare only what the Lord shall tell him; he consults the Lord on several occasions, and the Lord tells him what to say. However, the fact of his being called a "prophet" does not oblige us to regard him as a true prophet; for, the word "prophet" is not confined to the good; we find it applied to others, (*v.g.*) "prophets of Baal."—(3 Kings, xviii. 19).

17. He points out the utter worthlessness and hypocrisy of these men, "fountains without water." From a distance the dried wells promise water; but, the hopes of the traveller end in disappointment. So, these men promise, or pretend to promise, the refreshing waters of grace and Christian knowledge, which they are unable to give; hence, their hypocrisy. "Clouds tossed with whirlwinds," light, empty clouds, tossed about by the wind, not permitting the wholesome waters of heaven to irrigate the earth, nor the genial rays of the sun to warm it. The Greek for "whirlwinds" is ὑπο λαιλα-πος, *tempest*. These words also show the inconstancy of the heretics, and the ever fleeting varying nature of their doctrines, like clouds tossed here and there, by the winds. "To whom," that is, the heretics, as is clear from the Greek, οἷς, "the midst of darkness is reserved." St. Jude adds, "for ever." He refers to the everlasting darkness of hell.

18. "For speaking proud words of vanity." This is an illustration of the dried empty fountains (verse 17), they speak pompous and high sounding, but empty words. This is the constant practice of heretics, as St. Jerome tells us (on Isaias, xxii.) "They allure by the desires of fleshly riotousness;" they allure through the desires of the flesh, prone to lasciviousness, which they indulge in themselves, and teach their followers to regard as lawful; "those who for a little while escape such as converse in error," that is, those who have, for a short time, or imperfectly, left the society of such as still cling to the errors of Paganism.

19. The Apostle points out the mode, in which they insnare weak souls, "promising them liberty," a gift which always sounds sweet to our ears; they promise and proclaim an exemption from the restraint of all laws, whether of the church or state—a license to do whatever men may please; and this they term Christian liberty, or the liberty into which Christ asserted man. St. Jude more clearly expresses it, "turning the grace of our Lord God into riotousness;" verse 4.

"Whereas, they themselves are the slaves of corruption," that is to say, it is preposterous to see men, themselves slaves, promise true liberty to others. They are "the slaves of corruption," that is, of their corrupting, debasing passions, and carnal desires.

Text.

20. For if, flying from the pollutions of the world through the knowledge of our Lord and Saviour JESUS CHRIST, they *be* again entangled in them and overcome; their latter state is become unto them worse than the former.

21. For it had been better for them not to have known the way of justice, than after they have known it, to turn back from that holy commandment which was delivered to them.

22. For, that of the true proverb has happened to them. The dog is returned to his vomit: and, The sow that was washed to her wallowing in the mire.

Paraphrase.

20. Far from bestowing on them liberty, they reduce them to the worst description of slavery. For if, after having escaped, and being rescued from the defilements of this world, through the grace of God, that is to say, through the knowledge of our Lord and Saviour Jesus Christ, and faith in him, which is the first grace in the order of justification—they become again entangled in these corrupt practices, and are overcome—their latter state is worse than the former.

21. For it would have been a lesser evil for such persons never to have known the way of the gospel, which points out the mode of leading a life of justice, than, after having known it, to turn back from that law—every mandate of which is holy, and enjoins sanctity of life—delivered to them by the Apostles and preachers of the Gospel.

22. For, in their case is illustrated and fully verified the truth of the proverb: the dog is returned to his vomit; and the sow that was washed, to her wallowing place.

Commentary.

" For by whom a man is overcome, of the same also is he a slave." According to a fixed maxim observed, and universally admitted between contending parties, those who are conquered in war become the slaves of the victors; and hence, these men, being subdued by their own corrupt passions, are become the slaves of passion.

20. He proves in this verse that these false teachers, far from giving true liberty to their followers, on the contrary, involve them in a corrupt servitude, worse than that from which they were originally emancipated.

" If flying from the pollutions of the world," that is, the corrupt practices in which they were immersed, while in Paganism; the idea is the same as that conveyed—verse 18—" escape such as converse in error."

" Through the knowledge," &c., through the grace of God justifying them; and in the order of justification, faith, or " the knowledge of Christ," is the first grace. " They be again entangled in them, and overcome," by yielding to their solicitations. " Their latter state is worse than the first;" because their knowledge being now greater, they are not left the excuse of ignorance, and their ingratitude, consequently increased. Similar is the saying of our Divine Redeemer: " the last state of that man (viz., of the relapsing sinner) is worse than the first."

21. " It had been better," that is, a lesser evil, " for them not to have known the way of justice," *i.e.*, the truths of the gospel, which point out the road of a just and holy life, " than after they had known it, to turn back from that holy commandment;" that is, the Christian law, every commandment of which is " holy," points out, what is holy, and begets holiness, if observed. This " holy commandment" includes the precepts of faith and morality. It was a greater evil to have fallen away from this law, than never to have received it; for, they now sin with greater knowledge, and greater ingratitude; and they commit sin, by their very relapse. " To turn back;" " back," is not in the Greek. It is, however, found in the Alexandrian and other manuscripts.

22. He illustrates the base and filthy conduct of such sinners, by referring to the expressive proverbs, which are verified in their regard. " The dog is returned to his vomit," is taken from the Book of Proverbs. " As a dog that returneth to his vomit, so is the fool that repeateth his folly," (chap. xxvi. 11), The second proverb is probably added by St. Peter himself, according to Bede; at least, it was current and in vogue among the people of the East; it is a form of expression found in the writings of every country. " Give not that which is holy to dogs, nor cast ye your pearls before swine." (Matthew, chap vii.)

CHAPTER III.

Analysis.

In this chapter, the Apostle tells the faithful, that this is the second Epistle he addressed to them, in which, as well as in the former, he wished to remind them of the truths of faith, predicted by the prophets, and inculcated by the Apostles. He probably refers, in a particular manner, to the doctrine regarding the coming of Christ, in due time, to judge the world—a doctrine questioned by the false teachers (1, 2). In order to put them on their guard, he tells them that such persons would come amongst them, and at all times trouble the Church (3). The principal error of these men will consist in ridiculing the great doctrine of Christ's coming to judge the world. This is, indeed, the practical teaching of the impious at all times (1).

He refutes the teaching of those men, who probably ridiculed the idea of fire—one of the most active principles or elements of the present world—being made instrumental in its ruin, by showing that an element, which equally entered into the constitution of the present system—viz., water, was employed for its destruction, formerly. He thus refutes their assertion, that things continued in the same way from creation (5, 6). He next refutes their deduction from analogy, that things would continue as they were for ever, by showing, that the world is to be destroyed by fire (7). The scoffs of the impious regarding the tardiness of Christ's coming, he shows to be groundless ; since the measure of time with God is quite different from that adopted by us (8). And, in truth, this delay is intended by God as a judgment of mercy, to give men time for repentance, and to enable the number of the elect to be filled up (9). He again repeats his assertion, that the present system of the world is to be changed and renovated (10). and draws moral conclusions from thence—viz., that we should, by sanctity of life, prepare and fit ourselves for the renovated heavens and earth, the abode of the blessed (11-13), and endeavour to be found, in the presence of our Judge, free from spot (15).

He refers to the Epistle of St. Paul, as inculcating the same things, and observes regarding them, that they are difficult and hard to be understood ; to persons not fit to read them, they are like all other inspired scriptures, a source of spiritual ruin (15, 16).

In conclusion, he cautions them against being led astray by the erroneous doctrines of the impious scoffers in question, and exhorts them to endeavour to advance in grace and faith.

Text.

1. BEHOLD this second Epistle I write to you, my dearly beloved, in which I stir up by way of admonition your sincere mind :

Paraphrase.

1. Behold, dearly beloved, after having addressed to you a former Epistle, I write to you this second also, in both one and the other of which, I have endeavoured to stir up and stimulate to greater fervour your pure minds, already sincerely imbued with true piety, by reminding you of the truths of our holy faith.

Commentary.

1. "Behold." For this we have in the Greek, ηδη, *now ;* "this second Epistle I write to you." Hence, this Epistle was addressed, like the former, to the Christians of Asia Minor. "In which." This word is read in the plural, both in the Greek text εν αἱς, and in the Vulgate, *in quibus ;* and, hence, it refers to both Epistles ; I have written this second Epistle after the first, "in which," that is, both one and the other,

Text.

2. That you may be mindful of those words which I told you before from the holy prophets, and of your apostles, of the precepts of the Lord and Saviour.

3. Knowing this first, that in the last days, there shall come deceitful scoffers, walking after their own lusts,

Paraphrase.

2. That you may be mindful of the words of the holy prophets, which I have mentioned before, or, mindful of the words foretold by the holy prophets, and of the precepts of your Apostles, which are also the precepts of our Lord and Saviour (or, of the precepts given by us, the Apostles of the Lord and Saviour Jesus Christ).

3. This you should know in the first place, and attend to, as a matter of vital importance, that in this last stage of the world, on which we have entered, there shall come deceitful scoffers, deriding all true religion, seducing and leading astray the unwary; men, who shall freely indulge and follow the lust of their carnal corrupt passions;

Commentary.

" I stir up," that is stimulate to greater fervour, "by way of admonition," by reminding you of the truths of faith. ("I will begin to put you always in remembrance of the things;" chap. i. 12). As pastor of souls, he feels it his duty always to instruct his flock, both "in season and out of season."—(2 Tim. iv. 2).

"Your sincere mind;" your mind, sincerely imbued with feelings of religion, pure and undefiled. This he adds to gain their good will, in order to render them more docile to his instructions.

2. "That you may be mindful of those words which I told you." The Greek, μνησθηναι των προειρημενων ρηματων, should properly be rendered thus, and are rendered so by the Vulgate (St. Jude, verse 17) :— " *That you may be mindful of the words which have been spoken before,*" &c. He wishes them to keep in mind the predictions of the prophets, the reading of whose writings he recommended to them (chap. i. 19), particularly, so far as they regard the Divinity, and the glorious coming of our Lord Jesus Christ.

"And of your Apostles, of the precepts of the Lord and Saviour." The common Greek reading runs thus : και της των αποστολων ημων εντολης του κυριου και σωτηρος, *and of the precepts of us, Apostles of the Lord and Saviour*, or, *of the precepts of us Apostles* (which are also the precepts) *of the Lord and Saviour*. The sense is the same in either construction ; because the precepts of the Apostles of our Lord and Saviour Jesus Christ, are the precepts of Christ himself, "*qui vos audit, me audit.*" The *Codex Vaticanus* has ὑμων, for, ἡμων. The precepts to which he refers, are those concerning their perseverance in the faith, originally communicated to them, particularly as regards the promises and glorious coming of our Lord, and the shunning of false teachers.

3. "Knowing this first," or, as a matter of great importance to their salvation ; for, being forewarned of their approach, they will the more easily guard against the snares of the false teachers. "That in the last days." These words specify no particular time, except that, it is future—to come on hereafter—they most probably refer to the term during which the Christian religion is to last, called the last. time, and frequently "the last hour ;" because no other form of true religion is to exist, no other dispensation to be promulgated, until the day of judgment. Hence, St. Paul says (1 Cor. x.), "that upon us the ends of the world have come."

The words may refer to the time preceding the day of judgment ; and St. Peter, as supreme pastor of God's Church, addressing her now in her infancy, wishes also to warn her of the errors which will assail her, in her old age. Men shall arise to delude the people, and persuade them that the doctrine of the coming of Christ to judgment, is a mere chimerical idea ; this error will open the way to the apostasy, which St. Paul says, will usher in the day of judgment (2 Thes. ii. 3).

"There shall come deceitful scoffers," men who shall scoff at all religion, particularly the truths regarding Christ's second coming (verse 4), and will deceitfully insnare the faithful. In some Greek copies, there is no word for "deceitful." The chief MSS. have the words, ἐν εκπαιμονη εμπαικται, "scoffers *in deceit*, " " walking after their own

Text.

4. Saying: Where is his promise or his coming? for since the time that the fathers slept, all things continue as they were from the beginning of the creation.

5. For this they are wilfully ignorant of, that the heavens were before, and the earth, out of water, and through water, consisting by the word of God.

6. Whereby the world that then

Paraphrase.

4. Asking in a derisive tone, what is become of the promised coming of the Lord to judgment? It is a mere delusion ; for, since our fathers have slept—the first according to yourselves, to believe in and announce this, his second coming—all things have gone on in the way that they did from the creation of the world (and no doubt will continue so for ever).

5. For of this they are wilfully and culpably ignorant, viz., that the heavens were first, and then the earth, emerging from the water, and consisting by means of water, which bounds it, circulates freely through it, imparts to it fertility and prevents it from flying off in particles of dust ; and both the heavens and the earth owe their form and existence to the word or will of God (and can, therefore, perish by the FIAT of the same omnipotent will).

6. By which, viz., the heavens and the earth—the

Commentary.

lusts," indulging without scruple or restraint their corrupt passions. This is a general characteristic of heresy. Those who have made a shipwreck of faith, are always men of loose and dissolute morals.

4. " Saying, where is his promise or his coming?" in Greek, ἡ επαγγελία της παρουσιας *the promise of his coming*, or his promised coming, what is become of it? This question is equivalent to a denial, that he shall ever come. " For since the time," or, from the day, " that the fathers slept," that is, since the death of the patriarchs, who were the first to believe, and proclaim their belief in this truth—and since then a long interval has elapsed—" all things continue as they were from the beginning of the creation;" all things continue in their usual course, as from the " beginning of creation." (The Greek word for " creation," κτισεως, will also mean, *creature*), that is, since creation, when creatures began to exist. The apparent immutability and unchangeable course of nature, the same vicissitudes of seasons, alternations of day and night, the orderly courses and revolutions of the heavenly bodies, are put forward by the scoffing heretics in question, as an argument against the second coming of Christ, promised everywhere in the Scriptures, as if things would go on in the same way for ever.

5. " For, this they are wilfully ignorant of." They are culpably and wilfully ignorant of the following fact, which they might easily ascertain from the books of sacred Scripture, and the great book of nature herself, viz., " that the heavens were before," or, as in the Greek, εκπαλαι, *of old*, that is, from the beginning, at first created, " by the word" or, omnipotent will " of God," " and the earth out of water," that is standing forth from the water, out of which it emerged, on the third day of creation. when " the waters under the heavens were gathered together into one place, and the dry land appeared."—Genesis, i. 9. " And through the water," to which, most likely, the word, " consisting" should be joined. The earth consists " through water," because it is the water which surrounds the earth, circulating through it, like blood through the veins of a body, that gives it a consistency, preventing it from flying off in particles of dust, and imparting to it fertility and powers of production.

The term " consisting," as appears from the Greek, regards the earth only, γη συνεστωσα, but, both earth and the heavens exist by " the word" or omnipotent will " of God."

The Apostle confutes those deceitful scoffers by showing first, that their assertion, to the effect that all things continued in the same way from creation, was false, and that the same alternate course of dying and living did not proceed regularly since creation. In the following part, commencing at verse 7, he shows their conclusion from analogy—viz., that things would go on in the same way for ever, to be equally false.

6. " Whereby ;" the Greek words, δι ὦν, means, *by which*, in the plural number, that

Text.

was, being overflowed with water, perished.

7. But the heavens and the earth, which are now, by the same word are kept in store, reserved unto fire against the day of judgment and perdition of the ungodly men.

8. But of this one thing, be not ignorant, my beloved, that one day with the Lord is as a thousand years, and a thousand years, as one day.

Paraphrase.

one opening their cataracts, and the other, the great fountains of its abyss ; the then, or antediluvian world, perished, being deluged by water.

7. But the firmament, or regions of the air, and the earth, which now remain in their present deteriorated state after the deluge, are treasured up by the same omnipotent will of God, and preserved to be burned by the fire of conflagration, on the day of general judgment, a day also of eternal destruction to the impious, whom the fire of God's wrath shall carry with it to the lowest hell.

8. But as for the railleries of these impious scoffers regarding the tardy performance of God's promises to come and judge the world, they are to be unheeded; for, if the measure of time in the designs of God be considered, there is no room whatever for objection on this point. With him a thousand years and one day are the same ; viewed in comparison with eternity, both are a mere point.

Commentary.

is, through which heavens and earth, bursting loose their cataracts, and throwing open their great fountains (Genesis, vii. 11), "the world that then was," viz., the antediluvian world, "being overflowed with water, perished." Not alone had mankind, with all the living creatures on the earth, perished ; but, the earth itself and the atmosphere underwent a great change for the worse, in the universal deluge.—St. Augustine (*de Civitate Dei*, *libro* xx. 11).

7. After having refuted the assertion of the ungodly, that the world had remained always in the same state of alternate dying and living, by referring to the history of the universal deluge, of which these impious scoffers were wilfully ignorant, the Apostle proceeds, in this verse, to refute their conclusion, or rather deduction, from analogy—viz., that things would always continue, as they are and have been. He says, "the heavens that now are," by which is very probably meant, the firmament or atmosphere surrounding the earth (the space between us and the starry heavens is frequently called "heaven" in the Scripture ; thus, we say "*volucres cœli*"), but not the starry or empyrean, the abode of the blessed ; for, the starry heavens will be changed for the better ; but not burned by the fire of conflagration. "By the same words are kept in store," that is, are treasured up in the storehouse of God's providence, who will execute his decrees in due time, "reserved unto fire," to be burned by the fire of conflagration.

"Against the day of judgment ;" kept waiting for the day of general judgment, "and perdition of the ungodly men,' whom the fire of God's justice shall carry with it and plunge for ever into the bottomless pit of hell. It is not unlikely, that the impious scoffers in question had asserted the utter impossibility of the earth perishing by fire, one of the principal elements which should conspire with the others for the preservation of the universe. This the Apostle refutes by the example of the destruction of the former earth, by the deluge ; for, looking merely to natural principles, what greater repugnance can we have in believing, that the present earth and heavens should be destroyed by the element of fire, than that the former earth, which subsisted by water, and was rendered fertile, and kept compact thereby (verse 5), should be destroyed by the very same element (verse 6) which appeared to insure for it eternal duration.

8. The Apostle now proceeds to point out how devoid of all foundation are the scoffs and railleries of those impious men with regard to the slowness and tardiness of Christ's coming. With him, who beholds eternity at one glance, the longest and shortest periods of time are all the same ; a thousand years as well as a single day compared with eternity are the same, infinitely distant from it ; and hence, any delay in the coming of Christ, is, according to *their* computation of time, but not according to the measure adopted by *Him*.

Text.

9. The Lord delayeth not his promise, as some imagine; but dealeth patiently for your sake, not willing that any should perish, but that all should return to penance.

10. But the day of the Lord shall come as a thief, in which the heavens shall pass away with great violence, and the elements shall be melted with heat, and the earth and the works which are in it shall be burnt up.

Paraphrase.

9. The Lord does not put off, beyond the determined time, the execution of his promise, as some persons imagine, but he endures patiently and with long-suffering on your account, not willing that any persons should be lost, but that all should return to penance.

10. But the day of the Lord, like the nightly and sudden approach of a thief, shall come unexpectedly; in it the heavens will pass away with a great crash, such as is occasioned by a violent storm of wind or the pealing of thunder, and the elements changing their figure and appearance, shall, all on fire, be dissolved with great heat, and the earth, with all its productions, natural and artificial, as well as the works of mankind shall be burnt up.

Commentary.

9. What men are apt to consider a delay on the part of God to fulfil his promise, is not a delay at all; but rather a gracious judgment of his mercy, an exercise of his long-suffering, wishing to give his people time for repentance; "not willing that anyone should perish, but that all should return to penance;" the meaning of which words is, that, by a sincere, *antecedent* will, God wishes no one to perish, but that all men should be saved; He also gives all men sufficient means of salvation. The words, "the Lord delayeth not his promise," admit of this construction also, according to the Greek, ου βραδυνει κυριος επαγγελιας, *the Lord of the promise is not slow.* "As some imagine," are thus read in the Greek, ως τινες βραδυτητα ηγουνται, *as some compute slowness.* "For your sake." In the common Greek, *for our sake.* The *Codex Vaticanus* has, εἰς ὑμας, the Alexandrian, δι' ὑμας. Both support the Vulgate. How calculated is not the serious meditation on these words of the Apostle, "A thousand years with God is but as a single day," to raise our thoughts to eternal enjoyments, and make us undervalue all the pleasures and riches and honours of this life, which, be it ever so prolonged, when compared with eternity, is but a mere point. "A thousand years in his sight is but as yesterday which is past and gone." (Psalm lxxxix.) With the Psalmist we should frequently, in the day of trial and affliction, "*keep in mind the eternal years.*" (Psalm lxxvi.) Our conversation, our thoughts, should be in heaven, whence we are to expect, in his own good time, a deliverer; and we should rest assured, that if he appear tardy in coming to our relief, it is to give us time for penance, and to enable us to hoard up greater treasures of merit.

10. The day on which the Lord Jesus is to judge the world, will come unexpectedly, "as a thief," to which, in the common Greek, is added (*in the night*). These latter words are not found in either the Alexandrian or Vatican manuscripts, and were, most likely, added here and taken from 1 Thess. verse 2, where the day of judgment is described. "In which the heavens shall pass away," that is, the regions of the air, in Sacred Scriptures often called "heavens," shall pass away, and, purged of all their present grossness and imperfection, shall be changed into a more perfect and incorruptible form. "With great violence." The Greek word, ροιζηδον, means the hissing or crashing noise caused by a violent storm of wind or thunder. The fire of conflagration will, most probably, precede the coming of the judge, and causing the death of such men as will have survived the other precursory evils of the day of judgment, viz., famine, the sword, &c., shall continue to pass with great noise from hemisphere to hemisphere, and continue during the holding of the judgment, devouring and purging the elements, until, after the sentence of the judge, increasing in ardour and violence, it shall precipitate the impious into hell.

"And the elements shall be melted with heat." Some understand these of the four elements, viz., fire, air, earth, and water. They shall be melted away, not in such a way, as to be utterly destroyed, but merely changed, just as melted gold loses its dross and form, while its substance remains. Others say, the "elements" refer only to the earth and water; for, the Apostle treated already of the element of air, when saying "the heavens shall pass away," and as for the element of fire, they say it is hard to conceive how

Text.	Paraphrase.
11. Seeing then that all these things are to be dissolved, what manner of people ought to be in holy conversation and godliness,	11. Since, then, all things, heaven, the elements, and the works that are found in creation, are to be dissolved, and a new and perfect order of things to be introduced, how pure and holy should you not be both in the sanctity of your intercourse with your neighbour and in acts of piety towards God ;
12. Looking for and hasting unto the coming of the day of the Lord by which the heavens being on fire shall be dissolved, and the elements snall melt with the burning heat ?	12. Firmly hoping for, and hastening on to meet, or anticipating by your diligent preparation, the coming of the day of the Lord, by which the heavens, being set on fire, will be dissolved, and the elements shall melt away with a burning heat ?
13. But we look for new heavens and a new earth according to his promises, in which justice dwelleth.	13. But, although the present system of creation be dissolved, we look for and expect new and renovated heavens, a newly renovated earth, in which perfect justice and immaculate sanctity will dwell.

Commentary.

the fire of conflagration can destroy the elementary fire. To this it might, however, be replied, that it will only dissolve it, and depriving it of all grossness and imperfection, purify and render it a fit ingredient of the new creation, which is to be the dwellingplace of the glorified children of God.

"And the earth, and the works which are in it." He again repeats the burning of "the earth," though contained under the words, "elements shall be destroyed," because it has this peculiar to itself, that on its surface, men have made the most valuable improvements, and from its bowels come forth these treasures which worldlings prize most. "And the works which are in it," that is to say, its animal and vegetable productions, as also the works of art, such as, buildings, gold, &c. ; very likely he refers also to the moral works of man, which will be consumed by, and afford fuel to, the fire of conflagration.—(1 Cor. iii. 15). "If any one's work burn," &c.; and the Apostle wishes to stimulate the faithful to perform works which will stand the test of this devouring fire ; such is the moral exhortation clearly expressed in the following verses.

11. "What manner of people ought you to be," that is, how perfectly elevated above all terrestrial ideas and affections should you not be, to fit you for the new and perfect order of things which is to succeed the present ; "in holy conversation," in your several relations with men, "and godliness," and your piety, acts of faith, hope, love, religion, &c., towards God. "Conversation and godliness," are read in the plural in the Greek.

12. "Looking for," that is, by firm hope, looking forward to, "and hastening unto," or, anticipating, in the fervour and zeal of your preparation, "the coming of the day of the Lord," acting each day as you would, were the day of the Lord immediately at hand. "By which, that is, either day, or coming of the Lord. "The heavens being on fire shall be dissolved." The meaning of this is the same as that of verse 10 ; here, it is merely added, that the heat by which all things will be dissolved is the heat of fire. "The heavens will be dissolved." This refers to the lower heavens or regions of the air ; although it is most likely that the starry heavens will not be dissolved, it is still very probable, they will be changed or perfected, so as to suit the glorified condition of the children of God. "The powers of heaven·(the stars) shall be moved." and the Church sings in her Office, *quando cœli movendi sunt et terra.*" "And the elements shall melt away with a burning heat." They shall melt away like wax, with the form changed, the substance shall remain. "*Transit figura hujus mundi.*" (1 Cor. vii.)

13. "But we look for new heavens," that is, heavens renovated and perfected, into which the present heavens shall be changed, including both the lower air, or atmosphere, and the starry heaven For, "*the light of the moon shall be as the light of the sun, and the light of the sun shall be sevenfold, as the light of seven days.*"—(Isaias, xxx. 26).

Text.	Paraphrase.
14. Wherefore, dearly beloved, seeing that you look for these things, be diligent that ye may be found undefiled and unspotted to him in peace :	14. Wherefore, dearly beloved, as you are firmly hoping for this renovated state of things, this new heaven and new earth, exert all your care and diligence to be found by the Lord, at his coming, free from all gross crimes, particularly such as are practised by the deceitful scoffers, and, as far as possible, free from lesser defects, in a state of peace both with God and your neighbour, thus calmly prepared to meet your judge.
15. And account the long-suffering of our Lord salvation, as also our most dear brother Paul, according to the wisdom given him, hath written to you :	15. And look upon the long-suffering of the Lord, in deferring his coming, as solely intended for your salvation, to give you time for repentance and merit; as our most dear brother in the Apostleship, Paul, according to the divine and heavenly wisdom, given him from above, has written to you.

Commentary.

And a new earth," the present earth renovated and changed in its qualities and purified of all the dross and imperfection, which it contracted from the "slavery of corruption."—(Rom. viii.) "According to his promises." The new heavens, &c., are promised (Isaias, lxv. 17, lxvi. 22); or, the words may refer to the general promises of eternal happiness, made to the saints. "In which justice dwelleth," that is, which will be the seat and habitation of the blessed, free from all stains or defilements. "There shall not enter into it anything defiled."—(Apoc. xxi. 27).

14. "Wherefore, dearly beloved, seeing that you look for these things," seeing that you expect a new heaven and a new earth, and a total renovation of all things, at the coming of Christ to judgment, and that you thus turn a deaf ear to the incredulous, and to the scoffing questions of the impious, asking, "*where is his promise or his coming?*" verse 4), "be diligent," exert your utmost care and diligence, "that you may be found undefiled," that is, free from the grosser crimes, such as the Simonites, Gnostics, and other heretics had fallen into, ("walking after their own lusts," verse 3); "and undefiled," free from lesser or venial faults, as far as possible. "To him," in his presence, "in peace," by being in peace both with God and your neighbour. Thus you will calmly and peaceably be prepared to meet the judge.

15. "And account the long suffering of our Lord, salvation," that is to say, regard the long-suffering of God in deferring his coming to judge the world, not in a spirit of captious and deceitful inquiring, "where is his promise or his coming?" (verse 4), but, rather as intended, in the gracious designs of Providence, to secure your salvation, by giving you time for repentance, or for heaping up a treasure of merit. "As also our most dear brother Paul." By "brother," is meant, associate in the Apostolical ministry. "According to the wisdom," that is the heavenly and divine knowledge, "given to him," from above, "hath written to you." The Apostle praises the Epistles of St. Paul for the wisdom displayed in them, but in such a way, that the glory of it should be ultimately referred to God, from whom every good gift comes. "Written to you." It is disputed among Expositors of Sacred Scriptures, what Epistle of St. Paul St. Peter alludes to here—for, that he refers to some particular Epistle, is clear from the words next verse, "as also in all his Epistles." Some, with Œcumenius, say, it is that to the Romans; others, with Cajetan, the Epistles to the Galatians, Ephesians, and Colossians, addressed to the people of Asia Minor, as is also this Epistle of St. Peter's. The more probable opinion, however, appears to be, that he alludes to the Epistle to the Hebrews; for, throughout that Epistle, the principal object of the Apostle seems to be, to exhort the Hebrews to patience amidst trials and persecutions, by proposing to them the coming of our Lord, and by placing before them the example of the saints of old (x. 35-39; xi. to the end of the Epistle), and he occasionally, in the first part of the Epistle, treats of the same (iii. iv. vi.) The words, "as also our most dear brother Paul hath written to you." are to be connected with verse 14, "be diligent," &c.

Text.

16. As also in all _his_ epistles, speaking in them of these things; in which are certain things hard to be understood, which the unlearned and unstable wrest, as they do also the other Scriptures, to their own destruction.

Paraphrase.

16. As indeed, he has in all his Epistles, referring to the same subjects of which I have been treating, viz., regarding patience under afflictions in the hope of Christ's coming, steadfastness in resisting the aggressive attacks of the heretics, &c. In which writings of St. Paul, or among which subjects treated of by him, there are some hard to be understood, which, those unacquainted with spiritual things, as well as those who are not firmly grounded in the faith, distort by false interpretations, as indeed they do the other inspired Scriptures, to their own spiritual and eternal ruin.

Commentary.

16. As also in all his Epistles." This shows that in the preceding words, "hath written to you," he refers to a particular Epistle addressed to them. "Speaking in them of these things," wherein you have been instructed by me, regarding the necessity of patiently waiting for the coming of the Lord to judgment, of firmly expecting the performance, in due time, of his promise, of resisting the lures and temptations held out by false teachers, and of keeping yourselves pure and immaculate from the world, by the performance of good works. These appear to be the general subjects treated of in the Epistles of St. Paul.

"In which." These words are of a different gender from " Epistles " in the common Greek, ἐν οἷς. Hence, according to this reading, they mean, _in which things treated of by him_, or, _in which writings._ · The Vatican and Alexandrian MSS. have ἐν αἷς (_i.e._) Epistles. "There are certain things hard to be understood," that is, absolutely obscure, and, of themselves, difficult for all persons. "Which the unlearned," men not versed in spiritual things—" _The sensual man_," be he ever so wellversed in secular knowledge, "_perceiveth not the things that are of the spirit of God_" (1 Cor. ii. 14)—" and unstable," such as are not firmly grounded in the principles and foundation of religion; "wrest," distort their meaning by false interpretations ; "as they do also the other Scriptures "—hence, the Epistles of St. Paul are divine Scriptures, for, of such, St. Peter speaks—"to their own destruction."

· The Scriptures, therefore, are difficult and hard to be understood, and not only obscure with reference to all persons, but ruinous to some, both "unlearned" and learned. For, "the unstable" may embrace the learned classes also. Hence, the wisdom of the Catholic Church in not permitting the indiscriminate reading of the sacred Scriptures to all classes of persons, without distinction. The Scriptures are not clear and plain to every capacity, as modern heretics pretend. They are, in themselves, really difficult, we are assured here by St. Peter ; their reading, far from being attended with profit to all, is ruinous to some ; and hence, the Church of Christ, actuated by the same Holy Spirit which inspired St. Peter, restricts the reading of them to such as bring to their perusal the proper dispositions ; but particularly, docility to the teachings and interpretations of the Church, to whom alone belongs the duty of explaining God's holy word. Every one who knows anything of the history of modern heresies, will at once perceive that the assumption of the independent right to read the obscure and difficult oracles of God's truth, and interpret them, according to each one's private spirit, or rather, whim or caprice, has been the prolific source of the most monstrous errors and has split up the heretical communities themselves into countless sections, all differing in faith, from one another.

What the passages in the Epistles of St. Paul, containing peculiar difficulties and the source of perdition to some, are, cannot be asserted for certain. It is, however, probable, that he refers to the doctrine of justification by faith, as we are told by St. Augustine (_Libro de Fide et Operibus_, c. 14). From this, the heretics inferred the sufficiency of faith alone, without good works. We are assured by the same Father, that it was to correct this fundamental error, so fatal to the purity of Christian morality, to which the false interpretation of the words of St. Paul gave rise, the Catholic Epistles of the four Apostles were written (_Libro de Fide et Operibus_, c. 14).

Text.	Paraphrase.
17. You therefore, brethren, knowing these things before, take heed, lest being led aside by the error of the unwise, you fail from your own steadfastness.	17. Do you therefore, beloved brethren, admonished beforehand of these things, be on your guard, lest, forced aside from the path of truth, by the erroneous teaching of these men, you fall away from the steadfast profession of Christian faith, and the practice of Christian virtues, in which the grace of God has established you.
18. But grow in grace, and in the knowledge of our Lord and Saviour JESUS CHRIST. To him be glory both now and unto the day of eternity. Amen.	18. But (by the zealous performance of good works), endeavour to increase in grace, both actual and habitual, and in the more perfect faith and knowledge of our Lord and Saviour Jesus Christ. To him be rendered glory both in this life and during the never-ending ages of eternity. Amen.

Commentary.

17. The Apostle concludes this Epistle by cautioning them against being deceived by the erroneous teachings of the false scoffers. "Take heed, lest being led aside," from the path of truth. The Greek word for "led aside," συναπαχθεντες, means *being carried* or *forced forward*, as if by a crowd. "By the error of the unwise," in Greek, των ὁθεσμων, *of the lawless.* He refers to these scoffers who trample on all laws, human and divine. "You fall from your own steadfastness," both in the profession of faith and its inward belief, and the practice of virtues. Hence, faith is not inamissible. St. Paul assures us also, that Hymeneus and Philetus had fallen away from it (1 Tim. i. 20).

18. "But grow in grace," that is, by advancing from virtue to virtue, endeavour to acquire an increase of grace, both actual and habitual. "And the knowledge of our Lord," &c. This he says in opposition to those who, from an affectation of superior knowledge, were called *Gnostics*, though really ignorant and wandering from truth. The Apostle closes the Epistle with words almost the same as those with which he began it. "Grace to you and peace be accomplished in the knowledge of God, and of Christ Jesus our Lord" (chap. i. 2). "To him be glory both now," in this world, "and unto the day," the never-ending moment, "of eternity. Amen."

FIRST EPISTLE OF ST. JOHN.

————◆————

Introduction.

CANONICITY OF.—The Canonicity, or Divine authority of this Epistle, as well as its authenticity, have never been questioned in the Church. It is, therefore, ranked among the Proto-canonical Books of Scripture. The only persons who ever questioned its authenticity, and denied it to be the genuine production of St. John, were Marcion and some other early heretics. Such denial, however, avails little; for, it bears all the marks, both intrinsic and extrinsic, of authenticity.

WHEN AND WHERE WRITTEN.—Both points are matters of great uncertainty. According to some, it was written about the year, 68, before his Gospel. According to others, after his Gospel, about the year 99, of the Christian Era; and the frequent repetition of the terms, "my little children," throughout the entire Epistle, would seem to confirm the latter opinion, and show that this Epistle was written, at the close of the patriarchal age, which the Apostle reached. The place from which it was written cannot be ascertained with any degree of probability, unless we hold, that it was written about the year, 99. Ephesus might, in that case, be fixed upon, with very great probability, as it was there St. John closed his life.

OBJECT OF.—The chief object, which the Apostles had in view, in all the Catholic Epistles, as we are informed by St. Augustine (*Libro de Fide et Operibus*, ch. xiv.), was, to refute the pernicious and demoralizing error of Simon Magus, regarding the inutility of good works, and the sufficiency of faith alone for salvation. St. John devotes this Epistle, in a special manner, to the refutation of this error (i. 6, ii. 4, iii. 7, 8, &c., iv. 20). Besides this general object, he had specially in view to refute the errors which had sprung up in the very infancy of the Church, regarding the divinity and humanity of our blessed Lord. Hence, against Ebion and Cerinthus, who denied the divinity of Christ (his Gospel was also written against the same heretics), he asserts that Jesus is the Christ, the eternal Son of God, himself, true God. Against Basilides, who erred regarding his humanity, by asserting, that he assumed not a real, but a fantastical body, he declares Him to be true man, our advocate and intercessor with the Father. These, and all other heretics, who, at a future day, were to spring forth and promulgate errors; regarding the attributes of our divine Redeemer, whether in his divine or human nature, he terms, "antichrists;" "spirits that dissolve Jesus." He dwells much in proving the truth of the two great fundamental mysteries of the Trinity and Incarnation; but, his zeal is principally directed against the errors of Simon Magus. He also, in a special manner, insists on the precept of loving our neighbour; and repeats the same frequently, and in different ways, as being the most necessary and meritorious work we could perform.

STYLE OF.—The style of this Epistle is of the most simple and unadorned character.   The sentences, viewed in themselves, quite easy and intelligible ; but, viewed with reference to the context, it is not quite so easy to trace their connexion. A spirit of unction, benevolence, and charity, breathes throughout, to which is united a certain degree of parental authority, quite suited to the character of the aged Apostle of love.

TO WHOM ADDRESSED.—St. Augustine (*lib. 2do Quest. Evangel.*, ch. 39), Pope Hyginus (*Epist.* 1), and others quote from it, as the Epistle to the Parthians, that is to say to the Christians scattered throughout the extent of country that lies between the Tigris and the Indus ; and some assert, it was principally addressed to the converted Jews in these regions, whose fathers had been led into captivity under Salmanazar and Nebuchodonozor.   It may be, that the Apostle himself preached among the Parthians, as Baronius and others assert   and although these nations were converted by other Apostles, viz., Thomas, Simon, and Jude ; still, it is not unlikely, that St. John wished, after their death, to confirm their converts in the faith.   A similar course was pursued by St. Paul, with reference to those who were converted by other Apostles ; the Romans, converted by St. Peter, and the Colossians, by Epaphras, a disciple of his own.   To whomsoever, addressed, the Epistle is commonly reckoned among the *Catholic* Epistles, as being *Catholic*, in doctrine, and suited, at all times, to Christians of every age and character.

FIRST EPISTLE OF ST. JOHN.

CHAPTER I.

Analysis.

The Apostle commences this Epistle, omitting the usual salutation and inscription, as he also commences his Gospel, by entering at once on the most sublime of all subjects, the Divinity, and eternal generation of the Son of God; who, though existing from eternity, was still, in time, manifested to the world: of the reality of his assumed nature, the united testimony of all the senses gave his Apostles the most complete knowledge and the firmest certainty. It is with the announcement of the great mystery of God's love, in manifesting himself to the world, the Apostle commences this Epistle; his object in doing so is to bring men to a union and fellowship with God (verses 1, 2, 3).

In the next place, he declares, that in addressing them, and expounding the great mysteries of the Divinity and Humanity of Jesus Christ, and wishing them a fellowship with God, he only wishes to secure to them the fulness of spiritual joy (4).

He then enters on the great subject of all the Catholic Epistles, which is to inculcate the necessity of good works. This he does, first, by representing God, as the pure, unalloyed light, having no communication with the works of darkness (5); whence he infers, that those who live in the habitual commission of sin, are guilty of a lie, when they assert they have any fellowship with God (6); while, on the other hand, those who perform good works enjoy the union and fellowship with him. The Apostle, however, takes care to refer this blessing to its meritorious cause, viz., the blood of Christ, which merited for us the remission of our sins (7). He next points out the necessity of availing ourselves of the merits of Christ, since we all have sins to be remitted (8); and he shows the mode in which their actual remission is to be obtained, viz., by confessing them in the way in which the law of God prescribes confession to be made (9).

He shows, in conclusion, that by adopting the opposite course of confessing our sins, and denying that we have any sins to confess, we not only deceive ourselves (9), but that we also make God a liar (10).

Text.	Paraphrase.
1. THAT which was from the beginning, which we have heard, which we have seen with our eyes, which we have looked upon, and our hands have handled, of the word of life :	1. We declare unto you (verse 3) the Word of life, which existed from eternity, which, in His assumed nature, we, Apostles, have heard speak, which we have seen with our eyes, which we have closely and minutely examined, which our hands have touched and handled.

Commentary.

1, 2, 3. From the absence of the usual salutation, some expositors call this a treatise, rather than, an Epistle. The same, however, might be said of the Epistle of St. Paul to the Hebrews, which has no preface either ; it may also be said, that the announcement contained (verse 3), " and our fellowship may be with God the Father," &c., holds the place of the usual form of salutation ; for, in substance, it is a most desirable one.   The

Commentary.

construction of the words in these three verses, is rather intricate and complicated. The common interpretation, followed in the Paraphrase, includes the second verse within a parenthesis, and makes the words, "*we declare*" (verse 3), the first words in the arrangement of the sentence. The meaning of the passage, to verse 3, is kept suspended. "We declare unto you" (verse 3), "that," viz., "the word of life......" which was from the beginning," &c. (verse 1). "For the life was manifested," &c. (verse 2). In this construction the "terms of the word of life" ("*de verbo vitæ,*") are put for the accusative case, "the word of life" ("*verbum vitæ.*") With the Hebrews, it was not unusual, to employ the ablative with a preposition for the accusative or nominative (*v.g.*) "*effundam de spiritu meo, i.e., spiritum meum,*" (Acts, ii.), "*dabitur ei de auro Arabiæ, i.e. aurum Arabiæ,*" "*adorabunt de ipso i.e., ipsum,*" (Psalm lxi).

This construction, however, is totally opposed to the Greek reading, wherein, ὅ "that which," is of a different gender from, λογος "the word." On which account, others arrange the words thus, "we declare unto you (3) of," or *concerning* "the word of life, that which was from the beginning," viz., his Divinity, "which we have heard, which we have seen," &c., viz., his Humanity, assumed at his Incarnation ; in other words, we announce to you concerning the eternal Son of God that he possesses two natures —one, the Divine, which he had from eternity ; the other, the Human, which he had assumed at his Incarnation. Both constructions amount to the *same*, in sense.

"That which was from the beginning." From these words, as well as from the first words of St. John's gospel, "In the beginning was the word," is inferred the eternity of the Son of God. By the word "beginning," some understand, *the beginning of time*, or, *of creation;* and even from the words understood in this sense, they infer his eternity ; for, at the beginning of all time, *before* any object was created, the Word "WAS," and to what other moment can it refer, but the permanent, indivisible moment of eternity. This interpretation derives probability from the clear parallelism that exists between the description given by Moses of the Genesis of creation, and that given by St. John, both here, and in his gospel, of the eternal Genesis of the Son of God. In the one, it is said, "*in principio creavit Deus cœlum et terram;*" in the other, "*in principio a principio erat verbum;*" the difference being, that at the beginning of time, the world received existence, but at the same beginning the Word already WAS; hence, existing before all time, before anything was created, which would be untrue, if he himself were a creature. Therefore, he was uncreated and from eternity. By "the beginning," then, according to these, is meant, the beginning of any time, whether actual or imaginary, and even then the Word "WAS ;" hence, eternal. In scriptural language, "*to be from the beginning,*" expresses eternity, thus, in Isaias (xliii. 13), God says of himself, "*and from the beginning I am the same.*"

Others understand the word "beginning," as well here, as in the commencement of the gospel, to refer directly to eternity, which is a beginning without a beginning; termed, "beginning," to suit the weak conceptions of our obscure and limited understandings.

"Which we have heard, have seen with our eyes," &c. This refers to the human nature of the Son of God, of the reality of which, the united testimony of all the senses, viz., the hearing, sight, touch, &c., had conspired to assure the Apostles, "heard, seen, handled," &c.; "which we have looked upon," *i.e.*, leisurely examined, and closely viewed, and not in a mere passing way, which is expressed by the words, "have seen him;" "which our hands have handled," may be allusive to the practice usual with our divine Redeemer, of kissing his disciples when returning to him after any considerable absence ; hence, it was with a kiss, when saluting him as usual, that Judas betrayed him ; or, to the words addressed to them after his resurrection, *palpate et videte, quia spiritus carnem et ossa non habet,* &c.

From this verse, is proved the unity of person in Christ with two distinct natures ; for, the Apostle declares, that it was the same word which existed from eternity, he and the Apostles saw, heard, &c., of course, in his human nature.

"Of the word of life," *i.e.*, the eternal Son of God, the Second Person of the Adorable Trinity. The Son of God is called in Scripture, "*the Word,*" *i.e.*, the thought or conception of God. For, as our thought, or, the internal word of our mind, is generated and remains in the mind, even after it is externally expressed by the voice ; so, in like manner (as far as human and divine things admit of comparison), is the Son of God

Text.

2. For the life was manifested: and we have seen, and do bear witness, and declare unto you the life eternal, which was with the Father, and hath appeared to us:

3. That which we have seen and have heard, we declare unto you, that you also may have fellowship with us, and our fellowship may be with the Father, and with his son JESUS CHRIST.

Paraphrase.

2. For this essential life, who is also the source of all life both natural and supernatural in creatures, was manifested in his incarnation, and we have seen him, and testify regarding him even by our sufferings, and we declare him to you to be the essential life (the cause also of eternal life in us), that existed from eternity in the bosom of the Father, and in time has been manifested to us, in his assumed nature.

3. The Eternal Word, I say, which we have both seen and heard, we declare unto you, and our object in doing so is, that you may have a fellowship with us Apostles, in the profession of the same faith, and in the bonds of charity springing therefrom and that this fellowship may be the foundation of a more perfect fellowship, and more exalted union, between us and God the Father, together with his Son Jesus Christ.

Commentary.

begotten of Him, by an eternal generation, the substantial expression of His divine mind, consubstantial with Him, yet still existing in Him, as a distinct divine person. This, and other such comparisons, by which it is attempted to illustrate the eternal generation of the Son of God, his identity of nature and distinction of person with the Father, are, however, so imperfect and obscure, that it is better for us to contemplate, and firmly believe, rather than curiously pry into what faith proposes regarding him, both with respect to his divine nature, or his eternal generation, as God, begotten of the Father; and his human nature, assumed by him, as man, in time, being born of a virgin.

2. *For the life was manifested,* &c. This verse is, according to the commonly received construction, included in a parenthesis; "the life," *i.e.,* essential life in himself, and the author of all life, but particularly of spiritual and supernatural life in us, "was manifested," in his assumed nature. This is added by the Apostle to show how it is that he, and the other Apostles, could have *heard, seen him,* &c. (verse 1); "and we have seen." The heavenly love with which the heart of the Apostle glowed, makes him fond of repetition in everything connected with the great mystery of the Incarnation; hence, in these three verses, he repeatedly asserts, that he saw him, in his assumed nature; "and do bear witness," we are become true martyrs by our sufferings; and declare unto you the life eternal," that is, we declare him unto you to be the life eternal. These words evidently refer to a person, who is the essential life in himself, and the cause of life eternal, of which the life of grace here is the seed, in others.

"Which was with the Father," shows him to be a distinct person from the Father: "and hath appeared to us." "Manifested" and "appeared," have the same corresponding word in the Greek, εφανερωθη. Here, too, the fondness for repetition, the effect of divine love, in the heart of the Apostle, is observable.

3. "That which we have seen and heard, we declare unto you." These latter words, "we declare unto," are the first in the construction of these three verses.—(*Vide* Paraphrase).

"That you also may have fellowship with us." He says, his object in announcing to them this eternal Word, which existed from eternity, and was manifested in time, was, that they should have a fellowship with the Apostles, both in the profession of the same faith, of which he had announced the two leading articles in the preceding verses, viz., the Trinity and Incarnation, involved in the Divinity of the Word, and in the bonds of charity springing from faith; "and our fellowship may be with the Father, &c.," and this union may be with the Father and Son; for, this society between the faithful and the Apostles must not rest there; it must be the foundation of a further union with God. Hence, in order to enjoy the union of sanctifying grace or charity with God, it is necessary beforehand to be united with the true Church, and no one, who is outside the true Church by a voluntary act, can enjoy such a union with God—"*non potest habere Deum patrem, qui Ecclesiam noluerit habere matrem,*" (St. Cyprian *de Un. Eccl.*) In some copies, for "may be with the Father," we have, *is with the Father,* as if the Apostle

Text.

4. And these things we write to you, that you may rejoice, and your joy may be full.

5. And this is the declaration which we have heard from him, and declare unto you : that God is light, and in him there is no darkness.

6. If we say that we have fellowship with him, and walk in darkness, we lie, and do not the truth.

7. But if we walk in the light, as he also is in the light ; we have

Paraphrase.

4. And the things which we have spoken regarding the eternal and incarnate Word, announced to you by us, in order that you may enjoy a union with us and God, we write to you for this end, that you may rejoice with true and spiritual joy, on account of the prospects of future blessings, which this union will bring you, and that this your joy may be perfected in the sure possession of future glory.

5. And the announcement or declaration, which we have heard from him, while with us here on earth, and which we, in turn, make to you, is this : that God is the essential light of grace and glory, the source of all light and unalloyed sanctity in creatures, and that in him there is no fellowship or communication with the foul and darksome works of ignorance and sin, or with the workers of iniquity.

6. If, then, we say, that we have fellowship with God, while we habitually perform, and live subject to, the dominion of the works of sin and darkness, we announce what is false ; and our actions are not made to square with our words ; so that we lie both in word and act.

7. But, if, on the other hand, we live in the performance of good works, or the works of light, imitating

Commentary.

meant to show the value of a union with the Church, which is no less than a union with God himself. The Greek admits either. Commentators notice the exact parallelism which exists between the opening of this Epistle and that of the Gospel of St. John. "*In principio erat verbum,*" (Gospel) ; "*quod erat ab initio de verbo vitæ,*" (in this place) ; "*in ipso vita erat—et verbum caro factum est,*" (Gospel) ; "*et vita manifestata est,*" (here) ; "*erat lux vera quæ illuminat omnem hominem,*" (Gospel) ; "*Deus lux est,*" (here,) perfectly correspond.

4. In the Greek, the words, "that you may rejoice," are wanting.

5. "The declaration," means the subject matter of the declaration ; "no darkness." may either refer to the *works* of sin, or, the *workers* of sin, "*et tenebræ eum non comprehenderunt.*"—(Gospel of St. John, chap. i.) Both meanings are given in the Paraphrase. As "light" is the symbol of sanctity, grace, and glory ; so, "darkness," symbolizes ignorance and sin. By calling God, "light," the Apostle clearly intimates, what the nature of the "life" of which God is the essence and the cause in creatures, is. He clearly refers to the spiritual life, of which the light of faith is the chief and primary ingredient.

6. These words are an inference drawn from the general proposition, announced in the foregoing verse. If God be light, having no communication with darkness, *i.e.*, either with the *works* or *doers* of ignorance and sin, whosoever, therefore, says, that he has society or fellowship with God, at the same time "walking in," that is, habitually performing the works, and living subject to the passions, of "darkness," such a person "tells a lie," he announces what is false ; "and does not the truth," that is, speaks not the truth ; or, does not that in practice, which his words announce ; so that his actions do not verify his words. In this verse, the Apostle enters on the great object of all the Catholic Epistles, which is, to inculcate the necessity of works of sanctity, and to correct the error regarding the sufficiency of faith alone without good works ; he introduces the subject, by saying that evil works performed, under what pretext soever, whether by persons professing the faith of Christ, or otherwise, will destroy the fellowship which should subsist between the faithful and God.

7. He shows the effect of the opposite conduct. "If we walk in the light," that is, live in the performance of the works of light and sanctity, "as he also is in the light," by becoming assimilated to him in his uncreated, infinite, unchangeable sanctity, as

Text.

fellowship one with another, and the blood of JESUS CHRIST his Son cleanseth us from all sin.

8. If we say that we have no sin; we deceive ourselves, and the truth is not in us.

9. If we confess our sins; he is

Paraphrase.

his infinite and unchangeable sanctity, and becoming assimilated to him, as far as sinful creatures can approach a Creator of infinite perfection, we have fellowship with one another, that is, with God's Church, and consequently, with God himself; and the blood of Jesus Christ his Son, by being applied to us, in the performance of good works. in the sacraments, and other channels of grace, marked out by him, cleanses us from all sin.

8. If we say, that we commit no sin whatever, even indeliberate venial sins in the course of our lives, or, that we have not incurred the liability of punishment due to sin, we deceive ourselves, by stating what is false, and the truth is not in us.

9. If we confess our sins, with the proper dispositions

Commentary.

far as, in a limited way, our condition, as sinful creatures, will admit. "We have fellowship one with another," may mean—we have fellowship with God and ourselves; or rather, we have fellowship with God's Church, and as a consequence, with God himself; "and the blood of Jesus Christ his Son cleanses us from all sin;" that is, the merits of Christ purchased by his blood, after being applied in the performance of good works, through the sacraments, and other channels of grace marked out by him, cleanse us from all sin, original and actual, whether they be mortal sins, or *deliberate* venial sins. From falling into either mortal sins, or the venial sins referred to, the grace of Christ preserves us, and remits these *indeliberate* venial faults, into which all persons *must* fall without an extraordinary grace from God.—(Council of Trent, SS. vi. Can. 23). Of course, in saying "that the blood of Christ cleanses us from all sin, the Apostle can, by no means, be understood to exclude our own co-operation by good works; for, so, he would be contradicting his own exhortation in the preceding verse, regarding the performance of good works. He only attributes to the grace of God, purchased by the blood of Christ, which is the principal means of our justification, the entire effect, although the will of man has its subordinate share too, a thing quite usual in SS. Scripture, (v.g.) "*Unctio Dei vos omnia docebit.*" "*Non vos estis qui loquimini, sed spiritus, qui loquitor in vobis.*"

8. "If we say," either say in word, or think in our minds, "that we have no sin," that during our lives we commit no sin whatever, not even venial sin; or, the words may mean, that we have not incurred the liability of punishment due to sin; and hence, have no need of the redeeming blood of Christ to cleanse us from sin (verse 7), "we deceive ourselves," by asserting, or, thinking not only what is inconsistent with Christian humility, but, what is untrue, "and the truth is not in us," when we entertain such a thought, or make such an assertion. It is a point of Catholic faith, defined in the Council of Trent (SS. 6, Canon 23), "*that no person can, during the whole of his life, avoid all, even venial sins, unless by a special privilege of God, as the Church holds regarding the Blessed Virgin.*" Hence, by the ordinary aids of grace, no one can be free from all *indeliberate* venial sins; and the saints can say, with truth, "*forgive us our trespasses.*" There is one, however, the most perfect pure creature whom God ever created, who, by a special privilege of grace, was preserved from all sin, both original and actual. This is the glorious Queen of Heaven, in whom no spot could be found —"*tota pulchra es, et macula non est in te,*" the solemn proclamation of whose glorious preservation, by the grace of Her Son, from the state of original sin—now a point of faith—has filled the earth with universal joy and jubilee. St. Augustine (*libro de Nat. et Grat.*, c. 68), says, that when there is question of sin, there should be no mention whatever made of Her. Blessed be the God of all grace, who has provided so powerful a Protectress for His Church, through whose hands He deigns to transmit all the graces conferred on the human race—"*omnia voluit nos habere per Mariam.*"— St. Bernard.

9. The Apostle now points out the mode of receiving the remission of those sins

Text.

faithful and just, to forgive us our sins, and to cleanse us from all iniquity.

10. If we say that we have not sinned; we make him a liar, and his word is not in us.

Paraphrase.

of penance, God is faithful in the fulfilment of his promises, and just in his engagements, so as to forgive us our sins, and, by his sanctifying and justifying grace, to cleanse us from all iniquity.

10. If we say, that we have not sinned, and that we avoid all sins during our lives, we not only deceive ourselves by being liars ourselves (verse 8), but we also make a liar of God, who, in many places of sacred Scripture, tells us, that all have gone astray, and have sinned, and commands all to pray for the remission of their sins; and his doctrine does not reside in us by faith.

Commentary.

into which we all fall; it is, by confessing them, in whatever way this confession may be appointed by God; from other passages of Scripture, we know the ordinary way to be, confession to a priest, in the tribunal of penance. But, although St. John must refer here to auricular confession, made to a priest—since we know from other passages of SS. Scripture, that this is, under ordinary circumstances, a necessary means of obtaining forgiveness for our sins—still, it does not appear, that the passage, of itself, furnishes a proof of the necessity of such confession. He puts confession for the entire process of penance, of which confession is but a part, and it is in external confession, interior sorrow manifests itself. The Apostle refers to the confession prescribed in the sacred Scriptures, whether made to a priest or to God, according to circumstances. "He is faithful and just," regards that justice, which consists in fulfilling promises, and God promised to remit sin for the truly penitent; or, it may regard the congruity on the part of God to remit sin in the case of real penance; for, of strict justice there can be no question, only inasmuch as it may refer to the remission of sin, in consideration of the just claims, not of the sinner, but of Christ, who merited it for us.

"And cleanse us from all iniquity," proves *inherent*, and refutes the doctrine of *imputative*, justice. The words of the Apostle requiring of us to confess our sins, show, that the blood of Christ does not "*cleanse us*" immediately of itself (verse 7), without being applied through our own good works and co-operation, and through the channels of grace, instituted by God for that purpose.

10. In this verse, he, probably, repeats the same thing expressed by him (verses 6 and 8), in order to confound human pride; or it may bear a different signification from the foregoing, and mean, if we say, not only, that we have no sin at present, but that we never sinned in our past lives, "we make him (God) a liar;" who, in many places, charges all mankind with being under sin; "and his word is not in us," that is, we have not true faith in his revealed word, which condemns and convicts the whole world of sin.

CHAPTER II.

Analysis.

In this chapter, the Apostle points out the object which he had in view in reminding them, in the foregoing, of their weakness and liability to sin; and that was, to prevent them from committing sin any longer. He strengthens such as may have committed sin, against the horrors of despair, by pointing to the powerful advocacy of Jesus Christ in heaven (verse 1). He explains in what sense he is our advocate—viz., an advocate of redemption and propitiation (2). He next proceeds to point out the necessity of good works, the performance of them being the surest sign that we love God (3); and whosoever says he loves him, and observes not his commandments, is a liar, and asserts what is untrue (4); while, on the other hand, whosoever keeps his law, gives the clearest proof of the sincerity of his love for God, and a probable conjectural mark of being in his love and friendship (5). He requires for a continuance in God's friendship and grace, a moral assimilation with Christ in the performance of good works (6).

He says that the precept which he is inculcating, is not a "new" precept, but an "old" one, with which they were familiar from the very beginning of their conversion, although, under a different respect, it might be termed "new," also (7, 8). He shows what the precept is, to which he is referring—viz., the precept of loving our neighbour, and he points out the evils of its infraction, and the advantages flowing from its observance (9, 10 11).

He next addresses the faithful in general, and congratulates them on the spiritual gifts which they received (12); and having referred to the different stages of spiritual life, he congratulates them on their spiritual perfections, analogous to the natural gifts in which men, in the different stages of human life, are prone to glory (13, 14).

The Apostle next guards them against the greatest obstacle to fraternal charity—viz., the love of the world, and the things of the world, and assigns reasons for shunning all inordinate attachment to both one and the other—viz., their incompatibility with the love of God (15), their innate deordination (16), and the transient, fleeting condition of their enjoyment and possession (17).

The Apostle next proceeds to caution them against the snares of the heretics of the day. These heretics are the forerunners of the great Antichrist, and they deserted the Church, because they were not solid members of it (18, 19). But the faithful, who persevered in the unity of the Church, were sharers in the graces deposited with her (20).

He refers to one leading heresy of the day—viz., the denial of Jesus Christ, which involved a denial of his Father (22, 23). He exhorts them to perseverance in the profession of the old faith, from which the heretics wished to seduce them (24-26), and ascribes their perseverance to the grace of God, left in his Church, of which grace they were sharers (27).

He again exhorts them to perseverance (28), and closes the chapter by entering on a new subject—viz., a description of the sons of God (29).

Text.

1. MY little children, these things I write to you that you may not sin.

Paraphrase.

1. My little children, and dearly beloved, I write these things which I have now alluded to concerning

Commentary.

1. "My little children," a term of affection and endearment frequently employed by

Text.

But if any man sin, we have an advocate with the Father, JESUS CHRIST the Just :

2. And he is the propitiation for our sins : and not for ours only, but also for those of the whole world.

Paraphrase.

our common weakness and sinfulness, in order that, mindful of human frailty, you may guard against temptation and against adding still more to your natural weakness, by the habit of committing sin. But if any man commit sin, let him not despair of pardon ; because, we have a Mediator in heaven with God the Father, possessing all the qualities of a powerful advocate, who can allege sufficient grounds for obtaining the remission of our sins, viz., his own merits, and the ransom paid for them, and who has also a right to be heard. This is Jesus Christ the Just.

2. For, he is a victim of propitiation for our sins ; and not only for our sins, but for those of the entire world.

Commentary.

St. John in this Epistle, as also by our Redeemer himself (Mark, x.; John xiii., and by St. Paul, Gal. iv.), "these things I write to you, that you may not sin." By "these things," some understand the entire Epistle, the object of which is to keep them from sinning. Others make them refer immediately to the preceding chapter,—viz., I write these things regarding the liability in which we are all involved, of committing sin; and also regarding the sins into which we all fall, in order that, acknowledging your weakness and sinfulness, you may thus avoid the sins of pride or presumption ; or, in order that, mindful of human frailty, you may be the more on your guard against exposing yourself to temptation, and against adding to your natural weakness by habits of sin. Hence, the sinfulness in which we are all involved, and the facility of obtaining remission (verse 9, of the foregoing chapter), should be no reason for our committing sin anew. There is no contradiction between this and verse 10 of foregoing chapter ; for, here there is question of grievous sins, or sins for the commission of which, or continuance in them, the preceding words of St. John might be misconstrued, as a motive. "But if any man sin," that is, commit sin, whether mortal or venial, "we have an advocate," &c. Such a person should not despair of pardon, knowing that Jesus Christ has all the qualities of a powerful advocate in heaven. In the first place, he can adduce reasons for satisfying justice, without involving the condemnation of the criminal ; these reasons he has in his own merits. In the next place, he intercedes for guilty man, whose humble confession he presents to his Father (Rom. viii. 34 ; Heb. vii.), and thus applies his merits to us. "An advocate with the Father." The Greek word for "advocate," παρακλητον, also means, *a comforter, helper, intercessor.* The literal translation from the Greek *(paraclete)* expresses all these meanings together.

2. The Apostle explains in what sense Christ is our "advocate;" it is, as advocate, or *Mediator of Redemption,* who made atonement for our sins, paid the ransom, and substituted himself in our place, as a *vicarious* offering, αντιλυτρον, as St. Paul expresses it.—(1 Tim. ii. 5, 6.)

Is not the Catholic doctrine respecting the invocation of angels and saints opposed to this ?

By no means, since we invoke them, in quite a different sense, merely as *mediators,* or advocates of *intercession,* to obtain for us a share in the merits and graces which the one *Mediator of Redemption* purchased with his precious blood.

But is it not derogatory to the efficacy of Christ's advocacy, to have recourse to any others ?

Certainly not, in the sense in which this is done by Catholics; for so, St. Paul would have derogated from Christ's advocacy, by begging a share in the prayers of the faithful on earth (Rom. xv. 30 ; 1 Thes. v. 25 ; Heb. xiii. 12, &c., &c.) ; so would St. James, in recommending the faithful, to pray for one another (chap. v. 16). Moreover, if it be derogatory to the merits of Christ, for us to *beg* the intercession of the saints, it must be equally so for them, to *intercede* ; hence, the angel (Zacharias, i 12,) who

Text.

3. And by this we know that we have known him, if we keep his commandments.

4. He who saith that he knoweth him, and keepeth not his commandments, is a liar, and the truth is not in him :

Paraphrase.

3. And the probable test or mark, whereby we can ascertain, as far as can be ascertained in this life, that we have known him with a practical and effective knowledge of love and charity is, if we observe his commandments.

4. Whosoever says that he knows him, in the sense already expressed, and keepeth not his commandments, is a liar, and the truth is not in him.

Commentary.

prayed for Jerusalem, and Michael, the archangel (Daniel, x. 12), and Raphael (Tobias, xii. 12), and the saints, of whose prayers there is question (Apoc. viii. 4), must have derogated from the merits of Christ. The Church of England, on the Feast of St. Michael and all angels, employs a form of prayer as expressive of intercession, as any Catholic prayer can be.—*See* Book of Common Prayer.

But who can tell that the angels and saints hear us, or know our wants ?

RESP.—Our Divine Redeemer *can* tell, and actually tells us they do know our wants (Luke, xv. 10) : " there shall be *joy* before the angels of God upon one sinner doing penance ;" also, Tobias (xiii. 12 , and Daniel (x. 12). And we are told in the Gospel (Luke, xx. 36), that the saints in heaven are equal to the angels. How, then, could they *rejoice* over the sinner's conversion, unless they *knew* of it ? But, *how* can they know it ? We cannot say. Whether it be through the medium of visual rays or undulating sounds, or (which is more probable) in God, who may make this knowledge a part of their beatitude, we know not. We merely know and believe the *fact*. *How* the fact takes place, we know not, any more than we know the *how* of every other truth of faith, or of many phenomena of nature, which we firmly believe and know with undoubted certainty ; although, utterly ignorant of *how* they exist or take place.

Do Protestants understand the *how* of the fundamental Christian mysteries, Trinity, Incarnation, &c. ?—of several undoubted, natural truths ?

But do not Catholics worship saints and angels? Yes, with a worship, quite different from that paid to God. The word " worship " is expressive not only of the *supreme* adoration paid to God, which, according to Catholic doctrine, we could pay no creature, ever so exalted, without being guilty of the most heinous crime ; but, also of the *inferior* respect, paid the saints and angels, which is, however, ultimately referred to God himself, and is a homage to his grace and gifts, resplendently displayed in them. Thus, the children of the prophets at Jericho, " *worshipped* " Eliseus (4 Kings, ii. 15). In the very marriage ceremony of Protestants the word is, or, at all events, *was* employed, to denote respect quite different from divine adoration—"*and with my body I thee worship.*" Hence, the fairest rule for knowing whether the word is employed in a sense expressive of supreme worship, is, to ascertain the meaning attached to it by the society, among whom it is in use, and the acts expressed by it, practised. Should this fair test be applied to the worship of saints by Catholics, there can be no grounds whatever for the clumsy charge of idolatory, on this head. They ought themselves to be the best judges of what their Church teaches, and of what they themselves believe and practise, on this and on every other subject.

3. The Apostle proceeds to inculcate the necessity of good works against the heretics who put forward the sufficiency of faith only. " By this we know," as far as it is given us here below to ascertain, that is to say, with great probability, "that we have known him "—the word " known " expresses a knowledge of love and affection ; it means, that we have *loved* him, a signification the word frequently bears in sacred Scripture (Jeremiah, xxxi. 34 ; Wisdom, xv. 2 ; and Gospel of John, x. 14) ; " if we keep his commandments ;" but as no one can be infallibly sure that he observes God's commandments, in every respect : so, neither can he be infallibly sure that he enjoys the charity and friendship of God.—*See* Council of Trent, SS. vi. 9.

4. " He who saith that he knoweth him " (in Greek, ὁ λεγων, ὅτι εγ νωκα αὐτον, *he who saith I have known him*), with the effective knowledge of love already explained ;

5. But he that keepeth his word, in him in very deed the charity of God is perfected : and by this we know that we are in him.	5. But, on the other hand, whosoever observeth his commandments, in him the charity or love which we bear to God is genuine and sincere ; and it is by observing his word, we can form a very probable conjecture, that we are united to him by charity, and have society with him.
6. He that saith he abideth in him, ought himself also to walk even as he walked.	6. Whosoever says that he is united with God in the bonds of charity and operative love, should prove the truth of his assertion, by becoming morally assimilated to Christ in the performance of works of sanctity, such as he performed.
7. Dearly beloved, I write not a new commandment to you, but an old commandment which you had from the beginning. The old commandment is the word which you have heard.	7. Dearly beloved brethren, in inculcating the observance of God's commandments, alluded to in the foregoing, or rather, in inculcating the love of our neighbour, to which I am about to make special allusion, I do not mean to burthen you with a multiplicity of new precepts ; I only repeat an old precept, with which you have been familiar, from the very beginning of your conversion. That old precept is, the word of doctrine, or the commandment regarding the love of our neighbour, which you have received from the very beginning of your conversion.

Commentary.

in other words, he who saith that he loves God or Christ, "and keepeth not his commandments, is a liar;" for the test of his love (verse 3) is wanting; and hence, his pretences are proved to be false, "and the truth is not in him," he asserts what is untrue.

5. In this verse, the Apostle, by an antithesis, confirms his assertion, made in the preceding one. "But he that keepeth his word," that is, his commandments, particularly that which regards the love of our neighbour, including the love of our enemy, "in him in very deed, the charity of God," that is, the charity or love we have for God, "is perfected," that is, sincere and genuine ; it is as sincere and genuine as our love of God can be in this life, notwithstanding the numerous venial sins and frailties to which we are all subject (chap. i. 8). Others understand "perfected" of the external manifestation of our charity. In such a person the charity or love he bears to God is not merely confined to the mind, it is externally manifested in its fruits, which is the perfection of charity ; for, all charity, which is externally manifested, is more perfect than that which is confined to the mind. It is in the same sense that sin is said by St. James to be perfected or "completed," (chap. i. 15). "And by this," that is, by observing his word, "we know," as far as we can know in this life—viz., by a probable conjecture, "that we are in him," united to him by love and friendship.

6. He continues the same idea expressed in the preceding verses ; to "abide in God," and "to be in him," signify the same thing—viz., to be united with God, in the bonds of friendship and sanctifying grace. Whosoever then, says that he holds the endearing relation of a friend with God, "ought himself also to walk," that is, should prove the truth of this assertion, and the sincerity of such a pretence, by "walking, even as he walked," by habitually living and progressing in the practice of good works, and the observance of God's commandments, as Christ did. Of course, the Apostle only requires a moral assimilation, such as can subsist between man and God, just as the words, "be ye perfect as your heavenly Father is perfect," regard a likeness, not an equality of perfection. The verse may also mean, if any man pretend to enjoy God's friendship, he must, in order to remain in such a state, continue to perform good works, as Christ also performed good works, when here on earth.

7. "Dearly beloved," (in some Greek copies, *brethren ;* but the chief MSS. have αγαπητοι, the Vulgate reading). Both readings are united in the Paraphrase—"I write

Text.	**Paraphrase.**
8. Again a new commandment I write unto you, which thing is true both in him and in you : because the darkness is passed, and the true light now shineth.	8. Again, the same precept already designated as old, when considered under a different respect, I call a *new* precept, and that this precept is new, is a thing true both in reference to Christ himself, who has observed it in an extraordinary manner, dying for his enemies ; and in reference to you ; because, the darkness and mists of infidelity are dissipated by the promulgation of the gospel, and the true light of faith, which proposes new motives for this love of our neighbour, is already shining in the hearts of the faithful.
9. He that saith he is in the	9. Whosoever congratulating himself on having

Commentary.

not a new commandment to you," when inculcating the observance of God's commandments, to which I have been alluding in the foregoing part of the Epistle ; or rather, in inculcating that precept by which the whole law is fulfilled—viz., the love of our neighbour (which he specifies immediately after), " but an old commandment," a commandment with which you have been familiar, "which you had from the beginning." By the " beginning," some understand the beginning of creation, the love of our neighbour being a precept of the natural law ; others, from the beginning of the Mosaic law, transmitted to you by your fathers. The word, however, most probably refers to the beginning of the gospel, or, of their conversion to the faith, as St. Augustine understands it, and as the following words, which are a further explanation of the preceding, render very probable. "The old commandment is the word which you have heard ;" (to which is added in the Greek, *from the beginning* ; but there are wanting in the chief MSS. ; and hence, although implied in sense, expunged by modern critics). These words explain what the " beginning " in the foregoing refers to. It refers to the beginning of their conversion, when they first, " heard the word " of faith, and embraced the gospel.

8. "Again," although he called this precept of loving our neighbour, "an *old* commandment," as having been received from the beginning of their conversion ; or, according to others, as having been as old as creation ; still he calls it "a *new* commandment," considered in a different light. It was called " new " by our Divine Redeemer himself, when he first promulgated it, and made it the distinctive badge of his followers (Gospel of St. John, xiv. 35, 36) ; and it may have been termed " new " by him, either on the grounds of *new* and more exalted motives for its observance and its heavier obligation ; or *new*, as to its standard of fulfilment (" as I have loved you ") ; or, *new*, with reference to the persons to whom it was first promulgated, in regard to whom the precept of loving their neighbour was unheeded both *speculatively* (for, the false grossary of the Pharisees was " thou shalt love thy neighbour ; therefore, thou shalt hate thine enemy "), and *practically*, owing to the universal corrupt selfishness prevailing, when the Gospel began to be preached.

"Which thing," viz., that this precept is new, " is true both in him," viz., Christ, with whom St. John was so fully engaged, as not to permit his expressing who it was ; for, who else but Christ could it be that thus filled his soul, and engrossed his thoughts ? It was true in reference to Christ ; for, he fulfilled the precept of loving his neighbour in, an extraordinary way, by dying for his enemies, and praying for his very executioners ; and even now, as head of the Church, he loves us intensely.

"And in you," the same thing is true in reference to you also, " because the darkness is passed," the night of infidelity is rapidly passing away, owing to the preaching of the Apostles, who in a particular manner, inculcate the precept of charity ; " and the true light shineth now," the true light of faith is now shining in our hearts, and in the hearts of the faithful ; who, owing to the dictates of faith, love their neighbour from new and more exalted motives : hence, the precept is observed, in a new manner in them also. Some translate the Greek words corresponding with "true both in him," αληθες εν αυτω thus : *true in itself ;* because, the precept of loving our neighbour is a precept of the law of nature.

9. The man, whoever he be, that pretends to enjoy the possession of the true light

Text.

light, and hateth his brother, is in darkness even until now.

10. He that loveth his brother, abideth in the light, and there is no scandal in him.

11. But he that hateth his brother is in darkness, and walketh in darkness, and knoweth not whither he goeth: because the darkness hath blinded his eyes.

12. I write unto you, little children, because your sins are forgiven you for his name's sake.

Paraphrase.

received the Christian faith, and on being a true follower of Christ, still hates his brother, is grievously mistaken. He is still, at least equivalently, in the darkness of infidelity.

10. While, on the other hand, whosoever loveth his brother, equally enjoys the light of the gospel, and the love and friendship of God ; and such a person offends not against the commandments and the holy law of God.

11. But whosoever hateth his brother is in a state of darkness, even when he refrains from action, and walks in darkness, whenever he performs any work, his actions being generally infected by the state of sin and hatred in which he lives ; nor does he know whither he is going, for want of duly considering his actions in a proper light ; because the darkness of sin and ignorance in which he exists, blinds the eyes of his soul.

12. I write unto you, my spiritual children of every age and degree of advancement in Christian virtue, because your sins are remitted on account of the merits of Christ, which is a subject of the deepest congratulation.

Commentary.

of Christian faith and friendship with God, and, at the same time "hates his brother," which word embraces every fellow-creature, not excluding our very enemy ; such a person "is in darkness even until now ;" still involved in the darkness of Paganism, at least, equivalently and practically ; his faith will not avail him ; for, as charity or brotherly love is the great leading virtue of Christianity ; so, is the opposite vice a leading characteristic of Paganism.

10. In this verse, the Apostle specifies what the precept is to which he has been referring in the foregoing, viz., the precept of loving our brethren. "He that loveth his brother," embracing every human being ; for, all mankind are united in one common bond of brotherhood ; "abideth in the light," that is, really enjoys the true light of the gospel, and is united in friendship with God ; the love of our neighbour is the surest mark, that we are loved by God. "And there is no scandal in him." Such a person does not himself *impinge* or offend against the weighty commandments of God, which is *passive* scandal ; nor does he serve as an occasion for others to do so, which is *active* scandal ; a man walking in the light will not fall in with the obstacles placed in the way. The Apostle most probably alludes to the words of the Psalmist : "*Much peace have they that love thy law, and to them there is no stumbling block,*" or scandal.—Psalm cxviii.

11. This point regarding the love and hatred of our neighbour is so important, that St. John is not tired of repeating it. "Is in darkness," is always, even when performing no particular action, in a state of sin and spiritual darkness, "and walketh in darkness ;" whenever he acts, his actions are generally infected with the hatred and sin in which he exists ; for, although such a person may and does perform some good actions ; still, while hating and retaining feelings of hatred for his neighbour, he will, probably, render his actions vitiated by this evil passion. "And knoweth not whither he is going," which is understood by some thus : He knoweth not, that he is on the straight road to hell ; but it more likely means (as in Paraphrase) that he does not weigh his actions properly or consider them in the true light. "Because the darkness (of sin and ignorance) hath blinded his eyes." Hence, every sin is the result of a practical error, which precedes it.

12. "Little children,' τεχνία. It is disputed what class of Christians is designated by the words, "little children." By some they are understood of those who have not yet left their childhood, and have received the remission of sin in baptism. These also

Text.

13. I write unto you, fathers, because you have known him, who is from the beginning. I write unto you, young men, because you have overcome the wicked one.

14. I write unto you, babes, because you have known the Father. I write unto young men, because you are strong, and the word of God abideth in you, and you have overcome the wicked one.

Paraphrase.

13. I write to you, who are perfect in the Christian faith, able to instruct and bring forth others spiritually in the gospel; because, you have known and loved him, who was from eternity. I write to you also, and congratulate you, who have arrived at the stage of spiritual youth and manly vigour; because, in your spiritual strength, you have been proof against the temptations of the wicked one, viz., the devil, and have overthrown both him and his leagued auxiliaries, the flesh and the world.

14. I write to you who have lately received the faith, and require still to be fed with the milk of babes and to be assisted in your Christian progress; and congratulate you, on having known your heavenly Father, and lisped forth his sacred and endearing name. I once more, as I have done already (v. 13) congratulate you, who have attained a state of spiritual youth, on the strength which God has imparted to you, on becoming armed with his word and your having conquered the devil.

Commentary.

understand the words, "fathers," "young men," and "babes," in the following verses, of the different ages of men and their advancement in years. This opinion derives probability from the circumstance of the Apostle attributing to the different ages, what forms the peculiar matter for glorying, pertaining to each; old men, or "fathers," glory in their knowledge (verse 13)—"young men," in their bodily vigour and strength, and in their active feats; and "babes" or children in fawning on, and lisping the names of their fathers.

It is, however, more probable, that the Apostle refers to the different periods or stages of advancement in the spiritual life (as St. Augustine understands the passage), and to Christians placed in each of these, he ascribes perfections, and congratulates them on qualities, in the spiritual order, analogous to the natural perfections, in which men, during the several stages of physical existence, are prone to glory. Even following the opinion of St. Augustine, interpreters are divided about the meaning of "little children," in this verse. Some understand the word to mean the same as "babes," as in verse 14, where, according to them, the idea is repeated; and refer it to a state of spiritual childhood. Others, more probably, understand the word of Christians generally, as in verse 1, and verse 28, which is again subdivided into "fathers," "young men," and "babes," in the following verses.

The Apostle, then, writes to all Christians in general, congratulating them on having received the remission of their sins, and all graces through the merits of Christ, "for his name's sake." The heart of the Apostle was so full of Christ, that he does not express his name. Who else could it be but Christ that thus occupied all his thoughts?

13. He now divides "little children," or Christians in general, into "fathers," or, such as are for a long time professing the faith, and able to instruct and spiritually beget others; and "young men," or Christians advanced in virtue and spiritual knowledge, who though not so far advanced, as the class termed "fathers," still need not the milk of babes to support them. He congratulates this class, on their spiritual strength.

14. The next class of Christians are those whom he terms "babes," or persons in their spiritual infancy, who require to be fed with the milk of babes, and to be supported and propped up in their spiritual progress. These he congratulates on having known the father. Their lisping accents in the spiritual life show that they acknowledge God by faith to be a Father in their regard; and as it is the glory of infants, in the order of nature, to lisp and know the name of father; so, it is likewise in the spiritual order of grace. Some say, these words, "I write unto you, babes,"

Text.

15. Love not the world, nor the things which are in the world. If any man love the world, the charity of the Father is not in him.

16. For all that is in the world, is the concupiscence of the flesh, and the concupiscence of the eyes, and the pride of life, which is not of the Father, but is of the world.

Paraphrase.

15. What I write to you, and exhort you to, Christians of every age and degree, is this—love not this world, as your fixed, permanent dwelling-place, as your final end, nor the riches, pleasures, honours, &c., that are found therein. If any one love the world in the prohibited sense now explained, the love of the Father, who cannot endure a divided heart, or partial service, is not in him.

16. (Neither love the things that are in the world); for, all that is in the world are, the corrupt pleasures and inordinate gratification of sense; the greedy acquisition of wealth, and other goods of this life; and the inordinate desire of procuring honours, dignities, and elevated stations—this triple concupiscence in its present sinful state has not God for author; but, has its origin in the corruption of the world.

Commentary.

&c., are only a repetition of the words (verse 12), "I write unto you, little children," with an additional reason for addressing them. The interpretation now given is the more probable, and accords better with the order observed by the Apostle in marking out the different ages. (In the Greek, we find inserted here, a repetition of the words (verse 13), *I have written to you, fathers, because you have known that which was from the beginning*).

"I write" (in Greek, ἔγραψα, *I have written*), "unto you, young men," or such as have arrived at the stage of spiritual youth—it is a repetition of the words (verse 13), with a fuller reason, "because you are strong," and I congratulate you on being valiant in grace; "and the word of God abideth in you." You have taken the shield of faith and the sword of the spirit to resist your enemies (Ephes. chap. v.)—"and you have overcome the wicked one," the devil and his leagued auxiliaries, the flesh and the world.

It is, then, most likely, as St. Augustine maintains, that the Apostle is referring to the different stages of spiritual life; and to those constituted in each, he attributes the perfections, in the *spiritual* order, analogous to those of which men in the different stages of life are apt to boast, in the *natural* order. The old men, or those advanced in spiritual life, have acquired an exalted knowledge of him who existed from eternity. Those who had attained the state of spiritual youth, he congratulates on their active feats; they overcame their enemy, the devil; and the "babes," or those lately converted, he congratulates on having known and lisped the name of their common Father, whom they are taught by faith to address as such.

15. The Apostle now explains what it is he writes to the different classes of Christians, whom he congratulates on the good qualities suited to each, and furnishing an earnest, that they will attend to the injunction he is now about giving them, viz., to avoid the greatest obstacle to their advancement in Christian virtue, and to the perfect fulfilment of the precept of fraternal charity. "Love not the world." This is understood by some to refer to men of worldly habits and principles, who are not to be loved as such; although, as creatures of God, capable of eternal beatitude, they are to be loved by us. Others understand it (as in Paraphrase), of making this world our final resting-place; making it, instead of God, our last end. The following words, "nor the things that are in the world," render this interpretation very probable. "If any man love the world," fixing his heart and affections on it, as his last end; "the charity of the Father is not in him;" because, God cannot endure a divided heart. The world and God are two rivals, that cannot be served at the same time.

16. The Apostle having already, in the preceding verse, given a reason why they should not "love the world," now in this, shows why they should not love "the things that are in the world," by describing what these things are, and their utter worthlessness and opposition to the things of God. "For all that is in the world," or all the things that corrupt and worldly men set their heart upon, all the things that

Text.

17. And the world passeth away, and the concupiscence thereof. But he that doth the will of God, abideth for ever.

18. Little children, it is the last hour: and as you have heard that Antichrist cometh; even now there

Paraphrase.

17. And, moreover, the world passes, and is daily becoming more and more subject to decay ; so will all the darling objects of worldly esteem, viz., pleasures, riches, and honours, also pass away ; but, the man who does the will of God, and observes his commandments, will remain for ever, and his works will entitle him to an everlasting reward.

18. My dearly beloved children, we have now fallen upon the last age of the world, and as you have heard, and been informed, that the famous Antichrist,

Commentary.

they prize or value, "is the concupiscence of the flesh," the inordinate gratification of their carnal and impure passions. In this member of the sentence, as well as in the following, the *act* of passion or concupiscence is employed, for the *objects* of concupiscence.

"The concupiscence of the eyes," commonly understood of avarice or "The inordinate affection for the sensible goods of this life, viz., the riches and worldly substance of any kind, which fall beneath the sense of seeing; in Eccles. iv. 8, the eyes of the covetous man are said to be insatiable. Others, with St. Augustine, understand the words to refer to curiosity of every kind, of which the eyes are the principal inlets, not even excluding knowledge, when pursued from a mere spirit of curiosity, and from a desire of acquiring the reputation of learning. The former is, however, the more common interpretation of the words.

"And the pride of life," understood commonly of the inordinate desire of honours, dignities, elevated stations, &c. From the words of St. John, then, it is clear, that these great ruling maxims of the world, which are the sources of all other sins, and the bane of fraternal charity, are, the inordinate desire of sensual gratification, avarice, and ambition. Hence it is, that those who renounce the world, and serve God in a religious state, having their conversation and all their cares centered in another and a better world, take care to renounce altogether, and at once, all connexion with these corrupt maxims of the world. By vows of chastity, they renounce all carnal pleasures ; by vows of poverty, they renounce avarice ; and by vows of humble obedience, they renounce ambition ; and our Redeemer has proposed to all the faithful in general a triple remedy against these three corrupt principles, viz., fasting, alms-deeds, and prayer (Matthew, vi.)

"Which," triple concupiscence (as appears from the Greek, ὅτι πᾶν τὸ ἐν τῷ κοσμῷ, η επιθυμία της σαρκος......ουκ εστιν εκ του πατρος, *because everything in the world, the concupiscence of the flesh, &c., is not of the Father*), "is not of the Father," in its present corrupt state, as the *fomes peccati* impelling us to the violation of God's holy law ; "but is of the world," it is the effect of fallen human nature corrupted by sin ; for, "*God created man right*" (Eccles. vi. 30). This concupiscence, to which the Apostle refers, is evil ; and hence, our Redeemer, who assumed our common infirmities, was not subject to it.

In the Greek, the verb "is" is wanting in the words, "all that is in the world," as appears from the foregoing. The Syriac supports the Vulgate.

17. Another reason why they should not love the world nor the things of the world is derived from the fleeting, transitory nature of their existence and enjoyment. "The world passeth." The "world" may refer either to the present creation, daily approaching decay and dissolution ; or, to worldly men, who daily die and relinquish all their present enjoyments. This latter meaning is rendered probable by the contrast between the world and the man "who doth the will of God." "The concupiscence," the darling objects, prized by the world, such as pleasures, riches, honours. "But he that doth the will of God," that observes God's commandments, and renounces all inordinate attachment to the objects of this threefold concupiscence, "abideth for ever," will enjoy for ever eternal life, as the reward of his good works, and of his resistance to his corrupt passions.

18. The Apostle now passes from the subject of fraternal charity, to inculcate the

Text.

are become many Antichrists: whereby we know that it is the last hour.

19. They went out from us: but they were not of us. For if they had been of us, they would no doubt have remained with us: but that they may be manifest, that they are not all of us.

Paraphrase.

the man of sin and son of perdition, is to come; so now, many precursory Antichrists have made their appearance, ushering in his approach: whence we infer, that the last stage of time, which the persecuting reign of this man of sin is to close, has arrived.

19. They went from amongst us: but they did not possess the true spirit of God's faithful, or, they did not belong to those on whom God had designs of predestinating grace and glory. For, if they possessed the true spirit of the faithful of Christ, or, if they belonged to the elect, they would have remained with us united in the Church; but God permitted their departure and open separation, that it might be made manifest that He has not designs of grace and mercy on all.

Commentary.

necessity of avoiding the contagious influence of the nascent heresies of the day. " My little children," παιδία; a term of affection and endearment. " It is the last hour," by which is commonly understood, the last stage of the world—different hours or ages, have elapsed from Adam to Christ; but the period from Christ to the end of all things is called the last stage; because it will not be replaced by any other form of religion, or succeeded by any other dispensation, until the end of all arrives. " And as you have heard," both from the prediction of our Redeemer (John, v. 43; 2 Thess. ii. 3; and Apostolical tradition), "that Antichrist cometh," or will come. The present is often, in scriptural usage, put for the future; the words may also mean, " he is on the eve of coming; for, the age or hour of the world, at the close of which he is to come, has arrived. " Antichrist." The word means, the enemy of Christ, and by this name St. John designates him, whom St. Paul terms, " the man of sin," " the son of perdition" (2 Thess. ii), whose impiety he there fully details.

" Even now." The construction of the words appear to be. "*As* Antichrist is to come, *so* even now, there are become many Antichrists," precursors of this man of sin, who are promulgating and endeavouring to enforce separately regarding both the Humanity and Divinity of the Lord Jesus, these errors, which Antichrist will attempt to establish all at once, by endeavouring to blot out the name of Christ, and abolish all divine worship. Hence, these Antichrists, the precursors of *the Antichrist* (as the Greek has it), are the heretics, by whom *is worked*, in every age, " *the mystery of iniquity*" (2 Thess. ii.), " whereby we know;" from the appearance of these heretics we can see, that the last age of the world, which the persecuting reign of the famous Antichrist, or " man of sin," is to close, has already arrived.

19. These heretics " went out from us;" they separated themselves from the Church, of which they were before members; but, they had not the spirit of the true faithful of Christ; " but they were not of us." These words may also mean, they did not belong to those whom God had predestined for eternal salvation; since it seldom or ever happens, that Heresiarchs, such as St. John here refers to, return to the bosom of the Church. " For, if they had been of us," if they had the true spirit of the followers of Christ, or, if they belonged to the elect, " they would, no doubt, have remained with us." " But that they may be made manifest." God permitted their departure and open separation from us, in order to make it manifest, that they did not all belong to us.

The words of this verse furnish no grounds whatever for the heretical doctrine, that faith is *inamissible;* for, the words, " they were not of us," by no means imply, that these separatists had not true faith before their separation. They only convey, that the heretics in question were not, before their separation, solid, profitable members of the Church; for, St. Paul expressly declares, that many " will depart from the faith " (1 Tim. iv.); that some persons " suffered a shipwreck of their faith"

Text.	Paraphrase.
20. But you have the unction from the Holy one, and know all things.	20. But you, who have remained firm, are sharers in the unction and grace of the Holy Ghost, through the merits of Christ, promised to his Church; and owing to the enlightenment it bestows, you know all the truths necessary for salvation, and are strengthened against the delusive errors of these heretics.
21. I have not written to you as to them that know not the truth, but as to them that know it, and that no lie is of the truth.	21. Hence, in writing thus to you, I am far from wishing to imply, that you are ignorant of the truth; on the contrary, I only wish to recall to your mind the truths with which you have been thoroughly acquainted, and among the rest, you are aware that no lie, or error in faith, can proceed from the spirit of truth.
22. Who is a liar, but he who denieth that JESUS is the Christ? This is Antichrist, who denieth the Father and the Son.	22. And is there a liar in existence unless he be one, who denies that Jesus is the promised Messiah? Such a person is one of the precursory Antichrists, whoever he be, that denies to the Father and Son, the true and eternal relations between both.

Commentary.

1 Tim. i. 19); and that "Hymeneus and Philetus fell away from the truth" (1 Tim. ii.)

Neither does the passage furnish any grounds for the erroneous teaching that sinners are not in the Church; the words, "they went out *from* us," prove them to have been in the Church, previously; for, how go forth *from* us, if they were not heretofore *with* us; and the words, "but they are not of us," are only a rhetorical correction, giving the words, "*ex nobis*," a different signification in the second place, from what they had in the first. Again, the words, "they were not of us," might also mean, that they were private heretics, long before they openly separated from the body of the faithful, in which interpretation, the words, as is evident, furnish no grounds for asserting, that sinners are not in the Church.

20. "But you have the unction," that is, the grace of the Holy Ghost, enlightening your intellects, confirming and strengthening your will in the faith, without which grace, no one can have faith—no matter in how clear or convincing a manner, the external motives of credibility may present themselves to his mind. "From the holy one;" from the merits of Christ, "who is anointed the saint of saints" (Daniel, ix. 24), "and know all things;" all the truths necessary for salvation, and all things required to guard you against the false and delusive teaching of these heretics; or, if "all things" regard all points of faith; then, they know them implicitly, by receiving all things proposed to our belief by the Church. To this "*unction*" or grace of the Holy Ghost, is their faith, as well as steadfastness in the same, attributed, as being the principal cause of both. The words, then, mean, that while remaining in the Church, subject to the pastors appointed by Christ to govern them, they share in the grace of the Holy Ghost promised to the Church of Christ; and that they have, through the pastors of the Church, all the necessary knowledge, so as not to be obliged to look for it elsewhere, since it is in the Church alone, of which they continue members, it can be found.

21. He here wishes to conciliate their good will, and to guard against any prejudices which the weak amongst them might conceive against him, for teaching them, as if they were ignorant of the truth. He says, far from supposing them ignorant of the necessary truths, on the contrary he supposes them to be already instructed, and his object in writing is, merely to remind them of what they already know, and among the rest, that "no lie is of the truth," or consistent with truth; or, that no lie in faith can proceed from the spirit of truth.

22. "Who is a liar, but he who denieth?" &c. As if to say, if there be a liar in existence, one guilty of a lie, "*which is not of the truth*" (verse 21), he must be one who denies Jesus to be the long expected Messiah. Reference is, probably, made to the

Text.

23. Whosoever denieth the Son, the same hath not the Father. He that confesseth the Son, hath the Father also.

24. As for you, let that which you have heard from the beginning abide in you. If that abide in you, which you have heard from the beginning, you shall also abide in the Son and in the Father.

25. And this is the promise which he hath promised us, life everlasting.

26. These things have I written to you, concerning them that seduce you.

27. And as for you, let the unction, which you have received from him, abide in you. And you have no need that any man teach

Paraphrase.

23. Every man that denieth the Son, or that errs regarding his eternal filiation, denieth also, or errs regarding the eternal paternity of God the Father.— And he who confesseth the Son, as he ought, holds the true faith regarding the Father also.

24. I, therefore, exhort you, to persevere unto the end in the belief and profession of what you heard from the beginning of your conversion, and if you thus persevere, you will enjoy a union of friendship, and of permanent grace both with the Son and with the Father.

25. And the value of such a union is, that you will enjoy the object promised to those who are in God's friendship, which is, life everlasting.

26. These things I have written to guard you against the false teachers, who are endeavouring to lead you astray, and to destroy your faith.

27. But as for you, you are indebted for your stability in the faith and your resistance to their efforts to the grace of the Holy Ghost, which resides within you, and which is abundantly imparted to the Church,

Commentary.

errors of the Judaizantes, or of the heretics, Ebion and Cerinthus, who broached pernicious errors regarding the Divinity of Christ, even in the Apostle's own lifetime. "This is Antichrist," or one of the precursory Antichrists, to whom I have referred (verse 18). "Who denieth the Father and the Son," &c. Such a person is an Antichrist; for, by erring regarding the Son, he also falls into error, both regarding Father and Son, and denies the high and eternal attributes and relations of both.

"23. "Whosoever denieth the Son, the same hath not the Father." The denial of the Son involves a denial of the Father. They are correlative terms. Hence, the relation of paternity is destroyed, if filiation be denied; for, if Jesus be not the Son of God, neither can we attribute to the Father the relation of paternity; and hence, these heretics, by erring regarding the Son, fall into error, consequently, regarding the Father. "He that confesseth the Son, hath the Father also." These words are not read in the ordinary Greek copies, although they are found in the three principal Greek manuscripts, and in all Latin copies, and in many of the Fathers. Their omission can be easily ascribed to *homoioteleuton*, that is to say, to a desire, on the part of the Greek transcriber, to avoid the repetition of the same words, with which two successive sentences concluded; but their insertion, if not genuine, could not be so easily accounted for.

24. "As for you, let that which you have heard," &c. The Greek runs thus: "Let that, *therefore*, which you have heard," &c., which words convey an inference deduced from verse 21, as if he said, I have written nothing new to you, nothing but what you already know; persevere, then, in what you have known from the beginning of your conversion. The chief MSS. have not the word, *therefore*. "If that abide in you," or, if you do persevere thus, "you shall also abide in the Son," &c., you shall permanently enjoy the friendship of the Father and of the Son.

25. He shows the value of this union and friendship with God; it is the secure attainment of eternal life, the reward or inheritance promised to God's friends—"This is the promise," or, *the thing promised.*

26. These things he has written regarding the false teachers, who endeavour to corrupt the integrity of their faith.

27. "Let the unction which you have received abide in you," according to which reading, he wishes them to persevere in the "unction," or, doctrine taught and impressed upon them by the grace of the Holy Ghost. In the Greek, it runs thus: μενει εν ὑμιν, "The unction......*abideth in you*," and to this you owe your faith and stability in the same. "And you have no need that any man teach you," that is, you have no

Text.	Paraphrase.
you: but as his unction teacheth you of all things, and is truth, and is no lie. And as it hath taught you, abide in him.	and you have no need of being taught as ignorant persons, by these false teachers; but as the grace of God has wrought inward conviction and faith in your minds, regarding the things taught you exteriorly, through the ministry of your pastors (for what the grace of the Holy Spirit has taught you is true, without any admixture of falsehood); as it has taught you, I say, *so* persevere in believing and professing regarding him.
28. And now, little children, abide in him: that when he shall appear, we may have confidence, and not be confounded by him at his coming.	28. And now, dearly beloved children, continue united with him in the bonds of true faith, and in the profession of true doctrine; that when he shall make his appearance to judge the world, we may all stand with great confidence in his presence and not be confounded at his coming (we Pastors, by being deprived of the accidental glory of seeing the fruits of our labours in your salvation, and you, by being subjected to the eternal confusion of the damned.)

Commentary.

need to be taught by any of these false teachers, to whom allusion is made (verse 28), as endeavouring to seduce them; or, you nave no need to be taught by any one, as ignorant persons, unacquainted with the elementary truths of your religion. "But as his unction teaches you of all things (and is truth...) and as it has taught you, so abide in him;" for "in him," the Greek, εν αυτῷ, may also be translated, *in it.* Others arrange the sentence without including any part in a parenthesis, thus: As his unction has taught you concerning all things, so it is true, and there is no falsehood in what it taught you. St. John repeats the same truth negatively, a thing quite usual with Hebrew writers, who, after making an assertion, confirm the same by a denial of the contrary. The grace of God is called "unction," or anointing, on account of the effects produced by it in the spiritual order, analogous to those produced by ointment in the natural. It cools and refreshes, it exhilarates, strengthens, heals, enriches, &c.; and it is said "to teach them concerning all things," because, it is the principal cause of our faith; and hence, the entire effect is attributed to it, a thing quite usual in sacred Scripture. The words of this verse convey the same idea with the words of verse 20, "but you have unction from the holy one, and know all' things." "And as it has taught you, abide in him;" for "in him," the Greek might be rendered, *in it,* in the unction, or rather doctrine, impressed in you by the grace of the Holy Ghost. That the Apostle does not here exclude the external ministry of teachers, is clear from his writing this Epistle; for, why write it, if the external ministry of teaching were not required? In writing it, he would be contradicting his own words: and from the whole context it is quite evident that he is only encouraging the faithful to persevere in the doctrine which they originally believed—of course, from the preaching of the Apostles, and aided by Divine grace—and to shun the new doctrines of error from which the grace of God, confirming in their minds the truths which they originally received, will preserve them. The necessity of an external ministry is abundantly proved from other passages of Scripture (1 Cor. xii. verse 28), where he mentions "Doctors," in the third place—Ephes. iv. 11, 12, 13; Rom. x. 14, &c.

28. "And now"—a term ordinarily used in urging an earnest request—"little children," shows his love for them; "abide in him," εν αυτῷ, may also be rendered "abide *in it,*" and both may be united in sense thus: "Continue united to him by the steady profession of the faith which the grace and unction of God has enabled you to conceive—(*vide* Paraphrase); "that when he shall appear" in majesty to judge the world, "we may have confidence," that is, great intrepidity in standing before him, "and not be confounded by him at his coming." Estius understands the word "we" to refer to the Apostles, who would be subject to the slight confusion of losing the accidental crown of witnessing the success of their labours, in the salvation of their people. Of course, the essential reward is attached to the labour itself; this reward the Apostles and all teachers would enjoy independently of the fruits produced—which

Text.	**Paraphrase.**
29. If you know, that he is just; know ye, that every one also, who doth justice, is born of him.	29. And, since you have known him to be just by excellence, know also this, that every man who doth good works has contracted with God the relation of Son, having been regenerated by his spirit; it is only in virtue of the grace and strength, received at this second spiritual birth, that he performs good works.

Commentary

are not theirs but God's—should they discharge their functions properly. "Every man shall receive his own reward according to his own *labour*."—(1 Cor. iii. 8). The fruits result from God's grace; the *labour* is ours. It is likely, that the Apostle included the people also, when he says "we," and their confusion by falling away from the faith, would be the eternal confusion of the damned (as is explained in the Paraphrase).

29. The Apostle, after cautioning the faithful against the seductions of error, now proceeds to describe the sons of God. "If you know" (as you know, certainly, from faith) "that he is just," that Christ is by excellence "just," "know ye that every one also that doth justice" (to "do justice," means in every part of sacred Scripture, to perform just or good works, *v.g.*, Psalm xiv. 2; Rom. ix. 30; 1 John, iii. 7), "is born of him." It is not in virtue of the strength or natural powers received at his birth from the first Adam, that he does good works; but in virtue of the spiritual and supernatural strength received at his second birth from the second Adam, by sanctifying grace; for, through sanctifying grace, we receive a new existence, and are made partakers of the Divine nature.—(2 Peter, i. 4). And, as the morals and complexion of the son in the order of nature, show his earthly parentage and the seed from which he sprang; so, does the performance of good works point out the heavenly seed of grace, and the spiritual birth from God.

CHAPTER III.

Analysis.

In this chapter, the Apostle continues the subject, upon which he entered in the last verse of the preceding, and extols the great love of God, manifested in our spiritual regeneration by sanctifying grace (verse 1). He shows the great privilege of Divine Sonship, conferred on us at present, and points out the glory we are to enjoy in future (2); and also what we are to do here, in order to enjoy this glory hereafter (3). He next shows how opposed the commission of sin is to the sanctity of the Christian state, to the economy of the Incarnation of the Son of God, and to the true knowledge and love of God (4-6).

He then guards them against the leading error of the heretics of the day, respecting the sufficiency of faith without good works, and declares, that the performance of good works, and the avoidance of sin, are the real qualities and characteristics, whereby the sons of God are distinguished from the children of the devil, and among the principal sins of the latter, he specifies hatred of our brethren (7-10).

He points out, how stringent, from the very beginning of the gospel, has been the precept of loving one another (11), and cautions them against following the example of the fratricide, Cain (12). The love of our neighbour is a probable sign that we are in a state of spiritual life, while the man who loves not his neighbour is in a state of spiritual death (14); and the man who hates his brother, with a hatred involving a wish for his death, the Apostle calls a murderer like Cain. In such a person, the grace of God cannot reside (15).

In continuation, he points out the extent to which the precept of charity obliges. It binds us to lay down our lives for the spiritual good of our brethren, after the example of the charity of Christ for us; and also to relieve his corporal wants out of our worldly substance (16, 17). In every case, our sympathy should be practically manifested in works of beneficence (18). It is by the possession of this beneficent charity, we can tranquillize our conscience against all fears, and feel confidence that God will rescue us from damnation on the day of judgment (19-21); and we shall merit to obtain all our requests, because we observe his commandments regarding our believing in Christ and loving our neighbour (23). He concludes, by showing the advantages of keeping God's commandments.

Text.

1. BEHOLD what manner of charity the Father hath bestowed upon us, that we should be called, and should be the sons of God. Therefore the world knoweth not us, because it knew not him.

Paraphrase.

1. Reflect again and again, how great a proof of his unbounded love the Father has given us, by conferring upon us the exalted title of sons of God, and rendering us such in reality; and it is because the world neither knows nor loves this your bountiful Father, that it does not love you either; but on the contrary, persecutes you, and treats you with the greatest contempt.

Commentary.

1. "Behold," diligently consider, "what manner of charity the Father hath bestowed upon us," that is, how great is the love of God the Father for us, as manifested in this, viz., "that we should be called," or, should receive the exalted appellation and epithet, of "sons of God," and "should be," in reality, such, viz., adopted sons of God,

Text.

2. Dearly beloved, we are now the sons of God; and it hath not yet appeared what we shall be. We know, that, when he shall appear, we shall be like to him : because we shall see him as he is.

3. And every one that hath this hope in him, sanctifieth himself, as he also is holy.

Paraphrase.

2. Dearly beloved, we are even now in the midst of the persecution and contempt with which we are treated, the sons of God. But what we shall be, what glory we shall enjoy at a future day, hath not yet appeared. But when Christ shall come in majesty to judge the world, we know that our bodies, clad with all the properties of glorification, shall be assimilated to his, because we shall then see him, not as we see him now ("*through a glass, in a dark manner,*") but, as he really is, *face to face.*"—(1 Cor. xiii.)

3. And every one that hath a true and well grounded hope, through the merits of Christ, of thus seeing him, and of being, consequently, assimilated to him in glory, must, in this life, purify and sanctify himself, as Christ is pure and holy, as far as a creature can imitate God.

Commentary.

owing to our new spiritual birth by grace, and owing to his adopting us, as co-heirs of his Son. "Therefore, the world knows us not," does not recognise, or love us as his sons; on the contrary, it contemns and persecutes us, "because it knew not him," it is because the world, that is to say, worldly, carnal men, neither knew nor loved him, that, therefore, they prize not your exalted privilege of divine filiation, through sanctifying grace. The words, "should be,' are not in the ordinary Greek copies, but they are implied in "should be called," and are found και εσμεν, in the chief manuscripts and ancient versions.

2. Even at the present moment, in the midst of the opprobrium heaped upon us, by those who know not God, we enjoy the lofty prerogative of divine sonship ; and "what we shall be, hath not yet appeared," it is only at a future day it will be seen, to how great a degree of glory we are to be raised. "We know, that when he shall appear," when Christ shall appear in majesty to judge the world, "we shall be like to him." This is commonly understood to regard a likeness in the glorified bodies of the elect to Christ's glorified body. Some interpreters translate the words, "when he shall appear," εαν φανερωθῇ "when *it* shall appear," namely, when it shall appear, what we will be, as if reference were made to the words immediately preceding. The other, however, is the far more common construction. The words have the same meaning, as in chap. ii. verse 28. "Because we shall see him as he is," not obscurely, as now, but "*face to face*" (1 Cor. xii.), the LUMEN GLORIÆ shall enable us to see, "*face to face*," the glory of God ; for this, the grace of the present life would be insufficient ; and from the beatific vision of God, or the glory of our souls, shall flow the glorification of our bodies. Hence, the Apostle assigns our "seeing him as he is," as the cause why we will be like him as to the glorification of our bodies, when he shall appear in judgment, "because we shall see him as he is."

3. "And every one that hath this hope," or, a well grounded confidence "in him," through the merits of Christ, of seeing him as he is, and of consequently being assimilated to him in his glorified body. "Sanctifieth himself, as he also is holy." The Greek for "sanctifieth," αγνιζει, means, *purifieth*, and renders himself chaste, by imitating his purity and sanctity, as far as this imitation can be carried by creatures. The resemblance in glory between Christ and the elect, in order to be the object of solid and legitimate hope, must be commenced in this life by grace.

"He now shows, how opposed to this sanctity and purity, which should characterize every Christian, is the commission of sin, "whosoever committeth sin committeth also iniquity, and" (*i.e. for*), "sin is iniquity." The interpretation of the verse depends on the meaning of the words "sin" and "iniquity. St. Ambrose and St. Augustine think that "sin" is more grievous than "iniquity." Others, among whom is St. Gregory, understand them to mean the same thing, although there may be some difference in the signification of both words. It is, however, more probable, that "sin," is employed to denote every grievous departure from the rule of right reason, or the

Text.

4. Whosoever committeth sin, committeth also iniquity : and sin is iniquity.

5. And you know that he appeared to take away our sins : and in him there is no sin.

6. Whosoever abideth in him, sinneth not : and whosoever sinneth, hath not seen him, nor known him.

Paraphrase.

4. To this purity, which should characterize every Christian, sin is opposed ; for, all who commit sin, or in any way grievously violate the moral law, or the dictates of right reason, are guilty of iniquity, and violate the law of God ; since every grievous departure from the law of right reason is a violation of the law of God.

5. And you know from the principles of your faith that the object of Christ appearing on earth in his assumed nature, was, to take away or abolish sin, by offering a sufficient ransom to obtain pardon for our past, and to merit grace to prevent our future, transgressions ; for, he was fit to make satisfaction for our sins, having been himself free from all sin.

6. And whosoever is united to him, by sanctifying grace, receives the spiritual influences which, as head, he imparts to his members, commits no grievous sin, and whosoever commits mortal sin, has not practically seen him, nor known him with a knowledge joined with love.

Commentary.

dictates of the moral law, although not punishable with penalties by human law (*v. g.*), sins of uncleanness and impurity ; and it is likely that the followers of Simon Magus, and the Nicolaites, regarded sins of impurity, and other sins, not punished by human laws, as trifling, and thus indulged in them freely. Hence, St. John says, that all such sins are violations of God's law, and are opposed to the sanctity of the Christian state. The Greek word for iniquity is, ανομια, that is, the transgression, or prevarication of a law. Of course, St. John, when calling "sin" iniquity, speaks of grievous violations of the natural or moral law.

5. The Apostle gives, in this verse, a reason, grounded on the very economy and plan of the incarnation, why we should not sin ; "to take away our sins," is understood by some to mean, to carry or take upon him our sins, as to their imputability, in the sense of the prophet, "*vere languores nostros ipse tulit et dolores portavit ; ipse peccata multorum tulit.*" The interpretation of abolishing sin, adopted in the Paraphrase, is the most probable. The words, "and in him there is no sin," are understood *causatively*, by some—he made atonement for sin ; *because*, being a victim free from all sin, his atonement should be accepted. Others make these words have reference to the preceding words, "our sins," he took away *our* sins ; for, he had no sins of *his own* to atone for.

6. "Whosoever abideth in him," or, is united to him by sanctifying grace, "sinneth not." How can this be reconciled with the doctrine of the Church, viz., that without an extraordinary privilege of grace, every person will fall into venial sins ? Some Expositors, with St. Agustine (*lib 2do de Bap. Parvul.* ch. viii., *et Epistola* 95), say, the words mean, that such a person, *inasmuch*, as he received the grace of Christ, and shares in the influence of his headship on his members, does not commit any sin whatever : although, as a son of the world, he may often fall into sins. This interpretation, they contend, best accords with the scope of the Apostle in this verse, which is to prove the foregoing assertion, viz., that "in him (Christ) there is no sin ;" for, if his members, deriving the vital influence of his grace from him, do not commit any sin whatsoever ; therefore, in him there can be no sin. Others, with St. Jerome (*lib. 2do contra Jovinianum,* ch. i., *et libr.* 1 *contra Pelagianos,* ch. i.), say, the words, "sinneth not," refer to mortal sin, on account of which, alone, a person ceases to be a living member of Christ ; and, it is clear from the following verses, that the Apostle is referring to the sin which makes us "children of the devil," and that is mortal sin only. And, moreover, it is only of a person sinning mortally, that the words could be verified in the next member of the sentence, " whosoever sinneth, hath not seen him nor known

Text.

7. Little children, let no man deceive you. He that doth justice, is just : even as he is just.

8. He that committeth sin, is of the devil : for the devil sinneth from the beginning. For this purpose, the Son of God appeared, that he might destroy the works of the devil.

Paraphrase.

7. My dearly beloved children, let no one seduce or lead you astray (as is attempted by the heretics) ; *he only*, who does the works of justice, and no body else, is just before God, possessing the true justice similar to the justice of Christ.

8. Whosoever commits grievous and deadly sins is of the devil ; for, the devil sinned soon after his creation, or, was the first to commit sin, in which he still perseveres, and tempts others thereto. It was for the purpose of destroying sin, or the works of the devil, that Christ assumed human flesh, wherein he could offer atonement for our sins, and merit grace to prevent our future relapse into them.

Commentary.

him " practically, with an affective vision, a knowledge joined with love, he knows God, as if he knew him not ; for, had he known God as he ought, had he considered his love and goodness, and the rewards and punishments which he holds out, such a knowledge would have restrained him from the commission of sin. The words, "seen " and "known," mean the same thing. Oh ! that men had known God, how ardently would they love him, how zealously would they fulfil his holy law, and run in the way of his holy commandments !

7. " Little children," a term of endearment, "let no one deceive you," as the heretics of the day were attempting to do, viz., the Nicolaites and Simonians, whose fundamental error, as is also the case with modern heretics, was, that faith, without good works, confers justification. "He that doth justice," *i.e.*, performs the works of justice or good works, "is just, even as he is just," *i.e.*, as far as a comparison can be instituted between the Creator and the creature.

But, it may be asked, how can this be ? May not a catechumen, before baptism, or a penitent, before the reception of the Sacrament of Penance, " do justice," *i.e.*, perform good works, observe the commandments, have faith, hope, initial love, sorrow, such as is insufficient to remit sin without the sacrament, and still not be just before God, his sins being yet unremitted ?

Some interpreters say, the word "just " does not here imply the state of sanctifying grace or friendship with God. The word, according to them, means, the man who does the works of justice, is just, as far as the justice of works is concerned, as far as they can confer justice ; and they confer *initial* justice, which serves as a disposition for consummate justice, or sanctifying grace ; or, if there be question of persons already in the state of sanctifying grace, then, these works of justice will preserve that state in the soul ; for, by the contrary works, the state of justice would be lost. So, then, the words mean, according to them, such a person is in *perfect* justice, if a state of sanctifying grace be united to his good works ; in *imperfect* justice, unless sanctifying grace be added.

It is, however, far more probable, that the proposition is to be understood in an *exclusive* sense, (as in Paraphrase). HE ONLY, who doth the works of justice, and nobody else, is just, and one of the sons of God ; as contradistinguished from the children of the devil, in the following verses. This is what the Apostle intended to convey, when he employed the words, "let no one deceive you," with reference to the sufficiency of faith only ; nobody will be justified, except he do the works of justice. In this interpretation, there is not a shadow of ground for the preceding objection ; for, according to it, the Apostle does not say, that every one, who does good works, is, *eo ipso*, justified, but only that good works are indispensably necessary conditions for justification, the point he intended to prove against the heretics.

8. "He that committeth sin is of the devil," *i.e.*, whosoever commits mortal sin is one of " the children of the devil" (as in verse 10). Similar are the words of our Redeemer to the Jews (John, chap. vii.), "you do the works of your father ;" you are of your father the devil." It is the devil that tempts to sin, and even in cases where

Text.

9. Whosoever is born of God, committeth not sin : for his seed, abideth in him, and he cannot sin, bacause he is born of God.

10. In this the children of God are manifest, and the children of the devil. Whosoever is not just, is not of God, nor he that loveth not his brother.

11. For this is the declaration, which you have heard from the beginning, that you should love one another.

Paraphrase.

9. But every one who receives of God a new birth, through sanctifying grace, commits no grievous sin ; for, the seed of this new generation, which is sanctifying grace, resides in him by way of a permanent habit, and he cannot sin mortally, and, at the same time, continue a son of God ; the state of divine sonship and mortal sin, being perfectly incompatible.

10. It is by their committing or avoiding mortal sins, that the children of God, and the children of the devil, are manifested and distinguished. whosoever is not just by the justice of works, or whosoever does not perform good works, is not a son of God, and he especially is not a son of God who does not love his fellow-creature.

11. For the precept which was announced to you from the beginning of your conversion to the gospel is, to love one another.

Commentary.

the temptation proceeds immediately from our own concupiscence, it proceeds, still, from the devil, as its remote cause ; for, it was owing to the sin, to which he first tempted man, that we are troubled with this corrupt concupiscence, this FOMES PECCATI, "For the devil sinneth from the beginning," or, soon after, but not at his creation, having been created just ; or, the words may mean, the devil was the first who sinned. "*He was a murderer from the beginning*" (John, viii. 44). He says, the devil "sinneth," rather than, *sinned* : because, now he tempts and impels men to sin, and is himself obdurate and hardened in his hatred of God. "For this purpose the Son of God," &c. So far is such a person from being a son of God, when he commits sin, that it was to destroy and abolish his sins, which are the works of the devil, that Christ assumed human flesh.

9. "Whosoever is born of God," that is, receives of him the new nativity of sanctifying grace, "committeth not sin"—*mortal* sin—for, it alone destroys the divine sonship resulting from sanctifying grace. "For his seed abideth in him ;" "his seed" is commonly understood to refer to sanctifying grace, which is the seed of future glory and the principle of our new spiritual nativity ; and this grace abideth, PERMANENTLY in the soul. This is a point of faith. That it abides, or adheres, by WAY OF HABIT, is not defined as a matter of faith ; but, it is a most probable theological opinion. "And he cannot sin, because he is born of God ;" the words "cannot sin" are to be understood, as logicians say, *in sensu composito*, in the sense, that he cannot continue in mortal sin, and be at the same time, a son of God, both being as incompatible as "*the association of light with darkness, or of Christ with Belial*."—(2 Cor. chap. vi. verse 14, &c.) This verse, however, by no means conveys that grace is *inamissible ;* for, if so, that is to say, if men could not fall away from the state of divine sonship, why should St. John so often exhort the sons of God not to sin ? Did not David, although a son of God, fall into sin, as he himself humbly confesses and deplores in his Psalms ?

10. "In this," viz., in their committing sin (verse 8), and their not committing sin (verse 9), the children of the devil, and the children of God, are manifested ; such is the mark for distinguishing them. "Whosoever is not just," that is, does not perform the works of justice or good works. That such is the meaning of "just," is clear from the following words, "for he that loveth not his brother," in which is specified a particular instance of the injustice to which he refers in the words, " not just," which must, therefore, refer to not doing good works, or to doing evil works. The words of this verse also throw an additional light on the *exclusive or negatively exceptive* meaning of the proposition, "he that doth justice," &c. (verse 7).

11. One of the leading precepts which was announced to you from the very beginning of the gospel—a precept which was to be the great test of your love of God, and a

Text.

12. Not as Cain, who was of the wicked one, and killed his brother. And wherefore did he kill him? Because his own works were wicked: and his brother's, just.

13. Wonder not, brethren, if the world hate you.

14. We know that we have passed from death to life, because we love the brethren. He that loveth not, abideth in death.

15. Whosoever hateth his brother, is a murderer. And you know that no murderer hath eternal life abiding in himself.

Paraphrase.

12. And not act as Cain did, who was a child of the devil, and killed his brother, Abel; and wherefore did he do so? Was it in self-defence? No, but from feelings of the blackest envy, because his own works were wicked, and those of his brother accepted by God.

13. Let it not be a subject of wonder to you, my brethren, if the corrupt votaries of the world, instead of respecting your virtues, hate and persecute you.

14. For, although they may persecute us, we can calculate with very great probability, from the fact of loving our brethren, that we have been translated from a state of sin and spiritual death, to a state of grace and spiritual life. The man who loves not his brother, still remains in a state of sin, and spiritual death.

15. But whosoever not only omits loving his brother, but positively hates him, is a murderer in heart and wish; and you know, from the principles of your faith, that no murderer can have the seed of eternal life, or sanctifying grace, abiding in him.

Commentary.

sign, that you were his true disciples—is, that " you should love one another." And hence, the man who fails to love, or who hates his brother, transgresses in a particular way, the most important and the most stringent of God's commandments.

12. We should love one another, and not act as Cain acted, who was a son of the devil, and slew his brother, Abel. According to the Greek, *ου καθως Κάϊν εκ του πονηρου ην*, the construction runs thus : " *not as Cain was of the wicked one*," that is, we should not be of the devil, as Cain was, who killed his brother ; and to prove that the murder of Abel by Cain was at the instigation of the devil, the Apostle assigns the motive or impulsive cause of the act. Did he kill him from necessity or in self-defence? No, but he did so from the feelings of the blackest jealousy and envy. " Because his own works "—the offering which he made—" were wicked," and not pleasing to God, " and his brother's just," their acceptance by God publicly and visibly attested. It is commonly believed, that God showed his approval of Abel's sacrifice, by sending fire from heaven to burn it ; whereas, in Cain's case, no such approval was manifested. It is likely that either his intention was not pure, or that the fruits of the earth, presented by him, were not of the choicest kind, whereas Abel offered up the firstlings of his flocks.

13. The hatred of the good, by the wicked, is almost as old as creation, as is seen in the foregoing example. In these words of St. John, is contained an allusion to the saying of our Redeemer, " if the world hate you, know that it first hated me."—(John, xv. 13). Several reasons are assigned by Commentators, why the wicked hate the just : 1st, dissimilarity of morals ; " He is grievous unto us even to behold ; for, his life is not like other men's, and his ways are very different," (Wisdom, ii. 15, 16, &c.) ; 2ndly, envy at their superior virtues ; 3rd, their avoidance of worldly society and intercourse ; " because you are not of the world......therefore, the world hateth you," (John xv. 19) ; 4th, the censure which their morals reflect, by the contrast, on the corruption of worldlings. " *contrarius est operibus nostris.*"—(Wisdom, ii. 12).

14. " We know......because we love the brethren ;" the love of our brethren is the sign whereby we may know that we are in this happy state of spiritual translation. Of course, it can be no more than a probable sign or conjecture in any individual case ; for, as no one can know with an absolute certainty that he has this love of his brethren in the required degree, so, neither can he be absolutely certain that he is in the state of grace. He cannot have a greater certainty of the existence of the thing signified, than he has of the existence of the sign itself. " He that loveth not,

Text.

16. In this we have known the charity of God, because he hath laid down his life for us: and we ought to lay down our lives for the brethren.

17. He that hath the substance of this world, and shall see his brother in need, and shall put up his bowels from him: how doth the charity of God abide in him?

Paraphrase.

16. We have the clearest proof and manifestation of the charity and love of God for us in his having voluntarily and freely laid down his life for us; and we also, following the example of love which he, our predestined model, has set us, should lay down our lives for our brethren whenever the order of charity requires it.

17. And we are still more bound, under pain of grievous sin, to contribute out of our substance to his temporal wants); for, how can that man preserve the charity and grace of God, who, having it in his power to administer, out of his temporal substance, to the wants of his brother, of which he is conscious, will still refuse, and show no practical sympathy or commiseration for him?

Commentary.

abideth in death;" remains in the state of mortal sin and spiritual death, which involves a liability to eternal death, from which the others have been translated. Hence, the man who neglects to fulfil the positive precept of loving his neighbour, and fails to succour him in his necessities, lives in the state of mortal sin. After the words "loveth not," are added in the ordinary Greek, *his brother*. But these words are wanting in the chief manuscripts, the Vatican and Alexandrian.

15. The Apostle in this verse compares the man who hates his brother, to Cain the murderer of Abel; "whosoever hates his brother is a murderer." The hatred of which he speaks is a grievous hatred, containing a wish for the death and destruction of our neighbour; the man who entertains such a hatred is a murderer in heart and wish; the internal act derives its species and malignity from the external act to which it extends. Hence, our Redeemer says, *that every one who looks after a woman, to covet her, has committed adultery with her in his heart.*—(Matt. v. 28). "And you know," from your knowledge of Faith, "that no murderer has eternal life," that is, sanctifying grace, the pledge and seed of eternal life, "abiding in him."

16. He points out the extent or degree to which we should love our neighbour, after the example of Christ, who assigns his love for us, as the model of our love for our neighbour: *love one another, as I have loved you.*—(John, xv.) His charity has been manifested in his having so loved us, that, " he hath laid down his life for us;" and we, in turn, are bound by well regulated charity, "to lay down our lives for our brethren." The order of well regulated charity requires, that we should expose our lives for the souls of our brethren, if they be placed in *extreme* spiritual necessity. A *pastor*, who has charge of souls, is bound to expose his life for the salvation of his people, even in case of *grievous* spiritual necessity. "The charity of God." The Greek omits the words, "of God."

17. Not only are we bound to expose our lives for the *spiritual* wants of our neighbour; but we are also bound to administer to his *temporal* wants out of our worldly substance. If we are bound to sacrifice our lives for him, we are obliged to relieve his wants, out of our temporal substance, when necessary. "He that hath the substance of this world;" the Greek word for "substance," τον βιον, means, all the things required for the sustenance of human life, such as meat, drink, clothing, money, &c.; "and sees his brother in need," is aware of his wants, "and shall put up his bowels from him," steels his heart, against every feeling of pity for him, and refuses him all relief; "how doth the charity of God?" &c. The question is equivalent to a denial, that the charity or love of God, the common Father of all, for whom our neighbour is to be loved, can reside in the heart of the man, who neglects the precept of loving his neighbour. Hence, the obligation of the duty of almsdeeds, under pain of mortal sin, or of losing the charity and friendship of God. Two things are required to render us guilty of this mortal neglect—1st, that we have wherewith to relieve our neighbour, "he that hath the substance," &c.; and 2ndly, a knowledge of his wants, "and shall *see* his brother in need." Most likely, this extends to the common

Text.

18. My little children, let us not love in word, nor in tongue, but in deed, and in truth.

19. In this we know that we are of the truth : and in his sight shall persuade our hearts.

20. For if our heart reprehend us, God is greater than our heart, and knoweth all things.

21. Dearly beloved, if our heart do not reprehend us, we have confidence towards God :

Paraphrase.

18. Dearly beloved children, this love which we are all bound to manifest for our neighbour, should not be confined to mere bland expressions and kind words of condolence and pity, it should be manifested in works of alleviation, and acts of beneficence, which alone are the real test of true feelings of compassion.

19. And it is by the exhibition of such practical love of our neighbour, in acts of benevolence we can be sure that we are true sons of God, and by the recollection of such deeds of charity we will, in the presence of God, the searcher of hearts, tranquillize our conscience against whatever fears or scruples may arise.

20. But if our heart or conscience reprehend us for not loving our neighbour sincerely, and for not exhibiting acts of beneficence, how can we hope to escape the censure and condemnation of the all-seeing eye of God, whose knowledge far excels the obscure knowledge of our heart, and extends to all things even to the most refined motive of our most secret actions ?

21. Dearly beloved brethren, if our conscience do not reprehend us in this respect, we have a well grounded confidence of being heard by God in our petitions (verse 22) ; or, of being treated by him as genuine sons in the day of judgment.

Commentary.

necessities of our brethren, as it is not probable, that the Apostle contemplates cases so rare as those of extreme necessity generally are. It is on the neglect of this duty, that our Redeemer will, on the day of judgment, ground the sentence of reprobation on the wicked, " because I was hungry, and you gave me not to eat," &c.—(Matt. xxv.)

18. He points out the kind of charity we should show our neighbour—not the barren sympathy of bland words, like the man described by St. James (ii. 15, 16) ; but, we should evince the truth and sincerity of our professions of regard and pity, in actually relieving him by acts of practical benevolence.

19. " In this," that is, in loving our neighbour, " in deed and truth," we can have a moral certainty, or great probability, " that we are of the truth," that is, true sons of God—himself the truth, the fountain from which all true love of our neighbour springs—abiding in him, and united to him. Some make " in this " refer to the following, but it is better refer it to the foregoing, as in Paraphrase. " And in his sight," who unlike men, judges not by appearances, but searches the very heart ; " we shall persuade our hearts," that is, tranquillize and set at rest our consciences, by calling to mind the true charity of benevolence which we have shown our neighbour.

20. But if, on the other hand, " our heart reprehend us," that is, if our conscience censure us, for mere hypocritical, simulated love of our neighbour, not exhibited in active beneficence, " God is greater than our heart ;" we cannot expect that we will escape the keen and penetrating glance of divine omniscience, whose knowledge far exceeds the obscure knowledge of our blind hearts, " and knoweth all things," even to our most secret actions and intentions.

21. " If our heart do not reprehend us," in this matter of charity towards our neighbour, whom we love, " in deed and truth ;" or, if it reprehend us in no respect, " we have confidence towards God ;" we have probable, well founded grounds for hoping in God. This may regard the effects of our petitions, as in next verse, or, the saving of us, in the day of judgment (chap. iv. 17). Of course, as the knowledge which we have, that we love our neighbour practically, as we should, is only a probable knowledge ; so, neither can our confidence and knowledge of our being heard by God, or treated by him as sons, on the day of judgment, pass beyond the bounds of probability or moral certainty.

Text.

22. And whatsoever we shall ask, we shall receive of him : because we keep his commandments, and do those things which are pleasing in his sight.

23. And this is his commandment, that we should believe in the name of his Son JESUS CHRIST : and love one another, as he hath given commandment unto us.

24. And he that keepeth his commandments, abideth in him, and he in him. And in this we know that he abideth in us, by the Spirit which he hath given us.

Paraphrase.

22. And whatever we shall ask of him, with the proper conditions, we shall obtain ; because, aided and assisted by divine grace, we observe his commandments, and do the things that are pleasing in his sight.

23. And this is his great commandment, or the summary of his commandments, both with regard to faith and morality, viz., that we believe in his Son, Jesus Christ, and love one another, as he has repeatedly enjoined upon all his followers.

24. And whosoever observeth his commandments with the proper dispositions, and from a proper motive, abideth in God by a union of charity, and God, or, the Blessed Trinity, abides in him as in a dwelling place, by a communication of sanctifying gifts and grace. And we can know, with a high degree of moral certainty, that God abides in us, and is united to us in friendship, from the spirit of grace and love which he has given us to keep his commandments.

Commentary.

22. We will obtain the object of our petitions from him ; of course, it is always implied, that the object sought for is good and conducive to our salvation, and that the prayer itself is accompanied with humility, confidence and perseverance ; then, we will obtain, whenever it may be pleasing to God, the objects of our petitions, should He see it expedient for our salvation to grant them. Sometimes, he refuses, for their greater good, to grant the just the object of their petitions, as in the case of St. Paul (2 Cor. xii. 8) : and sometimes, he grants the wicked their demands, for their greater ruin. From this verse it is clear, that the Apostle refers, in the foregoing verse, to the just and pious, whose conscience does not reprehend them ; and, even in their case, this absence of the consciousness of sin, is not an infallible sign, that they are in the state of grace ; for, St. Paul tells us (1 Cor. chap. iv.), that although conscious to himself of no fault, he was still unable to discern the state of his soul before God, and could not regard himself as certain of his justification. We are assured here, that "God is greater than our heart," (verse 20), and may, therefore, see in us, sins which escape ourselves. From this verse it follows, that the commandments of God are not impossible ; as also the refutation of the heretical doctrine, that we sin in all our actions.

23. And his great commandment, or rather the sum of his commandments, is to "believe in the name of his Son, Jesus Christ." Believing "in the name," is the same as, believing, in the person of Jesus Christ. Thus it is said : "there is no other *name* (*i.e.*, person) under heaven," &c. "Hallowed be thy *name*," *i.e.*, person. To believe in Jesus Christ, is to believe in his divine and human natures. This, of course, involves a belief in the Trinity. It is the great foundation of the Christian religion, and was attacked by the early heretics. This is his great precept as regards *faith*, and as regards *morals*, his great commandment is, "that we love one another ;" for, this involves the love of God ; and in these two points, the love of God and of our neighbour, depend "the entire law and the prophets."—(Matthew, xxii. 30).

"As he hath given commandment unto us," These words are added by the Apostle to show how repeatedly our Divine Redeemer inculcated this precept.

24. "And in this we know that he abideth in us," which may refer to the *faithful* in general. Then, the moral evidence of his abiding in us is, "the spirit which he hath given us." From the spirit of grace, which he has given us, to love one another, and observe his commandments, we know, that he resides in us, as in his friends. Or, if the words "abideth in us," refer to *the Apostles*, the word "spirit" is to be understood of the visible gifts of the Holy Ghost, and the power of miracles, imparted to them to confirm their doctrine. From this, they were certain that they came from God ; for, they had his seal. In this sense, the words may also be extended to the different

Commentary.

members of the infant Church, founded by the Apostles, who, from the several "*gratiæ gratis datæ*," imparted to them, and to the Apostles, were sure that they were in the true Church.   In latter ages, these visible gifts are not abundantly imparted, being now unnecessary ; moreover, the former miracles still *morally* continue and retain their full force, to prove the truth of the Christian doctrine, in favour of which they were originally wrought ; the power of miracles, however, has never ceased in the Church, and may be brought into operation, whenever it becomes necessary.

CHAPTER IV.

Analysis.

In this chapter, the Apostle cautions the faithful against embracing, too readily, any doctrine proposed to them, or against attaching themselves, without due consideration, to every teacher that may pretend to a divine inspiration; because, many false teachers even in his day, went forth to deceive the people (verse 1). *He gives a special mark for distinguishing true doctrine or true teachers from the false, derived from the doctrine of Christ's Incarnation* (2, 3).

He attributes the stability of the faithful, and their resistance to the false teachers, to the grace and power of God dwelling in them (4). *He next accounts why these false teachers have followers in the world, on the ground, that they please the world in their preaching* (5). *He assigns a general note, accommodated to all times, for distinguishing true and false teachers, viz., their rejecting or receiving the doctrine of the Church, and submitting to the authority of her chief Pastors* (6).

The Apostle resumes the subject of brotherly love, from which he digressed (iii. 2, 3), *and while exhorting them to love one another, shows the advantages of loving our neighbour* (7), *and the evils of not loving him; and how incompatible the hatred of our brother is with the love of God* (8). *He extols the charity of God for us, on account of the great sacrifice it involved* (9), *and on account of its utter gratuitousness, being wholly unmerited on our part* (10); *from this he draws a conclusion containing an exhortation to us, after the example of the great love of God for us* (11). *He says that, although no one ever saw God; and hence, no one could either love him as he deserves, or make him a return of love; still, God dwells in us intimately, if we love our brethren* (12). *God has given another proof of his love, and of his abiding in us, in the spiritual gifts bestowed on the Church* (13).

From the testimony of the senses, he demonstrates the certainty of God having sent his Son to redeem us: this point, and the necessity of believing it, he dwells on particularly, owing to its great importance (14, 15). *The Apostle again refers to the great charity of God in sending his Son to redeem us, and asserts that God is himself the increated charity, from which all created charity flows* (16). *He shows the effect of charity, viz., to give us confidence in the day of judgment* (17). *He shows how this charity excludes all servile or perplexing fear* (18).

He next exhorts us to love God, and assigns the reason of this (19), *and proves that no one can love God and hate his neighbour—first, because the thing is impossible* (20); *and, secondly, because the man who hates his neighbour, violates God's precepts, and, therefore, cannot love God* (21).

Text.

1. DEARLY beloved, believe not every spirit, but try the spirits if

Paraphrase.

1. Dearly beloved, beware of lending too ready an assent to every doctrine proposed to you as inspired

Commentary

1. "Every spirit," may regard either *doctrine* or *preachers* of doctrine, as coming from God; "but try the spirits," by comparing them with the *general* test given (*v.* 6.) by examining whether their teaching be in accordance with the doctrine of the Church,

Text.	Paraphrase.
they be of God : because many false prophets are gone out into the world.	by God—or to every teacher who pretends to a divine inspiration ; but, in every case of this sort, try and examine if such persons or doctrines be from God or from the devil ; for, many false teachers pretending to a knowledge of the secrets of God, have gone forth into the world
2. By this is the spirit of God known. Every spirit, which confesseth that JESUS CHRIST is come in the flesh is of God :	2. There is one sign or test, whereby you may know at the present day, whether a person or doctrine be from God or not, viz., every doctrine or person that proposes the true faith regarding the Divinity and Humanity of Jesus Christ, is from God.
3. And every spirit that dissolveth JESUS is not of God : and this is Antichrist, of whom you have heard that he cometh, and he is now already in the world.	3. While, on the other hand, every doctrine or person (that does not confess that Jesus came into the flesh) ; and, therefore, dissolveth Jesus by expressing an error, regarding either his divine or human nature, such a doctrine or person is not from God ; and such is either the doctrine or the forerunner of Antichrist, of whom you have heard it said, that he is on the eve of coming (this being the last stage of the world), and that he is already in the world, in the persons of his precursors ; for even now there are many Antichrists —(chap. ii. 18).

Commentary.

"if they be of God." In this there is no license given to the faithful to subject to examination, the *defined* doctrines of faith proposed to them by their pastors ; for, here there is question of new doctrines not hitherto propounded, or of teachers not commissioned by the Apostles. "Because many false prophets are gone out," &c. By "prophets" are frequently meant in Scripture, not persons who can predict future events (the strict meaning of the word), but persons who pretended to a knowledge of the Divine mind, and to the faculty of explaining the doctrines of revelation, under the influence of Divine inspiration.—(1 Cor. xii. xiii. xiv.) Hence, by "false prophets," here are meant, men who propounded their own private errors, as doctrine divinely inspired.

2. "By this is known." The Greek is γινωσκετε, "*know ye*." The Vulgate, however, is supported by many manuscripts and versions. Here is assigned, a *particular mark* accommodated to the circumstances of the time and the errors then broached, viz. :—"Every spirit which confesseth that Jesus Christ is come in the flesh is of God," that is, every doctrine that propounds the true faith regarding the Humanity and Divinity of Jesus Christ, or every teacher that holds this faith, is from God.

OBJECTION.—Would not the Calvinists or Protestants, in general, admit this ?

ANSWER.—The Apostle gives this note merely in reference to the errors of the early heretics, who either erred regarding the Divinity (as Ebion and Cerinthus), or the Humanity of Jesus Christ (as was done by Simon Magus, and many heretics in after days) ; it *is* in reference to such only, that this note holds ; just in the same way as, talking of heretics now-a-days, pastors of the Church, referring to leading modern errors, might give as a mark of the orthodox believers : "Whosoever admits Transubstantiation, or the Primacy of the Roman Pontiff is of God." It might, however, be truly said that the note now given by the Apostle applies, in a certain sense, to all times ; for all heretics err in something connected with either the Divinity or Humanity of Jesus Christ. His Divinity is asserted in the words, "is come." Hence, he must have been previously existing ; and the reality of his flesh in the words, "come into the flesh."

3. In this verse, he gives the same remark, negatively "and every spirit that dissolveth Jesus." In the Greek it is, "*and every spirit that confesses not Jesus*," (to which is added, in the ordinary Greek text, "*to have come in the flesh*"), is not of God." St. Augustine employs both readings, the reading of the Vulgate, and that of the

Text.

4. You are of God, little children, and have overcome him. Because greater is he that is in you, than he that is in the world.

5. They are of the world : therefore of the world they speak, and the world heareth them.

6. We are of God. He that knoweth God, heareth us. He that is not of God, heareth us not. By this we know the spirit of truth, and the spirit of error.

Paraphrase.

4. But you, my dearly beloved children, are sons of God, and, therefore, have conquered this wicked one in his precursors, whose efforts to pervert your faith you have frustrated, owing to the grace and assistance of God, whose spirit, impressing on your minds the truths of faith, is more powerful than the spirit of the devil who dwells in and rules the impious.

5. These false teachers are of the number of worldlings, whose hopes and aspirations are confined to this world ; and, therefore, they propose things pleasing to the world, and in a style accommodated to the wisdom of worldlings, and hence it is that the world hears them and attends to them.

6. But, we, Apostles and divinely inspired teachers, are of God. Whosoever belongs to God by faith operating through charity hears us. And he that is not of God, does not hear us. By this general test, then, accommodated to all times and all circumstances, can we know who the person or what the doctrine is, that is from God ; and who the person or what the doctrine is, that comes from the devil, viz., by their conformity with the doctrine of the Catholic Church or otherwise.

Commentary.

Greek copies ; it is probable both readings were originally found in the sacred text. They have the same meaning expressed in different words. " He is said to " dissolve Jesus," who either denies his Humanity, or Divinity, or his unity of Person, and the distinction of natures in him ; in one word, he who broaches any error regarding his Humanity or Divinity, " is not of God," and, therefore, to be rejected. " And this is Antichrist " (in Greek, το του αντιχριστου, *this is that of Antichrist*), or, this is the spirit of Antichrist, either his doctrine or forerunner, according to the meaning given to the word " spirit." " Of whom you have heard that he cometh ; " or, is on the eve of coming, as the " last hour " has arrived (ii. 18), "and is now already in the world," in the persons of his precursors. " Even now there are become many Antichrists," (ii. 18). The fame of Antichrist's coming was known throughout the entire Church (St. John, chap. v. verse 45 ; 2 Thes. ii.) In the Greek, for, *of whom you have heard*, it is, ò ακηκοατε, *which* (spirit) *you have heard ;* the meaning of which would be, of which spirit of Antichrist, you have heard that it has come and is in the world, in the person of his precursors.

4. You have nothing in common with such, having been born of God, " and have overcome him " in his precursors. The Greek expresses this more clearly, *you have overcome them.* " Because greater is the spirit," &c. He refers their victory to the proper source, viz., the grace of God's spirit residing in them.

5. " They are of the world." These false teachers belong to the rank of worldlings, whose hopes and aspirations are centred in the goods of this world. " Therefore of the world they speak"—they propound doctrines pleasing to flesh and blood, discarding the more difficult and austere—or, the words may regard their mode of treating religious and sublime truths of faith. They treat of them in a philosophical way, reducing them to the rules of human reason, to suit the incredulity of worldlings.

" And the world heareth them," therefore, because religion is made to suit their corrupt passions and intellectual caprices.

6. " We," Apostles, and our successors in the government of the Church, " are of God," aided by his grace, and divinely commissioned by him, we propound to you the doctrine which he has revealed to us. " He that knoweth God " practically, and is

Text.

7. Dearly beloved, let us love one another : for charity is of God. And every one that loveth is born of God, and knoweth God.

8. He that loveth not, knoweth not God : for God is charity.

9. By this hath the charity of God appeared towards us, because God hath sent his only begotten Son into the world, that we may live by him.

Paraphrase.

7. Dearly beloved brethren, let us love one another, for this fraternal charity is of God—it is a singular gift emanating from his grace ; it has God for author, who unites in one common bond of charity all the members of the Church, militant and triumphant, and is a work singularly pleasing to him ; every one that loveth his neighbour is a son of God and co-heir of Christ, and has that affective knowledge of God, which is the fruit of his adoption.

8. And he that loveth not his neighbour has not the affective or practical saving knowledge of God ; for, God is the increated fountain of charity from which all created charity in creatures, like so many rivulets, flows.

9. In this, has the boundless charity of God the Father been singularly conspicuous towards mankind, viz., in his having sent his consubstantial and only begotten Son into the world, that we, who were in a state of spiritual death, might live through him.

Commentary.

united with him, "heareth us"—obeys us, and assents to the doctrine which we propose. "He that is not of God, heareth us not." "By this we know the spirit of truth, and the spirit of error," viz., by their receiving or rejecting our doctrine.

In this verse, the Apostle gives a second note, and a *general* one, for distinguishing true from false teachers ; a note accommodated to all circumstances, and true to the end of the world. It is this : the teacher who obeys the voice of the chief Pastors of the Church, the successors of the Apostles, is a true teacher ; or, the doctrine which is comfortable to the doctrine of the Church is true doctrine ; while on the other hand, he who obeys not the Church, and is not sent by the supreme Pastors, with whom Christ promised to remain, "to the end of the world," is a false teacher, and one inspired by the spirit of error. *He who hears you, hears me, and he who despises you, despises me.*— (Luke, x. verse 16).

7. The Apostle now resumes his favourite subject of fraternal charity, of which he had been treating (iii. 23), and from which he had digressed at the commencement of this. "Let us love one another, for charity is of God ;" fraternal charity is of God—(*vide* Paraphrase). "And every one that loveth is born of God," is a son of God, and co-heir of Christ—absolutely so, if he be already in sanctifying grace, but only remotely and so far as this love of his neighbour, under the influence of actual grace, disposes for justification, if he be not already justified. "And knoweth God" practically, with the affective knowledge joined to love.

8. "He that loveth not" his neighbour—for there is question of the love of our neighbour—"knoweth not God," has not the affective, saving knowledge of God, joined with the divine love ; although such a person may have true and divine faith.—"For God is charity." He is that increated charity, the source of charity in us—the fountain from which all created charity flows.

From this, it by no means follows, as Peter Lombard, commonly called *" The Master of Sentences,"* maintains, that charity is not a created habit, but the increated love of God residing in the soul, as in his temple ; because he resides there through the medium of created charity, expressed in the clearest terms by St. Paul (Rom. v.) : *" Charitas Dei diffusa est in cordibus nostris per spiritum sanctum qui datus est nobis."* Hence, it is distinct from the Holy Ghost.

9. The greatest proof of his boundless charity for man, that "God who is charity" (verse 8), has given us, is, "his having sent his only begotten Son into the world." It is thought by many interpreters, that the Apostle here gives Christ the title of " Only

Text.	**Paraphrase.**
10. In this is charity: not as though we had loved God, but because he hath first loved us, and sent his Son to be a propitiation for our sins.	10. His charity also has another distinguishing quality, viz., its gratuitousness. In this also is his charity much commended, that he did not love us by way of return for our having loved him; for, it was he who first loved us, and, in consequence thereof, sent his Son into the world to be a victim of propitiation for our sins.
11. My dearest, if God hath so loved us; we also ought to love one another.	11. If, then, my dearest children, God loved us even when we were his enemies, to the extent of delivering up his Son for us; we ought, in imitation of him, love one another, not even excepting our enemies.
12. No man hath seen God at any time. If we love one another, God abideth in us, and his charity is perfected in us.	12. No one has ever in this life seen God, nor his adorable perfections as they are, and as they merit our love; hence, no one can have the motives of sensible presence and familiarity to excite him to love God, as he has in reference to his fellow-creatures; but if we love one another from the proper motive of charity, God abides in us by the communication of his grace, and makes us his dwelling place, and the charity by which we love him is fully and perfectly accomplished in us.

Commentary.

Begotten Son," in refutation of the errors of Ebion and Cerinthus, who held that Christ was not the *natural*, but, like other good men, the *adoptive* Son of God. "That we may live by him"—we who before were dead in sin, and liable to eternal death, might receive through him spiritual life, and a title to an eternal inheritance. The words of this verse are similar to those addressed by our Redeemer to Nicodemus (John, iii.), "God so loved the world, as to give his only begotten Son," &c.—(iii. 16).

10. Another distinguishing feature of God's love for us, whereby it is most commended, is, its gratuitousness; he did not love us by any way of return for a love beforehand shown him, thus challenging him to love us in turn. "Not as though," might be more clearly rendered from the Greek, *ουχ ότι, not that.* "Because he hath first loved us," even when we were his enemies by sin; "and sent his Son to be a propitiation," may either mean, a *victim* of propitiation, or a *propitiator* "for our sins," these sins, so many rebellions against himself. By them we hurled defiance at him in Heaven. Oh! blessed be his boundless goodness and charity for ever. Similar is the idea conveyed in the words of St. Paul (Rom. v. 8, 9): "*God commendeth his charity towards us, because when as yet we were sinners......Christ died for us.*" "*When we were enemies, we were reconciled to God by the death of his Son.*"

11. In this verse, is drawn a conclusion and exhortation, founded on the preceding verses: If God loved us to the extent of dying for us when we were his enemies, we ought, after his example, love one another, not excepting our enemies. Similar is the exhortation (Ephes. v. 1): "Be ye imitators of God, and walk in love," &c.

12. "No man hath seen God at any time." The connexion of this with the preceding appears to be, no mortal has ever, in this life, seen God "*facie ad faciem,*" such as he is in himself; and so, has not seen his adorable perfections, which would force men to make a return of love in the most exalted degree; nor has any man the motive of sensible presence and familiarity to excite him to love God, as he has in reference to the love of his neighbour. Hence, no one can love God as he deserves to be loved, or make a return of love to him in this life. The inference from which is, that he should be loved, and a return made to him in our brethren, whom we see, as is expressed (verse 20).

"If we love one another, God abideth in us"—that is, if we make to one another a return of the love which we owe, and of which we cannot, in this life, make a return, to the invisible God, He will abide in us as intimately by sanctifying grace, as if we

Text.

13. In this we know that we abide in him, and he in us; because he hath given us of his spirit.

14. And we have seen and do testify, that the Father hath sent his Son *to be* the Saviour of the world.

15. Whosoever shall confess that Jesus is the Son of God, God abideth in him, and he in God.

16. And we have known, and have believed the charity, which

Paraphrase.

13. And by this we know that we abide in God by the close union of charity and love, and he in us, by sanctifying grace, viz., by the abundance of spiritual gifts which he has poured forth on the Church to which we belong—or by the spirit of charity for one another, which can only be the fruit of his grace and Holy Spirit.

14. And we, Apostles, have seen it with our eyes, and we bear testimony to the fact, that God the Father hath sent his Son to be the Saviour of the world.

15. Whosoever, then, shall confess, that Jesus is the Son of God, and the Saviour sent by him into this world, such a person abides in God, is united to him in friendship, and God abides in him by sanctifying grace.

16. And we have all known, from undoubted proofs, and we have believed in, the great charity of God,

Commentary.

felt him palpably present. "And his charity," or the charity we owe him, "is perfected in us;" because, unless we loved our neighbour, our love would be imperfect, and would not fully extend to all the objects contemplated by the precepts of charity. Again, by loving our neighbour, we perfect the love of God; for, by loving our neighbour supernaturally, we wish for him the greatest spiritual goods; and hence, we wish him to enjoy the knowledge and love of God, the greatest of spiritual advantages; and we, thereby, wish that God would be loved and known by his creatures, which is nothing else than an act of the love of God on our part. Hence, the love of God, and the love of our neighbour, have the *same formal* motive; the former is perfected by the latter.

"No man hath seen God at any time." It is disputed whether Moses, or St. Paul saw him in the sense of these words of the Apostle; and if they did, we can only say that their case was an exception to the general assertion here made. Similar are the words of the Apostle in the 1st chapter of his Gospel (verse 18), "no man hath seen God at any time;" but in the Gospel, his words have reference to the perfect *knowledge* of God; here, they have reference to the perfect *love* of him.

13. "Because he hath given us of his spirit," is referred by some, among the rest by Estius, to the spiritual gifts, or *gratiæ gratis datæ* (*v.g.*) miracles, tongues, &c., abundantly poured forth on the first Christians—which is a proof, that they belonged to God's Church, and that his sanctifying spirit resided in some of them—or, on the Apostles themselves. Others understand the words of the spirit, which he imparted to them, whereby they were enabled to love one another. This opinion is very much in accordance with the context, as it contains an encomium on the excellence of fraternal charity, which is a proof of the presence of God's Spirit.

14. This has reference to verse 9. St. John here proves what might be questioned, regarding God's sending his Son to save the world, from the very evidence of the senses on the part of the Apostles themselves. The words, "we have seen," &c., are the same as those of the 1st chapter (verses 1, 2). He insists on this point particularly, because it was called in question by the early heretics; and besides, it is the basis and foundation of all Christian faith and charity.

15. "Abideth in God, and God in him." Of course, the Apostle speaks of that faith and confession of Jesus Christ, which is animated by charity and has the other conditions accompanying it. In the same way, St. Paul says, "Christ dwells by faith in your hearts."—(Ephes. iii. 17). In these and other such affirmative proposiions, it is supposed, that all the other requisites are not wanting, the *attribute* of an *affirmative proposition* being always employed *particularly*.

16. "And we have known, and have believed the charity, which God hath to us."

Text.

God hath to us. God is charity : and he that abideth in charity, abideth in God, and God in him.

17. In this is the charity of God perfected with us, that we may have confidence in the day of judgment : because as he is, we also are in this world.

18. Fear is not in charity : but perfect charity casteth out fear, because fear hath pain. And he that feareth, is not perfected in charity.

Paraphrase.

manifested towards us in sending his Son to redeem us. God is the essential uncreated charity, from whom, as from its fountain, all created charity flows ; and he who abides in created charity, and through it, adheres to uncreated charity, abides in God, and God in turn abides in him, through the medium of sanctifying grace and in the bonds of mutual friendship.

17. In this is the charity by which we love God, perfected in us—a charity which will have the effect of begetting in us confidence on the day of judgment— viz., that as he is showering down his blessings on all, enemies as well as friends, so we also are in this world doing good to all, not excepting our enemies.

18. True and genuine charity begets confidence on the day of judgment, and, is therefore, incompatible with that servile fear, which dreads God's justice on account of past sins, and is so opposed to confidence ; perfect or genuine charity excludes every such fear ; because, this fear has joined to it an anxiety and torture of mind quite incompatible with the calm peace and confidence, which accompany charity. He, then, that is agitated and influenced by this fear, has not true and genuine charity.

Commentary.

The Apostle again repeats what he had said in the preceding verses. *The charity of God,* or, " the charity which God hath to us," regards the exhibition of his charity in sending his Son to redeem us. The Apostle is not tired of repeating the great charity of God for us, in order to induce us, after his example, to love one another. Some say that in the words, "we have known," &c., he speaks in the person of all the faithful in general, who, from the preaching and testimony of the Apostle, and the abundant gifts of the Holy Ghost, have known of the great love of God in sending his Son. " God is charity," the uncreated fountain, from which all created charity flows, " and he that abideth in charity," that is, adheres to uncreated charity, through the bond of created charity, which is a gift " poured by the Holy Ghost into our hearts " (Rom. v. 5), "abideth in God," is united to him by sanctifying grace and friendship, "and God in him," making his soul his habitation and the dwelling place of his Spirit.

17. "In this is the charity of God perfected in us." The words, "of God," are not in the Greek ; by "charity of God," some understand the charity God has for us, the effect of which is, the confidence we shall have in appearing before him on the day of judgment. Others, more probably, understand it of the charity or love we bear him, or rather bear our neighbour on his account ; and it is also disputed, what the words, " in this," refer to, whether to the words immediately following, " that we may have confidence," as if he said, the sincere and genuine love of our neighbour for God's sake will have this effect, viz., that it will beget confidence on the day of judgment—similar is the idea (chap. iii. 21) ; or, to the words, " because as he is," &c., as if he had said, in this is the charity by which we love God, or rather our neighbour for his sake, perfected in us, viz., that as he does good to all, " raining on the just and unjust," so we also should love our neighbour, and do good to our very enemies. This perfect beneficent charity shall afford us confidence on the day of judgment. The latter construction (which has been adopted in the Paraphrase), seems more in accordance with the Greek reading of the text, ὅτι καθὼς ἐκεῖνος ἐστιν καὶ ἡμεῖς ἐσμεν ἐν τῷ κόσμῳ τούτῳ.

18. The object which the Apostle has in view in this verse, is to prove that charity gives us confidence in the day of judgment (verse 17). " Fear is not in charity." The word " fear," may be understood either of *human* fear, produced by the apprehension of bodily punishment, loss of goods, &c., or of *perplexing* fear, which makes us dread the justice of God, on account of our past or present state of sin ; or of *servile* fear, which

Text.

19. Let us therefore love God, because God first hath loved us.

20. If any man say, I love God, and hateth his brother; he is a liar. For he that loveth not his brother, whom he seeth, how can he love God, whom he seeth not?

Paraphrase.

19. Let us, then, love God, since he first loved us, even when we were his enemies, having sent his Son to redeem us.

20. The best proof that we love God, is the love of our neighbour. If any person say, or even think in his mind, that he has the prescribed love for God, and at the same time hate his brother and exclude him from his affection; such a man is a liar and grossly deceives himself; for, he that loveth not the visible image of God, viz., his brother, whom he sees—whose wants he knows—with whom he shares the same common nature—on whom he depends for mutual aid and assistance—how can he love God whom he seeth not, who lies far beyond the reach of the senses? The thing is impossible.

Commentary

makes men avoid sin, solely from the dread of punishment. Now, charity excludes all such fear, but particularly the perplexing fear of God's judgment on account of our sins; for, those who are in charity have no such fear, exclusive of confidence, hanging over their heads. "Perfect charity," real, genuine charity, whether initial or more perfect, "casteth out fear, because fear hath pain," that is a torture and anxiety of mind, incompatible with the calm and peace which charity carries with it. Others understand the words, "hath pain," to mean, hath pain, or punishment, for object. "And he that feareth, is not perfected in charity," that is, the man who observes God's commandments, solely from fear of punishment, and acts under the influence of *servile* fear, such a person has not that genuine and perfect charity, which the Christian Law requires, and cannot "have confidence in the day of judgment" (verse 17).

The question which the Apostle here considers, does not regard how far fear may influence those who are perfected in charity, in avoiding the offence of God; but it regards either the avoidance of sin, *solely* from fear of punishment, or the fear and anxiety regarding God's judgment, on account of past and present sins. Of course, the Apostle does not here consider *filial* fear, or, the fear of displeasing God; for, the more we love God, the more we reverence him and fear to offend him. The very *powers tremble*, and are seized with reverential awe, in his presence; are we not all recommended to "work out our salvation with fear and trembling?"

19. "Let us, therefore, love God." The Greek has not "therefore," nor "God," it runs thus: "let us love him, because *he* first loved us." The Alexandrian MS. supports the Vulgate. According to our reading, the Apostle now addresses to us the same exhortation to love God, which, in verse 11, he addresses to us, regarding the love of our neighbour, grounded on the same reason, viz., the pure and gratuitous love of God for us, manifested, in a special manner, in the Incarnation of his Son—"Because he first loved us," which shows the inseparable connexion that exists between the love of God and of our neighbour. The Greek for, "let us love," αγαπωμεν, may be also rendered, *we love*.

20. In this verse, the Apostle points out the test which God requires of our love for himself, and he shows by an argument, *a minore ad majus*, that no one can love God and hate his brother.

"If any man say, I love God, and hateth his brother," if he say it, either in word, or conceive it in his mind, such a man "is a liar," he both says and conceives what is perfectly untrue; he imagines two things to co-exist, which are perfectly incompatible, "for he that loveth not his brother whom he sees," (the Apostle puts *loving not*—when and where it is a matter of duty to manifest our love for our neighbour—and *hating him*, on the same footing), if a man cannot love the visible image of God, viz., "his brother whom he sees," whom the knowledge of his wants, together with a sense of mutual dependence, as well as the participation of the same common nature, should induce him to love and relieve in his necessities; if, in one word, he cannot

Text.

21. And this commandment we have from God, that he, who loveth God, love also his brother.　.

Paraphrase.

21. Moreover, no one can love God and violate his commandments; now, it is a commandment of God, that we should love our brother. Hence, no one can hate his brother and love God.

Commentary.

comply with the more easy, and to him, the more natural branch of the precept of charity, how can he discharge the more difficult, in loving "God whom he sees not," who is placed far beyond the reach of the senses? And, although the supernatural love of our neighbour be not more easy than the love of God, since it is on account of God we love our neighbour, and hence, the supernatural love of him involves the love of God; still, as natural affection would appear to precede in the mind the love of charity, the man who has not natural affection proves that he is wholly indisposed for the love of charity.

21. Another reason why a man cannot love God and hate his neighbour, is that the best proof we can give of our love of God is, the observance of his commandments. "If you love me," says our blessed Lord, "keep my commandments." Now, it is one of God's commandments, that we should love our brethren, as we love ourselves. The man, therefore, who hates his brother, or does not love him as he ought, that is to say, "in deed and truth," or relieve him in his necessities, such a man violates the commandments; and, therefore, cannot love God.

CHAPTER V.

Analysis.

In this chapter, the Apostle continues his exhortation to brotherly love ; he considers our brethren as sons of God, and under this respect, he exhorts us to love them, since our love of the Father involves the love of his sons (verse 1). He gives a mark for knowing that we love our neighbour, viz., if we love God himself and observe his commandments (2). The surest test of our loving God himself is to keep his commandments, and this duty is not too grievous to the sons of God, aided by his actual graces (3). He shows that His commandments are not grievous to the sons of God, since, every description of persons born of Him have conquered the world, and thus observed his precepts, and the instrumental cause of this victory is faith (4), viz., the faith in Christ, as God and man (5).

The Apostle next proves Christ to be Saviour of the world, of whom the Prophets predicted, that he would redeem mankind by water and blood,—and the Holy Ghost also, on divers occasions, testified that he was true God and true man (6). He next adduces three undoubted witnesses in heaven (7), and three witnesses on earth, to prove the Divinity and Humanity of Jesus Christ (8). He contrasts the superior excellence of the Divine testimony with the testimony of men, which is considered, in some cases, as final and decisive (9).

He tacitly exhorts and stimulates them to persevere in the faith of Christ, by pointing out the advantage of this faith, and the spiritual and eternal ruin which its rejection entails on us (10). One of the fruits of this true faith is, eternal life (11, 12). Another result of this faith is, a firm confidence of obtaining from God the objects of our lawful petitions (14, 15).

He takes occasion, from the mention of the confidence with which all true Christians should approach the throne of God, to recommend the exercise of charity in behalf of their sinning brethren. He tells them to pray confidently for such persons ; for, in certain cases, their prayers will be attended to. He does not hold out the same encouragement in case our brethren may fall into sins of a certain description which he calls " sins unto death" (16). He points out the blessings exclusively enjoyed by the children of God—they are preserved from sin and the tyranny of the devil, and they only are thus favoured (18, 19). He shows the source of these blessings—Christ our Saviour (20). He cautions them against idol worship (21).

Text.

1. WHOSOEVER believeth that Jesus is the Christ, is born of God. And every one that loveth him who begot, loveth him also who is born of him.

Paraphrase.

1. Every one who believes that Jesus is the long expected Messiah promised by the prophets, is spiritually born of God by sanctifying grace, and every one who loves the Father, loves also his Son, whether natural or adopted.

Commentary.

1. The Apostle here inculcates brotherly love, on the ground, that our brethren are sons of God, but this does not exclude from our love such of them as are not sons of

Text.

2. In this we know that we love the children of God : when we love God, and keep his commandments.

3. For this is the charity of God, that we keep his commandments : and his commandments are not heavy.

4. For whatsoever is born of God, overcometh the world : And this is

Paraphrase.

2. And by this we can know that we love the children of God, viz., by our loving God himself and observing his commandments.

3. And the surest test we can have that we love God is, the observance of his commandments, and these commandments, whether viewed in contrast with the heavy yoke of the ceremonial law of the Jews, or considered in themselves, are not onerous to the sons of God, aided by actual grace.

4. For, every description of persons, spiritually born of God, be they young or old, male or female,

Commentary.

God ; for, these are to be loved so as to be made sons of God and true brethren in Christ. " Whosoever believeth that Jesus is the Christ," that is, the long-expected Messiah, and of course reduces this faith to practice ; "is born of God," has received of him the new spiritual birth through sanctifying grace which imparts to him a new essence, and makes him "partaker of the divine nature," (2 Peter, i.) Under the faith that " Jesus is the Christ," is most probably contained the belief in all the other points of revealed doctrine ; and the truths of Christ's divine mission is prominently put forward, because called in question by the heretics of the day. " Is born of God ;" this being an affirmative proposition, of course, only implies, that he is such. all other conditions being observed ; " and every one that loveth him who begot," that is, the Father, " loveth him also who is born of him," viz., the Son, be he natural or adopted. Some persons restrict the words, " him who is born of him," to Christ, the natural Son of God. It is better, however, to give it a general signification of an adage or maxim, in use among men, referring to fathers and sons generally.

2. The Apostle, in this verse, applies to a particular case, viz., as regards the children of God, the adage employed in a general sense, as regarding all fathers and sons in the preceding. In the foregoing part of this Epistle, he gave it as a sign and argument of our loving God, if we loved our neighbour. Now, by an argument, *e converso*, he shows, that if we love God, we love our neighbour, the love of both being inseparable ; for, the motive of both is the very same, as has been shown (iv. 12). It may often happen, that the love of God may be better known at one time, and the love of our neighbour at another, according to the nature of our immediate occupation; according as we may be engaged in acts immediately affecting the divine honour, or, in relieving human misery. "And keep his commandments ;" this he adds to the words, " we love God," lest any person should deceive himself by imagining that he can love God, without fulfilling his precepts.

3. The best proof we can afford that we love God is to keep his commandments ; for, whosoever sincerely loves God, will, influenced by that love, observe all his other precepts. And lest any one should be disheartened by the test of God's love required by the Apostle, he says, " his commandments are not heavy," which words are understood by some, in a relative sense, as compared with the heavy yoke of the Ceremonial Law of the Jews, " which neither they nor their fathers could bear," and was abrogated by Christ ; the precepts of the New Law are not heavy. Or, although many precepts in the New Law be repugnant to the feelings of corrupt nature (*v.g.*)—taking up our cross, renouncing ourselves, losing our lives, &c. ; still, they are rendered light by God's grace, and the stimulating examples of Christ and his saints. Moreover, it is likely, as appears from the entire context, that the Apostle refers to such as are sons of God, and in sanctifying grace, and love him ; and to such, persons nothing is " *heavy*," or burdensome. Hence, St. Paul calls all present tribulations, as compared with eternal bliss, "*light and momentary*" (2 Cor. iv. 17). If the commandments of God are not " *heavy*," none of them, therefore, is *impossible*, as has been taught by Jansenius.

4. " For whatsoever is born of God." " Whatsoever," that is, every description of persons born of God—and this favours the interpretation of the preceding verse, which understands it of all the sons of God—" overcometh the world," with all its

the victory which overcometh the world, our faith.

Jew or Gentile, have overcome the world, and renounced all its false maxims—to such, therefore, the commandments of God are not heavy—and the instrumental cause by which this victory over the world is obtained, is our faith.

5. Who is he that overcometh the world, but he that believeth that Jesus is the Son of God?

5. And what faith is it that overcomes the world, but Christian faith, of which the belief in the Divinity of Jesus Christ, the eternal Son of God, is the foundation?

6. This is he that came by water and blood, Jesus Christ: not by water only, but by water and blood. And it is the Spirit which testifieth, that Christ is the truth.

6. This is he, who has come into the world, Jesus Christ, God and man, to save us according to the prediction of the Prophets, by the water of baptism and the blood of his passion, and not by water only, as came the Baptist, whose baptism had only the effect of preparing men for penance, but by water and blood. And we have also the testimony of the Holy Ghost, bearing witness to the truth of Christ's Divinity and Humanity.

Commentary.

temptations, seductive maxims, and ruling principles, "the concupiscence of the flesh," &c. (ii. 16). To such, therefore, the commandments of God are not heavy. He next points out the source of victory, viz., "our faith," since faith alone is the foundation of all those graces which enable us to overcome the world; it alone obtains for us those necessary graces; without it no one can ever have the means necessary for overcoming the world.

5 "Who is he that overcometh the world," &c.—In other words, no one can have the faith whereby the world is overcome except he who believes "that Jesus is the Son of God." The Apostle shows, in this verse, what the faith is, to which he refers, it is the faith of which the belief in Christ's Divinity is the foundation. Of course, he supposes this Christian, victorious faith, to be an operative faith, a faith enlivened by charity, and he refers to the article regarding the Divinity of Christ in a special manner, both here and in other parts of this Epistle, in consequence of the leading errors of the day being specially levelled against this—the foundation of the Christian religion.

6. The Apostle here proves, that Christ is the long expected Messiah, the Son of God. "Jesus Christ," God and man, the Saviour of the world, who, as the prophets predicted, was about to redeem mankind by his blood, and expiate their sins in the waters of Baptism (Ezechiel, xxxvi. 25, &c., xlvii.; Zach. xii. 13). "This is he that came" (or, as the Greek, ὁ ἐλθών implies, *this is the man long expected to come*), "by water and blood," to redeem the world, and spiritually regenerate mankind "by water" of baptism "and blood" of his passion, of which the baptism in water, and purifications by the shedding of blood, among the Jews, were so many significant types and figures. "Not by water only," in which allusion is evidently made to the Baptist, of whom it is everywhere pointedly asserted by the Evangelist—and the same is repeatedly asserted by himself—that he came to baptize in water only, and that he was sent by God for this purpose, and his baptism did not of itself remit sin, as it most probably, was a mere preparation for penance, and for the true baptism instituted by Christ. "But by water and blood." He came "by water," because he instituted baptism of water, whereof that which issued from his side while hanging on the cross was a sign; and "by blood," poured forth on the cross, from which baptism, and all the other channels of divine grace, derive their efficacy. "And it is the Spirit that testifieth, that Christ is the truth"; to the testimony of the water and blood, the Apostle adds that of the Holy Ghost, who testified to the Divinity of Christ, during his sacred life, working wonders in proof thereof; and after his death and resurrection, when descending on the Apostles, in the form of fiery tongues, he filled them with his graces, he also bore testimony to the same. in the many gifts which he bestowed on the faithful. In the Greek reading the words run thus : καὶ τὸ πνεῦμα ἐστιν τὸ μαρτυροῦν, ὅτι τὸ πνεῦμα

Text.

7. And there are three who give testimony in heaven, the Father, the Word, and the Holy Ghost. And these three are one.

8. And there are three that give testimony on earth : the spirit, and the water and the blood, and these three are one.

Paraphrase.

7. For, there are three *divine* and *uncreated* witnesses, who, in heaven and from heaven, bear testimony both to angels and men, that Christ is true God and true man, and the Saviour of the world, viz. ; the Father, the Word (or Son), and the Holy Ghost, and these, although three in Person, are one in Nature.

8. And there are three *earthly* and *created* witnesses that bear testimony on earth to the reality of the same Divinity and Humanity in Jesus Christ, viz., the water, and blood, that issued from his side on the cross. and his soul which he breathed forth, when expiring ; and these three witnesses concur in one and the same testimony.

Commentary.

εστιν, η αληθεια "and it is the Spirit that testifieth, because the *Spirit* is truth," according to which the meaning is : the Holy Ghost also bears testimony, that Christ is the expected Messiah and Saviour of the world, and this testimony is of the greatest weight, because the Holy Ghost is essential truth. The Vulgate reading is, however, preferable, since the question regards the truth of Christ's Divinity and Humanity ; both of which are necessary to constitute him the true Saviour of the world.

7. The Apostle now adduces the most incontrovertible evidence of the truth of his assertion made in the foregoing verse, viz., that Jesus Christ was the long-expected Messiah, true God and true man, who was to come and redeem mankind. The witnesses here adduced are *divine* witnesses. (Such is the meaning of "in heaven," as contradistinguished from "on earth," next verse), viz., the three Adorable Persons of the Trinity, "the Father," who bore testimony to Christ (Matthew, i. 21 ; iii. 17 ; xvii. 5 ; John, xii. 28) :—"the Word," that is, the Son. He bore testimony that he was himself the Messiah promised by the Father, and proved it by repeated miracles (John, chap. v., verses 17, 36 ; viii. 14, 25 ; x. 25) ;—and finally, he testified that he was the Son of God in presence of the High Priest, during his sacred Passion. "And the Holy Ghost." The Holy Ghost testified, that Christ was the only begotten Son of God, and in his assumed nature, the Saviour of the world, viz., at his baptism by John, on the day of Pentecost ; and in the abundant effusion of his heavenly gifts, on many occasions.

"And these three are one." These three witnesses, who "in heaven," and from heaven, give a testimony certain beyond all doubt, regarding Christ's Divinity and Humanity, His Mediatorial and Redemptory qualities, as man-God, although distinct in Person, are one and indivisible in the same divine nature and essence. The word "one" is taken in the same sense in which it is taken in chap. x. of John, where our Redeemer says, "*I and the Father are* ONE," that is, we possess the same power and the same divine essence. Hence, the evidence which St. John here adduces is that of the Godhead, three in Person and one in nature.

8. And there are three *earthly* and *created* witnesses (such is the meaning of "on earth," as contrasted with "in heaven," in the preceding verse), viz., "the Spirit," that is, the *created soul* of Christ, which he breathed forth with a loud cry upon the cross ; from the mode in which this happened, the Centurion cried out, "*truly this man was the Son of God.*" (Mark, xv. 39), "and the water and the blood." The "water"—the first and chiefest of material elements—which flowed from his side extended on the cross, and the "blood"—the first of the four humours whereby animated creatures live—which likewise flowed therefrom, and which he abundantly shed during his entire Passion, proved him to have a true body. He had, then, a true body and a soul ("spirit,") These three witnesses, therefore, prove him to be a real man. They also prove him to be truly God also ; since the very mode in which he expired convinced the Centurion at the foot of the cross of this ; and his laying down his life *freely*, and reuniting, by an astonishing effort of his own power. his soul and body in his Resurrection, the circumstances, and mode, and time of which he predicted before-

Commentary.

hand, also proves the same. "And these three are one," that is (as is more clearly expressed in the Greek, εἰς τὸ ἕν εἰσιν, *unto one*); they conspire together and concur in one and the same testimony, viz., that Jesus Christ is both God and man.

The authenticity of this passage, from the words of verse 7, "in heaven," to the words of verse 8, "on earth," inclusively, has been disputed, and has given rise to several learned critical dissertations, for and against. It may be fairly asserted that, at the opening of the present century, there existed a preponderance of Protestant opinion both at home and abroad, in favour of its genuineness. The preponderance of Protestant opinion, however, of late years has been the other way. This change of opinion among Protestants is attributable to the prevalence of the rationalistic and infidel spirit, which of late has so generally infected the cultivated Protestant mind.

But as regards Catholics, while freely indulging in critical researches, which, fairly followed up, only serve to throw additional light in every department of science, on God's revelation, to which natural truth can never be opposed (for, God, the source of all truth, it is that "enlightens every man ")—whether naturally or supernaturally—"that cometh into this world ;)" they feel that the genuineness of the above passage is clearly decided for them, after the twofold Decree of the Council of Trent; one, on the subject of inspired Scriptures (" *De Canonicis Scripturis* "); the other, on the authenticity of the Vulgate, " *De Editione et usu Sacrorum librorum* " (SS. iv.) The Decree regarding the Canonical Scriptures, after enumerating the several books which are to be regarded as inspired Scripture, concludes with these words : " *But should any one not receive as Sacred and Canonical the entire books themselves, with all their parts, as they were wont to be read in the Catholic Church, and are found in the old Latin Vulgate edition......let him be anathema.*" Now, whatever latitude of interpretation may be allowed in regard to the words, " *with all their parts,*" as also in regard to the authenticity of the Latin Vulgate, as decreed by the Council, one thing seems beyond all question or doubt, viz., that all texts or passages establishing a doctrine of faith or a precept of morals must be included. For, the very object which the Council professes (*loco citato*) to have in view, in issuing the above Decree in its present form, as well as the subjoined Decree on the authenticity of the Vulgate, was to show that, in its future definitions regarding faith or morals, the Council employed the revealed word of God. Hence, dogmatic texts, like the one in question, are clearly included. Now, the disputed words, " *were wont to be read in the Catholic Church.*" They are solemnly read in the Epistle of Low Sunday and in the 8th Responsory of Matins, in the office of all Sundays, from Trinity to Advent. They are also "*found in the old Vulgate Latin edition.*" The definition of the Council regarding the integrity of the several books, contained in the Canon of SS. Scriptures, and the authenticity of the Vulgate was grounded on the constant and public use made by the Church of these books, as contained in the Vulgate Edition ; and considering the divine constitution of the Church, and the promises of inerrancy divinely accorded to her, we cannot suppose, for a moment, that, consistently with such promises, she could admit on the Canon of SS. Scriptures, or venerate as the word of God, to be employed, as such, in her definitions of faith, in her instructions to the people, in her ritualistic Decrees, &c., what was, in reality, but the word of man.

But, apart from the unerring authority of the Church, the genuineness of this passage regarding the three heavenly witnesses can be proved from the most unexceptionable testimony.

In the Western Church it has been quoted as Divine Scripture from the earliest period. In the 3rd century, we have Tertullian *adv. Praxeam* (ch. xxv.) " ita connexus Patris in Filio et Filii in Paracleto tres efficit coherentes "..." qui tres *unum* sint," " non *unus.*" St. Cyprian (3rd century) ad *Jubaianum,* Ep. lxxiii., "cum tres unum sint," &c. The same Father, *de Unitate Ecclesiæ,* says, " Et iterum de Patre......Scriptum est." Et hi tres unum sunt (1 Joan, verse 7). We are assured by St. Fulgentius, in the beginning of the 6th century, that, in these words, St. Cyprian referred to the 7th verse of 5th chapter of St. John.

St. Jerome (5th century) in his prologue to the Canonical Epistles, refers to the genuineness of this verse, and to the clear proof of the Trinity which it contains.

In the *Speculum* of St. Augustine (contemporary of St. Jerome), the words of verse

Commentary.

7, are quoted more than once as Divine Scripture, and a proof of the Trinity founded on them. Some very learned critics assert that this *Speculum* is the genuine production of St. Augustine. At all events, the great antiquity of the work is admitted on all hands, and the text in question must surely be known to him, as it would be absurd to suppose him ignorant of a dogmatic text. quoted 50 years after his death by over 400 African Bishops in their Profession of Faith, in 484, addressed to King Hunneric. St. Augustine's *silence* elsewhere regarding this verse, may be accounted for on this ground, that it was the Italic version, which was but a *recension* of the African, St. Augustine used. It was in Italy, he first learned the Scriptures on his conversion, and it was the Italic recension, to which he was so partial, he used after he returned home. Now, in this latter, the words in question, from some accident, were wanting. In his *Speculum*, intended for the unlearned, he uses the African version, to which the people were accustomed, and in which these words are found. In his Tracts on the Epistles of St. John these words are wanting, as these Tracts concluded with the first verses of chapter 5, before he came to treat of verse 7.

Neither does he refer to the Second and Third Epistles of St. John for the same reason. Vigilius, of Thapsus (end of 5th century) quotes the words of verse 7, *De Trinitate.*

About the same time (A.D. 484), Eugene of Carthage, in obedience to the Edict of Hunneric, the Arian King of the Vandals. presented to him a Profession of Faith framed by a Council of more than four hundred Bishops, from Africa and the Islands of Corsica, Sardinia. &c., of whom many endured exile and tortures, as confessors of the Faith. In the *second* part of this Profession they quote the words of verse 7 (they make no reference to them in the *first* part of that Profession which referred to the Consubstantiality of the Word), and addressing this Arian persecutor, they unhesitatingly assert, that the refutation of Arianism which the words of verse 7 contained, was "*luce clarius*" (*clearer than light*). Surely, they would not have ventured to speak thus confidently, had the slightest doubt of the genuineness of the words existed in their minds, or even on the part of the Arians themselves. Nor is it to be supposed that the Arians. if any doubt existed on this head, would have allowed the words to pass unchallenged, as they did, without the slightest stricture or animadversion.

Fulgentius (6th century) quotes the words (*de Trinitate*) also in his "decima Responsio contra Arianos"—in which he refers to St. Cyprian as quoting this verse 7 in his Treatise, *de Unitate Ecclesiæ.*

Besides the African, we have other Churches of the West bearing testimony from the earliest date. In the Church of Spain, we have the words of verse 7 quoted in the "*Collectio testimoniorum Scripturæ et Patrum*" which most learned critics believe to be more ancient than St. Isidore ; they are quoted also in the famous *Codex Toletanus* of the Bible in the 8th century, also by Etherius, *Contra Elipandum.* They are also quoted by St. Isidore himself. "Testimonia Scripturæ *de distinctione personarum.*"

In Italy, towards the middle of the 6th century, Cassiodorus, the most learned man of his day, who evinced the greatest zeal and industry, and had the most ample opportunities, besides, in procuring the best MSS., Greek and Latin, and collating the most accurate readings, one with another, quotes verse 7, in his *Complexiones*, or brief notes on the Epistles, &c.

Italy, too, furnishes further most important evidence. We are informed by the learned Cardinal Wiseman (*Two Letters on* 1 *John, verse* 7, 1832-3), that in the Monastery *della Cava* between Naples and Salerno, was found an old Latin MS., which Cardinal Maia, and himself refer to the 7th or 8th century, in which this verse 7 was read. Cardinal Wiseman gives the quotation, of which the following is a portion :— Quia tres sunt qui testimonium dant in terra. Spiritus et aqua et sanguis ; et nii tres hunum sunt in Xho. ihu. Et tres sunt qui testimonium dicunt in cœlo. Pater verbum et Sps., et, hii tres hunum sunt. Si testimonium hominum, &c.

The Cardinal calls attention to the fact of the 8th verse being placed before the 7th in this MS. and he quotes the words of Griesbach to show that this is the case in the oldest MSS.—"Antiquiores fere anteponunt Comnia Octavum Septimo." This fully answers the negative argument founded by some adversaries on the

Commentary.

8th verse being found in some MSS. after the 6th. They should prove besides, that the 7th verse is not found after the 8th in the MSS. referred to, as is the case in the above quotation.

From time out of mind this verse 7 was recited in the Roman Liturgy as may be inferred from St. Bernard (*Sermo* II., *in Octava Paschæ.*) Rupertus (12th century), *de Divinis " Officiis Lib.* xiii. *c.* xvii. Durandus (13th century), *Rational. Div. Offic. Lib.* vi. *c.* xxvii.

The Fourth Council of Lateran, at which some Greek Bishops, and the Procurators of others, assisted, quotes it unhesitatingly, as SS. Scripture.

It is quoted as furnishing a dogmatic proof in the Decretals. Cap. *damnamus de Summa Trinitate, lib.* i. *tit.* i. *c.* i. ; also *de Celebratione Missæ.* Cap. *in quodam, lib.* iii. *tit.* xli., &c.

It is quoted in the prologue to the Canonical Epistles attributed to St. Jerome.

It was commented on by ancient Interpreters, without hesitation. St. Bernard, the Master of Sentences, St. Bonaventure, St. Thomas. It is to be observed that St. Thomas, in his Exposition of the Decretal, *de Summa Trinitate*, against the Abbot Joachim, says—as is stated in a marginal note of the Complutensian Polyglot—that the words, " hi tres unum sunt," in reference to the earthly witnesses, were added by the Arians, which shows he regarded the rest as genuine.

The clear and uniform testimony of the African Fathers and writers from the earliest date in favour of the genuineness of verse 7 is of the utmost importance, as it proves that these words were found in the early African Latin Version of the Vulgate, in existence before the days of Tertullian, who quotes from it. Now, this early African Latin Version represents a Greek MS., from which the version was made, of an earlier date than any Greek MS. of the Scripture now extant.

It is proved by Cardinal Wiseman, in one of the letters referred to, that Africa was the birth-place of the first Latin version of the Scriptures. In Africa, it was most needed. For, at Rome, Greek was extensively cultivated among all classes, as we are informed by Juvenal (*Sat.* 6). Greek was the language employed by the earliest Ecclesiastical writers in Rome. A Latin version of the Scriptures was not so much needed there as in Africa, whose earliest Ecclesiastical writers wrote in Latin. Moreover, Cardinal Wiseman (*loco citato*) adduces several examples of peculiar phrases and constructions, clearly *Africanisms*, or African idioms, employed in the Vulgate, for the purpose of showing that the original version was made in Africa, of which the Italian was a mere *Recension*. The fact of the words of verse 7 being found in this old African version, is the strongest argument in its favour. It being wanted in the Italian Vulgate, besides being a mere negative argument, might be accounted for on the grounds of its being passed over by the copyist. It is easier to suppose its omission on account of *Homoioteleuton* and other causes, than for its insertion, if it were not found in the original Greek MS. ; the more so, as there is question of a public record in public use from the earliest ages in the Church, containing a fundamental law of Christian faith, warmly disputed by heretics from the very beginning.

The arguments against are mostly, if not all, of a *negative* character. In view of the strong *positive* arguments in favour of this text, these negative arguments should contain the most overwhelming evidence, and considering that the text in question was a public document, in public use, it is sufficient to assign probable grounds for its omission in some MSS., and for the silence of some Fathers in regard to it. When our adversaries assert that a reading common to all the Church, and even to heretics and schismatics, is spurious and an interpolation, they should prove this to demonstration. Some Fathers, who omitted quoting these words in their disputations with heretics, did so, not because they were ignorant of its existence, but because they did not want it, having abundance of other texts to prove their point, and this in a special manner is true when the Divinity of the Son of God alone was questioned. It was only when speaking of the entire Trinity they used it. This is true of Iræneus, Clement of Alexandria, Dionysius of Alexandria, Leo in his Epistle to Flavian, although he must have well known the existence of such a leading Dogmatic text, quoted by Cassiodorus shortly after his death. Leo quotes verse 8 after verse 6 ; but this was the connection in his copy of the SS. Scriptures—moreover, verse 7 did not

Text.

9. If we receive the testimony of men, the testimony of God is greater. For this is the testimony of God, which is greater, because he hath testified of his Son.

10. He that believeth in the Son of God, hath the testimony of God in himself. He that believeth not the Son, maketh him a liar : because he believeth not in the testimony which God hath testified of his Son.

11. And this is the testimony,

Paraphrase.

9. But, if we admit the testimony of two or three men, as conclusive on any subject, how much more weight should we not attach to the undoubted testimony of God the Father. Now, the testimony of God has been pledged in favour of the divinity of his Son (Matthew, iii. 17 ; xvii. 25, &c.)

10. He that believeth that Jesus is the Son of God and the Word Incarnate, has within himself, and firmly assents to, the testimony of God the Father regarding him, and thus honours the Father ; whereas, he that does not believe him to be the Son of God, insults and outrages the veracity of God, by making him a liar, since he does not believe the testimony which he has borne regarding his son, but rather rejects it, as if it were false.

11. And a portion of the testimony of the Father

Commentary.

bear on his subject. Most likely, some Fathers omitted quoting it, seeing it was disputed, as they had other texts in abundance to prove their point.

Its disappearance from the leading Greek MSS., the Vatican (B), Alexandrian (A), and Sinaitic, which are generally referred to the fourth or fifth century, may be ascribed to the hurry or negligence of copyists, to *Homoioteleuton ;* possibly, to the artifices of heretics, who may have corrupted the copies that came into their hands, and these multiplied in the transcription. At all events, the positive arguments in its favour, and especially that founded on its being read in almost all Latin editions of the earliest date, far outweigh, putting the authority of the Church altogether aside, all the negative arguments against it. Its insertion, in case it were spurious, would be utterly unaccountable, as Catholics needed it not to prove Catholic doctrine, having an abundant supply of other texts for the purpose.—(*Vide* Franzelin, *de Deo Trino ;* Perrone, &c.)

9. By an argument, *a minori ad magus,* he sets forth, in a still clearer light the weight of the Divine testimony, which he adduces in verse 7. If the testimony of two or three witnesses, taken from among men, be regarded as final and decisive on any subject, " *in the mouth of two or three witnesses every word shall stand,*" (Deut. xix. 15), how much more authoritative must not the testimony of God the Father be, when joined to the concordant testimony of the two other Persons of the Adorable Trinity. Now, " this is the testimony of God, which is greater," viz., that which " he has borne concerning his Son," (*which is greater,* is not in the Greek). The ordinary Greek copies, in place of, " BECAUSE he hath testified," have, ην μεμαρτυρηκε, *which he hath testified,* as if he said the testimony of the Father, to which I refer, is that which regards the Son. When it was, that the Father had borne this testimony, has been already shown (verse 7). The Alexandrian and Vatican MSS. support the Vulgate, and have ὅτι μεμαρτυρηκεν.

10. In this verse is contained a tacit exhortation to embrace and retain the faith regarding Jesus Christ, which the Apostle has been proposing throughout this chapter, in refutation of the errors of the day, viz., that he is true God and true man, the Saviour and Mediator given by God to mankind—" he that believeth in the Son of God," in the sense now explained, " hath the testimony of God in himself," that is, firmly assents to what God testified, and thereby honours him by doing homage to his veracity. The words " of God," are omitted in the Greek, they are, however, found in the Alexandrian MS. On the other hand, " he that believeth not the Son," (in Greek, " he that believeth not *God,*" ὁ μὴ πιστευων τῳ Θεῳ· the Alexandrian MS. favours the Vulgate) ; he that refuses to believe that Jesus Christ is the Son of God, " maketh him a liar," proclaims by this unbelief that God is a liar, having borne testimony to what is false, " because he believeth not in the testimony which God had testified." He believes not what God has testified " of his Son," viz., that Jesus is his Son, and the Saviour of the world ; but rejects it as false, as if God were a liar.

11. " And this is the testimony," that is, the following is a part of the testimony

<table>
<tr><th>Text.</th><th>Paraphrase.</th></tr>
</table>

Text.

that God hath given to us eternal life. And this life is in his Son.

12. He that hath the Son, hath life. He that hath not the Son, hath not life.

13. These things I write to you, that you may know that you have eternal life, you who believe in the name of the Son of God.

14. And this is the confidence

Paraphrase.

regarding Jesus, is this, that he has given us, who believe in him, and obey his law, the life of grace here, which is a certain pledge of glory, and he will surely give us eternal life hereafter, and this life of grace and of glory is attributable to the saving merits of his Son.

12. He that has the Son residing in him, owing to his lively operative faith, has within himself the fountain of all grace, and the source of eternal life. On the other hand, he that has not this lively operative faith in the Son of God, has no claim or title to eternal life.

13. These things I have written to you, regarding the utility and necessity of faith in Christ, in order that you who believe in the Son of God, may know that you have here a sure claim to eternal life, and may thus be stimulated to perseverance in the same faith.

14. Another result of our sincere faith in Christ is,

Commentary.

which the Father "hath testified of his Son," (verse 10), or the result of our faith in this testimony is, "that God had given to us eternal life," in its certain seed, viz., sanctifying grace, in hope here, and in the actual possession of it hereafter. "And this life is in his Son," that is, his Son is the meritorious cause of the graces which God imparts to us here, and of our glory hereafter. The practical advantage, resulting to us from God's testimony, concerning his Son, and from our faith in it, is life eternal, which is to be obtained through his merits ; he, therefore, is justly entitled to be termed our Saviour.

12. The Apostle, here, again exhorts them to have faith in Jesus Christ, on the grounds both of its great utility, "hath life," and of its necessity, "he that hath not," &c., "hath not life."

"He that hath the Son," means, he that believes in the Son of God, and, of course, it is understood, obeys his law, thus having a faith that worketh by charity , hath life, has within himself the source, and a sure pledge of eternal life. Whereas, " he that hath not the Son of God," either by not believing in him, or who, although he believes, still, obeys not his law, whose faith, therefore, is dead and inoperative, such a man "hath not life." *There is no other name under heaven, given to men, wherein they may be saved* (Acts, iv. 12), "*no one comes to the Father but by me,*" (John, xiv.) The Apostle thus particularly insists on the necessity of faith in Christ, owing to the errors of the time, which were specially directed against this fundamental point of belief.

13. "These things," which have been mentioned in the preceding verse, "I write to you," (in Greek, ἔγραψα, *I have written to you*), " that you may know, that you have eternal life," that is, a claim to eternal life, and a sure earnest here, which, however, is not inamissible ; "you who believe in the name of his Son," or, in his Son himself. *Name*, is used for the person named. In some Greek copies, these words, *and that you may believe in the name of the Son of God*, are added, and must mean, unless we fall into a useless tautology, that you may persevere in the same belief, which you hold at present. The same is, however, sufficiently implied in our version, since it was to encourage them to persevere in the faith, notwithstanding the allurements of pleasure and the pressure of persecution, that he writes these things. The words are wanting in the Alexandrian and Vatican MSS., which support the Vulgate reading. Similar are the words of the gospel : " *These things are written that you may believe that Jesus is the Christ the Son of God ; and that believing you may have life in his name.*— (John. xx. 31).

14. Another fruit of our sincere faith in the testimony of the Father regarding his Son, Jesus Christ, is a strong feeling of confidence, which springs from this faith, that

Text.	Paraphrase.
which we have towards him : That, whatsoever we shall ask according to his will, he heareth us.	an assured confidence which we have regarding him, that whenever we ask anything of him, which is conformable to his will, both as to the object and manner of petition, he hears us, as far as it may be expedient for our true welfare.
15. And we know that he heareth us whatsoever we ask : we know that we have the petitions which we request of him.	15. And not only have we confidence, but we know that he will hear us in regard to whatever we shall ask of him (of course, according to his will), for, we know that he has granted the petitions which we have heretofore made to him.

Commentary.

whatever we ask of him, he will hear us, provided it be "according to his will." In order that our prayers should have the effect of infallible impetration, certain conditions are required ; for, sometimes, we do not obtain the fruit of our prayers, "*because we ask amiss*" (St. James, chap. i.) One general condition, in which all the others are included, is, that our prayers "*be according to God's will*," and the will of God is, first, as regards the *object* of petition, that it be necessary or useful for our salvation ; if there be a question of temporal blessings, they should be petitioned for always *conditionally*, with a spirit of conformity to God's holy will. Spiritual blessings, whether necessary or useful, are to be petitioned for absolutely. Secondly, as regards the *mode* of offering up our prayers, "the will of God" is, that they be presented with *piety* and *perseverance ; piety* implies, first, a certain and undoubted faith in all that God had revealed in general, as also a particular faith that God would grant us the effect of our lawful petitions, as far as it may be expedient for us—a firm confidence in obtaining the effect of our petition grounded on God's fidelity, liberality, and mercy—attention and devotion in presenting our petition—also, the virtue of humility. Piety also implies, that a man is in the state of grace, or at least, disposed to return to God by penance. It is needless to add, that the condition of *perseverance* in prayer is almost everywhere recommended and inculcated in the SS. Scriptures. Besides the above mentioned conditions, St. Augustine and St. Thomas require, in order that prayer would be *infallibly* impetratory, that a man pray for *himself ;* for, says St. Augustine, the promise is, "*dabit vobis*," "he will give it to *you*" (John, xvi.) And, moreover, our neighbour, in whose behalf we offer up our prayers, may place an obstacle to its effect. Hence, according to them, it is only to prayer in behalf of one's self, the promise of infallibly granting a request is made. Others do not require this latter condition for the infallible efficacy of prayer. In a just man, prayer, as a work supernaturally good, is meritorious of a reward *de condigno*, but whether, in a just man or sinner, who wishes to be converted, it is infallibly impetratory, if accompanied with the requisite conditions ; and this infallible effect is not founded on God's justice, but on his mercy and simple fidelity.

15. Here he repeats the same thing asserted in verse 14 ; and, he says, that we have not only confidence, but we know, that he hears us "whatsoever we ask." Of course, it is implied, that we ask "according to God's will." This knowledge is grounded on the experience which we have, that our past prayers have been heard, and our past petitions granted by him, "we know that we have the petitions which we request of him ;" for, "we request," it is in the ordinary Greek, ητηκαμεν, "*we requested*," as if we had a certain guarantee of being heard in future, in the fact of our having been heard by him on past occasions. In the Greek, the particle "if," is used in the first part of the verse, thus, και ἐάν οιδαμεν, "*and if we know, that he heareth us, whatsoever we ask, we know that we have the petitions which we have requested of him.*" Estius supposes, that the same particle "if," is understood in the latter member of this verse also, and that the whole sense is completed in verse 16, according to the Greek reading, thus : "*If* we know that he heareth us..., and *if* we know that we have the petitions," &c., then the conclusion is, "*that if any man know his brother to sin*," verse 16, "*let him ask*" for him. This would appear to be the construction and meaning according to the

Text.

16. He that knoweth his brother to sin a sin *which is* not to death, let him ask, and life shall be given to him, who sinneth not to death. There is a sin unto death : for that I say not that any man ask.

Paraphrase.

16. Should, then, a person know that his Christian brother has committed a mortal sin, which is not a sin unto death, let him pray for him, and the spiritual life of grace, whereof the commission of such a sin has deprived his brother, will be restored to him, whose sin does not contain the peculiar malignity of being unto death. I say, *whose sin is not unto death ;* for, there is such a thing as a sin unto death ; in case a brother commit a sin of this sort, I do not tell every one to pray for such a person with the same confidence he would have in praying for the remission of the sin which is not unto death.

Commentary.

Greek reading referred to. The Vatican MS. has *και αν οιδαμεν*, in support of the Vulgate.

16. This verse is a conclusion drawn from the two preceding verses, thus : since we have confidence, and know that God will hear our petitions in future, as he has heard them on former occasions, I recommend to you, therefore, the exercise of fraternal charity towards your sinning brethren ; "he that knoweth his brother to sin " (in Greek, *εαν τις ιδη τον αδελφον αυτου αμαρτανοντα if any one shall see his brother sinning*) "a sin which is not unto death, let him ask, and life shall be given " to such a brother, at his request. The great difficulty in this passage is, to determine what is meant by "a sin unto death," and by "a sin not unto death." In the first place, it is clear the difference between them cannot consist in this, that one is venial, and the other mortal : for, St. John supposes the sin "not unto death," to take away spiritual life, "life shall be given to him who sinneth not unto death ;" and hence, to be a *mortal* sin. The "sin," therefore, "which is unto death," must be a mortal sin, of some peculiar enormity or aggravation. Some interpreters understand it of wilful apostasy from the faith ; others of any mortal sin, wherein a person obstinately intends to persevere, and owing to which he refuses to do anything towards extricating himself from the wretched state in which he is ; so that it refers to a sort of temporary impenitence in sin. Some understand it of final impenitence ; but, this opinion is improbable ; for, final impenitence is known only at death ; but with reference to the sin, of which there is question here, St. John supposes, that we can know that our brother has fallen into it. The Greek is more expressive, *if any one see his brother sinning*, &c. Moreover, St. John would not have a person free to pray for one who died in final impenitence ; whereas, here, he neither commands nor prohibits it, "I say not that any man ask."

"There is a sin unto death." He uses these words to show that it is not without reason he made mention in the preceding, of a man sinning not unto death.

"For that I say not that any man ask." The Apostle does not command us to pray for such a sinner, with the firm confidence of being heard in his behalf, with which we ordinarily present our petitions to God. The conversion of such a person is the result of a very great grace on the part of God, and requires an abundant degree of favour and acceptability with Him, on which every person cannot, without a certain degree of presumption, calculate. The Apostle does not prevent our praying for such a person ; for, we ought to pray for our enemies and persecutors, be they ever so obstinate in evil ; he only abstains from holding out certain hopes, that our prayers will be always heard, in the case of a sinner of this sort. Of course, whatever interpretation we adopt of this passage, we know from faith, that God wishes not the death of any sinner, but "that he be converted and live " (Ezech. xxxiii. 11 ; Isaias, iii. 18). There is no sin, for the remission of which, the Lord has not left power with his Church.

"A sin unto death," probably refers to the sin of apostasy from the faith, and some other heinous sins, which are seldom, and with difficulty, remitted. The Apostle gives very little encouragement to such as pray for sinners like these, to expect that their petitions will be heard.

Text.

17. All iniquity is sin. And there is a sin unto death.

18. We know that whosoever is born of God, sinneth not: but the generation of God preserveth him, and the wicked one toucheth him not.

19. We know that we are of God, and the whole world is seated in wickedness.

20. And we know that the Son

Paraphrase.

17. Every violation of the equity and rectitude of God's law, or every injustice or injury done to God, is a sin; and the sin which is unto death contains an injury against God of greater enormity, than is ordinarily contained in mortal sins.

18. We know from the principles of our faith, that whosoever is become the adopted son of God, and receives of him a spiritual birth through sanctifying grace, commits no grievous sin; the infusion of sanctifying grace, whereby he was begotten of God, will, however, preserve him, and the devil cannot reach him, so as to tempt him to commit grievous sin.

19. We know that we and all good Christians are born of God, and we only; for, all the rest of mankind, lovers of the world and earthly pleasures, are placed under the power of the devil.

20. We know as a certain matter of faith, that the

Commentary.

17. "All iniquity," *i.e.*, every violation of the rectitude and equity of God's law, "is sin;" for, sin is defined to be, "*factum, dictum vel concupitum contra legem Dei eternam.*" (St. Augustine, lib. ii. 27, *contra Faustum.*) "And there is a sin unto death," *i.e.*, although every violation of God's law be a sin, there is a peculiar violation of his eternal law, which is called and is, "a sin unto death." There is a difference of degree both in intensity and effect between the sin unto death, and others. In the Greek, instead of "there is sin unto death," it is, εστιν ὑμαρτια ου προς θανατον, *there is a sin not unto death.* However, there is no difference in the sense, because in the expression, "there is a sin unto death," is implied the existence of such a thing as "a sin *not* unto death," and *vice versa.*

18. The Apostle having digressed, at verse 14, from the subject of recommending persevering and practical faith in Jesus Christ, which he had been inculcating throughout the chapter, now returns to the same, and shows the advantages of this persevering faith. Not only will the remission of past sins, but also preservation against future sins, be the fruit of it. "Whosoever is born of God," *i.e.*, has been partaker, in a certain sense, of the divine nature, and received a new nativity of him, by sanctifying grace, "sinneth not," *i.e.*, commits no grievous sin, so long as he remains a son of God; for, with a state of grievous sin, the state of divine sonship is incompatible. And hence, every one should strive to persevere in that state, "but the generation of God preserveth him," *i.e.*, the sanctifying grace whereby he was born of God, and the spiritual strength therein imparted to him, will preserve him. In the ordinary Greek it is, αλλ' ὁ γεννηθεις εκ του Θεου τηρεῖ ἑαυτον, *he that is begotten of God keepeth himself.* The Vatican reading is "keepeth him," τηρεῖ αυτον. Of course, this does not imply inamissibility of grace (*vide* iii. 6–9). "And the wicked one," *i.e.*, the devil, "toucheth him not," *i.e.*, cannot induce him to commit sin.

19. "We know," *i.e.*, we Apostles know, "that we are of God," *i.e.*, that we, and all good Christians, are born of God; and hence, safe from sin, and out of the reach of the fraud and violence of the devil, as long as we preserve in ourselves this heavenly seed of sanctifying grace, "and the whole world," *i.e.*, all the rest of mankind, lovers of the world and of earthly pleasures, solely influenced by its leading corrupt maxims, viz., "the concupiscence of the flesh, the concupiscence of the eyes," &c. (chap. ii. 16), "is seated in wickedness," *i.e.*, are placed under the dominion of the wicked one, who is called in Sacred Scripture, "the prince of this world" (John, xii. 31; and Ephes. chap. ii.), "the prince of the power of this air, that now worketh on the children of unbelief"—(*see* also Colos. chap. i.) Hence, as all the world besides are under the power of the devil, we are stimulated to persevere in the true faith, which alone will rescue us from his dominion.

20. The Apostle closes the Epistle by proposing anew the great subjects of faith which pervade the entire Epistle, viz., the Divinity and Humanity of Jesus Christ—

Text.

of God is come : and he hath given us understanding, that we may know the true God, and may be in his true Son. This is the true God, and life eternal.

21. Little children, keep yourselves from idols. Amen.

Paraphrase.

eternal son of God has come amongst us, by assuming human nature, to be our Redeemer ; and has given us a supernatural knowledge, so as to know the true God, and to be united and incorporated with his true and consubstantial Son, Jesus Christ. This Son is true God, of the same divine essence with his Father, and is both the object in the fruition, as well as the meritorious cause, of eternal life.

21. Dearly beloved children, carefully guard against joining in any way in the worship of idols. Amen.

Commentary.

articles which the heretics of the day had specially impugned ; and he also shows the source to which we are indebted for our being rescued from the dominion of the wicked one, and segregated from the rest of men, viz., faith in Jesus Christ. "We know that the Son of God is come," *i.e.*, that Jesus Christ, who is the eternal Son of God, "is come," has assumed human nature, to redeem us, "and hath given to us understanding to know the true God." (The word "God," is not in the Greek. It is, however, found in the Alexandrian MS.) Unlike the unconverted Pagans, who adore idols, and obey their passions like brute beasts, we have received from Jesus Christ "understanding," reason, and spiritual faculties and knowledge, whereby we "know," by a supernatural knowledge, and obey and serve "the true God," viz., God the Father, "and may be in his true Son," *i.e.*, incorporated with him by sanctifying grace, and ingrafted on him, as branches of the same tree. In the Greek the reading is, καὶ ἐσμὲν ἐν τῷ ἀληθινῷ, ἐν τῷ υἱῷ αὐτοῦ Ἰησοῦ Χριστῷ, *and we are in the true one, in his Son Jesus Christ.* The first member probably refers to God the Father. "This is the true God, and life eternal," refers to the words immediately preceding, and must refer to them only ; for, to say that it refers to the words, "true God," as is asserted by Erasmus, would be quite absurd, since it would mean : "*this true God is true God.*' Hence, it refers to Jesus Christ, who, therefore, is "true God," and "eternal life," *i.e.*, the object of the beatific vision in heaven, and the meritorious cause of eternal life.

21. "Keep yourselves from idols," *i.e.*, idol worship of every kind, or from externally joining in any way in the worship of idols—a crime which was frequently committed by partaking of idolothytes, or meats offered to idols, in circumstances calculated to scandalize their weaker brethren, or endanger their own faith. Hence it is, that St. Paul strongly cautions the early Christians in this matter (1 Cor. chap. viii. and x.) ; and hence, also, the occasion of the decree of the Council of Jerusalem on the same subject (Acts, chap. xv.) This verse furnishes an instance of Protestant perversion of the Sacred Text. In some Protestant editions of the Bible, the verse is translated thus : "my little children, keep yourselves *from images.*" Whereas, the text is, ἀπὸ τῶν εἰδώλων, "from idols." The object of such corruption obviously was to bring an argument against the Catholic practice of venerating images and sacred relics.

THE

SECOND EPISTLE OF ST. JOHN.

CHAPTER I..

Introduction.

CANONICITY OF.—This, as well as the Third Epistle of St. John, is reckoned among the *Deutero-canonical* Books of Scriptures, that is to say, those books the Divine authority of which was not always admitted in the Church. Their authenticity also had been questioned. Many among the ancients, whose opinion is embraced by Erasmus, looked upon them as the production of another John, called the Senior, of whom there is mention made in the writings of Papias (*vide Eusebium lib.* 3). *Historiæ, cap. ultim., St. Jerome, de Script. Eccles*). However, it is now a point of Catholic faith, defined by the Council of Trent (SS. 4), that they are both divinely inspired Scripture, written by St. John, the Apostle. The Councils of Carthage (3rd) and of Laodicea, preceded the Fathers of Trent, in the same declaration. The earliest among the Fathers quote from them, as inspired Scripture. Tertullian (*de Præscriptionibus, ch.* 33, *et libro* iii. 14, *et lib.* iv. 5, *contra Marcionem*), says, the author of these, and of the Apocalypse, is the same—viz., John the Apostle. Clement, of Alexandria, commented on both Epistles, as the production of the Apostle. Innocent I. (*Ep.* 3, *ad Exuperium*) places them on the catalogue of inspired books. St. Augustine (*lib.* 2, *de Doctrina Christiana*), St. Jerome (*Epistola* 85) quote them, as the inspired production of the same. Since the fourth or fifth century they have been regularly received by the Church as divinely inspired, and written by St. John.

To WHOM ADDRESSED.—It is addressed to "*the lady Elect and her children,*" (ch. i. 1).—But it is warmly controverted, whether, by "*the lady Elect,*" is meant a particular person, or some particular Church, to which St. John wishes to impart encouragement and consolation, and wishes to put on their guard, against the prevailing heresies of the day. Mauduit, in a learned dissertation, endeavours to prove the latter supposition to be the more probable. The former opinion, which understands the word of a certain lady of quality, is the more common. Whether "*Elect*" was her proper name, or an epithet given her for her superior virtues and endowments, is a matter not determined upon either. By some it is contended that it was her proper name, and that the article was omitted in the Greek, on this account. Others maintain it was only an epithet given her on account of her virtues, and, particularly, her generous charity towards the preachers of the gospel, and distressed Christians, so much commended by St. Paul in his first Epistle to Timothy, "*si pedes sanctorum lavit.*" The Greek construction, which places "*elect*" before "*lady,*" εκλεκτῇ κυρια, favours this opinion ; so does the application of the same term to her sister (verse 13) ; for, it is not likely there were two of the same name in one family. Moreover, the Latin interpreter, who rendered the Greek word "εκλεκτα," in Latin, "*Electa*," seems to favour the same opinion. However, nothing can be determined for certain, on this subject.

WHEN AND WHERE WRITTEN.—Both are uncertain. It is likely, it was written at Ephesus, where St. John died in the the third year of Trajan, and ninety-ninth year of the Christian era. And it is equally probable, that it was written at the close of his life.

SECOND EPISTLE OF ST. JOHN.

CHAPTER I.

Analysis.

The Apostle conveys to Electa and her children the love and spiritual affection not only of himself, but also of all true Christians, who are incorporated with them in the profession of the same faith (ver. 1, 2). He wishes them the fulness of all heavenly and spiritual blessings (3). He next congratulates her and her children on their progress in Christian virtue (4); and exhorts them to the performance of good works, especially the works relating to fraternal charity (5). He thus confutes the demoralizing error of Simon Magus, regarding the sufficiency of faith only. He then exhorts them to fulfil God's commandments; and, in a particular manner, specifies his commandment to persevere in the true faith (6).

He enters on the second part of the Epistle, which is to warn them against being seduced from the faith by the heretics who then sprang forth. He alludes to Basilides, Ebion and Cerinthus, &c., who erred regarding the human and divine natures of Jesus Christ (7). He cautions them against forfeiting eternal life, by following these heretics (8). He shows the disadvantage and ruin entailed by the doctrine of the heretics, and the reward, both here and hereafter, of perseverance in the true faith (9). He next tells them to deny all entrance into their houses, to all false teachers, as also to refuse them the common civilities of life (10)—lest they might be chargeable with countenancing or approving of their wicked works (11).

He puts off many things of importance which he wished to impart to her, not desiring to commit them to writing; he hopes soon to see her (13). He conveys to her the salutation of her sister's children (13).

Text.

1. THE ancient to the lady Elect, and her children, whom I love in the truth, and not I only, but also all they that have known the truth,

Paraphrase.

1 The ancient bishop (salutes) the lady Electa and her children, whom I love with a sincere spiritual affection, and whom not only I, but also all true Christians united with me in the profession of the Christian faith, embrace with true Christian love and regard.

Commentary.

1. "The ancient." St. John suppresses his title of Apostle, through modesty, in writing to a single individual, and calls himself "the ancient," in Greek, Ὁ Πρεσβύτερος which is a term not only employed to express age, but also ecclesiastical dignity in the Church. He was the oldest Christian and Bishop in the Church. Hence, he might be termed "the ancient," by excellence. "To the lady Elect;" in the Greek it is, ἐκλεκτῇ κυρίᾳ, *to Electa, lady*. Hence, it probably refers to an epithet which had been given to the lady in question, in consequence of her superior virtues and charity;

Text.

2. For the sake of the truth, which dwelleth in us, and shall be with us for ever.

3. Grace be with you, mercy, and peace from God the Father, and from Christ Jesus the Son of the Father, in truth and charity.

4. I was exceeding glad, that I found of thy children walking in truth, as, we have received a commandment from the Father.

5. And now I beseech thee, lady, not as writing a new commandment to thee, but that which we have had from the beginning, that we love one another.

6. And this is charity, that we walk according to his commandments. For this is the command-

Paraphrase.

2. On account of a conformity in the profession of the same true faith which dwells in us now, and shall remain with us in its effects for ever, or which shall remain in the Church until the end of the world.

3. May the abundance of all spiritual blessings, and of divine mercy, and the undisturbed possession of the same, be conferred on you by their efficient cause, God the Father, and their meritorious cause, Jesus Christ, the true Son of the Father, being of the same nature with him, and the beloved Son, in whom he was always well pleased.

4. It has been to me a subject of great spiritual joy to find your children advancing and progressing in the profession of the true faith, and in the practice of Christian virtue, as we have been commanded by the Father.

5. And now, lady, I entreat you, and I also entreat your children, to attend to a precept by no means new (for I have no idea of proposing to you any such), but to a precept which you have heard from the very beginning of your conversion—viz., that we love one another.

6. And the true test of our love of God, with which the love of our neighbour is inseparably connected, is the observance of his commandments. Now, one of

Commentary.

"lady," a title of respect, which shows that she was a person of quality, "and her children," both sons and daughters, "whom," both mother and children, "I love in the truth," with a true Christian love, whereby I wish for them all spiritual blessings, "and not only I, but also all who have known the truth," *i.e.*, all true and sincere Christians hold them in the like sincere and spiritual regard.

2. "For the sake of the truth," *i.e.*, they and I love Electa and her children, on account of professing the same unchangeable Catholic faith, which abides in us, and in the Church at present, and shall abide with the Church to the end, and continue with us in its effects for ever, even in the life to come.

3. This is the usual form of Apostolical salutation, "be with you;" in Greek it is, ἐσται μεθ' ὑμων, *shall be with you.* By a Hebrew idiom, however, the future indicative is used for the imperative. Hence, the sense is expressed in our version. "In truth and charity," are connected by some (as in Paraphrase), with "the Son of the Father." Others connect them with the preceding words, "grace, mercy," &c., thus: may grace, mercy, be bestowed on you, together with an increase of true faith and charity.

4. He now enters on the subject of the Epistle, "that I found of thy children," which some understand to mean, by a Hebrew idiom, *I found thy children,* as "*adorabunt de ipso,*" *i.e., ipsum* (Psalm lxxi. 16), "*dabitur ei de auro Arabiæ, i.e., aurum Arabiæ,* "*docebit vos de viis suis,*" *i.e., vias suas* (Isaias, ii. 3). Others understand the words to mean, *some of your children,* "walking in truth," *i.e.,* progressing, as the word "walking" implies, in Christian faith and virtue. "as we have received a commandment from the Father," *i.e.,* as the Father has commanded all to walk and progress. Of course, this congratulation for their past virtue, is a tacit admonition to her and them to persevere in the same praiseworthy course.

5. "And I now beseech thee, lady,"—of course, the admonition is through her conveyed to her children and all Christians—"not as writing a new precept," when recommending that which he beseeches them to practise, "but that which we have heard from the beginning," viz., of their conversion (*vide* 1 Ep. ii. 7). What he beseeches of her and her children, and proposes to them as an old precept is, "that we love one another."

6. The charity of God is inseparably connected with the love of our neighbour,

Text.

ment, that, as you have heard from the beginning, you should walk in the same:

7. For many seducers are gone out into the world, who confess not that JESUS CHRIST is come in the flesh: this is a seducer and an antichrist.

8. Look to yourselves, that you lose not the things which you have wrought: but that you may receive a full reward.

Paraphrase.

his chief commandments is, that we should persevere in the same faith which we have heard from the beginning, through the preaching of the Apostles.

7. (It is not without cause I exhort you to perseverance in the faith, and wish to put you on your guard); for, many deceitful seducers have gone forth into the world, who deny that Jesus Christ, descending from the bosom of the eternal Father, assumed real flesh; the leader of this heretical swarm is a deceiver, and one of the principal precursors of Antichrist.

8. Take heed, therefore, and beware, lest, seduced by these, you may lose the reward of the good works which you have heretofore wrought; rather strive to secure the full and abundant reward which is in store for you.

Commentary.

since the love of God must be the motive of the love of our neighbour, and without it we could not love our neighbour as we ought (1 Ep. v. 2); and our love of God is most sincerely attested by observing his commandments (1 Ep. v. 3). "For this is the commandment." "For," is not in the Greek, and the sense will be more clearly expressed without it, by substituting either, *and*, or, *but*, for it, thus: "*but* this is the commandment," or one of the commandments, the observance of which will be a sincere test of our love for God, it is, "that as you have heard from the beginning," &c., *i.e.*, that you persevere in the faith which has been taught from the beginning of your conversion. This perseverance in the true faith he insists on, in consequence of the pernicious errors then disseminated, of which he treats in the following.

7. In this verse he commences the second part of the Epistle, wherein, after exhorting them to charity and good works in the preceding part, he encourages them to perseverance in the true faith, and cautions them against the wiles of the heretics. He, in a particular manner, alludes to Basilides and his followers, who denied that Christ assumed real flesh; they asserted that he assumed merely fantastical flesh; and hence, they subverted the mystery of the Incarnation and Redemption. What he says applies also to the heretics, who erred either regarding Christ's Divinity or Humanity. "This is a seducer and antichrist." He employs the singular number to mark out the leader of these heretics; or, to show that each of them is a precursor of Antichrist (*vide* 1 Epistle, ii. 18), "are gone out." In the ordinary Greek, εισηλθον εις τον κοσμον, *are entered into the world*. The Vatican supports the Vulgate, εξηλθον εις τον κοσμον.

8. "Look to yourselves," and be cautious, "that you lose not the things which you wrought," lest being seduced by them, you lose the merit and fruit of the good works which, aided by divine grace, you heretofore performed; "but that you may receive a full reward," *i.e.*, but rather endeavour, by persevering in the true faith, to secure the possession of the reward, the "full," *i.e.*, copious and abundant reward which is reserved for you in heaven. The word "full" does not imply that, should they not persevere, they would receive a reward, *not full*; it only expresses the quality of the reward they would receive in case of perseverance, and forfeit altogether, should they be seduced by the heretics from the true faith. From this verse it follows—first, that good works merit a reward with God; secondly, that charity, as also the merit of our former good works, may be lost. In the ordinary Greek, the reading is in the first person thus: μη απολεσωμεν......απολαβωμεν. (The Alexandrian and Vatican MSS. have these verbs in the second person; and, thus, support the Vulgate), "that *we* lose not......we have wrought......that *we* may receive," &c. The meaning is, however, the same, since the Apostle identifies himself with them, as is frequently done by orators when speaking of disagreeable or saddening matters; or, it may be, that he refers to the accidental reward, the *aureola*, which the preachers of the gospel enjoy from seeing their people saved (*see* 1 Peter, v. 4).

Text.

9. Whosoever, revolteth, and continueth not in the doctrine of Christ, hath not God. He that continueth in the doctrine, the same hath both the Father and the Son.

10. If any man come to you, and bring not this doctrine, receive him not into the house, nor say to him, God speed you.

11. For he that saith unto him, God speed you, communicateth with his wicked works.

Paraphrase.

9. Whosoever recedes from the Church, and passes over to the heretics, and perseveres not in professing the doctrine and obeying the precepts of Christ, has not God as his friend, neither has he him residing in him, and united to him by sanctifying grace; but, on the other hand, whosoever perseveres in the doctrine and precepts of Christ, the same is united to the Father and Son, by sanctifying grace here, and shall be eternally united to them in glory hereafter.

10. If any man come to you and express anything opposed to the doctrine which you have received, admit him not into your houses, nor manifest in his regard the common civilities of saluting him, or bidding him God speed.

11. For every person that shows any civility in the way of salutation, or expresses friendly feelings for such a person, countenances to a certain extent, and is, therefore, a sharer in, his wicked doctrines and works.

Commentary.

9. "Whosoever revolteth;" for which the ordinary Greek is, πας ὁ παραβαινων, *passes over*, and means, whosoever deserts the standard of God, and *passes over* to the camp of the heretics, Basilides, Ebion, Cerinthus, &c. The Vat can has, πας ὁ προαγων, "and continueth not in the doctrine of Christ," including faith and morals, "hath not God" dwelling in him, by sanctifying grace. "He that continueth in the doctrine," to which is added in the ordinary Greek, *of Christ*, *i.e.*, whosoever professes his faith, and obeys his precepts, "the same hath the Father and the Son" (*see* 1 Epistle, ii. 23). *Of Christ*, is wanting in the Alexandrian and Vatican MSS.

10. "And bring not this doctrine." There is in these words, a *meiosis*, *i.e.*, they express *less* than they are meant to convey; they mean: "If any man brings," that is, expresses any doctrine *opposed* or *contrary* to what you have received; for, the Apostle would not prevent them from harbouring in their houses or paying the ordinary civilities to a Pagan, who never heard of Christ, and says nothing opposed to his Divine or Human nature. Hence, he speaks of the seducers and antichrists, of whom he treats in the foregoing verses, "receive him not into the house," *i.e.*, deny him all entrance into your houses, and what is more, "say not to him, God speed you." The word for "God speed you," χαιρειν, means, *hail*, or *joy be with you*.

11. The Apostle assigns the reason of the precept given above, "he that saith to him, God speed you, communicateth with his wicked works." He is supposed, by manifesting friendship and civility towards him, to approve of his heresy and wicked actions. Of course, this prohibition of the Apostle does not extend to showing charity and offering relief to heretics in distress; they are all our neighbours, and we are ordered by the God of charity himself, in such cases to imitate the good Samaritan. But, most undoubtedly, the words of the Apostle convey a strict precept to avoid, as much as possible, all intercourse with such heretics, as make any attempt at perversion. They should then be treated by us, as the heathens and publicans were treated by the Jews, *i.e.*, we should know nothing of them; we should have nothing to do with these traffickers in human souls; and this holds in a particular way, when there is question of proselytizing ministers, "whose speech spreadeth like a canker."—(2 Tim. ii. 17). St. John himself, although the Apostle of love, gives us a striking example of the abhorrence all should feel in coming in contact with heresiarchs, or disseminators of false doctrine : "*Fugiamus*," said he, when he heard that Cerinthus was in the same bath with him—"*ne cadat et opprimat nos balneum in quo lavatur Cerinthus*" (St. Ireneus, lib. 3, ch. iii.) —and Polycarp, when at Rome, refused to return the "*ave*" of Marcion, calling him "*primogenitus diaboli*." Such conduct, far from being uncharitable, is the perfection of the charity, which we owe our own souls, and the souls of others.

Text.	Paraphrase.
12. Having more things to write unto you, I would not by paper and ink: for I hope that I shall be with you, and speak face to face: that your joy may be full.	12. Having many matters of importance to write to you, I have not thought fit to communicate them through the medium of writing ; for, I hope soon to be enabled to be with you, and speak to you personally, that, from the more free communication of spiritual blessings, your joy may be full.
13. The children of thy sister Eect salute thee.	13. The children of thy sister Elect, wish thee the abundance of all spiritual blessings.

Commentary.

12. " Having more," in the Greek it is, πολλα εχων ὑμιν γραφειν, "*having many things to write to you*," doubtless, matters of great importance, worthy of the aged Apostle of love; "I would not by paper and ink," *i.e.*, I would not wish to make writing with paper and ink, the medium of conveying them, " for,"—the Greek is, ἀλλὰ, *but ;* the Alexandrian and other MSS. have the causal particle—"I hope I shall be with you." Hence, she lived not far from Ephesus. The ordinary Greek has, ελθειν προς ὑμας, "to·*come* to you." The chief manuscripts have the Vulgate reading. " And speak face to face," *i.e.*, speak to you in person, not, as now, by writing, "that your joy may be full," *i.e.*, the joy which the treating more freely on spiritual subjects is calculated to beget, may be perfect and full. The ordinary Greek has, ἡμων χορα, *our joy ;* the Vatican and Alexandrian Manuscripts have ὑμων χαρα, *your joy.* From this verse it appears there were many things of importance, communicated orally by the Apostles, which they did not commit to writing.

13. "The children of thy sister Elect " may mean, taking "elect" for a common noun, the children of thy excellent sister, who may have been herself dead, or absent from Ephesus, "salute thee," *i.e.*, wish thee the abundance of all spiritual gifts and blessings. In the Greek the word, "*Amen,*" is added. It is, however, commonly rejected by critics.

THIRD EPISTLE OF ST. JOHN.

Introduction.

THIS Epistle is addressed to Gaius, whom St. John commends for his faith, for his charity and hospitality towards strangers and the ministers of the Gospel. Who this Gaius is, cannot be known for certain. Some, with the Venerable Bede, say, that he is the Corinthian referred to by St. Paul (Rom. xvi., and 1 Cor. i.), and commended for the virtues on account of which St. John here eulogizes the person whom he addresess. Others say it was Gaius of Derbe, mentioned in Acts, xx.; while others infer from verse 4, of this Epistle, that he was neither one nor the other; since the Apostle here regards him as one of his children, whom he either instructed in the faith or baptized. Nothing certain can be known regarding him.

THIRD EPISTLE OF ST. JOHN.

CHAPTER I.

Analysis.

After addressing Gaius, the Apostle expresses the interest and concern which he feels in his temporal and spiritual welfare (verses 1, 2). He congratulates him on his faith, and the charity manifested by him towards the poor and indigent Christians, and the different ministers of the gospel (3, 4, 5). He exhorts him to persevere in the same meritorious course of charity towards the visible representatives of God (6), who, having been bereft of all temporal means in his holy cause (7), have, therefore, a claim for support on all Christians, whom God has blessed with the means of doing charity. Such deeds of charity will render the doers of them sharers in the merits of those to whose support they contribute (8.)

He next says, he would have addressed the entire Church on the subject of alms-giving, were it not that Diotrephes refuses to recognise his authority (9) ; and he threatens, on his arrival, to expose his misdeeds before the assembly of the faithful (10). He cautions Gaius against following so pernicious an example. He eulogises the charity of Demetrius (11, 12). He concludes the Epistle in verses 13, 14.

Text.

1. THE ancient to the dearly beloved Gaius, whom I love in truth.

2. Dearly beloved, concerning all things I make it my prayer that thou mayest proceed prosperously, and fare well as thy soul doth prosperously.

3. I was exceeding glad when the brethren came, and gave testi-

Paraphrase.

1. The ancient Bishop (salutes) the dearly beloved Gaius, whom I love with a sincere spiritual affection.

2. I make it the subject of my prayer to God, dearly beloved, that you may prosper in all your undertakings, and enjoy health of body, as your soul prospers and progresses in sanctity, by the exercise of charity and good works.

3. It has been to me a source of great spiritual joy, to hear the testimony which the brethren, coming

Commentary.

1. "The ancient," &c. (*See* 2nd Epistle, chap. i.)

2. "Concerning all things," is understood by some to mean, *above all things.* However, it is better understand it to mean, *in all thy undertakings, and in all thy concerns,* namely, in thy family, wealth, &c., which thou renderest subordinate to the works of charity. "I make *it* my prayer that (in all these things) you should prosper." "And fare well." The Greek word for this, ὑγιαίνειν, means, *enjoy bodily health.* "As thy soul doth prosper," *i.e.,* I pray that in other things you may be as prosperous, as I know you to be with regard to the health and prosperity of your soul, which progresses every day more and more in grace and virtue, owing to your charity and hospitality.

3. In this and the following verse, the Apostle congratulates Gaius, on his past hospitality, so as to refer the glory of it to God, and exhort him to perseverance in the same meritorious course. "When the brethren," *i.e.,* the poor Christians, and probably Christian ministers of the gospel.

Text.

mony to the truth in thee, even as thou walkest in the truth.

4. I have no greater grace than this, to hear that my children walk in truth.

5. Dearly beloved, thou dost faithfully whatever thou dost for the brethren, and that for strangers.

6. Who have given testimony to thy charity in the sight of the church : whom, thou shalt do well to bring forward on their way in a manner worthy of God.

7. Because, for his name they went out, taking nothing of the gentiles.

8. We therefore, ought to receive

Paraphrase.

hither from thy country, have borne regarding thy true faith, and good works of mercy. as indeed in all thy actions thou dost display true faith and sincere charity.

4. Nothing can afford me greater satisfaction and joy than to hear, that those whom I have spiritually begotten in Christ, advance in faith and Christian love.

5. Dearly beloved, thou dost act a part worthy of a Christian when ministering to the necessities of our indigent Christian brethren, and particularly when exercising charity towards strangers.

6. Who have borne testimony to thy works of charity in the presence of all the faithful here. and in all places, and thou wilt act a meritorious part by continuing a course of charity towards such persons, not only by entertaining them at thy house, but also when they leave thee, by having them escorted out of the reach of danger, and by furnishing them with provisions for their journey, thus treating them in a manner suited to the ministers and representatives of God.

7. For. they went forth, as it were, into voluntary exile, in his behalf, and to propagate his faith, refusing to receive anything for their support from the Gentiles, whom they converted.

8. All of us, therefore. whom God has blessed with

Commentary.

4. "Grace," in Greek, χαρίν. The word, "joy," differs in Greek only by a single letter (χαραν, "joy," is the word used in the ordinary Greek reading). The Vatican MS. supports the Vulgate. "My children," that is, those spiritually begotten by him. Hence, Gaius was either converted, or more fully instructed by him.

5. "Faithfully," *i.e.,* a thing worthy of a Christian instructed in. the true faith, "Whatever thou dost," *i.e.,* in thy charitable ministrations towards the "brethren," *i.e.,* the Christian converts, "and that for strangers," and particularly towards such as come to thee from other regions, and are the most friendless and unpitied.

6. These Christian strangers whom thou hast befriended and aided by your charity, have announced thy praises publicly here, in presence of the assembled faithful, and they do the same wherever they go. "Whom thou shalt do well," not only to entertain at thy house, but also "to bring forward on their way," by having them escorted out of the reach of danger, and furnished with the necessary viatic for the journey. "In a manner worthy of God." In a manner befitting in us to treat those who are engaged in God's service, and have renounced everything for him ; or, in the same respectful way in which we would treat God himself, whose visible representatives they are, "he who receives you receives me."—(Matt. x. 40).

7. "Because they went forth in his name." You should treat them with the respect due to the visible representatives of God ; because in going forth from their home and in suffering the loss of everything else. it was on his account, and for the advancement of his holy cause. "Taking nothing of the Gentiles," *i e.,* declining all remuneration, as did St. Paul (1 Cor. ix. &c.), lest they should obstruct the spread of the gospel and give the Gentiles any pretext for charging them with mercenary motives. If we understand the word "Gentiles" to refer to the unconverted Gentiles, then, the word will mean, that the poor ministers of the gospel did not wish to receive any support from the Pagans, lest they might be scandalized at the want of charity in the Christian converts, who permitted their ministers to be in distress ; or, the words may mean, that the Gentiles robbed them of their possessions.

8. "We, therefore," *i.e.,* all who are blessed with means ; he joins himself, either be-

<table>
<tr><td>

Text.

such that we may be fellow-helpers of the truth.

9. I had written perhaps to the church : But Diotrephes, who loveth to have the pre-eminence among them, doth not receive us.

10. For this cause, if I come, I will advertise his works which he doth ; with malicious words prating against us. And as if these things were not enough for him, neither doth he himself receive the brethren, and them that do receive them he forbiddeth, and casteth out of the church.

11. Dearly beloved, follow not that which is evil, but that which is good. He that doth good, is of God : he that doth evil, hath not seen God.

</td><td>

Paraphrase.

the means of exercising charity, should receive such poor Christian ministers, in order that we may share in their merits by co-operating with them, and enabling them to announce the true faith.

9. I would have written to the faithful at large of your Church, recommending to them the same, and not throw the burden of supporting the brethren on any single individual, if it were not that Diotrephes, who wishes to hold the chief place among them, refuses to recognise our authority.

10. On this account, should I come amongst you, I will expose in presence of the faithful his past misdeeds, maliciously indulging in detraction against us, and endeavouring to injure our good name by calumnious imputations. And as if he were not content with these things, he not only refuses to afford any aid to the distressed brethren, but he also prohibits others from doing so, and casts out from the assembly of the faithful, such as perform these works of charity.

11. Dearly beloved, follow not the example of this wicked man, but follow the example of the good. He that does good, is a son of God, he that doth evil, hath not seen God nor known him practically, as he ought.

</td></tr>
</table>

Commentary.

cause he had alms for distribution ; or, he speaks in the first person as is often usual with those addressing others, even when the matter may apply solely to those to whom the the discourse is addressed. "Ought to receive such," *i.e.,* help and relieve them, "that we may be fellow-helpers in the truth," *i.e.,* share in the merits of the preachers of the faith. "He who receives a prophet in the name of a prophet, receives the reward of a prophet," (Matt. x. 42). It is likely these poor ministers of the gospel were the bearers of this Epistle.

9. "I had written perhaps to the Church." This he says, to excuse himself for throwing the burden of supporting the poor Christian ministers on one individual. In the ordinary Greek, the reading is absolute, ἔγραψα τῃ εκκλησια—*I have written to the Church.* In many Greek manuscripts is found the reading, ἐγραψα αν—"I had perhaps written." Both readings may be easily connected in this way : I have written to the Church, but in vain, and would have written perhaps on the same subject. The Vatican MS. has, ἔγραψας τι τῃ εκκλησια. "But Diotrephes, who loves to have the pre-eminence, does not receive us." Some say, this Diotrephes was bishop of the Church in question ; others, with Venerable Bede, that he was a heretic who had great influence in that particular Church ; a man probably of consideration amongst them. It is conjectured by many that he was one of the "*Judaizantes,*" who endeavoured to unite with he gospel the ceremonial law of the Jews. Against the opinion of Bede, it may, however, be fairly objected, that St. John does not speak of expelling him from the Church, as he certainly would have done, if this haughty man were a heretic ; so strong were the feelings of the Apostle with regard to such persons (2 Ep. verse 10).

10. St. John threatens to expose publicly his misdeeds. "With malicious words prating against us." He wished to lessen the authority of the Apostle, and by calumnious rumours to damage his character. And still more, he refuses to give the poor distressed Christian ministers any support ; and prevents others from doing so, and even excludes from the Church such as exceed his prohibition. This, probably, was a sort of unjust excommunication, and a fearful abuse of power. These are the heads of the charges, which the Apostle will bring against this wicked man.

11. He tells Gaius not to follow the bad example of this man, but to follow rather

Text.

12. To Demetrius testimony is given by all, and by the truth itself, yea and we *also* give testimony: and thou knowest that our testimony is true.

13. I had many things to write unto thee : but I would not by ink and pen to write to thee.

14. But I hope speedily to see thee, and we will speak mouth to mouth. Peace be to thee. Our friends salute thee. Salute the friends by name.

Paraphrase.

12. To Demetrius testimony is borne by all Christians, and by the evidence of his good works, nay, even we ourselves bear testimony to his goodness, and thou knowest that our testimony is true.

13. I had many things of importance to impart to you, but I do not wish to do so through the medium of writing.

14. But I shortly hope to see you, and speak to you in person. Peace be to you. Our friends salute you. Salute the friends by name.

Commentary.

the good example, of which he gives an instance, next verse, in the case of Demetrius. *He that doth good is of God*, &c.—(*Vide* 1 Ep. iii. 10, iv. 7 and 8).

12. "To Demetrius testimony," of his charity and hospitality, "is given by all" Christians coming hither ; or, by all men, whether Christians or infidels, who admire his charity; "and by the truth itself," that is, by the public notoriety of the fact ; and by ourselves, "yea, and we also," &c. ; "and thou knowest that our testimony is true." Similar are his words in the gospel (xxi. 24). The Greek reading for "thou knowest," is, *οίξαrε, ye know ; οιδας,* "thou knowest," is found in the three chief MSS. Who this Demetrius was, cannot for certain be known.

13. *See* verse 12, of 2nd Epistle ; *σoι,* "to thee," is omitted in the ordinary Greek ; but it is found in the Alexandrian and Vatican MSS.

14. "But I hope speedily to see thee, and we will speak mouth to mouth," *i.e.* I shall speak to thee in person. "Peace," *i.e.*, the secure possession of all spiritual blessings, "be to thee." "Our friends salute thee." *i.e.*, wish thee the abundance of all graces and blessings. "Salute the friends by name" *i.e.*, convey our regards and Christian love to all the Christians who are with thee, severally and individually, which is expressive of greater respect.

EPISTLE OF ST. JUDE, THE APOSTLE.

Introduction.

AUTHOR OF.—St. Jude, the author of this Epistle, also called Thaddeus, to distinguish him from the traitor Iscariot, was brother of James the Lesser, also of Simon, the successor of St. James in the See of Jerusalem, and of Joseph, surnamed the Just. These four were the sons of Alpheus, likewise called Cleophas, and of Mary, the cousin of the Blessed Virgin ; they are termed in Scripture "the brethren of our Lord," in accordance with the usage of the time, designating those, who were merely cousins, by the title of brethren. The Sacred Scriptures are quite silent regarding the particular of St. Jude's call to the Apostleship. We find his name introduced for the first time (Matthew, chap. x.), where there is mention made of the names of the twelve Apostles. After he had gone forth to preach the gospel, we are informed by Nicephorus and the Martyrologies, that he preached throughout Judea, Samaria, Idumea, Syria, and, especially, in Mesopotamia ; some persons state that he preached in Lybia. Fortunatus, and several Martyrologies, informs us, that he went from Mesopotamia to Persia ; the same tells us, that he was martyred there. The Menology of the Emperor Basil, and other Greek authorities, say it was at Ararat, in Armenia, then subject to the Parthian Empire, his death occurred.

The writer of this Epistle is not to be confounded with another Thaddeus, who, as we are informed by Eusebius, was sent by St. Thomas, the Apostle, to Odessa, and died in peace at Phenicia, as is stated by the Menæa. Our Apostle is, according to the common opinion, of quite a different person.

CANONICITY OF.—The Canonicity or Divine authority of this Epistle was not universally admitted in the Church until the fourth century ; since then, it has been admitted universally, both by the Latin and Greek Churches. It has been quoted by such of the Holy Fathers, as since that time, furnished catalogues of the inspired Scriptures, viz., Innocent I., Pope Gelasius, Athanasius, Jerome, Ambrose, Augustine, Isidore, &c. ; and by the Councils of Laodicea, Carthage, Florence, and Trent. Its inspiration is believed, by every Catholic, as undoubtedly as that of the four Gospels. We have in its favour, the only certain means by which, in the present order of things, the inspiration of any book can be known, viz. : the infallible authority of the Catholic Church. The principal reasons for questioning its Canonicity on the part of some persons, were founded on certain points to which it refers, regarding the contest of the devil with Michael the Archangel, for the body of Moses (verse 9), and the prophecy of Enoch, which are not found in any part of the ancient Scriptures. But it will be shown in the Commentary, that the mention of these is no argument against its claims to inspiration and Canonical authority—(*see* verses 9 and 14).

OCCASION OF.—The occasion of this Epistle was the same as that of the other Catholic Epistles. We are informed by St. Augustine (*Libro de Fide*, &c., ch. xiv.), that all the Catholic Epistles had for object, to meet the unsound doctrine and perverse principles of morality, put forward by the early heretics, viz., the Simonians, the Valentinians, and the whole swarm, comprised under the general denomination of Gnostics. All these erred regarding either the Divine or Human Nature of Christ; and their principles and practices of immorality were too shocking to be mentioned. St. Jude graphically describes them, in this short Epistle.

TIME OF.—From the similiarity, and, in many cases, identity, that exists between certain words and phrases in this and the Second Epistle of St. Peter (chap. ii.), it is inferred by some, that St. Peter, in the chapter referred to, borrowed from this Epistle of St. Jude. In that supposition, this Epistle must have been written before the year 66, the date to which the Second Epistle of St. Peter is generally referred. The common opinion, however, appears to be, that St. Jude has borrowed from St. Peter, and this opinion has some foundation in the words of St. Jude (verse 17), where he speaks of the words of the Apostles, words almost identical with those of St. Peter (2 Ep. iii. 3). In this supposition, this Epistle must have been written after the year 68, the date of St. Peter's death, under Nero.

LANGUAGE OF.—It is commonly believed that it was written in Greek—the language then most generally diffused, and consequently the best adapted for a circular Epistle like the present—the language, too, in which almost all the New Testament was written.

THE

EPISTLE OF ST. JUDE, THE APOSTLE.

CHAPTER I.

Analysis.

St. Jude commences this Epistle with the usual form of Apostolical salutation (verses
1, 2). *He next enters on its subject, and says, that to his anxious desire of writing to
the faithful, was superadded a sense of duty to do so, in order to exhort them to firmness
and perseverance against the machinations of the corrupt teachers, whom he describes,
both as to morals and faith* (2, 3). *He then points out some of the instances in which
their crimes, and the punishment which is to await these false teachers, were prefigured*
(5, 6, 7); *and shows how these heretics followed the pernicious example of the wicked
sinners of old* (8).

*He contrasts their blasphemous conduct with the forbearance exhibited by Michael, the
Archangel, towards the devil, when disputing about the body of Moses* (9, 10); *and
denounces against them the punishment of eternal destruction, prefigured in the signal
punishment of the wicked of old, whose perverse ways they followed* (11).

He next describes their corrupt morals, and the awful doom reserved for them (12, 13).
*He quotes a prophecy of Enoch, to prove the truth of the menaces denounced against
those heretics* (14, 15). *He continues to describe their corrupt morals* (16), *and cautions
the faithful against them, by referring to the words of the other Apostles, graphically
describing beforehand their impiety in religion, and corruption of morals* (17, 18).
*The Apostle himself gives a further description of their disobedience and wicked
works* (19.

*He exhorts the faithful to persevere, and to rear themselves into a spiritual edifice, of
which the foundation was to be faith; the superstructure, hope, and charity, joined
to earnest prayer* (20, 21). *He points out what line of conduct they should pursue with
reference to the heresiarchs and their deluded followers* (22, 23), *and concludes with an
appropriate doxology.*

*It will be seen by comparing both Epistles, that the 2nd chapter of the Second Epistle of
St. Peter and this Epistle of St. Jude, perfectly coincide in their description and denunciation of the early heretics; one Epistle throws great light on the other.*

Text.	Paraphrase.
1. JUDE the servant of JESUS CHRIST, and brother of James : to	1. Jude, who has been engaged in the service of Jesus Christ, as minister of his gospel, and the brother

Commentary.

1. "Jude," (*see* Introduction), "the servant of Jesus Christ," refers to the special
engagement of preaching the Gospel. Similar is the introduction of the Epistle
of St. James, "and brother of James." This he adds, as well to be distinguished

Text.

them that are beloved in God the Father, and preserved in Jesus Christ, and called.

2. Mercy unto you, and peace and charity be fulfilled.

3. Dearly beloved, taking all care to write unto you concerning your common salvation, I was under a necessity to write unto you: to beseech you to contend earnestly for the faith once delivered to the saints.

4. For certain men are secretly entered in (who were written of

Paraphrase.

of James, the lesser (writes), to the called, that is to say, to all Christians, who are beloved and sanctified by God the Father, the author of all sanctity, and are guarded by Jesus Christ, against being led astray by the spirit of error.

2. May the gifts of God's mercy, and peace, and charity, abound and be multiplied in you.

3. Dearly beloved, having been heretofore exceedingly anxious to write to you, concerning our common salvation, I felt it has become now a duty of necessity to do so, for the purpose of beseeching and exhorting you to contend earnestly for the unchangeable deposit of the faith once left with the Church.

4. (It behoves you earnestly to exert yourselves in the good cause), because, certain men have surrep-

Commentary.

from the traitor, Judas Iscariot, as also to conciliate the good will of those whom he addresses ; for, St. James the Lesser was held in the highest esteem by all. "To them that are beloved," the ordinary Greek for which is, τοις ηγιασμενοις, *to them that are sanctified.* The Vatican and Alexandrian MSS. support the Vulgate, τοις ηγαπημενοις, "beloved," "in God the Father and preserved......and called." The particle "and," before "called," is not in the Greek. Hence "called," being a noun, is given as a peculiar epithet of all Christians ; and the words "beloved of God and preserved," &c., are predicted of them (as in Paraphrase). The Greek ordinary reading, which for "beloved in God," has, *sanctified in God,* is preferred by many, because it conveys to the Christians an exhortation to shun and hold in abhorrence the impurities of the Gnostics, as opposed to the spirit of sanctity which they received. Both readings are employed in the Paraphrase.

2. "Mercy unto you," *i.e.,* the abundant gifts of God's grace, which to wretched sinners are a great mercy. Hence the form of salutation here employed by St. Jude, is substantially the same with "grace and peace," the form usually adopted by the other Apostles. "And charity," which may mean either the love of God, or of our neighbour. The former is the effect of mercy ; the latter, the cause of peace. "Be fulfilled ;" the Greek word, πληθυνθειη, also means, *to abound and be multiplied.*

3. He introduces in this verse the subject of the Epistle, "taking all care to write to you concerning your common salvation," ("your," is not in the ordinary Greek according to which it is, *concerning the common salvation.* The Vatican and Alexandrian MSS. have, περι της κοινης ὑμων σωτηριας, "concerning *our* common salvation,") which may either mean—that his desire of writing to them concerning their common salvation, was so great, that he felt himself constrained by this desire, as by a kind of necessity ; or, according to others, that he formerly had an anxious desire of writing to them, but, that it now became a matter of duty or necessity to do so, owing to the dangers to which they are exposed, "to beseech you to contend earnestly for the faith once delivered to the saints," *i.e.,* for the integrity of the deposit of faith, "once delivered," as a deposit in its unchangeable entirety, incapable of increase or diminution ; no point of faith can be added to it, or taken from it. Hence, in her Dogmatic Definitions, nothing *new* is defined by the Church. She only formulates revealed doctrines ; "to the saints," *i.e.,* left with the Church, the assembly of the saints.

4. "For certain men," &c. The Apostle, in this verse, shows the cause of the necessity, which he was under, of writing to them, viz., because certain men covertly insinuated themselves amongst them ; ("who were written of long ago unto this judgment) ;" these words, which are to be read within a parenthesis, mean, that all the punishment inflicted on the wicked in the Old Law, were so many types and figures of the punishment to be inflicted on the heretics, in the New. Similar is the idea conveyed (Rom.

Text.

long ago unto this judgment) un-godly men, turning the grace of our Lord God unto riotousness, and denying the only Sovereign Ruler, and our Lord JESUS CHRIST.

5. I will therefore admonish you, *though* ye once knew all things, that JESUS, having saved the people out of the land of Egypt, did after-wards destroy them that believed not :

Paraphrase.

titiously insinuated themselves amongst you (whose judgment of obduracy here, as well as of eternal punishment hereafter, was long since predicted and prefigured by the punishment of the wicked in the Old Law), impious men, who have no regard for religion ; who convert the grace and liberty of the gospel into a licentious system of impurity, and deny the divine nature and Sovereign lordship of the only supreme Lord and God, Jesus Christ.

5. I will, therefore, remind you, who have already known all the things necessary for your salvation, that the Lord Jesus, after having rescued the Hebrew people from the Egyptian bondage, did afterwards destroy those amongst them, who were incredulous.

Commentary.

xv. 4 ; Gal. iii. 1) ; "this judgment" refers to their present punishment of obduracy and insensibility in this life, as described, verses 10, 11, 12, 13, of this chapter (for, sin is the most dreadful punishment of sin) ; and to their eternal punishment here-after. Similar are the words of St. Peter regarding them (2 Ep. ii. 3) : "ungodly men," who have no regard for the relations towards God, which religion prescribes ; "turning the grace of our Lord God," *i.e.*, abusing the grace of the gospel and converting it "into riotousness," *i.e.*, into a system of licentious impurity ; thus, looking on the gospel liberty, unto which Christ asserted us, as a perfect freedom from restraint, and a per-mission to indulge all their corrupt passions. This refers to their errors in morality. He next describes their errors in faith, "and denying the only sovereign ruler, and our Lord Jesus Christ." The first part is made by some to refer to God the Father ; but, it is better refer both members of the sentence to "Jesus Christ." For, looking to the Greek, τον μονον ἱεσποτην και κυριον ἡμων, we find the two nouns are pre-ceded by only one article, and followed by the pronoun, and should therefore, refer to the same subject, viz., "Jesus Christ." Moreover, the errors of the Ebionites, Simonians, Nicolaites, and Gnostics, regarded the divine nature of Christ, whom they admitted to be the expected Messiah, but denied to be God, this inter-pretation is confirmed by a reference to 2 Epistle ii. 1, of St. Peter, where the idea conveyed is the same as that intended here by St. Jude, and is understood only of Christ. The heretics referred to did not deny one sovereign ruler ; they only denied Christ to be such. Of course, when Christ is termed, "the only sovereign ruler," the Father and the Holy Ghost, who possesses the same Divine nature and essence with him, are not excluded from a participation in the Supreme sovereignty. After "sovereign ruler," the ordinary Greek adds ("God"), but, it is wanting in the chief MSS.

5. "I will, therefore, admonish you," *i.e.*, recall to your remembrance, "though ye once knew all things" *i.e.*, you were formerly instructed in all things appertaining to the knowledge of salvation. In the ordinary Greek, we have for "all things," τουτο, *this.* The chief MSS. have, παντα, the Vulgate reading. The Apostle now instances a few of the cases in which the heretics, to whom he alludes, "were written of long ago unto this judgment" (verse 4), *i.e.*, in which their condemnation, as well as their crimes were prefigured. The first is, the example of the incredulous Hebrews. "That Jesus having saved the people," &c. ; by "Jesus" (for which in the ordinary Greek we have, κυριος, *the Lord ;* but the Vatican and Alexandrian MSS. have Ιησους, is evidently meant our Lord Jesus Christ ; since Josue, to whom, some think, reference to be made, did not save the people out of Egypt, nor did he destroy the unbelievers. "Did afterwards destroy them that believed not." Caleb and Josue were the only persons, out of 600,000, whose carcasses were not overthrown in the desert (Heb. chap. iii. ; Numbers xiv. and xxvi.) Reference is made to the same (1 Cor. xiv.) It was our Lord Jesus, according to his Divine Nature, which existed from eternity, tha inflicted

Text.

6. And the angels, who kept not their principality, but forsook their own habitation, he hath reserved under darkness in everlasting chains, unto the judgment of the great day.

7. As Sodom and Gomorrha, and the neighbouring cities, in like manner, having given themselves to fornication, and going after other flesh, were made an example, suffering the punishment of eternal fire.

8. In like manner these men also defile the flesh, and despise dominion, and blaspheme majesty.

Paraphrase.

6. And the angels, who, by falling into sin, forfeited their excellence and the primitive state of justice and innocence, in which they were created, and forsook, or rather were forcibly expelled from, their heavenly habitation suited to their former dignity, he hath reserved under darkness, in everlasting chains, unto the judgment of the great and terrible day, when all things shall be brought to a close.

7. As Sodom and Gomorrha, and the neighbouring cities, which, like Sodom and Gomorrha, had committed fornication, and indulged in unnatural lusts, were made an example of the eternal torments of fire, when suffering the dreadful punishment described in the book of Genesis (chap. xix. 24).

8. In the same way, these senseless men (notwithstanding the examples of divine vengeance set before their eyes) defile the flesh by their lusts and impurities ; they, moreover, despise all divine and earthly dominion, and blaspheme the celestial majesties.

Commentary.

those punishments, and effected the deliverance of the Israelites; both acts were common to the Son, with the Father and the Holy Ghost. On this account it may be, that "Lord" was substituted in the ordinary Greek text.

6. The second example of divine wrath, which, also, prefigured the punishment of the heretics, is that of the fallen angels, whom our Lord, after they "kept not their principality," *i.e.*, forfeited the original justice and excellence in which they were created ; "but forsook their own habitation," *i.e.*, were hurled from their heavenly habitation, "their own," alone suited to their former excellence and dignity—"hath reserved under darkness and everlasting chains," &c. The idea conveyed here, is the same with that expressed in the 2nd Epistle, chap. ii. of St. Peter. Although the words of this passage would appear to afford grounds for the opinion that the devils are confined to hell ; it is, however, the far more probable opinion, that they were first hurled into hell ; and that some of them were, by divine dispensation, as St. Thomas expresses it, allowed to come forth to tempt and carry on their fiendish war against mankind. Wherever they are, they carry their torments with them. St. Jerome expressly assures us, "*omnium Doctorum est opinio, quod aer iste, qui cœlum et terram medium dividens inane appellatur, contrariis fortitudinibus sit plenus,*" (in cap. 6 *Ep ad Ephes.* ; *see* 2 Ep. of St. Peter, ch. ii. 4).

7. The next example (which is also adduced by St. Peter, ii. 6), is that of Sodom and Gomorrha, and the neighbouring or surrounding cities, Adama and Seboim "in like manner having given themselves to fornication." The words, "in like manner," as appears from the Greek, τον ὁμοιον τουτοις τρόπον, mean, that the other cities gave themselves up, like Sodom and Gomorrha, to fornication, "and going after other flesh." The words, "other flesh," are commonly understood to express the unnatural lusts of these sinful cities, to which the Apostle refers (Rom. i.) and which derive their odious name from sinful Sodom ; "other," means contrary to nature ; "were made an example, suffering the punishment of eternal fire." The connexion adopted in the Paraphrase seems the most probable ; it is admitted by the Greek, and it connects the words, "eternal fire," with "example ;" they were made an example and clear type of eternal fire, "suffering punishment," of fire and brimstone, showered down upon them from heaven (Genesis, xix. 24).

8. "In like manner." In this verse, the Apostle applies to the men in question, the awful example of the Sodomites. These heretics, like the men of Sodom, "who went after other flesh" (verse 7), "also defile the flesh," by their impure lusts ; and hence, will be involved in the eternal fire, of which the punishment of the Sodomites was an expressive type. In the Greek, we have the words, ὁμοιως και ουτοι ενυπνιοζομενοι, "in like manner, *these dreamers* also," &c., which word, "*dreamers,*" refers to the

Text.

9. When Michael the Archangel, disputing with the devil, contended about the body of Moses, he durst not bring against him the judgment of railing speech, but said: The Lord command thee.

Paraphrase.

9. When Michael, the Archangel, disputing with the devil, contended about the body of Moses, he durst not pronounce against him, in reproachful language, the harsh sentence of condemnation, so justly called for; he merely contented himself with saying: May the Lord command, and foil thee in thy attempt.

Commentary.

delusive, idle fancies of these men, imagining themselves secure, while opposing the holy will of God. "And despise dominion," understood by some, of the lofty and supreme dominion which God exercises over creation, and which these bring into contempt, by their foolish, ridiculous fables; by others, of ecclesiastical authorities, whom the heretics, in all ages, make it a merit to despise; by others, of civil authority, which the first Christians were accused of undervaluing, owing to the insubordination of the early heretics. "And blaspheme majesty," (in Greek, ἐοξας (*majesties*), this, most probably, refers to the angels, regarding whom the Gnostics held so many disparaging and ridiculous opinions; they are called "*majesties*," owing to the exalted nature of their office, while assisting before the throne of God. This verse is the same as verse 10, chap. ii. of St. Peter. The latter words of the verse, "and despise dominion," &c., are not intended as applications of the foregoing examples, they are added to express the crimes of these men; the particle "and" means "*moreover*, they despise dominion."

9. The Apostle, in this verse, contrasts the blasphemies of these heretics, with the forbearance exhibited by Michael, the Archangel, under circumstances of the greatest provocation, "When Michael the Archangel, &c." As the circumstance recorded here by St. Jude, is not mentioned in any other part of Scripture, it is likely, he learned it from the tradition of the Jews, as St. Paul learned the names of the Egyptian Magicians, Jannes and Mambres (2 Tim. iii. 8); or, it may be, that he found it in some of the Apocryphal books, and having been quoted by St. Jude, it became a divinely revealed fact of Scripture. Everything in the Apocryphal work need not be untrue. We even find St. Paul quoting some true passages from Pagan authors, and having been quoted by him, they have all the authority of divinely inspired Scriptures (Titus, i. 12; 1 Cor. xv. 33; and Titus, chap. i.) It is stated in the last chapter of Deuteronomy, that when Moses died, "the Lord," *i.e.*, Michael, the Archangel, in the name of the Lord, "buried him in the valley of the land of Moab, over against Phogor, and no man hath known of his sepulchre until this present day," (Deut. xxxiv. 6). The most probable reasons of this dispute between Michael and the Devil appear to be—1st, Because the devil wished to have Moses buried publicly, in order to serve as a rock of offence to the Jews, who, already prone to idolatry, might, at some future day, be tempted to pay him divine honours. 2ndly, Because the devil would prevent the sepulture of Moses in the land of Moab, in a special manner his own, on account of the gross idolatry of the people; his reason being lest the presence of the saint's body should obstruct the permanence of his reign, in that land of darkness and idolatry. Michael, on the occasion of the altercation in question, through reverence for a creature, though a fallen creature of God, refrained from cursing him, as he deserved, or from uttering against him maledictory or reproachful language, such as, "*Begone to the infernal abyss, wicked devil, proud, haughty rebel,*" or the like. The Tradition, from which the knowledge of this fact has been derived, represents Michael merely as saying, "May the Lord command thee," *i.e.*, prevent thee from succeeding in thy attempt. This altercation, or rather the reasons assigned for it above, are, by no means opposed to the Catholic worship of images or relics of the saints. The first reason assigned, is not opposed to us, since it supposes that the object of the Archangel was, to guard against paying divine worship to the body of Moses—and Catholics never intend any such worship for images; nor is the second reason—on the contrary, it favours us; for, if the devil feared so much from the presence of the body of Moses, has he not equal reason to fear from the presence of the relics and images of the saints, which are, therefore, entitled to a certain degree of religious respect from us?

Text.

10. But these men blaspheme whatever things they know not: and what things soever they naturally know, like dumb beasts, in these they are corrupted.

11. Wo unto them, for they have gone in the way of Cain : and after the error of Balaam they have for reward poured out themselves, and have perished in the contradiction of Core.

12. These are spots in their

Paraphrase.

10. But these wretched men blaspheme the things, which they neither understand nor know, as they are far above their comprehension; and what things soever they know, like senseless beasts, from mere animal instinct, in these things they are corrupted, by reducing and degrading the dignity of human nature to the level of the brute creation.

11. An eternal malediction is in store for them, because they have, like the fratricide Cain, murdered the souls of their brethren, by infusing into them the poison of corrupt doctrines. They eagerly rush into the sin committed by Balaam, from the same motives of sordid avarice ; and by their disobedience to the divinely constituted authorities, they have become faithful followers of Core, and involved themselves in the like punishment.

12. These men are spots, and a disgrace both to

Commentary.

10. " But, these men," far from following the example set them by the Archangel, " blaspheme whatever things they know not," which may refer to the ridiculous opinions and idle fables regarding the divine and angelic natures, so far above their comprehension ; such opinions are nothing else than blasphemies ; or, perhaps he refers to some mysteries of the Christian faith, and certain arduous precepts of Christian morality, which they treat disrespectfully ; " and what things soever they naturally know," i.e., know from the senses and from mere animal instinct, " like dumb beasts," i.e., senseless beasts, " in these they are corrupted," i.e., in following and obeying the instincts of carnal concupiscence, they degrade and destroy the dignity of rational nature, reducing it to a level with the beasts.

11. " Woe unto them." He denounces against them the merited sentence of eternal punishment ; for, having imitated Cain, Balaam, and Core in their crimes, they shall be involved in their ruin. " For they have gone in the way of Cain," by becoming spiritual murderers of their brethren, infusing into them the deadly poison of their corrupt doctrines ; they have also imitated Cain in his irreligion and impiety, reserving to himself the best gifts of the earth, because they seek after their own advantage, without any regard for the interests of God ; "and, after the error of Balaam, they have for reward poured out themselves," i.e., they have ardently and eagerly encouraged immorality, to advance their own private ends. Balaam, whose history is given (Numbers, xxii., xxiv.) counselled Balac, King of Moab, as is inferred from Numbers (xxiv. 14, xxxi. 16), and Apocalypse (chap. ii. verse 14), and is attested by Josephus (lib. 4, Antiq. chap. 6), to send the beautiful women of Moab and Madian into the Hebrew camp, in order to entice the Hebrews to commit fornication, and afterwards worship Beelphegor ; this counsel had the intended effect, as appears from Numbers, chap. xxv. 1, 2. So, in like manner, the Simonites and Gnostics corrupt the people, from motives of avarice and sensuality. "And have perished in the contradiction of Core," the punishment of Core is a clear type of the punishment in store for them, on account of murmuring and rebelling like him and his associates, (Numbers xvi.) against the authority appointed by God to rule them. Whether Core was swallowed down to hell by the opening of the earth, or was merely destroyed with the two hundred and fifty Levites, by fire from heaven, is disputed. It is quite clear, from Numbers, xvi. 33, and Deuteron. xi., and Psalm cv., that Dathan and Abiron were swallowed down in the opening of the earth. In the three examples adduced, St. Jude marks out three leading vices of the heretics, viz. : envy, avarice, and ambition, besides the vice common to them with all sinners of old, viz., hostility towards the true worshippers of God, as in the case of Cain, who hated Abel ; of Balaam, who hated God's people ; and of Core, who rejected the authority of Moses and Aaron.

12. The Apostle now describes, in glowing metaphorical language, the immoralities of these heretics. "These are spots in their banquets ;" the Greek is, ἐν ταῖς ἀγαπαῖς

Text.

banquets, feasting together without fear, feeding themselves, clouds without water which are carried about by winds, trees of the autumn, unfruitful, twice dead, plucked up by the roots,

13. Raging waves of the sea, foaming out their own confusion, wandering stars : to whom the storm of darkness is reserved for ever.

Paraphrase.

religion and humanity in your Agapes or feasts of Christian love, feasting with you in such a way as to show by their excesses that they have neither reverence for God, nor fear of man, seeking their own gain and emolument, while pretending to be concerned for the spiritual progress of others ; they are clouds without water, which neither irrigate the earth, nor permit the genial rays of the sun to warm it, changeable as the winds, and inconsistent in their teachings ; they are autumnal trees, that never bring fruit to maturity ; they are without any fruit whatever; altogether dead ; plucked up from the very roots.

13. Like raging waves of the sea, they are turbulent and boisterous in their conduct, foaming out, in the obscenity of their acts and language, their own confusion and shame. They are wandering stars, shedding a false light, ever wandering from the true path of the gospel, whose end is to be utterly extinguished in that storm of darkness, whither they are hurrying, reserved in punishment of their iniquities, for ever and ever.

Commentary.

ὑμῶν, *in your Agapes.* The Apostle, most probably, alludes to their improper conduct at the AGAPES, or feasts of charity, so common in the infancy of the Church, as preparatory to the holy communion, and to which the rich and poor were indiscriminately admitted (*vide* 1 Cor. xi.) These heretics insinuated themselves into the edifying meetings of the Christians, of which they were the disgrace, owing to their misconduct. The Greek word for "*spots*," also signifies "*rocks*" of scandal, but the other meaning assigned it accords better with the words of St. Peter (chap. ii. verse 13), which St. Jude closely follows in this Epistle. "Feasting together without fear," *i.e.*, without reverence for God or fear of man—"feeding themselves ;" while pretending to seek the spiritual good of their people, of whom they constitute themselves teachers, they, in reality, only seek their own gain and emolument. "Clouds without water," which, far from serving the earth by the wholesome irrigation of the waters of heaven, on the contrary, injure it by intercepting the genial warmth of the sun. "Which are carried about by the wind ;" these words show the fickleness of heretics, and the ever varying inconsistency of their doctrines. "Trees of the autumn," *i.e.*, trees which produce leaves and fruit at the close of the autumn, which never come to maturity ; "unfruitful," *i.e.*, it should rather be said they produce no fruit at all. The word "unfruitful," intensifies the word "autumnal ;" "twice" (*i.e.*, altogether) "dead." "Twice," bears this meaning frequently in SS. Scripture (*v.g.*, Jeremias, xvii., xviii. ; Proverbs, xli. 21 ; Isaias, lx. 2 ; 1 Tim. verse 17). Altogether dead, and without any hope of ever recovering life or vegetation, for they are "plucked up by the roots." The last words add in intensity to the words "twice dead." They strongly convey the utter hopelessness, nay, almost impossibility, of deriving any good from an heresiarch.

13. "Raging waves of the sea," shows the restless, boisterous, turbulent conduct of these heretics, "foaming out their own confusion," expressive of their impotent rage against the immovable rock of Christ's Church, and of their obscene, filthy language and conduct. Similar are the words of Isaias, lvii. 20. "Wandering stars ;" pretending to give light to their followers, a false light, however, "wandering" from the unchangeable and fixed course marked out by the gospel.

"To whom the storm of darkness is reserved for ever." In Second Epistle, ii. 17, of St. Peter, the same Greek words are translated in our English version, "to whom the mist of darkness is reserved." The Apostle, to express their eternal punishment, employs the words "storm of darkness," rather than eternal fire, in allusion to the spiritual darkness in which these heretics kept their duped followers, whereof eternal

Text.

14. Now of these Enoch also, the seventh from Adam, prophesied saying: Behold, the Lord cometh with thousands of his saints,

15. To execute upon all judgment, and to reprove all the ungodly for all the works of their ungodliness, whereby they have done ungodly, and of all the hard things which ungodly sinners have spoken against God.

16. These are murmurers, full of complaints, walking according to their own desires, and their mouth speaketh proud things, admiring persons for gain's sake.

Paraphrase.

14. Now, of these, Enoch also, the seventh patriarch inclusively in a direct line from Adam, prophesied, when he said: "Behold the Lord cometh with thousands or myriads of his holy angels,"

15. To execute judgment upon all the reprobate and to convict the impious and ungodly of all their wicked deeds, and of all the blasphemous language, which they uttered against him and his holy mysteries.

16. These men are always murmuring against authority, always discontented with their own lot, finding fault with their neighbours, and especially their superiors; following their carnal desires, indulging in pompous, swelling, and empty words, flattering, and paying court to the wealthy, for the sake of private gain and emolument.

Commentary.

darkness is the appropriate punishment. All the foregoing metaphors represent the corrupt morals of those heretics.

14. The Apostle quotes a prophecy of the patriarch Enoch, the seventh in a direct line from Adam inclusively, in proof of this assertion, that these impious men shall be subjected to everlasting punishment. "Behold the Lord cometh," or, *will come* (the present is, in a prophetic style, employed for the future, on account of the certainty of the predicted event), "with thousands of his saints." The Greek is, *εν αγιαις μυριασιν αυτου, with his holy myriads.* The Vulgate has, *in sanctis millibus ejus, with his holy thousands.* He refers to the angels who will, at his second coming, to which reference is here made, accompany our Lord to judgment; for, the just men will be rapt up into the air, to meet him at his descent.

15. "To execute judgment upon all" the reprobate, "and reprove all the ungodly of all the works of their ungodliness." The Greek is, "*and reprove all the impious* AMONG THEM *of all the works of their impiety,*" according to which the meaning is, that although judgment would be executed on all the wicked, still against the impious in particular, such as were the heretics whom St. Jude addresses, a special judgment of more severe exposure and scrutiny would be instituted for their impious actions; "among them," is wanting in the chief MSS.; "and of all the hard things which ungodly sinners have spoken," *i.e.*, of all the words of unbelief, impiety and blasphemy, which they uttered against God and his precepts, and the truths of his heavenly revelation. "Against God," in Greek, *κατ' αυτου, "against him."* This prophecy of Enoch must have been known by St Jude, either from tradition, if it was merely verbally announced by the patriarch, or taken from some writing now lost, which the Apostle, from inspiration, knew to be true, so far as this prophecy is concerned; this, being quoted by St. Jude here, becomes a portion of divine Scripture, and is attested by the authority of the Holy Ghost; and even, though it were quoted from the apocryphal book of Enoch, it furnishes no argument against the inspiration of this Epistle, any more than quoting from Pagan writers (1 Cor. xv. 23; Titus, i. 12), does against the inspiration of these Epistles of St. Paul (*vide* verse 9).

16. The Apostle continues the description of their corrupt morals; "murmurers," *i.e.*, passing censure on their superiors. "Full of complaints," the Greek, *μεμψιμοιροι,* means, *finding fault with and blaming their lot or condition,* probably finding fault with the disposition of Providence and the arrangement of their superiors in their regard; "walking according to their own desires," *i.e.*, indulging in passions, or pertinaciously adhering to their own opinions; "and their mouth speaketh proud things," (*vide* 2 chap. 2 Ep. verse 18, of St. Peter, where the same words are employed). "Admiring persons," *i.e.*, paying court to, and flattering persons in power and influence, "for gain sake," *i.e.*, from motives of selfish gain and private emolument.

Text.

17. But you, my dearly beloved, be mindful of the words which have been spoken before by the apostles of our Lord JESUS CHRIST.

18. Who told you, that in the last time there should come mockers, walking according to their own desires in ungodliness.

19. These are they, who separate themselves, sensual men, having not the Spirit.

20. But you, my beloved, building yourselves upon your most holy faith, praying in the Holy Ghost,

21. Keep yourselves in the love

Paraphrase.

17. But do you, dearly beloved keep in mind the words which have been told to you beforehand, by the Apostles of our Lord Jesus Christ.

18. Who told you, that in the last age of the world, on which we have already entered, there would come men whose religion would consist in scoffing at everything sacred; and their morality, in freely indulging their own base and grovelling passions.

19. These are the men, who now are causing separation and exciting schisms, both in their own case and that of others, who lead a sensual and animal life, and are destitute of the spirit of God.

20. But do you, dearly beloved, rear yourselves into a spiritual edifice, of which the sure foundation will be your most holy faith, and the superstructure, prayer offered up with the proper dispositions, inspired by the Holy Ghost.

21. Persevere in the love and grace of God and

Commentary.

17. The Apostle now enters on an exhortation to them to continue firm in the faith, by reminding them of the words of the Apostles. Reference is, probably, made to the words of St. Paul to Timothy (2 chap. iii. and iv.), and to St. Peter (2 Epistle, chap. iii.), whose words are perfectly the same with the following words of St. Jude himself.

18. The things which they predicted are, "that in the last time there should come mockers," (similar are the words of St. Peter, 2 Ep. iii. 3, the Commentary on which *see*) *i.e.*, men who would mock at everything sacred and hallowed in religion; "walking according to their own desires in ungodliness." These words point out the corruption of their morals.

19. The Apostle gives further marks of the impious and immoral men who were spoken of beforehand by the other Apostles; "who separate themselves," ("*themselves*," is not in the Greek), men who cause schisms in the Church, from which they go out themselves, and influence others to do the same. "Sensual men, having not the spirit;" these words may, also, besides the meaning assigned them in the Paraphrase, have the same signification that the words "*sensual man*," have in the 1st Epistle to the Corinthians (ii. 14), signifying, a man who regulates all his faith by reason, and rejects whatever he cannot see, according to reason. With such men those are contrasted who *have the spirit* ("spiritual man,") who, practised in the principles of faith, are always prepared to submit to authority—(see 1 Cor. ii. 14).

20. In this verse, the Apostle resumes his exhortation; "but you, building yourselves upon your most holy faith." He exhorts them to rear themselves into a spiritual edifice, of which "our most holy faith" is to be the foundation. He calls faith "most holy," because it emanates from the Divine mind, which is the fountain of all sanctity, and by saying, "your faith," he shows they should have no connexion with the impure faith of the Gnostics. The Apostles frequently represent the soul of each Christian in particular, as well as the entire assemblage of Christians in general, under the expressive image of a spiritual edifice (*v.g.* 2 Ephes. xxi. ; 1 Cor. vi. ; 1 Peter, ii. 1 . "Praying in the Holy Ghost," the first part of the superstructure is prayer, accompanied with the requisite dispositions; "in the Holy Ghost," since, without, we cannot obtain the necessary graces, nor above all, the all necessary grace of *final perseverance*, which if we obtain, we are saved, if we fail to obtain, we are certainly eternally lost; and it can only be obtained by suppliant prayer, "*suppliciter emereri potest.*"—St. Augustine. We should pray for this necessary gift unceasingly.

21. The next part of the superstructure in this spiritual edifice is "the love of God," in which he exhorts them to persevere. "Keep yourselves in the love of God," which

Text.

of God, waiting for the of mercy our Lord JESUS CHRIST unto life everlasting.

22. And some indeed reprove being judged :

23. But others save, pulling *them* out of the fire. And on others have mercy, in fear ; hating also the spotted garment which is carnal.

Paraphrase.

the patient hope in God's mercy until, through the merits of our Lord Jesus Christ, you shall obtain life everlasting.

22. And reprove some, who by their pertinacious defence of false doctrines and obstinate perseverance in error, show that they are already condemned, and their conversion morally hopeless ; and make manifest to all the absurdity of their tenets.

23. But others, who are in the proximate danger of perversion and spiritual ruin, rescue from destruction in the eternal fire which is prepared for them ; and on others, who, through weakness have been entangled in the snares of these wicked deceivers, have compassion, by representing beforehand to them the terrors of the divine vengeance, which they have been treasuring, up for themselves ; at the same time taking care to hate and detest the errors of these impious men and their sensual and corrupt morals, which defile both soul and body.

Commentary.

may either mean, the love of God for us, or our love for him, or both ; for one follows from the other. Hence, the words mean, persevere in the grace and love of God. "Waiting for the mercy of our Lord Jesus Christ." This refers to patient, enduring hope, amid the trials and difficulties of life, until the reward of our sufferings shall be given us, viz., life everlasting, through the gracious merits of our Lord Jesus Christ. Hence, this spiritual edifice will have faith for its foundation ; hope and charity producing the good works which the grace of God, obtained by fervent prayer, will enable them to perform, for its superstructure.

22, 23. "And some indeed reprove, being judged," *i.e.*, the heresiarchs and others amongst them who obstinately persevere ; reprove," *i.e.*, publicly convict and show the absurdity of their errors, in order to render their teaching innocuous to others. "Being judged." Such persons are self-condemned by the notoriety and evidence of their perversity, and their conversion morally hopeless. Similar is the idea expressed by St. Paul ('Titus, iii. 11) :—"*Subversus est, cum sit proprio judicio condemnatus.*' "But others save, pulling them out of the fire," *i.e.*, such as are in imminent danger of perversion and ruin, like a thing cast into the fire, and about to burn, these save and rescue from spiritual destruction. "Pulling them out of the fire," expresses the immediate risk, in which they are placed. "And on others have mercy in fear." This is a third class, who had been inveigled by false teachers. On this class he recommends them to have compassion, and to show them mercy, "in fear," *i.e.*, by pointing out the fear of divine judgment, in order that they may avoid it in time, which is the greatest mercy. The words "in fear," may be also understood to mean, with a spirit of mildness and consideration for their weakness, mindful of your own liability to fall, as is recommended by St. Paul (Gal. vi. 1). It is to be observed that there is a diversity between our reading and that of the present Greek copies. Instead of *three* classes of persons, regarding the treatment of whom the Apostle here speaks, and *three* members of a sentence, as in our Vulgate, the ordinary Greek only treats of *two* classes of persons, and contains only *two* members in the sentence. It runs thus : και ους μεν ελεειτε διακρινομενοι, ους δε εν φοβω σωζετε εκ του πυρος αρπαζοντες·— *and on some have compassion, making a distinction, but others save in fear, snatching them out of the fire,* in which there is no reference made to the first class of persons mentioned in our Vulgate, viz., "others reprove, being judged." In some Greek copies, however, instead of "have mercy," we find "*reprove*" in the first member of the sentence, as in our Vulgate. Beza testifies that he found the Vulgate reading in three Greek copies, and Œcumenius, as appears from his Commentary, evidently found the same reading. In both the ordinary Greek and Latin Vulgate, the second member is the same, except that in the Greek, the words "in fear," are added to the

Text.

24. Now to him, who is able to preserve you without sin, and to present you spotless before the presence of his glory with exceeding joy in the coming of our Lord Jesus Christ,

25. To the only God our Saviour through Jesus Christ our Lord, be glory and magnificence, empire and power before all ages, and now, and for all ages of ages. Amen.

Paraphrase.

24. Now to God, who alone is able, and knows how to preserve you unto the end without sin, and bestow on you the great gift of final perseverance, and to present you free from all guilt and stain of sin, when you shall appear with exceeding great exultation before the glory of our Lord Jesus Christ, when he shall come to judge the world.

25. To the only true God our Saviour (Father, Son, and Holy Ghost), through Jesus Christ our Lord, are due, glory and magnificence, dominion and power, from all eternity, and now, and unto the never-ending ages of eternity. So be it.

Commentary.

second member, thus : "*But others save in fear*," &c. The reason, then, why three members are found in our version seems to be, that the Latin interpreter, finding in one Greek copy the wo rd, "*reprove*," and in another, the words "have mercy," united these several readings ; and thus made out a third member by fusing these distinct readings into one. The reading of the *Codex Vaticanus* runs thus : και ους μεν ελεᾶτε διακρίνομενους, σωζετε, εκ πυρος αρπαζοντες ; Ους δε ελεᾶτε εν φοβψ. *And some, indeed, compassionate, being judged, save, snatching from the fire, but on others, have compassion in fear.* "Having also the spotted garment which is carnal." In these words, the Apostle instructs them to observe circumspection and prudence, in their charitable intercourse with the deluded followers of the Gnostics, to shun and detest their errors and their corrupt morals—which is the external garment in which they appear—as they would the garment of one who had been suffering from an infectious distemper. Allusion is probably also made to the command of the Jewish law (Leviticus, xv.), prohibiting all contact with the clothes of a person infected with leprosy, &c. Some persons understand the words in their literal signification, as implying the avoidance of all unnecessary communication with the heretics in question.

24. The Apostle closes with a magnificent doxology, opposed to the errors of the Gnostics, in which he shows from what source we are to obtain the graces necessary for a holy life and final perseverance, and in which is also implied a prayer that God would bestow these gifts on us. "To preserve you without sin," so as to persevere unto the end, "and to present you spotless," &c., which refers to their being presented to our Lord Jesus Christ, when he comes in his glory to judge the world. "With exceeding joy," expresses the great exultation and transport of the blessed in meeting their Judge at the last day, when, exempt from all sin, and freed from all liability to temporal punishment, they are about to enter on glory, both as to soul and body. The words, "in the coming of our Lord Jesus Christ," are not in the Greek.

25. To the only God, our Saviour." In the ordinary Greek, *to the only wise God*. &c. *Wise*, is, however, wanting in the chief manuscripts, and is rejected by critics generally. The words, most probably, refer to the entire Trinity—Father, Son, and Holy Ghost. "Through Jesus Christ our Lord." These words are not in the ordinary Greek ; they are, however, found in the chief MSS., and now generally received. "Be glory," &c., express the majesty and high dominion of God over all creatures, and the consequent glory and honour which are due him.

The End.

DUBLIN: PRINTED BY SEALY, BRYERS & WALKER,

(A. THOM & CO., LTD.).